Table of Equivalent Weights an...

Weight

1 Gramm = 0.03 ounces
1 Pfund (500 Gramm) = 1.1 pounds
1 Kilogramm *oder* Kilo (1 000 Gramm) = 2.2 pounds

1 ounce = 28 Gramm
1 pound = 0,45 Kilo
1 U.S. ton (2,000 lbs) = 900 Kilo

Liquid Measure

1/4 Liter = 0.53 pints
1/2 Liter = 1.06 pints
1 Liter = 1.06 quarts

1 pint = 0,47 Liter
1 quart = 0,95 Liter
1 gallon = 3,8 Liter

Distance

1 Zentimeter (10 Millimeter) = 0.4 inches
1 Meter (100 Zentimeter) = 39.5 inches *or* 1.1 yards
1 Kilometer (1 000 Meter) = 0.62 miles

1 inch = 2,5 Zentimeter
1 foot = 0,3 Meter
1 yard = 0,9 Meter
1 mile = 1,6 Kilometer

Temperature

0° Celsius (centigrade) = 32° Fahrenheit
100° Celsius = 212° Fahrenheit

$$°C = \frac{10(°F - 32)}{18}$$

$$°F = \frac{18 \times °C}{10} + 32$$

Neue Horizonte

Neue Horizonte

A First Course in German Language and Culture

Fourth Edition

David B. Dollenmayer
Worcester Polytechnic Institute

Thomas S. Hansen
Wellesley College

D. C. HEATH AND COMPANY
Lexington, Massachusetts   Toronto

Address editorial correspondence to:

D. C. Heath
125 Spring Street
Lexington, MA 02173

Acquisitions:	Denise St. Jean
Development:	Katherine Gilbert / Harriet Dishman
Editorial Production:	Renée M. Mary
Design:	Kenneth Hollman
Photo Research:	Billie Porter / Sue McDermott
Art Editing:	Carol Reid
Production Coordination:	Lisa Merrill / Charles Dutton
Permissions:	Margaret Roll

International Standard Book Number: 0-669-35528-3 (Student's Edition).
35529-1 (Instructor's Edition).

Library of Congress Catalog Number: 95-81613.

10   9   8   7   6   5   4   3   2   1

About the Authors

David B. Dollenmayer is Associate Professor of German at the Worcester Polytechnic Institute (Worcester, Massachusetts). He received his B.A. and Ph.D. from Princeton University and was a Fulbright fellow at the University of Munich. He has written on the 20th-century writers Alfred Döblin, Joseph Roth, Christa Wolf, and Ingeborg Bachmann, and is the author of *The Berlin Novels of Alfred Döblin* (Berkeley, CA: University of California Press, 1988).

Thomas S. Hansen is Professor of German and Chairman of the German Department at Wellesley College (Wellesley, Massachusetts). He received his B.A. from Tufts University, studied six semesters at the University of Tübingen, and received his Ph.D. from Harvard University. His current research focuses on the 20th-century writer Arno Schmidt and on German-American literary relations. He is the author (with Burton R. Pollin) of *The German Face of Edgar Allan Poe: A Study of Literary References in His Works* (Columbia, SC: Camden House, 1995).

PREFACE

Neue Horizonte, Fourth Edition, is a comprehensive first-year German program for college and university students. With it you will learn the basic structures and vocabulary of German by practicing the four skills of speaking, listening, reading, and writing. In addition, you will learn about the culture of contemporary Germany, Austria, and Switzerland.

The goal of the program is to help you achieve a basic level of linguistic proficiency in German. Such proficiency includes both communicative competence — that is to say, speaking the language in order to communicate thoughts, ideas, and feelings — and grammatical accuracy. *Neue Horizonte* prepares you either to continue with an intermediate course in German or to go directly to a German-speaking country. There, after a period of acclimatization, you will be able to communicate in most everyday situations and to continue to build on what you have already learned.

In addition, the text aims to excite your curiosity and help you view your own culture through the prism of another, thereby expanding your intellectual horizons in the spirit of the Austrian philosopher Ludwig Wittgenstein when he wrote, "Die Grenzen meiner Sprache sind die Grenzen meiner Welt" (*The boundaries of my language are the boundaries of my world.*).

The Student Text

Neue Horizonte consists of a short introductory chapter and sixteen regular chapters.

Einführung *(Introductory chapter)*

From the very first day of the course, you can begin talking with your fellow students in German. In this chapter you will learn greetings and farewells. You will also learn basic vocabulary such as the names of classroom objects, the days of the week, and the months of the year. In addition, you will learn how to spell, count to twenty, tell time, talk about the weather, and tell how you feel and where you are from.

Chapter Organization

Each of the sixteen regular chapters contains the following sections:

Dialoge und Variationen *(Dialogues and Variations)*

The **Dialoge** introduce new vocabulary and structures through idiomatic conversations in everyday situations. There are two or three dialogues per chapter, most short enough to be memorized, with English translations printed on the following page. The **Variationen** follow up with activities that encourage you to build on and vary the material in the dialogues. When a dialogue is closely related to the *Neue Horizonte* video, this is signaled by a video icon that appears in the margin.

Wortschatz 1 und Wortschatz 2 *(Vocabulary 1 and Vocabulary 2)*

Each chapter contains two lists of words and phrases for you to learn. **Wortschatz 1** (*Vocabulary 1*) comes early in the chapter, following the dialogues. **Wortschatz 2** comes later, just before the reading selection. Words are arranged alphabetically by parts of speech. In addition, nouns are arranged by gender to facilitate learning. Each **Wortschatz** also includes useful expressions (**Nützliche Ausdrücke**), antonyms (**Gegensätze**), as well as a section called **Mit anderen Worten** (*In other words*). Here some of the colorful idioms frequent in the everyday speech of native Germans are defined using German you already know. These include, for instance, intensified forms of adjectives such as **blitzschnell** (*quick as lightning*) and colloquialisms such as **prima** (*great!*). By the end of *Neue Horizonte* you will have acquired a total active lexicon of about 1600 words and phrases.

Lyrik zum Vorlesen *(Poetry for reading aloud)*

Each chapter includes a poem related to its cultural theme. This may be used both for pronunciation and intonation practice and for simple interpretive discussion. Unfamiliar vocabulary is glossed in the margins.

Grammatik *(Grammar)*

Grammar explanations in *Neue Horizonte* are brief but complete and do not presuppose familiarity with English grammatical terms. So that class time can be devoted to communication, you should study the grammar carefully outside of class.

The sequence of in-class activities moves from theory to practice. The **Übungen** (*Exercises*) are directed by your instructor and briefly reinforce the grammar you have studied on your own. These are followed by activities called **Gruppenarbeit** and **Partnerarbeit** (*Group Work and Work with Partners*) in which you use German with more freedom and creativity on your way toward communicative competence.

Tips zum Lesen und Lernen *(Tips for reading and studying)*

This pre-reading section offers tips for learning and expanding your German vocabulary. Lists of easily recognized cognates (e.g., **Universität**) are given under the heading **Leicht zu merken** (*Easy to remember*). Strategies for approaching the reading selection that follows are also provided.

Lesestück *(Reading selection)*

The **Lesestück** is the core of the cultural presentation of each chapter. In Chapters 1–8 it provides basic information on daily life in the German-speaking countries. Topics include the family, secondary schools, geography and climate, work and professions, university study, travel, and urban life. The readings of Chapters 9–16 address important topics in twentieth-century German history and culture. These include the Weimar era, the legacy of World War II, and German reunification, as well as issues of intense current concern such as the environment, foreigners living and working in Germany, and the status of women in modern society. The readings in Chapters 13 and 14 are devoted to Switzerland and Austria, respectively. Chapters 12 and 15 present authentic, unedited nonfiction texts by the modern writers Anna Seghers and Şinasi Dikmen. Following each reading, the **Fragen zum Lesestück** (*Questions on the reading*) check your understanding of the content of the reading and sometimes ask for interpretive responses.

Situationen aus dem Alltag *(Situations from everyday life)*

This section contains activities and optional vocabulary that emphasize "survival skills" for everyday situations such as using public transportation, eating in restaurants, introducing oneself in various social situations, and expressing feelings. When these situations are the subject of a *Neue Horizonte* video module, this is indicated by the video icon (shown on the left).

Zum Schluß *(In conclusion)*

The oral and written exercises in this section integrate and combine the grammatical, lexical, and cultural material of the chapter in communicative and interactive contexts. The final written exercise of each chapter, entitled **Wie sagt man das auf deutsch?** (*How do you say that in German?*), asks you to translate brief colloquial conversations from English to German. In this way you can verify your mastery of the grammar and vocabulary you have learned in the chapter.

Videoecke *(Video corner)*

The **Videoecke** is a new feature that follows the **Zum Schluß** section in every even-numbered chapter of *Neue Horizonte*, Fourth Edition. It contains pre-viewing and viewing activities that will increase your understanding and enjoyment of the *Neue Horizonte* video program that accompanies the text. You can find an answer key to these activities in Appendix 1 at the end of this book.

Almanach *(Almanac)*

The final section provides more detailed information in English on the cultural topic of the chapter or presents authentic material in German related to the chapter's theme. For example, in Chapter 3 you will learn more about the school system in German-speaking countries, while in Chapter 8 you will work with a city bus brochure.

Student Annotations

A new feature of **Neue Horizonte**, Fourth Edition, are the student annotations printed in red in the margins. These annotations serve several purposes. They not only provide cross-references to the Workbook / Laboratory Manual and Cassette Program, but also offer learning hints, cultural and historical notes, contrasts and similarities to English, interesting word histories, and statements of communicative and cultural goals.

End Matter

Neue Horizonte includes the following appendices:

Appendix 1   An answer key to the **Videoecke** exercises that appear in every even-numbered chapter.

Appendix 2   A table of the principal parts of the strong and irregular verbs introduced in the book.

Both the German-English and the English-German end vocabularies include all the active vocabulary in the **Wortschatz** sections, as well as the optional vocabulary from the **Situationen aus dem Alltag** and the **Videoecke** sections.

For quick reference, the book ends with a comprehensive index to grammatical and communicative topics included in the text.

The Workbook / Laboratory Manual and the Cassette Program

The Workbook / Laboratory Manual and the Cassette Program for **Neue Horizonte**, Fourth Edition, are fully integrated with your Student Text. Further, this edition of the textbook includes an extensive system of cross-references to the text ancillary components. Because the audio program (the Laboratory Manual plus the Cassette Program) is an integral part of the **Neue Horizonte** program and is essential to the learning process, the cassettes are available for purchase at a special student price.

Using these components correctly will enhance the learning process for you. It is important that you do the work in the Workbook / Laboratory Manual in the sequence suggested in the marginal cross-references in order to derive the maximum benefit from this important supplemental material. Each cross-reference is accompanied by an icon identifying it as a reference to either the Workbook or to the Laboratory Manual and Cassette Program.

 The pen icon directs you to exercises in the Workbook. These exercises supply further written practice of the vocabulary and grammar studied in each Student Text chapter.

In addition, **Zusammenfassung und Wiederholung** (*Summary and review*) sections appear after every four chapters in the Workbook. These sections contain condensed grammar summaries and review useful vocabulary expressions. They also contain a self-correcting test called *Test Your Progress* that you can use to review the preceding quarter of the book.

The headphone icon directs you to material in the Laboratory Manual and the Cassette program. All the **Dialoge**, **Lyrik zum Vorlesen**, and **Lesestücke** from the Student Text are recorded on the cassettes. Abundant exercises are also recorded and keyed to supporting written work in the Laboratory Manual. Some of these exercises are identical to the exercises in the Student Text while others are variations on exercises in the Student Text.

The *Neue Horizonte* Video

Shot entirely on location in Berlin, the *Neue Horizonte* video is a new feature of the *Neue Horizonte* program. Each module of the video corresponds to two chapters of the Student Text.

Each module opens with scenes of Germany related to the module's cultural theme. There follow several minutes of a continuing story, performed by German actors using idiomatic language. Each module concludes with a **Welle Magazin** segment in which further footage shows aspects of German culture and life. For students who wish to view the video at their own convenience, the *Neue Horizonte* video is available for purchase at a special discount price.

The eight **Videoecke** sections in the Student Text correspond to, and are meant to be used in conjunction with, the eight modules of the *Neue Horizonte* video. In addition, when a video module is particularly closely related to a dialogue or a **Situation aus dem Alltag** section in the Student Text, a video icon (shown here on the left) signals that fact and alerts you to the possibility of viewing this module again at this point.

The *Neue Horizonte* Tutor

Available in MS-DOS® (3 1/2" disks), Macintosh®, and Windows® formats, this text-specific software package offers additional, computer-aided practice of the structures and vocabulary of the Student Text. It also provides helpful error correction and automatic scoring. The software is available for student purchase at a special low price.

Acknowledgments

We wish to express our special gratitude to Ellen Crocker of the Massachusetts Institute of Technology for countless suggestions for improvement of the text and better coordination with the Workbook / Laboratory Manual and Cassette Program. Thanks to Harriet Dishman, Kirk Smith, and Christina Ortmeier of Elm Street Publications for their unfailing attention to detail, as well as to the expert editorial team at D. C. Heath: Denise St. Jean, Katherine Gilbert, Renée Mary, and copyeditor Karen Hohner. Thanks also are due our colleagues and students at Wellesley College, Worcester Polytechnic Institute, and the Massachusetts Institute of Technology, who have used and improved *Neue Horizonte* along with us, as well as to our users whose comments and criticisms have helped to make it better from edition to edition.

We wish to thank especially the following colleagues for their advice and help.

Prof. Jutta Arend, College of the Holy Cross
Prof. John Austin, Georgia State University
Prof. Sharon Di Fino, University of Florida at Gainesville
Dr. Diethild Harrington, Worcester Polytechnic Institute
Prof. Wighart von Koenigswald, Universität Bonn
Prof. Jean Leventhal, Wellesley College
Prof. Michael Resler, Boston College
Frau Uta Trevor, Arbeitskreis DaF in der Schweiz
Prof. Margaret Ward, Wellesley College

In addition, we would like to thank the following colleagues who reviewed the manuscript at various stages of its development:

Prof. Edwin Arnold, Clemson University
Prof. Brigitte Bjorn, Everett Community College
Prof. William Langdon, Washburn University of Topeka
Prof. Joseph Magedanz, University of Nebraska, Lincoln
Prof. Herman Teichert, Western Michigan University

We welcome reactions and suggestions from teachers and students using **Neue Horizonte**. Please feel free to contact us.

Prof. David B. Dollenmayer
Department of Humanities and Arts
Worcester Polytechnic Institute
Worcester, Massachusetts 01609-2280
E-mail: dbd@wpi.wpi.edu

Prof. Thomas S. Hansen
Department of German
Wellesley College
Wellesley, Massachusetts 02181
E-mail: thansen@wellesley.edu

CONTENTS

KAPITEL 10   **Deutschland im 20. Jahrhundert**   **280**

KAPITEL 13 Die Schweiz   378

KAPITEL 14 Österreich   404

Maps

Neue Horizonte

(Introduction)

Communicative Goals

- Greeting people and asking their names
- Identifying classroom objects
- Saying good-bye
- Learning the days of the week and months of the year
- Spelling in German
- Describing how you feel
- Talking about the weather
- Counting to 20
- Telling time
- Telling where you are from

Guten Tag! *(Hello!)*

The shaded boxes in this **Einführung** *(Introduction)* contain useful words and phrases that you should memorize. You will find a complete list of this vocabulary on pp. 20–21.

German speakers greet each other in various ways. What greeting you use depends on the time of day:

Guten Morgen!	*Good morning!* (until about 10:00 A.M.)
Guten Tag!	*Hello!* (literally: "*Good day.*" Said after 10:00 A.M.)
Guten Abend!	*Good evening!* (after 5:00 P.M.)

where you live:

Grüß Gott!	*Hello!* (in southern Germany and Austria)

and how well you know each other and what the social situation is:

Hallo! **Tag!**	*Hi!* (informal greetings)

Lab Manual
Einführung dialogues in Stufe 1. Complete introduction to the sounds of German at the end of the **Einführung** cassette.

1 Gruppenarbeit: Guten Tag!

(Group work)

When German speakers meet friends and acquaintances, they not only greet each other, but they also shake hands. Greet the students next to you in German. Don't forget to shake hands!

2 Partnerarbeit: Was sagen diese Leute?

(Work with partners: What are these people saying?)

With a partner, complete the following dialogues by saying them aloud.

German has no equivalent to English **Ms.** One can avoid **Fräulein** by using **Frau** for all young women. In restaurants a waitress is frequently called by saying **Bedienung, bitte!** *(Service, please!).*

Herr	=	*Mr.*
Frau	=	*Mrs. or Ms.*
Fräulein	=	*Miss*

1. _____ , Herr Lehmann!
   _____ , Frau Schmidt!

2. _____ , Brigitte!
   _____ , Heinz!

3. _____ , Fräulein Schröder!
   _____ , Frau Königstein!

4. _____ , Peter!
   _____ , Ute!

5. _____ , Franz!
   _____ , Joseph!

Wie heißen Sie? *(What's your name?)*

you: *du* or *Sie?*

German has two forms of the pronoun *you*. If you're talking to a relative or good friend, use the familiar form **du**. University students call each other **du** even when they're meeting for the first time. If you're talking to an adult whom you don't know well, use the formal **Sie**.

When you meet people for the first time, you want to learn their names. Listen to your instructor, then repeat the following dialogue.

A: Hallo, ich heiße Anna. Wie heißt du?	*Hello, my name is Anna. What's your name?*
B: Hallo Anna. Ich heiße Thomas.	*Hello Anna. My name's Thomas.*
A: Freut mich, Thomas!	*Pleased to meet you, Thomas.*

You can hear these dialogues on the tape accompanying the **Einführung**.

If you're meeting an adult who is not a fellow student, the dialogue would go like this:

A: Ich heiße Schönhuber, und wie heißen Sie?
B: Guten Tag, Herr Schönhuber. Ich heiße Meyer.
A: Freut mich, Herr Meyer.

heißen: _____ 's name is

German verbs have endings that must agree with the subject of the sentence:

ich heiß**e**	*my name is* (literally: *I am called*)
du heiß**t**	
Sie heiß**en** }	*your name is*
er heiß**t**	*his name is*
sie heiß**t**	*her name is*
Wie heißt du? }	*What's your name?* (literally: *How*
Wie heißen Sie?	*are you called?*)

3 Partnerarbeit: Wie heißt du?

Practice the first dialogue at the bottom of p. 0 with a partner. Substitute your own names for Anna and Thomas, and don't forget to switch roles.

4 Gruppenarbeit: Ich heiße . . .

Now introduce yourself to three or four people in class you don't know. Use **du** and don't forget to shake hands.

Wie heißt du?   Wie heißt er?

Wie heißt sie?

5 Gruppenarbeit: Wie heißt . . . ?

Your instructor will ask you the names of other students. If you can't remember someone's name, just ask that person, **Wie heißt du?**

Wie geht's? *(How are you?)*

> **dir or Ihnen?**
>
> **informal** Wie geht's **dir**? ⎫ (literally) *How goes it for*
> **formal**   Wie geht es **Ihnen**? ⎬ *you?*

After you've said hello, you want to find out how someone is. With a relative or fellow student, the conversation goes like this:

A: Wie geht es dir, Franz?   *How are you, Franz?*
B: Sehr gut, danke. Und dir?   *Very well, thanks. And you?*
A: Prima, danke.   *Great, thanks.*

With other adults, the exchange goes like this:

A: Wie geht es Ihnen heute,   *How are you today, Mrs.*
       Frau Müller?   *Müller?*
B: Leider nicht so gut.   *Unfortunately, not so well.*
A: Oh, das tut mir leid.   *Oh, I'm sorry.*

6 Partnerarbeit: Wie geht's?

With a partner, practice the two preceding dialogues several times until you can say them with books closed.

7 Partnerarbeit: Wie geht's dir?

Complete this dialogue with a new partner. You're both students or good friends and so say **du** or **dir** to each other.

A: Hallo! Wie geht's dir heute, _____ ?
B: _____ , danke. Und _____ ?
A: _____ , danke.

8 Partnerarbeit: Wie geht es Ihnen?

Now you have a more formal relationship. Use **Sie** and **Ihnen**.

A: Guten Tag, Frau / Herr _____ . Wie geht es Ihnen heute?
B: Leider _____ .
A: Oh, _____ .

Was ist das? *(What is that?)*

In items 1–4, the first word refers to a university classroom (professor and student), while the second word in parentheses refers to a secondary school classroom (teacher and pupil). **Student** in German *always* means *university student*.

1. der Professor
   (der Lehrer)
2. die Professorin
   (die Lehrerin)
3. der Student
   (der Schüler)

4. die Studentin
   (die Schülerin)
5. die Tafel
6. der Tisch
7. die Uhr
8. die Wand
9. das Fenster

10. der Stuhl
11. die Tür
12. die Landkarte
13. das Poster
14. die Kreide
15. der Wischer

1. das Buch
2. das Heft
3. das Papier
4. der Bleistift
5. der Kugelschreiber
6. der Radiergummi

A: **Was ist das?**
B: **Das ist der Tisch.**
        das Buch.
        die Tafel.

What is that?
That's the table.
     the book.
     the blackboard.

The = *der, das* or *die*

Every German noun belongs to one of three classes, traditionally called *masculine*, *neuter*, and *feminine*. The form of the definite article (**der**, **das**, **die** = *the*) shows which class each noun belongs to. This article *must* be learned with each noun.

masculine	**der** Mann	*the man*
	der Stuhl	*the chair*
neuter	**das** Kind	*the child*
	das Buch	*the book*
feminine	**die** Frau	*the woman*
	die Tafel	*the blackboard*

A:	**Wer ist das?**	*Who is that?*
B:	**Das ist Thomas.**	*That's Thomas.*
	die Professorin.	*the (female) professor.*
	der Professor.	*the (male) professor.*
	die Studentin.	*the (female) student.*
	der Student.	*the (male) student.*

The **-in** suffix denotes a female.

9 Partnerarbeit: Was ist das?

Work together and see how many people and things in the room you can identify.

A:	Was ist das?		A:	Wer ist das?
B:	Das ist der/das/die _____ .		B:	Das ist _____ .

Question Words	
wie?	*how?*
was?	*what?*
wer?	*who?*

Auf Wiedersehen! *(Good-bye!)*

There are several expressions you can use when leaving.

Tschüs is derived from Spanish adios.

Auf Wiedersehen!	*Good-bye!*
Tschüs!	*So long!* (informal, among friends)
Schönes Wochenende!	*(Have a) nice weekend!*
Danke, gleichfalls!	*Thanks, same to you! (You too!)*
Bis morgen!	*Until tomorrow!*
Bis Montag!	*Until Monday!*

Die Wochentage *(Days of the week)*

Montag	*Monday*
Dienstag	*Tuesday*
Mittwoch	*Wednesday*
Donnerstag	*Thursday*
Freitag	*Friday*
Samstag (in southern Germany)	
Sonnabend (in northern Germany)	*Saturday*
Sonntag	*Sunday*

10 Gruppenarbeit: Auf Wiedersehen!

At the end of class, turn to your neighbors and say good-bye until next time. Tell your instructor good-bye too.

STUFE 2

Das Alphabet

Lab Manual
Einführung, The Alphabet.

In addition to this alphabet, German also has three vowels modified by a symbol called the **Umlaut: ä, ö, ü.**

The name of almost every letter in German contains the sound ordinarily represented by that letter. You should memorize the German alphabet. Listen to the alphabet on the tapes and to your instructor.

a	ah	**j**	jot	**s**	ess
b	beh	**k**	kah	**t**	teh
c	tseh	**l**	ell	**u**	uh
d	deh	**m**	emm	**v**	fau
e	eh	**n**	enn	**w**	weh
f	eff	**o**	oh	**x**	iks
g	geh	**p**	peh	**y**	üppsilon
h	hah	**q**	kuh	**z**	tsett
i	ih	**r**	err	**ß**	ess-tsett

Notes on capitalization:

- All nouns are capitalized, wherever they occur in the sentence.
- Adjectives denoting nationality are *not* capitalized.

deutsch	*German*
amerikanisch	*American*
kanadisch	*Canadian*

11 Partnerarbeit: Wie schreibt man das? *(How do you spell that?)*

A. Ask each other how you spell your names. Write the last name as your partner spells it, then check to see whether you've written it correctly.

A: Wie heißt du?
B: Ich heiße Jay Schneider.
A: Wie schreibt man Schneider? *How do you spell*
                                 "Schneider"?
B: Man schreibt das S-C-H-N-E-I-D-E-R. *You spell it . . .*

B. Now turn to the classroom objects pictured on p. 7. One partner spells four or five of the objects pictured; the other partner says each word as it is spelled. Then switch roles.

BMW = Bayerische Motorenwerke (*Bavarian Motor Works*), **MP** = Militärpolizei, **ISBN** = Internationale Standardbuchnummer, **EKG** = Elektrokardiogramm, **BASF** = Badische Anilin- und Sodafabrik (*Baden Aniline and Soda Factory*).

12 Gruppenarbeit: Wie sagt man das? *(How do you say that?)*

Here are some abbreviations used in both English and German. Take turns saying them in German:

VW	BMW	ISBN	BASF
IBM	MP	EKG	TNT
USA	PVC	CD	

13 Gruppenarbeit: Wie spricht man das aus? *(How do you pronounce that?)*

A. Let's move from individual letters to pronouncing entire words in German. Here are some well-known German surnames. Take turns saying them aloud.

Fahrenheit	Kissinger	Nietzsche	Bach
Jung	Freud	Luther	Schönberg
Diesel	Ohm	Zeppelin	Schwarzenegger
Beethoven	Röntgen	Bunsen	Goethe
Hesse	Mozart	Schiffer	Pfeiffer

B. Now here are some words that English has borrowed from German. Caution: in English, their pronunciation has been anglicized. Be sure to pronounce them in German, and see if you know what they mean.

Flak = acronym for **Fliegerabwehrkanone** (*anti aircraft gun*).

Angst	Kindergarten	Strudel
Ersatz	Kitsch	Wanderlust
Gestalt	Poltergeist	Weltanschauung
Gesundheit	Rucksack	Zeitgeist
Hinterland	Spiel	Zwieback
Flak	Leitmotiv	Schmalz

Wie geht's?

Now let's move beyond the basics of "How are you?" "I'm fine" and find out more detail about how you're feeling.

A: **Wie geht's heute? Bist du guter Laune?**

B: **Nein, ich bin nicht guter Laune. Ich bin schlechter Laune.**

How are you today? Are you in a good mood?

No, I'm not in a good mood. I'm in a bad mood.

You will learn the complete present tense of **sein**, including plural forms, in **Kapitel 1**.

---

sein **to be**

The most frequently used verb in German is **sein**. It is very irregular in the present tense.

ich bin	*I am*
du bist }	*you are*
Sie sind ⌡	
er ist	*he is*
sie ist	*she is*

Negation

Nicht (*not*) is placed in front of the adjective it negates:

A: Bist du müde?

B: Nein, ich bin **nicht** müde.

Are you tired?

No, I'm not tired.

Wie geht's? (How are you?)

Es geht mir gut. (*I'm fine.*)

Ich bin . . .
    guter Laune (*in a good mood*).
    munter (*wide-awake, cheerful*).
    fit (*in good shape*).

Das freut mich! (*I'm glad!*)

Es geht mir nicht so gut. (*I'm not so well.*)

Ich bin . . .
    schlechter Laune (*in a bad mood*).
    müde (*tired*).
    krank (*sick*).
    sauer (*ticked off, sore*).

Das tut mir leid. (*I'm sorry.*)

14 Gruppenarbeit

Describe these six people in German.

Er *(oder)* sie ist _____ .

15 Partnerarbeit

With a partner, complete the following dialogues.

GERTRUD: Grüß Gott, Melanie! Wie geht's _____ heute?

MELANIE: Hallo, Gertrud. Leider geht's mir _____ gut. Ich bin heute _____ .

GERTRUD: Oh, _____ .

FRAU PABST: Guten Tag, Herr Hauser! Wie geht es _____ ?

HERR HAUSER: Guten Tag, Frau Pabst! Sehr gut, danke. Ich bin heute _____ !

FRAU PABST: Oh, _____ !

16 Gruppenarbeit: Bist du . . . ?

Form groups of three or four for this guessing game. Each person in turn acts out one of the adjectives listed on page 11. The others ask questions until they guess what the mood is.

A: Bist du müde?
B: Nein, ich bin nicht müde.
C: Bist du . . . ?
B: Ja, ich bin . . .

Das Wetter (The weather)

The weather is a frequent topic of conversation everywhere.

A: Wie ist das Wetter heute?
B: Es ist **herrlich** (*great, terrific*).   ODER (*or*)   Es ist **furchtbar** (*terrible*).

Es ist kühl.   **Es ist warm.**   **Es ist kalt.**   **Es ist heiß.**

Scheint die Sonne heute?   *Is the sun shining today?*

Ja, die Sonne scheint.   *Yes, the sun is shining.*

Nein, es regnet.   *No, it's raining.*

17 Partnerarbeit: Wie ist das Wetter heute?

Chat briefly with a partner about today's weather. Use the words and phrases above.

More Weather Words

Es ist heute wolkig.	*Today it's cloudy.*
neblig.	*foggy.*
sonnig.	*sunny.*
windig.	*windy.*
Es regnet.	*It's raining.*
Es schneit.	*It's snowing.*

Guess the meaning of **Aufgang** and **Untergang**. What season is this?
Ist es heiß oder kalt? (Die Temperatur ist Celsius!)

Wie ist das Wetter in Berlin?
Ist es Sommer oder Winter?

18 Gruppenarbeit: In Oslo ist es . . .

Describe the weather in the following places.

Wie ist das Wetter in . . .

Oslo?

Cannes?

Boston?

Berlin?

Hamburg?

Lab Manual
Einführung, The Numbers.

Wie viele? *(How many?)*

0	null	11	elf
1	eins	12	zwölf
2	zwei	13	dreizehn
3	drei	14	vierzehn
4	vier	15	fünfzehn
5	fünf	16	sechzehn
6	sechs	17	siebzehn
7	sieben	18	achtzehn
8	acht	19	neunzehn
9	neun	20	zwanzig
10	zehn		

19 **Gruppenarbeit: Wie ist die Telefonnummer?** *(What is the telephone number?)*

Read these business telephone numbers aloud.

Two of these numbers include an area code beginning with 0. When dialing German numbers from abroad, the zero is omitted. For example, to dial the Dortmund number from the U.S., dial 011 (international operator), 49 (country code), then the area code 231 (without zero), and then the local number 82 34 45. 49 is the country code for Germany, 43 for Austria, 41 for Switzerland.

NATURKOST · NATURKOSMETIK
belladonna
BERGMANNSTR. 101   694 3731

mitfahr zentrale Berlin 15
030-8827606

Dortmund 0231/82 34 45
82 20 67

SCHALLPLATTEN + CD's
ANKAUF · VERKAUF · TAUSCH
Ständiger Barankauf von LP's + CD's (Sammlungen)
LP's ab 4 DM
Sl ab 1 DM
Mo–Fr 12.00–18.30
Sa 10.00–14.00
Bergmannstraße 10
Telefon: 6 93 19 98

EIGENER ABSCHLEPPDIENST
K. Walter vorm. ZINNEKER
1230 WIEN, BREITENFURTERSTR. 213
☎ 804 21 42
KAROSSERIE-FACHWERKSTÄTTE
Einbrenn- und Sonderlackierung
Autokosmetik

Lab Manual
Einführung dialogues in Stufe 3.

20 **Kettenreaktion: Wie ist deine Telefonnummer?** *(Chain reaction: What's your telephone number?)*

Follow the model. One student asks the next.

BEISPIEL: A: Wie ist deine Telefonnummer?
(Example) B: Meine Telefonnummer ist _____ . Wie ist *deine* Telefonnummer?
C: _____ .

Wie spät ist es bitte? *(What time is it, please?)*

Es ist drei Uhr.

Es ist Viertel nach sieben.

Es ist Viertel vor zehn.

Es ist ein Uhr. *or* **Es ist eins.**

Es ist elf (Minuten) nach zehn.

Es ist vierzehn vor acht.

The half hour is counted in German in relation to the following full hour, not the preceding hour as in English.

Es ist halb acht.
(literally) *It is halfway to eight.*

„Wie spät ist es?" (Turmuhr [**tower clock**] und Sonnenuhr in Würzburg)

Einführung

21 Partnerarbeit: Wie spät ist es bitte?

Take turns asking each other for the time.

1   2   3   4   5

Persönliche Fragen *(Personal questions)*

Question Words	
woher?	*from where?* (origin)
wo?	*where?* (location)

When you meet people, you usually want to find out some basic facts about them, such as where they come from. Listen to the following dialogue and repeat it after your instructor.

Woher kommst du? connotes *Where were you born?*

The only American states with separate German names are **Kalifornien** and **Pennsylvanien**, and states beginning with **Nord-** or **Süd-**, as in **Südkarolina.**

A: **Woher kommst du?**	*Where do you come from?*
B: **Ich komme aus Minnesota.**	*I come from Minnesota.*
A: **Wo wohnst du jetzt?**	*Where do you live now?*
B: **Ich wohne jetzt in Kalifornien.**	*I'm living in California now.*

kommen *to come*		**wohnen** *to live*	
ich komme	*I come*	ich wohne	*I live*
du kommst		du wohnst	
Sie kommen	*you come*	Sie wohnen	*you live*
er kommt	*he comes*	er wohnt	*he lives*
sie kommt	*she comes*	sie wohnt	*she lives*

22 Gruppenarbeit: Woher?

Walk around the classroom and find out what cities, states, or foreign countries your classmates are from. Your instructor can help you with the German names of other countries. Then find out where your classmates live, on campus or otherwise.

A: Woher kommst du?
B: Ich komme aus _____ .
A: Wo wohnst du jetzt?
B: Ich wohne in Davis Hall.

Listen to the dialogue and repeat it after your instructor.

A: Wann hast du Geburtstag?

When is your birthday?
(literally: When do you have birthday?)

B: Ich habe im Januar Geburtstag.

My birthday is in January.

Lab Manual
Einführung, The Months.

The stress is on the second syllable in **April** and **Augúst**.

haben	*to have*	
ich	**habe**	*I have*
du	**hast**	*you have*
Sie	**haben**	
er	**hat**	*he has*
sie	**hat**	*she has*

Die Monate (The months)

im Januar	im Juli
im Februar	im August
im März	im September
im April	im Oktober
im Mai	im November
im Juni	im Dezember

23 Kettenreaktion

Find out in what months your classmates were born.

BEISPIEL: A: Wann hast du Geburtstag?

B: Ich habe im _____ Geburtstag. Wann hast *du* Geburtstag?

C: _____ .

Lab Manual
Einführung, The Sounds of German and Useful Classroom Expressions.

This is useful classroom vocabulary. You need not memorize these expressions.

Useful Classroom Expressions

Wie sagt man „the book" auf deutsch?
How do you say "the book" in German?

Man sagt „das Buch".
You say "das Buch."

Übersetzen Sie bitte.
Please translate.

Wiederholen Sie bitte.
Please repeat.

Üben wir!
Let's practice!

Machen Sie Nummer drei, bitte.
Please do number three.

Alle zusammen, bitte.
All together, please.

Sie sprechen zu leise.
You're speaking too softly.

Sprechen Sie bitte lauter.
Please speak more loudly.

Sie sprechen zu schnell.
You're speaking too fast.

Sprechen Sie bitte langsamer.
Please speak more slowly.

Wie bitte?
I beg your pardon? What did you say?

Antworten Sie bitte auf deutsch!
Please answer in German.

Das ist richtig.
That's correct.

Das ist falsch.
That's incorrect.

Verstehen Sie das?
Do you understand that?

Wortschatz

(Vocabulary)

The following list contains all the words and expressions from the **Einführung** that you need to know.

Greetings

Grüß Gott! Hello! (*in southern Germany and Austria*)
Guten Abend! Good evening!
Guten Morgen! Good morning!
Guten Tag! Hello!
Hallo!
Tag! } Hi!

Partings

Auf Wiedersehen! Good-bye!

Bis morgen. Until tomorrow.
Schönes Wochenende! Have a nice weekend!
Danke, gleichfalls! Thanks, same to you!
Tschüs! So long!

Days of the Week

Montag Monday
Dienstag Tuesday
Mittwoch Wednesday
Donnerstag Thursday
Freitag Friday
Samstag / Sonnabend Saturday
Sonntag Sunday

Courtesy Titles

Frau Mrs. / Ms.
Fräulein Miss
Herr Mr.

Question Words

was? what?
wann? when?
wer? who?
wie? how?
wie viele? how many?
wo? where?
woher? from where?

Personal Questions, Feelings, and Emotions

Wie heißen Sie?
Wie heißt du? } What's your name?

Wie geht es dir?
Wie geht es Ihnen? } How are you?

Ich bin guter / schlechter Laune. I'm in a good / bad mood.
Ich bin munter / müde. I'm wide-awake, cheerful / tired.
    fit in good shape.
    krank sick.
    sauer ticked off, sore.

Das freut mich. I'm glad.
Das tut mir leid. I'm sorry.

Time and Place

Wie spät ist es bitte? What time is it please?
Woher kommst du? Where do you come from?
Wann hast du Geburtstag? When is your birthday?

Classroom Words

der Lehrer, die Lehrerin   (school) teacher
der Professor, die Professorin   professor
der Schüler, die Schülerin   pupil, student (*pre-college*)
der Student, die Studentin   (university) student
der Bleistift   pencil
das Buch   book
das Fenster   window
das Heft   notebook
die Kreide   chalk
der Kugelschreiber   ballpoint pen
die Landkarte   map
das Papier   paper
das Poster   poster
der Radiergummi   rubber eraser
der Stuhl   chair
die Tafel   blackboard
der Tisch   table
die Tür   door
die Uhr   clock, watch
die Wand   wall
der Wischer   blackboard eraser

Months of the Year

Januar	**Juli**
Februar	**August**
März	**September**
April	**Oktober**
Mai	**November**
Juni	**Dezember**

The Weather

Wie ist das Wetter heute?	How's the weather today?
Es regnet / schneit.	It's raining / snowing.
Es ist herrlich / furchtbar.	It's great / terrible.
heiß	hot
kalt	cold
kühl	cool
warm	warm
neblig	foggy
sonnig	sunny
windig	windy
wolkig	cloudy

Profile of the Federal Republic of Germany

Area:	357,000 square kilometers; 138,000 square miles
Population:	81 million, or 227 people per square kilometer (586 per square mile)
Currency:	Deutsche Mark; 1 DM = 100 Pfennige
Major Cities:	Berlin (largest city, official capital, pop. 3.5 million); Bonn (pop. 311,000); Munich (pop. 1.3 million); Frankfurt am Main (pop. 629,000); Hamburg (pop. 1.6 million); Cologne (pop. 1 million); Düsseldorf (pop. 577,000); Leipzig (pop. 500,000); Stuttgart (pop. 581,000); Dresden (pop. 481,000)
Religions:	Protestant: 45%; Catholic: 37%; other: 18%

In 1945 the victorious Allies divided defeated Germany into four zones of occupation: American, British, French, and Soviet. Their original intention was to denazify and reunite Germany. But by 1949 the ideological tensions of the Cold War led to the creation of two German states. The Federal Republic of Germany in the West and the German Democratic Republic in the East existed side by side for 41 years. The reunification of 1990 merged one of the most affluent capitalist countries with one of the most prosperous socialist countries from the Eastern bloc. The former GDR was divided into five new states (*Länder*) of the Federal Republic.

Today, the unified nation has an area slightly smaller than Montana. The Federal Republic is the most populous and economically one of the strongest countries in the European Union.

But the revolutionary changes in Germany are still difficult to assess. Forty years of state ownership and lack of competition left eastern Germany's industry obsolete and unable to compete in the Western marketplace. The infrastructure of the former GDR is being modernized and its industry privatized, a process that has caused inflation in the entire country and high rates of unemployment in the former East German workforce. Unification has thus come at a high price to German taxpayers. Germans east and west must continue to make economic sacrifices to resolve their differences and achieve genuine national unity.

NORDSEE

OSTSEE

SCHLESWIG-
HOLSTEIN

Kiel

MECKLENBURG-
VORPOMMERN

HAMBURG
Hamburg

Schwerin

BREMEN
Bremen

BRANDENBURG

NIEDERSACHSEN

Berlin
Potsdam
BERLIN

Hannover

Magdeburg

SACHSEN-ANHALT

NORDRHEIN-
WESTFALEN

Düsseldorf

Dresden

Erfurt

SACHSEN

HESSEN

THÜRINGEN

Wiesbaden
Mainz

RHEINLAND-
PFALZ

SAARLAND
Saarbrücken

Stuttgart

BAYERN

BADEN-
WÜRTTEMBERG

München

0   120 Km.

0   80 Mi.

Wie geht es Ihnen?

Communicative Goals

- Making statements
- Asking yes / no questions
- Asking for information: when, why, who, where, what, etc.

Cultural Goal

- Understanding the social implications of German forms of address

Chapter Outline

Lyrik zum Vorlesen Kinderreime, Zungenbrecher

Grammatik Personal Pronouns • Verbs: Infinitive and Present Tense • Noun Gender and Pronoun Agreement • Noun Plurals • Nominative Case • The Sentence: German Word Order • The Flavoring Particle *ja*

Lesestück Wie sagt man you auf deutsch?

Situationen aus dem Alltag Sie **oder** *du*?

Almanach Where Is German Spoken?

In colloquial German **guten Morgen!**, **auf Wiedersehen!**, and **guten Tag!** are often shortened to **Morgen!**, **Wiedersehen!**, and **Tag!**

In Eile

HERR LEHMANN:	Guten Morgen, Frau Hauser!
FRAU HAUSER:	Morgen, Herr Lehmann. Entschuldigung, aber ich bin in Eile. Ich fliege um elf nach Wien.
HERR LEHMANN:	Wann kommen Sie wieder zurück?
FRAU HAUSER:	Am Mittwoch . . . also dann, auf Wiedersehen!
HERR LEHMANN:	Wiedersehen! Gute Reise!

Die Mensa

KARIN:	Tag, Michael!
MICHAEL:	Hallo, Karin! Wie ist die Suppe heute?
KARIN:	Sie ist ganz gut. . . Übrigens, arbeitest du viel im Moment?
MICHAEL:	Nein, nicht sehr viel. Warum fragst du?
KARIN:	Ich gehe heute abend zu Horst. Du auch?
MICHAEL:	Ja, natürlich.
KARIN:	Prima! Also tschüs, bis dann.

Typisch für September

FRAU BACHMANN:	Guten Tag, Frau Kuhn! Wie geht's?
FRAU KUHN:	Tag, Frau Bachmann! Sehr gut, danke, und Ihnen?
FRAU BACHMANN:	Danke, auch gut. Was machen die Kinder heute?
FRAU KUHN:	Sie spielen draußen, das Wetter ist ja so schön.
FRAU BACHMANN:	Ja, endlich scheint die Sonne. Aber vielleicht regnet es morgen wieder.
FRAU KUHN:	Das ist typisch für September.

„Wie ist die Suppe heute?"

In a Hurry

MR. L.: Good morning, Ms. Hauser.

MS. H.: Morning, Mr. Lehmann. Forgive me, but I'm in a hurry. I'm flying to Vienna at eleven.

MR. L.: When are you coming back again?

MS. H.: On Wednesday. . . . Well then, good-bye.

MR. L.: Bye. Have a good trip!

The University Cafeteria

K.: Hi, Michael!

M.: Hello, Karin! How's the soup today?

K.: It's pretty good. . . . By the way, are you working a lot at the moment?

M.: No, not very much. Why do you ask?

K.: I'm going to Horst's tonight. You too?

M.: Yes, of course.

K.: Great! Well, so long until then.

Typical for September

MRS. B.: Hello, Mrs. Kuhn. How are you?

MRS. K.: Hi, Mrs. Bachmann. Very well, thanks, and you?

MRS. B.: Thanks, I'm fine too. What are the kids doing today?

MRS. K.: They're playing outside—the weather is so nice.

MRS. B.: Yes, the sun is finally shining. But maybe it will rain again tomorrow.

MRS. K.: That is typical for September.

Wortschatz 1

(Vocabulary 1)

Verben *(Verbs)*

arbeiten to work
fliegen to fly
fragen to ask
gehen to go; to walk
kommen to come
machen to make; to do
regnen to rain
scheinen to shine; to seem
sein to be
spielen to play
wohnen to live; to dwell

Substantive *(Nouns)*

der **Herr, -en** gentleman
  Herr Lehmann Mr. Lehmann
der **Morgen**, - morning
der **September** September
der **Tag, -e** day
das **Büro, -s** office
das **Kind, -er** child
das **Wetter** weather
(das) **Wien** Vienna
die **Frau, -en** woman; wife
  Frau Kuhn Mrs./Ms. Kuhn
die **Mensa** university cafeteria
die **Sonne** sun
die **Straße, -n** street, road
die **Suppe, -n** soup

In this book, nouns are grouped by gender for easier learning. Always learn the article and the plural along with the singular of each noun. Don't just learn **Kind** = *child*, but rather **das Kind, die Kinder**.

City names are neuter in German but are seldom used with the article. In such cases, the article is given in parentheses in the **Wortschatz.**

Adjektive und Adverbien *(Adjectives and adverbs)*

auch also, too
da there
dann then
draußen outside
endlich finally
gut good; well
  ganz gut pretty good; pretty well
heute abend this evening, tonight
hier here
morgen tomorrow
natürlich natural(ly); of course
schön beautiful(ly)
sehr very
typisch typical(ly)
vielleicht maybe, perhaps
wieder again

German has no equivalent for the English adverbial ending *-ly.* For example, the German word **natürlich** can mean both *natural* and *naturally* (similarly, **gut** means both *good* and *well*).

Andere Vokabeln *(Other words)*

aber but
also well
bis until; by

bis dann until then; by then
danke thanks
für for
in in
ja yes; *untranslatable "flavoring particle," see pp. 39–40.*
nach to (*with cities and countries*)
nein no
nicht not
übrigens by the way
um (*prep.*) at (*with expressions of time*)
und (*conj.*) and
usw. (= **und so weiter**) etc. (= and so forth)
viel (*pron.*) much, a lot
warum? why?
wie (*conj.*) how; like, as

zu (*prep.*) to (*with people*); too (*as in* "too much")
zurück back

There is a complete list of abbreviations on p. 495.

Nützliche Ausdrücke
(Useful expressions)

am Mittwoch (Donnerstag usw.) on Wednesday (Thursday, etc.)
Entschuldigung! Pardon me! Excuse me!
Gute Reise! (Have a) good trip!
im Moment at the moment
in Eile in a hurry
Prima! Terrific! Great!

Gegensätze (Opposites)

gut ≠ schlecht good ≠ bad
hier ≠ da here ≠ there
schön ≠ häßlich beautiful ≠ ugly
der Tag ≠ die Nacht day ≠ night
viel ≠ wenig much, a lot ≠ not much, little

Study hint: learn antonyms in pairs. They are all active vocabulary.

Mit anderen Worten
(In other words)

prima = sehr gut
wunderschön = sehr schön

Variationen (Variations)

A **Persönliche Fragen** (Personal questions)

1. Wo wohnen Sie?
2. Wie geht es Ihnen heute?
3. Arbeiten Sie viel im Moment?
4. Was machen Sie heute abend?

B **Partnerarbeit** (Work with a partner)

Asking for information is a communicative goal.

Now ask each other the same questions as in **Variation A**. Use the **du**-form.

Partnerarbeit: Wann fliegst du?

The clock faces show departure times from the Frankfurt airport. Ask each other when you're flying to various places.

> BEISPIEL: Wann fliegst du nach Sydney?
> Ich fliege um halb acht.

1. nach Prag

2. nach Moskau

3. nach Kopenhagen

4. nach Madrid

5. nach Toronto

6. nach Singapur

D Übung *(Exercise)*

Respond to these greetings and farewells.

1. Guten Morgen!
2. Wie geht es Ihnen?
3. Guten Tag!
4. Auf Wiedersehen!
5. Gute Reise!
6. Tschüs, bis dann.
7. Tag!
8. Hallo!
9. Schönes Wochenende!

E Übung: Und Sie?

To each question, respond that you feel the same way.

> BEISPIEL: Richard ist heute guter Laune. Und Sie?
> Ja, *er* ist guter Laune, und *ich* bin es auch.

1. Maria ist fit. Und Sie?
2. Herr Schrödinger ist krank. Und Sie?
3. Frau Bachmann ist munter. Und Sie?
4. Christian ist guter Laune. Und Sie?
5. Wir sind schlechter Laune. Und Sie?
6. Ich bin heute sauer. Und Sie?

In each chapter this section presents some short selections of original German poetry (**Lyrik**), rhymes, or song texts for your enjoyment. Read them aloud. Don't worry about understanding everything. The emphasis here is on the *sound* of German.

Kinderreime *(Children's rhymes)*

Traditional Counting-out Rhymes

Eins zwei drei,	
du bist frei.°	free
Vier fünf sechs,	
du bist weg.°	out
Sieben acht neun,	
du mußt's sein.°	you are it

Ich heiße Peter, du heißt Paul.	
Ich bin fleißig,° du bist faul.°	hard-working/lazy

Children's Alphabet Rhyme

A b c d e f und g,	
h i j k l m n o p,	
q r s t u v w,	
x y z und o weh,°	**o weh** = oh my
jetzt kann ich das ABC.°	now I know the ABC

Zungenbrecher°

Tongue twisters

In Ulm, um Ulm°	In Ulm, around Ulm,
und um Ulm herum.°	and round about Ulm.

Fischers Fritz fischt frische Fische,	Fischer's (boy) Fritz fishes fresh fish,
frische Fische fischt Fischers Fritz.°	Fresh fish is what Fischer's Fritz fishes.

Ulm lies on the Danube River in the southern state of Baden-Württemberg. Its famous Gothic church has the highest spire in the world at 161.6 meters.

Grammatik

(Grammar)

Personal Pronouns

Personal pronouns as the subject of a sentence:

	Singular		Plural	
1st person	ich	*I*	wir	*we*
2nd person	du	*you* (familiar)	ihr	*you* (familiar)
	Sie	*you* (formal)	Sie	*you* (formal)
3rd person	er	*he, it*		
	es	*it*	sie	*they*
	sie	*she, it*		

Understanding the social implications of German forms of address is the cultural goal of this chapter.

The Three Ways to Say *You* in German

German has three words for the subject pronoun *you:* **du, ihr,** and **Sie.**

The familiar pronouns **du** (*singular*) and **ihr** (*plural*) are used when addressing children, family members, close friends, animals, and the deity. Members of certain groups (students, blue-collar workers, soldiers, athletes) converse among themselves almost exclusively with **du** and **ihr.** People on a first-name basis usually use **du** with each other. In conversation with German speakers, allow them to establish which form is used.

The formal **Sie** is used when addressing one or more adults who are not close friends of the speaker. In writing, **Sie** meaning *you* is distinguished from **sie** meaning *they* by always beginning with a capital letter.

The pronoun **ich** is not capitalized except when it is the first word in a sentence.

„Tag, Frau Breitenkamp! Wie geht es Ihnen?"

The Infinitive

German verbs are found in a dictionary in the infinitive form. In English the infinitive is usually preceded by *to*.

> *to play*   *to hike*

In German, the infinitive consists of the verb stem plus the ending **-en** or **-n**.

spiel-	**spielen**	*to play*
wander-	**wandern**	*to hike*

Present Tense Endings

A German verb has various endings in the present tense, depending on its subject.

Das Kind spiel**t** draußen.	*The child plays outside.*
Die Kinder spiel**en** draußen.	*The children play outside.*

In order to form the present tense of a German verb, first find the stem by dropping the infinitive ending **-en** or **-n**:

> komm- ~~en~~

Then add the personal endings:

Stem + Ending			Present Tense		
ich	komm- **e**		ich	komme	*I come*
du	komm- **st**		du	kommst	*you come*
Sie	komm- **en**		Sie	kommen	
er/es/sie	komm- **t**		er/es/sie	kommt	*he, it, she comes*
wir	komm- **en**		wir	kommen	*we come*
ihr	komm- **t**		ihr	kommt	*you come*
Sie	komm- **en**		Sie	kommen	
sie	komm- **en**		sie	kommen	*they come*

The verb ending will help you distinguish between **sie** = *she* (**sie kommt**) and **Sie/sie** = *you/they* (**Sie/sie kommen**). The verb ending for third-person plural and the polite *you*-form is always the same. From now on they will be listed together in verb paradigms: **sie, Sie kommen**.

Prima leben und sparen

Lab Manual Kap. 1, Üb. 1, 3; Var. (Variationen) zur Üb. 1, 3.

Workbook Kap. 1, A, B.

1 Übung: Wer kommt morgen?

Say who is coming tomorrow, using the pronouns cued.

> BEISPIEL: ich
> Ich komme morgen.

1. er
2. Sie (*you*)
3. wir
4. sie (*they*)
5. sie (*she*)
6. du
7. ich
8. ihr

2 Kettenreaktion: Wo wohnst du?

Say where you live and then ask the next student.

> BEISPIEL: Ich wohne in Atlanta. Wo wohnst du?
> Ich wohne in _____ .

Regular Variations in Personal Endings

Verbs with stems ending in **-d, -t,** or a consonant cluster such as **-gn** require an **-e-** before the **du, er,** and **ihr** endings to make them pronounceable.

arbeiten	stem: **arbeit-**			regnen	stem: **regn-**
ich	arbeite	wir	arbeiten		
du	arbeit**est**	ihr	arbeit**et**		es regnet
er/es/sie	arbeit**et**	sie, Sie	arbeiten		

3 Übung: Wer arbeitet heute?

Tell who is working today, using the cued pronoun or name.

> BEISPIEL: wir
> Wir arbeiten heute.

1. ich
2. Herr Lehmann
3. sie (*they*)
4. du
5. ihr
6. Sie (*you*)
7. wir
8. Michael

4 Gruppenarbeit: Was machst du heute? (*4 Studenten*)

Ask each other what you're doing today.

> A: Was machst du heute, Katrin?
> B: Ich fliege nach Wien. Was machst *du* heute?
> C: Ich _____ . Was machst du heute?

English and German Present Tense Compared

German present tense is equivalent to three English forms:

ich gehe $\begin{cases} \textit{I go} \\ \textit{I am going} \\ \textit{I do go} \end{cases}$

Present Tense with Future Meaning

In German the present tense often expresses future meaning, especially when another element in the sentence makes the future meaning clear.

Ich fliege um elf nach Wien.	*I'm flying to Vienna at eleven.*
Mittwoch bin ich wieder zurück.	*I'll be back Wednesday.*

Note that English often uses the present progressive (*I'm flying*) for the same purpose.

The Verb *sein*

Like *to be* in English, the verb **sein** is irregular; its forms must be memorized.

ich	**bin**	*I am*	wir	**sind**	*we are*
du	**bist**	*you are*	ihr	**seid**	*you are*
er/es/sie	**ist**	*he, it, she is*	sie, Sie	**sind**	*they, you are*

Noun Gender and Pronoun Agreement

You have learned that German has three genders for nouns, shown by the definite article (**der, das, die**). When a pronoun replaces a noun *(the chair = it)*, it must have the same gender.

Wo ist **der** Stuhl?	**Er** ist hier.	*It's here.*
Wo ist **das** Buch?	**Es** ist hier.	*It's here.*
Wo ist **die** Tafel?	**Sie** ist hier.	*It's here.*

Note that **er, es,** and **sie** can all mean *it*.

Note also the similarities between the definite article and its corresponding pronoun.

der Stuhl → **er**
das Buch → **es**
die Tafel → **sie**

Plural forms do not show gender. The definite article **die** is used with all plural nouns, and the pronoun **sie** replaces all plural nouns.

Wo sind **die** Stühle?		
Wo sind **die** Bücher?	**Sie** sind hier.	*They are here.*
Wo sind **die** Tafeln?		

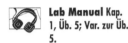
5 Übung

Answer the questions affirmatively. Use a pronoun.

> BEISPIEL: Ist Rolf heute guter Laune?
> Ja, er ist heute guter Laune.

1. Ist das Buch gut?
2. Ist Frau Schmidt sehr müde?
3. Spielen die Kinder draußen?
4. Ist das Wetter typisch für September?
5. Scheint die Sonne heute?
6. Sind Karin und Michael Studenten?
7. Ist die Suppe gut?
8. Ist der Tag schön?

6 Partnerarbeit: Hier oder da?

Partner A asks where the things in the left-hand column are. Partner B answers with the correct pronoun, pointing to the object. Reverse roles for the right-hand column.

> BEISPIEL: A: Wo ist die Tafel?
> B: Sie ist da.

das Buch	der Radiergummi
das Heft	das Fenster
die Tür	der Professor/die Professorin
der Bleistift	der Tisch
die Wand	der Stuhl
die Landkarte	das Poster

Here are the nouns you learned in the **Einführung** with their plurals:

der Lehrer, - / die Lehrerin, -nen
der Professor, -en / die Professorin, -nen
der Schüler, - / die Schülerin, -nen
der Student, -en / die Studentin, -nen
der Bleistift, -e
das Buch, ¨er
das Fenster, -
das Heft, -e
der Kugelschreiber, -
das Poster, -
der Stuhl, ¨e
die Tafel, -n
der Tisch, -e
die Tür, -en
die Uhr, -en
die Wand, ¨e

Noun Plurals

The most common plural ending for English nouns is *-s* or *-es*: chair, chairs; dish, dishes. Some nouns have irregular plurals: man, *men*; mouse, *mice*; child, *children*; sheep, *sheep*.

German has a much greater variety of plural forms. There is no one basic rule, nor is any one form the most common. The following list gives examples of all the plural forms.

	singular	*plural*
No change	der Lehrer	die Lehrer
Umlaut added to stem vowel	die Mutter	die Mütter
Add ending **-e**	der Tisch	die Tische
Umlaut + ending **-e**	der Stuhl	die Stühle
Add ending **-er**	das Kind	die Kinder
Umlaut + ending **-er**	das Buch	die Bücher
Add ending **-en**	die Frau	die Frauen
Add ending **-n**	die Straße	die Straßen
Add ending **-s**	das Büro	die Büros

Dictionaries and vocabulary lists customarily use an abbreviation to indicate the plural. An umlaut above the hyphen indicates that the stem (stressed) vowel is umlauted in the plural.

Dictionary Entry	You Must Learn
der **Lehrer, -**	der **Lehrer**, die **Lehrer**
die **Mutter, ̈**	die **Mutter**, die **Mütter**
der **Tag, -e**	der **Tag**, die **Tage**
der **Stuhl, ̈e**	der **Stuhl**, die **Stühle**

Lab Manual Kap. 1, Üb. 7, 8.

Workbook Kap. 1, E.

Turn to the German–English glossary at end of book, pp. 495–537, for more practice with plurals.

7 Übung

Look at the following nouns and say aloud both the singular and plural forms with their articles.

1. das Kind, -er
2. das Büro, -s
3. der Tisch, -e
4. die Mutter, ̈

5. die Tafel, -n
6. die Straße, -n
7. der Stuhl, ̈e
8. die Frau, -en

8 Übung

Make the subjects plural. Change the verbs accordingly.

BEISPIEL: *Der Herr kommt um elf.*
Die Herren kommen um elf.

1. Das Büro ist sehr schön.
2. Die Frau fliegt nach Wien.
3. Das Kind kommt heute abend.
4. Die Straße ist sehr schön.

5. Das Buch ist gut.
6. Der Lehrer arbeitet morgen im Büro.

The definite article in German, unlike English *the*, shows the *gender* (masculine, neuter, or feminine), *number* (singular or plural), and *case* of the noun it is used with. As a result, German has many forms that all correspond to *the* in English.

Nominative Case

The case of a noun or a pronoun signals its function in the sentence. German has four cases: nominative, accusative, dative, and genitive. The article used with the noun shows its case.

Der Schüler fragt den Lehrer.   *The pupil asks the teacher.*
Der Lehrer fragt **den** Schüler.   *The teacher asks the pupil.*

Nominative Case		*Accusative Case*
der Schüler		**den** Schüler
subject	vs.	direct object
person asking		person being asked

This chapter uses only the nominative case, which is the case for the subject of a sentence and for a predicate nominative (see page 36).

Definite Article in the Nominative Case

You have already learned the definite articles (*the*) in the nominative:

	Singular	*Plural*
masculine	**der** Mann	**die** Männer
neuter	**das** Kind	**die** Kinder
feminine	**die** Frau	**die** Frauen

Indefinite Article in the Nominative Case

Like the definite article, the indefinite article (*a, an*) shows the gender, number, and case of the noun it is used with. Here are the indefinite articles in the nominative:

	Singular	*Plural*
masculine	**ein** Mann	Männer
neuter	**ein** Kind	Kinder
feminine	**eine** Frau	Frauen

Note: Masculine and neuter singular indefinite articles are identical in the nominative: **ein** Mann, **ein** Kind. The indefinite article has no plural:

Ein Kind ist hier. → Kinder sind hier.

The personal pronouns you have learned in this chapter (**ich, du**, etc.) are all in the nominative case.

9 Übung: Was ist das?

Say what your instructor is pointing to. Use the indefinite article.

> BEISPIEL: PROFESSORIN: Was ist das?
> STUDENTIN: Das ist **ein** Fenster.

Use of the Nominative Case

The subject of the sentence is always in the nominative case. Notice that the subject does not have to come at the beginning of the sentence.

Der Herr ist in Eile.	*The gentleman is in a hurry.*
Endlich kommt **die Suppe.**	*The soup is finally coming.*
Morgen fliegt **sie** zurück.	*She's flying back tomorrow.*

Other linking verbs (**bleiben** *to remain*; **heißen** *to be called*; **werden** *to become*) also take the predicate nominative. You will learn them later.

A predicate nominative is a noun that refers to the same person or thing as the subject of the sentence. It follows the subject and the linking verb **sein**.

| Das ist **Frau Schmidt.** | *That is Mrs. Schmidt.* |
| Paul ist **ein Kind.** | *Paul is a child.* |

Remember to always use nominative case after the verb **sein**.

Lab Manual Kap. 1, Var. zur Üb. 10.

Workbook Kap. 1, F.

10 Gruppenspiel *(Group game)*: Was ist das? Wer ist das?

One student leads the game. The rest are divided into two teams. The leader points to an object or a person in the room and asks:

> Wer / Was ist das?
> Das ist ein(e)/der/das/die _____ .

Teams answer alternately. The team with the most correct answers wins.

The Sentence: German Word Order

Making statements is a communicative goal.

Statements: Verb-Second Word Order

In declarative sentences (statements) in English, the subject almost always comes immediately before the verb phrase.

> *subject verb*
> **We are going** to Richard's tonight.

Other elements may precede the subject-verb combination:

> Tonight **we are going** to Richard's.

In German statements, only the verb has a fixed position. *The verb is always the second element.*

> *1*   *2*   *3*   *4*
> Wir   **gehen**   heute abend   zu Richard.

This is an ironclad rule that must be learned well. If an element other than the subject begins the sentence, the verb *remains* in second position and the subject then *follows* the verb. Note the difference from English, where the subject always precedes the verb.

> *1*   *2*   *3*   *4*
> Heute abend   **gehen**   wir   zu Richard.
> Zu Richard   **gehen**   wir   heute abend.

A time phrase (**heute abend**) or a prepositional phrase (**zu Richard**) may consist of two or more words, but counts as *one* grammatical element.
Initial **ja**, **nein**, **und**, and **aber** do *not* count as first elements.

> *0*   *1*   *2*   *3*
> Ja,   wir   gehen   zu Richard.
> Aber   wir   gehen   zu Richard.

First position is generally used to restate what's being talked about. A new element with information value—the answer to a question, for instance—is usually placed at the end of the statement.

Was machen wir?	Wir gehen **zu Claudia**.
Was machen wir heute abend?	Heute abend **gehen wir zu Claudia**.
Wann gehen wir zu Claudia?	Zu Claudia gehen wir **heute abend**.

Wie geht es Ihnen?   **37**

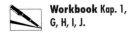

Workbook Kap. 1, G, H, I, J.

11 Übung

Restate the sentences, beginning with the word or phrase in italics.

> BEISPIEL: Ich arbeite *übrigens* viel.
> *Übrigens* arbeite ich viel.

1. Die Lehrerin geht *morgen* zu Frau Bachmann.
2. Die Sonne scheint *endlich* wieder.
3. Es regnet *heute*.

4. Wir fliegen *um elf* nach Wien.
5. Das ist *vielleicht* die Straße.
6. Ich arbeite viel *im Moment*.
7. Die Suppe ist *heute* ganz gut.
8. Es regnet *natürlich* viel.

Questions

Asking yes/no questions and asking for information are communicative goals.

There are two main types of questions in German:

- Yes/no questions are answered by **ja** or **nein**. In a yes/no question, the verb is always the first element.

Ist Andrea hier?	*Is Andrea here?*
Arbeitet sie in Berlin?	*Does she work in Berlin?*
Kommst du wieder zurück?	*Are you coming back again?*

- Questions asking for information start with a question word (*what, how, when*, etc.) and have the same verb-second word order as statements.

1	*2*		
Was	macht	er?	*What is he doing?*
Wie	geht	es Ihnen?	*How are you?*
Wann	kommen	Sie wieder zurück?	*When are you coming back again?*

Here are some question words:

wann	*when*	**Wann** kommt sie zurück?
warum	*why*	**Warum** fragst du?
was	*what*	**Was** macht er?
wer	*who*	**Wer** ist das?
wie	*how*	**Wie** geht es dir?
wo	*where*	**Wo** wohnen Sie?
woher	*from where*	**Woher** kommt ihr?

Do not confuse **wer** (*who*) and **wo** (*where*)!

Lab Manual Kap. 1, Üb. 12.

Workbook Kap. 1, H, I, J.

12 Übung

Change these statements to yes/no questions.

> BEISPIEL: Stefan arbeitet in Stuttgart.
> Arbeitet Stefan in Stuttgart?

1. Das ist typisch für September.
2. Ihr geht wieder zu Karin.
3. Es regnet.
4. Herr Hauser fliegt nach Berlin.
5. Frau Kuhn kommt auch.
6. Du arbeitest viel im Moment.
7. Er ist sehr in Eile.
8. Der Herr kommt am Mittwoch zurück.

13 Übung

Ask the questions for which the following statements are answers:

> BEISPIEL: Das ist der Professor.
> Wer ist das?

1. Er fliegt um elf.
2. Die Lehrer sind im Büro.
3. Das ist Frau Bachmann.
4. Das ist die Mensa.
5. Die Suppe ist gut, danke.
6. Sie kommt aus Deutschland.

Time before Place

In German, adverbs like **heute** and adverbial phrases like **nach Wien** *must* come in the sequence *time before place*. The usual sequence in English is exactly the reverse: *place before time.*

	time	*place*
Sie fliegt	morgen	nach Wien.
Wir gehen	heute abend	zu Horst.

	place	*time*
She's flying	*to Vienna*	*tomorrow.*
We're going	*to Horst's*	*tonight.*

14 Übung: Heute oder morgen?

Answer with a complete sentence, using either **heute** or **morgen**.

> BEISPIEL: Wann gehen Sie zu Stefanie?
> Ich gehe heute zu Stefanie.

1. Wann fliegt Stefan nach Wien?
2. Wann geht Frau Bachmann zu Frau Kuhn?
3. Wann spielen die Kinder draußen?
4. Wann kommt Herr Lehmann zurück?

The Flavoring Particle *ja*

German adds various kinds of emphasis to sentences by using intensifying words known as "flavoring particles." These can seldom be directly translated into English, but it is important to become familiar with them and understand the intensity, nuance, or "flavor" they add to a sentence.

One flavoring particle frequently used in declarative sentences (i.e., statements) is **ja**. As a flavoring particle, **ja** does not mean *yes,* but rather adds the sense of *after all, really.*

In the third dialogue at the beginning of this chapter, Frau Kuhn says about her children:

Sie spielen draußen, das Wetter ist **ja** so schön.

They're playing outside—the weather really is so beautiful.

The flavoring particle **ja** is usually placed immediately after the verb and personal pronouns. Here is how **ja** might be added to some other sentences from the dialogues:

Ich bin **ja** in Eile.
Ich gehe **ja** heute abend zu Horst.

I'm in a hurry, after all.
I'm going to Horst's tonight, you know.

Wie sagt man *you* auf deutsch?

Tips zum Lesen und Lernen *(Tips for reading and studying)*

Tips zum Vokabelnlernen *(Tips for learning vocabulary)*

The feminine suffix *-in*   You've learned that German has two different nouns to distinguish between a male and a female.

Professor/Professorin   Lehrer/Lehrerin
Schüler/Schülerin   Partner/Partnerin
Student/Studentin

The suffix **-in** always denotes the female, and its plural is always **-innen.**

-in
die Studentin

-innen
die Studentinnen

Partnerarbeit: Wie heißt der Mann, wie heißt die Frau?

With a partner, fill in the blanks. Say the words aloud as you write them.

Mann	eine Frau?	zwei Frauen?
1. Amerikaner	*Amerikanerin*	*Amerikanerinnen*
2. Tourist	_____	_____
3. Nachbar (*neighbor*)	_____	_____
4. Lehrer	_____	_____
5. Professor	_____	_____
6. Schüler	_____	_____
7. Student	_____	_____
8. Partner	_____	_____

Note the stress shift:
Profes'sor / Professo'rin.

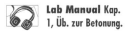

Lab Manual Kap. 1, Üb. zur Betonung.

Leicht zu merken (Easy to remember)

German has many words that look so much like their English equivalents that you can easily guess their meanings. Both languages have borrowed many of these words from Latin or French. When such words occur in the readings, they are previewed in this special section called **Leicht zu merken**. If the German word is stressed on a different syllable than the English, this will be indicated to the right. You should have no trouble guessing the meanings of these cognates:

formell	for<u>mell</u>
die **Solidarität**	Solidari<u>tät</u>
der **Tourist**	Tou<u>rist</u>

These pre-reading exercises help you to acquire the skill of reading a text in a foreign language. Always work through them carefully before beginning to read the **Lesestück**. The most valuable technique is *re*-reading a foreign language text as many times as possible.

Einstieg in den Text (Getting into the text)

Here are some tips to help you get the most out of the reading (**Lesestück**) in each chapter.

- Read the title. How does it anticipate the text? The title „Wie sagt man *you* auf deutsch?," for example, lets you know that the text is about the various forms of second-person address. You have already used these.

- Read out loud the new active vocabulary for the reading (**Wortschatz 2**). Try to identify similarities between English and German forms that will help you remember the words; for example, **grüßen** (*greet*), **Haus** (*house*), **Gruppe** (*group*); **freundlich** (*friendly*), **oft** (*often*).

- Read the text once aloud without referring back to the vocabulary. Do not try to translate as you read. Your purpose is to get a rough idea of content from the key words you recognize in each paragraph. For example, in the first paragraph of the following reading, you will recognize the words **Touristen**, **Deutschland**, and **Amerikaner**. A good working assumption is that the paragraph deals with tourists in Germany—perhaps American tourists.

- Once you have a general idea of the content of each paragraph, read the text at least one more time, again without trying to translate. Your object this time is to begin to understand the text on the sentence level.

The marginal glosses (marked by the degree sign°) will help you to understand words and phrases not for active use.

- Read and try to answer the content questions (**Fragen zum Lesestück**). Refer back to the text only if necessary.

Wortschatz 2

Verben

bedeuten   to mean, signify
   Was bedeutet das?   What does that mean?
grüßen   to greet, say hello
meinen   to be of the opinion, think
sagen   to say; to tell
(stimmen) das stimmt   that's right, that's true
studieren   to attend a university; to study (*a subject*); to major in

Substantive

der **Amerikaner, -**   American (*m.*)
der **Deutsche, -n**   German (*m.*)
der **Schüler, -**   primary or secondary school pupil (*m.*)
der **Student, -en**   university student (*m.*)

Note the abbreviations *m.* (for *masculine*) or *f.* (for *feminine*) after **Amerikaner**, **Deutsche**, and other nouns. There is a complete list of abbreviations on p. 495.

der **Tourist, -en**   tourist (*m.*)
(das) **Deutschland**   Germany
das **Haus, ̈er**   house
die **Amerikanerin, -nen**   American (*f.*)
die **Deutsche, -n**   German (*f.*)
die **Gruppe, -n**   group
die **Klasse, -n**   class; grade
die **Schülerin, -nen**   primary or secondary school pupil (*f.*)
die **Studentin, -nen**   university student (*f.*)
die **Touristin, -nen**   tourist (*f.*)

Note the plural form of **Haus—Häuser**: the first vowel of a diphthong is umlauted.

Adjektive und Adverbien

freundlich   friendly
höflich   polite(ly)
immer   always
oft   often
so   so; like this
viele   many
wahrscheinlich   probably
ziemlich   fairly, quite

Andere Vokabeln

einander (*pron.*)   each other
man   one (*indefinite pronoun*)
miteinander   with each other
oder (*conj.*)   or

Note on **man**: This pronoun is often best translated with *we*, *you*, or *they*: **Das sagt man oft.** = *They (people) often say that.* See p. 89 for a complete explanation.

Nützliche Ausdrücke

zum Beispiel   for example
auf deutsch   in German

Gegensätze

immer ≠ nie   always ≠ never
oft ≠ selten   often ≠ seldom

Wie sagt man *you* auf deutsch?

 Lab Manual Kap. 1, Lesestück.

Touristen in Deutschland sagen oft, die Deutschen sind sehr freundlich und höflich. Das stimmt, aber wahrscheinlich meinen viele Amerikaner auch, die Deutschen sind ziemlich formell.

Frau Bachmann und Frau Kuhn sind zum Beispiel Nachbarinnen.°   *neighbors*
5 Sie wohnen im selben° Haus und sind auch miteinander befreundet,°   **im selben** = *in the same* / *on* aber Frau Bachmann fragt nicht: „Wie geht es dir, Gisela?" Nein, sie   *friendly terms* sagt: „Wie geht es Ihnen, Frau Kuhn?" Sie grüßen einander formell.

Die Lehrer duzen° die Schüler von Klasse eins bis Klasse zehn.   *address with* **du** Aber ab° Klasse elf sagen sie „Sie". Die Schüler siezen° die Lehrer   *beginning in* / *address with* **Sie** 10 natürlich immer.

Das „Du" ist auch ein Ausdruck der° Solidarität. Für die Studen-   **Ausdruck der** = *expression of* ten bedeutet es: Wir sind eine Gruppe. Karin und Michael, zum Beispiel, studieren.[1] Sie sagen von Anfang an° „du" zueinander.   **von . . .** = *from the beginning*

Fragen zum Lesestück *(Questions on the reading)*

1. Wer meint, die Deutschen sind ziemlich formell?
2. Was sagt Frau Bachmann zu Frau Kuhn?
3. Sagen Lehrer und Schüler „du"?
4. Was sind Karin und Michael?
5. Sagen Karin und Michael „Sie"?
6. Was bedeutet das „Du" für Studenten?

Diese Studenten sagen „du" zueinander.

---

[1]Note that **studieren** means to attend college or university and is not used to describe a student's daily activity of studying. Thus, *I'm studying* (i.e., doing homework) *tonight* is translated as **Ich *arbeite* heute abend,** or **Ich *lerne* heute abend.**

Partnerarbeit: *Sie* oder *du*?

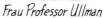

Frau Professor Ullman   Herr Kuhn   Karoline und Dieter Flessner   Niklas Schuhmacher

1. Take turns asking the people pictured
   a. what their names are.
   b. whether they're working at the moment.
   c. whether they're tired today.
   d. where they live.
   e. where they work.

2. Partner A plays one of the people pictured above and responds to Partner B's questions. Then Partner B plays another of these people and answers Partner A's questions.

   BEISPIEL: A: Wo wohnen Sie, Herr Kuhn?
                  B: Ich wohne in Wien.

3. Now ask each other three personalized questions using the **du**-form.

Zum Schluß

(In conclusion)

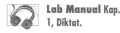

Lab Manual Kap. 1, Diktat.

Sprechen wir miteinander! *(Let's talk together!)*

A   Partnerarbeit: Ist es wahrscheinlich?

Partner A uses the cues to ask questions. Partner B responds, beginning with one of the three adverbs in the right-hand column.

BEISPIEL: fliegen / Berlin?

       A: Fliegst du nach Berlin?
       B: Vielleicht fliege ich nach Berlin.

Partner A	*Partner B*
gehen / zu Marion?	Natürlich . . .
studieren / in Konstanz?	Wahrscheinlich . . .
arbeiten / im Moment?	Vielleicht . . .
kommen / zurück?	
wohnen / hier?	
fliegen / nach Leipzig?	

Review the days of the week together as a class. Then use the cues below to ask each other questions. Your partner answers with any day of the week, beginning the sentence with **Am . . .**

BEISPIEL: wann / kommen / zurück?
PARTNER A: Wann kommst du zurück?
PARTNER B: Am Dienstag komme ich zurück.

1. wann / arbeiten?
2. wann / haben / Deutsch?
3. wann / gehen / zu Gisela?
4. wann / fliegen / nach Hamburg?
5. wann / kommen / zurück?
6. wann / spielen / Tennis?

C **Partnerarbeit: Seid ihr auch so?**

With your partner, look at the following adjectives you can use to describe your personality. You shouldn't have trouble understanding them, because they all have English cognates. Ask each other questions to find out which of these characteristics you have in common. Make a list of three or four characteristics you share.

BEISPIEL: Ich bin sehr emotional. Bist du auch emotional?
Ja, ich bin (immer / oft / ziemlich / sehr) emotional.
or: Nein, ich bin (selten / nicht / nie) emotional.

emotional	modern	kreativ	konservativ
sentimental	aktiv	dynamisch	objektiv
subjektiv	kompetent	progressiv	optimistisch
pessimistisch	naiv	athletisch	exzentrisch
intelligent	clever		

D **Gruppenarbeit**

Now go with your partner to another pair of students and ask questions to find out how they describe themselves. Use the words listed in exercise C.

BEISPIEL: GRUPPE A: Seid ihr auch emotional?
GRUPPE B: Nein, wir sind nicht emotional, wir sind . . . Und ihr?

E **Übung: Wie ist das Wetter im Januar? Was machen Sie am Montag?**

Answer the following questions. The lists of vocabulary will give you some ideas.

BEISPIEL: Wie ist das Wetter im Januar?   Was machen Sie am Montag?
Es ist kalt. / Es schneit viel.   Ich arbeite mit Karl.

1. Wie ist das Wetter im _____ ?

schön	kalt	herrlich	heiß	kühl
windig	sonnig	neblig	wolkig	

2. Was machen Sie am _____?

arbeiten	fliegen	spielen	gehen

Schreiben Sie zu Hause *(Write at home)*

F **Zwei Studenten im Gespräch** *(Two students in conversation)* Write a dialogue using the following cues. You will need to provide verb endings, correct word order, etc.

> ULLI: Tag / Dieter! du / arbeiten / morgen?
> DIETER: Nein. warum / du / fragen?
> ULLI: morgen / wir / gehen / zu Hans. du / kommen / auch?
> DIETER: natürlich / ich / kommen

G **Was machst du?** Answer each question according to the cue in English. Answer appropriately for the way you're addressed (**Was machst du? Ich fliege . . . Was macht ihr? Wir fliegen . . .**)

> BEISPIEL: Was machst du morgen? *(flying to Vienna)*
> Ich fliege morgen nach Wien.

1. Was macht ihr heute? *(going to Stefan's)*
2. Was machst du im Moment, Richard? *(working a lot)*
3. Was machen Sie, Frau Gruber? *(attending the university)*
4. Was machst du, Regina? *(playing outside)*
5. Was macht ihr am Mittwoch, Rolf und Helene? *(flying to Hamburg)*
6. Was machen Sie, Frau Bachmann? *(greeting Mrs. Kuhn)*

H **Antworten Sie bitte auf deutsch!** *(Please answer in German.)* Answer the yes/no questions affirmatively and with complete sentences.

1. Was machst du heute abend?
2. Bist du in Eile?
3. Fliegt der Professor nach New York?
4. Wer wohnt hier?
5. Regnet es wieder?
6. Was machen wir im Moment?
7. Arbeitest du vielleicht morgen?
8. Ist das typisch?

I **Wie sagt man das auf deutsch?**

1. When are you coming back, Jürgen and Katrin?
2. We are coming back tomorrow.

3. Excuse me, are you in a hurry?
4. Yes, I'm going to Helene's.

5. She says the Germans are friendly.
6. Yes, that's right.

7. How are you, Herr Beck?
8. Fine thanks, and you?

9. The sun is shining again.
10. Good! We'll work outside.

Where is German spoken?

German is the language of the Federal Republic of Germany, Austria, Liechtenstein, and portions of Switzerland, Luxembourg, the South Tirol in northern Italy (until 1919 part of Austria), and Belgium. Linguistic enclaves of German speakers in the U.S.A. (notably the Amish in Pennsylvania), Canada, Brazil, Africa (especially in Namibia, once the German colony of South West Africa), and Australia bring the number of native German speakers to around 121 million. In 1993, 20 million people were studying German as a second language. Of these, 13 million were eastern Europeans.

The following statistics on the world's major languages include both native and second-language speakers in 1994. Notice that the names of almost all languages in German end with **-sch.**

Chinesisch	1 Milliarde 18 Millionen
Englisch	470 Millionen
Hindustani	418 Millionen
Spanisch	381 Millionen
Russisch	288 Millionen
Arabisch	219 Millionen
Portugiesisch	182 Millionen
Japanisch	126 Millionen
Französisch	124 Millionen
Deutsch	121 Millionen
Italienisch	63 Millionen

eine Milliarde = (American) *billion;* **eine Billion** = (American) *trillion.*

Familie und Freunde

Communicative Goals

- Talking about the family
- Saying what belongs to whom
- Counting above 20

Cultural Goal

- Learning about German family life

Lab Manual Kap. 2, Dialoge, Fragen, Hören Sie gut zu!, Üb. zur Aussprache [z / s].

Wer liest die Zeitung?

Viste (handwritten)

VATER: Kurt, ich suche meine Zeitung. Weißt du, wo sie ist?
zuhe (handwritten)

SOHN: Deine Zeitung? Ich lese sie im Moment.

VATER: Was liest du denn?

SOHN: Ich lese einen Artikel über unsere Schule.

Ich hab' eine Frage

ANNETTE: Katrin, ich hab' eine Frage. Kennst du den Mann da drüben?

KATRIN: Wen meinst du denn?

ANNETTE: Er spricht mit Stefan. Ich sehe, er kennt dich.

KATRIN: Natürlich kenn' ich ihn—das ist mein Bruder Max!

ANNETTE: Ach, du hast auch einen Bruder! Ich kenne nur deine Schwester.

Listen carefully to the tapes and your instructor for the difference in the pronunciation of **denn** (short vowel) and **den** (long vowel).

Georg sucht ein Zimmer

The video screen icon signals that related material appears in the video program.

GEORG: Kennst du viele Leute in München?

STEFAN: Ja, meine Familie wohnt da. Warum?

GEORG: Ich studiere nächstes Semester dort und brauche ein Zimmer.

STEFAN: Unser Haus ist ziemlich groß. Sicher haben meine Eltern ein Zimmer frei.

GEORG: Phantastisch! Vielen Dank!

STEFAN: Bitte, bitte. Nichts zu danken.

Pronunciation of **hab'**: **b** becomes unvoiced **p**.

Notes on Usage: Unstressed *e* and *denn*

Dropping Unstressed *e* In informal conversation, Germans often drop the unstressed ending **-e** in the first-person singular.

Katrin, ich **hab'** eine Frage.
Natürlich **kenn'** ich ihn.

The Flavoring Particle *denn* Probably the most frequently used flavoring particle is **denn**. It adds an element of personal interest to a question. **Denn** is never stressed and usually comes immediately after the verb and personal pronouns.

Was liest du **denn**?
Wen meinst du **denn**?
Wer ist **denn** das?

Who's Reading the Newspaper?

FATH.: Kurt, I'm looking for my newspaper. Do you know where it is?

SON: Your newspaper? I'm reading it at the moment.

FATH.: What are you reading?

SON: I'm reading an article about our school.

I Have a Question

A.: Katrin, I have a question. Do you know that man over there?

K.: Whom do you mean?

A.: He's talking with Stefan. I see he knows you.

K.: Of course I know him—that's my brother Max!

A.: Oh, you have a brother too! I only know your sister.

Georg Is Looking for a Room

G.: Do you know many people in Munich?

S.: Yes, my family lives there. Why?

G.: I'm studying there next semester and need a room.

S.: Our house is pretty big. My parents surely have a room free.

G.: Fantastic! Thanks a lot!

S.: You're welcome. Don't mention it.

The preposition **über** means *about* with verbs like *to say, tell, write, read, laugh,* etc.

Wortschatz 1

Verben

brauchen to need
essen (ißt) to eat
haben to have
heißen to be called
  Er heißt Max. His name is Max.
kennen to know, to be acquainted with
lesen (liest) to read
  lesen über (+ *acc.*) to read about
meinen to mean
nehmen (nimmt) to take
sehen (sieht) to see
sprechen (spricht) to speak, to talk
  sprechen über (+ *acc.*) to talk about
suchen to look for; to seek
wissen (weiß) to know (*a fact*)

Substantive

der **Artikel, -** article
der **Bruder, ¨** brother
der **Freund, -e** friend
der **Mann, ¨er** man; husband
der **Sohn, ¨e** son
der **Vater, ¨** father

das **Fleisch** meat
das **Gemüse** vegetables
das **Obst** fruit
das **Semester, -** semester
das **Zimmer, -** room

die **Familie, -n** family
die **Frage, -n** question
die **Schule, -n** school
die **Schwester, -n** sister
die **Zeitung, -en** newspaper

die **Eltern** (*pl.*) parents
die **Leute** (*pl.*) people

Adjektive und Adverbien

(da) drüben over there
dein (*fam. sing.*) your
dort there
frei free; unoccupied
groß big; tall
mein my
nur only
sicher certain, sure
unser our

Andere Vokabeln

ach oh, ah
bitte you're welcome
denn *flavoring particle, see p. 49*
mit with
über (+ *acc.*) about
wen? whom?
wessen? whose?
wie viele? how many?

Nützliche Ausdrücke

Phantastisch! Fantastic!
vielen Dank many thanks, thanks a lot
nächstes Semester next semester
Nichts zu danken! Don't mention it!

Gegensätze

danke ≠ **bitte** thank you ≠ you're welcome
groß ≠ **klein** big; tall ≠ little; short

DIE BANK FÜR LEUTE VON HEUTE

Variationen

A Persönliche Fragen

1. Wie viele Studenten kennen Sie hier? Wie heißen sie?
2. Stefans Haus ist ziemlich groß. Ist Ihr Haus auch groß, oder ist es klein? Wie viele Zimmer hat es?
3. Stefan kommt aus München. Woher kommen Sie?
4. Kurt liest die Zeitung im Moment. Lesen Sie auch eine Zeitung? Oft oder nur selten? Wie heißt sie?

B Partnerarbeit: Wie heißt . . . ?

Help each other recall the names of other students in the class.

A: Wie heißt die Studentin *oder* der Student da drüben?
B: Sie/er heißt . . .

C Partnerarbeit: Wen kennst du hier?

Ask your neighbor whom he or she knows in class and how well.

A: Wen kennst du hier?
B: Ich kenne . . .
A: Kennst du ihn *(oder)* sie gut?
B: Ja, sehr gut. (*oder*: Nein, nicht sehr gut.)

Vielleicht sprechen die Frauen über das Wetter. Was sagen sie zueinander?

(handwritten top): Ich meinen meine / Du deinen deine deine

D **Partnerarbeit: Was suchst du?**

(handwritten): Er seinen sein seine / Ihr seinen sein seine

Tell what you're looking for. Try to remember the correct gender of these nouns, then put them into the corresponding column.

(handwritten): Sie Ihren

Buch   Stuhl   Professor
Bleistift   Kugelschreiber   Professorin
Heft   Landkarte   Zeitung
Uhr

(handwritten left): Du suchst / Ihr Sucht / Ich Suche / Er / Sie / ehre

Ich suche:

meinen (masculine)	**mein** (neuter)	**meine** (feminine)
Stuhl	Buch	Professorin
Professor	Heft	Landkarte
Bleistift		Zeitung
Kugelschreiber		Uhr

(handwritten left margin): Dein / Deinen / Deine

(handwritten bottom left): Ich mein m   M   P   m

Now use each of these objects in the following conversation.

A: Was suchst du?
B: Ich suche meinen / mein / meine _____.
A: Er / es / sie ist nicht hier.

E **Gruppenarbeit: Was brauchen wir?** *(4 Studenten)*

You and three friends are going to Munich to study. Decide together on some things you'll need.

Wir brauchen:

einen (masculine)	**ein** (neuter)	**eine** (feminine)

Lyrik zum Vorlesen

Lab Manual Kap. 2, Lyrik zum Vorlesen.

This is one of the earliest surviving love poems in German. It was found in the Latin text of a letter written ca. 1160 A.D. by a lady to her lover. The original medieval German has been translated into modern German.

Du bist mein, ich bin dein,
Des sollst du gewiß sein.°   **Des...** = of that you can be certain
Du bist verschlossen°   locked up
In meinem Herzen,°   heart
Verloren° ist das Schlüsselein:°   lost / little key
Du mußt immer drinnen° sein.   inside

The Accusative Case

In **Kapitel 1** you learned the forms and functions of the nominative case. In this chapter you will learn the accusative case. The direct object of a verb is in the accusative.

The Direct Object

The direct object is the thing or person acted upon, known, or possessed by the subject.

Subject (nominative)			Direct Object (accusative)	
Sie	lesen	→	das Buch.	*They're reading the book.*
Anna	kennt	→	meine Eltern.	*Anna knows my parents.*
Karl	hat	→	einen Bruder.	*Karl has a brother.*

The accusative is identical in form to the nominative *with the exception of the masculine singular articles.*

	Nominative	Accusative
masc:	Hier ist der / ein Bleistift.	Ich habe den / einen Bleistift.
neut:	Hier ist das / ein Zimmer.	Ich habe das / ein Zimmer.
fem:	Hier ist die / eine Zeitung.	Ich habe die / eine Zeitung.
plur:	Hier sind die / meine Bücher.	Ich habe die / meine Bücher.

The indefinite article **ein** has no plural form. Therefore, the possessive adjective **mein-** (*my*) is used to show the plural endings.

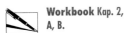 **Workbook** Kap. 2, A, B.

1 Übung: Wer hat ein Deutschbuch?

Your instructor asks who has various things. Say that you have them.

BEISPIEL: Wer hat ein Deutschbuch?
Ich habe ein Deutschbuch.

Suchen Sie einen Freund?

2 **Übung: Was sehen Sie?**

Name five things you see in the picture.

> BEISPIEL: Ich sehe einen Tisch.

3 **Kettenreaktion: Was brauchst du?**

Ask other students what things they need.

> BEISPIEL: A: Was brauchst du?
> B: Ich brauche den/das/die _____ . Und was brauchst du?
> C: Ich brauche . . .

Fragewort

The accusative form of the question word **wer** is **wen**:

> **Wen** kennst du in München?   *Whom do you know in Munich?*

Accusative of the Personal Pronouns

Be sure to learn all forms of the accusative personal pronouns.

	Singular			Plural	
nom.	**acc.**		**nom.**	**acc.**	
ich	**mich**	*me*	wir	**uns**	*us*
du	**dich**	*you*	ihr	**euch**	*you*
Sie	**Sie**		Sie	**Sie**	
er	**ihn**	*him, it*			
es	**es**	*it*	sie	**sie**	*them*
sie	**sie**	*her, it*			

Workbook Kap. 2, C, D, E.

Lab Manual Kap. 2, Var. zur Üb. 5.

4 Übung: Brauchen Sie etwas?

Your instructor asks whether you need something. Say that you do need it.

> BEISPIEL: Brauchen Sie den Stuhl?
> Ja, ich brauche ihn.

5 Partnerarbeit: Wen kennst du hier?

Conduct the following dialogue with your partner, naming as many students in your class as possible.

> A: Wen kennst du hier?
> B: Ich kenne Barbara/Robert.
> A: Ich kenne sie/ihn auch.
> B: Wen kennst *du* hier?

6 Übung: Fragen

Answer the questions affirmatively.

> BEISPIEL: Suchst du mich?
> Ja, ich suche dich.

1. Kennst du mich?
2. Brauchst du uns?
3. Seht ihr uns?
4. Kenne ich dich?
5. Kenne ich euch?
6. Fragst du mich?
7. Brauche ich dich?
8. Brauche ich euch?
9. Kennen Sie mich?
10. Kenne ich Sie?

Wir seht ms

Wickt kenne mkeu egel

More on Verbs in the Present Tense

Contraction of *du*-form: *heißen*

Verbs with stems ending in **-s, -ß,** or **-z** contract the **du**-form ending **-st** to **-t**. In these verbs, the **du**-form and the **er**-form are identical. You used some of the forms of **heißen** in the **Einführung**. Here is the complete conjugation in the present tense.

heißen	*to be called*		stem: **heiß-**
ich	heiße	wir	heißen
du	**heißt**	ihr	heißt
er/es/sie	heißt	sie, Sie	heißen

Verbs with Stem-Vowel Change *e* to *i* or *ie*

Some German verbs change their stem vowel in the **du-** and **er-**forms of the present tense.

e → i	sprechen	*to speak*	
ich	spreche	wir	sprechen
du	**sprichst**	ihr	sprecht
er/es/sie	**spricht**	sie, Sie	sprechen

e → ie	sehen	*to see*	
ich	sehe	wir	sehen
du	**siehst**	ihr	seht
er/es/sie	**sieht**	sie, Sie	sehen

e → ie	lesen	*to read*	
ich	lese	wir	lesen
du	**liest**	ihr	lest
er/es/sie	**liest**	sie, Sie	lesen

Stem-vowel change will be indicated in the **Wortschatz** sections by inclusion of the **er**-form: **sehen (sieht)** *to see.* Two other verbs in this group are **essen,** *to eat;* and **nehmen,** *to take.* They change not only their stem vowel, but also some consonants.

Digraph-s (ß), called **ess-zett** in German, regularly replaces **ss** (1) at the end of a word (**groß**); (2) before personal endings beginning with **t** (du **ißt,** ihr **eßt**); and (3) between vowels when the first vowel is long or a diphthong (**heißen**). For example, **Füße** (*feet*) has a long **ü,** but **Flüsse** (*rivers*) has a short **ü.**

essen	*to eat*	nehmen	*to take*
ich	esse	ich	nehme
du	**ißt**	du	**nimmst**
er/es/sie	**ißt**	er/es/sie	**nimmt**

Lab Manual Kap. 2, Var. zur Üb. 7.

Workbook Kap. 2, F.

7 Kettenreaktion

1. Say what you eat, then ask the next person.

   BEISPIEL: Ich esse Fleisch, was ißt du?

2. Say what you read, then ask the next person.

BEISPIEL: Ich lese den *Spiegel*, was liest du?

3. Say what languages you speak and then ask the next person.

BEISPIEL: Ich spreche _____ , was sprichst du?

Chinesisch	Schwedisch	Englisch	Spanisch
Italienisch	Deutsch	Japanisch	Russisch
Polnisch	Französisch		

4. Say what you see. The next student repeats what you see, then adds something new.

BEISPIEL: A: Ich sehe ein Fenster.
B: Sie sieht ein Fenster, und ich sehe eine Tafel.

The Verb *wissen*

The verb **wissen** (*to know*) is irregular in the present singular. Its forms must be memorized.

ich	**weiß**	wir	wissen
du	**weißt**	ihr	wißt
er/es/sie	**weiß**	sie, Sie	wissen

The difference between **wissen** and **kennen** parallels that between French **savoir** and **connaître** and Spanish **saber** and **conocer**. Cf. Scots English *ken: to know* (a person or thing); also "beyond my ken": *beyond my knowledge.*

Both the first person singular and the third person singular lack endings: **ich weiß, er weiß.**

wissen* vs. *kennen Both **wissen** and **kennen** may be translated as "to know," but **wissen** means "to know a fact" and **kennen** means "to be familiar, acquainted with" and is used when the direct object is a person or place.

Weißt du, wer das ist?   *Do you know who that is?*
Ja, ich **kenne** ihn sehr gut.   *Yes, I know him very well.*
Kennen Sie Berlin, Herr Brandt?   *Do you know Berlin, Mr. Brandt?*
Nein, nicht sehr gut.   *No, not very well.*

8 Übung: *Wissen* oder *kennen*?

BEISPIEL: ich / Georg   Ich kenne Georg.

1. er / Michael
2. wir / Berlin
3. Katrin / wo ich wohne
4. ihr / was sie macht

5. ich / Stefan und Annette
6. du / München
7. ich / wer das ist
8. die Schüler / was der Lehrer meint

The Verb *haben*

The verb **haben** (*to have*) is irregular in the present singular.

ich	habe	wir	haben
du	**hast**	ihr	habt
er/es/sie	**hat**	sie, Sie	haben

9 Übung: Wer hat die Zeitung?

Your professor asks you who has the newspaper, while pointing to somebody. Say that that person has the newspaper.

BEISPIEL: Wer hat die Zeitung? (*points to Sean*)
Sean hat sie.

Learn all forms of the possessive adjectives.

Possessive Adjectives

Singular		Plural	
personal pronoun	**possessive adjective**	**personal pronoun**	**possessive adjective**
ich	**mein** *my*	wir	**unser** *our*
du	**dein**	ihr	**euer**
Sie	**Ihr** } *your*	Sie	**Ihr** } *your*
er	**sein** *his; its*		
es	**sein** *its*	sie	**ihr** *their*
sie	**ihr** *her; its*		

Note that formal **Ihr** (*your*), like formal **Sie** (*you*), is always capitalized.

SPIEGEL-Leser wissen mehr

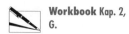

Possessive adjectives must agree with the nouns they modify in case, number, and gender. This agreement is shown by endings. As the following table shows, the endings of the possessive adjectives are the same as the endings of **ein**. Possessive adjectives are therefore called **ein**-words.

Endings of **ein**-words			
	masc.	**neut.**	**fem.**	**plur.**

	masc.	neut.	fem.	plur.
nom.	ein	ein	eine	(*no plural*)
	mein	mein	meine	meine
	ihr	ihr	ihre	ihre
	unser	unser	unsre	unsre
	euer	euer	eure	eure
acc. Ich	einen	ein	eine	(*no plural*)
	meinen	mein	meine	meine
	ihren	ihr	ihre	ihre
	unsren	unser	unsre	unsre
	euren	euer	eure	eure

The **e** *must* be dropped from **euer** (⟶ **euren**) and *may* be dropped from **unser**.

Note: The **-er** on **unser** and **euer** is *not* an ending, but part of the stem. When **euer** and **unser** take endings, the second **-e-** of the stem is dropped.

Das ist _{unser} / _{euer} Bruder. Das ist _{unsre} / _{eure} Schwester.

Note: The endings for nominative and accusative possessive adjectives are identical *except in the masculine.*

masculine nominative
Das ist mein Bruder.
Das ist ihr Bruder.
Das ist unser Bruder.
Das ist euer Bruder.

masculine accusative
Ich sehe mein**en** Bruder.
Sie sieht ihr**en** Bruder.
Wir sehen unsr**en** Bruder.
Ihr seht eur**en** Bruder.

Fragewörter

wer?	*who?*
wen?	*whom?*
wessen?	*whose?*

Woher kommen wir,
wohin gehen wir?

Lab Manual Kap. 2, Var. zur Üb. 10, 11.

Workbook Kap. 2, H, I, J, K.

Saying what belongs to whom is a communicative goal.

10 Übung: Wessen Buch ist das?

Tell your instructor whose book is being pointed to.

> BEISPIEL: Wessen Buch ist das?
> Das ist *mein* Buch.

11 Übung: Wessen Freund kennen Sie?

Tell your instructor whose friend you know.

> BEISPIEL: *Wessen* Freund kennen Sie?
> Ich kenne *seinen* Freund.

Zahlkarte		(Mit Schreibmaschine, Tinte oder Kugelschreiber deutlich ausfüllen)
DM	Pf	(DM-Betrag in Buchstaben wiederholen)
— 125 —	—	**- einhundertfünfundzwanzig -**

Cardinal Numbers above 20

Counting above 20 is a communicative goal.

The English nursery rhyme "Sing a Song of Sixpence" contains the phrase "four-and-twenty blackbirds." German forms the cardinal numbers above twenty in the same way: 24 = **vierundzwanzig**.

20	zwanzig	30	dreißig
21	einundzwanzig	31	einunddreißig (usw.)
22	zweiundzwanzig	40	vierzig
23	dreiundzwanzig	50	fünfzig
24	vierundzwanzig	60	sechzig
25	fünfundzwanzig	70	siebzig
26	sechsundzwanzig	80	achtzig
27	siebenundzwanzig	90	neunzig
28	achtundzwanzig	100	hundert
29	neunundzwanzig	1 000	tausend

4 982   viertausendneunhundertzweiundachtzig

German uses a period or a space where English uses a comma to divide thousands from hundreds, etc. German numbers above twelve (**zwölf**) are seldom written as words, except on checks. When they *are* written out, each number is one continuous word.

German	English
4.982 oder 4 982	4,982

German uses a comma where English uses a decimal point. The comma is read as **Komma**.

0,5	0.5
(null Komma fünf)	(zero point five)

Deutsche Bank Berlin
Aktiengesellschaft
Berlin

Zahlen Sie gegen diesen Scheck

einhundert sieben und zwanzig
Betrag in Buchstaben

an *Buchhandlung Gastehof Berlin,*
oder Überbringer

den 28.8.95
Datum

Währung Betrag

127,00

Markus Gerdes
Unterschrift

Der vorgedruckte Schecktext darf nicht geändert oder gestrichen werden. Die Angabe einer Zahlungsfrist auf dem Scheck gilt als nicht geschrieben.

Scheck-Nr. | X | Konto-Nr. | X | Betrag | X | Bankleitzahl | X Text

51987054 ⑆   5230289 ⑈   1007 0000 ⑆ 11 ⑈

Bitte dieses Feld nicht beschriften und nicht bestempeln

Workbook Kap. 2, L.

12 Übung

Read these numbers aloud in German.

26	1 066	3 001
69	533	0,22
153	985	3,45
4 772,08	48	71
1992	1971	1800

Sign directs drivers to **Ortsmitte** (*town center*), where tourist information (**i**) is available.

Weilheim 22 km
Peißenberg 14 km
Böbing 4 km
Ortsmitte i
23 Augsburg 79 km
Schongau 13 km
Garmisch-Part. 38 km
Oberammergau 19 km

Wie weit ist es nach Garmisch-Partenkirchen?

Fleurelle
Komplett-
Schlauch-
wagen
mit 50 m Ge-
webeschlauch
1/2'', mit
Kunststoff-
Armaturen
sowie 1,5 mm
Anschluß-
garnitur

89,95

Was kostet das?

Die Familie heute

Tips zum Lesen und Lernen

Lab Manual Kap. 2, Üb. zur Betonung.

Tips zum Vokabelnlernen

Compound Nouns   A characteristic feature of German is its formation of compound nouns from two or more nouns. You should get used to analyzing these words and should learn to identify their component parts. You will frequently see similarities to English compound nouns:

Hausfrau	*housewife*
Hausarbeit	*housework*

Often a connecting **-(e)s-** or **-(e)n-** is inserted between the components.

das **Eigentum** + die **Wohnung** = die **Eigentumswohnung**
(property)   *(apartment)*   *(condominium)*

der **Bund** *(federation)* + die **Republik** = die **Bundesrepublik**

die **Familie** + die **Diskussion** = die **Familiendiskussion**

The gender of the *last* component noun is *always* the gender of the entire compound.

das **Haus** + die **Frau** = die **Hausfrau**

das **Wort** + der **Schatz** = der **Wortschatz**
(word)   *(treasure)*   *(vocabulary)*

Leicht zu merken

die **Alternative, -n**	Alternative
der **Konflikt, -e**	Konflikt
(das) **Nordamerika**	
normal	normal
relativ	
sozial	sozial
traditionell	traditionell

Einstieg in den Text

- Review the tips for reading on pages 41–42 in **Kapitel 1**.
- The following text is entitled "Die Familie heute." This gives you a good idea of what sort of information to expect.
- Before reading, recall the vocabulary you already know that relates to the topic of family, e.g., **Bruder, Schwester**, etc.
- **Guessing from context**   The first sentence of a paragraph—the topic sentence—announces the primary topic of what follows. Look at page

64, line 9 of "Die Familie heute." **Die typische Familie** is the topic of this paragraph. Later in the paragraph comes this sentence:

Fast alle Familien besitzen ein Auto und einen Fernseher.

The words that are probably immediately comprehensible to you are **alle Familien** and **Auto.** Knowing the topic, you can make an educated guess at the meaning of **fast** and **besitzen.** Such educated guessing, or finding context clues, is very important when reading texts with many unfamiliar words.

Wortschatz 2

Verben

besitzen to own
bleiben to stay, remain
finden to find
geben (gibt) to give
kochen to cook
leben to live; to be alive
verdienen to earn

Substantive

der **Beruf, -e** profession, vocation
der **Fernseher, -** TV set
der **Großvater, ∷** grandfather
der **Onkel, -** uncle

das **Auto, -s** car
das **Essen** food; meal
das **Geld** money
das **Klischee, -s** cliché
das **Problem, -e** problem

die **Arbeit** work
die **Bundesrepublik (Deutschland)** the Federal Republic (of Germany)
die **BRD** the FRG
die **Diskussion, -en** discussion

die **Großmutter, ∷** grandmother
die **Hausfrau, -en** housewife
die **Mutter, ∷** mother
die **Rolle, -n** role
die **Stelle, -n** job, position
die **Tante, -n** aunt
die **Tochter, ∷** daughter

die **Großeltern** (*pl.*) grandparents

Adjektive und Adverbien

anders different
berufstätig employed
deutsch German
fast almost
jung young
manchmal sometimes
mehr more
  nicht mehr no longer, not any more
noch still
  noch ein another, an additional
sogar even, in fact
überall everywhere
wenigstens at least
wichtig important

Andere Vokabeln

alle (*pl.*) all; everybody
niemand nobody, no one
zwischen between

Nützliche Ausdrücke

es gibt (+ *acc.*) there is, there are
das sind (*pl. of* **das ist**) those are
zu Hause at home

Gegensätze

jung ≠ **alt** young ≠ old
niemand ≠ **jemand** no one ≠ someone
wichtig ≠ **unwichtig** important ≠ unimportant

Mit anderen Worten

Kinder sagen:
  Vati = Vater
  Mutti = Mutter
  Oma = Großmutter
  Opa = Großvater

Die Familie heute

„Der Vater hat einen Beruf und verdient das Geld, die Mutter ist Hausfrau. Sie bleibt zu Hause, kocht das Essen und versorgt° die Kinder." Die Klischees kennen wir schon. Heute stimmen sie aber nicht mehr, wenigstens nicht für junge[1] Familien in Deutschland.
5 Dort ist die Rollenverteilung° oft anders. Viele Frauen sind berufstätig oder suchen eine Stelle. Tagsüber° ist manchmal niemand zu Hause. Oft machen der Mann und die Frau die Hausarbeit gemeinsam,° und in Familiendiskussionen haben die Kinder heute auch eine Stimme.°

Die typische Familie ist relativ klein: ein oder zwei Kinder, das
10 ist normal. Manchmal wohnen auch die Großeltern mit ihnen zusammen.° Viele Familien in der Bundesrepublik haben ein Haus oder eine Eigentumswohnung.° Fast alle Familien besitzen ein Auto und einen Fernseher. Ihr Lebensstandard° ist sogar oft höher als° in Nordamerika.

15 Aber gibt es denn keine° Konflikte? Natürlich! Man findet in Deutschland, wie überall, Probleme zwischen Eltern und Kindern. Viele junge Leute suchen Alternativen. Sie wohnen manchmal in Wohngemeinschaften° oder Landkommunen.° Aber für die Mehrheit° bleibt die traditionelle Familie—Mutter, Vater und Kinder—noch die
20 wichtigste° soziale Gruppe.

takes care of

Learning about German family life is the cultural goal of this chapter.

assignment of roles

during the day

jointly

voice

mit... = with them

condominium

standard of living / **höher als** = *higher than*

no

communal living groups / rural communes / majority

most important

Fragen zum Lesestück

1. Was sind die Klischees über die traditionelle Familie?
2. Was suchen heute viele Frauen?
3. Haben Familien in Deutschland viele Kinder?
4. Wie heißt Deutschland offiziell?
5. Besitzen alle Familien in Deutschland ein Haus?
6. Ist die Familie auch heute noch wichtig?

HALLO KINDER!
DIE TOLLE KISTE
ZUM
BRIEFMARKENSAMMELN
IST DA!

Junge Familie aus Eibelstadt. Wie alt sind die Kinder?

---

[1]Line 4, **junge**: When German adjectives are used before nouns they have endings, most often **-e** or **-en**. You will learn how to use these endings actively in **Kapitel 9**.

Situationen aus dem Alltag

Die Familie

Here is some useful vocabulary for talking about your family. You already know some of these words. English equivalents are given for those you don't know yet.

die **Großeltern**	
die **Großmutter,** ⸚	
die **Oma, -s**	*grandma*
der **Großvater,** ⸚	
der **Opa, -s**	*grandpa*
die **Eltern**	
die **Mutter,** ⸚	
die **Mutti, -s**	*mama, mom*
der **Vater,** ⸚	
der **Vati, -s**	*papa, dad*
der **Sohn,** ⸚e	
die **Tochter,** ⸚	
die **Geschwister** (*pl.*)	*siblings, brothers and sisters*
der **Bruder,** ⸚	
die **Schwester, -n**	
der **Onkel, -**	
die **Tante, -n**	
die **Kusine, -n**	*cousin* (f.)
der **Vetter, -n**	*cousin* (m.)

Partnerarbeit: Fragebogen *(Questionnaire)*

You are a German sociologist studying American family life. Use the questionnaire below to interview your partner. Be ready to report the information that you collect to the class.

1. **Großeltern:** Leben sie noch?   ja / nein
2. **Mutter:** wie alt? _____ berufstätig? ja / nein Beruf? _____
3. **Vater:** wie alt? _____ berufstätig? ja / nein Beruf? _____
4. **Geschwister:** wie viele Brüder? _____ wie alt? _____
                wie viele Schwestern? _____ wie alt? _____
5. **Autos:** wie viele? _____
6. **Fernseher:** wie viele? _____
7. Wer kocht das Essen? _____
8. Wer macht die Hausarbeit? _____
9. Besitzt Ihre Familie ein Haus?   ja / nein

Gruppenarbeit: Familienfotos (*4 oder 5 Studenten*)

Bring to class photographs or your own drawing of some of your family members. Tell the others in the group about the people in the picture.

Sprechen wir miteinander!

Workbook Kap. 2, M, N, O.

Lab Manual Kap. 2, Diktat.

geb. = geboren (*born*)

A Übung: Wer ist in der Familie?

Answer the questions about Sylvie, Felix, and their families.

1. Das ist Sylvie Klein. Sie hat eine Mutter und . . .
   Wer is Peter Klein? . . . Er ist ihr Vater.
   Wer ist Elise Klein?
   Wer ist Jörg?
   Wer sind Anna und Anton Huber?
2. Das ist Felix Scheuch. Er hat einen Vater und . . .
   Wer sind Beate und Julie? Karsten Scheuch? Helene Scheuch? Elise Klein?

B Gruppenarbeit: Was gibt es hier?

Say what's in your classroom.

> BEISPIEL: Hier gibt es _____ .

C Partnerarbeit: Was siehst du?

Take turns saying what you see in the pictures on p. 67.

> BEISPIEL: Ich sehe einen Wagen.

D Gruppenarbeit (*3 oder 4 Personen*)

How many answers can you give to the following questions?

1. *Was liest du denn?*

   Ich lese _____ .

   _____ .

   _____ .

   _____ .

2. *Was kochst du?*

   Ich koche _____ .

   _____ .

   _____ .

   _____ .

3. *Wen kennst du?*

   Ich kenne _____ .

   _____ .

   _____ .

   _____ .

4. *Was suchst du?*

   Ich suche _____ .

   _____ .

   _____ .

   _____ .

5. *Was brauchst du denn?*

   Ich brauche _____ .

   _____ .

   _____ .

   _____ .

6. *Was siehst du denn?*

   Ich sehe _____ .

   _____ .

   _____ .

   _____ .

E Gruppenarbeit (*3 Personen*)

A German student from Rostock is visiting America and doesn't understand much English. Student A is a reporter asking questions. Student B interprets for the German visitor (student C).

BEISPIEL: A: Where is she from?
           B: Woher kommst du denn?
           C: Ich komme aus Rostock.

1. Where does his/her family live?
2. Does it rain there often?
3. What's his/her mother's name?
4. Is he/she employed?
5. Are his/her grandparents alive?
6. Whom does he/she know here?

Schreiben Sie zu Hause

F Write sentences using the cues provided. Add verbs, articles, and endings to verbs and possessive adjectives where necessary.

BEISPIEL: ich / suchen / mein / Geschwister
Ich suche meine Geschwister.

1. kennen / du / mein / Bruder?
2. Frau Huber / lesen / Artikel
3. unser / Mutter / haben / Beruf
4. dein / Eltern / auch / berufstätig?
5. mein / Familie / besitzen / Fernseher
6. Karin / suchen / ihr / Bruder
7. sehen / du / unser / Professor?
8. kennen / ihr / Mann / da drüben?

G Construct dialogues from the following cues (a double slash indicates a comma).

1. Sie / kennen / Berlin?
ja // mein / Familie / wohnen / dort. warum / Sie / fragen?
ich / studieren / im Oktober / da / und / suchen / Zimmer

2. wie / du / heißen?
ich / heißen / Klaus
wen / du / suchen / denn?
mein / Bruder. du / wissen // wo / er / sein?

H **Wissen** oder **kennen**?   Choose the correct equivalent of the verb *to know*.

A: _____ du den Mann da drüben?

B: Natürlich _____ ich ihn.

A: _____ du, wie er heißt?

B: Ja, er heißt Wolf Breisacher.

C: Ich _____ München gut.

D: Das _____ ich. Du kommst ja aus München!

C: _____ du Julian Wegener? Er studiert dort.

D: Wirklich? Ich _____ ihn nicht gut, aber ich _____, er wohnt in München.

I **Wie sagt man das auf deutsch?**

1. Her family is quite typical.
2. Their name is Schölz and they live in Munich.
3. Does her brother work, or is he looking for a job?
4. He's studying in Heidelberg.

5. I'm looking for my newspaper.
6. Fritz has it.
7. He's reading an article.

8. Where are your children, Mr. Asch?
9. They're at home.

10. When are you eating, children?
11. Probably at six.

VIDEOECKE

1 Ist das Zimmer noch frei? (00:00)

Katrin nimmt das Zimmer.

Katrin Berger aus Leipzig studiert in Berlin. Sie braucht ein Zimmer und findet eine Adresse, wo ein Zimmer frei ist. Das Zimmer ist in der Wohnung von Familie Bachmann. Katrin geht hin (there) und findet das Zimmer schön. Es kostet auch nicht viel, und sie nimmt es. Sie ist nicht in Eile und trinkt mit Bachmanns zusammen eine Tasse Kaffee.

Wortschatz zum Video

kosten	*to cost*
mieten	*to rent*
zeigen	*to show*
das **Bett, -en**	*bed*
der **Garten, ⸚**	*garden, yard*
der **Wandschrank, ⸚e**	*cupboard, closet*
gern	*gladly, with pleasure*
hell	*bright*
eine Tasse Kaffee	*a cup of coffee*
ein Stück Kuchen	*a piece of cake*

A **Was sehen Sie im Video?**

Watch video Module 1 (00:20–03:58) once without sound. Check off in the list below the things you see in the video.

Ich sehe . . .

____ 1. ein Auto   ____ 5. den Großvater

____ 2. einen Tisch   ____ 6. Bücher

____ 3. einen Fernseher   ____ 7. ein Fenster

____ 4. die Mutter   ____ 8. ein Radio

B **Was hören Sie?**

Now watch the same section with sound, checking off the words you hear. Try to guess the meanings of the ones you haven't yet learned.

____ 1. Universität   ____ 5. Rostock

____ 2. Bruder   ____ 6. Großvater

____ 3. Balkon   ____ 7. Sofa

____ 4. Biologie   ____ 8. Schwester

C **Wer macht das? Wer sagt das?**

Choose the person who does or says the following.

1. _____ zeigt Katrin das Zimmer.
   a. Herr Bachmann   b. Frau Bachmann   c. Sabrina

2. „Ich habe Zeit."
   a. Stefan   b. Herr Blum   c. Fräulein Berger

3. _____ studiert in Heidelberg.
   a. Frau Bachmanns Tochter   b. Frau Bachmanns Sohn   c. Katrin

4. „Kennst du Berlin schon?"
   a. Harald   b. Stefan   c. Herr Bachmann

Richtig oder falsch?

Indicate whether each statement is **richtig (R)** or **falsch (F)**.

1. Das Zimmer ist nicht groß genug (*enough*).	R	F
2. Die Kinder spielen draußen.	R	F
3. Das Zimmer kostet DM 400 im Monat.	R	F
4. Im Zimmer gibt es einen Fernseher.	R	F
5. Katrin ißt ein Stück Kuchen.	R	F
6. Katrin kommt aus Leipzig.	R	F

E **Welle Magazin: Was sehen Sie?**

Read through the list below. Then watch the **Welle Magazin** (04:03–05:26) and check off the rooms and things you see in the video.

Ich sehe . . .

____ 1. die Garage (*garage*)
____ 2. das Badezimmer (*bathroom*)
____ 3. den Garten
____ 4. eine Blumenvase (*vase of flowers*)
____ 5. das Eßzimmer (*dining room*)
____ 6. die Küche (*kitchen*)
____ 7. einen Schreibtisch (*desk*)
____ 8. den Keller (*cellar*)
____ 9. das Schlafzimmer (*bedroom*)
____ 10. einen Computer
____ 11. den Dachboden (*attic*)

This newspaper advertisement lists an apartment and a house for rent. How much of the descriptions can you guess from context?

Wohnungsmarkt

3-ZIMMER-WOHNUNG
zu vermieten, frisch gestrichen, moderne Küche, nahe Universität. Tel. 09 11/35 24 03

HAUS ZU VERMIETEN
4 Schlafzimmer, Möbel, Moltkestr. 66/Ecke Engelstr., Tel. 02 41/52 31 22

Die ganze Familie *(The whole family)*

Der Vater, der heißt Daniel,
der kleine Sohn heißt Michael,
die Mutter heißt Regine,
die Tochter heißt Rosine.

Der Bruder, der heißt Kristian,
der Onkel heißt Sebastian,
die Schwester heißt Johanna,
die Tante heißt Susanna.

Der Vetter, der heißt Benjamin,
die Kusine, die heißt Katharin,
die Oma heißt Ottilie—
nun kennst du die Familie!

In the early 1990s, these were the most popular first names for newborn children according to the **Gesellschaft für deutsche Sprache** (Society for the German Language):

Namen für Mädchen

Sarah	Julia	Maria
Katharina	Lisa	Laura
Anna / Anne	Franziska	Vanessa
Stefanie	Jessica	Jennifer

Namen für Jungen

Christian	Michael	Daniel
Alexander	Tobias	Kevin
Maximilian	Patrick	Philipp
Martin	Dennis	Paul

Parents do not have absolute freedom in choosing names for their children. A name may be rejected by the government registry office if it does not clearly indicate the child's sex or if it is deemed to "endanger the well-being of the child."

Die Familie ist zusammen. Sie trinken Kaffee und sprechen miteinander.

Ottilie
geb. 1918

Hermann
1917–1945

Daniel
geb. 1941

Regine
geb. 1947

Sebastian
geb. 1939

Susanna
geb. 1937

Kristian
geb. 1976

Rosine
geb. 1977

Michael
geb. 1986

Johanna
geb. 1987

Benjamin
geb. 1975

Katharin
geb. 1973

Der Stammbaum

The Family Tree

geb. (abbreviation for **geboren**) = *born*

Jugend und Schule

Communicative Goals

- Negating statements and questions
- Contradicting someone
- Requesting confirmation
- Expressing opinions
- Talking about clothing

Cultural Goal

- Learning about German schools

Lab Manual Kap. 3, Dialoge, Fragen, Hören Sie gut zu!, Üb. zur Aussprache [o / ö].

Two cities in Germany are named Frankfurt. They are distinguished by the rivers on which they are situated: Frankfurt am Main (Frankfurt a. M. or Frankfurt/Main) in the state of Hessen; and Frankfurt an der Oder (Frankfurt a. d. O. or Frankfurt/Oder) in the state of Brandenburg.

Du hast es gut!

Renate besucht ihre Freundin Monika.

MONIKA: In Frankfurt hast du es gut, Renate! Hier in Hinterwalden ist es stinklangweilig.

RENATE: Dann mußt du mich bald besuchen. Oder hast du keine Lust?

MONIKA: Doch, ich möchte schon nach Frankfurt, aber ich habe leider kein Geld.

RENATE: Das verstehe ich schon, aber bis Juni kannst du sicher genug verdienen.

Eine Pause

Kurt und Stefan fahren nach Innsbruck.

KURT: Wir müssen noch eine Stunde nach Innsbruck fahren.

STEFAN: Können wir eine Pause machen? Ich möchte ein bißchen laufen.

KURT: Ich auch. Da drüben kann man halten, nicht wahr?

STEFAN: Ja . . . (*Sie halten.*) Mensch! Der Berg ist wahnsinnig steil!

KURT: Was ist denn los? Bist du nicht fit?

STEFAN: Doch! Das schaff' ich leicht.

Innsbruck is the capital city of the mountainous Austrian province of Tyrol (German **Tirol**). German place names often have topographical significance. **Die Brücke** = *bridge*; this city was originally a settlement at "the bridge over the Inn River." See the map in the front of the book.

Heute habe ich leider keinen Wagen

CAROLA: Klaus, wie spät ist es denn?

KLAUS: Um Gottes Willen! Es ist schon halb zwölf.

CAROLA: Mußt du jetzt nach Hause?

KLAUS: Ja, und ich muß zu Fuß gehen. Heute habe ich leider keinen Wagen.

CAROLA: Warum denn nicht?

KLAUS: Mein Mitbewohner hat ihn heute abend. Er hat viel zu tun.

Um Gottes Willen! Although **Gott** means *God*, this exclamation is not offensive in German, but is the social equivalent of *For heaven's sake* or *Oh, my gosh*.

Note on Usage: The Flavoring Particle *schon*

As a flavoring particle, **schon** is often used to strengthen, confirm, or reinforce a statement. It adds the sense of "really," "indeed." In the first dialogue, Monika protests:

Ich möchte **schon** nach Frankfurt, aber ich habe leider kein Geld.	*I really would like to go to Frankfurt, but unfortunately I don't have any money.*

Renate answers:

Das verstehe ich **schon** . . .	*I certainly understand that . . .*

You've Got It Made

Renate is visiting her friend Monika.

M.: You've got it made in Frankfurt, Renate. It's really boring here in Hinterwalden.

R.: Then you have to visit me soon. Or don't you want to?

M.: Sure I do. I really would like to go to Frankfurt, but unfortunately I don't have any money.

R.: I certainly understand that, but surely you can earn enough by June.

A Break

Kurt and Stefan are driving to Innsbruck.

K.: We still have an hour to drive to Innsbruck.

S.: Can we take a break? I'd like to walk a bit.

K.: Me too. We can stop over there, can't we?

S.: Yes . . . (*They stop.*) Man, the mountain is really steep!

K.: What's the matter? Aren't you in shape?

S.: Sure! I can manage that easily.

Unfortunately, I Don't Have a Car Today

C.: Klaus, what time is it?

K.: Oh, my gosh! It's already 11:30.

C.: Do you have to go home now?

K.: Yes, and I have to walk. Unfortunately I don't have a car today.

C.: Why not?

K.: My roommate has it tonight. He has a lot to do.

Verben

besuchen   to visit
dürfen (darf)   may, to be allowed to
fahren (fährt)   to drive; to go (*by vehicle*)
halten (hält)   to stop (*intrans.*); to hold
können (kann)   can, to be able to
laufen (läuft)   to run; to go on foot, walk (*colloq.*)
ich möchte   I would like to
müssen (muß)   must, to have to
schaffen   (*colloq.*) to handle, manage; to get done
schlafen (schläft)   to sleep
sollen (soll)   should, to be supposed to
tragen (trägt)   to carry; to wear
tun   to do
verstehen   to understand
wollen (will)   to want to

Berg: cf. English *iceberg.*

Substantive

der **Berg, -e**   mountain
der **Wagen, -**   car
der **Mitbewohner, -**   roommate (*m.*)
die **Freundin, -nen**   friend (*f.*)
die **Minute, -n**   minute
die **Pause, -n**   break; intermission
  eine Pause machen   to take a break
die **Stunde, -n**   hour; class hour
  die **Deutschstunde**   German class

die **Mitbewohnerin, -nen**   roommate (*f.*)

Adjektive und Adverbien

bald   soon
fit   in shape
genug   enough
jetzt   now
langweilig   boring
leicht   easy; light (*in weight*)
leider   unfortunately
schon   already, yet
spät   late
steil   steep
wahnsinnig   (*colloq. adv.*) extremely, incredibly
wahr   true

Andere Vokabeln

doch   yes I *do*, yes I *am*, etc. (*contradictory*, see p. 88)
kein   not a, not any, no
nichts   nothing
wie lange?   how long?
wohin?   where to?

Kein has the same endings as **ein**. See p. 86.

Nützliche Ausdrücke

ein bißchen   a little; a little bit; a little while
Ich habe keine Lust.   I don't want to.
Mensch!   Man! Wow!
nicht (wahr)?   isn't it?, can't you?, doesn't he?, etc.
nach Hause   home (*as destination*)
  Ich fahre nach Hause.   I'm driving home.

Variationen

A Persönliche Fragen

1. Wo sind Sie zu Hause?
2. Gibt es da viel zu tun, oder ist es langweilig?
3. Brauchen Sie heute einen Wagen, oder gehen Sie zu Fuß?
4. Besitzen Sie einen Wagen?
5. Sind Sie fit oder nicht?
6. Haben Sie genug Geld?

So üben Sie mit Sicherheit richtig!

Das sind nur einige Beispiele aus FIT UND GESUND

Falsch   Richtig

B Übung

1. Kurt möchte ein bißchen laufen. Ich möchte zu Hause bleiben.
   Was möchten Sie denn machen?
   Ich möchte _____ .

2. Kurt und Stefan wollen da drüben halten. Ich will nach Hause laufen.
   Was wollen Sie denn machen?
   Ich will _____ .

3. Klaus muß morgen arbeiten. Ich muß kochen.
   Was müssen Sie denn morgen machen?
   Ich muß _____ .

C Partnerarbeit: Doch!

Contradict what your partner says, using **doch**.

BEISPIEL: Du besuchst mich nicht!
Doch, ich besuche dich!

1. Du bist nicht fit!
2. Der Tourist kommt nicht aus Amerika!
3. Du verstehst mich nicht!
4. Wir arbeiten heute nicht!
5. Die Studenten gehen nicht nach Hause!
6. Robert ist nicht dein Freund!
7. Der Berg ist nicht steil!
8. Es ist nicht spät!

Bruder Jakob

This round for four voices comes originally from France, but is sung by children all over the world. In German, **Frère Jacques** is called **Bruder Jakob**.

Lab Manual Kap. 3, Lyrik zum Vorlesen.

Bruder Jakob, Bruder Jakob!
Schläfst° du noch? Schläfst du noch?   sleep
Hörst du nicht die Glocken?°   bells
Hörst du nicht die Glocken?
Ding, ding, dong. Ding, ding, dong.

Rätsel *(Riddles)*

Rhyming riddles are very old forms of oral popular literature. The solutions to these two are shown by the accompanying illustrations.

(der Hummer)

Rot° und gut,   red
hat Fleisch° und kein Blut.°   flesh / blood

(die Schnecke)

Ich gehe alle Tage° aus   every day
und bleibe doch in meinem Haus.

Grammatik

The Predicate

In both German and English, all statements and questions contain a subject (S) and an inflected verb (V):

S V	S V
Ich arbeite viel.	*I work a lot.*

V S	V S
Schläfst du?	*Are you sleeping?*

The verb by itself, however, is not always adequate to express the entire action or condition in which the subject is involved. For example, consider the simple statement:

Stefan ist jung.

Stefan is the subject and **ist** is the verb. When taken by themselves, however, the words

Stefan ist

are not a meaningful utterance. The verb **sein** must be completed, in this case by the adjective **jung**. **Sein** may also be completed by a noun in the nominative case.

Stefan ist **mein Bruder.**

In both cases, the verb and its complement together make up the entire verbal idea, or predicate. That's why adjectives and nouns that follow the verb **sein** are called *predicate adjectives* and *predicate nominatives*.

Various kinds of words and phrases can complement verbs to form the complete predicate. For instance, in the sentence

Ich trage Jeans.

the verb **trage** is completed by the direct object **Jeans**. In the sentence

Ich möchte laufen.

the modal verb **möchte** is completed by the infinitive **laufen**. You will learn about modal verbs like **möchte** in the following section.

Modal Verbs

The English modal system has no past tense for verbs like *must* and *may*; instead, English speakers say *had to* and *was allowed to*. The German system is much more regular.

There is a group of six verbs in German called *the modal verbs*. They do not express an action or condition by themselves, but rather the subject's *attitude* or *relation* to the action expressed by another verb.

Wir **müssen** noch eine Stunde **fahren**.	*We still **have to drive** for an hour.*
Bis Juni **kannst** du genug **verdienen**.	*By June you **can earn** enough.*

The modal verb **müssen** (*have to*) indicates that it is *necessary* for the subject (**wir**) to perform the action of driving (**fahren**). **Müssen** is the first part of the predicate, and the infinitive **fahren** is the second part of the predicate. The German modals are:

		expresses
dürfen	*to be allowed to, may*	permission
können	*to be able to, can*	ability
müssen	*to have to, must*	necessity
sollen	*to be supposed to, should*	obligation
wollen	*to want to; to intend to*	desire; intention
(ich) **möchte**	*(I) would like to*	inclination, desire

Möchte (*would like to*) is a subjunctive form of the modal verb **mögen** (*to like*), which you will learn in the next chapter.

Lehrer und Schüler

The modal auxiliaries take no endings in the **ich-** and **er-**forms, and most have a changed stem vowel in the singular.

dürfen	to be allowed to
ich	**darf**
du	**darfst**
er/es/sie	**darf**
wir	dürfen
ihr	dürft
sie, Sie	dürfen

können	to be able to
ich	**kann**
du	**kannst**
er/es/sie	**kann**
wir	können
ihr	könnt
sie, Sie	können

Darf ich draußen **spielen**?
May I play outside?

Wir **können** da drüben **halten**.
We can stop over there.

Notice that only **sollen** does not have a stem-vowel change in the singular.

müssen	*to have to*
ich	**muß**
du	**mußt**
er/es/sie	**muß**
wir	müssen
ihr	müßt
sie, Sie	müssen

Heute **muß** ich zu Fuß **gehen**.
Today I have to go on foot.

sollen	*to be supposed to*
ich	soll
du	sollst
er/es/sie	soll
wir	sollen
ihr	sollt
sie, Sie	sollen

Sollen wir eine Pause **machen**?
Should we take a break?

Notice that **möchte** has endings different from the other modal verbs.

wollen	*to want to*
ich	**will**
du	**willst**
er/es/sie	**will**
wir	wollen
ihr	wollt
sie, Sie	wollen

Willst du jetzt **essen**?
Do you want to eat now?

ich möchte	*I would like to*
(infinitive: **mögen**)	
ich	möchte
du	möchtest
er/es/sie	möchte
wir	möchten
ihr	möchtet
sie, Sie	möchten

Ich **möchte** dich **besuchen**.
I would like to visit you.

In contrast to German, some English modals require a dependent infinitive with *to* (*I want to read*), while others do not (*I can read*).

The modal verb is *always* the inflected verb in the sentence. The complementary infinitive (which is the second part of the predicate) comes at the end of the sentence. Note the difference from English, in which the dependent infinitive immediately *follows* the modal verb.

Wir **können** da drüben **halten**.	We **can stop** over there.
Das **muß** ich für morgen **lesen**.	I **have to read** that for tomorrow.
Marie **soll** ihre Eltern **besuchen**.	Marie **is supposed to visit** her parents.

It is important to get used to this two-part predicate, since it is a central structural feature of German sentences.

Lab Manual Kap. 3, Var. zur Üb. 1, 4.

Workbook Kap. 3, A, B, C.

1 **Übung: Was möchten Sie heute tun?**

Here are some things people in the dialogues on p. 75 are doing.

Monika besuchen	Geld verdienen
nach Frankfurt fahren	eine Pause machen
ein bißchen laufen	da drüben halten
nach Hause fahren	zu Fuß gehen

Choose from these activities to answer the following questions.

> BEISPIEL: Was möchten Sie heute tun?
> Ich möchte Monika besuchen.

1. Was können Sie heute tun?
2. Was müssen Sie heute tun?
3. Was möchten Sie heute tun?

2 Gruppenarbeit: Was willst du machen? *(4 Studenten)*

Ask each other about what you intend to do or be. This list will provide some ideas. What others can you find?

> BEISPIEL: Was willst du denn machen?
> Ich will in Deutschland studieren, und du?

eine Familie haben	Freunde in Europa besuchen
viel Geld verdienen	fit sein
berufstätig sein	eine Pause machen
ein Haus besitzen	in Deutschland studieren
nach Hause fahren	

Omission of the Infinitive

Certain infinitives may be omitted from sentences with modal verbs when they are clearly implied.

- **haben**

  Möchten Sie ein Zimmer [**haben**]?

  Would you like (to have) a room?

- **machen, tun**

  Das kann ich leider nicht [**machen/tun**].

  Unfortunately I can't (do that).

- verbs of motion (**gehen, fahren, fliegen, laufen**) when destination is expressed

  Mußt du jetzt nach Hause [**gehen, fahren**]?

  Do you have to go home now?

- **sprechen**, in the following expression:

  Kannst du Deutsch?
  Ja, ich kann Deutsch.
  Ich kann auch Dänisch.

  Can you speak German?
  Yes, I can speak German.
  I can also speak Danish.

3 Übung: Wie sagt man das auf englisch?

1. Wollen Sie jetzt nach Hause?
2. Er kann das noch nicht.
3. Willst du meinen Bleistift?
4. Mein Vater will das nicht.
5. Sie können schon gut Deutsch.
6. Möchten Sie das Geld?
7. Darf man denn das?
8. Wann wollen Sie nach Amerika?

Wohin (*where to?*) is analogous to the question word **woher?** (*from where?*): **Woher kommst du?**

4 Partnerarbeit: Wohin wollen wir im Februar?

By the time the semester break comes in mid-February, many German students want to travel where it is warm. Use the map of Europe on the inside back cover to plan such a trip with your partner.

BEISPIEL: A: Wohin willst du im Februar?
            B: Ich will nach . . . Wohin willst du?

Verbs with Stem-Vowel Change *a to ä, au to äu*

Some verbs change their stem-vowel in the following ways:

a → ä	**fahren**		*to drive; to go by vehicle*	**halten**		*to hold; to stop*
ich	fahre	wir	fahren	ich halte	wir	halten
du	**fährst**	ihr	fahrt	du **hältst**	ihr	haltet
er/es/sie	**fährt**	sie, Sie	fahren	er/es/sie **hält**	sie, Sie	halten

Other verbs in this group are: **schlafen** (**schläft**), *to sleep*; **tragen** (**trägt**), *to carry, wear.*

au → äu	**laufen**		*to run*
ich	laufe	wir	laufen
du	**läufst**	ihr	lauft
er/es/sie	**läuft**	sie, Sie	laufen

Lab Manual Kap. 3, Var. zur Üb. 5.

Workbook Kap. 3, D.

5 Kettenreaktion

Say how you get home, then ask your classmates how they get home.

BEISPIEL: A: Ich fahre nach Hause. Fährst du auch nach Hause?
            B: Nein, ich laufe nach Hause. Läufst du auch nach Hause?
            C: Ja, ich laufe auch nach Hause. Läufst du . . .

6 Kettenreaktion

Wie lange schläfst du?

> BEISPIEL: Ich schlafe acht Stunden. Wie lange schläfst du?

7 Gruppenarbeit: Mit offenen Büchern (With open books)

Tell one thing that you're wearing, then one thing the person next to you is wearing.

> BEISPIEL: Ich trage _____ und er/sie trägt heute _____ .

eine Armbanduhr

ein T-Shirt

Jeans

eine Brille

eine Jacke

Turnschuhe

einen Rock

eine Mütze

einen Pulli

einen Rucksack

Negating statements and questions is a communicative goal.

Negation with *nicht* (not)

Nicht is used to negate a sentence.

Sabrina ist meine Schwester.	*Sabrina is my sister.*
Sabrina ist **nicht** meine Schwester.	*Sabrina is **not** my sister.*

For a preview and summary of German negation, see **Zusammenfassung und Wiederholung I**, in the Workbook.

In English, *not* almost always follows the inflected verb immediately.

Some expressions of definite time: **jetzt, heute, heute abend, morgen, am Mittwoch.**

In the preceding example, the position of **nicht** is exactly the same as the position of *not* in English. In most German sentences, however, this will not be the case. Here are some preliminary guidelines for the position of **nicht**.

- **Nicht** usually *follows* the subject, verb, and direct object.

Ich kenne deinen Freund **nicht**.	*I don't know your friend.*
Er sagt das **nicht**.	*He doesn't say that.*
Wir besitzen das Auto **nicht**.	*We don't own the car.*

- **Nicht** also usually follows expressions of definite time.

Sie können heute abend **nicht** kommen.	*They can't come tonight.*
Hans arbeitet jetzt **nicht**.	*Hans isn't working now.*

 Lab Manual Kap. 3, Üb. 8, 9.

Workbook Kap. 3, E.

8 **Übung**

Negate these sentences by adding **nicht**.

1. Kurt besucht seinen Bruder.
2. Ich kenne eure Mutter.
3. Frau Schmidt besucht uns morgen.
4. Monika macht das heute abend.
5. Ich verstehe ihn.
6. Am Donnerstag kochst du.
7. Er liest sein Buch.
8. Mein Großvater schläft.

Review the explanations of the predicate on p. 79 and of predicate nominatives on p. 36.

- **Nicht** *precedes* complements that constitute the second part of the predicate. These include:

1. Predicate adjectives

Der Berg ist **steil**.	*The mountain is **steep**.*
Der Berg ist **nicht** steil.	*The mountain is **not** steep.*

2. Predicate nominatives

Das ist **Herr Blum**.	*That is **Mr. Blum**.*
Das ist **nicht** Herr Blum.	*That is **not** Mr. Blum.*

3. Adverbs of manner, indefinite time, and place

Margit geht **zu Fuß**.	*Margit is going **on foot**.*
Margit geht **nicht** zu Fuß.	*Margit isn't going on foot.*
Er besucht mich **oft**.	*He **often** visits me.*
Er besucht mich **nicht** oft.	*He doesn't visit me often.*
Sie wohnt **hier**.	*She lives **here**.*
Sie wohnt **nicht** hier.	*She doesn't live here.*

Some expressions of indefinite time: **bald, spät, früh, immer, oft.**

4. Prepositional phrases that show destination (**nach Wien, nach Hause**) or location (**in Berlin, zu Hause**)

Sie geht **nach Hause**.	*She's going **home**.*
Sie geht **nicht** nach Hause.	*She's **not** going home.*
Er arbeitet **in Berlin**.	*He works **in Berlin**.*
Er arbeitet **nicht** in Berlin.	*He doesn't work in Berlin.*

5. Infinitives complementing modal verbs

Er kann mich **sehen**.	He can **see** me.
Er kann mich **nicht** sehen.	He can't see me.

9 Übung

Negate these sentences by adding **nicht**.

1. Das Wetter ist schön.
2. Ich kann dich besuchen.
3. Ich möchte Berlin sehen.
4. Der Berg ist steil.
5. Wir wollen halten.
6. Frau Mackensen ist unsere Lehrerin.
7. Ich muß nach Hause gehen.
8. Margit läuft gut.
9. Er kann mich sehen.

10 Partnerarbeit: Unsere neue Mitbewohnerin

You're both getting a new roommate. Take turns asking each other questions about her. Answer them all negatively.

BEISPIEL: A: Kennt unsere Mitbewohnerin Berlin?
            B: Nein, sie kennt Berlin nicht.

1. Kommt sie aus Dresden?
2. Ist sie freundlich?
3. Arbeitet sie heute abend?
4. Studiert ihr Bruder in Leipzig?
5. Kennst du ihn?
6. Muß sie nach Hause?
7. Fährt sie allein?
8. Schläft sie viel?
9. Ist das ihr Auto?
10. Ist sie oft schlechter Laune?

Negation with *kein*

Kein (*not a, not any, no*) is the negative of **ein**. It negates nouns preceded by **ein** or nouns not preceded by any article.

Morgen will ich ein Buch lesen.	*I want to read a book tomorrow.*
Morgen will ich **kein** Buch lesen.	*I don't want to read a book tomorrow.*
Hier wohnen Studenten.	*Students live here.*
Hier wohnen **keine** Studenten.	*No students live here.*

Kein is an **ein**-word and takes the same endings as **ein** and the possessive adjectives.

Das ist { **ein** Fernseher. / **kein** Fernseher. / **unser** Fernseher.

Er hat { **einen** Wagen. / **keinen** Wagen. / **meinen** Wagen.

Nicht and **kein** are mutually exclusive. In any given situation, only one will be correct. If a noun is preceded by the definite article or by a possessive adjective, use **nicht** rather than **kein** to negate it.

Ist das die Professorin?	*Is that the professor?*
Nein, das ist **nicht** die Professorin.	*No, that's not the professor.*
Ist das eure Professorin?	*Is that your professor?*
Nein, das ist **nicht** unsere Professorin.	*No, that's not our professor.*
Ist sie Professorin?	*Is she a professor?*
Nein, sie ist **keine** Professorin.	*No, she's not a professor.*

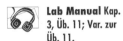

Lab Manual Kap. 3, Üb. 11; Var. zur Üb. 11.

Workbook Kap. 3, F, G.

11 Übung

Negate the sentence, using **kein**.

1. Meine Familie besitzt einen Wagen.
2. Maria hat heute Geld.
3. Hier gibt es ein Problem.
4. Hier wohnen Studenten.
5. Morgen gibt es eine Diskussion.
6. Herr Meyer hat Kinder.

12 Übung

Respond negatively to these questions, using **kein** or **nicht**.

BEISPIEL: Hat Barbara einen Freund? Nein, sie hat keinen Freund.
Ist das ihr Freund? Nein, das ist nicht ihr Freund.

1. Haben Sie einen Freund in Oslo?
2. Haben Sie Freunde in Washington?
3. Ist das der Professor?
4. Verdient er Geld?
5. Sehen Sie das Haus?
6. Ist das seine Freundin?
7. Suchen Sie das Buch?
8. Suchen Sie ein Buch?

13 Partnerarbeit: Meine Familie

Ask each other about your families. (For family members, see p. 65.)

BEISPIEL: A: Hast du einen Sohn?
B: Nein, ich habe keinen Sohn.

Requesting confirmation is a communicative goal.

Nicht wahr? can only follow positive statements.

Expecting an Affirmative Answer: *nicht wahr?*

Nicht wahr? (literally, "not true?"), when added to a positive statement, anticipates confirmation (English: *doesn't she? wasn't he? wasn't it? didn't you?* etc.). In spoken German, you may shorten it to **nicht?**

Heute ist es schön, **nicht wahr?**	*It's beautiful today, isn't it?*
Sie studieren in Freiburg, **nicht?**	*You're studying in Freiburg, aren't you?*
Gisela kennst du, **nicht wahr?**	*You know Gisela, don't you?*

Jugend und Schule

14 Übung: Das ist ein Tisch, nicht wahr?

Contradict your instructor if necessary.

> BEISPIEL: Das ist ein Tisch, nicht wahr?
> Nein, das ist kein Tisch, das ist ein(e) _____ .

15 Übung: Wie sagt man das auf deutsch?

1. You have a car, don't you?
2. You're learning German, aren't you?
3. You'll visit me soon, won't you?
4. He's in good shape, isn't he?
5. We can work today, can't we?
6. You can understand that, can't you?

Contradicting a Negative Statement or Question: doch

Contradicting someone is a communicative goal.

To contradict a negative statement or question, use **doch** instead of **ja**.

Ich spreche nicht gut Deutsch.	*I don't speak German well.*
Doch, Sie sprechen sehr gut Deutsch!	*Yes you do, you speak German very well.*
Kennst du Ursula nicht?	*Don't you know Ursula?*
Doch, ich kenne sie sehr gut!	*Sure, I know her very well.*

Lab Manual Kap. 3, Var. zur Üb. 16.

16 Übung: Doch!

Initial **doch** does not count as the first element in determining word order. See p. 37.

Contradict these negative statements and questions, beginning your response with a stressed **doch**.

> BEISPIEL: Schaffst du das nicht?
> Doch, ich schaffe das!

1. Wir wollen nicht halten.
2. Wir haben nicht genug Geld.
3. Hast du keinen Bruder?
4. Es ist nicht sehr spät.
5. Kannst du kein Deutsch?
6. Willst du nicht zu Fuß gehen?

17 Übung

Contradict your instructor if necessary.

> BEISPIEL: Das ist kein Tisch.
> Doch! Natürlich ist das ein Tisch!

[AUCH INSIDER BRAUCHEN INPUT.]

The Indefinite Pronoun *man*

The indefinite pronoun **man** refers to people in general rather than to any specific person. Although the English indefinite pronoun "one" may sound formal in everyday speech, **man** does not sound this way in German. It is used in both colloquial and formal language. It is often best translated into English as "people," "they," "you," or even "we."

You can use **man** only as the subject of a sentence, and only with a verb in the third person singular.

In Deutschland sagt **man** das oft.	*They often say that in Germany.*
Das muß **man** lernen.	*You've got to learn that.*
Das weiß **man** nie.	*One never knows.*

Do not confuse **man** with **der Mann** (*the man*).

Der Mann spricht Deutsch.

Hier spricht man Deutsch.

18 Übung

Change the subject to **man**.

1. In Hinterwalden können die Leute nicht genug verdienen.
2. Um elf Uhr machen wir eine Pause.
3. Hoffentlich können wir drüben halten.
4. Hier können Sie gut essen.
5. Dürfen wir hier schlafen?

19 Übung: Wie sagt man das auf deutsch?

Use **man** as the subject.

1. In America we don't say that.
2. You've got to stop here.
3. One has to do that.
4. People say there are problems here.
5. Can we go on foot?

Eine Klassendiskussion

Tips zum Lesen und Lernen

Tip zum Vokabelnlernen

Masculine nouns ending in **-er** have the same form in the plural.

Singular	*Plural*
der Lehrer	die Lehrer
der Amerikaner	die Amerikaner
der Schüler	die Schüler
der Europäer	die Europäer
der Pullover	die Pullover
der Computer	die Computer

Resist the temptation to add an **-s** as in the English plural (*two pullovers*). Remember that *very few* German nouns take **-s** in the plural.

Übung

Answer your instructor's questions with the plural form.

1. Wie viele Computer besitzt die Universität?
2. Wie viele Amerikaner sind hier im Zimmer?
3. Wie viele Schüler kennen Sie?
4. Wie viele Europäer studieren hier?
5. Wie viele Pullover besitzen Sie?

 Lab Manual Kap. 3, Üb. zur Betonung.

Leicht zu merken

international	internati<u>o</u>nal	**pessimistisch**	pessim<u>i</u>stisch
die **Jeans** (*pl.*)		das **System**, -e	Syst<u>e</u>m
optimistisch	optim<u>i</u>stisch	das **Schulsystem**	Sch<u>u</u>lsystem

Einstieg in den Text

1. The speakers in the following **Klassendiskussion** express opinions about their recent trip. Notice how often they preface opinions with such phrases as **Ich finde, . . .** or **Man meint, . . .** (*I think . . . , People think . . .*).
2. Remember that word order in German is in some ways freer than in English. It is true that the verb must be in second position in statements. In place of the subject, however, an object, an adverb, or some other element can be in first position. You will often find sentences beginning with the direct object:

Das finde ich auch.	*I think so too.* (literally: *I find that too.*)
Angst habe ich auch.	*I'm afraid too.* (literally: *I have fear too.*)

The clue to understanding such sentences is the personal ending of the verb. Words like **habe** and **finde** are obviously first person and go with the subject pronoun **ich**.

Wortschatz 2

Verben

besprechen (bespricht) to discuss
entscheiden to decide
hassen to hate
hören to hear
lachen to laugh
lernen to learn
schreiben to write
singen to sing

Substantive

der **Europäer, -** European (m.)
der **Fuß, ¨e** foot
  zu Fuß on foot
der **Mantel, ¨** coat
der **Pullover, -** pullover, sweater
  also: der **Pulli, -s**
der **Schuh, -e** shoe
  der **Turnschuh** sneaker, gym shoe
(das) **Amerika** America
(das) **Deutsch** German (*language*)
(das) **Englisch** English
(das) **Europa** Europe
das **Gymnasium,** die **Gymnasien** secondary school (*prepares pupils for university*)

Gymnasium derives from Greek for the place where athletes trained (**gymnos** = *naked*). The word was later generalized to mean *place of study*.

das **Hemd, -en** shirt
das **Kleid, -er** dress; *pl.* = dresses *or* clothes
die **Angst, ¨e** fear
  Angst haben to be afraid
die **Europäerin, -nen** European (*f.*)
die **Farbe, -n** color
die **Hausaufgabe, -n** homework assignment
die **Hose, -n** trousers, pants
die **Jacke, -n** jacket
die **Musik** music
die **Reise, -n** trip
  eine Reise machen to take a trip
die **Sprache, -n** language
  die **Fremdsprache** foreign language
die **Umwelt** environment
die **Welt, -en** world
die **Zeit, -en** time
die **Pommes frites** (*pl.,* pronounced *"Pomm fritt"*) French fries

Adjektive und Adverbien

ähnlich similar
also thus, for that reason
amerikanisch American
darum therefore, for that reason

Angst from Latin *angustiae* = a narrow constriction. English has borrowed **Angst** from German and uses it to mean *anxiety, existential fear*.

dunkel dark
ehrlich honest
eigentlich actually, in fact
fremd strange, foreign
neu new
schnell fast
toll (*colloq.*) great, terrific

Basic meaning of **toll:** *mad, crazy* (**das Tollhaus** = *madhouse*).

Farben

blau blue
braun brown
bunt colorful, multicolored
gelb yellow
grau gray
grün green
rot red
schwarz black
weiß white

Nützliche Ausdrücke

bitte please
Das finde ich auch. I think so too.
gar nicht not at all
Stimmt schon. That's right.

Eine Klassendiskussion

Last spring class 10a from the Kepler Gymnasium in Hannover visited a high school in California. Now they are discussing their impressions of the States with their teacher, Herr Beck; they also plan to write an article for their school newspaper.[1]

HERR BECK: Können wir jetzt unsere Amerikareise ein bißchen besprechen? Rolf, möchtest du etwas sagen? . . . Ach, er schläft ja wieder. *(Alle lachen.)*

ROLF: Meinen Sie mich? Entschuldigung! Unsere Reise? Sie war° doch toll.

KIRSTEN: Das finde ich auch. Die Amerikaner sind wahnsinnig freundlich, und jetzt weiß ich, die Schüler in Amerika sind eigentlich gar nicht so anders. Dort trägt man ja auch Jeans und Turnschuhe, hört Rockmusik, singt dieselben Schlager° und ißt Pommes frites.

HERR BECK: Stimmt schon, aber haben die amerikanischen Schüler auch ähnliche Probleme wie ihr?

ANDREAS: Ach, wissen Sie, alle Schüler hassen Hausaufgaben! *(Alle lachen.)* Nein, aber im Ernst,° wir sind alle manchmal pessimistisch. Man meint, man kann später° keine Arbeit finden, und auch die Umweltprobleme sind heute international. Überall haben die Schüler ein bißchen Angst.

HERR BECK: Angst habe ich auch, muß ich ehrlich sagen. Aber gibt es denn keine Unterschiede° zwischen hier und dort?

KIRSTEN: Doch, natürlich! Dort besuchen° alle Schüler die High-School, bis sie 18 sind. Mit zehn Jahren müssen wir aber entscheiden: Gymnasium, Realschule oder Hauptschule.[2] Die zwei Schulsysteme sind also ganz anders.

Lab Manual Kap. 3, Lesestück.

Learning about German secondary schools is the cultural goal of this chapter.

Notice the flavoring particle **ja** (lines 3 and 8) conveying the meaning *after all*.

war° — was

dieselben Schlager = the same hits

im Ernst° — seriously
später° — later

Unterschiede° — differences
besuchen° — *here:* attend

---

[1]Class 10a is one of several parallel 10th-grade classes in the **Gymnasium**. Students stay in the same group for several years and take all their classes together. German 10th-graders are 16 or 17 years old.

[2]See *Almanach*, p. 99

Die Schülerin hat eine Frage. (Hannover)

25	CHRISTA:	Ich finde, wir müssen hier mehr und schneller° lernen. Deutschland ist in Mitteleuropa° und hat viele Nachbarländer.° Darum müssen wir ja Fremdsprachen lernen. Viele Europäer können z.B. gut Englisch, aber relativ wenige Amerikaner lernen Fremdsprachen.	faster Central Europe neighboring countries
30	HERR BECK:	Jetzt haben wir leider keine Zeit mehr. Aber morgen können wir unseren Artikel über die Reise für die Schülerzeitung schreiben. Auf Wiedersehen bis dann.	

Fragen zum Lesestück

1. Wer bespricht die Amerikareise?
2. Wie war die Reise?
3. Sind die Schüler in Amerika sehr anders, oder sind sie ähnlich?
4. Was trägt man zum Beispiel in Amerika und auch in Deutschland?
5. Was ißt man auch dort?
6. Was hassen alle Schüler?
7. Warum sind viele Schüler manchmal pessimistisch?
8. Warum müssen die Deutschen Fremdsprachen lernen?
9. Was müssen die deutschen Schüler mit 10 Jahren machen?
10. Was schreibt die Klasse für ihre Schülerzeitung?

Talking about clothing is a communicative goal.

Was soll ich heute tragen?

You already know some of this vocabulary.

	die **Kleidung**	*clothing*
1.	der **Anzug, ⸚e**	*suit*
2.	die **Bluse, -n**	*blouse*
3.	die **Brille** (*sing.*)	*glasses*
4.	der **Handschuh, -e**	*glove*
5.	das **Hemd, -en**	
6.	die **Hose, -n**	
7.	der **Hut, ⸚e**	*hat*
8.	die **Jacke, -n**	
9.	das **Kleid, -er**	
10.	die **Krawatte, -n**	*tie*
11.	der **Mantel, ⸚**	
12.	der **Pulli, -s**	
13.	der **Rock, ⸚e**	*skirt*
14.	der **Schuh, -e**	
15.	die **Tasche, -n**	*pocket; handbag, shoulder bag*
16.	das **T-shirt, -s**	*T-shirt*
17.	der **Turnschuh, -e**	
18.	der **Regenschirm, -e**	*umbrella*
19.	die **Mütze, -n**	*cap*

Gruppenarbeit: Was tragen Sie heute?

BEISPIEL: PROFESSOR: Was tragen Sie heute, Mary?
                STUDENTIN: Ich trage _____ und _____ .

Partnerarbeit: Was trägst du heute?

BEISPIEL: A: Was trägst du heute, Mary?
            B: Ich trage _____ und _____ . Was trägst du?

Gruppenarbeit: Was tragen Sie in diesen Situationen?

BEISPIEL: Es regnet.
           Dann trage ich . . .

1. Es regnet. (Es schneit. Es ist windig.)
2. Die Sonne scheint, und es ist sehr warm.
3. Sie müssen eine Stelle suchen.
4. Sie und Ihre Mitbewohner machen heute abend eine Party.

Belgien

Dänemark

Griechenland

Großbritannien

Luxemburg

Niederlande

Portugal

Spanien

EG

Finnland[5]

Schweiz[5]

Japan

Kanada

USA

Welche Farbe hat das?

The prefixes **dunkel** and **hell** may be added to the colors you have learned in **Wortschatz 2**.

    dunkelblau = *dark blue*
    hellgrün   = *light green*

Three more colors that may be useful:

    rosa   *pink*
    lila   *violet, lavender*
    orange   *orange*

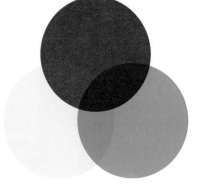

Übung

Welche Farben haben diese Fahnen (*flags*)?

BEISPIEL: Frankreich: rot, weiß, blau   **Frankreich**

Deutschland: _____ , _____ , _____ [*gold*]
Österreich: _____ , _____ , _____
Schweden: _____ , _____
Italien: _____ , _____ , _____
Irland: _____ , _____ , _____

Deutschland

Österreich[5]

Schweden[5]

Italien

Irland

Partnerarbeit

Ask each other about the colors of various things in the classroom and of clothing people are wearing.

> BEISPIELE: Welche Farben hat die Landkarte?
> Sie ist _____ .
>
> Welche Farbe hat Peters Hemd?
> Sein Hemd ist _____ .

Sprechen wir miteinander!

A Übung

Answer each question in the negative, making sure to use **nicht** or **kein** correctly.

1. Haben Sie heute abend Hausaufgaben?
2. Machen Sie Ihre Hausaufgaben heute abend?
3. Können wir jetzt arbeiten?
4. Sind Ihre Freunde fit? Sind Sie fit?
5. Machen Sie im Dezember eine Reise?
6. Wollen Sie das?
7. Hören Sie mich?
8. Lachen die Kinder laut?
9. Haben Sie Angst?
10. Tragen Sie eine Mütze?
11. Ist ihre Hose grün?
12. Fahren Sie oft nach Hause?

B Gruppenarbeit: Mit offenen Büchern (*3 oder 4 Studenten*)

Take turns changing each sentence by substituting the new elements provided.

> BEISPIEL: Ich möchte morgen nach Berlin. (wollen)
> A: Ich will morgen nach Berlin. (Wien)
> B: Ich will morgen nach Wien.

1. Ich möchte morgen nach Berlin.
   wollen
   München
   müssen
   wir
   Kopenhagen
   nächstes Semester

2. Im Juni kannst du viel Geld verdienen.
   müssen
   September
   ich
   haben
   wollen

3. Wir können da drüben halten.
   sollen
   eine Pause machen
   ich
   möchte
   arbeiten
   zu Hause

4. Er geht jetzt nach Hause.
   fahren
   morgen
   Max
   bald
   ihr

Unser Kind soll gesund sein.

C Gruppenarbeit: Was meinen Sie? (*4 Personen*)

Expressing opinions is a communicative goal.

Here are some topics of conversation and some adjectives. Using the verbs **meinen** and **finden**, take turns expressing opinions about these topics. Others in the group agree or disagree.

BEISPIEL: A: Ich finde (meine), die Umwelt ist wichtig.
            B: Das finde (meine) ich auch. *oder*
               Das finde (meine) ich nicht.

Schulen in Amerika	schön/häßlich
Schulen in Deutschland	wichtig/unwichtig
Rockmusik	interessant/langweilig
klassische Musik	toll
die Umwelt	prima
Fremdsprachen	stinklangweilig
Hausaufgaben	wahnsinnig gut

D Gruppenspiel: Stimmt nicht! (*3 Personen*)

Play this game with two other people. One says something obviously false. The others contradict that statement and give the correct information. Then the next player takes a turn.

BEISPIEL: —Kirsten trägt heute einen Pulli.
            —Stimmt nicht! Sie trägt keinen Pulli! Sie trägt eine Bluse.

E Partnerarbeit: Interview—*heute und morgen*

Interview each other. Give as many answers as possible to the following questions.

1. Was möchtest du heute abend machen? Ich möchte _____ .
2. Was mußt du morgen machen? Morgen muß ich _____ .
3. Was willst du in 10 Jahren (*in 10 years*) machen? In 10 Jahren will ich _____ .

Schreiben Sie zu Hause

F Udo is throwing a party, but nobody can come. Finish writing him the following note explaining why. There are some cues to help you.

Lieber Udo (*Dear Udo*),

Leider kann niemand zur Party kommen. Monika muß zu Hause bleiben. Klaus . . .

Klaus / müssen / für morgen / machen / seine Hausaufgaben
Ruth / möchten / fahren / nach Berlin
Peter und Ute / wollen / besuchen / ihre Tante / in Wien
Herr Beck / können / leider / finden / seinen Anzug / nicht
Andreas / dürfen / nicht so spät / kommen / nach Hause
ich / wollen / gar nicht / kommen

G Finish the following dialogue by completing the sentences.

ANNA: Hallo Klaus!

KLAUS: _____ , wie geht's?

ANNA: _____ . Was machst du denn heute?

KLAUS: Heute muß ich _____ . Und du?

ANNA: Heute soll ich _____ , aber ich will _____ . Also tschüs!

KLAUS: Tschüs Anna!

Now compose your own dialogue of three or four exchanges.

H Wie sagt man das auf deutsch?

1. Wouldn't you like to stay a bit?
2. Unfortunately, I have to work this evening.
3. What do you have to do?
4. I have to read a book and an article.

5. Don't you have any friends in Hinterwalden?
6. Yes, I do. Unfortunately they're quite boring.
7. Then you have to visit us soon.

8. You want to come to Berlin, don't you?
9. Yes. I can't stay in Hinterwalden.
10. Why not? Aren't there any jobs there?
11. Yes, but not enough. I want to look for a job in Berlin.

A Note About Schools in German-speaking Countries

The public school systems in Germany, Austria, and Switzerland all differ from American public schools in the degree to which they track pupils. Relatively early in their schooling, children are steered toward apprenticeships, commercial training, or preparation for university study. In the Federal Republic of Germany, each **Land** (state) has authority over its own school system. In all **Länder**, children attend four years of elementary school (**Grundschule**) together. At the end of the fourth, fifth, or sixth grade (depending on the **Land**), they are then tracked into separate schools. The decision is made on the basis of grades and conferences between teachers and parents.

There are three possibilities: the **Hauptschule**, the **Realschule**, or the **Gymnasium**. The first two are oriented respectively toward trades and business and prepare the pupils for various forms of apprenticeship and job training. The **Gymnasium** is the traditional preparation for university study. After passing their final examination, called the **Abitur** in Germany and the **Matura** in Austria and Switzerland, pupils may apply to a university.

Since 1971, there has been some experimentation in the Federal Republic with **Gesamtschulen** (unified schools) comprising all three types of secondary schools. These are schools designed on the American model, where pupils need not make their important decision at the age of ten, but can wait until they are sixteen. **Gesamtschulen**, however, comprise only a small percentage of the total number of secondary schools.

DUDEN
für
SCHÜLER

Land und Leute

Communicative Goals

- Making suggestions and giving commands
- Expressing likes, dislikes, and preferences
- Discussing weather, climate, and landscape

Cultural Goal

- Learning about the climate and geography of Germany

Chapter Outline

Lyrik zum Vorlesen „Die Jahreszeiten"

Grammatik Prepositions with the Accusative Case • Suggestions and Commands: The Imperative • The Verb *werden* • Negating *schon* and *noch* • Equivalents of English *to like* • Sentence Adverbs • *gehen* + infinitive

Lesestück Deutschland: Geographie und Klima

Situationen aus dem Alltag Klima, Wetter und Landschaft

Almanach The Common Origin of German and English

Lab Manual Kap. 4, Dialoge, Fragen, Hören Sie gut zu!, Üb. zur Aussprache [r].

Am See

FRAU MÜLLER: Wollen Sie noch einmal schwimmen gehen, Frau Brinkmann?

FRAU BRINKMANN: Nein, lieber nicht. Ich bin ein bißchen müde. Und das Wasser ist so wahnsinnig kalt. Gehen Sie doch ohne mich.

FRAU MÜLLER: Möchten Sie vielleicht lieber Karten spielen?

FRAU BRINKMANN: Ja, gerne!

Kitzbühel is a popular skiing and hiking resort in Tirol (Austria).

Winterurlaub

RICHARD: Möchtest du im Winter nach Österreich?

EVA: Super! Fahren wir doch im Januar nach Kitzbühel.

RICHARD: Hoffentlich können wir noch ein Hotelzimmer bekommen.

EVA: Ich glaube, es ist noch nicht zu spät.

Morgens um halb zehn

Das Frühstück originally meant the piece (**das Stück**) of bread eaten early (**früh**) in the morning.

ANITA: Also tschüs! Ich muß jetzt weg.

BEATE: Warte mal! Ohne Frühstück geht's nicht! Iß doch wenigstens ein Brötchen.

ANITA: Leider habe ich keine Zeit mehr. Mein Seminar beginnt um zehn, und unterwegs muß ich noch ein Heft kaufen.

BEATE: Nimm doch das Brötchen mit. Später wirst du sicher hungrig.

ANITA: Du hast recht . . . Also, bis nachher!

Beim Bäcker kauft man frische Brötchen.

Wortschatz 1

At the Lake

MRS. M.: Do you want to go swimming again, Mrs. Brinkmann?

MRS. B.: No, I'd rather not. I'm a little tired. And the water is so awfully cold. You go without me.

MRS. M.: Maybe you'd rather play cards?

MRS. B.: Yes, gladly!

Winter Vacation

R.: Would you like to go to Austria this winter?

E.: Great! Let's go to Kitzbühel in January!

R.: I hope we can still get a hotel room.

E.: I don't think it's too late yet.

9:30 in the Morning

A.: So long then. I've got to go now.

B.: Wait a second! Not without breakfast! Eat a roll at least.

A.: Unfortunately I have no more time. My seminar begins at ten, and on the way I still have to buy a notebook.

B.: Take the roll along. Later you're sure to get hungry.

A.: You're right . . . Well, see you later!

Brötchen (called **Semmeln** in southern Germany and Austria), crusty rolls baked fresh daily, are the most common breakfast food.

Verben

beginnen   to begin
bekommen   to receive
frühstücken   to eat breakfast
(etwas oder jemand) gern haben   to like something or someone
glauben   to believe; to think
kaufen   to buy
mögen (mag)   to like
schwimmen   to swim
warten   to wait
werden (wird)   to become, to get (*in the sense of "become"*)

Don't confuse **bekommen** (*to receive*) with **werden** (*to become*).

Substantive

der **See, -n**   lake
  am See   at the lake
der **Urlaub, -e**   vacation (*from a job*)
der **Winter, -**   winter
  im Winter   in the winter

das **Brötchen, -**   roll
das **Frühstück**   breakfast
  zum Frühstück   for breakfast
das **Hotel, -s**   hotel
(das) **Österreich**   Austria
das **Seminar, -e**   (*university*) seminar
das **Wasser**   water

die **Karte, -n**   card; ticket; map

Adjektive und Adverbien

einmal   once
  noch einmal   once again, once more
gern(e)   gladly, with pleasure

The final -e on **gerne** is optional; **gern** and **gerne** mean the same thing.

Gott sei Dank   thank goodness
hoffentlich   I hope . . .
hungrig   hungry
kalt   cold
lang(e)   long; for a long time
lieber (+ *verb*)   prefer to, would rather
  Ich spiele lieber Karten.   I'd rather play cards.
morgens (*adv.*)   in the morning(s)
müde   tired, weary
nachher   later on, after that
noch nicht   not yet
selbstverständlich   it goes without saying that . . ., of course
später   later
super (*colloq.*)   super, great
unterwegs   on the way; en route; on the go
weg   away, gone
zusammen   together

Andere Vokabeln

doch (*flavoring particle with commands, see p. 106*)
durch   through
gegen   against
mal (*flavoring particle with commands, see p. 106*)
mit   along (with me, us, etc.)
ohne   without
um   around; at (with times)

Nützliche Ausdrücke

Bis nachher!   See you later!
Es geht.   It's all right. It's possible. It can be done.
Es geht nicht.   Nothing doing. It can't be done.

Variationen

A Persönliche Fragen

1. Frau Brinkmann und Frau Müller spielen gern Karten. Was machen Sie gern?
2. Spielen Sie gern Karten, oder gehen Sie lieber schwimmen?
3. Frau Brinkmann sagt, sie ist ein bißchen müde. Sind Sie heute müde?
4. Wohin wollen Sie im Winter?
5. Essen Sie immer Frühstück, oder haben Sie manchmal keine Zeit?
6. Essen Sie gern Brötchen?
7. Wann beginnt die Deutschstunde?
8. Anita muß ein Heft kaufen. Was müssen Sie heute kaufen?

B Gruppenarbeit: Gegensätze (*Mit offenen Büchern*)

Contradict each other.

> BEISPIEL: A: Fremdsprachen sind unwichtig.
 B: Nein, sie sind wichtig.

1. 8.15 Uhr ist zu früh.
2. Dieses Buch ist langweilig.
3. Dieses Zimmer ist schön.
4. Wir kennen jemand in München.
5. Bernd haßt Rockmusik.
6. Du trägst oft Turnschuhe.
7. Sie sind immer müde.
8. Ich esse sehr langsam.

C Partnerarbeit: Wie kann man antworten?

For each sentence in the left column choose appropriate responses from the right column.

1. Gehen wir noch einmal schwimmen!	Super!
2. Das Wasser ist zu kalt!	Du hast recht.
3. Ohne Frühstück geht's nicht.	Stimmt schon.
4. Es gibt keine Hotelzimmer mehr.	Stimmt nicht.
5. Spielen wir zusammen Karten!	Das finde ich auch.
6. Das schaffst du leicht.	Gar nicht!
7. Bist du hungrig?	Es tut mir leid.
8. Ein Hotelzimmer mit Frühstück kostet DM 250!	Was ist denn los?
9. Du kommst wieder zu spät.	Um Gottes Willen!
10. Mensch, bin ich müde.	Nichts zu danken.
	Mensch!
	Phantastisch!
	Doch!
	Prima!
	Gerne!

Now choose one of the exchanges above and expand it into a mini-dialogue. Prepare to say it for the whole class.

BEISPIEL: A: Es gibt keine Hotelzimmer mehr.
B: Um Gottes Willen! Was machen wir denn?
A: Ich weiß nicht. Hoffentlich . . .

Mensch, bin ich todmüde!

Lyrik zum Vorlesen

Lab Manual Kap. 4, Lyrik zum Vorlesen.

Viele deutsche Kinder lernen dieses traditionelle Gedicht (*poem*) über die Jahreszeiten.

Die Jahreszeiten°	seasons
Es war° eine Mutter,	there was
Die hatte° vier Kinder:	who had
Den Frühling, den Sommer,	
Den Herbst und den Winter.	
Der Frühling bringt Blumen,°	flowers
Der Sommer bringt Klee,°	clover
Der Herbst, der° bringt Trauben,°	it / grapes
Der Winter bringt Schnee.°	snow

Grammatik

No German prepositions take nominative case, which is used only for the subject of a sentence and for predicate nominatives (see p. 36).

Prepositions with the Accusative Case

Prepositions are a class of words that show relationships of space (*through* the mountains), time (*until* Tuesday), or other relationships (*for* my friend, *without* any money). A preposition with the noun or pronoun that follows it is called a prepositional phrase. German prepositions are used with nouns in specific grammatical cases. Here is the list of prepositions that are always followed by the accusative case. Learn this list by heart.

bis	*until, by*	Wir warten **bis Dienstag.**
		Ich muß es **bis morgen** lesen.
durch	*through*	Er fährt **durch die Berge.**
für	*for*	Sie arbeitet **für ihren Vater.**
gegen	*against*	Was hast du **gegen mich?**
	around, about (with times)	Karl kommt **gegen drei.**
ohne	*without*	Wir gehen **ohne dich.**
um	*around* (the outside of)	Das Auto fährt **um das Hotel.**
	at (with times)	Karl kommt **um drei.**

In spoken German, **durch, für,** and **um** often contract with the article **das: durchs, fürs, ums.**

 Workbook Kap. 4, A, B.

1 Übung: Für wen?

Sie suchen eine Karte. Für wen suchen Sie sie?
Ich suche sie für mein-_____.
Sie machen heute das Frühstück. Für wen machen Sie es?
Ich mache es für mein-_____.

2 Übung: Ich mache das allein.

 Lab Manual Kap. 4, Var. zur Üb. 2.

Your instructor asks if you do things with other people in your class. Say that you do everything without them. Use pronouns in your answer.

1. Spielen Sie mit Richard Karten? Nein, ohne _____.
2. Arbeiten Sie morgen mit Ingrid zusammen? Nein, leider ohne _____.
3. Gehen Sie mit Robert und Susan schwimmen?
4. Frühstücken Sie am Mittwoch mit Patrick?

3 Übung: Wohin fährt Monika?

Monika is going to drive through various locations. Tell where she's driving. Use a complete sentence.

Sie fährt durch _____.
Dann fährt sie durch _____.

die Stadt

die Berge

das Dorf

der Wald

Übung: Wie sagt man das auf deutsch?

1. Are you for me or against me?
2. I'd like to take a trip around the world.
3. I hope I can do it without my parents.
4. She's looking for a card for her grandfather.
5. Let's drive through the mountains.

Making suggestions and giving commands are communicative goals.

Suggestions and Commands: The Imperative

The imperative form of German verbs is used either to make suggestions ("Let's go swimming") or to give commands ("Wait!").

"Let's do something": The *wir*-Imperative

Fahren wir nach Österreich.   ***Let's go** to Austria.*
Spielen wir Karten.   ***Let's play** cards.*

The **wir**-imperative has the same word order as a yes/no question, but at the end of the sentence, the voice drops instead of rising. Compare the following intonation curves:

Gehen wir nach Hause?   Gehen wir nach Hause!

*In the first dialogue on page 101, Frau Brinkmann uses the Sie-imperative: **Gehen Sie doch ohne mich.***

"Do something": The *Sie*-Imperative

Fahren Sie nach Österreich.   *Go to Austria.*
Bitte **besuchen Sie** mich im Mai.   *Please visit me in May.*

Note on Usage: Flavoring Particles *doch* and *mal*

doch **why don't you . . .** You can soften a command to a suggestion by adding the unstressed flavoring particle **doch.**

Gehen Sie nach Hause!   *Go home!*
Gehen Sie **doch** nach Hause.   *Why don't you go home.*

mal You can make a command more peremptory by adding the unstressed flavoring particle **mal.**

Warte!   *Wait!*
Warte **mal**!   *Wait a second!*
Hören Sie **mal**!   *Just listen here!*

*Bitte also turns an imperative into a polite request: **Gehen Sie bitte nach Hause.***

Note on punctuation: German uses an exclamation mark to add emphasis to commands.

---

5 Übung: Machen Sie das doch!

Encourage your instructor to go ahead and do something.

> BEISPIEL: Ich möchte eine Reise machen.
> Machen Sie doch eine Reise!

[handwritten: Kaufen Sie doch ein Brötchen]

1. Ich möchte Brötchen kaufen.
2. Ich möchte eine Pause machen.
3. Ich möchte nach Hause gehen.
4. Ich möchte Tennis spielen.
5. Ich möchte Frau Klein besuchen.
6. Ich möchte meinen Wagen verkaufen.

6 Übung: Nein, machen Sie das nicht!

Now tell your instructor *not* to do the things listed in **Übung 5.**

> BEISPIEL: Ich möchte nach Hause gehen.
> Nein, gehen Sie nicht nach Hause!

7 Gruppenarbeit: Ja, machen wir das!

Here are some activities you could do today. Take turns suggesting them to each other.

> BEISPIEL: schwimmen gehen
> A: Gehen wir heute schwimmen!
> B: Ja, machen wir das! *oder* Nein, lieber nicht.

jetzt frühstücken	eine Reise machen
Karten spielen	eine Pause machen
eine Zeitung kaufen	nach Hause laufen
zu Hause arbeiten	den Wagen verkaufen

Now suggest other things to do today.

8 Übung: Wie sagt man das auf deutsch? (*Mit offenen Büchern*)

Use the **Sie-** or **wir**-imperative.

1. Let's go swimming.
2. Buy a notebook.
3. Let's discuss our trip.
4. Learn a foreign language. *[handwritten: Lernen sie ein Fremdsprache]*
5. Please speak slowly.
6. Don't sleep now.
7. Let's walk a little bit.
8. Don't wear that.

Imperative Forms for *du* and *ihr*

To give commands or make suggestions to people whom you address with **du**, you need to learn the forms of the **du-** and **ihr-**imperatives.

The *du*-imperative The **du-**imperative of most verbs is simply the verb stem without ending.

KOMM IN DIE BERGE
... mach Ferien im Schnee!

Geh ohne mich.	*Go without me.*
Frag mich nicht.	*Don't ask me.*
Fahr schnell nach Hause!	*Drive home quickly!*
Sei nicht so langweilig.	*Don't be so boring.*

Note: The pronoun **du** is *not* used with the **du-**imperative!

If the verb changes its stem vowel from **e** to **i(e)**, the *changed* stem is used:

verb	statement	**du**-imperative
lesen	Du **liest** das für morgen.	**Lies** das für morgen.
geben	Du **gibst** Peter das Buch.	**Gib** Peter das Buch.
essen	Du **ißt** ein Brötchen.	**Iß** ein Brötchen.

Note that the stem-vowel change **a(u)** to **ä(u)** does *not* appear in the *du*-imperative:

fahren	Du **fährst** nach Hause.	**Fahr** nach Hause.
laufen	Du **läufst** zu schnell.	**Lauf** nicht so schnell!

Verb stems ending in **-d** or **-t** add an **-e** to the stem:

Arbeite nicht so viel.	*Don't work so hard.*
Warte doch!	*Wait!*

Lab Manual Kap. 4, Var. zur Üb. 9, 10; Üb. 11.

9 Übung: Ja, tu das doch!

Your instructor plays the part of your friend Beate. Tell her to go ahead and do the things she asks about.

> BIESPIEL: Soll ich da drüben halten?
> Ja, halte doch da drüben.

1. Soll ich Englisch lernen?
2. Soll ich mit Hans sprechen?
3. Soll ich Peter das Buch geben?
4. Soll ich schnell laufen?
5. Soll ich hier warten?
6. Soll ich Pommes frites essen?
7. Soll ich etwas singen?
8. Soll ich zu Fuß gehen?
9. Soll ich eine Zeitung lesen?
10. Soll ich eine Jacke tragen?

10 Partnerarbeit: Nein, lieber nicht.

Now tell your partner *not* to do the things listed in **Übung 9**. This time, do *not* use **doch**.

> BEISPIEL: Soll ich drüben parken?
> Nein, park nicht drüben.

Wie bitte? Was sollen wir essen?

Reminder: Sie- and **wir-**imperatives include the pronoun; **ihr-** and **du-**imperatives do not.

The *ihr*-imperative   The **ihr**-imperative is identical to the present-tense **ihr**-form, but without the pronoun.

present tense	*ihr* imperative
Ihr **bleibt** hier.	**Bleibt** hier.
Ihr **singt** zu laut.	**Singt** nicht so laut.
Ihr **seid** freundlich.	**Seid** freundlich.

11 Übung: Sollen wir das machen?

A. Your instructor plays one of a group of children and asks what they all should do.

> BEISPIEL: Sollen wir bald nach Hause kommen?
> Ja, kommt doch bald nach Hause.

1. Sollen wir Karten spielen?
2. Sollen wir das Buch lesen?
3. Sollen wir nach Hause laufen?
4. Sollen wir die Brötchen essen?

B. Now tell them what not to do.

> BEISPIEL: Sollen wir nach Hause kommen?
> Nein, kommt nicht nach Hause.

1. Sollen wir Jeans tragen?
2. Sollen wir heute kommen?
3. Sollen wir hier bleiben?
4. Sollen wir das sagen?

Imperative of *sein*

The verb **sein** is irregular in the **Sie**- and **wir**-imperatives (the **du**- and **ihr**-forms are regular):

Seien Sie bitte freundlich, Herr Kaiser.	*Please be friendly, Mr. Kaiser.*
Seien wir freundlich.	*Let's be friendly.*
Seid freundlich, Kinder.	*Be friendly, children.*
Sei freundlich, Rolf.	*Be friendly, Rolf.*

Lab Manual Kap. 4, Var. zur Üb. 12.

Workbook Kap. 4, C.

12 Übung: Sei doch . . . !

A. Tell the following people to be honest.

> BEISPIEL: Richard
> Sei doch ehrlich, Richard!

1. Kinder
2. Herr Bachmann
3. wir
4. Barbara

B. Now tell them not to be so boring.

> BEISPIEL: Herr Stolze
> Seien Sie doch nicht so langweilig, Herr Stolze!

1. Ute
2. Frau Klein
3. Thomas und Beate
4. wir

13 Übung: Wie sagt man das auf deutsch? (*Mit offenen Büchern*)

Use the **du**-imperative.

1. Please be honest.
2. Wear your jeans.
3. Please read the article.
4. Give Anita your notebook.

Now use the **ihr**-imperative.

5. Ask me later.
6. Please wait here.
7. Work together.
8. Don't be so pessimistic.

The only German verbs that are irregular in the present tense are **werden, sein, haben, wissen,** and the modal verbs. You have now learned them all.

The Verb *werden*

The verb **werden** (*to become*) is irregular in present tense **du-** and **er-**forms.

ich	werde	wir	werden
du	**wirst**	ihr	werdet
er/es/sie	**wird**	sie, Sie	werden

Werden is a frequently used verb. Its basic English equivalent is *to become, get.* It can be translated in various ways, depending upon context.

Es **wird** kalt.	*It's getting cold.*
Ihre Kinder **werden** groß.	*Your children are getting big.*
Meine Schwester will Professorin **werden**.	*My sister wants to become a professor.*
Am Montag **werde** ich endlich 21.	*I'm finally turning 21 on Monday.*

14 Übung: Wer wird müde?

Say who is getting tired.

BEISPIEL: Barbara
Barbara wird müde.

1. wir
2. die Kinder
3. meine Mutter
4. ihr
5. du
6. ich

15 Übung: Wie sagt man das auf englisch?

1. Morgen wird es heiß.
2. Wann wirst du denn zwanzig?
3. Draußen wird es warm.
4. Das Buch wird endlich interessant.
5. Meine zwei Freunde wollen Lehrer werden.

Negating *schon* and *noch*

The negations of **schon** (*already, yet*) are:

noch nicht	*not yet*
noch kein- [+ *noun*]	*not a* [+ noun] *yet*
	not any [+ noun] *yet*

Here are some examples of questions followed by negative answers.

Sind Sie **schon** hungrig?   *Are you hungry yet?*
Nein, **noch nicht.**   *No, not yet.*

Wollt ihr **schon** gehen?   *Do you want to leave already?*
Nein, wir wollen **noch nicht**   *No, we don't want to leave yet.*
 gehen.

Hast du **schon** Karten?   *Do you have tickets yet?*
Nein, ich habe **noch keine**   *No, I don't have any tickets yet.*
 Karten.

Kauft er **schon** einen Wagen?   *Is he already buying a car?*
Nein, er kauft **noch keinen**   *No, he's not buying a car yet.*
 Wagen.

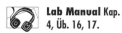

Lab Manual Kap. 4, Üb. 16, 17.

16 Übung: Nein, noch nicht.

Answer the following questions about Katrin Berger negatively, saying that things haven't happened yet.

1. Ist Katrin schon da?
2. Studiert sie schon in Berlin?
3. Kennt sie Frau Bachmann schon?
4. Beginnt das Semester schon?
5. Will sie schon essen?

17 Übung

Say you don't have any of these things yet.

1. Haben Sie schon Kinder?
2. Haben Sie schon eine Karte?
3. Haben Sie schon ein Hotelzimmer?
4. Besitzen Sie schon einen Wagen?
5. Haben Sie schon Angst?
6. Besitzen Sie schon einen Computer?

In **Übung 17**, the short answers would all be **Nein, noch nicht.** Complete-sentence answers, however, must use **noch kein-** [+ *noun*].

The negations of **noch** (*still*) are:

nicht mehr   *not any more, no longer*
kein- [+ *noun*] **mehr**   *no more* [+ noun], *not any more* [+ noun]

Here are some examples of questions followed by negative answers:

Regnet es **noch**?   *Is it still raining?*
Nein, **nicht mehr.**   *No, not any more.*

Studiert Rita **noch?**   *Is Rita still a student?*
Nein, sie studiert **nicht mehr.**   *No, she's no longer a student.*

Hast du **noch Geld**?   *Do you have any more money?*
Nein, ich habe **kein Geld mehr.**   *No, I haven't got any more money.*

Können wir **noch Karten**   *Can we still get tickets?*
 bekommen?
Leider habe ich **keine Karten**   *Unfortunately I have no more*
 mehr.   *tickets.*

Lab Manual Kap. 4, Üb. 18, 19; Var. zur Üb. 19.

Workbook Kap. 4, D.

18 Übung

Answer these questions negatively.

1. Wohnen Sie noch zu Hause?
2. Können Sie noch warten?
3. Ist es draußen noch kalt?
4. Ist Ihr Wagen noch neu?
5. Geht Ihre Uhr noch?
6. Können Sie uns noch besuchen?

19 Übung

Answer these questions negatively.

1. Hat er noch Arbeit?
2. Haben Sie noch Zeit?
3. Hat Ihre Großmutter noch einen Wagen?
4. Ist er noch ein Kind?
5. Gibt es noch Probleme?
6. Hören Sie noch Rockmusik?

Equivalents of English *to like*

Expressing likes, dislikes, and preferences is a communicative goal.

Gern is etymologically related to English *yearn*.

Verb + *gern(e)* = to like to do something

Ich **schwimme gern.**	*I like to swim.*
Sie **geht gern** zu Fuß.	*She likes to walk.*
Hören Sie **gerne** Musik?	*Do you like to listen to music?*

Gern(e) generally comes immediately after the subject and verb. The negation of **gern** is **nicht gern.**

Ich schwimme **nicht gern.**	*I don't like to swim.*

Lab Manual Kap. 4, Var. zur Üb. 20, 22.

20 Partnerarbeit: Ich höre gern Musik.

Take turns saying what you like to eat (**essen**), read (**lesen**), play (**spielen**), and listen to (**hören**). Here are some suggestions.

BEISPIEL: Ich höre gern Rockmusik. Und du?

Jazz	Fußball	Frühstück
Pizza	Brötchen	Volksmusik
Mozart	Zeitungen	Bücher
Tennis	Tischtennis	Lyrik (*poetry*)

21 Kettenreaktion: Was machen Sie gern? Was machen Sie lieber?

A: Ich spiele gern Tennis.

B: Sie spielt gern Tennis, aber ich lese lieber Bücher.

C: Er liest gern Bücher, aber ich _____ lieber _____.

usw.

Mögen or *gern haben* = to like someone or something

Ich **habe** dich sehr **gern.** } *I like you very much.*
Ich **mag** dich sehr.

Negation: Ich habe dich **nicht gern.**
Ich mag dich **nicht.**

Mögen is a modal verb. Its present-tense forms are:

mögen *to like (something)*			
ich	**mag**	wir	mögen
du	**magst**	ihr	mögt
er/es/sie	**mag**	sie, Sie	mögen

Use **mögen** or **gern** + *verb* to say what you like to eat: **Ich mag die Suppe heute** and **Brötchen esse ich gern.** Do not use **gern haben** for food.

Unlike the other modals, it is usually used without an infinitive.

Ich **mag** Maria.   *I like Maria.*
Mögen Sie die Suppe nicht?   *Don't you like the soup?*

22 Übung

Tell who likes Frau Brandt. Use the appropriate form of **mögen.**

BEISPIEL: die Schüler
            Die Schüler mögen Frau Brandt.

1. du   4. meine Eltern
2. wir   5. ich
3. Franz   6. ihr

23 Übung: Was haben Sie gern?

Say which things and people you like or dislike. Here are some ideas. Add some of your own. Use **gern haben** or **mögen.**

meine Mitbewohner   die Uni
das Mensaessen   meine Arbeit
den Winter   meine Geschwister
Hausaufgaben   Fremdsprachen

Summary: Three German Equivalents for *to like*

Distinguish carefully among the three German equivalents for English *to like*:

- **Möchte** means *would like to* do something and is used with a complementary infinitive (which may sometimes be omitted, see p. 82):

  Ich **möchte** Innsbruck besuchen.
  Ich **möchte** nach Innsbruck (fahren).

- A *verb* + **gern** means *to like to do something.*

  Ich spiele **gern** Karten.

Möchte expresses a wish for something, while a *verb* + **gern** makes a general statement about your likes or dislikes:

| Ich **möchte** Karten spielen. | *I would like to play cards.* |
| Ich spiele **gern** Karten. | *I like to play cards.* |

- **Mögen** or **gern haben** means *to like* people or things and is used with a noun or pronoun:

  Ich **mag** Professor Jaeger.
  Ich **habe** ihn **gern**.

24 Übung: Wie sagt man das auf deutsch?

1. I like the soup.
2. I like to eat soup.
3. I would like the soup.
4. They would like to study in Germany.
5. Karl doesn't like to wait.
6. Do you like Professor Lange?
7. Our children like to play outside.
8. We would like to drive home.
9. I don't like that.
10. I like her.

Sentence Adverbs

Sentence adverbs modify entire sentences and express the speaker's attitude toward the content of the whole:

Natürlich bin ich morgens müde.	*Of course I'm tired in the morning.*
Du hast **sicher** genug Geld.	*You **surely** have enough money.*
Leider habe ich keine Zeit mehr.	*Unfortunately I have no more time.*
Gott sei Dank ist es nicht mehr so heiß.	*Thank goodness it's not so hot any more.*
Du kannst mich **hoffentlich** verstehen.	*I hope you can understand me.*
Selbstverständlich mag ich Pizza.	*Of course I like pizza.*
Übrigens habe ich kein Geld mehr.	*By the way, I don't have any more money.*

Lab Manual Kap. 4, Var. zur Üb. 25.

Workbook Kap. 4, E.

25 Übung: Selbstverständlich!

Answer these questions emphatically. Show that your answer is obvious by beginning it with **Selbstverständlich** . . . or **Natürlich** . . .

BEISPIEL: Lernen Sie Deutsch?
Selbstverständlich lerne ich Deutsch!

1. Frühstücken Sie bald?
2. Sind Sie hungrig?
3. Haben Sie Zeit für mich?
4. Möchten Sie nach Österreich?
5. Schwimmen Sie gern?
6. Spielen Sie gern Karten?

Segelboot im Hafen von Lindau (Bodensee).

26 Übung: Leider!

Answer these questions. Show that you regret having to answer "yes" by beginning your answer with **Ja, leider . . .**

> BEISPIEL: Regnet es noch?
> Ja, leider regnet es noch.

1. Schneit es noch?
2. Haben Sie viele Fragen?
3. Sind Sie sehr müde?
4. Ist der Berg sehr steil?
5. Gehen Sie ohne mich?
6. Ist das Wasser zu kalt?

Gehen + infinitive

The verb **gehen** is often used with an infinitive as its complement.

Sie **geht** oft **schwimmen.**	*She often goes swimming.*
Gehen wir noch einmal **schwimmen!**	*Let's go swimming again!*
Ich **gehe** mit Dieter **schwimmen.**	*I'm going swimming with Dieter.*

The complementary infinitive **schwimmen** is the second part of the predicate and comes at the end of the sentence.

Note what happens when the entire verbal idea **schwimmen gehen** (*to go swimming*) is used as the complement of a modal verb:

Wir wollen heute **schwimmen gehen.**	*We want to go swimming today.*

27 Partnerarbeit: Dann geh doch . . . !

Partner 1 reads the sentences on the left. Partner 2 then tells partner 1 what to do, choosing an appropriate activity from the right-hand column.

> BEISPIEL: Ich bin müde.
> Dann geh doch schlafen!

1. Ich muß Geld verdienen.
2. Ich bin hungrig.
3. Ich möchte gern fit bleiben.
4. Ich bin müde!

arbeiten gehen
schlafen gehen
essen gehen
Tennis spielen gehen

Deutschland: Geographie und Klima

Tips zum Lesen und Lernen

Tips zum Vokabelnlernen

- Note that all four compass points are masculine:

der Norden	der Osten
der Süden	der Westen

  Remember that the days, seasons, and the months are also masculine:

der Montag	der Januar
der Dienstag	der Februar
der Mittwoch	der März
der Donnerstag	der April
der Freitag	der Mai
der Samstag (oder Sonnabend)	der Juni
der Sonntag	der Juli
	der August
der Frühling	der September
der Sommer	der Oktober
der Herbst	der November
der Winter	der Dezember

Haupt is derived from Latin *caput* (head).

- The prefix **Haupt-** is attached to nouns and adds the meaning *main, chief, primary, principal, most important.*

die **Haupt**regionen	*the principal regions*
die **Haupt**frage	*the main question*
die **Haupt**stadt	*the capital city*
die **Haupt**rolle	*the leading role*
die **Haupt**straße	*the main street*

Lab Manual Kap. 4, Üb. zur Betonung.

Kolonie: Both this word and the city name Cologne (German **Köln**) are derived from Latin *colonia.* The Roman emperor Claudius named the city Colonia Agrippinensis in A.D. 50 after his wife Agrippina. Its strategic position on the Rhine made it the capital of the Roman colony *Germania Inferior.*

Leicht zu merken

die **Alpen**
barbarisch
die **Geographie**   Geographie
geographisch
die **Kolonie, -n**   Kolonie
der **Kontrast, -e**   Kontrast
die **Kultur, -en**   Kultur
mild
die **Region**   Region
der **Rhein**
wild
zirka

Rivers in German are generally **die**. Exceptions are **der Rhein, der Main, der Inn, der Lech, der Neckar,** and foreign rivers (**der Nil, der Mississippi**) except those ending in *-a* or *-e* (**die Themse, die Rhone**).

das Meer
die Insel
die Küste
das Tiefland
der Hügel
der Fluß
der Baum
der Berg
der Wald
der See
das Gebirge
das Hochland

Einstieg in den Text

The reading in this chapter builds on familiar vocabulary about the weather (**das Wetter**) and discusses climate and geography (**Klima und Geographie**).

Study this map and try to guess the meanings of the new words.

The word **Wein** is not of Germanic origin but was introduced by the Romans (Latin *vinum*) along with viniculture. The word **Bier** comes from Latin *bibere* (*to drink*). The Germanic word for beer is preserved in English *ale*, which was brewed without hops. The medieval cloister breweries first added hops to the beverage.

Wortschatz 2

Verben

beschreiben   to describe
fließen   to flow
liegen   to lie; to be situated
trinken   to drink
wandern   to hike; to wander

Substantive

der **Baum, ⸚e**   tree
der **Fluß, Flüsse**   river
der **Frühling**   spring
der **Herbst**   fall, autumn
der **Hügel, -**   hill
der **Norden**   the North
der **Osten**   the East
der **Schnee**   snow
der **Sommer**   summer
der **Süden**   the South
der **Wald, ⸚er**   forest

The obvious cognates in points of the compass and seasons (**der Herbst**, English *harvest*) recall common Germanic designations for time and space.

der **Wein, -e**   wine
der **Westen**   the West

das **Bier, -e**   beer
(das) **Italien**   Italy
das **Klima**   climate
das **Land, ⸚er**   country
das **Leben**   life
das **Lied, -er**   song
   das **Volkslied, -er**   folk song
das **Märchen, -**   fairy tale
das **Meer, -e**   sea
das **Tal, ⸚er**   valley

die **Landschaft, -en**   landscape
die **Schweiz**   Switzerland
die **Stadt, ⸚e**   city

Adjektive und Adverbien

flach   flat
hoch   high
immer noch / noch immer
   still (*intensification of noch*)

modern   modern
naß   wet, damp
schrecklich   terrible
sonnig   sunny
trocken   dry

Andere Vokabeln

von   from

Nützliche Ausdrücke

im Süden (im Norden usw.)
   in the South (in the North, etc.)
im Winter (im Sommer usw.)
   in the winter (in the summer, etc.)

Gegensätze

naß ≠ trocken   wet ≠ dry
modern ≠ altmodisch
   modern ≠ old-fashioned

Deutschland: Geographie und Klima

Lab Manual Kap. 4, Lesestück.

Für die alten Römer° war° das Leben in der Kolonie Germania nicht sehr schön. Der Historiker° Tacitus (zirka 55 bis 115 n.Chr.°) beschreibt das Land als° kalt und neblig.° Über die Germanen° schreibt er: „Sie sind ohne Kultur, haben keine Städte und leben im Wald. Sie sind wild und barbarisch, wie ihr Land."

Das moderne Deutschland liegt in Mitteleuropa, und die „wilden Germanen" wohnen heute zum größten Teil° in der Stadt.[1] Es gibt keinen Urwald° mehr, aber der Wald ist immer noch typisch und wichtig für die Landschaft in Deutschland, Österreich und der Schweiz. Am Sonntag wandert man gern durch die Wälder, und die Kinder hören auch heute noch gern Märchen wie „Hänsel und Gretel" oder „Schneewittchen".[2] In solchen° Märchen und auch in deutschen Volksliedern spielt der Wald eine große Rolle.

Romans / was
*historian / **nach Christus** = A.D.*
as / foggy / Germanic peoples

Cultural goal: Learning about the climate and geography of Germany.

zum... = for the most part
primeval forest

such

Familienwanderung im Regen.

---

[1] **Die Germanen** were the ancient tribes that the Romans called collectively *germani*. The word **Deutsch** comes from Old High German **diot** (*people*). The French applied the name of one tribe, the *alemanni*, to the whole people: *les Allemands*.

[2] *Snow White.* Other folk tales are **Dornröschen** (*Sleeping Beauty*), **Rotkäppchen** (*Little Red Riding Hood*), **Aschenputtel** (*Cinderella*), and **Der Froschkönig** (*The Frog King*).

Auch das Klima in Deutschland ist Gott sei Dank nicht so
15 schrecklich, wie° Tacitus meint. Selbstverständlich ist es nicht so
warm und sonnig wie in Italien, aber das deutsche Klima ist eigentlich
ziemlich mild. In den Flußtälern wird es zum Beispiel im Winter nicht
sehr kalt. Die großen Flüsse—der Rhein, die Weser, die Elbe und die
Oder—fließen durch das Land von Süden nach Norden. Nur die
20 Donau° fließt von Westen nach Osten. Am Rhein und an der° Donau
trinkt man gern Wein; die Römer brachten° den Weinbau° nach
Deutschland. Die Deutschen trinken also nicht nur Bier.

Es gibt in Deutschland drei geographische Hauptregionen. Im
Norden ist das Land flach und fruchtbar und ohne viele Bäume. Hier
25 beeinflußt° das Meer—die Nordsee und die Ostsee—Landschaft und
Klima. Diese° Region nennt man das Norddeutsche Tiefland.° In der
Mitte des Landes° aber gibt es viele Hügel und kleine Berge. Man
nennt diese Region das Mittelgebirge.° Im Süden liegt das Hochge-
birge°—die Alpen. Hier gibt es natürlich viel Schnee im Winter, denn°
30 die Berge sind sehr hoch. Deutschlands höchster° Berg ist die
Zugspitze (2 963 m). Man sieht also, in Deutschland gibt es viele Kon-
traste: Stadt und Land, Wald und Feld,° Berge und Meer.

so . . . wie = as . . . as

the Danube River / **am** and **an
der** = on the
brought / viniculture

influences
this / North German lowlands
In... In the middle of the country
central mountains
high mountains / because
highest

field

Burgruine (*castle ruin*) Ehrenfels
am Rhein.

Fragen zum Lesestück

1. Wie beschreibt Tacitus die Kolonie
   Germania?
2. Was ist noch immer typisch für die
   Landschaft in Deutschland?
3. Was macht man gern am Sonntag?
4. Was spielt eine große Rolle in „Hänsel und
   Gretel"? Kennen Sie andere Märchen?
5. Wie ist das Klima in Deutschland?
6. Ist es so warm und sonnig wie in Italien?
7. Wo trinkt man viel Wein?
8. Wie ist das Land im Norden?
9. Wo gibt es viel Schnee im Winter?
10. Wie heißen die drei geographischen
    Hauptregionen?

Situationen aus dem Alltag

Discussing weather, climate, and landscape is a communicative goal.

Klima, Wetter und Landschaft

You already know some of these words from the introductory chapter (see pp. 13–14).

Klima und Wetter

die **Luft**   *air*
der **Regen**   *rain*
  regnerisch   *rainy*
  Es regnet.
der **Schnee**
  Es schneit.
der **Wind**   *wind*
  Es ist windig.
wolkig
neblig
sonnig
windig
kalt ≠ **heiß**
warm ≠ **kühl**
naß ≠ **trocken**
mild

Landschaft

der **Baum, ¨e**
der **Berg, -e**
  bergig   *mountainous*
der **Wald, ¨er**
das **Meer, -e**

der **Hügel, -**
  hügelig   *hilly*
das **Tal, ¨er**

Gruppenarbeit: Sprechen wir über Klima und Landschaft

Beschreiben Sie die Landschaft in diesen Fotos.

1.

2.

3.

Partnerarbeit: Landschaft und Klima, wo ich wohne.

Find out where your partner comes from and ask about the climate and geography there.

BEISPIEL: Woher kommst du denn?
  Wie ist das Klima dort im Sommer?
  Kannst du die Landschaft beschreiben?

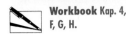

Zum Schluß

Sprechen wir miteinander!

Lab Manual Kap. 4, Diktat.

Workbook Kap. 4, F, G, H.

A Partnerarbeit: Sei doch (nicht) . . . !

Give your partner some ideas for self-improvement. Take turns telling each other how you should be (or not be).

> BEISPIEL: Sei doch ehrlich!
> Sei doch nicht sauer!

guter Laune	sauer	höflich
schlechter Laune	munter	fit
glücklich	freundlich	ehrlich

B Partnerarbeit: Nein, das darfst du nicht!

Ask your partner for permission to do something. Your partner tells you to do something else. The list will help you get started. Then try inventing some of your own exchanges.

> BEISPIEL: zu Hause bleiben? draußen spielen
> A: Darf ich zu Hause bleiben?
> B: Nein, spiel doch draußen!

nach Hause fahren?	zu Fuß gehen
Tennis spielen?	deine Hausaufgaben machen
jetzt Pizza essen?	bis heute abend warten

C Partnerarbeit: Macht das bitte für uns!

Machen Sie zusammen eine Liste: Was können andere Studenten für Sie machen? Seien Sie kreativ!

> BEISPIEL: Sie können für uns . . .
> die Bücher tragen
> die Hausaufgaben schreiben
> usw.

Sie und Ihr Partner sagen jetzt zu zwei anderen Studenten, sie sollen etwas für Sie machen. Die anderen antworten **ja** oder **nein**.

> BEISPIEL: A + B: Jennifer und Brian, tragt bitte die Bücher für uns.
> C + D: Ja, O.K., das machen wir gern für euch. *oder*
> Nein, das wollen wir nicht machen.

D Gruppenarbeit

Expressing likes and dislikes is a communicative goal.

Say what you like and don't like about university life. Also say what you like and don't like to do. Your instructor will write your responses on the board.

> BEISPIEL: Ich habe meine Mitbewohnerin sehr gern.
> Ich mag das Essen nicht.

E **Gruppenarbeit: Was wollen wir denn machen?**

Planen wir einen Urlaub. Lesen wir zusammen diese Anzeigen für Ferienorte. Hier gibt es sehr viel zu tun! Was machen Sie gerne? Was machen Sie lieber? Wollen wir schwimmen oder wandern gehen?

Die Landschaft für Aktivurlaub und echte Erholung

Lenzkirch Saig ○ Kappel Raitenbuch

Hochschwarzwald Titisee-Feldberg bei 800-1100 m

Wandern, Tennis, Reiten, Wintersport, heilklimatischer Jahreskurort, Luftkurort, Kur- und Höhenbäder, beheiztes Freibad, Schwarzwälder Gastlichkeit, sonnige Höhenlage.

Natur erleben
Kanu + Wandern
Ausgerüstete Touren in Skandinavien u. Grönland
Auch für Unerfahrene.
Informationen bei
SUN-TEAM, 2 HH 76
Lachnerstr. 1/1
Tel. 040/279 88 88

Schreiben Sie zu Hause

F **Phantasiefrage**   You are the Roman historian Tacitus. You have returned to contemporary Germany to update your impressions. Write in German about the country. What do people still (**noch**) do or no longer (**nicht mehr**) do? What plays a role in modern life? How are things nowadays, such as the cities, the wine, etc.?

 G   Write sentences using the elements below. You may have to add words.

1. wer / wollen / wandern / durch / Berge?
2. er / möchten / fahren / ohne / sein / Freund
3. leider / wir / haben / kein / mehr / Brötchen (*pl.*)
4. du / können / vier Uhr / gehen / schwimmen
5. wir / gehen / zusammen / durch / Tal
6. im Winter / ich / mögen / die Berge

 H   **Wie sagt man das auf deutsch?**

1. The sun is shining and the water is warm. Let's go swimming.
2. I don't want to go swimming yet. Go without me.
3. But I don't like to swim alone.
4. Do you like the winter, Stefan?
5. No, I don't like it any more.
6. I don't like to walk through the snow.
7. Wait here, Sabrina and Harald.
8. We don't want to wait.
9. I hope that you still have money.
10. Unfortunately, I don't have any more money.
11. Can you do something for me?
12. Unfortunately, I have to go home now.

With this chapter you have completed the first quarter of *Neue Horizonte*. For a concise review of the grammar and idiomatic phrases in chapters 1–4, you may consult the **Zusammenfassung und Wiederholung 1** *(Summary and Review 1)* on pages 35–47 of your Workbook. The review section is followed by a self-correcting test.

VIDEOECKE

2 Ohne Frühstück geht's nicht! (5:29)

Es ist schon acht Uhr, aber die Studentin Katrin Berger schläft noch. Harald will sie darum wecken (wake). Katrin ist in Eile und muß schnell weg — ihr Seminar beginnt ja um 10. Aber Herr Blum meint, sie muß noch etwas essen. Seinen Regenschirm soll Katrin auch mitnehmen (take along). Es soll heute regnen. Katrin geht weg, aber dann beginnt der Regen, und sie muß zurückkommen und den Schirm holen (get).

Wortschatz zum Video	
aufstehen	*to get up*
wecken	*to wake (someone) up*
die **Butter**	*butter*
das **Ei, -er**	*egg*
die **Erdbeermarmelade**	*strawberry jam*
die **Wurst, ¨e**	*sausage*
vorher	*before that*
Ich bin spät dran.	*I'm late.*
Setzen Sie sich.	*Sit down.*
eine Tasse Tee	*a cup of tea*

A Was sehen Sie im Video?

Watch video Module 2 (5:43–8:36) once without sound. Check off in the list below what you see in the video.

Ich sehe . . .

____ 1. ein Ei	____ 4. Tee	____ 7. einen CD-Spieler
____ 2. Pommes frites	____ 5. Kaffee	____ 8. Bier
____ 3. eine Zeitung	____ 6. Marmelade	____ 9. Frau Bachmann

B Was hören Sie?

Now watch the same section with sound, checking off the words you hear. Try to guess the meanings of the ones you haven't yet learned.

____ 1. früh	____ 4. Brötchen	____ 7. Regenmantel
____ 2. aufstehen	____ 5. Tee	____ 8. Regenschirm
____ 3. Brot	____ 6. Heft	

Land und Leute

Choose the person who does or says the following.

a. Harald   b. Katrin   c. Herr Blum
d. Frau Bachmann   e. Stefan

1. _____ schläft ein bißchen zu lange.
2. _____ sagt: „Ich muß weg!"
3. _____ sagt: „Nimm doch ein Brötchen mit."
4. _____ muß schnell ein Buch kaufen.
5. _____ besitzt keinen Regenschirm.

D **Richtig oder falsch?**

Indicate whether each statement is **richtig** (**R**) or **falsch** (**F**).

1. Es ist Viertel vor acht.	R	F
2. Harald geht Katrin wecken.	R	F
3. Katrin ißt ein Ei.	R	F
4. Vor ihrem Seminar muß Katrin ein Buch kaufen.	R	F
5. Herr Blum ist heute in Eile.	R	F
6. Katrin braucht keinen Regenschirm.	R	F

E **Was ist die beste Lösung?**

Complete the sentence with the best word or phrase.

1. Tschüs, Kinder. Ich muß jetzt _____ .
   a. kaufen   b. studieren   c. gehen

2. Nehmen Sie doch _____ ein Ei oder Butter und Wurst.
   a. hoffentlich   b. wenigstens   c. um 9 Uhr

3. Sie sollten aber einen Regenschirm _____ !
   a. vergessen   b. finden   c. mitnehmen

4. Ich habe ein Seminar _____ .
   a. am Donnerstag   b. um halb elf   c. um zehn

5. _____ muß ich noch ein Buch kaufen.
   a. Früher   b. Vor   c. Vorher

F **Welle Magazin: Was sehen Sie?**

Read through the list below. Then watch the **Welle Magazin** (8:38–9:30) and check off the words and things you see in the video.

Ich sehe . . .

_____ 1. Eduscho (*brand of coffee*)
_____ 2. Berliner Morgenpost (eine Berliner Zeitung)
_____ 3. eine Schule
_____ 4. Zum Imbiss (ein Restaurant, wo man schnell essen kann)
_____ 5. die Familie Bachmann im Garten
_____ 6. Konditorei (Hier kann man Kaffee und Kuchen bekommen.)
_____ 7. eine Küche

The Common Origin of German and English

Although Tacitus thought the Germanic tribes had "always been there," they in fact originated in the Baltic region around the second millenium B.C. As the Roman Empire began to collapse in the fourth century A.D., the Germanic peoples migrated south, a movement that continued for nearly two hundred years. The **Germani** (as they were called by the Romans) displaced the Celts from the heart of the European continent, pushing them as far west as Ireland. The Romans temporarily halted Germanic expansion southward by establishing their own northern frontier, a series of fortifications called the **limes,** literally the "limits" or boundaries of their empire. Remains of the **limes** can be seen in Germany today. Contemporary dialects and regional differences within the German-speaking countries have their origins in the various Germanic tribes of the early Middle Ages.

Thanks to the migration of the Germanic Angles and Saxons to the British Isles in the fifth century A.D., the Germanic language that was to evolve into modern English was introduced there. German and English thus share common origins. Some other languages included in the Germanic family are Yiddish, Dutch, Flemish, Norwegian, Swedish, Danish, and Icelandic. You will easily recognize cognates (words that have the same etymological root) in English and German, although different meanings may have developed. These words can be readily identified by some regularly occurring consonant shifts. Try guessing the English equivalents for the following words:

German	English	Related Words
z	t	zehn = ten
		Herz =
ss	t	Wasser =
		groß =
pf	p	Pflanze =
ff	p or pp	Schiff =
		Pfeffer und Salz =
ch	k	machen =
		Milch =
t	d	Tag =
		Tür =
d	th	du =
		drei =
		Pfad =

Land und Leute

Arbeit und Freizeit

Communicative Goals

- Talking about work and professions
- Showing, giving, and telling things to people
- Asking about prices in shops
- Saying when and for how long things happen

Cultural Goal

- Learning about the world of work in Germany

DIALOGE

🎧 **Lab Manual** Kap. 5, Dialoge, Fragen, Hören Sie gut zu!, Üb. zur Aussprache (I).

Der neue Bäckerlehrling kommt an

Morgens um 6:00. Georg macht die Bäckerei auf.

MARTIN: Morgen. Ich heiße Martin Holst. Ich fange heute bei euch an.

GEORG: Morgen, Martin. Mein Name ist Georg. Den Chef lernst du gleich kennen.

MARTIN: Ist gut. Seit wann arbeitest du denn hier?

GEORG: Erst seit einem Jahr. Komm jetzt mit, und ich zeige dir den Laden.

Beim Bäcker

DM 6,80 is pronounced sechs Mark achtzig.

VERKÄUFERIN: Was darf's sein, bitte?

KUNDE: Geben Sie mir bitte sechs Brötchen und ein Bauernbrot.

VERKÄUFERIN: (*Sie gibt ihm das Brot.*) So, bitte sehr. Sonst noch etwas?

KUNDE: Sind diese Brezeln frisch?

VERKÄUFERIN: Ja, von heute morgen.

KUNDE: Dann geben Sie mir doch sechs Stück. Wieviel kostet das bitte?

VERKÄUFERIN: Das macht zusammen DM 6,80, bitte sehr.

KUNDE: Danke. Auf Wiedersehen.

VERKÄUFERIN: Wiedersehen.

Schule oder Beruf?

Lehrling: apprentice in training, colloquially called **Azubi** (acronym for the official term **Auszubildender** = *person to be trained*).

VATER: Warum willst du denn jetzt die Schule verlassen? Deine Noten sind ja ganz gut, und du hast nur noch ein Jahr.

KURT: Aber das Abitur brauch' ich nicht. Ich will ja Automechaniker werden.

VATER: Sei nicht so dumm! Als Lehrling verdienst du schlecht.

KURT: Aber ich hab' die Nase einfach voll. Ich möchte lieber mit den Händen arbeiten.

VATER: Quatsch! Du schaffst das Abitur, und ich schenke dir ein Motorrad. Einverstanden?

KURT: Hmmm.

Note on Usage: *Seit wann?*

| Seit wann **arbeitest** du hier? | *How long **have** you **worked** here?* |

English uses perfect tense (**have worked**) for a situation beginning in the past but still continuing. German uses present (**arbeitest**).

The New Baker's Apprentice Arrives

Six A.M. Georg is opening the bakery.

M.: Morning. My name is Martin Holst. I'm starting here today.

G.: Morning, Martin. My name is Georg. You'll meet the boss soon.

M.: O.K. How long have you been working here?

G.: Only for a year. Now come with me and I'll show you the shop.

At the Baker's

*CL.: May I help you?

**CU.: Give me six rolls and one loaf of dark bread, please.

CL.: (*She gives him the bread.*) There you are. Anything else?

CU.: Are these pretzels fresh?

CL.: Yes, from this morning.

CU.: Then give me six of those. How much is that, please?

CL.: Together that comes to six marks eighty.

CU.: Thank you. Good-bye.

CL.: Bye.

School or Profession?

F.: Why do you want to leave school now? Your grades are pretty good and you've only got one more year.

K.: But I don't need the **Abitur**. I want to be an auto mechanic.

F.: Don't be so dumb. You won't earn much as an apprentice.

K.: But I'm fed up. I'd rather work with my hands.

F.: Nonsense! You pass your **Abitur** and I'll give you a motorcycle. Is it a deal?

K.: Hmmm.

*CL = Clerk

**CU = Customer

Wortschatz 1

See p. 139 for an explanation of the raised dot in **an·fangen** and other verbs.

Verben

an·fangen (fängt an) to begin, start

an·kommen to arrive

an·rufen to call up

auf·hören (mit etwas) to cease, stop (*doing something*)

auf·machen to open

auf·stehen to stand up; to get up; get out of bed

kennen·lernen to get to know; to meet

kosten to cost

mit·kommen to come along

schenken to give (*as a gift*)

stehen to stand

verlassen (verläßt) (*trans.*) to leave (*a person or place*)

zeigen to show

Substantive

der **Automechaniker, -** auto mechanic

der **Bäcker, -** baker

der **Bauer, -n** farmer

der **Chef, -s** boss

der **Kunde, -n** customer (*m.*)

der **Laden, ⁓** shop, store

der **Lehrling, -e** apprentice

der **Name, -n** name

das **Abitur** final secondary school examination

das **Brot** bread

das **Bauernbrot** dark bread

das **Jahr, -e** year

das **Motorrad, ⁓er** motorcycle

das **Stück, -e** piece

sechs **Stück** six (*of the same item*)

die **Bäckerei, -en** bakery

die **Brezel, -n** soft pretzel

die **Chefin, -nen** boss (*f.*)

die **Deutsche Mark (DM)** the German mark

die **Hand, ⁓e** hand

die **Kundin, -nen** customer (*f.*)

die **Nase, -n** nose

die **Note, -n** grade

die **Woche, -n** week

Adjektive und Adverbien

dumm dumb

einfach simple, easy

erst not until; only

fertig (mit) done, finished (with); ready

frisch fresh

gleich right away, immediately

heute morgen this morning

voll full

Andere Vokabeln

als as a

als Lehrling as an apprentice

als Kind as a child

dies- this, these

dir (to *or* for) you

euch (to *or* for) you (*pl.*)

jed- each, every

wem? to *or* for whom?

wieviel? how much?

Dies- and **jed·:** These words (*this, every*) always take endings (**dieser, jede**, etc.).

Präpositionen mit Dativ

The eight prepositions below are followed by dative case. See **Grammatik**, p. 137.

aus   out of; from
außer   except for; besides
bei   at; at the home of
   bei euch   with you, at your place (*i.e., where you work or live*)
mit   with
nach   after
seit   since (*temporal*)
von   from; of; by
zu   to

Nützliche Ausdrücke

Bitte sehr.   Here it is. There you are.

Einverstanden.   Agreed. It's a deal. O.K.
Ich habe die Nase voll.   I'm fed up. I've had it up to here.
Was darf es sein?   What'll it be? May I help you?
Sonst noch etwas?   Will there be anything else?
Das macht zusammen . . .   All together that comes to . . .
Ist gut. (*colloq.*)   O.K.; Fine by me.
Quatsch!   Baloney! Nonsense!

Gegensätze

an·fangen ≠ **auf·hören** to start ≠ to stop
auf·machen ≠ **zu·machen** to open ≠ to close
dumm ≠ **klug**   dumb ≠ smart, bright
einfach ≠ **schwierig** simple ≠ difficult
voll ≠ **leer**   full ≠ empty

Mit anderen Worten

das Abitur = **das Abi** (*Schülerslang*)
dumm = **blöd**

„bei Heinz Holl"
Spezialitäten Restaurant für Kenner
Geöffnet: Mo. - Sa. 19.00 -2.00 Uhr

1 Berlin 31
Damaschkestraße 26
Tel.: 32 31 40 04

Tischbestellungen erbeten!

Variationen

A Persönliche Fragen

1. Der Vater schenkt Kurt ein Motorrad. Was schenkt Ihnen Ihr Vater? Er schenkt mir _____.
2. Kurt sagt, das Abitur braucht er nicht. Was brauchen *Sie* nicht?
3. Kurt hat nur noch ein Jahr, und dann ist er mit der Schule fertig. Wie viele Jahre haben Sie noch an der Uni?
4. Kurt arbeitet gern mit den Händen. Arbeiten Sie auch gern mit den Händen?
5. Martin lernt den Chef gleich kennen. Wen möchten *Sie* kennenlernen?
6. Sechs Brezeln und ein Bauernbrot kosten DM 6,80. Was kosten 12 Brezeln und zwei Bauernbrote?

B Partnerarbeit: Was darf's sein? (*mit offenen Büchern*)

Partner A spielt den Verkäufer oder die Verkäuferin, Partner B spielt eine Kundin oder einen Kunden. Für das Semester müssen Sie viel kaufen. Spielen Sie diesen Dialog zusammen. Hier sehen Sie, was man kaufen kann.

A: Guten Tag. Was darf's denn sein, bitte?

B: Zeigen Sie mir bitte _____ .

A: Bitte sehr.

B: Was kostet denn _____ ?

A: Das kostet _____ .

B: Ich möchte gern _____ , _____ und _____ kaufen.

A: Das macht zusammen DM _____ , bitte sehr.

"The Germans have an inhuman way of cutting up their verbs. Now a verb has a hard enough time of it in this world when it's all together. It's downright inhuman to split it up. But that's just what those Germans do. They take part of a verb and put it down here, like a stake, and they take the other part of it and put it away over yonder like another stake, and between these two limits they just shovel in German."

Mark Twain

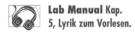
Richard Dehmel worked as a journalist in Berlin and was active in progressive literary circles. The language of his revolutionary lyric poetry was influenced by the philosopher Friedrich Nietzsche. In this poem an **Arbeitsmann** (*day laborer*) contrasts his family's life of toil and deprivation with the freedom, beauty, and fearlessness of the swallows that he and his child see on a Sunday walk.

Lab Manual Kap. 5, Lyrik zum Vorlesen.

Der Arbeitsmann

Wir haben ein Bett,° wir haben ein Kind,   bed
Mein Weib!°   **mein Weib = meine Frau**
Wir haben auch Arbeit, und gar zu zweit,°   **und**... = and even together
Und haben die Sonne und Regen und Wind.
Und uns fehlt nur eine Kleinigkeit,°   **uns**... = we lack only a small thing
Um so frei zu° sein, wie die Vögel° sind: **um ... zu** = in order to / birds
Nur Zeit.

Wenn wir sonntags° durch die Felder° gehn,   on Sundays / fields
Mein Kind,
Und über den Ähren weit und breit°   **über**... = above the grain far and wide
Das blaue Schwalbenvolk blitzen sehn,°   **Das**... = see flocks of blue swallows flashing
Oh, dann fehlt uns nicht das bißchen
Kleid,
Um so schön zu sein, wie die Vögel sind:
Nur Zeit.

Nur Zeit! wir wittern° Gewitterwind,°   smell / stormwind
Wir Volk.°   common folk
Nur eine kleine Ewigkeit;°   eternity
Uns fehlt ja nichts, mein Weib, mein Kind,
Als all das, was durch uns gedeiht,°   **als**... = except for all that prospers through us
Um so kühn° zu sein, wie die Vögel sind.   daring
Nur Zeit!

Richard Dehmel (1863–1920)

Grammatik

Dative Case

The dative case is the case of the indirect object in German. An indirect object is the person or thing *for* whom an action is performed or *to* whom it is directed.

> Sie gibt **ihm** das Brot.   *She gives him the bread.* or
>   *She gives the bread to him.*

English shows the indirect object by means of word order and in some cases also uses a preposition (*to* him, *for* the teacher).

1 | Übung

Identify the direct object and the indirect object in the following English sentences.

1. We owe him a debt of gratitude.
2. I'm buying my father a necktie.
3. Tell me what you think.
4. We're cooking spaghetti for the kids.
5. Peel me a grape.
6. To whom did you say that?

German versus English Indirect Object

You can recognize the dative case by the form of the personal pronoun (e.g., **dir** = to/for you) or of the article or possessive adjective used with a noun (**dem** Lehrer = *to/for the teacher*, **ihrer** Tochter = *to/for her daughter*).

Die Arbeit in der Bäckerei fängt früh an.

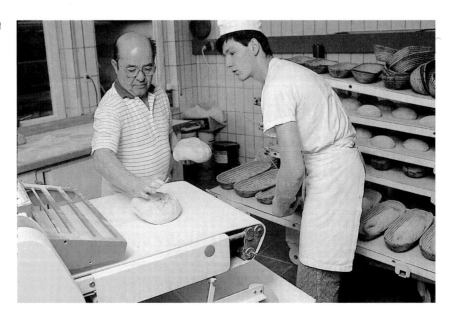

German does *not* use a preposition to show the indirect object. It is signalled by case alone.

ind. obj. dir. obj.

Ich kaufe **dir das Motorrad**. { *I'll buy you the motorcycle.*
I'll buy the motorcycle for you.

ind. obj. dir. obj.

Sag **dem Lehrer guten Morgen**. { *Tell the teacher good morning.*
Say good morning to the teacher.

ind. obj. dir. obj.

Sie gibt **ihrer Tochter das Geld**. { *She's giving her daughter the money.*
She's giving the money to her daughter.

The German case system allows more flexibility in word order than does English. The following sentences all say basically the same thing, with some minor shifts in emphasis.

Sie gibt **ihrer Tochter das Geld**.
Sie gibt **das Geld ihrer Tochter**.
Das Geld gibt sie **ihrer Tochter**.
Ihrer Tochter gibt sie **das Geld**.

By mastering the case endings, you can always find your way through such sentences and understand what they mean.

Forms of the Dative Case

The definite article, indefinite article, possessive adjectives, and **dies-** all share the same set of dative endings. The chart below shows these dative forms, as well as the nominative and accusative forms of the definite article (the cases you have already learned).

	masc.	neut.	fem.	plural
nom.	der Vater }	das Kind	die Frau	die Leute
acc.	den Vater }			
dat.	-em	-em	-er	-en -n
	dem Vater	**dem** Kind	**der** Frau	**den** Leuten
	dies**em** Vater	dies**em** Kind	dies**er** Frau	dies**en** Leuten
	ein**em** Vater	ein**em** Kind	ein**er** Frau	kein**en** Leuten
	unser**em** Vater	dein**em** Kind	sein**er** Frau	mein**en** Leuten

Note: *All nouns* in the dative plural add an **-n** to the noun itself (**den** Leuten, **den** Händen), except those nouns already ending in **-n** (**den** Frauen) and those ending in **-s** (**den** Hotels).

> Here are some verbs you already know that can take a dative and an accusative object in the same sentence: **sagen (Sag mir etwas); geben (Ich gebe dir 2 Mark); kochen; tragen; schreiben; singen; kaufen; verkaufen; beschreiben; schenken; zeigen.**
>
> Showing, giving, and telling things to people are communicative goals.

Fragewörter

wer?   *who?*
wen?   *whom?* (direct object)
wessen?   *whose?*
wem?   *to* or *for whom?* (indirect object)

Wem geben Sie das Geld?   ***To whom** are you giving the money?*

Lab Manual Kap. 5, Var. zur Üb. 2.

Workbook Kap. 5, A.

2 Übung: Wem soll sie es geben?

Beate kann ihr Brötchen nicht essen. Wem soll sie es geben?

BEISPIEL: die Lehrerin
Sie soll es der Lehrerin geben.

feminine	*neuter and masculine*	*plural*
1. ihre Freundin	5. ein Kind	10. die Kinder
2. ihre Schwester	6. ihr Freund	11. diese Leute
3. die Professorin	7. der Lehrer	12. die Studenten
4. die Chefin	8. mein Vater	13. ihre Freunde
	9. dieser Automechaniker	

3 Kettenreaktion: Wem schenkst du den Pulli?

Sie kaufen einen schönen Pulli für jemand in Ihrer Familie. Wem schenken Sie ihn?

BEISPIEL: A: Wem schenkst *du* den Pulli?
B: Meiner Schwester. Wem schenkst *du* den Pulli?
C: Mein- —————— . Wem . . . ?

To review family vocabulary, see p. 65.

Das gebe ich dir, aber was gibst du mir?

4 Übung: Wie sagt man das auf deutsch?

Benutzen Sie (*Use*) den du-Imperativ.

BEISPIEL: *Read the child a book.*
Lies dem Kind ein Buch.

1. Buy your sister a book.
2. Give my parents the money.
3. Describe the problem to the mechanic.
4. Write your mother a card.
5. Cook the food for your friends.
6. Show my friend the city.

Dative Personal Pronouns[1]

The following table lists the dative personal pronouns and reviews their nominative and accusative forms as well.

Singular			Plural		
nom.	**acc.**	**dat.**	**nom.**	**acc.**	**dat.**
ich	mich	**mir**	wir	uns	**uns**
du	dich	**dir**	ihr	euch	**euch**
Sie	Sie	**Ihnen**	Sie	Sie	**Ihnen**
er	ihn	**ihm**			
es	es	**ihm**	sie	sie	**ihnen**
sie	sie	**ihr**			

Note the similarities between the third-person dative pronouns and the dative endings of the articles and possessive adjectives.

ihm → **dem** Mann, **meinem** Kind
ihr → **der** Frau, **seiner** Schwester
ihnen → **den** Freunden, **unseren** Kindern

5 Übung: Kaufen wir Brot.

Sie wollen Brot kaufen. Ihre Professorin möchte wissen, **wem** Sie es kaufen.

BEISPIEL: Wem kaufen Sie das Brot? (*points to another student*)
Ich kaufe es *ihm/ihr.*

Lab Manual Kap. 5, Var. zur Üb. 6.

Workbook Kap. 5, B, C.

6 Partnerarbeit: Kaufst du mir etwas?

Taking turns and using the cues below, ask your partner what he or she will do for you.

BEISPIEL: Kaufst du mir eine Brezel?
Ja, ich kaufe dir eine Brezel *oder*
Nein, ich kaufe dir keine Brezel.

dein Motorrad verkaufen   Geld schenken
deine Fotos zeigen   eine Karte kaufen
deine Reise beschreiben   ein Brötchen geben (gibst)

---

[1]Note that English pronouns do not have different forms for the direct object and the indirect object, whereas German pronouns (except **uns** and **euch**) do.

I see **him**.   Ich sehe **ihn**.
I'm giving **him** the book. Ich gebe **ihm** das Buch.

Word Order of Noun and Pronoun Objects

Verbs such as **geben, schenken, kaufen, beschreiben, sagen,** and **zeigen** often have two objects. The first is usually the person (in the dative case) *to whom* something is given, shown, etc., or *for whom* something is done. The second object is the thing (in the accusative case) that is being given, shown, bought, etc.

> Ich zeige **meiner Freundin den Laden**.
> *I'm showing my girlfriend the shop.*

If one of the objects is a pronoun, it precedes the noun object.

> Ich zeige **ihr den Laden**.
> *I'm showing her the shop.*
> Ich zeige **ihn meiner Freundin**.
> *I'm showing it to my girlfriend.*

If both objects are pronouns, the accusative must precede the dative. (Note the similarity to English word order.)

> Ich zeige **ihn ihr**.
> *I'm showing it to her.*

Any personal pronouns that are not in the first position are placed *immediately after the inflected verb.*

Note the third example: the direct-object pronoun (**uns**) even precedes the noun subject (**dein Opa**).

> Ich gebe **ihm** mein Buch.
> *I'm giving **him** my book.*
> Ich gebe **es** meinem Bruder.
> *I'm giving **it** to my brother.*
> Kann **uns** dein Opa anrufen?
> *Can your grandpa phone **us**?*

If more than one personal pronoun follows the verb, they come in the order *nominative, accusative, dative.* Again, this is just like English word order: *subject pronoun, direct-object pronoun, indirect-object pronoun.*

> Ich gebe **es Ihnen** heute.
> *I'm giving **it to you** today.*
> Heute gebe **ich es Ihnen**.
> *Today **I'm** giving **it to you**.*

Lab Manual Kap. 5, Var. zur Üb. 7.

Workbook Kap. 5, D.

7 | **Übung: Wem schenken Sie das Buch?**

You've bought copies of your favorite novel as presents. Your instructor will ask whom you're giving it to. Answer the questions affirmatively, using pronouns.

BEISPIEL: Wem schenken Sie das Buch? Schenken Sie es Ihrer Mutter?
Ja, ich schenke es ihr.

Schenken Sie es . . .

1. Ihrem Vater?
2. den Kindern?
3. Ihrem Freund?
4. Ihrer Mitbewohnerin?
5. mir?
6. uns?

MERIAN zeigt Ihnen die Welt.

Prepositions with Dative Case

The dative case is also used for the object of the following prepositions.

aus	*out of*	Sie sieht **aus** dem Fenster.	*She's looking out of the window.*
	from (native country, city or region)	Ich komme **aus** Amerika.	*I'm from America.*
außer	*except for*	**Außer** ihm sind wir alle hier.	*We're all here except for him.*
	besides, in addition to	**Außer** ihm wohnt auch sein Bruder hier.	*Besides him, his brother lives here too.*
bei	*in the home of*	Ich wohne **bei** meiner Tante.	*I live at my aunt's.*
	at	Er ist **bei** der Arbeit.	*He's at work.*
mit	*with*	Ich arbeite **mit** den Händen.	*I work with my hands.*
nach	*after*	**Nach** der Arbeit bin ich manchmal müde.	*After work I'm sometimes tired.*
	to (with country and city names)	Wir fahren **nach** England.	*We're going to England.*
seit	*since* (referring to time)	**Seit** dem Tag mag ich ihn nicht mehr.	*Since that day I haven't liked him.*
	for	Ich arbeite **seit** einem Jahr hier.	*I've worked here for a year.*
von	*from*	Das Buch habe ich **von** meiner Mutter.	*I got that book from my mother.*
	of	Er ist ein Freund **von** mir.	*He's a friend of mine.*
	by	Das ist ein Buch **von** Hermann Hesse.	*That's a book by Hermann Hesse.*
zu	*to* (people and some locations)	Ich gehe **zur** Schule und dann **zu** meinen Freunden.	*I'm going to school and then to my friends' house.*

Contractions

The following contractions are standard.

bei dem	→	**beim**	Brezeln kaufe ich immer **beim** Bäcker.
von dem	→	**vom**	Ich komme gerade **vom** Chef.
zu dem	→	**zum**	Ich muß schnell **zum** Professor.
zu der	→	**zur**	Ich gehe jetzt **zur** Schule.

Lab Manual Kap. 5, Var. zur Üb. 8.

Workbook Kap. 5, E.

8 Übung: Bei wem wohnen Sie?

Sie sind alle Studenten in Tübingen. Sie wohnen aber nicht im Studenten-wohnheim (*dormitory*). Sagen Sie Ihrem Professor oder Ihrer Professorin, bei wem Sie wohnen.

BEISPIEL: Bei wem wohnen Sie?
Bei meinem Freund.

Tante	Freundin	Bruder	Großeltern
Familie	Vater	Freund	Frau König

9 Kettenreaktion: Zu wem gehst *du*?

Say whom you are going to see, then ask another student.

Automechaniker	Bäckerin	Lehrling
Professorin	Automechanikerin	Amerikaner
Professor	Eltern	Familie
Chef	Amerikanerin	Bäcker

BEISPIEL: PROFESSOR/IN Zu wem gehen Sie?
A: Ich gehe zu meiner Familie. Zu wem gehst *du*?
B: Ich gehe zum Bäcker. Zu wem . . .

10 Übung: Mit wem gehen Sie schwimmen?

Sie gehen mit Freunden aus der Deutschstunde schwimmen. Sagen Sie, mit wem Sie schwimmen gehen.

BEISPIEL: PROFESSOR/IN: Mit wem gehen Sie schwimmen?
STUDENT/IN: (*points to one or more other students in the class*)
Mit ihr/ihm/ihnen.

Verbs with Separable Prefixes

The meanings of many English verbs can be changed or modified by the addition of another word.

to find	→	*to find out*
to look	→	*to look up*
to burn	→	*to burn down*
to hang	→	*to hang around*

Likewise, the meanings of many German verbs are modified—or even changed completely—by the addition of a prefix to the root verb.

stehen	*to stand*	→	**auf**stehen	*to stand up; get out of bed*
kommen	*to come*	→	**mit**kommen	*to come along*
hören	*to hear*	→	**auf**hören	*to cease, stop*
fangen	*to catch*	→	**an**fangen	*to begin*

Similarly:

ankommen	*to arrive*
anrufen	*to call up*
aufmachen	*to open*
kennenlernen	*to get to know, meet*
zurückkommen	*to come back*

Such verbs are called *separable-prefix verbs.* Separable-prefix verbs have the primary stress on the prefix (**an**kommen, **auf**hören).

In the present tense and the imperative, the prefix is *separated* from the verb and placed at the end of the sentence or clause. It is the second part of the predicate.

Ich **stehe** morgen sehr früh **auf.**	*I'm getting up very early tomorrow.*
Wann **stehst** du **auf?**	*When are you getting up?*
Stehen Sie bitte **auf!**	*Please get up!*
Steht ihr denn bald **auf?**	*Are you getting up soon?*

When a verb with a separable prefix complements a modal verb, the separable prefix is again attached to the root verb infinitive at the end of the sentence or clause.

without a modal	*with a modal*
Er **fängt** morgen **an.**	Er soll morgen **anfangen.**
Ich **lerne** sie **kennen.**	Ich möchte sie **kennenlernen.**

Note: Separable prefixes will be indicated in the **Wortschatz** sections by a raised dot between prefix and root verb: **an·fangen.** This symbol is often used in textbooks, though *not* in conventional German spelling.

Lab Manual Kap. 5, Var. zur Üb. 11, 12.

Workbook Kap. 5, F, G, H.

11 Übung

Ihre Professorin sagt, Sie sollen etwas machen. Antworten Sie, Sie können es nicht machen.

BEISPIEL: Fangen Sie doch heute an.
            Ich kann heute nicht anfangen.

1. Hören Sie doch auf.
2. Kommen Sie doch mit.
3. Machen Sie den Laden auf.
4. Rufen Sie doch Ihre Mutter an.
5. Stehen Sie bitte auf.
6. Kommen Sie bitte heute zurück.

Ihr Professor sagt, Sie müssen etwas machen. Sie antworten, Sie sind einverstanden.

> BEISPIEL: Sie müssen um sieben aufstehen.
> Einverstanden, ich stehe um sieben auf.

1. Sie müssen jetzt anfangen.
2. Sie müssen früh aufstehen.
3. Sie müssen um acht aufmachen.
4. Sie müssen Helena anrufen.
5. Sie müssen aufhören.
6. Sie müssen gleich mitkommen.

13 Partnerarbeit: Mach das bitte für mich.

1. **aufmachen**   Partner A asks partner B to open various things, and B agrees.

> BEISPIEL: A: Mach doch _____ auf.
> B: Gut, ich mache _____ auf.

| Buch | Laden | Rucksack | Zeitung |
| Fenster | Tür | Tasche | |

2. **anrufen**   Partner B tells A to call up various relatives and friends. Partner A doesn't want to.

> BEISPIEL: B: Ruf doch dein- _____ an.
> A: Aber ich will mein- _____ nicht anrufen.

Onkel	Tante	Freundin	Lehrer
Bruder	Schwester	Großeltern	Professorin
Mutter	Vater	Geschwister	

3. **Um 7 Uhr**   Partner A wants to know when B is going to do various things. Partner B answers with the time.

> BEISPIEL: A: Wann kommst du denn zurück?
> B: Um 7 komme ich zurück.

ankommen	mit deiner Arbeit aufhören
zurückkommen	morgens aufstehen
anfangen (fängst . . . an)	den Chef kennenlernen

Verbs with Inseparable Prefixes

There are also German verbs with *inseparable* prefixes. These prefixes *never* separate from the root verb. You can tell them from separable prefixes in these ways:

- They are *never* stressed.
- They have no independent meaning of their own, while separable prefixes resemble other parts of speech such as prepositions (**mit**kommen) and adverbs (**zurück**kommen).

The inseparable prefixes are: **be-, ent-, er-, ge-, ver-**, and **zer-**. Here are the verbs with inseparable prefixes that you have already learned: **bedeuten, beginnen, bekommen, beschreiben, besitzen, besprechen, besuchen, entscheiden, verdienen, verlassen, verstehen.**

14 Übung

Say these verb pairs aloud to practice the difference between stressed separable prefixes and unstressed inseparable prefixes. Then complete the following sentences with the appropriate verb.

inseparable	*separable*
verstehen	**auf**stehen
beschreiben	**auf**schreiben (*to write down*)
gehören (*to belong to*)	**auf**hören
bekommen	**mit**kommen
erfahren (*to find out*)	**ab**fahren (*to depart*)

1. Ich _____ dich nicht. (*understand*)
   Ich _____ um 7 Uhr _____ . (*get up*)

2. _____ Sie es bitte! (*describe*)
   _____ Sie es bitte _____ ! (*write down*)

3. Harald _____ heute ein Motorrad. (*is getting*)
   Bernd _____ heute _____ . (*is coming along*)

Saying when and for how long things happen is a communicative goal.

Remember that when a time phrase uses a preposition, that preposition will govern the case of the noun: **seit dem Tag** *since that day;* **nach einer Stunde** *after an hour.*

Time Phrases in Accusative Case

Here are some time phrases telling *when* or *how often* something occurs or *how long* it goes on. The nouns in these phrases are in the *accusative case.*

Wann?

diesen Freitag	dieses Semester	diese Woche
diesen Herbst	dieses Jahr	
diesen März		

Ich studiere **dieses Semester** in Konstanz.

I'm studying in Konstanz this semester.

Diese Woche ist Thomas krank.

Thomas is sick this week.

Wann / Wie oft?

jeden Morgen	jedes Semester	jede Minute
jeden Abend	jedes Jahr	jede Stunde
jeden Tag		jede Woche
jeden Montag		
jeden Mai		
jeden Sommer		

Wir gehen **jeden Tag** zum Bäcker.

We go to the baker's every day.

Er fährt **jedes Jahr** nach Amerika.

He goes to America every year.

Wie lange?

einen Tag	ein Jahr	eine Minute	drei Tage
		eine Stunde	zwei Semester

Wir bleiben **einen Tag** in London.

We're staying in London for a day.

Ich studiere **ein Semester** in Köln.

I'm studying in Cologne for a semester.

Note that the German equivalent of "*for* a day" is simply **einen Tag** without a preposition.

Remember that expressions of time (**jeden Tag**) precede expressions of place or destination (**zum Bäcker**).

15 **Übung:** *Mit offenen Büchern*

Supply the missing time phrases cued in English.

1. Wie oft stehen Sie um 7 Uhr auf?
   Ich stehe ⎯⎯⎯ um 7 Uhr auf. (*every day*)
   jeden Tag

2. Wann rufen Sie Ihre Eltern an?
   Ich rufe sie ⎯⎯⎯ an. (*this Wednesday*)
   jeden Mittwoch

3. Wie lange bleiben Sie in Tübingen?
   Ich bleibe ⎯⎯⎯ dort. (*a year*)
   ein Jahr

4. Wann arbeitest du denn mit Karl zusammen?
   Wahrscheinlich arbeite ich ⎯⎯⎯ mit ihm zusammen. (*this week*)
   diese Woche

5. Wie lange wartet ihr noch?
   Wir warten noch ⎯⎯⎯ vor der Bäckerei. (*for an hour*)
   eine Stunde

6. Hoffentlich kannst du lange bei uns bleiben.
   Nein, leider kann ich nur ⎯⎯⎯ bei euch sein. (*one day*)
   einen Tag

7. Wann ist das Klima bei euch besonders schön?
   Das Wetter ist ⎯⎯⎯ mild und kühl. (*every October*)
   jeden Oktober

8. Wann kann ich Sie besuchen, Herr Wahrig?
   ⎯⎯⎯ um 9 Uhr bin ich frei. (*every Tuesday*)
   jeden Dienstag

Drei Deutsche bei der Arbeit

Tips zum Lesen und Lernen

Tips zum Vokabelnlernen

Remember that singular masculine nouns ending in **-er** have the same form in the plural: **der Arbeiter, die Arbeiter.** Feminine forms ending **-erin,** however, do have a plural ending: **die Arbeiterin, die Arbeiterinnen.**

Agent Nouns   Both English and German add the suffix **-er** to a verb stem to form a noun that denotes a person who performs the action (agent). In German, the additional ending **-in** indicates that the agent is female.

arbeiten → **der Arbeiter / die Arbeiterin**   *to work* → *worker*
lesen   → **der Leser / die Leserin**   *to read* → *reader*

Sometimes an umlaut is added in the agent noun:

anfangen	→	**Anfänger**	*to begin*	→	*beginner*
tragen	→	**Briefträger**	*to carry*	→	*letter carrier*
backen	→	**Bäcker**	*to bake*	→	*baker*
handeln	→	**Buchhändler**	*to trade, deal*	→	*bookseller*

Übung

Was machen diese Leute?

1. Herr Kropf ist Kaffeetrinker.
2. Frau Baumann ist Zeitungsleserin.
3. Wir sind alle Anfänger.
4. Albert ist Frühaufsteher.
5. Frau Hanselmann ist Buchhändlerin.

Facharbeiterin [*technician*] in der Optikindustrie.

Adverbs of Time German adds an **-s** to the names of the days or parts of the day to form adverbs showing regular or habitual occurrence.

morgens	*in the mornings, every morning*
nachmittags	*in the afternoons, every afternoon*
abends	*in the evenings, every evening*
nachts	*at night, every night*
montags	*Mondays, every Monday*
dienstags	*Tuesdays, every Tuesday*
usw.	*etc.*

Note: These words are *adverbs*, not nouns, and are therefore not capitalized.

Übung

Wann machen Sie das?

> BEISPIEL: Wann essen Sie Brötchen?
> Morgens esse ich Brötchen.

1. Wann haben Sie Deutsch?
2. Wann trinken Sie Kaffee?
3. Wann machen Sie Ihre Hausaufgaben?
4. Wann gehen Sie zum Bäcker?
5. Wann rufen Sie Ihre Familie an?

Lab Manual Kap. 5, Üb. zur Betonung.

Korsika (*Corsica*) is a French island in the Mediterranean. See map on the inside of the back cover.

Leicht zu merken

campen	(pronounced **kämpen**)
die **Industrie, -n**	Industrie
der **Journalist, -en**	Journal<u>i</u>st
(das) **Kanada**	
der **Korrespondent, -en**	Korrespond<u>e</u>nt
(das) **Korsika**	
der **Partner, -**	
realistisch	
der **Sport**	
der **Supermarkt**	
die **Universität, -en**	Universit<u>ä</u>t
die **USA** (*pl.*)	

Einstieg in den Text

The title "Drei Deutsche bei der Arbeit" lets you know that the reading will focus on three individuals and their work. What sorts of things would you expect to learn about people's personal and professional lives from such a reading? You can apply to this text the familiar question words that you have been using to ask about each other's lives.

Before reading the whole text, skim the third portrait and see if you can quickly find answers to the following questions:

Wie heißt dieser Mann?
Wie alt ist er?
Was macht er?
Wo wohnt er?
Wer sind die anderen (*other*) Menschen in seiner Familie?

Let these questions guide your reading for information as you work through the entire text.

Wortschatz 2

Verben

ab·holen   to pick up, fetch, get
aus·sehen (sieht aus)   to appear, look (happy, tired, fit, etc.)
  Du siehst schrecklich aus. You look terrible.
berichten   to report
ein·kaufen   to shop for; to go shopping
fern·sehen (sieht fern)   to watch TV
reisen   to travel
schließen   to close
spazieren·gehen   to go for a walk
sterben (stirbt)   to die
vergessen (vergißt)   to forget
vorbei·kommen   to come by, drop by

schließen: *synonym = zumachen.*

Substantive

der **Arbeiter, -**   worker
der **Fußball**   soccer
der **Reiseführer, -**   (travel) guide book
der **Roman, -e**   novel
der **Stadtplan, ¨e**   city map
der **Streß** (*no plural*)   stress

das **Bild, -er**   picture; image

das **Dorf, ¨er**   village
(das) **Frankreich**   France
das **Geschäft, -e**   business; store
das **Mittagessen**   midday meal, lunch
das **Schaufenster, -**   store window
das **Wochenende, -n**   weekend
  am Wochenende   on the weekend
das **Wort**   word (*2 plural forms:* **die Worte**: words in a context; **die Wörter**: unconnected words, as in a dictionary)
das **Wörterbuch, ¨er**   dictionary

die **Buchhandlung, -en**   bookstore
die **Fabrik, -en**   factory
die **Freizeit**   free time
die **Mannschaft, -en**   team
die **Muttersprache, -n**   native language
die **Postkarte, -n**   postcard
die **Stimme, -n**   voice
die **Wanderung, -en**   hike

The word **Frankreich** recalls the original empire of the Franks (**die Franken**), a Germanic tribe that settled mainly west of the Rhine. The greatest Frankish king was Charlemagne (**Karl der Große**), 747–814 A.D.

die **Zeitschrift, -en**   magazine
die **Lebensmittel** (*pl.*)   groceries

Adjektive und Adverbien

abends   (in the) evenings
aktuell   current, topical
besonders   especially
bunt   colorful
französisch   French
meistens   mostly, usually

Gegensätze

fleißig ≠ **faul**   industrious ≠ lazy

Mit anderen Worten

stressig (*colloq.*) = **mit viel Streß**

Am Schreibtisch arbeiten

Drei Deutsche bei der Arbeit

Lab Manual Kap. 5, Lesestück.

Learning about the world of work in Germany is the cultural goal of this chapter.

Man sagt über die Deutschen, sie leben für ihre Arbeit. Stimmt das heute noch? Unsere Beispiele zeigen ein anderes° Bild.

different

Christine Sauermann, Buchhändlerin

Christine Sauermann ist 35 Jahre alt, geschieden,° und hat einen jun-
5 gen Sohn Oliver (10 Jahre alt). Sie ist seit sieben Jahren berufstätig und besitzt seit fünf Jahren eine Buchhandlung in der Altstadt° von Tübingen.[3] Zwei Angestellte° arbeiten für sie im Laden.

divorced

old city
employees

Das Geschäft geht gut, denn° viele Touristen gehen durch die Altstadt spazieren, und Studenten kommen auch jeden Tag vorbei. Mit
10 den neuesten° Romanen sieht ihr Schaufenster immer bunt aus. Den Studenten verkauft sie Wörterbücher und Nachschlagewerke,° aber die Touristen kaufen meistens Reiseführer, Stadtpläne und Postkarten von der Stadt.

because

newest
reference works

Morgens macht sie um 9 Uhr auf und abends um 6 Uhr zu. Von
15 1 Uhr bis 3 Uhr macht sie Mittagspause.° Sie schließt den Laden, holt Oliver von der Schule ab und geht mit ihm nach Hause. Dort kocht sie das Mittagessen und kauft später dann noch Lebensmittel im Supermarkt ein.[4]

midday break

Außer sonntags arbeitet Christine Sauermann jeden Tag sehr
20 fleißig in ihrem Laden. In ihrer Freizeit möchte sie also Erholung° vom Streß. Darum macht sie gern Wanderungen mit ihrem Sohn zusammen. Diesen Sommer zum Beispiel gehen sie zusammen in Schottland° campen.

relaxation

Scotland

Es ist schon spät, aber die Buchhandlung ist noch offen. (München)

---

[3]Most German cities and towns have an **Altstadt** (*old city*) in their centers, which may date from the Middle Ages. They are often pedestrian zones. **Tübingen** is a university town on the Neckar River about twenty miles south of Stuttgart. The university was founded in 1477.

[4]Many small shops and businesses close from 1:00 to 2:30 or 3:00 P.M., but this practice is less common nowadays in large cities. The noon meal is traditionally the main meal of the day.

Jörg Krolow (22 Jahre alt), Fabrikarbeiter

25 Jörg Krolow arbeitet seit einem Jahr als Mechaniker in einer Autofabrik in Dortmund.[5] Die Arbeit ist schwer, aber gut bezahlt.°   paid
Arbeit trinkt er oft ein Bier mit Freunden zusammen oder sieht fern.
Am Wochenende spielt er im Sportverein° Fußball.   sports club
    Wie die meisten° deutschen Arbeiter in der Schwerindustrie ist   most
30 Krolow in einer Gewerkschaft.° Sie sichert° jedem Mitglied° einen   union / assures / member
guten Lohn° und gibt den Arbeitern eine Stimme im Aufsichtsrat.[6]   wage
    Krolow hat wie die meisten Deutschen° fünf Wochen Urlaub im   **wie**... = like most Germans
Jahr. Dieses Jahr will er im Sommer mit seiner Freundin nach Korsika. Im Oktober fährt seine Fußballmannschaft nach Amiens,[7] der
35 Partnerstadt von Dortmund, und spielt dort gegen einen französischen Fußballklub.

Klaus Ostendorff (53 Jahre alt), Journalist

Klaus Ostendorff ist Korrespondent bei der Deutschen Presseagentur°   wire service
in Nordamerika. Seit fünfzehn Jahren berichtet er über die USA und
40 Kanada für Zeitungen und Zeitschriften in Deutschland. Seine Artikel
geben den Lesern ein realistisches Bild von beiden° Ländern.   both

---

[5]An industrial city in North Rhine-Westphalia. See map on the inside of the front cover.

[6]**Aufsichtsrat** = board of directors. Historically, the ability of West German trade unions to elect up to 50% of the board of directors of large companies brought a high degree of cooperation between management and labor, very few strikes, and a high standard of living for union members. West Germany's economic growth ensured low unemployment rates. Since German unification in 1990, however, unemployment in the new eastern **Bundesländer** has been high, and many workers have left the unions.

[7]Northern French city on the Somme River. Many such partnerships exist between European cities.

Im Moment schreibt Ostendorff einen Artikel über das Waldster-
ben° in Nordamerika. Dieses Problem ist in Deutschland besonders
aktuell: Der saure° Regen bedroht° auch die Wälder in Europa.

45 Ostendorff lebt mit seiner Frau Martina und ihren drei Kindern in
Washington. Die Kinder sollen ihre Muttersprache nicht vergessen,
und darum spricht die Familie zu Hause meistens Deutsch. Die Kinder
besuchen das deutsche Gymnasium in Washington und reisen im
Sommer nach Deutschland. Dort macht die ganze° Familie Urlaub bei
50 den Großeltern. Sie wohnen in einem Dorf in den Bayerischen° Alpen.

death of the forests
acid / threatens

whole
Bavarian

Fragen zum Lesestück

1. Wo arbeitet Christine Sauermann? Buchha
2. Wie lange ist sie schon berufstätig?
3. Wer sind ihre Kunden, und was kaufen
   sie bei ihr?
4. Wie sieht ein typischer Tag für
   Frau Sauermann aus?
5. Was macht sie gern in ihrer Freizeit?
6. Was macht Jörg Krolow in seiner Freizeit?
7. Wohin fährt er im Urlaub?
8. Über was schreibt Klaus Ostendorff im Moment?
9. Wie ist seine Familie anders als die Familie
   von Christine Sauermann oder Jörg Krolow?
10. Warum sprechen Ostendorff und seine Frau zu Hause
    meistens Deutsch?

MIT FREUNDEN, SURFBRETTERN, PICKNICK-KOFFER, MOUNTAIN-BIKES UND EINEM HUND.

Situationen aus dem Alltag

Berufe

Was sind Sie von Beruf?   *What is your profession?*

Diese Berufe wissen Sie schon auf deutsch:

der **Bäcker**, -	die **Bäckerin**, -nen
der **Fabrikarbeiter**, -	die **Fabrikarbeiterin**, -nen
der **Hausmann**, ¨er	die **Hausfrau**, -en
der **Journalist**, -en	die **Journalistin**, -nen
der **Lehrer**, -	die **Lehrerin**, -nen
der **Mechaniker**, -	die **Mechanikerin**, -nen
der **Professor**, -en	die **Professorin**, -nen

Wer arbeitet hier? Lesen Sie die Schilder [signs].

Here are some other professions you can use in the following exercises.

der **Arzt**, ̈e	die **Ärztin**, -nen	*physician*
der **Elektrotechniker**, -	die **Elektrotechnikerin**	*electrician or electrical engineer*
der **Geschäftsmann** (*pl.*) **Geschäftsleute**	die **Geschäftsfrau**	*businessman/ business- woman*
der **Ingenieur**, -e	die **Ingenieurin**, -nen	*engineer*
der **Kellner**, -	die **Kellnerin**, -nen	*waiter/ waitress*
der **Krankenpfleger**, -	die **Krankenschwester**, -n	*nurse*
der **Künstler**, -	die **Künstlerin**, -nen	*artist*
der **Landwirt**, -e	die **Landwirtin**, -nen	*farmer*
der **Politiker**, -	die **Politikerin**, -nen	*politician*
der **Rechtsanwalt**, ̈e	die **Rechtsanwältin**, -nen	*lawyer*
der **Schriftsteller**, -	die **Schriftstellerin**, -nen	*writer*
der **Verkäufer**, -	die **Verkäuferin**, -nen	*salesperson*

Talking about work and professions is a communicative goal.

Fragen: Was wissen Sie über diese Berufe?

1. Wer braucht das Abitur?
2. Wer muß für seinen Beruf studieren?
3. Wer macht eine Lehre (*apprenticeship*)?
4. Wer verdient gut? Wer verdient relativ schlecht?
5. Wer hat viel Freizeit? Wer hat nicht viel Freizeit?
6. Wer hat flexible Arbeitszeiten?
7. Wer arbeitet oft nachts / morgens / abends?
8. Wer arbeitet draußen?
9. Wer braucht vielleicht einen Computer bei der Arbeit?
10. Wer arbeitet meistens allein, wer mit anderen Menschen zusammen?

Mit Menschen zu tun haben

Handwerklich arbeiten

Im Labor arbeiten

Note on Usage: Stating profession or nationality

| Ich will Automechaniker werden. | *I want to become **an** auto mechanic.* |
| Frau Gerhard ist Amerikanerin. | *Ms. Gerhard is **an** American.* |

German does not use an indefinite article before the noun.

Gruppendiskussion: Was willst du werden, und warum? (4 Studenten)

First tell each other what you want to do after college. Then ask questions about each other's career plans.

BEISPIEL: A: Ich möchte Lehrer werden.
B: Verdienen Lehrer genug Geld?
C: Sind deine Eltern Lehrer?
D: Wo möchtest du denn arbeiten?
usw.

Partnerarbeit mit dem Almanach: Suchen wir eine Stelle.

Sie und Ihr Partner brauchen Geld und suchen Stellen für den Sommer. Im Almanach (S. 155) sind einige Stellenangebote (*job offers, help wanted ads*) aus deutschen Zeitungen. Besprechen Sie sie zusammen. Was möchten Sie gern machen? Was möchten Sie lieber nicht machen?

Zum Schluß

Lab Manual Kap. 5, Diktat.

Workbook Kap. 5, J.

Sprechen wir miteinander!

A Gruppenarbeit: Was zeigst du mir? (4 oder 5 Personen)

Use a verb from the list below to ask other students what they are going to do for you. Other students use a noun from the list to answer. After asking each person in the group, a new questioner starts over with a different verb.

BEISPIEL: Was kaufst du mir, Joanne?
Ich kaufe dir einen Fernseher.
Vielen Dank! Was _____ du mir, Steve?

verbs	*nouns*	
kaufen	Mantel	Hemd
beschreiben	Wagen	Mittagessen
kochen	Artikel	Buch
geben	Stadtplan	Stadt
schenken	Fernseher	Roman
zeigen	Brot	Tasche
verkaufen	Auto	Zeitung
	Brötchen	Zeitschrift
	Wörterbuch	Uhr
	Motorrad	

WIR SUCHEN AZUBIS!

Wir bieten jungen Leuten eine solide Ausbildung in krisenfesten Berufen als

KAUFMANN/KAUFFRAU
im Einzelhandel
VERKÄUFER/VERKÄUFERIN

B Partnerarbeit: Nein, das stimmt nicht! (Mit offenen Büchern)

Take turns contradicting each other.

> BEISPIEL: Dieser Wagen ist *neu*!
> Nein, das stimmt nicht. Dieser Wagen ist *alt*!

1. Wir holen die Kinder *früh* ab.
2. Hamburg liegt in *Süddeutschland*.
3. Jetzt *fangen* wir *an*.
4. Der Lehrling *schließt* den Laden.
5. Der Chef möchte *etwas* sagen.
6. Wir essen *viel*.
7. Ich glaube, *jemand* wohnt da drüben.
8. Meine Nase ist *häßlich*.
9. Diese Jacke ist *altmodisch*.
10. Diese Übung ist *schwer*.

C Gruppenarbeit: Mit anderen Worten

With books closed, the class forms two teams. The instructor says a sentence, and the first team to think of a more colorful or colloquial way to say the same thing gets a point.

> BEISPIEL: Heute ist es *sehr sehr* kalt.
> Heute ist es *wahnsinnig* kalt.

1. Der Film ist *sehr langweilig*.
2. Ich schenke meiner *Großmutter* ein Foto von mir.
3. Roberts VW ist *sehr alt*.
4. Die Autos fahren *sehr schnell* durch die Stadt.
5. Heute bin ich *sehr sehr müde*.
6. Die Berge in Österreich sind *sehr schön*.

D Partnerarbeit: Sprechen Sie miteinander!

Take turns asking each other the following questions. Choose your responses from the list of words below. Then ask some questions of your own.

(der) Tag, Morgen, Nachmittag, Abend
       Montag, Dienstag usw.
       Januar, Februar, März usw.
       Winter, Frühling, Sommer, Herbst

(das) Semester, Jahr, Wochenende

(die) Stunde, Woche

1. Wie oft gehst du schwimmen?
   Ich gehe jed-_____ schwimmen.

2. Wie oft ißt du Brezeln?
   Brezeln esse ich _____ .

3. Wann fährst du nach Europa?
   Ich fahre dies-_____ nach Europa.

4. Wann studierst du in Konstanz?
   Ich studiere _____ in Konstanz.

5. Wie lange bleibst du in München?
   Ich bleibe ein-_____ da.

6. Wie viele Stunden schläfst du am Wochenende?
   Am Wochenende schlafe ich _____ .

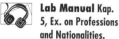

Lab Manual Kap. 5, Ex. on Professions and Nationalities.

E Gruppenarbeit: Bist du Amerikaner/in?

Choose a profession or nationality (**Bäcker, Studentin, Amerikaner,** etc.). Don't tell anyone else what you are. Speak to as many of your classmates as possible and guess what they are until you find the right answer.

BEISPIEL: Bist du Bäckerin?
            Nein, ich bin nicht (oder) keine Bäckerin.
            Bist du _____?

Schreiben Sie zu Hause

F Der Arbeitstag
Gerd hat eine neue Stelle. Er schreibt seinen Eltern und beschreibt ihnen einen typischen Arbeitstag. (Use the cues to reconstruct his letter.)

Liebe Mutti, lieber Vati!

aufstehen / morgens / 7.00
Arbeit / anfangen / 8.30
ich / arbeiten / mit / mein Freund Kurt / zusammen
Laden / zumachen / 6.00
nach / Arbeit / ich / gehen / Bier / trinken
nach / Essen / fernsehen / oft / ein bißchen
abends / ich / sein / todmüde

Euer Gerd

G Fill in the blanks with the correct dative ending or dative personal pronoun.

1. Ich wohne seit ein-_____ Monat bei mein-_____ Tante in Tübingen.
2. Mit _____ (*her*) gehe ich fast jeden Tag einkaufen.
3. Sie bekommt oft Briefe von ihr-_____ Freunden und ihr-_____ Bruder.
4. Sie schreibt _____ (*them*) oft Postkarten mit Bilder-_____ von d-_____ Stadt.
5. Nach d-_____ Seminar gehe ich mit mein-_____ Freunden Fußball spielen.

H **Berufsberatung** (*Career Counseling*) Frau Friedrichsen, a career counselor (**Berufsberaterin**), is advising her client, Herr Liebig. Fill in Herr Liebig's answers to her questions.

FRAU F: Also Herr Liebig, sagen Sie mir bitte, arbeiten Sie lieber mit Menschen oder allein?

HERR L: _____

FRAU F: Sagen Sie mir etwas über Ihre Familie. Wie viele Kinder haben Sie?

HERR L: _____

FRAU F: Ist Ihre Frau auch berufstätig?

HERR L: Ja.

FRAU F: Und was ist sie von Beruf?

HERR L: _____

FRAU F: Was machen Sie besonders gern in Ihrer Freizeit?

HERR L: _____

FRAU F: Wieviel wollen Sie verdienen?

HERR L: _____

FRAU F: Also, Herr Liebig, vielleicht sollen Sie _____ werden.

I Aufsatzthema (*Essay Topic*): **Beschreiben Sie Ihre Arbeit!** You have read about the lives of three working Germans. Write a page about your own job or your parents' jobs. How is working in this country different from what you have read about working in Germany?

J Wie sagt man das auf deutsch?

1. When are you getting up tomorrow?
2. At six. I have to leave the house early.
3. Why? What are you doing?
4. I'm driving with my girlfriend to Munich.

5. What are you doing on the weekend?
6. I don't know yet. Why do you ask?
7. Can you come by? A student from Germany is visiting me.
8. Gladly. I'd like to meet him.
9. I want to show him the city tomorrow.
10. Good. I'll come by at ten.

Stellenangebote (Help Wanted Ads)

These help-wanted ads from the German press range from unskilled labor (**Zeitungsträger/in**) to highly specialized professionals (**Statistiker/in**). Note the English business and computer jargon in the technical fields.

An der Universität

Communicative Goals

- Talking about events in the past
- Writing a letter in German

Cultural Goal

- Learning about German student life and the university system

Lab Manual Kap. 6, Dialoge, Fragen, Hören Sie gut zu!, Üb. zur Aussprache (**b, d, g / p, t, k**).

Karin sucht ein Zimmer

STEFAN: Hast du endlich ein Zimmer gefunden?

KARIN: Nee, ich suche noch. Leider habe ich keinen Platz im Studentenwohnheim bekommen.

STEFAN: Du! Gestern ist bei uns in der WG die Helga ausgezogen. Also, jetzt ist ein Zimmer frei. Willst du zu uns?

KARIN: Super! Meinst du, das ist möglich?

STEFAN: Selbstverständlich!

Dormitory space is scarce in Germany. Students frequently live together in apartments called **Wohngemeinschaften** (abbreviated **WG**).

Am Semesteranfang

CLARA: Wo warst du denn so lange?

EVA: In der Bibliothek und später in der Buchhandlung.

CLARA: Hast du mir ein Vorlesungsverzeichnis mitgebracht?

EVA: Ja, ich hab's auf den Schreibtisch gelegt.

CLARA: Ach ja, da liegt es unter der Zeitung. Wieviel hat's denn gekostet?

EVA: Vier Mark fünfzig, aber ich schenk's dir.

CLARA: Das ist wirklich nett von dir! Vielen Dank!

German students buy their course catalogues every semester in local bookstores.

An der Uni in Tübingen

PETRA: Hast du den Peter schon kennengelernt?

KLAUS: Ist das der Austauschstudent aus Kanada?

PETRA: Ja. Er kann phantastisch Deutsch, nicht?

KLAUS: Ich glaube, er hat schon zwei Semester in Konstanz studiert.

PETRA: Ach, darum!

German students calculate time spent at the university in semesters rather than years.

Konstanz is a city on Lake Constance (**der Bodensee**) with a university founded in 1966.

Note on Usage: Definite Article with Names

In informal, colloquial speech, Germans often use the definite article with proper names. The dialogues contain two examples of this:

Gestern ist bei uns in der WG **die** Helga ausgezogen.	*Yesterday Helga moved out of our apartment.*
Hast du **den** Peter schon kennengelernt?	*Have you met Peter yet?*

Karin Looks for a Room

S.: Have you finally found a room?

K.: Nope, I'm still looking. Unfortunately I didn't get a place in the dorm.

S.: Hey! Yesterday Helga moved out of our apartment. So now there's a room free. Do you want to move in with us?

K.: Terrific! Do you think it's possible?

S.: Of course.

At the Beginning of the Semester

C.: Where were you for so long?

E.: In the library and later at the bookstore.

C.: Did you bring me a course catalogue?

E.: Yes, I put it on the desk.

C.: Oh yeah, it's lying under the newspaper. How much did it cost?

E.: Four marks fifty, but I'll give it to you for free.

C.: That's really nice of you! Thanks a lot.

At the University in Tübingen

P.: Have you met Peter yet?

K.: Is that the exchange student from Canada?

P.: Yes. He speaks fantastic German, doesn't he?

K.: I think he's already studied two semesters in Konstanz.

P.: So that's why!

Verben

aus·ziehen, ist ausgezogen[1] to move out

bringen, hat gebracht to bring

legen to lay, put down

mit·bringen, hat mitgebracht to bring along, take along

ziehen, hat gezogen to pull

Substantive

der **Anfang, ⁼e** beginning
  am Anfang at the beginning

der **Austauschstudent, -en, -en**[2] exchange student

der **Mensch, -en, -en** person, human being

der **Platz, ⁼e** place; space; city square

der **Schreibtisch, -e** desk

das **Bett, -en** bed

(das) **Kanada** Canada

das **Studentenwohnheim, -e** student dormitory

das **Vorlesungsverzeichnis, -se** university course catalogue

die **Bibliothek, -en** library

die **Universität, -en** university
  an der Universität at the university

die **Vorlesung, -en** university lecture

die **Wohngemeinschaft, -en** communal living group, co-op apartment

Adjektive und Adverbien

gestern yesterday
möglich possible
nett nice
so lange for such a long time
wirklich real; really

Präpositionen mit Dativ oder Akkusativ

an to, toward; at, alongside of

auf onto; on, upon, on top of

hinter behind

in into, to; in

neben beside, next to

über over, across; above

unter under; beneath

vor in front of

zwischen between

Gegensätze

am Anfang ≠ am Ende at the beginning ≠ at the end

ausziehen ≠ einziehen to move out ≠ to move in

möglich ≠ unmöglich possible ≠ impossible

Mit anderen Worten

die **Uni, -s** (*colloq.*) = **Universität**

die **WG, -s** (*colloq.*) = **Wohngemeinschaft**

nee (*colloq.*) = **nein**

---

[1]For an explanation of the form **ist ausgezogen**, see **Grammatik**, pp. 161–168.

[2]For an explanation of the second ending, see **Grammatik**, p. 173.

Variationen

A Persönliche Fragen

1. Wo wohnen Sie: im Studentenwohnheim, bei einer Familie, in einer WG oder zu Hause bei Ihren Eltern?
2. Stefan wohnt in einer WG. Kennen Sie Studenten in WGs? Was ist dort anders als im Studentenwohnheim?
3. Eva kauft ein Vorlesungsverzeichnis. Was müssen Sie am Semesteranfang kaufen?
4. Eva schenkt Clara das Vorlesungsverzeichnis. Was schenken Sie Ihrem Mitbewohner oder Ihrer Mitbewohnerin?
5. An der Uni in Tübingen gibt es viele Austauschstudenten. Gibt es auch an Ihrer Uni Austauschstudenten? Woher kommen sie?

B Übung: Das möchte ich auch.

Your instructor tells you something he has done. Say you would like to do that too.

> BEISPIEL: A: Ich habe in Berlin gewohnt.
> B: Ich möchte auch in Berlin wohnen.

1. Ich habe einen Sportwagen gekauft.
2. Ich habe um acht Uhr gefrühstückt.
3. Ich habe Karten gespielt.
4. Ich habe Russisch gelernt.
5. Ich habe eine Reise gemacht.

C Übung: Was meinen Sie?

Antworten Sie mit dem Gegensatz.

> BEISPIEL: Finden Sie den Film *gut*?
> Nein, ich finde ihn *schlecht*.

1. Soll man *spät* aufstehen?
2. Ist dieses Klassenzimmer zu *groß*?
3. Sind Fremdsprachen *unwichtig*?
4. Ist Deutsch *schwer*?
5. Soll man *immer* in Eile sein?
6. Spricht der Professor zu *langsam*?
7. Soll man *allein* arbeiten?
8. Sind die Studenten hier meistens *faul*?

Lyrik zum Vorlesen

Lab Manual Kap. 6, Lyrik zum Vorlesen.

This brief poem from 1780 is perhaps the most famous in the German language. Goethe first wrote it on the wall of a forest hut where he was spending the night. The simplicity of its three main images (mountains, trees, and birds) and the evocative language of stillness make this a profound statement of the relationship between man and nature.

Wanderers Nachtlied

Der junge Goethe

Über allen Gipfeln°	mountain peaks
Ist Ruh,°	peace
In allen Wipfeln°	tree tops
Spürest° du	feel
kaum° einen Hauch;°	hardly / breath
Die Vögelein° schweigen° im Walde.	little birds / are silent
Warte nur, balde°	**balde = bald**
Ruhest° du auch.	rest

Johann Wolfgang von Goethe
(1749–1832)

Many composers have set this text to music. One of the most famous settings is Franz Schubert's Opus 96, No. 3 (D 768).

NATIONALE FORSCHUNGS-
UND GEDENKSTÄTTEN DER KLASSISCHEN
DEUTSCHEN LITERATUR IN WEIMAR

**GOETHEHAUS
GOETHEMUSEUM**

209198 ✲

EINTRITTSKARTE 5,00

Simple Past Tense of *sein*

Talking about events in the past
is a communicative goal.

Up to now, you have been using the present tense of verbs to talk about events in the present. To talk about events in the past, German has two tenses. One is called the *perfect tense* and the other, the *simple past tense*. In spoken German, the perfect tense is usually used to talk about the past. You will learn how to use it in this chapter. The frequently occurring verb **sein**, however, is used more often in the simple past than in the perfect. It is therefore very useful for you to learn the following conjugation.

ich	**war**	*I was*	wir	**waren**	*we were*
du	**warst**	*you were*	ihr	**wart**	*you were*
er/es/sie	**war**	*he/it/she was*	sie, Sie	**waren**	*they, you were*

Lab Manual Kap. 6, Var. zur Üb. 1.

Workbook Kap. 6, A.

1 **Übung: Wo waren sie?**

Ihr Professor fragt, wo diese Menschen waren. Sagen Sie ihm, sie waren alle in der Buchhandlung.

> BEISPIEL: Wo war Eva?
> Sie war in der Buchhandlung.

1. Wo war Clara?
2. Wo war Franz?
3. Wo warst du?
4. Wo waren die Studenten?

5. Wo war ich?
6. Wo wart ihr?
7. Wo waren wir?
8. Wo waren Sie?

Perfect Tense

The perfect tense is composed of an *auxiliary verb* ("helping" verb) and a form of the main verb called the *past participle*. The auxiliary verb, either **haben** or **sein**, is conjugated to agree with the subject of the sentence. The past participle is a fixed form.

Conjugation with *haben*

Most German verbs use **haben** as their auxiliary verb. Here is a sample conjugation:

aux.		*part.*	
Ich **habe** das Buch **gekauft**.			*I bought the book. (or: I have bought the book.)*
Du **hast** es **gekauft**.			*You bought it.*
Sie **hat** es **gekauft**.			*She bought it.*
Wir **haben** es **gekauft**.			*We bought it.*
Ihr **habt** es **gekauft**.			*You bought it.*
Sie **haben** es **gekauft**.			*They bought it.*

An der Universität

161

Past Participles of Weak Verbs

There are two basic classes of verbs in German: the *weak* verbs and the *strong* verbs. They are distinguished by the way they form their past participle.

The weak verbs form their past participle by adding the unstressed prefix **ge-** and the ending **-t** or **-et** to the verb stem. Here are some examples of weak verbs you have already learned:

infinitive	*stem*	*auxiliary + past participle*
arbeiten	arbeit-	hat **gearbeitet**
kaufen	kauf-	hat **gekauft**
kosten	kost-	hat **gekostet**
legen	leg-	hat **gelegt**
meinen	mein-	hat **gemeint**

Verbs ending in **-ieren** are *always* weak verbs. They do *not* add the prefix **ge-** in the past participle, just a **-t** to the stem.

studieren → studier- → hat studiert

Er hat in Freiburg studiert.   He studied in Freiburg.

2 Übung: Was haben Sie gekauft, und was hat das gekostet?

You went on a shopping spree yesterday. Tell your instructor which of the things listed below you bought and what they cost.

1. eine Schreibmaschine (DM 949)
2. einen Taschenrechner (DM 39)
3. ein Vorlesungsverzeichnis (DM 4,50)
4. eine Espressomaschine (DM 129)

> BEISPIEL: A: Was haben Sie gestern gekauft?
> B: Ich habe ein- _____ gekauft.
> A: Was hat das denn gekostet?
> B: Das hat DM _____ gekostet.

Solar-Digital Taschenrechner nur 39,-

3 Partnerarbeit: Austauschstudenten

Say where the exchange students come from and where they studied.

> BEISPIEL: Nicole kommt aus Frankreich, und sie hat in Leipzig studiert.

Name	*Heimat* (homeland)	*Universitätsstadt*
Nicole	Frankreich	Leipzig
Yukiko	Japan	Tübingen
Pedro	Spanien	Zürich
Cathleen	Irland	Wien
Matthew	Kanada	Berlin
Beth	USA	Konstanz

Past Participles of Strong Verbs

Beginning in **Wortschatz 1** of this chapter, the past participle (and present-stem vowel change, when applicable) of each new strong verb is given following the infinitive.

Strong verbs in English also form past tenses by changing their root vowels and sometimes add the ending *-n: give, gave, given; see, saw, seen; stand, stood, stood; drink, drank, drunk; do, did, done.*

The strong verbs form their past participle by adding the prefix **ge-** and the suffix **-n** or **-en** to the verb stem. In addition, many strong verbs change their stem vowel. Some verbs also change consonants in the stem. For this reason, *the past participle of each strong verb must be memorized.* Here are some examples of strong verbs you have already learned:

infinitive	*auxiliary + past participle*
geben	hat **gegeben**
sehen	hat **gesehen**
stehen	hat **gestanden**
trinken	hat **getrunken**
tun	hat **getan**

4 Übung: Was haben Sie gesehen?

Was haben Sie gestern gesehen? Sagen Sie es der Gruppe.

BEISPIEL: A: Sagen Sie uns, was Sie gestern gesehen haben.
B: Ich habe ———— , ———— und ———— gesehen.

5 Kettenreaktion: Was hast du getrunken?

You and your friends were thirsty yesterday. Each person says what he or she drank, then asks the next person.

BEISPIEL: A: Gestern habe ich ———— getrunken. Was hast du getrunken?
B: Ich habe ———— getrunken.

Kaffee   Milch   Tee

Conjugation with *sein*

Some German verbs use **sein** rather than **haben** as their auxiliary verb in the perfect tense.

Gestern **ist** die Helga ausgezogen.   *Helga moved out yesterday.*

To take **sein**, a verb must fulfill two conditions:

1. It must be *intransitive* (i.e., it *cannot* take a direct object).

2. It must indicate *change of location or condition.*

Here are some examples of verbs with **sein** as their auxiliary:

infinitive	*auxiliary + participle*	
ausziehen	**ist ausgezogen**	
fliegen	**ist geflogen**	
gehen	**ist gegangen**	*change of location*
wandern	**ist gewandert**	
reisen	**ist gereist**	
aufstehen	**ist aufgestanden**	
sterben	**ist gestorben**	*change of condition*
werden	**ist geworden**	

As you can see, verbs with **sein** may be either weak (**gereist**) or strong (**geflogen**).

Two frequently used verbs are exceptions to the second rule: **sein** itself and **bleiben**. In the perfect tense, these verbs use **sein** as their auxiliary even though they don't show change of location or condition:

Wo **bist** du so lange **gewesen**?　　*Where were you for so long?*
Wir **sind** bei unseren　　　　　　*We stayed with our friends.*
　　Freunden **geblieben**.

6 Kettenreaktion: Wohin bist du gereist?

Alle haben sicher Reisen gemacht. Wohin sind *Sie* einmal gereist?

BEISPIEL:　A: Ich bin nach Mexiko gereist. Wohin bist du gereist?
　　　　　　B: Ich bin _____ gereist.
　　　　　　　(usw.)

7 Übung: Was ist sie geworden?

You've all lost touch with your old school friend Karoline. Tell your instructor what you think she became.

BEISPIEL:　Was glauben *Sie*?
　　　　　　Ich glaube, sie ist Ärztin geworden.

Table of Strong Verbs

The table on p. 165 contains all the strong verbs that you have learned so far.[1] Review your knowledge of the infinitives and stem-vowel changes in

There are about 200 strong or irregular verbs in German, many of low frequency. In *Neue Horizonte* you will learn about 70 frequently used ones. The strong verb forms are the result of a linguistic development in the Germanic languages that was completed hundreds of years ago. New verbs coined in German today are always regular weak verbs, often borrowed from English: **interviewen, formattieren.**

---

[1]Except for **anfangen, anrufen, besitzen, entscheiden, vergessen,** and **verlassen,** this list includes only the basic verb (e.g., **stehen** but not **aufstehen** or **verstehen**). See pp. 166–167 for the formation of past participles of verbs with separable and inseparable prefixes.

the present tense. Note that the verbs with stem-vowel change in the present-tense **du-** and **er-**forms are *always* strong verbs. *Memorize the past participles.*

infinitive	stem-vowel change	aux. + participle	English
anfangen	fängt an	**hat angefangen**	*to begin*
anrufen		**hat angerufen**	*to call up*
beginnen		**hat begonnen**	*to begin*
besitzen		**hat besessen**	*to possess*
bleiben		***ist** geblieben*	*to stay*
entscheiden		**hat entschieden**	*to decide*
essen	ißt	**hat gegessen**	*to eat*
fahren	fährt	***ist** gefahren*	*to drive*
finden		**hat gefunden**	*to find*
fliegen		***ist** geflogen*	*to fly*
fließen		***ist** geflossen*	*to flow*
geben	gibt	**hat gegeben**	*to give*
gehen		***ist** gegangen*	*to go*
halten	hält	**hat gehalten**	*to hold; to stop*
heißen		**hat geheißen**	*to be called*
kommen		***ist** gekommen*	*to come*
laufen	läuft	***ist** gelaufen*	*to run*
lesen	liest	**hat gelesen**	*to read*
liegen		**hat gelegen**	*to lie*
nehmen	nimmt	**hat genommen**	*to take*
scheinen		**hat geschienen**	*to shine; to seem*
schlafen	schläft	**hat geschlafen**	*to sleep*
schließen		**hat geschlossen**	*to close*
schreiben		**hat geschrieben**	*to write*
schwimmen		***ist** geschwommen*	*to swim*
sehen	sieht	**hat gesehen**	*to see*
sein	ist	***ist** gewesen*	*to be*
singen		**hat gesungen**	*to sing*
sprechen	spricht	**hat gesprochen**	*to speak*
stehen		**hat gestanden**	*to stand*
sterben	stirbt	***ist** gestorben*	*to die*
tragen	trägt	**hat getragen**	*to carry; to wear*
trinken		**hat getrunken**	*to drink*
tun		**hat getan**	*to do*
vergessen	vergißt	**hat vergessen**	*to forget*
verlassen	verläßt	**hat verlassen**	*to leave*
werden	wird	***ist** geworden*	*to become*
ziehen		**hat gezogen**	*to pull*

8 Übung: Heute und gestern

Sie hören etwas über heute. Sie sagen, auch gestern ist es so gewesen.

> BEISPIEL: A: Heute scheint die Sonne.
>   B: Auch gestern hat die Sonne geschienen.

1. Heute trägt Thomas einen Pulli.
2. Heute liegt die Zeitung da.
3. Heute tun wir das.
4. Heute singt er zu laut.
5. Heute nimmt Vater den Wagen.
6. Heute schließe ich den Laden.
7. Heute steht Markus draußen.
8. Heute liest du einen Artikel.
9. Heute essen wir um sieben.
10. Heute abend wird es kalt.
11. Heute finden wir die Vorlesung gut.
12. Heute schlafen wir bis acht.
13. Heute läuft Christian durch den Wald.
14. Heute kommt ihr um neun Uhr.
15. Heute geben wir dem Kind ein Brötchen.
16. Heute hält das Auto hier.

Past Participles of Separable-Prefix Verbs

Verbs with separable (stressed) prefixes form their past participles by inserting **-ge-** *between* the prefix and the verb stem.

anfangen   → hat **angefangen**
aufmachen   → hat **aufgemacht**

Das Konzert hat um acht Uhr **angefangen**.	*The concert began at eight o'clock.*
Wann bist du denn **aufgestanden**?	*When did you get up?*
Wer hat den Laden **aufgemacht**?	*Who opened the store?*

9 Übung: Ich habe das schon gemacht!

Ihr Professor sagt Ihnen, Sie sollen etwas tun. Sagen Sie, Sie haben es schon getan.

> BEISPIEL: A: Machen Sie doch die Tür auf.
>   B: Ich habe sie schon aufgemacht.

1. Fangen Sie doch an.
2. Hören Sie doch auf.
3. Stehen Sie doch auf.
4. Kaufen Sie doch ein.
5. Machen Sie doch die Tür zu.
6. Rufen Sie doch Robert an.

To review inseparable prefixes, see p. 141.

Past Participles of Inseparable-Prefix Verbs

Verbs with inseparable (unstressed) prefixes do *not* add the prefix **ge-** in the past participle.

berichten → hat **berichtet**
verstehen → hat **verstanden**

Sie hat uns über Amerika **berichtet**.	*She reported to us about America.*
Das habe ich nicht **verstanden**.	*I didn't understand that.*

10 Übung: Ich habe das schon getan!

Ihr Professor sagt Ihnen, Sie sollen etwas tun. Sagen Sie, Sie haben es schon getan.

BEISPIEL: A: Beginnen Sie bitte.
            B: Ich habe schon begonnen.

1. Beschreiben Sie die Landschaft.
2. Vergessen Sie das.
3. Besuchen Sie Ihre Großeltern.
4. Berichten Sie über Ihre Reise.
5. Besprechen Sie das Problem.
6. Verlassen Sie das Zimmer.

Perfect Tense of Mixed Verbs

A handful of German verbs have the weak participle form **ge—t** but also change their stem. They are called "mixed verbs." The ones you have learned so far are:

bringen	hat **gebracht**
mitbringen	hat **mitgebracht**
kennen	hat **gekannt**
wissen	hat **gewußt**

Schon gehört? . . . Nee, hab' ich nicht gewußt.

11 Partnerarbeit: Das habe ich schon gewußt!

Take turns telling each other things. Respond either that you did or did not know that already.

BEISPIEL: A: Mark kommt aus Kanada.
            B: Das habe ich schon gewußt! (*oder*)
               Wirklich? Das habe ich nicht gewußt.

12 Kettenreaktion: Was hast du heute mitgebracht?

Say what you've brought with you to class today, then ask what the next student has brought.

BEISPIEL: A: Ich habe heute einen Bleistift mitgebracht. Was hast du mitgebracht?
             B: Ich habe ein- _____ mitgebracht.

The Use of the Perfect Tense

The perfect tense is used much more frequently in German than it is in English. In spoken German, the perfect is the most frequently used tense for talking about events in the past. It is therefore often referred to as the "conversational past." English uses the simple past tense (one-word form) for the same purpose.

Sie **sind** gestern nach Berlin **geflogen**.	*They **flew** to Berlin yesterday.*
Ich **habe** die Zeitung um sieben **gelesen**.	*I **read** the newspaper at seven.*

There are no German equivalents for English past-tense progressive and emphatic forms.

$$\text{Ich habe } \textbf{gesprochen.} = \begin{cases} \textit{I spoke.} \\ \textit{I have spoken.} \\ \textit{I was speaking.} \\ \textit{I did speak.} \end{cases}$$

Two-Way Prepositions

Review accusative prepositions, p. 104; dative prepositions, p. 137.

You have learned that some prepositions in German are always followed by an object in the accusative case, while others are always followed by an object in the dative case. A third group, called the "two-way prepositions," all show spatial relationships. They are followed by the *accusative* case when they signal *destination*, and by the *dative* when they signal *location*. In the example sentences in the table on p. 169, notice how the verb determines location or destination. Verbs like **stehen** and **sein** show location (*dative*); verbs like **fahren** and **gehen** show destination (*accusative*).

Memorize the list of two-way prepositions.

Preposition	Destination (accusative) Answers Wohin?	Location (dative) Answers Wo?
an	**to, toward** Hans geht **ans Fenster**. *Hans is walking toward the window.*	**at, alongside of** Hans steht **am Fenster**. *Hans is standing at the window.*
auf	**onto** Wohin legt Inge das Buch? Sie legt es **auf den Tisch**. *She's putting it on the table.*	**on, on top of** Wo liegt das Buch? Es liegt **auf dem Tisch**. *It's lying on the table.*
hinter	**behind** Das Kind läuft **hinter das Haus**. *The child is running behind the house.*	**behind** Das Kind steht **hinter dem Haus**. *The child is standing behind the house.*
in	**into, in** Wo gehen die Studenten hin? Sie gehen **in die Mensa**. *They're going (in)to the cafeteria.*	**in** Wo sind die Studenten? Sie sind **in der Mensa**. *They're in the cafeteria.*
neben	**beside, next to** Leg dein Buch **neben die Zeitung**. *Put your book next to the newspaper.*	**beside, next to** Dein Buch liegt **neben der Zeitung**. *Your book is next to the newspaper.*
über*	**over, across** Wir fliegen **über das Meer**. *We're flying across the ocean.*	**over, above** Die Sonne scheint **über dem Meer**. *The sun is shining over the ocean.*
unter**	**under** Die Katze läuft **unter das Bett**. *The cat runs under the bed.*	**under, beneath** Die Katze schläft **unter dem Bett**. *The cat sleeps under the bed.*
vor	**in front of** Der Bus fährt **vor das Hotel**. *The bus is driving up in front of the hotel.*	**in front of** Der Bus hält **vor dem Hotel**. *The bus is stopping in front of the hotel.*
zwischen	**between** Er läuft **zwischen die Bäume**. *He's running between the trees.*	**between** **Er steht zwischen den Bäumen**. *He's standing between the trees.*

*Some two-way prepositions can sometimes show nonspatial relationships, e.g., **über** = *about* with verbs like **sprechen, lachen, schreiben**. In this meaning, **über** is always followed by accusative case: **Wir haben über unsere Amerikareise gesprochen**.

Note: The prepositions **an** and **in** are regularly contracted with the articles **das** and **dem** in the following way:

an das $\rightarrow$ **ans**   in das $\rightarrow$ **ins**
an dem $\rightarrow$ **am**   in dem $\rightarrow$ **im**

Fragewörter

The question words **wohin** and **woher** can be separated in the following way:

| **Wohin** gehst du? | oder | **Wo** gehst du **hin**? |
| **Woher** kommen Sie? | oder | **Wo** kommen Sie **her**? |

Lab Manual Kap. 6, Var. zur Üb. 16.

Workbook Kap. 6, G–J.

13 Übung: *Wo oder wohin?*

Ihre Professorin fragt Sie, **wo** einige (*some*) Leute sind, oder **wohin** sie gehen. Antworten Sie mit **In der Mensa** oder **In die Mensa**.

1. Wo ist Karin?
2. Wo geht ihr jetzt hin?
3. Wo habt ihr gestern gegessen?
4. Wo sind Horst und Petra?
5. Wo hast du Wolf gesehen?
6. Wohin läuft Peter so schnell?

14 Übung: *Wo oder wohin?*

Answer the questions about where things are lying or where they are being placed. Answer with **Auf dem Tisch** or **Auf den Tisch** as appropriate.

1. Wo liegt meine Zeitung?
2. Wohin soll ich das Geld legen?
3. Wo liegen die Karten für heute abend?
4. Wohin hast du das Buch gelegt?
5. Wo liegt denn das Vorlesungsverzeichnis?

An jeder Universität Berlins

Kiepert

Bücher Für Alle

15 Übung: Wo war Martina heute?

Martina war heute viel unterwegs. Sagen Sie, wo sie war.

BEISPIEL: Sie war in der Stadt.

16 Gruppenarbeit (*Mit offenen Büchern*)

Take turns replacing the verbs in the sentences below with new verbs from the list. Change the case of the prepositional object according to whether the verb you use shows destination or location. Choose three or four new verbs for each sentence.

gehen	liegen	warten	laufen	halten
arbeiten	fahren	lesen	wohnen	sein

1. Wir fahren in die Stadt.
2. Jutta steht hinter dem Haus.
3. Das Kind läuft unter den Tisch.
4. Hans steht am Fenster.
5. Wir sind im Zimmer.

Note on the Prepositions *an* and *auf*

The prepositions **an** and **auf** do not correspond exactly to any English prepositions.

- **an** generally signals motion *toward* or location *at* a border, edge, or vertical surface.

Gehen Sie bitte **an die Tafel**.	*Please go to the blackboard.*
Wir fahren **ans Meer**.	*We're driving to the ocean.*
Sie steht **am Tisch**.	*She's standing at the table.*

- **auf** generally signals motion *onto* or location *upon* a horizontal surface.

Leg das Buch **auf den Tisch**.	*Put (or lay) the book on the table.*
Das Buch liegt **auf dem Tisch**.	*The book is (lying) on the table.*

17 Übung: Wo ist Hans? Wohin geht er?

Sagen Sie, wohin Hans geht oder wo er steht.

18 Übung: *an* oder *auf?*

Complete each sentence with **an** or **auf** and the appropriate article.

Wohin? Antworten Sie mit Präposition + *Artikel im Akkusativ.*

1. Karl geht _____ Tafel.
2. Legen Sie Ihren Mantel _____ Stuhl.
3. Marga fährt im Sommer _____ Meer.
4. Ich habe die Zeitung _____ Schreibtisch gelegt.

Wo? Antworten Sie mit Präposition + *Artikel im Dativ.*

5. Das Kind steht _____ Stuhl.
6. Karl wartet _____ Tür.
7. Das Haus liegt _____ Meer.
8. Das Essen ist schon _____ Tisch.

Masculine N-nouns

A few masculine nouns take the ending **-en** or **-n** in all cases except the nominative singular. They are called "N-nouns."

	singular	**plural**
nom.	der Student	die Student**en**
acc.	den Student**en**	die Student**en**
dat.	dem Student**en**	den Student**en**

Dieser Student kennt München sehr gut.
Kennst du diesen Student**en**?
Ich habe diesem Student**en** einen Stadtplan verkauft.

A good rule-of-thumb is that a noun that is masculine, refers to a person or animal, and has the plural ending **-en** or **-n** is an N-noun. Here are the N-nouns you have already learned. The first ending is for all cases in the singular *except* nominative; the second ending is for all cases in the plural.

When **Herr** is used as a title (*Mr.*), it also must have the N-noun singular ending: **Das ist Herr Weiß;** *but* **Kennen Sie Herrn Weiß?**

der **Bauer, -n, -n**	*farmer*
der **Herr, -n, -en**	*gentleman; Mr.*
der **Journalist, -en, -en**	*journalist*
der **Kunde, -n, -n**	*customer*
der **Mensch, -en, -en**	*person, human being*
der **Student, -en, -en**	*student*
der **Tourist, -en, -en**	*tourist*

19 Partnerarbeit: Wer ist das? Ich kenne ihn nicht.

Lab Manual Kap. 6, Var. zur Üb. 19.

Workbook Kap. 6, K, L.

Partner A asks who one of these men is; partner B answers. Partner A says he doesn't know this person. Switch roles for the next man.

BEISPIEL:
A: Wer ist das?
B: Das ist ein Bauer.
A: Ich kenne diesen _____ nicht.
B: Wer ist das? (usw.)

Ein Brief aus Freiburg

Tips zum Lesen und Lernen

Writing a letter is a communicative goal.

Wie schreibt man eine Postkarte oder einen Brief auf deutsch?

Salutation: **-e** with a female name, **-er** with a male name

Place and date: day / month / year

All second-person forms capitalized: Euch, Euer, Du, Dein, etc.

Jena, den 20.5.95

Liebe Sabine, lieber Markus!
Hallo! Wie geht's Euch denn? Gestern sind wir hier angekommen und haben schon Eure Kusine Gertrud besucht. Sie und ihre Freunde sind wahnsinnig nett und haben uns sehr viel von Jena gezeigt.
Morgen fahren wir nach Berlin und sind am Freitag wieder zu Hause. Bis dann.
Viele herzliche Grüße von Tanja und Fabian

Standard closing = *many cordial greetings*

Lab Manual Kap. 6, Üb. zur Betonung.

Leicht zu merken

automatisch	
der **Film**, -e	
finanzieren	finanzieren
das **Foto**, -s	
das **Konzert**, -e	Konzert
die **Party**, -s	
die **Philosophie**	Philosophie
praktisch	
privat	privat
das **Programm**, -e	Programm
das **Theater**, -	Theater

Einen Brief lesen The following text is a letter written by a German student named Claudia in response to a letter from her American friend Michael, who is coming to Germany as an exchange student. Such informal letters between friends are more loosely structured and associative than formal prose. They tend to be halfway between spoken and written style. In Claudia's letter, for instance, you'll find conversational phrases and slang (e.g., „Ich kann Dir eine Menge erzählen" or „Da staunst Du wohl, oder?").

Claudia writes first about what she's studying, then tells a bit about student life in Freiburg and compares it to America. Then she describes the difficulty of finding a place to live and talks about the rich cultural life in Freiburg. It is clear that her letter is a response to what Michael has written her. She refers to his letter with the following phrases:

„Dein Brief ist gestern angekommen, . . ." (line 6)

„Du schreibst, . . . " (line 7)

What do you think Michael wrote in his original letter? Claudia also asks some questions of him:

„Wie ist es denn bei Dir? Bekommst Du . . . " (line 41)

How might Michael respond in his next letter to her?

In einer Vorlesung

Wortschatz 2

Verben

antworten (+ *dat.*) to answer (*a person*)
   Ich kann dir nicht antworten. I can't answer you.
aus·geben, hat ausgegeben to spend (*money*)
belegen to take (*a university course*)
bezahlen to pay for
enttäuschen to disappoint
erzählen to tell, recount
feiern to celebrate, have a party
schicken to send
sitzen, hat gesessen to sit
staunen to be amazed, surprised

Substantive

der Ausweis, -e I.D. card
   Studentenausweis student I.D.
der Brief, -e letter
der Bürger, - citizen
der Krieg, -e war
der Termin, -e appointment

Glück haben means *to be lucky*, but **glücklich sein** means *to be happy*.

das Ende, -n end
das Glück happiness; luck
   Glück haben to be lucky
das Haar, -e hair
das Hauptfach, ⸚er major field (*of study*)
das Kino, - movie theater
   ins Kino gehen to go to the movies
das Nebenfach, ⸚er minor field (*of study*)
das Referat, -e oral report; written term paper
das Stipendium, Stipendien scholarship, stipend

das Studium (university) studies
das Tempo pace, tempo
die Antwort, -en answer
die Geschichte, -n story; history
die Klausur, -en written test
die Kneipe, -n tavern, bar
die Wohnung, -en apartment
die Ferien (*pl.*) (school or university) vacation
   die Semesterferien semester break

Der Urlaub is a vacation from a job. **Die Ferien** (always plural) is the term for school and university vacations.

Adjektive und Adverbien

billig inexpensive, cheap
gerade just, at this moment
je ever
kostenlos free of charge
lieb dear, nice, sweet
   Das ist lieb von dir! That's sweet of you!
niedrig low
schlimm bad
sofort immediately, right away
sonst otherwise, apart from that
verantwortlich (für) responsible (for)
wohl probably

Andere Vokabeln

alles (*sing.*) everything
einige some
ein paar a couple (of); a few
selber or **selbst** by oneself (myself, yourself, ourselves, etc.)

Remember: **alle** (*pl.*) = *everybody*.

Nützliche Ausdrücke

das heißt that means, in other words
   d.h. i.e. (= that is)
Herzlich willkommen! Welcome! Nice to see you!
letzte Woche last week

Gegensätze

billig ≠ **teuer** cheap ≠ expensive
Glück haben ≠ **Pech haben** to be lucky ≠ to be unlucky
je ≠ **nie** ever ≠ never
der Krieg ≠ **der Frieden** war ≠ peace

Mit anderen Worten

die Bude, -n (*Studentenslang*) = **das Studentenzimmer**
eine Katastrophe = **eine schlimme Situation**
eine Menge (*colloq.*) = **viel**

Ein Brief aus Freiburg[2]

Learning about German student life and
the university system is the cultural goal
of this chapter.

Claudia Martens hat gerade einen Brief von ihrem amerikanischen
Freund Michael Hayward bekommen. Claudia war ein Jahr in Amerika als Austauschschülerin an Mikes High-School in Atlanta. Sie schickt
ihm sofort eine Antwort.

Freiburg, den 20.2.96

5 Lieber Michael,
Dein Brief ist gestern angekommen, und ich möchte ihn sofort
beantworten.° Du schreibst, Du willst zwei Semester an der Uni in
Freiburg Geschichte studieren. Das finde ich super! Ich studiere auch
Geschichte, aber nur im Nebenfach. Mein Hauptfach ist eigentlich
10 Philosophie. Letztes° Semester habe ich ein sehr interessantes Seminar über den Ersten Weltkrieg belegt. Vielleicht können wir im Herbst
zusammen in die Vorlesung über Bismarck und die Gründerjahre[3]
gehen.
Habe ich Dir je über unser Universitätssystem und das Studenten-
15 leben bei uns berichtet? Die Semesterferien[4] haben gerade begonnen,
also habe ich endlich ein bißchen Freizeit und kann Dir eine Menge
erzählen. Im allgemeinen° ist das Tempo bei uns etwas langsamer und
das Studium weniger° stressig als bei Euch. Wir schreiben nicht so
viele Klausuren und Referate, und man ist als Student mehr für sich
20 selbst° verantwortlich. Das heißt zum Beispiel, Du kannst abends zu
Hause sitzen und Bücher wälzen° oder mit Freunden in die Kneipe
gehen. Erst am Semesterende mußt Du für das Seminar ein Referat
schreiben; dann bekommst Du einen Schein.° Bei einer Vorlesung gibt
es weder Referate noch° Klausuren! Da staunst Du wohl, oder?°
25 Wie Du vielleicht schon weißt, sind unsere Unis staatlich;° das bedeutet, sie sind für uns Studenten fast kostenlos. Die Studienge-
bühren° sind sehr niedrig. Ansonsten° muß man praktisch nur für
Wohnung, Essen, Bücher und Kleidung Geld ausgeben. Außerdem°
bekommen viele Studenten auch das sogenannte° BAföG.[5] Wie fi-
30 nanzierst Du eigentlich Dein Jahr in Deutschland? Mit einem
Stipendium, oder mußt Du alles selber bezahlen?

answer (*trans.*)

last

im allgemeinen = in general
weniger = nicht so

für... = for oneself
Bücher wälzen = hit the books

certificate of course credit
weder . . . noch = neither . . .
    nor / = nicht wahr?
state-run

tuition fees / otherwise
in addition
so-called

---

[2]City in Baden-Württemberg between the Black Forest and the Rhine. The Albert-
Ludwigs-Universität was founded in 1457.

[3]Otto von Bismarck (1815–1898): German statesman and Prussian Chancellor,
under whose leadership the German states were united into the German Empire in
1871. Gründerjahre: the "Founders' Years" refers to the period of 1870–1900,
when many German businesses were established.

[4]The German academic year has a Wintersemester that begins in mid-October and
ends in mid-February. The Sommersemester begins in late April and ends in mid-
July. The Semesterferien come between the two semesters.

[5]Inexpensive government loans for university students in Germany are mandated
by the Federal Education Support Law, or Bundes-Ausbildungsförderungsgesetz
(BAföG). This acronym has entered the university vocabulary.

Wo möchte dieser Student wohnen? Kann man ihn anrufen?

Jedenfalls° ist das Essen in der Mensa immer billig und relativ gut, aber mit dem Wohnen ist es manchmal eine Katastrophe. Es gibt nicht genug Studentenwohnheime für alle Studenten, und private Buden
35 sind wahnsinnig teuer geworden. Die Wohnungsnot° ist besonders schlimm: Wir sind seit der Wiedervereinigung° überflutet von° Deutschen aus der ehemaligen° DDR und von den Aussiedlern aus Osteuropa.⁶ Übrigens habe ich letztes Semester einigen Schulkindern aus zwei Aussiedlerfamilien Nachhilfestunden° in Deutsch gegeben,
40 denn° diese neuen Bürger können oft nur wenig Deutsch.

Wie ist es denn bei Dir? Bekommst Du durch das Austauschprogramm automatisch einen Platz im Studentenwohnheim? Wenn nicht,° dann hast Du Glück: Du kannst zu uns in die WG! Wir haben nämlich° nächstes Semester ein Zimmer frei, und Du bist herzlich
45 willkommen. Michael, Du bist immer so gern ins Kino und Konzert gegangen. Ich bin sicher, die Filme und Konzerte hier werden Dich nicht enttäuschen.° Mit Deinem Studentenausweis bekommst Du im Theater, Kino und Museum immer eine Ermäßigung.°

Jetzt habe ich aber einen Termin beim Arzt und muß nachher für
50 eine Party einkaufen. Wir feiern nämlich heute abend das Semesterende. Also, genug für heute, aber ich schreibe Dir bald wieder. Viele herzliche Grüße an Dich und Deine Familie.

Deine

Claudia

P.S. Ich hab' Dir einen Stadtplan und ein paar Postkarten von der Alt-
55 stadt beigelegt,° und dazu° ein neues Foto von mir. Kennst Du mich noch mit kurzen Haaren?

in any case	
housing shortage	
reunification / inundated by	
former	
tutoring	
because	
wenn nicht = if not	
you see	
werden... = will . . . disappoint	
discount	
enclosed / in addition	
mit kurzen Haaren: The plural form is usually used to describe someone's hair: **Jetzt hat sie kurze Haare.**	

---

⁶Citizens of the former German Democratic Republic and the **Aussiedler** (*emigrants*, ethnic Germans from other Eastern European countries) have a constitutional right to German citizenship. Many of them have flooded the German housing and employment markets since the dissolution of the Soviet bloc in the late 1980s.

Fragen zum Lesestück

1. Wo hat Claudia Michael kennengelernt?
2. Was möchte Michael in Freiburg studieren?
3. Wie ist das Tempo im Studentenleben in Freiburg?
4. Warum kostet das Studium in Deutschland nicht sehr viel?
5. Wie finanziert man das Studium?
6. Wo können Studenten billig essen?
7. Warum sind Studentenzimmer manchmal wahnsinnig teuer?
8. Wo kann man sonst leben?
9. Was hat Claudia letztes Semester in ihrer Freizeit gemacht?
10. Wo kann Michael in Freiburg wohnen?
11. Was hat ihm Claudia außer einem Brief geschickt?
12. Was war für Michael neu auf dem Foto von Claudia?

Situationen aus dem Alltag

Das Studium

Einige Wörter kennen Sie schon.

studieren an (+ *dat.*)	*to study at*
Ich studiere an der FU.	
(= **Freien Universität**, Berlin).	
die **Bibliothek, -en**	
das **Fach, ̈er**	*area of study, subject*
das **Hauptfach**, das **Nebenfach**	
die **Klausur, -en**	
das **Labor, -s**	*lab*
das **Referat, -e**	
ein Referat halten	*to give an oral report*
ein Referat schreiben	*to write a paper*
das **Semester, -**	
das **Sommersemester**	*spring term (usually April to July)*
das **Wintersemester**	*fall term (usually October to February)*
das **Seminar, -e**	
die **Vorlesung, -en**	
die **Wissenschaft, -en**	*science; scholarship; field of knowledge*

Note stress: **Labór.**

An der Universität

Einige Studienfächer

Note that most academic disciplines are feminine.

die **Anglistik**	Anglistik	*English studies*
die **Betriebswirtschaft**		*management, business*
die **Biologie**	Biologie	*biology*
die **Chemie**	Chemie	*chemistry*
die **Elektrotechnik**		*electrical engineering*
die **Germanistik**	Germanistik	*German studies*
die **Geschichte**		*history*
die **Informatik**	Informatik	*computer science*
Jura (used without article)		*law*
die **Kunstgeschichte**		*art history*
die **Landwirtschaft**		*agriculture*
die **Linguistik**	Linguistik	*linguistics*
die **Mathematik**	Mathematik	*mathematics*
die **Medizin**	Medizin	*medicine*
die **Musikwissenschaft**		*musicology*
die **Pädagogik**	Pädagogik	*education*
die **Philosophie**	Philosophie	*philosophy*
die **Physik**	Physik	*physics*
die **Politikwissenschaft**		*political science*
die **Psychologie**	Psychologie	*psychology*
die **Soziologie**	Soziologie	*sociology*
die **Wirtschaftswissenschaft**		*economics*

Talking about university life is a communicative goal.

Jetzt sprechen wir über das Studium:

Gruppenarbeit: Was studierst du denn?

Was ist Ihr Hauptfach und was belegen Sie dieses Semester?

BEISPIEL: Mein Hauptfach ist _____ . Dieses Semester belege ich _____ , _____ und _____ . Was studierst denn du?

Partnerarbeit: Interview

Interview each other in more detail about your studies. Take notes if necessary, and be prepared to report to the whole class. Ask each other questions such as the following:

1. Was tust du lieber: Referate schreiben oder Referate halten? Wie oft mußt du das tun?
2. Schreibst du deine Referate auf einem Computer?
3. Arbeitest du oft in der Bibliothek, oder mehr im Labor?
4. Was willst du nach dem Studium machen?
5. Brauchst du Deutsch für dein Studium oder für deinen Beruf?
6. Wie finanzierst du das Studium? Bekommst du ein Stipendium?
7. Wohnst du im Studentenwohnheim oder privat?

Das Studentenzimmer

Die Möbel (*pl.*)   *furniture*

Dieses Zimmer ist **möbliert** (*furnished*).

1. das Telefon, -e
2. das Bett, -en
3. die Lampe, -n
4. der Teppich, -e
5. der Computer, -
6. der CD-Spieler, -
7. die CD, -s
8. das Radio, -s
9. das Bücherregal, -e
10. das Poster, -
11. der Spiegel, -
12. der Wecker, -
13. der Kleiderschrank, ⸚e
14. der Schlüssel, -
15. die Decke, -n
16. der Boden, ⸚

Gruppenarbeit: Beschreiben wir dieses Zimmer.

Wie finden Sie dieses Zimmer? Ist es typisch für die Studentenzimmer bei Ihnen? Kann man hier gut wohnen? Wie sieht *Ihr* Zimmer aus? Was gibt es zum Beispiel *nicht* bei Ihnen?

Sprechen wir miteinander!

A Gruppenarbeit: Was hat Maria letzte Woche gemacht?

Maria studiert Philosophie an der Uni in Tübingen. Sie ist sehr gut organisiert. Das sieht man an ihrem Terminkalender für letzte Woche. Wo war sie letzte Woche, und was hat sie gemacht?

BEISPIEL: Am Montag hat sie mit Thomas im Café Völter Kaffee getrunken.

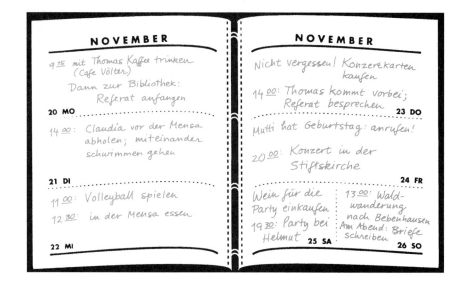

B Gruppenarbeit: Was haben Sie letzte Woche gemacht?

Jetzt machen Sie *Ihren* Terminkalender auf. Was haben *Sie* letzte Woche getan?

C Gruppenarbeit: Wo im Klassenzimmer?

Answer the questions about where the people and things are located in the classroom shown on p. 183. Then describe the locations of other people and objects.

BEISPIEL: Wo sitzt Herr Schröder?
Er sitzt auf dem Tisch (vor Marie usw.).

1. Wo sitzt Marie?
2. Wo steht Jutta?
3. Wo steht Karl?
4. Wo steht Gertrud?
5. Wo sitzt der Lehrer?
6. Wo steht Emil?
7. Wo liegt die Zeitung?
8. Wo sind diese Leute?

D Gruppenarbeit

Jetzt beschreiben Sie *Ihr* Klassenzimmer. Wo stehen oder sitzen die Menschen?

E Gruppenarbeit

Here is another picture of the same classroom, but now everyone is moving around and doing things. Tell where they are going and what they are doing. Describe any other actions you can.

1. Wohin legt Gertrud ihr Buch?
2. Wo geht Karl hin?
3. Wohin legt der Lehrer das Buch?
4. Wo geht Emil hin?
5. Wo geht Anna hin?

An der Universität

Gruppenarbeit: Wir möchten in die WG. (4 Personen)

Zwei Studenten sind schon Mitbewohner in einer WG, und zwei andere Studenten wollen in diese WG. Die Mitbewohner interviewen die neuen Studenten über ihr Studium und ihre Interessen (*interests*).

> Was studiert ihr?
> Habt ihr je in einer WG gewohnt?
> Warum wollt ihr bei uns wohnen? usw.

Die neuen Studenten haben auch einige Fragen:

> Wie sehen die Zimmer aus?
> Gibt es schon einen Schreibtisch im Zimmer? usw.

Schreiben Sie zu Hause

G **Was habe ich letzte Woche gemacht?** In exercise A above you used Maria's appointment calendar to help you describe what she did last week, then in exercise B you described your own activities. Now write a paragraph in German describing what you did last week.

Letter-writing is a
communicative goal.

H **„Liebe Claudia, . . .“** Claudias Brief an Michael Hayward haben Sie schon gelesen. In diesem Brief hat sie ihm das Studentenleben in Freiburg beschrieben. Jetzt spielen Sie die Rolle von Michael Hayward und schreiben Sie eine Antwort an Claudia. Beantworten Sie ihre Fragen und schreiben Sie über das Studentenleben bei Ihnen. Haben Sie andere Fragen an Claudia über Freiburg und das Studium dort? (Review „Wie schreibt man eine Postkarte oder einen Brief auf Deutsch“ on p. 174.)

I **Wie sagt man das auf deutsch?**

1. I've brought you a course catalogue.
2. Did it cost much?
3. No, it was cheap. Shall I put it on your desk?

4. The lecture began at ten o'clock.
5. Unfortunately, I arrived too late.
6. I stood behind my friends and didn't hear anything.

7. What did you study in Dresden?
8. History was my major but I also studied German.

9. Tonight we're going to the movies together.
10. I hope you haven't forgotten your student I.D.
11. No, it's in my pocket.
12. Good, let's go! We have to be there before 8:00 o'clock.

3 Wie war deine Vorlesung? (09:33)

Was macht ihr denn heute abend?

In der Bibliothek lernt Stefan Su-Sin (eine Studentin aus China) kennen. Sie besprechen ihr Studium an der Uni. Dann kommt Katrin mit zwei Freunden vorbei. Heute abend läuft ein neuer Film, und sie wollen zusammen essen und dann ins Kino gehen. Eigentlich soll Stefan pauken (cram), aber dann geht er doch mit.

Wortschatz zum Video

pauken	*cram (student slang)*
Mathe	*math*
Echt?	*Really? (slang)*
Setz dich.	*Sit down.*
Viel Spaß noch!	*Have fun!*

A Was sehen Sie im Video?

Watch video Module 3 (9:38–12:43) once without sound. Check off in the list below the words, things, and people you see in the video.

—— 1. Universitätsbibliothek
—— 2. Studenten liegen in der Sonne
—— 3. eine Familie am Frühstückstisch

—— 4. Stefan und Katrin in der Mensa
—— 5. Hörsaal (*lecture hall*)
—— 6. einen Mann auf einem Fahrrad (*bicycle*)

B Wissen Sie die Antwort?

Now watch video Module 3 with sound (9:38–12:43). Then answer these questions about what happens.

1. Wo lernt Stefan Su-Sin kennen?
2. Woher kommt Su-Sin?
3. Was studiert Stefan?
4. Wie war seine Vorlesung bei Professor Klemm?
5. Was wollen Katrin und ihre Freunde heute abend machen?

C Wer sagt das?

Choose the person who does or says the following.

a. Su-Sin   b. Stefan   c. Katrin   d. Professor Klemm

1. —— sagt: „Meine Familie wohnt seit zwei Jahren in Berlin."
2. —— sagt: „Ich muß lesen."
3. —— fragt: „Wie war deine Vorlesung heute?"
4. —— sagt: „Ich hab' so die Nase voll."
5. —— sagt: „Ich hab' keine Zeit. Muß pauken. Mathe."
6. —— sagt: „Wir können ja vorher zum Italiener essen gehen."

D Richtig oder falsch?

Indicate whether each statement is **richtig (R)** or **falsch (F)**.

1. Stefan findet seine Mathevorlesung langweilig.   R   F
2. Die Freunde wollen zusammen ins Theater gehen.   R   F
3. Su-Sin macht dieses Semester Biologie.   R   F
4. Stefan geht nicht mit ins Restaurant.   R   F
5. Professor Klemm scheint freundlich zu sein.   R   F
6. Stefan ist erst eine Stunde in der Bibliothek.   R   F

E Conversational exchanges

For each sentence in the left column, find the appropriate response in the right column.

_____ 1. Was studierst du denn?

_____ 2. Das ist Su-Sin. Sie kommt aus Beijing.

_____ 3. Stefan, kommst du mit?

_____ 4. Wie findest du Berlin?

_____ 5. Viel Spaß noch.

a. Leider nicht. Ich muß pauken.

b. Anglistik im Hauptfach und Geschichte im Nebenfach.

c. Danke, gleichfalls.

d. Freut mich, Su-Sin. Ich heiße Katrin.

e. Echt toll!

Some Statistics on University Study

The graph and table below show some interesting facts about education and employment in Germany.

Wie weit haben sie's gebracht?
Von je 100 vollzeitbeschäftigten Erwerbstätigen in den alten Bundesländern

mit diesem Berufsabschluß...

...haben diese Berufsstellung erreicht:

Universität, Fachhochschule | **Betriebliche Lehre oder Fachschule** | **Ohne Berufsausbildung**

Gehobene oder leitende Stellung, Selbständigkeit

91 | 77 | 24 | 11 | 20 | 10

58 | 54 | 24 | 20

35 | 56 | 70

Mittlere Stellung — 8 | 22

Hilfsarbeiter, einfache Angestellte — 1 | 1 | 18

Männer | Frauen | Männer | Frauen | Männer | Frauen

© Globus

Wie weit haben sie's gebracht? (*How Far Did They Get?*) correlates employment level with level of education. Three levels of educational achievement are shown:

- degree from a university or technical institute (**Fachhochschule**)
- apprenticeship or degree from a technical secondary school (**Fachschule**)
- no job training

Males and females are compared within each level. The numbers show the percentage of each group at the following employment levels:

- upper-level managers or self-employed
- middle managers
- employees and unskilled laborers

Hitliste der Studienfächer (*List of Favorite Fields of Study*) shows the 20 fields most popular among Germans beginning university study in the fall of 1988.

Hitliste der Studienfächer Deutsche Studienanfänger im WS 1988/89 in den 20 beliebtesten Studienfächern			
	Insgesamt	*Männer*	*Frauen*	*Anteil der Frauen in Prozent*
Betriebswirtschaftslehre	16 643	10 449	6 194	37,2
Elektrotechnik	13 452	12 985	467	3,5
Maschinenbau	12 401	11 986	415	3,3
Wirtschaftswissenschaften	10 186	6 463	3 723	36,6
Rechtswissenschaften	9 959	5 118	4 841	48,6
Informatik	7 120	6 032	1 088	15,3
Germanistik	6 366	1 236	5 130	80,6
Medizin	5 991	3 173	2 818	47,0
Chemie	5 754	3 736	2 018	35,1
Mathematik	4 926	2 814	1 637	33,2
Physik	4 837	4 262	575	11,9
Biologie	4 553	1 854	2 699	59,3
Architektur	4 357	2 540	1 817	41,7
Bauingenieur	3 930	3 289	641	16,3
Anglistik	3 045	585	2 460	80,8
Volkswirtschaftslehre	2 599	1 680	919	35,4
Wirtschaftsingenieur	2 323	2 023	300	13,0
Pädagogik	2 303	528	1 775	77,1
Psychologie	1 973	583	1 390	70,5
Geschichte	1 843	897	946	51,3

Quelle: Statistisches Bundesamt

Communicative Goals

- Expressing opinions, preferences, and polite requests
- Making travel plans and talking about traveling
- Talking on the telephone
- Telling time with the 24-hour clock

Cultural Goal

- Learning about traveling in Germany and Europe

Chapter Outline

Lyrik zum Vorlesen Wilhelm Müller, „Wanderschaft"

Grammatik Der-words and ein-words • Coordinating Conjunctions • Verbs with Dative Objects • Personal Dative • Using *würden* + infinitive • More on Two-Way Prepositions • Perfect Tense of Modal Verbs • Official Time-Telling

Lesestück Unterwegs per Autostop oder mit der Bahn

Situationen aus dem Alltag Reisen und Verkehr

Almanach Jugendherbergen (*Youth Hostels*)

Am Bahnhof

Lab Manual Kap. 7, Dialoge, Fragen, Hören Sie gut zu!, Üb. zur Aussprache [u / ü].

Ein Student sieht eine alte Dame mit viel Gepäck und will ihr helfen.

STUDENT:	Darf ich Ihnen helfen?
TOURISTIN:	Ja, bitte! Würden Sie mir den Koffer tragen?
STUDENT:	Gerne. Wohin müssen Sie denn?
TOURISTIN:	Gleis drei. Mein Zug fährt um 15.00 Uhr ab.

Vor der Urlaubsreise

die Flasche: English cognate: *flask.*

MARION:	Suchst du die Thermosflasche?
THORSTEN:	Nein, nicht die Thermosflasche, sondern den Straßenatlas. Ich glaube, ich habe ihn auf den Tisch gelegt.
MARION:	Ja, hier liegt er, unter meiner Jacke.
THORSTEN:	Häng die Jacke doch auf, dann haben wir mehr Platz. Wir müssen unsere Reise nach Venedig planen.

der Straßenatlas: Most German drivers carry a bound road atlas of Western Europe rather than folding maps.

→ Am Telefon

Marion ruft ihren Vater an. Es klingelt lange, aber endlich kommt Herr Krogmann ans Telefon.

HERR KROGMANN:	Krogmann.
MARION:	Hallo Papa! Hier ist Marion. Warum hast du nicht gleich geantwortet?
KROGMANN:	Ach, Marion, seid ihr wieder zurück? Ich habe auf dem Sofa gelegen und bin eingeschlafen.
MARION:	Oh, tut mir leid, Papa.
KROGMANN:	Das macht nichts. Ich habe sowieso aufstehen wollen. Wie war denn eure Reise?
MARION:	Alles war wunderbar.

Mit dem Kofferkuli *(luggage cart)* am Bahnhof kann man viel Gepäck allein tragen (Frankfurter Hauptbahnhof).

191

At the Train Station

A student sees an elderly woman with a lot of luggage and wants to help her.

S.: May I help you?

T.: Yes, please. Would you carry my suitcase?

S.: Gladly. Where do you have to go?

T.: Track three. My train leaves at 3:00 P.M.

Before the Trip

M.: Are you looking for the thermos bottle?

T.: No, not the thermos, but the road atlas. I think I put it on the table.

M.: Yes, here it is, under my jacket.

T.: Hang up the jacket, then we'll have more room. We've got to plan our trip to Venice.

On the Telephone

Marion is calling up her father. The phone rings a long time, but Mr. Krogmann finally comes to the telephone.

MR. K.: Krogmann.

M.: Hello, Dad. This is Marion. Why didn't you answer right away?

MR. K.: Oh, Marion, are you back? I was lying on the sofa and fell asleep.

M.: Oh, sorry, Dad.

MR. K.: That doesn't matter. I wanted to get up anyway. How was your trip?

M.: Everything was wonderful.

Wortschatz 1

Verben

ab·fahren (fährt ab), ist abgefahren to depart, leave (*by vehicle*)

danken (+ *dat.*) to thank

ein·schlafen (schläft ein), ist eingeschlafen to fall asleep

gefallen (gefällt), hat gefallen (+ *dat.*) to please

Das Buch gefällt mir. I like the book.

gehören (+ *dat.*) to belong to (a person)

hängen, hat gehängt (*trans.*) to hang

auf·hängen to hang up

hängen, hat gehangen (*intrans.*) to be hanging

helfen (hilft), hat geholfen (+ *dat.*) to help

klingeln to ring

reservieren to reserve

setzen to set (down), put

stellen to put, place

würden (+ *infinitive*) would (do something)

Substantive

der **Bahnhof, ¨e** train station

der **Koffer, -** suitcase

der **Straßenatlas** road atlas

der **Zug, ¨e** train

das **Gepäck** luggage

das **Gleis, -e** track

das **Telefon, -e** telephone

(das) **Venedig** Venice

die **Flasche, -n** bottle

die **Thermosflasche** thermos bottle

Adjektive und Adverbien

sowieso anyway

wunderbar wonderful

Andere Vokabeln

sondern but rather, but . . . instead

welch- which

Nützliche Ausdrücke

Es tut mir leid. I'm sorry.

Das macht nichts. That doesn't matter.

Das ist (mir) egal. It doesn't matter (to me). I don't care.

Das macht (mir) Spaß. That's fun (for me).

Wieviel Uhr ist es? = Wie spät ist es?

Often shortened in spoken German: **Tut mir leid; Macht nichts; Mir egal.**

Gegensätze

ab·fahren ≠ an·kommen to depart ≠ to arrive

auf·stehen ≠ ins Bett gehen to get up ≠ to go to bed

ein·schlafen ≠ auf·wachen to fall asleep ≠ to wake up

The verbs in **Gegensätze** illustrate the meanings of some separable prefixes: **ab** = *away from;* **an** = *at;* **auf** = (*here*) *up.*

Mit anderen Worten

Das ist mir Wurscht. (*colloq.*) = **Das ist mir egal.**

Variationen

A Persönliche Fragen

1. Sind Sie oft mit dem Zug gefahren? Wohin?
2. Fahren Sie gern mit dem Zug?
3. Die Touristin muß zu ihrem Zug. Wohin müssen Sie heute?
4. Thorsten und Marion brauchen einen Straßenatlas für ihre Reise. Was brauchen Sie für eine Reise?
5. Thorsten plant eine Reise nach Venedig. Planen Sie eine Reise in den Ferien? Wohin?
6. Schlafen Sie gern nachmittags wie Herr Krogmann?
7. Herr Krogmann schläft auf dem Sofa. Wo schlafen Sie lieber am Nachmittag, auf dem Sofa oder im Bett?

B Reaktionen

Respond to the statements and questions on the left with an appropriate phrase from the right.

1. Ich kann den Koffer nicht tragen.	Einverstanden!
2. Würden Sie mir bitte helfen?	Doch!
3. Hast du das nicht gewußt?	Oh, das tut mir leid!
4. Wo fährt denn Ihr Zug ab?	Das macht nichts!
5. Waren die Hausaufgaben besonders schwer?	Gerne!
6. Wie war die Reise?	Auf dem Tisch.
7. Wohin hast du den Atlas gelegt?	Gar nichts.
8. Wo liegt denn der Stadtplan?	Auf das Sofa.
9. Gehen wir zusammen einkaufen?	Das finde ich auch.
10. Was ist denn los?	Bitte sehr.
	Auf Gleis zehn.
	Nee, gar nicht.
	Wunderbar!

C Übung: Im Reisebüro *(At the travel agency)*

Im Reisebüro fragt man, ob Sie etwas machen wollen. Antworten Sie, Sie würden das gerne tun.

BEISPIEL: A: Wollen Sie ein Hotelzimmer reservieren?
　　　　　　 B: Ja, ich würde gern ein Hotelzimmer reservieren.

1. Wollen Sie Ihren Mantel aufhängen?
2. Wollen Sie morgen abfahren?
3. Wollen Sie morgen abend in Venedig ankommen?
4. Wollen Sie im Zug schlafen?
5. Wollen Sie mir Ihr Gepäck geben?
6. Wollen Sie Ihre Familie anrufen?

German Romantic literature uses nature images to evoke themes of yearning for the unknown, wandering, and love. The Romantic poets were obsessed with the illusory world of appearances expressed in moonlit nights, fog, and the forest. In the early 19th century **das Wandern** described the life of an itinerant journeyman. These were artisans who journeyed from town to town, gaining experience with different master craftsmen.

Wilhelm Müller's poem cycle „Die schöne Müllerin" (1820) is unified by the theme of the love of the journeyman for the miller's daughter. In this poem the youth is moved to **Wanderlust** by the mill itself with its rushing water and turning wheels. He ends by asking the miller and his wife for permission to depart.

Lab Manual Kap. 7, Lyrik zum Vorlesen.

Set to music by Franz Schubert, this poem is the first song in his cycle „Die schöne Müllerin," op. 5, no. 1 (D 795).

Wanderschaft°

journeying

Das Wandern ist des Müllers Lust,°
Das Wandern!
Das muß ein schlechter Müller sein,
Dem niemals fiel das Wandern ein,°
Das Wandern.

des... = the miller's desire

dem... = who has never thought of wandering

Vom Wasser haben wir's gelernt,
Vom Wasser!
Das hat nicht Rast° bei Tag und Nacht,
Ist stets° auf Wanderschaft bedacht,°
Das Wasser.

rest
stets = immer / intent

Das sehn wir auch den Rädern ab,°
Den Rädern!
Die gar nicht gerne stille stehn
Und sich mein Tag nicht müde drehn,°
Die Räder.

sehn... see also from the wheels

Und... = never tire of turning

Die Steine selbst,° so schwer sie sind,
Die Steine!
Sie tanzen mit den muntern Reihn°
Und wollen gar noch schneller sein,
Die Steine!

Steine selbst = even the stones

cheerful dance

O Wandern, Wandern, meine Lust,
O Wandern!
Herr Meister und Frau Meisterin,
Laßt mich in Frieden weiterziehn°
Und wandern!

Laßt... = let me go in peace

Wilhelm Müller (1794–1827)

Der-words and ein-words

You have learned the definite and indefinite articles (**der** and **ein**) and similar words that precede nouns (**dies-, jed-, mein, kein, alle**). Such words are divided into two groups, the **der**-words and the **ein**-words, because of slight differences in their endings:

der-words		*ein*-words	
der, das, die	*the*	**ein**	*a, an*
dies-	*this, these*	**kein**	*no, not a*
jed-	*each, every*		
welch-	*which*		
all-	*all*		

mein	*my*	
dein	*your*	
sein	*his, its*	
ihr	*her*	} *possessive adjectives*
unser	*our*	
euer	*your*	
ihr	*their*	
Ihr	*your*	

Since the endings of the definite article (**der, das, die**) are slightly irregular, **dieser** is used here to review the **der**-word endings in the three cases you know so far.

der-word endings				
	masc.	**neut.**	**fem.**	**plural**
nom.	dieser Stuhl ⎫	dieses Buch	diese Uhr	diese Bücher
acc.	diesen Stuhl ⎭			
dat.	diesem Stuhl	diesem Buch	dieser Uhr	diesen Büchern

The **ein**-words have the same endings as **der**-words *except in three cases* where they have *no* endings, as highlighted in the following table.

ein-word endings				
	masc.	**neut.**	**fem.**	**plural**
nom.	**mein** Stuhl	**mein** Buch ⎫	meine Uhr	meine Bücher
acc.	meinen Stuhl	**mein** Buch ⎭		
dat.	meinem Stuhl	meinem Buch	meiner Uhr	meinen Büchern

1 Übung

Your instructor makes a statement. Student A asks which thing is meant. Student B answers.

BEISPIEL: Das Zimmer ist klein.
A: Welches Zimmer ist klein?
B: Dieses Zimmer ist klein.

1. Das Hemd ist teuer.
2. Die Turnschuhe sind neu.
3. Der Lehrling heißt Martin.
4. Die Gruppe fährt nach Europa.
5. Der Pulli ist häßlich.
6. Die Brötchen sind frisch.

Lab Manual Kap.
7, Var. zur Üb. 2.

Workbook Kap.
7, A.

2 Übung

Respond to each statement as in the example.

BEISPIEL: Dieser Berg ist steil.
Ja, aber nicht jeder Berg ist steil.

1. Dieser Koffer ist schwer.
2. Dieses Studentenwohnheim ist neu.
3. Dieser Zug fährt pünktlich ab.
4. Dieses Telefon klingelt zu laut.
5. Diese Thermosflasche ist teuer.
6. Dieser Tourist kann Deutsch.
7. Diese Vorlesung ist langweilig.

Tempelhofer Ufer 32
10963 Berlin
Tel. 030 / 264 95 2-0
Fax 030 / 262 04 37

JUGENDHERBERGE

3 Übung

Your instructor wants to know what belongs to whom. Answer as in the examples.

BEISPIEL: I: Ist dieses Buch Ihr Buch?
S: Nein, dieses Buch ist sein Buch.
I: Welches Buch ist Ihr Buch?
S: Dieses Buch ist mein Buch.

Coordinating Conjunctions

A clause is a unit containing a subject and an inflected verb. A simple sentence consists of one clause; a compound sentence has two or more clauses.

Coordinating conjunctions are words that join clauses that could each stand alone as a simple sentence. The coordinating conjunction joins them into a compound sentence.

Christa ist achtzehn.   Ihr Bruder ist sechzehn.
Christa ist achtzehn, **und** ihr Bruder ist sechzehn.

Kannst du das Fenster aufmachen?   Soll ich es machen?
Kannst du das Fenster aufmachen, **oder** soll ich es machen?

Do not confuse the conjunction **denn** with the flavoring particle used with questions: **Wo bist du denn so lange gewesen?**

The most common coordinating conjunctions in German are

und	*and*
oder	*or*
aber	*but, however*
sondern	*but rather, instead*
denn	*for, because*

Remember the iron-clad rule: The verb is always in second position in German statements. A coordinating conjunction is *not* counted as being in first position in its clause. The word order of the second clause is *not* affected by the coordinating conjunction.

0   1   2

Ute kommt nicht zu Fuß, **sondern** sie fährt mit dem Auto.

0   1   2

Ich kann dich erst am Abend anrufen, **denn** ich bin bis 7 in der Bibliothek.

0   1   2

Klaus muß bis drei arbeiten, **aber** dann kann er nach Hause.

The coordinating conjunctions are also used to join units smaller than a clause.

Ich habe einen Bruder **und** eine Schwester.
Möchtest du Wein **oder** Bier?
Dieser Laden ist gut, **aber** sehr teuer.
Barbara ist nicht hier, **sondern** in Italien.

Note on punctuation: There is *always* a comma before **aber, sondern,** and **denn.** Before **und** and **oder,** there is only a comma if a complete clause (with subject) follows.

Jens geht in die Stadt **und** kauft Lebensmittel ein.
Jens geht in die Stadt, **und** Maria kauft Lebensmittel ein.

Lab Manual Kap. 7, Var. zur Üb. 4, Üb. 5.

Workbook Kap. 7, B, C.

4 Partnerarbeit

Use **und, aber, oder,** or **denn** to join each sentence from column A to one from column B. Try to find the most logical pairings. Compare results with other students.

A   B

Meine Eltern kommen morgen.   *und*   Ich möchte sie dort besuchen.
Bist du heute krank?   Willst du in einer WG wohnen?
Gisela studiert in Freiburg.   Ich zeige ihnen meine Wohnung.
Ich bringe das Buch mit.   Mein Bruder wohnt auf dem Land.
Ich wohne in der Stadt.   Du sollst es lesen.
Ich bin jetzt in Eile.   Sie hat mir nicht geantwortet.
Willst du in der Mensa essen?   Mein Zug fährt gleich ab.
Willst du allein wohnen?   Wollen wir bei mir etwas kochen?
Ich habe Sabine gefragt.   Geht es dir gut?

Aber versus sondern

Aber and **sondern** are both translated with English *but*. Both express a contrast, but they are *not* interchangeable. **Sondern** <u>must</u> be used when *but* means *but . . . instead, but rather.*

Er bleibt zu Hause, **aber** sie geht einkaufen.	*He's staying home, but she's going shopping.*
Er bleibt nicht zu Hause, **sondern** geht einkaufen.	*He's not staying home, **but** is going shopping **instead**.*

Sondern *always* follows a *negative* statement and expresses *mutually exclusive alternatives*. Note that the clause following **sondern** often leaves out elements it has in common with the first clause. Such deletion is called *ellipsis*.

> Er bleibt nicht zu Hause, sondern [er] geht einkaufen.
> Das ist kein Wein, sondern [das ist] Wasser.
> Käthe hat es nicht getan, sondern die Kinder [haben es getan].

[handwritten: aber = have to be mutually exclusive]

5 Übung: *Aber* oder *sondern*?

Combine each pair of simple sentences into a compound sentence, using **aber** or **sondern** as appropriate. Use ellipsis where possible.

1. Sie fliegt nach Italien. Ihr Mann fährt mit dem Zug.
2. Sie haßt mich nicht. Sie liebt mich.
3. Es ist noch nicht sieben Uhr. Er ist schon zu Hause.
4. Ich fahre nicht mit dem Auto. Ich gehe zu Fuß.
5. Ich trage keinen Mantel. Ich trage meine Jacke.
6. Bernd mag dieses Bier nicht. Lutz trinkt es gern.

Mit dem Fahrrad *(bicycle)* kann man billig reisen und auch fit bleiben. Woher kommen diese Radfahrer?

Word Order: *nicht x, sondern y*

Notice how the position of **nicht** shifts when it is followed by **sondern**.

Ich kaufe den Mantel nicht.   *but*   Ich kaufe **nicht den Mantel**, sondern die Jacke.

Johanna arbeitet heute nicht.   *but*   Johanna arbeitet **nicht heute**, sondern morgen.

6 Übung: Nein, nicht x, sondern y.

Answer these questions negatively, using **sondern**.

BEISPIEL: Wollen Sie *um sieben* frühstücken?
            Nein, ich will nicht um sieben frühstücken, sondern um zehn.

1. Suchen Sie *die Thermosflasche?*
2. Gehen Sie *am Mittwoch* ins Kino?
3. Gehen Sie *mit Ursula* in die Stadt?
4. Gehen Sie mit Ursula *in die Stadt?*
5. Wollen Sie mir *die Fotos* zeigen?
6. Waren Sie *gestern* in der Bibliothek?

Verbs with Dative Objects

Review dative endings for **der**-words, p. 133, and dative forms of the personal pronouns, p. 135.

A few German verbs require an object in the dative case rather than the accusative. Two of these are **helfen** and **antworten**.

Ich sehe den Mann.   *I see the man.*
    but:
Ich helfe **dem** Mann.   *I'm helping the man.*

Du fragst die Frau.   *You ask the woman.*
    but:
Du antwortest **der** Frau.   *You answer the woman.*

This chapter introduces the following verbs with dative objects:

Glauben takes an accusative inanimate object, but a dative personal object: **Ich glaube das.** but **Ich glaube dir.** One can thus say: **Ich glaube dir das.** = *I believe you when you say that.*

antworten	*to answer* (someone)
danken	*to thank*
gefallen	*to please*
gehören	*to belong to*
glauben	*to believe* (someone)
helfen	*to help*

The dative object is usually a person.

Marie dankt **ihrem Lehrer**.   *Marie thanks her teacher.*
Wem gehört dieser Wagen?   *Who owns this car?* (Literally: *To whom does this car belong?*)

Diese Stadt gefällt **mir**.   *I like this city.* (Literally: *This city pleases me.*)

Note that **gefallen** is another way of saying *to like something*. However, since its literal meaning is *to please* (*someone*), the subject and object are the reverse of English. Remember that the verb must agree in number with the singular.

Die Vorlesungen gefallen **mir**.   literally: *The lectures please me.*

I like the **lectures**.

 Lab Manual Kap. 7, Var. zur Üb. 7.

 Workbook Kap. 7, D, E.

7 Übung: Was gefällt Ihnen?

Your instructor asks if you like various things. Say whether you do or do not.

> BEISPIEL: Gefällt Ihnen das Wetter heute?
>   Ja, es gefällt mir. *oder* Nein, es gefällt mir nicht.

1. Gefällt Ihnen diese Stadt?
2. Gefällt Ihnen Ihr Hauptfach?
3. Gefällt Ihnen mein Hemd?
4. Gefällt Ihnen das Wetter heute?
5. Gefallen Ihnen die Vorlesungen an der Uni?
6. Gefallen Ihnen diese Bilder?
7. Gefallen Ihnen meine Schuhe?
8. Gefällt Ihnen dieser Film?

8 Übung: Wem helfen diese Leute?

Diese Leute wollen heute helfen. Sagen Sie, wem sie helfen.

9 Übung: Wem gehört das Buch?

Say what belongs to whom.

> BEISPIEL: A: Wem gehört dieses Buch?
>   B: Es gehört mir.

10 Gruppenarbeit: Wer kann mir helfen? (Mit geschlossenen Büchern)

Your instructor asks a general question. Redirect the question to a neighbor, who may answer positively or negatively.

> BEISPIEL: Wer kann mir helfen?
>   A: Kannst *du* ihr helfen?
>   B: Nein, ich kann ihr nicht helfen.

1. Wer glaubt mir?
2. Wer kann mir antworten?
3. Wem gehört dieser Rucksack?
4. Wem gefällt das Wetter heute?
5. Wer kann mir heute helfen?

Personal Dative

The dative case is also used to indicate a person's involvement in or reaction to a situation. This *personal dative* is often translated by English *to* or *for*.

Ist es **Ihnen** zu kalt?   *Is it too cold **for you**?*
Es wird **mir** zu dunkel.   *It's getting too dark **for me**.*

Wie geht es **dir**?	*How are you?* (Literally: *How is it going for you?*)
Wie geht es **deiner Mutter**?	*How is your mother?*
Das ist **mir** egal.	*It's all the same to me.*
Das macht **mir** Spaß.	*That's fun for me.*

When personal dative is omitted, a statement is more absolute. Contrast **Es ist zu dunkel** with **Es ist mir zu dunkel**.

The personal dative may often be omitted without changing the basic meaning of the sentence.

Ist es zu kalt?   Es wird zu dunkel.   Wie geht es?   Das macht Spaß.

It may *not* be omitted in the following idiom:

Das tut mir leid.   *I'm sorry about that.*

Lab Manual Kap. 7, Var. zur Üb. 11.

Workbook Kap. 7, F.

auch nicht = *not . . . either.*

11 Übung: Ist es Ihnen zu kalt?

Your instructor asks how you feel about something. Give your opinion, then ask your neighbor for an opinion.

> BEISPIEL: Ist es Ihnen hier zu kalt?
> A: Mir ist es nicht zu kalt. Und dir?
> B: Mir ist es auch nicht zu kalt.

1. Ist es Ihnen zu dunkel hier?
2. Ist Ihnen dieses Zimmer zu heiß?
3. Ist Ihnen dieses Buch zu teuer?
4. Ist Ihnen dieser Stuhl hoch genug?
5. Macht Ihnen Deutsch Spaß?
6. Ist Ihnen der Winter hier zu kalt?

12 Partnerarbeit: Reaktionen

Make at least three statements (invented or real) about how things are going for you, what you're doing at the moment, etc. Your partner must decide whether to respond with indifference, sympathy, or enthusiasm. Then switch roles.

> BEISPIEL: Ich habe morgen eine Klausur.
> Oh, das tut mir leid. *oder* Das ist mir egal.
>
> Am Dienstag fahren wir nach Venedig.
> Das finde ich toll!

Expressing opinions, preferences, and polite requests is a communicative goal.

To express opinions, preferences, and polite requests the verb **würden** is used with an infinitive.

Ich **würde** das nicht **machen**.   *I wouldn't do that.*
Was **würdest** du gerne **tun**?   *What would you like to do?*
Würden Sie mir den Koffer   *Would you carry my suitcase?*
    tragen?

The German equivalent of English *would* is **würden**. It functions like a modal verb, with a dependent infinitive in final position. **Würden** is conjugated like **möchten** (see p. 81):

Ich **würde** sagen, . . .   Wir **würden** sagen, . . .
Du **würdest** sagen, . . .   Ihr **würdet** sagen, . . .
Er/sie **würde** sagen, . . .   Sie/sie **würden** sagen, . . .

13 Gruppenarbeit: Würden Sie bitte . . . ?

Ask your instructor to do a favor for you. Some possibilities are listed below.

BEISPIEL: Würden Sie bitte das Fenster schließen?

mir den Koffer tragen   für uns ein Foto machen
mir eine Brezel kaufen   Lebensmittel einkaufen
das Mittagessen kochen   Ihre Arbeit beschreiben
mir den Bahnhof zeigen   mir den Straßenatlas geben

14 Kettenreaktion: Ich würde gern . . .

Was würden Sie heute abend gerne machen? Sagen Sie es, und dann fragen Sie weiter.

BEISPIEL: Heute abend würde ich gern _____ . Und du?
             Ich würde gern _____ .

Verbs with Two-Way Prepositions

There is an important group of verb pairs used with the two-way prepositions. One verb shows destination and always takes the accusative case. The other shows location and always takes the dative case.

Destination (accusative)	Location (dative)
Weak Transitive Verbs	**Strong Intransitive Verbs**
legen, hat gelegt *to lay (down), put*	**liegen, hat gelegen** *to lie, be lying*
Ich lege das Buch **auf den Schreibtisch.** *I'm putting the book on the desk.*	Das Buch liegt **auf dem Schreibtisch.** *The book is (lying) on the desk.*
setzen, hat gesetzt *to set (down), put*	**sitzen, hat gesessen** *to sit, be sitting*
Sie setzt das Kind **auf den Stuhl**. *She's putting the child on the chair.*	Das Kind sitzt **auf dem Stuhl**. *The child is (sitting) on the chair.*
stellen, hat gestellt *to place (down), put*	**stehen, hat gestanden** *to stand, be standing*
Ich stelle die Flasche **auf den Tisch.** *I'll put the bottle on the table.*	Die Flasche steht **auf dem Tisch.** *The bottle is (standing) on the table.*
hängen, hat gehängt *to hang up*	**hängen, hat gehangen** *to be hanging*
Er hat die Karte **an die Wand** gehängt. *He hung the map on the wall.*	Die Karte hat **an der Wand** gehangen. *The map hung on the wall.*

Note that **hängen** has one infinitive form but a weak participle (**gehängt**) and a strong participle (**gehangen**).

Legen and **liegen** are used when objects are *laid down* or are *lying* in a horizontal position. **Stellen** and **stehen** are used when objects are *stood up* or are *standing* in a vertical position.

Ich **lege** das Buch auf den Tisch.	*I'm putting the book (down flat) on the table.*
but:	
Ich **stelle** das Buch ins Bücherregal.	*I'm putting the book (upright) in the bookcase.*

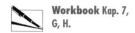 **Workbook** Kap. 7, G, H.

15 Übung: Bei Frau Schneider zu Hause

Frau Schneider is working around the house. Describe what she is doing in the left-hand pictures, then the results of her efforts in the right-hand pictures.

You know that modal verbs are used with a dependent infinitive.

Ich muß meinen Freund **anrufen**.	*I have to call my friend.*
Wir wollen nach Hause **gehen**.	*We want to go home.*

Here are the same sentences in the perfect tense:

Ich habe meinen Freund **anrufen müssen**.	*I had to call my friend.*
Wir haben nach Hause **gehen wollen**.	*We wanted to go home.*

A modal verb with a dependent infinitive uses its own *infinitive* form instead of a past participle to form the perfect tense.[1] The infinitive of the modal verb *follows* the dependent infinitive. This construction is called a "double infinitive."

Note that the modal verbs always use **haben** as their auxiliary in the perfect tense, regardless of the dependent infinitive.

Wir **sind** nach Hause gegangen.	*We went home.*
but:	
Wir **haben** nach Hause gehen wollen.	*We wanted to go home.*

Lab Manual Kap. 7, Üb. 16.

Workbook Kap. 7, I.

16 Übung

Change these sentences from present to perfect tense.

> BEISPIEL: Wir dürfen nicht laut singen.
> Wir haben nicht laut singen dürfen.

1. Ich will meinen Stadtplan finden.
2. Meine Freundin muß ich heute anrufen.
3. Sie muß viel Geld ausgeben.
4. Ich kann den Bahnhof nicht finden.
5. Darf man Fotos machen?
6. Ich muß kein Referat schreiben.
7. Ich will dich nicht enttäuschen.

Urlaub auf dem Bauernhof
Ferien auf dem Lande

Seite 140 Marlene Jensen, Steinbergkirche
Einzelhof, ruhig und schön gelegen, Spielplatz, Tischtennis, Fahrräder, 7 km zur Ostsee, BAB-Abfahrt Tarp, Bahnstation Sörup.

---

[1]All the modal verbs are mixed verbs and have past participles on the pattern **ge-** + stem + **-t** (**dürfen–gedurft, können–gekonnt, mögen–gemocht, müssen–gemußt, sollen–gesollt, wollen–gewollt**). These past participles, however, are used *only* when there is *no* dependent infinitive.

Das hat er nicht **gekonnt**.	*He wasn't able to do that.*
Sie hat mich nicht **gemocht**.	*She didn't like me.*
Das habe ich nicht **gewollt**.	*I didn't want that (to happen).*

Lab Manual Kap. 7, Üb. 17.

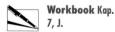 **Workbook** Kap. 7, J.

Telling time with the 24-hour clock is a communicative goal.

You already know how to tell time in German (see p. 17). For official time-telling, however, there is another system. One gives the full hour and the number of minutes past it. In addition, rather than A.M. or P.M., the twenty-four hour clock is used. This is the way the time is given in the media, in train schedules, on announcements of events, etc. Subtract 12 to get the P.M. time as expressed in English.

Midnight can be both **0 Uhr** and **24.00 Uhr.** However, one minute past midnight is **0.01** (**null Uhr eins**).

written	spoken	English
1.40 Uhr	ein Uhr vierzig	1:40 A.M.
7.55 Uhr	7 Uhr 55	7:55 A.M.
13.25 Uhr	13 Uhr 25	1:25 P.M.
20.00 Uhr	zwanzig Uhr	8:00 P.M.

17 Übung: Wieviel Uhr ist es?

Sagen Sie die Uhrzeit auf deutsch.

BEISPIEL: 11:20 P.M.
Es ist 23.20 Uhr (dreiundzwanzig Uhr zwanzig).

1. 1:55 P.M.
2. 6:02 P.M.
3. 11:31 A.M.
4. 9:47 P.M.
5. 10:52 P.M.
6. 2:25 A.M.

Wann kann man Dr. Mehler donnerstags im Büro besuchen?

Lesestück

Unterwegs per Autostop oder mit der Bahn

Tips zum Lesen und Lernen

Tips zum Vokabelnlernen

Translating English *to spend* The reading passage in this chapter talks of spending time and money. Note the different verbs that German uses to distinguish between these two kinds of *spending*.

Zeit: verbringen

Wir **verbringen** unsere Ferien in den Alpen.

We're spending our vacation in the Alps.

Sie hat den Nachmittag zu Hause **verbracht**.

She spent the afternoon at home.

Sparen (*to save*) is used with both time <u>and</u> money.

Geld: ausgeben

Wieviel muß man für ein Zimmer **ausgeben**?

How much do you have to spend for a room?

Wir haben sehr viel Geld **ausgegeben**.

We spent a lot of money.

Note the verbal noun in Wilhelm Müller's poem on p. 194: ***Das Wandern*** ist des Müllers Lust.

Verbal Nouns   Any German infinitive may act as a noun. It is then capitalized and is always neuter.

reisen $\rightarrow$ **das Reisen** (*traveling*)

Das Reisen ist heutzutage leicht.   *Traveling is easy nowadays.*

These verbal nouns correspond to English gerunds (the form ending in **-ing**); some have additional, more specific meanings. For instance, **das Essen** means *eating* but also *food* and *meal*. Here are some other examples:

das **Lernen**	*learning, studying*	das **Wissen**	*knowing;*
das **Leben**	*living; life*		*knowledge*
das **Sein**	*being; existence*	das **Fliegen**	*flying*

Lab Manual Kap. 7, Üb. zur Betonung.

Das Ticket has been borrowed from English and is used mainly for airline tickets and international train travel. In a train, however, the conductor will say **Fahrkarten, bitte** (*Tickets, please*).

Leicht zu merken

hektisch
der **Horizont, -e**   Horiz<u>on</u>t
das **Instrument, -e**   Instrum<u>ent</u>
die **Kamera, -s**
packen
spontan
das **Ticket, -s**
die **Wanderlust**

Einstieg in den Text

„Unterwegs per Autostop oder mit der Bahn" describes how German young people travel in Europe. To gain a first impression of this text, simply skim it, do not read it. Look for familiar vocabulary that is related to travel. In addition, watch for context clues that point to new travel-related vocabulary. As you skim, also keep an eye out for obvious cognates such as **Instrument**.

After skimming the text, go back and read it through once completely. Use the following questions as a guide to highlight some main ideas. See whether you can answer them after a first reading.

Wie kann man durch Europa reisen?
Warum reisen diese Menschen gern?

Wie kann man beim Reisen Geld sparen?
Wo kann man unterwegs Menschen kennenlernen?
Wo kann man auf der Reise übernachten?

Wortschatz 2

Verben

aus·steigen, ist ausgestiegen to get out (*of a vehicle*)
benutzen to use
hoffen to hope
mit·nehmen (nimmt mit), hat mitgenommen to take along
quatschen (*colloq.*) to talk nonsense; to chat
sparen to save (*money or time*)
trampen (*pronounced „trämpen"*), **ist getrampt** to hitchhike
übernachten to spend the night
verbringen, hat verbracht (+ *time phrase*) to spend (*time*)

Substantive

der **Abend, -e** evening
  am Abend in the evening
der **Platz, ⸚e** seat
der **Rucksack, ⸚e** rucksack, backpack

das **Ausland** (*sing.*) foreign countries
  im Ausland abroad (*location*)
  ins Ausland abroad (*destination*)
das **Ding, -e** thing
das **Flugzeug, -e** airplane
das **Foto, -s** photograph
  ein Foto machen to take a picture
das **Ziel, -e** goal
  Reiseziel destination
die **Bahn** railroad; railway system
die **Fahrkarte, -n** ticket (*for means of transportation*)
die **Freiheit, -en** freedom
die **Jugendherberge, -n** youth hostel
die **Tasche, -n** pocket; hand *or* shoulder bag

Adjektive und Adverbien

bequem comfortable
pünktlich punctual, on time

so so
sympathisch friendly, congenial, likeable
verrückt crazy, insane

Nützliche Ausdrücke

in der Nähe von near, nearby
egal wohin (wer, warum usw.) no matter where (who, why, etc.)

Gegensätze

aussteigen ≠ einsteigen to get out ≠ to get in

Mit anderen Worten

per Autostop reisen = trampen

Unterwegs per Autostop oder mit der Bahn

Lab Manual Kap. 7, Lesestück.

Mit dem Sommer kommt wieder die Wanderlust, Dann packt man den Koffer oder den Rucksack und macht eine Reise. Viele Menschen fahren mit dem eigenen° Wagen oder mit dem Flugzeug. Aber junge Leute mit wenig Geld in der Tasche wollen nicht so viel ausgeben. Sie
5 fahren lieber mit der Bahn oder reisen per Autostop. Ein paar erzählen uns hier von ihren Reiseerfahrungen.°

Learning about traveling in Germany and Europe is the cultural goal of this chapter.

own

travel experiences

Adrienne, 18, Azubi° aus Kaisersaschern

= Lehrling

„Trampen erweitert° den Horizont. Ich bin in den Sommerferien mit
meinem Freund Markus nicht nur in Deutschland, sondern auch im
10 Ausland getrampt. Wir haben Glück gehabt: Überall waren die Menschen sympathisch, und wir haben auch eine Menge Geld gespart. In
Italien war es einfach super. Ein Autofahrer hat uns von Venedig nach
Florenz² mitgenommen. Er hat ein bißchen Deutsch verstanden, und
wir haben dann drei Tage bei seiner Familie gewohnt. Mit meiner
15 Kamera habe ich ein paar schöne Fotos von seinen Kindern gemacht.
Das hat uns Spaß gemacht, und ich hoffe, wir können sie nächstes
Jahr wieder besuchen. Ja, im Zug lernt man die Menschen einfach
nicht so gut kennen.“

broadens

Thomas, 21, Student aus Tübingen

20 „Ich trampe schon in der Nähe von Tübingen, aber für eine lange
Reise würde ich immer ein Interrail-Ticket kaufen. Das kostet unter
DM 500 für vier Wochen, und man kann durch ganz Europa reisen.
Mit diesem Ticket habe ich viel Freiheit: Da kann man spontan weg,
egal wohin.
25   Freunde von mir benutzen den Zug als ‚rollendes° Hotel‘. Am Tag
besuchen sie eine neue Stadt. Am Abend steigen sie wieder ein und
schlafen dann im Zug unterwegs zum nächsten° Reiseziel. Dieses
Tempo ist mir aber zu hektisch. Ich übernachte lieber in der Jugendherberge und verbringe ein paar Tage in jeder Stadt.“

rolling

next

Trämper in der
Nähe von Heidelberg.

---

²Florence: city in Tuscany famous as a center of Italian Renaissance culture.

Herbert, 29, Assistenzarzt° aus Ulm   resident (physician)

„Früher bin ich viel per Autostop gereist, aber heute würde ich das nicht mehr machen. Die Unsicherheit° ist mir zu stressig, und ich   uncertainty
habe nicht mehr so viel Freizeit. Das Reisen mit der Bahn gefällt mir, denn es ist sehr praktisch und bequem. Man geht einfach zum Bahn-
35 hof, kauft eine Fahrkarte, und steigt in den Zug ein. Und man weiß, man kommt pünktlich an.

Im Abteil quatsche ich gern ein bißchen mit den Mitreisenden°   fellow passengers
über viele Dinge. Letztes Wochenende bin ich zum Beispiel nach Berlin gefahren. Neben mir hat ein Musikstudent aus Leipzig gesessen.
40 Er ist in Wittenberg³ ausgestiegen, und ich habe ihm mit seinem Gepäck geholfen. Er hatte° nicht nur einen Rucksack und einen Koffer   had
mit, sondern auch eine Baßgeige.° Für sein Instrument hat er einen   double bass
zweiten° Platz reservieren müssen. Verrückt, nicht?"   second

Unterwegs mit der Bahn.

Fragen zum Lesestück

1. Warum reisen viele Leute so gern im Sommer?
2. Wie kann man im Urlaub Geld sparen?
3. Wohin ist Adrienne getrampt?
4. Hat es ihr Spaß gemacht? Warum?
5. Wo kann man Menschen unterwegs kennenlernen?
6. Wie kann man mit der Bahn billig reisen?
7. Wie kann man den Zug als „rollendes Hotel" benutzen?
8. Wo kann man billig übernachten?
9. Warum würde Herbert heutzutage nicht mehr trampen?
10. Wem hat er im Zug geholfen?

---

³The composer Johann Sebastian Bach (1685–1750) spent the greater part of his life in **Leipzig** (in the state of Saxony). The church reformer Martin Luther (1483–1546) is buried in **Wittenberg** (in the state of Saxony-Anhalt).

Reisen und Verkehr   *(Travel and traffic)*

Some of these words are already familiar.

Verben

abfahren ≠ **ankommen**
einsteigen ≠ **aussteigen**
um·steigen   to transfer, change (*buses, trains, etc.*)

Substantive

der **Bahnhof**, ¨e
der **Bus**, -se   *bus*
der **Flughafen**, ¨   *airport*
der **Verkehr**   *traffic*
der **Wagen**, -
der **Zug**, ¨e
das **Auto**, -s
das **Flugzeug**, -e
die **Autobahn**, -en   *expressway, high-speed highway*
die **Fahrkarte**, -n

ERHOLUNG AUF DEM RHEIN.
DIE BAHN BRINGT SIE ZUM SCHIFF.
KD Köln-Düsseldorf Deutsche Bundesbahn

Debate continues about whether to impose a speed limit on the **Autobahn.** Many claim the present lack of a speed limit contributes to Germany's high accident rate.

Nützliche Ausdrücke

Ich fahre **mit dem Wagen.**   . . . *by car.*
          mit dem Bus.   . . . *by bus.*
          mit der Bahn.   . . . *by train.*
Ich fliege.

Partnerarbeit: Was habe ich zuerst gemacht?

Here are eight statements about a train trip. Number them in the order that the events most likely happened. Then read them aloud in order.

_____ Ich habe im Zug mit der Frau neben mir gequatscht.
_____ Ich habe mir eine Fahrkarte gekauft.
_____ Ich habe im Zug einen guten Roman gelesen.
_____ Ich habe eine Reise ins Ausland machen wollen.
_____ Ich bin in den Zug eingestiegen.
_____ Ich habe mir eine Landkarte gekauft.
_____ Ich bin zum Bahnhof gegangen.
_____ Ich bin pünktlich angekommen.

Gruppenarbeit: Planen wir unsere Reise. (4 Personen)

Planen Sie eine Reise nach Europa. Besprechen Sie diese Fragen zusammen. Benutzen Sie die Landkarte.

Welche Länder wollen wir besuchen?
Wie lange wollen wir bleiben?

Making travel plans and talking about traveling is a communicative goal.

Wie wollen wir durch Europa reisen? Mit der Bahn? Per Autostop?
Wo wollen wir übernachten? In einer Jugendherberge? Im Hotel?
Was wollen wir mitnehmen? Machen wir eine Liste.
Haben wir etwas vergessen?

Jetzt berichtet jede Gruppe über ihre Pläne.

Partnerarbeit: Rollenspiel

Spielen Sie diese Situation mit Ihrem Partner. Partner A spielt den Auto-fahrer, Partner B spielt den Tramper. Der Tramper steht seit einer Stunde im Regen. Endlich hält ein Auto. Der Tramper steigt ein und spricht mit dem Fahrer über das Trampen und die Ferien.

Sie können Ihr Gespräch (*conversation*) dann vor der ganzen Klasse spielen.

Partnerarbeit: Wann kommt der Zug an?

Sie arbeiten am Hauptbahnhof in Mannheim und geben Auskunft über die Züge. Eine Touristengruppe bittet um (*asks for*) Auskunft. Sie müssen die Antworten auf dem Fahrplan finden.

BEISPIEL: A: Entschuldigung, wann kommt der Zug aus Hamburg in Mannheim an?
               B: Er kommt um 14.22 Uhr an.
               A: Um wieviel Uhr fährt er in Hamburg ab?
               B: Um 9.33 Uhr.

Mannheim Hbf (Hauptbahnhof)					
Ankunft (arrivals)			*Abfahrt* (departures)		
Zug-Nr.	ab[1]	an[1]	Zug-Nr.	ab	an
6342	Hamburg 9.33 Uhr	Mannheim 14.22 Uhr	1338	Mannheim 5.42 Uhr	Zürich 8.12 Uhr
7422	München 10.03 Uhr	Mannheim 13.10 Uhr	2472	Mannheim 6.06 Uhr	Nürnberg 9.33 Uhr
1387	Frankfurt 11.20 Uhr	Mannheim 12.01 Uhr	6606	Mannheim 7.55 Uhr	Straßburg 8.40 Uhr
7703	Wien 10.10 Uhr	Mannheim 17.56 Uhr	2203	Mannheim 10.12 Uhr	Innsbruck 15.46 Uhr
9311	Berlin 11.05 Uhr	Mannheim 19.16 Uhr	3679	Mannheim 13.23 Uhr	Prag 20.09 Uhr

[1]**ab:** time and place of departure; **an:** time and place of arrival.

Zum Schluß

Sprechen wir miteinander!

Lab Manual Kap. 7, Diktat.

Workbook Kap. 7, K.

A Gruppenarbeit: Was gefällt euch hier?

Was gefällt Ihnen an Ihrer Uni? Was gefällt Ihnen nicht? Machen Sie miteinander zwei Listen (*lists*).

das Essen in der Mensa
das Leben im Studentenwohnheim
die Vorlesungen

die Hausaufgaben
der Streß
die Studentenzeitung
usw.

B Gruppenarbeit: Was mache ich jetzt?

The class is divided into two groups. The instructor does various things, and each team in turn tries to describe the action. A correct answer scores a point. If your team answers incorrectly, the other team has a chance to describe the same action.

> BEISPIEL: Was mache ich jetzt?
> Sie stellen die Flasche auf den Stuhl.

C Partnerarbeit: Am Telefon

Talking on the telephone is a communicative goal.

Situation: Barbara Hinrich phones her father to tell him when she's arriving this evening. He asks where she is and whether she's going to have dinner at home tonight. She says she's going to a restaurant with friends and won't be home until late. Her father says he'll see her later. They say good-bye (on the telephone: **Auf Wiederhören**).

Complete this conversation with your partner.

VATER: Hallo? Hinrich.

BARBARA: Hallo _____ ! Hier ist _____ .

VATER: Ach _____ ! Wo _____ ?

BARBARA: _____ .

VATER: Wirklich? _____ ?

BARBARA: _____ .

VATER: Also, _____ .
Auf Wiederhören, bis _____ !

BARBARA: _____ !

Freude für
Tante Erna:
Die ganze
Familie ruft an.

Now choose one of the following situations and invent your own telephone conversation. Since long distance rates are expensive, be brief and convey as much information as efficiently as you can.

1. Phone a friend to report about your vacation abroad.
2. Phone home to say you have arrived somewhere.
3. Phone your roommate to say you've forgotten something.
4. Find out whether a youth hostel or hotel has room for you.

E **Gruppeninterview: Wer ist schon weit gereist?**

Wie viele Studenten haben schon eine lange Reise gemacht? Die anderen (*other*) Studenten interviewen sie und fragen zum Beispiel:

Wann?   **Wohin?**   **Mit wem?**   **Warum?**

F **Partnerarbeit: Was würdest du lieber machen?**

Here are some choices you might make when traveling. Ask each other which you would rather do. State a preference and give a reason.

Expressing preferences is a communicative goal.

BEISPIEL:

┌──── **sprechen** ────┐
Ihre Muttersprache?   eine Fremdsprache?

Ich würde lieber eine Fremdsprache sprechen, denn das macht mehr Spaß.

┌──── **übernachten** ────┐
im Hotel?   in einer Jugendherberge?

┌──── **reisen** ────┐
per Autostop?   mit der Bahn?

┌──── **mitbringen** ────┐
einen Rucksack?   einen Koffer?

┌──── **eine Woche verbringen** ────┐
in der Stadt?   auf dem Land?

┌──── **kennenlernen** ────┐
Touristen aus Ihrem Land?   Studenten aus dem Ausland?

┌──── **sitzen** ────┐
im Konzert?   im Café?

Schreiben Sie zu Hause

G **Wanderlust**   Complete the sentences below to form a short essay on traveling inexpensively.

1. Manchmal will ich einfach . . .
2. Natürlich braucht man Geld für . . .
3. Ohne viel Geld in der Tasche kann . . .
4. Man kann aber immer . . .

5. Das ist manchmal schön, denn . . .
6. Mit meinem Interrail-Ticket kann . . .
7. Ich würde wahnsinnig gern . . .
8. Nächstes Jahr . . .
9. Hoffentlich ist . . .

H **Die Reise war super.   Ein Brief nach Hause.**

Auf Seite 209 im Lesestück hat Adrienne von ihrer Reise mit ihrem Freund
erzählt. Natürlich hat sie im Ausland eigentlich viel mehr gemacht. Was hat
sie ihren Eltern aus Italien geschrieben? Wie war es bei dieser Familie,
warum hat es soviel Spaß gemacht usw.? Schreiben Sie Adriennes Brief
nach Hause. (*Review letter-writing conventions in Kapitel 6, p. 174.*)

I Schreiben Sie das Gespräch (*conversation*) im Zug zwischen Herbert
und dem Musikstudenten aus Leipzig. (Siehe S. 210.)

J **Wie sagt man das auf deutsch?**

1. Did you take a trip this year?
2. Yes, we went to Venice.
3. Did you take the children along?
4. Yes, and they liked Italy very much. (*use* **gefallen**)

5. Does this suitcase belong to you?
6. Not to me, but to my brother.
7. Where should I put it?
8. Would you please put it under the table?

9. How's your husband?
10. He's not very well.
11. Oh, I'm sorry.

Ausflugschiff *(excursion boat)*
auf dem Bodensee.

A l m a n a c h

Jugendherbergen (Youth Hostels)

There are about 670 Jugendherbergen in Germany, 110 in Austria, 85 in Switzerland, and 13 in Luxembourg. They are meeting places for young travelers from all over the world. In addition to providing inexpensive food and lodging, they offer a variety of courses and organized trips.

Membership in the AYH (American Youth Hostels) entitles the cardholder to privileges in hostels all over the world. Membership costs as of 1995: under 18 years of age, $10.00; 18–54, $25.00; over 54, $15.00. In Bavaria you must be under 26 years of age to stay in a youth hostel. To apply for membership, write to:

American Youth Hostels, Inc.
P.O. Box 37613
Washington, D.C. 20013–7613
(202) 783-6161

Here are some excerpts from the 1994–95 Youth Hostel handbook for Germany.

Erklärung der Piktogramme

Sportplatz	Fußball	Basketball	Tennis
Sporthalle	Volleyball	Kegeln	Reitsport

	Sportplatz	Sporthalle	Fußball	Volleyball	Basketball	Kegeln	Tennis	Reitsport
Bayern								
Bayerisch-Eisenstein			◆	◆				
Bayreuth			◆	◆				
Bayrischzell			◆	◆	◆		◆	
Benediktbeuern "Don-Bosco"			◆	◆	◆			
Bodenmais			◆	◆				
Furth im Wald			◆	◆				
Garmisch-Partenkirchen								
Berlin								
Berlin, JGH Wannsee								

Anschrift: JGH Berlin, Kluckstraße 3, 10785 Berlin, ☎ 030/2611097, Fax: 030/2650383.
Herbergsväter: Hans-Martin Schwarz und Ingolf Keil.
Anreise: Auto: Stadtautobahn (Richtung Wilmersdorf/Schöneberg: Ausfahrt Innsbrucker Pl.), links. über Hauptstr. und Potsdamer Str. bis Lützowstr., dort links, Kluckstr. rechts einbiegen. Bahn: Bahnhof. Zoo-U-Bahn-Linie 1 (Richtung Schlesisches Tor) bis Kurfürstenstr. und 5 Min. Fußweg oder Bhf. Zoo und Bus 129 ab Haltestelle Kurfürstendamm/Joachimstaler Str. (Richtung Hermannplatz) bis JGH, Haltestelle "Gedenkstätte".
Lage: Innenstadt, am Rande des Tiergarten, nahe des Kulturforums.
Geeignet für: Familien (bedingt), Seminare, Tagungen, Lehrgänge (nach Absprache), Gruppen, Einzelgäste.
Raumangebot: 364 Betten, 5 Tagesräume, 6 Familienzimmer.
Freizeitmöglichkeiten: Fahrradausleihe (500 m entfernt), TT-Platten, Spaziergänge durch den Tiergarten mit Reichstag, Brandenburger Tor, Siegessäule, Kulturforum. Stadterkundungen auf kulturellem und historischen Gebiet, Gedenkstätte: Widerstand im 3. Reich,

"Alternativszene" Kreuzberg, Berlin-Ost: historisches Zentrum (Nikolai-Viertel, Unter den Linden, Museumsinsel, Pergamonmuseum).

⚲ Fahrrad-Verleih am Ort	🤸 Leichtathletik	✈ Flugsportarten	⛷ Wintersport	⛵ Segeln/Surfen	🚣 Kanu/Kajak/Rudern	◺ Hallenbad	〰 Freibad/Gewässer

⚲	🤸	✈	⛷	⛵	🚣	◺	〰	Besonderes:
			♦				♦	
				♦			♦	
			♦				♦	
♦					♦		♦	Billard
			♦				♦	
♦					♦	♦	♦	
			♦		♦		♦	Bergsport
				♦	♦		♦	

Das Leben in der Stadt

Communicative Goals

- Talking about food and shopping
- Discussing city life
- Asking for directions
- Ordering in a restaurant

Cultural Goal

- Learning about life in German cities

Im Restaurant: Zahlen bitte!

In this context, the response **danke** = *No thank you.* **Bitte sehr** = *Yes, please.*

Remember: **DM 25,80** is spoken **fünfundzwanzig Mark achtzig.** Note on tipping: German restaurants automatically add 15% for service to the bill. When paying, however, it is customary to round up the bill.

KELLNERIN:	So, hat es Ihnen geschmeckt?
GAST:	Ausgezeichnet!
KELLNERIN:	Möchten Sie noch etwas bestellen?
GAST:	Danke, ich möchte zahlen, bitte.
KELLNERIN:	Sie haben Schnitzel, Pommes frites, einen Salat und ein Bier gehabt, nicht wahr?
GAST:	Ja, und auch eine Tasse Kaffee.
KELLNERIN:	Das macht zusammen DM 25,80, bitte sehr.
GAST:	(*Gibt ihr DM 30*) 27 Mark.
KELLNERIN:	Danke sehr, und drei Mark zurück.

Hat es Ihnen geschmeckt? (*How was everything?*) means literally *Did it taste good to you?*

Was brauchen wir noch?

Most Germans eat a hot meal at noon and a simple supper of cold cuts, bread, cheese, and salad in the evening.

DORA:	Heute morgen habe ich Max zum Abendessen eingeladen. Weißt du, ob er kommt?
FRANZ:	Ja, aber er hat mir gesagt, daß er erst um halb sieben kommen kann. Wieviel Uhr ist es jetzt?
DORA:	Halb sechs. Also muß ich noch schnell zum Supermarkt, um ein paar Sachen einzukaufen. Was brauchen wir noch?
FRANZ:	Ein Kilo Kartoffeln, 200 Gramm Leberwurst, Käse, eine Flasche Rotwein und Obst zum Nachtisch.
DORA:	Ist das alles?
FRANZ:	Ich glaube schon.

Ein Stadtbummel

Marianne besucht ihren Freund Helmut in Köln. Er hat ihr die Stadt noch nicht gezeigt, weil es geregnet hat.

Du is used here as an attention-getter, equivalent to *hey, look.*

HELMUT:	Du, der Regen hat endlich aufgehört! Hast du jetzt Lust, einen Stadtbummel zu machen?
MARIANNE:	Ja gerne. Aber ich hab' jetzt Hunger. Können wir zuerst essen?
HELMUT:	Selbstverständlich! In der Nähe des Doms gibt es ein Lokal, wo wir griechisch essen können.
MARIANNE:	Hmm, das klingt lecker!
HELMUT:	Nachher können wir dann den Dom besuchen, und von da ist es nicht mehr weit zum Kunstmuseum.

In a Restaurant: Check please!

WAIT.: How was everything?

P.: Excellent!

WAIT.: Would you like to order anything else?

P.: No thanks. I'd like the check, please.

W.: You had a cutlet, French fries, a salad, and a beer, right?

P.: Yes, and also a cup of coffee.

WAIT.: All together that comes to 25 Marks 80, please.

P.: (Gives her DM 30) 27 Marks.

WAIT.: Thank you, and three Marks change.

What Else Do We Need?

D.: This morning I invited Max to supper. Do you know if he's coming?

FR.: Yes, but he told me that he couldn't come until 6:30. What time is it now?

D.: 5:30. So I need to make a quick trip to the supermarket to buy a few things. What else do we need?

FR.: A kilo of potatoes, 200 grams of liverwurst, cheese, a bottle of red wine, and fruit for dessert.

D.: Is that all?

FR.: I think so.

A Stroll Through Town

Marianne is visiting her friend Helmut in Cologne. He hasn't shown her around town yet, because it's been raining.

H.: Hey look, the rain's finally stopped! Do you want to take a stroll through town now?

M.: Sure. But I'm hungry now. Can we eat first?

H.: Of course. Near the cathedral there's a place where we can eat Greek food.

M.: Hmm, that sounds delicious!

H.: Then we can visit the cathedral afterwards, and from there it's not far to the art museum.

Wortschatz 1

Verben

bestellen   to order

ein·laden (lädt ein), hat eingeladen   to invite

klingen, hat geklungen   to sound

schmecken   to taste; to taste good

Wie schmeckt es dir?   How does it taste? How do you like it?

zahlen   to pay

Dom comes from Latin *domus ecclesiae* (house of the congregation).

Substantive

der **Bummel, -**   stroll, walk

einen Stadtbummel machen   to take a stroll through town

der **Dom, -e**   cathedral

der **Durst**   thirst

der **Gast, ¨e**   guest; patron

der **Hunger**   hunger

der **Kaffee**   coffee

der **Kellner, -**   waiter

der **Liter**   liter

der **Nachtisch**   dessert

zum Nachtisch   for dessert

der **Salat, -e**   salad; lettuce

das **Abendessen**   supper, evening meal

zum Abendessen   for dinner

das **Gebäude, -**   building

das **Glas, ¨er**   glass

das **Gramm**   gram

das **Kilogramm** (*or* das **Kilo**)   kilogram

(das) **Köln**   Cologne

das **Lokal, -e**   neighborhood restaurant or tavern

das **Museum, Museen**   museum

das **Restaurant, -s**   restaurant

das **Schnitzel, -**   cutlet, chop

die **Kartoffel, -n**   potato

die **Kellnerin, -nen**   waitress

die **Kunst, ¨e**   art

die **Sache, -n**   thing; item

die **Tasse, -n**   cup

die **Wurst, ¨e**   sausage

die **Leberwurst**   liverwurst

Adjektive und Adverbien

ausgezeichnet   excellent

griechisch   Greek

lecker   tasty, delicious

weit   far; far away

zuerst   first, at first

Andere Vokabeln

daß   (*sub. conj.*) that

noch etwas   something else, anything more

ob   (*sub. conj.*) whether, if

um . . . zu   in order to

Nützliche Ausdrücke

Ich glaube schon.   I think so.

griechisch (italienisch, französisch usw.) essen   to eat Greek (Italian, French, etc.) food

Hunger haben   to be hungry

Durst haben   to be thirsty

Lust haben (etwas zu tun)   to want to (do something)

Käse des Monats:

Echter Käse aus Holland

holländischer Schnittkäse, 30% Fett i.Tr., 100 g   **1.99**

Granny Smith Äpfel
Chile, Kl. I, neuerntig
1 kg   **2.99**

Unser SB-Wurst-Angebot:
Pfälzer Leberwurst
400-g-Packung   **3.49**

Obstabteilung!

Griech. Victoria-Trauben
Hkl. I
1 kg   **2.99**

Südafrik. Outspan-Orangen
Hkl. I
7er Netz   **2.99**

Variationen

A Persönliche Fragen

1. Haben Sie heute gefrühstückt? Was haben Sie denn gegessen? Hat's Ihnen geschmeckt?
2. Kennen Sie ein Lokal, wo man sehr gut essen kann? Wie heißt es?
3. Essen Sie gern griechisch? italienisch? französisch? deutsch?
4. Trinken Sie viel Kaffee? Was trinken Sie sonst?
5. Was essen Sie gern zum Nachtisch?
6. Laden Sie oft Freunde zum Abendessen ein?
7. Kaufen Sie im Supermarkt ein? Wie oft?
8. Marianne hat Lust, einen Stadtbummel zu machen. Haben Sie Lust, heute etwas zu machen? Was denn?
9. Gehen Sie gern ins Kunstmuseum? Welche Künstler (*artists*) mögen Sie?

B Übung: Raten Sie mal! *(Take a guess!)*

Marianne und Helmut wollen einen Stadtbummel machen. Das heißt, sie haben ein bißchen Freizeit und können langsam durch die Stadt gehen. Um einen Bummel zu machen, braucht man also Zeit. Raten Sie mal, was diese Wörter bedeuten:

1. Sie machen einen **Schaufensterbummel.**
2. Ich hab' ein bißchen Geld in der Tasche. Machen wir doch einen **Einkaufsbummel.**
3. Der Zug hat an jedem kleinen Bahnhof gehalten. Ich fahre nie wieder mit diesem **Bummelzug!**
4. Fritz studiert seit 13 Semestern an der Uni und ist immer noch nicht fertig. Er ist ein **Bummelstudent!**
5. Die Arbeiter arbeiten immer noch, aber sehr langsam. Sie machen einen **Bummelstreik.**

```
        15-08-90 #0000

GAST/TISCH # 161
 2 PAELLA VAL.   *40.00
 1 SCHNITZEL PA  *14.00
 1 KINDERTELLER   *9.00
 1 FL WASSER      *3.50
 1 FL LIMO        *3.50
 1 MÄRZEN 0.5     *2.80
 1 WEIZEN         *3.50
 1 MÄRZEN 0.3     *1.80
BROT             *2.00
BAR    *80.10
ENTH.MWST14%     *9.59

BESTEN DANK
COSTA DEL SOL
```

C Partnerarbeit: Schmeckt es dir?

Fragen Sie Ihren Partner, ob ihm etwas schmeckt.

> BEISPIEL: A: Ißt du gern Tomatensuppe?
> B: Nein, das schmeckt mir nicht. (*oder*)
> Ja, das schmeckt mir.

Talking about food is a
communicative goal.

Käse	Kaffee	Pommes frites
Bier	Brot	Leberwurst
Pizza	Salat	griechisches Essen
Kartoffeln	Wiener Schnitzel	Wein

Lyrik zum Vorlesen

The cliff called the Loreley is on the Rhine River at its deepest spot. In his famous poem „Ich weiß nicht, was soll es bedeuten" (1823), Heinrich Heine invented a Romantic myth about a siren who lures boatmen to their deaths at this place. Set to music by the composer Silcher, it achieved the status of a folk song.

Lab Manual Kap.
8, Lyrik zum Vorlesen.

Ich weiß nicht, was soll es bedeuten („Die Loreley")

Ich weiß nicht, was soll es bedeuten,	
daß ich so traurig° bin;	sad
ein Märchen aus alten Zeiten,	
das kommt mir nicht aus dem Sinn.°	**das... = das kann ich nicht vergessen**
Die Luft ist kühl und es dunkelt,°	**es dunkelt = es wird dunkel**
und ruhig° fließt der Rhein;	peacefully
der Gipfel° des Berges funkelt°	mountain top / glistens
im Abendsonnenschein.	
Die schönste Jungfrau° sitzet°	most beautiful maiden /**sitzet = sitzt**
dort oben° wunderbar,	high above
ihr goldenes Geschmeide° blitzet,°	jewelry / glistens
sie kämmt° ihr goldenes Haar.	combs
Sie kämmt es mit goldenem Kamme,°	comb
und singt ein Lied dabei;°	while doing so
das hat eine wundersame,°	**= wunderbare**
gewaltige° Melodei.	powerful
Den Schiffer° im kleinen Schiffe°	sailor / boat
ergreift es° mit wildem Weh;°	is gripped / longing
er schaut° nicht die Felsenriffe,°	**= sieht** / submerged rock
er schaut nur hinauf in die Höh.°	up to the heights
Ich glaube, die Wellen° verschlingen°	waves / swallow
am Ende Schiffer und Kahn;°	boat
und das hat mit ihrem Singen	
die Loreley getan.	

Heinrich Heine (1797–1856)

Heinrich Heine

Subordinate Clauses and Subordinating Conjunctions

When it answers a question, a subordinate clause can stand alone as a complete utterance: **Wie lange müssen wir warten? Bis der Regen aufhört.**

Subordinating conjunctions, like coordinating conjunctions, join two clauses together. The clause beginning with a subordinating conjunction, however, is *subordinate to*, or *dependent on*, the main clause. A subordinate clause is *not* an independent sentence.

main clause	*subordinate clause*
I know	*that they still remember me.*

In the example above, the subordinate clause "that they still remember me" is not a complete sentence. In this chapter you will learn the following subordinating conjunctions:

Causal meaning of *since*: Since it's raining . . . (**Da es regnet** . . .); temporal meaning of *since*: Since November . . . (**Seit November** . . .).

bis	*until*
da	*since* (causal, not temporal)
daß	*that*
ob	*whether, if* (when it means *whether*)
weil	*because*
wenn	*if*

...für meine Familie tu' ich alles.
Aber was passiert, wenn mir was passiert?

Verb-Last Word Order in the Subordinate Clause

Review the coordinating conjunctions **und, oder**, etc. on pp. 196–198, which do *not* change word order in the second clause.

Unlike coordinating conjunctions, which do not affect word order, subordinating conjunctions *move the inflected verb to the end of the subordinate clause.*

Wir **essen** um halb sieben.

Ich glaube, **daß** wir ▬ um halb sieben **essen**.
I think that we're eating at 6:30.

Brauchen wir noch etwas?

Weißt du, **ob** ▬ wir noch etwas **brauchen?**
Do you know whether we need anything else?

Ich **habe** gerade gegessen.

Ich habe keinen Hunger, **weil** ich ▬ gerade gegessen **habe**.
I'm not hungry because I've just eaten.

Ich **habe** Zeit.

Ich helfe dir, **wenn** ich ▬ Zeit **habe**.
I'll help you if I have time.

Lab Manual Kap. 8, Üb. 1, 2, 7; Var. zur Üb. 3, 5, 8.

Workbook Kap. 8, A–D.

1 Übung: Ich weiß, daß . . .

Sie planen miteinander ein Abendessen. Ihre Professorin sagt Ihnen etwas. Sagen Sie, daß Sie das wissen.

> BEISPIEL: Die Wurst ist teuer.
> Ich weiß, daß sie teuer ist.

1. Wir essen um sieben.
2. Wir brauchen Rotwein.
3. Der Käse schmeckt gut.
4. Die Kinder wollen essen.
5. Tante Marie kommt zum Abendessen.
6. Wir haben keinen Salat.
7. Wir brauchen etwas zum Nachtisch.
8. Tante Marie trinkt keinen Kaffe.

2 Übung: Ich weiß nicht, ob . . .

Ihr Professor ist neu in dieser Stadt. Er hat viele Fragen, aber Sie wohnen auch nicht lange hier und können ihm keine Antworten geben.

> BEISPIEL: Ist dieses Restaurant teuer?
> Ich weiß nicht, ob es teuer ist.

1. Gibt es hier einen Automechaniker?
2. Ist dieses Hotel gut?
3. Ist die Uni weit von hier?
4. Gibt es eine Buchhandlung in der Nähe?
5. Kann man den Dom besuchen?
6. Kann man hier einen Stadtplan kaufen?

3 Partnerarbeit: Warum lernst du Deutsch?

Ask each other why you do the things listed below. Give your reason, then ask the next question.

> BEISPIEL: Warum lernst du Deutsch?
> Ich lerne Deutsch, *weil* es interessant ist. Warum . . . ?

Deutsch lernen	einen Rucksack tragen
zur Buchhandlung gehen	bis 9.00 schlafen
trampen	draußen sitzen
jetzt essen	keine Leberwurst essen
viel Kaffee trinken	früh aufstehen

WENN ALLES EGAL IST...

Conditional Sentences: If *x* is true, then *y* is true

A clause introduced by **wenn** is called a *conditional clause* because it states a condition. The main clause is then called the *result clause* because it states the expected result of the condition. The result clause may begin with an optional **dann** which does not affect word order.

> Wenn ich Zeit habe, helfe ich dir.
> Wenn ich Zeit habe, **dann** helfe ich dir.

4 Übung: Wenn . . . , dann . . .

A. Complete these sentences by supplying a result clause:

1. Wenn wir Hunger haben, dann . . .
2. Wenn du griechisch essen willst, dann . . .
3. Wenn du mich morgen einlädst, dann . . .

B. Now supply the conditional clause:

1. Wenn . . . , dann können wir einen Stadtbummel machen.
2. Wenn . . . , dann kannst du einen Nachtisch bestellen.
3. Wenn . . . , dann müssen wir noch schnell einkaufen.

Question Words as Subordinating Conjunctions

The question words (**wann, warum, was, wer,** etc.) act as subordinating conjunctions when they introduce an indirect question (i.e., a question restated as a subordinate clause).

> *question:*   Was brauchen wir zum Abendessen?

> *indirect question:*
> Weißt du, **was** wir zum Abendessen brauchen?
> *Do you know what we need for supper?*

> Wer ist das?

> Ich kann Ihnen nicht sagen, wer das ist.
> *I can't tell you who that is.*

5 **Übung: Die Tramper**

Ein Freund von Ihnen will mit anderen Studenten eine Reise per Autostop machen. Ihr Professor hat Fragen über ihre Reise, aber Sie wissen die Antworten nicht.

> BEISPIEL: Wer plant die Reise?
> Ich weiß nicht, wer die Reise plant.

1. Wohin fahren die Tramper?
2. Wo wollen sie übernachten?
3. Warum trampen Ihre Freunde?
4. Wen wollen sie besuchen?

5. Wann kommen die Tramper zurück?
6. Was packen sie in den Rucksack?
7. Welche Städte besuchen sie?

Verbs with Separable Prefixes in Subordinate Clauses

You know that when a verb with a separable prefix is used in a main clause, the prefix is separated from the verb and placed at the end of the clause.

> Dort **kaufe** ich immer **ein.**

In a subordinate clause, the verb moves to the end of the clause and the prefix is attached to it.

> Weißt du, warum ich ▬▬▬▬ immer dort einkaufe?

6 **Partnerarbeit: Wie lange müssen wir warten?**

Sie warten zusammen vor der Mensa. Sagen Sie einander (*each other*), bis wann Sie warten müssen. (*Use the cues below.*)

> BEISPIEL: Wie lange müssen wir noch warten?
> (der Bus / kommen)
> Wir müssen warten, bis der Bus kommt.

1. der Regen / aufhören
2. Max / uns abholen
3. unsere Freunde / ankommen

4. die Vorlesung / anfangen
5. die Buchhandlung / aufmachen

7 **Übung: Was hat sie gefragt?**

Die Professorin spricht zu leise (*quietly*). Student A hört sie nicht richtig, und fragt Student B, was sie gesagt hat. Student B antwortet.

> BEISPIELE: Wann stehen Sie auf?
> A: Was hat sie gefragt?
> B: Sie hat gefragt, wann du aufstehst.
>
> Kommt Bernd vorbei?
> A: Was hat sie gefragt?
> B: Sie hat gefragt, ob Bernd vorbeikommt.

1. Wann fängt das Semester an?
2. Kommt Ingrid vorbei?

3. Warum geht Regine weg?
4. Bringt Maria die Kinder mit?
5. Hört die Musik bald auf?
6. Mit wem geht Hans spazieren?

7. Wo steigt man in die Straßenbahn ein?
8. Wo steigen wir aus?
9. Wer macht das Fenster zu?

Order of Clauses in the Sentence

*A **da**-clause is almost always the first clause in its sentence.*

Subordinate clauses may either follow or precede the main clause.

> *1   2*
> Ich spreche langsam, da ich nicht viel Deutsch gelernt habe.

> *1   2*
> Da ich nicht viel Deutsch gelernt habe, spreche ich langsam.

When the subordinate clause comes first, the *entire* subordinate clause is considered the first element in the sentence. The verb of the main clause therefore follows it immediately in second position. The two inflected verbs are directly adjacent to each other, separated by a comma.

> *subordinate clause   main clause*
> Wenn ich Zeit **habe, gehe** ich ins Museum.
> Ob er sympathisch **ist, weiß** ich nicht.

8 Übung

Ihr Professor hat Fragen, aber Sie wissen die Antworten nicht.

> BEISPIEL: Wie ist das Wetter?
>   Wie das Wetter ist, weiß ich nicht.

1. Wer ist das?
2. Wem gehört das?
3. Wohin fährt er?
4. Was kostet das?

5. Wie heißt sie?
6. Warum ist er müde?
7. Wessen Koffer ist das?
8. Wen kennt sie?

9 Übung: Ich mache heute keinen Stadtbummel.

You've decided not to take a stroll through town today. Use the cues below to explain why.

> BEISPIEL: Es regnet noch.
>   Da es noch regnet, mache ich keinen Stadtbummel.

1. Ich habe keine Zeit.
2. Das Wetter ist schlecht.
3. Ich brauche nichts in der Stadt.
4. Ich gehe nicht gern allein.
5. Ich bin heute spät aufgestanden.
6. Ich habe zu viel Arbeit.

When used in a sentence, the German infinitive is sometimes preceded by **zu**. For the most part, this construction parallels the use of the English infinitive with *to*:

Was gibt's hier **zu sehen**?	*What's there to see here?*
Hast du Zeit, diesen Brief **zu lesen?**	*Do you have time to read this letter?*

Note especially the second sentence above. In German, the infinitive with **zu** comes at the end of its phrase. In English, the infinitive with *to* comes at the beginning of its phrase.

When a separable-prefix verb is used, the **zu** is inserted between the prefix and the stem infinitive.

    ab**zu**fahren   spazieren**zu**gehen

Ich hoffe, bald **abzufahren.**	*I hope to leave soon.*
Hast du Lust, mit mir **spazierenzugehen?**	*Would you like to go for a walk with me?*

Here are some cases in which the infinitive with **zu** is used:

- as a complement of verbs like **beginnen, anfangen, aufhören, helfen, hoffen, lernen, planen, scheinen,** and **vergessen.**

Ich fange an, **einen Brief zu schreiben.**[1]	*I'm starting to write a letter.*
Sie hofft, **Geschichte zu studieren.**	*She's hoping to study history.*
Ich habe vergessen, **dir von meiner Reise zu erzählen.**	*I forgot to tell you about my trip.*

- as a complement of constructions like **Lust haben, Zeit haben,** and **Spaß machen.**

Hast du Lust, **einen Stadtbummel zu machen?**	*Do you want to take a walk through town?*
Ich habe keine Zeit, **einkaufen zu gehen.**	*I have no time to go shopping.*

- as a complement of many adjectives such as **dumm, einfach, schön,** and **wichtig.**

Es ist sehr wichtig, **das zu verstehen.**	*It's very important to understand that.*
Es ist schön, **dich wiederzusehen.**	*It's nice to see you again.*

---

[1]Note on punctuation: Infinitive constructions with **zu** are always set off by a comma, unless they consist only of **zu** + *infinitive*: **Ich fange an, einen Roman zu lesen** BUT **Ich fange an zu lesen.**

Lab Manual Kap. 8, Var. zur Üb. 10, 13; Üb. 14.

Workbook Kap. 8, E, F.

10 Übung: Es macht mir Spaß . . .

Ihr Professor fragt, ob Sie etwas gerne machen. Antworten Sie, daß es Ihnen Spaß macht.

BEISPIEL: Gehen Sie gern ins Museum?
Ja, es macht mir Spaß, ins Museum zu gehen.

1. Trampen Sie gern?
2. Reisen Sie gern mit der Bahn?
3. Essen Sie gern im Restaurant?
4. Quatschen Sie gern am Telefon?
5. Spielen Sie gern Tennis?
6. Leben Sie gern in der Stadt?

11 Kettenreaktion: Was hast du vergessen?

Sie haben alle vergessen, etwas zu tun. Sagen Sie, was Sie vergessen haben, dann fragen Sie den nächsten Studenten.

BEISPIEL: A: Ich habe vergessen, meine Hausaufgaben zu schreiben.
Was hast du vergessen?
B: Ich habe vergessen, . . .

Diese Liste gibt Ihnen einige Möglichkeiten (*possibilities*):

to invite my friends	to shop
to order tickets	to buy potatoes
to order dessert	to show you my photographs

Infinitives with *um . . . zu* and *ohne . . . zu*

um . . . zu = *in order to*

Ich muß in die Stadt, **um Lebensmittel einzukaufen.**

Ich fahre nach Deutschland, **um Deutsch zu lernen.**

I have to go to town (in order) to buy groceries.

I'm going to Germany in order to learn German.

ohne . . . zu = *without . . . -ing*

Sie ist abgefahren, **ohne mich zu besuchen.**

Ich habe das Buch gelesen, **ohne es zu verstehen.**

She left without visiting me.

I read the book without understanding it.

12 Übung

Restate each sentence, changing the **weil**-clause to an **um . . . zu** phrase and eliminating the modal verb and its subject.

BEISPIEL: Ich gehe in die Stadt, weil ich einkaufen will.
Ich gehe in die Stadt, *um einzukaufen.*

1. Ich gehe ins Lokal, weil ich etwas essen will.
2. Sie sitzt am Fenster, weil sie die Straße sehen möchte.
3. Oft trampen Studenten, weil sie Geld sparen wollen.
4. Manchmal fährt man ins Ausland, weil man mehr lernen möchte.

13 Übung

Sagen Sie, warum Sie etwas machen.

> BEISPIEL: Warum gehen Sie zum Supermarkt?
> Um Brot zu kaufen.

1. Warum gehen Sie zur Uni?
2. Warum gehen Sie nach Hause?
3. Warum arbeiten Sie diesen Sommer?
4. Warum sparen Sie Geld?
5. Warum rufen Sie Ihre Eltern an?
6. Warum gehen Sie ins Museum?

14 Übung

Combine these sentences, changing the second one to an **ohne . . . zu** phrase.

> BEISPIEL: Er hat den Koffer genommen. Er hat mich nicht gefragt.
> Er hat den Koffer genommen, ohne mich zu fragen.

1. Sie sind abgefahren. Sie haben nicht „auf Wiedersehen" gesagt.
2. Ich arbeite in einem Geschäft. Ich kenne den Chef nicht.
3. Karin hat ein Zimmer gefunden. Sie hat nicht lange gesucht.
4. Geh nicht spazieren. Du trägst keinen Mantel.
5. Geh nicht weg. Du hast kein Frühstück gegessen.
6. Sie können nicht ins Konzert. Sie haben keine Karten gekauft.

Genitive Case

The genitive case is the fourth and last case to be learned. It expresses possession (*John's books*) or a relationship between two nouns marked in

English by the preposition *of* (*the color **of your eyes***). Here are some examples of genitive phrases:

der Wagen **meiner Mutter**	***my mother's*** *car*
die Freunde **der Kinder**	***the children's*** *friends*
das Haus **meines Bruders**	***my brother's*** *house*
das Ende **des Tages**	*the end **of the day***
Egons Freundin	***Egon's*** *girlfriend*

Review **der-** and **ein**-words on p. 195.

Forms of the Genitive Case

The **der**-words and the **ein**-words all share the same set of genitive endings. Nominative, accusative, and dative—the cases you have already learned—are included in the following table for comparison and review.

Genitive Case			
masc.	**neut.**	**fem.**	**plural**
nom. der Mann ⎫			
acc. den Mann ⎭	das Kind	die Frau	die Leute
dat. dem Mann	dem Kind	der Frau	den Leuten
gen. -es -(e)s	-es -(e)s	-er	-er
des Mannes	**des** Kindes	**der** Frau	**der** Leute
eines Mannes	**eines** Kindes	**einer** Frau	**keiner** Leute
meines Mannes	**eures** Kindes	**Ihrer** Frau	**unserer** Leute
dieses Mannes	**jedes** Kindes	**welcher** Frau	**dieser** Leute

In addition to the genitive ending of the **der**- or **ein**-word, in the masculine and neuter singular *the noun itself adds the ending* **-s** (de**s** Bahnhof**s**). Monosyllabic nouns such as **Mann** and **Kind** usually take the ending **-es** (des Mann**es**).

Review N-nouns on p. 173.

The masculine N-nouns, however, do *not* add an **-s** to the noun, but rather the same **-en** or **-n** ending as in the accusative and dative.

Kennen Sie die Freundin **meines Studenten?**	*Do you know my student's friend?*
Kennen Sie die Frau **dieses Herrn?**	*Do you know this gentleman's wife?*

Use of the Genitive Case

In German, the genitive generally *follows* the noun it modifies, but in English, the possessive precedes the noun: **das Haus meines Bruders** (*my brother's house*). Proper names and kinship titles used as names, however, usually *precede* the nouns they modify, as in English: **Egons Freundin** (*Egon's girlfriend*), **Muttis Wagen** (*Mom's car*). Proper names simply add **-s** without an apostrophe in the genitive.

Das Leben in der Stadt

German uses the genitive case for both persons and things, whereas English usually reserves the possessive ending 's for people and animals and uses *of* for things.

das Haus **meiner Großmutter**   *my grandmother's* house
die Häuser **der Stadt**   *the houses of the city*

Lab Manual Kap. 8, Üb. 15; Var. zur Üb. 16.

Workbook Kap. 8, G, H.

15 Übung

Change these noun phrases from nominative to genitive.

> BEISPIEL: der Zug
>   des Zuges

1. ein Arzt
2. mein Freund
3. unser Vater
4. die Lehrerin
5. das Kind
6. die Leute
7. jede Uni
8. deine Mutter
9. der Student
10. dieser Herr
11. das Essen
12. diese Zimmer

Note on Usage: von + Dative

German uses **von** + *dative* where English uses **of** + *possessive*:

a friend of my brother's	**ein Freund von meinem Bruder**
a cousin of mine	**eine Kusine von mir**
Is Max a friend of yours?	**Ist Max ein Freund von dir?**

---

16 Übung: Wie sagt man das auf deutsch?

> BEISPIEL: *your girlfriend's sister*
>   die Schwester deiner Freundin

1. the walls of my room
2. the end of the week
3. Karl's major
4. the children's pictures
5. the history of the war
6. his brother's house
7. her sister's boyfriend
8. the cities of Switzerland
9. a student's letter
10. the rooms of the house
11. Maria's students
12. the cities of Europe
13. the windows of this room
14. your mother's car
15. the history of these countries
16. Grandpa's clock
17. a friend of yours
18. a student of mine

Prepositions with the Genitive

You've already memorized the accusative, dative, and two-way prepositions on pp. 104, 137, and 169. Remember that no prepositions take the nominative case.

There is a small group of prepositions that take the genitive case.

statt or **anstatt**	*instead of*	Schreib eine Karte **statt eines Briefes.**
trotz	*in spite of, despite*	**Trotz des Wetters** sind wir ans Meer gefahren.
während	*during*	**Während der Woche** fährt er oft in die Stadt.
wegen	*because of, on account of*	**Wegen meiner Arbeit** kann ich nicht mitkommen.

Note: **Statt** and **anstatt** are interchangeable and equally correct.

17 Übung

Form prepositional phrases with the elements provided and give English equivalents. Then complete the sentences in your own words.

BEISPIEL: während / Sommer
während des Sommers (*during the summer*)
Während des Sommers habe ich gearbeitet.

1. trotz / Wetter
2. während / Ferien
3. statt / Stadtplan
4. wegen / mein / Mutter
5. wegen / mein / Studium
6. trotz / Arbeit
7. während / Tag
8. anstatt / Hotel

18 Übung: Warum tun Sie das?

Ihre Professorin möchte wissen, warum Sie etwas tun. Sagen Sie es ihr. Die Liste von Gründen (*reasons*) hilft Ihnen.

BEISPIEL: Warum arbeiten Sie so viel?
Wegen meines Studiums.

Studium	Eltern	Wetter
Klausur	Schnee	Klima
Arbeit	Regen	Streß

1. Warum bleiben Sie heute zu Hause?
2. Warum wollen Sie im Süden wohnen?
3. Warum dürfen Sie heute abend nicht mitkommen?
4. Warum brauchen Sie Ferien?
5. Warum brauchen Sie manchmal Aspirin?
6. Warum wollen Sie heute draußen sitzen?

Nouns of Measure, Weight, and Number

German noun phrases indicating measure and weight do not use a preposition. Equivalent English phrases use *of*.

ein Glas Bier	*a glass **of** beer*
eine Flasche Wein	*a bottle **of** wine*
eine Tasse Kaffee	*a cup **of** coffee*
ein Kilo Kartoffeln	*a kilo **of** potatoes*
ein Liter Milch	*a liter **of** milk*
ein Stück Brot	*a piece **of** bread*
eine Portion Pommes frites	*an order **of** French fries*

Masculine and neuter nouns of measure *remain in the singular*, even following numerals greater than one.

See table of equivalent weights and measures on the inside of the back cover.

drei **Glas** Bier	*three glasses of beer*
zwei **Kilo** Kartoffeln	*two kilos of potatoes*
vier **Stück** Brot	*four pieces of bread*

Feminine nouns of measure, however, *do* use their plural forms.

zwei Tass**en** Kaffee	*two cups of coffee*
drei Flasch**en** Wein	*three bottles of wine*
drei Portion**en** Pommes frites	*three orders of French fries*

19 Übung: Im Lokal

Ordering in a restaurant is a communicative goal.

Sie reisen durch Deutschland mit einer Gruppe und essen in einem Lokal. Die anderen in der Gruppe können kein Deutsch. Sie müssen der Kellnerin sagen, was sie bestellen wollen.

BEISPIEL: *I'd like a cup of coffee.*
Bringen Sie uns bitte eine Tasse Kaffee.

1. . . . a glass of wine and two cups of coffee.
2. . . . three glasses of water and two glasses of beer.
3. . . . a bottle of wine and two orders of French fries.
4. . . . three glasses of beer, two glasses of wine, and a cup of coffee.

Equivalents of English *to*

The all-purpose English preposition indicating destination is *to*: We're going *to Germany, to the ocean, to the train station, to the movies, to Grandma's*. German has several equivalents for English *to*, depending on the destination:

- Use **nach** with cities, states, and most countries

> Wir fahren **nach Wien.**
> **nach Kalifornien.**
> **nach Deutschland.**
> **nach Europa.**

and in the idiom: **nach Hause.**

Remember also that **an** + *acc.* signals motion toward a border, edge, or vertical surface: **Ich gehe ans Fenster / an die Tafel / an die Tür. Wir fahren ans Meer / an den See.** (Review p. 171.)

- Use **zu** with people and some locations.

> Ich gehe **zu meinen Freunden.**
> **zu meiner Großmutter.**
> **zum Arzt.**
> **zum Bahnhof.**
> **zur Buchhandlung.**
> **zur Post** (*to the post office*).

- Use **in** with countries whose names are feminine or plural, and with some locations.

> Ich fahre **in die Schweiz.**
> **in die Bundesrepublik.**
> **in die USA.**

> Wir gehen **ins Kino.**
> **ins Bett.**
> **ins Konzert.**
> **ins Museum.**
> **ins Restaurant/ins Lokal.**
> **ins Theater.**
> **in die Stadt** (*downtown*).
> **in die Kirche** (*to church*).
> **in die Mensa.**

Here is a rough rule-of-thumb for deciding whether to use **zu** or **in** with a destination within a city: **in** is usually used with destinations where one will spend a relatively long time (**ins Kino, in die Kirche, ins Bett**); **zu** is usually used with destinations involving a briefer visit (**zum Bahnhof, zur Post**).

Lesestück

Aspekte der Großstadt

Tips zum Lesen und Lernen

Tips zum Vokabelnlernen

The topic of this chapter is **die Stadt**. Compound nouns with **Stadt** define various kinds of cities. You have already encountered, for example, **Altstadt,** the "old city" or medieval core of modern German cities. In the following reading, other kinds of cities are mentioned: **Großstadt, Kleinstadt,** and **Hafenstadt** (*port city*).

Übung

Try to describe in German the following kinds of cities:

BEISPIEL: Industriestadt
Eine Stadt mit viel Industrie. (*oder*)
Eine Stadt, wo es viel Industrie gibt.

Touristenstadt
Universitätsstadt
Kulturstadt
Weltstadt
Ferienstadt

Lab Manual Kap.
8, Üb. zur Betonung.

Leicht zu merken

der **Aspekt, -e**	As<u>pekt</u>
elegant	ele<u>gant</u>
die **Generation, -en**	Genera<u>tion</u>
historisch	
katastrophal	katastro<u>phal</u>
die **Restauration, -en**	Restaura<u>tion</u>
der/die **Sozialarbeiter/in**	So<u>zial</u>arbeiter
die **Tour, -en**	

Einstieg in den Text

The following reading is called **Aspekte der Großstadt.** In it, an American exchange student and a German social worker talk about their lives in Hamburg and Munich, two of Germany's largest cities. Before reading it, think about your own experiences in or impressions of cities. Write a few sentences in German about what you find good or bad about big cities.

Das Stadtleben

Das gefällt mir   Das gefällt mir nicht

_____   _____

_____   _____

Wortschatz 2

Verben

ärgern to annoy, offend
bauen to build
rad·fahren (fährt Rad), ist radgefahren to bicycle
ski·fahren (fährt Ski), ist skigefahren (*pronounced* „Schifahren") to ski

steigen, ist gestiegen to climb
zerstören to destroy

Substantive

der **Alltag** everyday life
der **Eindruck, -̈e** impression

der **Fußgänger, -** pedestrian
der **Hafen, -̈** port, harbor
der **Preis, -e** price

das **Jahrhundert, -e** century
(das) **München** Munich
das **Rad, -̈er** wheel; bicycle
  das **Fahrrad, -̈er** bicycle
(das) **Rußland** Russia

die **Ecke, -n** corner	**Adverbien**	**viele** (*pl. pronoun*) many people
an der Ecke at the corner	**geradeaus** straight ahead	
um die Ecke around the corner	**links** to *or* on the left	**Nützliche Ausdrücke**
die **Fußgängerzone, -n** pedestrian zone closed to vehicles	**rechts** to *or* on the right	**auf dem Land** in the country (i.e., rural area)
die **Großstadt, ¨e** large city (*over 500,000 inhabitants*)	**trotzdem** in spite of that, nevertheless	**aufs Land** to the country
die **Kleinstadt, ¨e** town (*5,000 to 20,000 inhabitants*)	Links, rechts, and geradeaus are adverbs, *not* adjectives.	**im Gegenteil** on the contrary
die **Luft** air	**Andere Vokabeln**	**Mit anderen Worten**
die **Luftverschmutzung** air pollution	**gar kein . . .** no . . . at all, not a . . . at all	**riesengroß = sehr sehr groß**
	obwohl (*sub. conj.*) although	

Aspekte der Großstadt

 Lab Manual Kap. 8, Lesestück.

Die meisten° Deutschen leben in Städten mit über 80 000 Einwohnern. Welche Vorteile und Nachteile° gibt es, wenn man in einer Großstadt wohnt?

°most
°advantages and disadvantages

Learning about life in German cities is the cultural goal of this chapter.

Eindrücke eines Amerikaners

5 *Mark Walker, Student:* Dieses Jahr verbringe ich zwei Semester als Austauschstudent an der Universität Hamburg.[2] Da ich aus einer Kleinstadt in Colorado komme, schien° mir Hamburg zuerst riesengroß. Es war schwer zu verstehen, wie die Deutschen so dicht zusammengedrängt° leben können.

°seemed

dicht zusammengedrängt = crowded together

10 Aber das heißt nicht, daß Hamburg mir nicht gefällt. Im Gegenteil! Ich finde es phantastisch, daß es in der Stadt so viel zu tun gibt. Wenn ich Lust habe, kann ich jeden Tag ins Konzert, ins Kino oder ins Museum gehen. Hamburg ist die zweitgrößte° Stadt der Bundesrepublik. Weil es eine Hafenstadt ist, gibt es seit Jahrhunderten Verbindungen° mit dem Ausland.

°second largest
°ties

15 Wenn das Stadtleben mir zu viel wird, dann ist es sehr leicht, mein Fahrrad zu nehmen, in die Bahn zu steigen und aufs Land zu fahren. In der Lüneburger Heide[3] südlich von° Hamburg kann man schöne Radtouren machen. Dieser Kontrast zwischen Stadt und Land scheint mir typisch für Deutschland. Das Land ist den Einwohnern° der Städte sehr wichtig als Erholung° vom Streß des Alltags.

°south of
°inhabitants
°relaxation

---

[2] A deep-water port on the Elbe River, population 1.6 million.

[3] **Die Lüneburger Heide** (*heath*) is an extensive nature preserve on the North German plain between Hamburg and Hannover.

Einkaufen am Markt
(München)

„Ich wohne gern hier"

Beate Kreuz, Sozialarbeiterin in München:[4] Ich arbeite mit Ju-
gendlichen°. Sie haben oft keinen Schulabschluß° und können keine
25 Arbeit finden. Ich sehe also jeden Tag die Probleme der Großstadt.
Trotz dieser Probleme wohne ich sehr gerne hier. Obwohl die Woh-
nungsnot° schlimm ist, habe ich eine Wohnung in einem alten
Gebäude finden können. Ich kann mit der S-Bahn° überall hinfahren°
und brauche gar kein Auto. Im Sommer gehen wir in der Isar schwim-
30 men oder im Englischen Garten[5] radfahren, und im Winter fahren wir
in den Alpen Ski. In der Kaufinger Straße gibt es eine große Fußgängerzone, wo viele gern einen Schaufensterbummel machen. An
jeder Ecke gibt es ein elegantes Geschäft, aber in meinem Beruf sehe
ich so viel Arbeitslosigkeit,° daß mich der Konsumzwang° und die
35 hohen° Preise ärgern. Trotzdem kann man auch ohne viel Geld in der
Tasche gut leben.

**mit Jugendlichen = mit jungen
Leuten** / diploma

housing shortage
Stadtbahn = commuter rail
service / **überall hin-** =
everywhere

unemployment / pressure to buy
high

---

[4]*Munich:* capital city of Bavaria (**Bayern**), population 1.2 million.

[5]**Die Isar:** a tributary of the Danube. **Englischer Garten:** large park in the center of Munich designed by the American-born Benjamin Thompson, Count Rumford (1753–1814).

Aufbauarbeit° im Osten

Carsten Oberosler, 52; Steinmetz° in Dresden: Seit Generationen wohnen meine Vorfahren° in Sachsen,° aber meine Eltern sind erst nach dem Krieg nach Dresden[6] gekommen. Wie mein Vater bin ich Steinmetz und habe auch jahrelang° an der Restauration meiner Heimatstadt° gearbeitet.

Dresden war immer ein kunsthistorisches Juwel° Deutschlands, aber die eine Bombennacht° im Februar 1945 hat die ganze Innenstadt° zerstört. Bis heute haben wir immer noch nicht alles wiederaufgebaut,° und dazu° bedroht° die katastrophale Luftverschmutzung Menschen und Gebäude. Ich bin aber optimistisch, weil die Stadt seit der Vereinigung Deutschlands 1990 endlich mehr Geld für die wichtige Restaurationsarbeit bekommt.

reconstruction work
stone cutter
Vorfahren = Eltern, Großeltern, usw. / Saxony
for years
home town
jewel
night of bombing
center of the city
reconstructed / in addition / threatens

Fragen zum Lesestück

1. Woher kommt Mark Walker?
2. Welchen Eindruck hat Hamburg zuerst auf ihn gemacht? Warum?
3. Wie gefällt ihm die Stadt jetzt?
4. Was kann er jeden Tag tun, wenn er Lust hat?
5. Was können die Menschen in der Stadt machen, wenn ihnen der Streß des Alltags zu viel wird?
6. Was ist Beate Kreuz von Beruf?
7. Warum braucht sie gar kein Auto?
8. Was macht sie in ihrer Freizeit im Sommer? im Winter?
9. Welche Probleme des Stadtlebens sieht sie in ihrer Arbeit?
10. Was ist Herr Oberosler von Beruf?
11. Warum ist seine Arbeit in einer Stadt wie Dresden besonders wichtig?
12. Warum ist er optimistisch?

Seals of the five new federal states created from the former German Democratic Republic; from left to right:

Mecklenburg-Vorpommern
Sachsen-Anhalt
Thüringen
Sachsen
Brandenburg

[6]**Dresden** on the river Elbe is the capital of the federal state of Saxony (**Sachsen**). Under the 18th-century Saxon kings it reached its zenith as a center of art and culture. It is renowned for its beautiful public buildings and art treasures.

Hamburg

Unterwegs in der Stadt

Gebäude und Orte (*Buildings and places*)

die **Apotheke, -n**	*pharmacy*
die **Brücke, -n**	*bridge*
das **Café, -s**	*café*
die **Haltestelle, -n**	*streetcar or bus stop*
das **Kaufhaus, ¨er**	*department store*
die **Kirche, -n**	*church*
die **Konditorei, -en**	*pastry café*
die **Post**	*post office*
das **Rathaus, ¨er**	*city hall*

Verkehrsmittel (*Means of transportation*)

der **Bus, -se**	*bus*
das **Taxi, -s**	*taxicab*
die **Straßenbahn**	*streetcar*
die **U-Bahn**	*subway*

U-Bahn: short for **Untergrundbahn.**

Fragen wir nach dem Weg. (*Let's ask for directions.*)

Entschuldigung, wie komme ich **zur Post?**

... **zum Bahnhof?**

Das ist gleich in der Nähe.
Das ist nicht weit von hier.
Gehen Sie über die Straße und dann geradeaus.

... nach links.

... nach rechts.

... um die Ecke.

Asking directions is a communicative goal.

Partnerarbeit: Wie komme ich zu . . . ?

Partner A ist fremd in dieser Stadt. Er oder sie benutzt den Stadtplan, um nach dem Weg zu fragen. Partner B ist hier zu Hause und sagt Partner A den Weg durch die Stadt. Dann tauschen Sie die Rollen (**tauschen** = *exchange*).

1. Sie stehen vor der Post und wollen zum Marktplatz.
2. Sie sind im Museum und müssen zum Hotel zurück, um zu Mittag zu essen.
3. Sie sind in der Fußgängerzone und haben Hunger. Sie brauchen Hilfe (*help*), um ein Restaurant zu finden.

Gruppendiskussion: Was machen wir denn morgen?

Mit einer Studentengruppe machen Sie eine Reise durch Deutschland. Heute abend sind Sie in einer Großstadt angekommen und übernachten im

Das Leben in der Stadt

Hotel Sommerhof (siehe Stadtplan). Besprechen Sie, was Sie morgen machen wollen.

Wohin wollen wir gehen?

Was gibt es dort zu tun oder zu sehen?

Wo wollen wir essen?

Was machen wir denn am Abend?

Wie kommen wir hin (*get there*)? Zu Fuß, mit einem Taxi oder mit der Straßenbahn?

In der Konditorei

Am Tisch

1. die Serviette, -n
2. die Gabel, -n
3. der Teller, -
4. das Messer, -
5. der Löffel, -
6. das Glas, ¨er
7. die Speisekarte, -n

Was gibt's zum Essen und zum Trinken?

Das wissen Sie schon:

das Bier	die Kartoffel, -n	die Tasse
das Brot	der Käse	das Wasser
das Brötchen, -	der Nachtisch	der Wein
die Flasche, -n	die Pommes frites	die Wurst
der Kaffee	der Salat	

A **Konditorei** is a bakery-café serving pastries and sometimes light fare such as cold cuts and egg dishes.

Auf der Speisekarte der Konditorei finden Sie auch:

die **Butter**	*butter*
das **Ei, -er**	*egg*
das **Eis**	*ice cream*
das **Kännchen, -**	*small (coffee or tea) pot*

der **Kuchen**, -	cake
die **Milch**	milk
die **Portion**, -en	serving of, order of
der **Saft**, ⸚e	juice
die **Sahne**	cream
der **Schinken**	ham
der **Tee**	tea

Kaffee Hag is decaffeinated coffee; **Glühwein** is *hot mulled wine*; **Zitrone natur** is *fresh lemonade*; **Konfitüre** = **Marmelade**.

❖ Café-Konditorei Reidel

Warme Getränke

Tasse Kaffee	2,30
Kännchen Kaffee . . .	4,60
Tasse Mocca	4,40
Kännchen Mocca . . .	5,40
Tasse Kaffee Hag. . . .	2,40
Kännchen Kaffee Hag . .	4,80
Tasse Kakao mit Sahne . .	2,40
Kännchen Kakao mit Sahne .	4,80
Glas Tee mit Milch oder Zitrone .	2,30
Glas Tee mit Rum . . .	4,50
Glas Pfefferminztee . . .	2,30
Glas Grog von Rum 4 cl . .	5,00
Glas Glühwein 0,2l . . .	4,50
Glas heiße Zitrone . . .	2,60

Eis und Eisgetränke

Portion gemischtes Eis . .	3,20
Portion gemischtes Eis mit Sahne	3,90
Früchte-Eisbecher ‚Florida‘ . .	6,50
Eis-Schokolade	4,00

Kalte Getränke

Flasche Mineralwasser . . .	2,10
Flasche Coca Cola . . .	2,10
Flasche Orangeade . . .	2,10
Pokal Apfelsaft	2,40
Glas Orangensaft . . .	2,80
Glas Tomatensaft . . .	2,80
Glas Zitrone natur . . .	2,60

Frühstück

Kleines Gedeck	6,00
1 Kännchen Kaffee, Tee od. Schokolade, 2 Brötchen, Butter, Konfitüre	
Großes Gedeck	7,90
1 Kännchen Kaffee, Tee od. Schokolade, 2 Brötchen,Butter, Konfitüre, 1 gek. Ei, 1 Scheibe Schinken od. Käse	

Ergänzung zum Frühstück

1 gekochtes Ei	1,00
1 Portion Konfitüre	0,80
1 Portion Butter	0,80
1 Scheibe Käse	1,60
1 Scheibe Schinken . . .	1,80
1 Brötchen oder 1 Scheibe Brot	0,60

Talking about food and ordering in a restaurant are communicative goals.

Gruppenarbeit: In der Konditorei (3 oder 4 Personen)

Sie sitzen zusammen in der Café-Konditorei Reidel und bestellen etwas zu essen und trinken. Jemand in der Gruppe spielt den Kellner oder die Kellnerin. Die anderen bestellen von der Speisekarte.

Wo gehen wir hin?
Essen & Trinken · Freizeit & Unterhaltung

Zum Schluß Sprechen wir miteinander! **Lab Manual** Kap. 8, Diktat.

 Workbook Kap. 8, I–L.

A Übung: Wann machen Sie das?

Ihr Professor fragt, wann Sie etwas machen. Die Liste der Zeitangaben (*time phrases*) hilft Ihnen mit der Antwort.

BEISPIEL: Wann haben Sie Zeit, eine Reise zu machen?
Während der Ferien. / Im Sommer. / usw.

You can also use phrases such as **nach meiner Vorlesung** and **vor dem Frühstück**.

am	*im*	*während*
Morgen	Frühling	Woche
Abend	Herbst	Ferien
Wochenende	Winter	Vorlesung
Montag (usw.)	Januar (usw.)	Konzert

1. Wann gehen Sie zur Deutschstunde?
2. Wann haben Sie Zeit einzukaufen?
3. Wann schreiben Sie Briefe?
4. Wann schlafen Sie gern?
5. Wann haben Sie Lust, ins Ausland zu fahren?
6. Wann haben Sie keine Zeit, ins Kino zu gehen?

B Partnerarbeit: Wie findest du das?

On the left are some adjectives you can use to describe your attitude toward the activities listed on the right. Take turns telling each other what you think.

BEISPIEL: Ich finde es wunderschön, schwimmen zu gehen.

altmodisch	einen Stadtbummel zu machen
bequem	Deutsch zu lernen
barbarisch	schwimmen zu gehen
blöd	Hausaufgaben zu schreiben
einfach	meine Eltern anzurufen
furchtbar	um 6 Uhr aufzustehen
gut	Frühstück zu essen
interessant	Romane zu lesen
klug	ins Museum zu gehen
leicht	Geld zu sparen
nett	im Sommer zu arbeiten
phantastisch	Freunde einzuladen
schwierig	Kaffee zu trinken
stinklangweilig	ein Zimmer zu finden

C Partnerarbeit: Wessen . . . ist das?

Pictured below are Ute's family and some things that belong to them. Take turns asking what belongs to whom.

BEISPIEL: **Wessen Buch ist das?**
Das ist das Buch ihrer Schwester.

Ute   Schwester   Bruder   Eltern

D Gruppenarbeit: Warum tun Sie das?

Ask each other why you do certain things. Answer with an **um . . . zu** phrase.

BEISPIEL: A: **Warum gehst du in die Altstadt?**
B: **Um einen Schaufensterbummel zu machen.**

1. Warum gehst du ins Wasser?
2. Warum lernst du Deutsch?
3. Warum fahren Studenten oft per Autostop?
4. Warum bringt man eine Kamera mit, wenn man reist?
5. Warum fährt man im Winter in die Alpen?
6. Warum rufst du deine Freunde an?

Jetzt fragen Sie andere Studenten in der Klasse, was sie gern machen und warum. Sie antworten mit **um . . . zu** oder **weil**.

> BEISPIEL: So fängt es an: A: Was machst du denn gern?
> B: Ich gehe oft gern in die Stadt.
> A: Warum?
> B: *Um* ins Kino *zu* gehen. *oder*
> *Weil* ich gern ins Kino gehe.

Schreiben Sie zu Hause

In exercises F and G avoid using adjectives attributively (before nouns). Attributive adjectives need endings that are taught in Kap. 9.

F **Die ideale Stadt** Sie sind Städteplaner/in von Beruf und kennen viele Städte. Einige haben Ihnen sicher gefallen, einige nicht. Jetzt dürfen Sie die ideale Stadt planen. Beschreiben Sie diese Stadt. Was würde sie haben, was würde sie nicht haben? Warum?

G **Ein Brief nach Hause** Sie kennen schon die Stadt auf Seite 241. Sie haben den Tag dort verbracht. Jetzt sitzen Sie am Abend im Hotel und schreiben einen Brief nach Hause. Beschreiben Sie Ihrer Familie, wie der Tag war. Was sind Ihre Eindrücke von der Stadt und von den Menschen?

H **Wie sagt man das auf deutsch?**

1. Can you please tell me where the cathedral is?
2. It isn't far from here. If you go around the corner, you'll see it.
3. Thanks very much.

4. What do you do when city life gets too stressful for you?
5. Sometimes I go to the country and go for a walk.

6. Do I still have time to go shopping?
7. Yes, of course. If we can go right away, I'll come along.
8. My brother's girlfriend has a birthday tomorrow and I want to give her something.

9. During the week I don't have time to go to the museum.
10. Therefore I'd like to stay here until it closes.

With this chapter you have completed the second quarter of **Neue Horizonte.** For a concise review of the grammar and idiomatic phrases in chapters 5–8, you may consult the **Zusammenfassung und Wiederholung 2** *(Summary and Review 2)* on pages 79–92 of your Workbook. The review section is followed by a self-correcting test.

Rudern [*rowing*] auf der Alster (*Hamburg*).

VIDEOECKE

4 Gehen wir doch einkaufen! (13:19)

Die Metzgerei schließt um 18.00 Uhr.

Katrin und Stefan müssen für ein Picknick Lebensmittel einkaufen. Das Wetter sieht aber nicht gut aus. Sie müssen laufen, denn es regnet vielleicht am Nachmittag. Sie gehen zuerst zum Tante-Emma-Laden (Mom and Pop grocery store) und finden dort fast alles. Es ist schon 18.00 Uhr, und die Läden in der Stadt haben zugemacht. Also müssen sie zum Türkenmarkt (open-air Turkish market); dort kann man nach 18.00 Uhr noch einkaufen.

Wortschatz zum Video

empfehlen	*to recommend*
probieren	*to sample, try*
schmecken	*to taste; to taste good*
wünschen	*to wish for, want to have*
die Flasche, -n	*bottle*
das Pfund	*500 grams (about 1 pound)*
die Tüte, -n	*paper bag; small cardboard carton*
welch-?	*which?*
Welchen Käse können Sie mir empfehlen?	*Which cheese can you recommend to me?*
Ich hätte gern . . .	*I'd like to have . . .*
Könnt' ich . . .	*Could I . . .*
Das war's.	*That's it. That's everything.*

 A **Was sehen Sie im Video?**

Watch the video episode (13:25–16:41) once without sound. Check off in the list below what you see in the video.

Das habe ich gesehen:

_____ 1. einen Bus
_____ 2. ein Kind auf einem Dreirad (*tricycle*)
_____ 3. eine Bäckerei
_____ 4. Zeitungen
_____ 5. Frau Bachmann
_____ 6. einen Regenschirm
_____ 7. ein Computergeschäft
_____ 8. Geld

B **Wer sagt das?**

Choose the person who says the following.

a. Katrin   b. Stefan   c. Verkäuferin im Laden
d. Verkäufer am Türkenmarkt

1. _____ sagt: „Ich komm' mit. Gehen wir doch zusammen einkaufen."
2. _____ sagt: „Du kaufst den Orangensaft, ich kaufe den Käse und die Leberwurst."
3. _____ fragt: „Welches Brot wünschen Sie bitte?"
4. _____ fragt: „Welcher Saft schmeckt besser?"
5. _____ sagt: „Das war's."
6. _____ sagt: „Wir gehen zum Türkenmarkt. Der hat länger offen."
7. _____ sagt: „Sechs Mark und achtzig."

C Einkaufsliste (shopping list)

Watch what Katrin and Stefan buy. Then fill in their shopping list with the amounts they need. What are these items in English?

English

_____ Brot

_____ Leberwurst

_____ Käse

_____ Orangensaft

_____ gegrilltes Hähnchen

D Die Metzgerei hat schon zugemacht.

Use the shop sign pictured on page 247 to answer these questions.

1. An welchen Tagen kann man hier nicht einkaufen?
2. Wann macht das Geschäft am Mittwoch auf?
3. An welchem Tag macht das Geschäft um 13.00 Uhr zu?
4. Bis wann ist das Geschäft am Donnerstag auf?

E Was haben Sie gesehen?

Read through the list below. Then watch the **Welle Magazin** (16:43–18:14) and check off the words you have seen.

___ 1. Taxi
___ 2. Anprobe (*fitting room*)
___ 3. Lederjacke (*leather jacket*)
___ 4. Sparpreise (*low prices*)

___ 5. Parkhaus (*parking garage*)
___ 6. Ausgang (*exit*)
___ 7. Toiletten (*rest rooms*)
___ 8. Kasse (*cashier*)

SEIT 1390
HISTORICHES

**Hotel-Restaurant
Goldener Adler**

GOETHE-STUBE · BATZENHÄUSL

Besitzer · Familie Cammerlander
Direktion Karl Pokorny

6020 INNSBRUCK
Herzog Friedrich Str. 6. Tel. 26 3 34

Mit dem Bus durch Berlin

Most German cities have superb public transportation systems that make it easy to get around. Berlin, for instance, has a comprehensive system of subways, buses, streetcars, and commuter trains. These pages from a brochure give information about touring the city with the double-decker buses of the **BVG** (Berlin's public transportation authority). The map of bus line 100 (**die Hunderter Linie**) through the heart of Berlin (**Berlin Mitte**) and the accompanying photos show points of interest along the route. These include the Brandenburg Gate (**das Brandenburger Tor**) and Museum Island (**die Museumsinsel**).

Brandenburger Tor ⑧

Wahrzeichen für die Stadt Berlin und seit dem Mauerfall auch Symbol für die Einheit Deutschlands. 1788-91 wurde das Brandenburger Tor von Langhans nach antikem Vorbild erbaut. 1793 wurde Schadows Quadriga mit der Siegesgöttin aufgestellt.

Staatsoper Unter den Linden ⑨

Die Lindenoper feierte 1992 ihr 250-jähriges Jubiläum. Mendelssohn-Bartholdy, Furtwängler und Richard Strauss feierten hier große künstlerische Triumphe. Der 1742 eingeweihte Knobelsdorf-Bau ist ein Zeugnis des norddeutschen Rokoko.

Touristen-Information

BUS

DER HUNDERTER

100 PRENZLAUER BERG MICHELANGELOSTR.

**100% Berlin.
Auf der ganzen Linie.**

BVG Gut für Sie. Und Berlin.

Berliner Dom

Im Stil der Neorenaissance wurde die Hof-
kirche der Hohenzollern in den Jahren 1893
bis 1905 erbaut. Im Krieg stark zerstört,
wurde der größte Kirchenbau Berlins 1993
nach 18jähriger Renovierung wiedereröff-
net. Hörenswert sind die Konzerte auf der
historischen Orgel des Doms

(11)

(10)

Museumsinsel

Zwischen dem Alten Museum und dem
Bodemuseum erstreckt sich auf einer Insel
zwischen Spree und Kupfergraben einer
der weltweit bedeutendsten Museums-
komplexe. Unter anderem befindet sich
hier auch das Pergamonmuseum. Attrak-
tionen sind der beeindruckende Perga-
mon-Altar und das berühmte Markttor von
Milet. Nehmen Sie sich Zeit für einen
Spaziergang in einer Welt von Kunst und
Geschichte.

Unsere Umwelt

Communicative Goals

- Using adjectives to describe things
- Giving the date
- Discussing ecology and recycling
- Talking about sports

Cultural Goal

- Learning about German and global environmental issues

Lab Manual Kap. 9, Dialoge, Fragen, Hören Sie gut zu!

Haus also = *apartment house, building.*

Recycling in unserem Wohnhaus

Frau Berg trifft Herrn Reh auf der Treppe.　　Discussing recycling is a communicative goal.

FR. BERG:　Mensch, wohin mit dem riesengroßen Sack?

HR. REH:　In den Keller. Die neuen Container sind da. Jetzt können wir Altglas und Altpapier hier im Haus sammeln.

FR. BERG:　Na, endlich! Jetzt brauche ich meinen Müll nicht mehr zum Recycling zu schleppen.

HR. REH:　Ja, das ist jetzt nicht mehr nötig. Wenn alle mitmachen, dann ist das ein großer Fortschritt.

Ein umweltfreundliches Geburtstagsgeschenk

DANIEL:　Was hat dir Marianne zum Geburtstag geschenkt?

FRANK:　Ein neues Fahrrad, weil wir unseren Zweitwagen verkauft haben.

DANIEL:　Wieso denn?

FRANK:　Er war ja sowieso kaputt, und da wir in die Stadt umgezogen sind, kann ich mit dem Rad zur Arbeit fahren.

DANIEL:　Da sparst du aber viel Geld.

FRANK:　Ja, und ich habe auch ein gutes Gefühl, weil ich etwas gegen die Luftverschmutzung mache.

Treibst du Sport?　　Talking about sports is a communicative goal.

JUNGE:　Sag mal, treibst du gern Sport?

MÄDCHEN:　Klar. Ich verbringe das ganze Wochenende auf dem Tennisplatz. Spielst du auch Tennis?

JUNGE:　Ja, das ist mein Lieblingssport, aber ich bin kein guter Spieler.

MÄDCHEN:　Da kann ich dir einen wunderbaren Tennislehrer empfehlen.

Notes on Usage: Adverb **da** and Flavoring Particle **aber**

The Adverb *da* At the beginning of a clause, the adverb **da** often means *then, in that case, under those circumstances, for that reason:*

> **Da** sparst du aber viel Geld.
> **Da** kann ich dir einen wunderbaren Tennislehrer empfehlen.

The Flavoring Particle *aber* As a flavoring particle, **aber** is often used to intensify a statement. It adds the sense of *really, indeed.*

> Da sparst du **aber** viel Geld.　　*Then you'll **really** save a lot of money.*

The particle **aber** can add a note of surprise or admiration:

> Mensch, das ist **aber** teuer!　　*Wow, that's **really** expensive!*

Recycling in Our Apartment Building

Ms. Berg meets Mr. Reh on the stairs.

MS. B.: Wow, where to with that huge sack?

MR. R.: To the cellar. The new trash containers are here. Now we can collect (old) glass and waste paper here in the building.

MS. B.: At last! Now I don't have to haul my trash to the recycling center anymore.

MR. R.: Yes, that's not necessary anymore. If everyone participates, then that's great progress.

An Ecological Birthday Present

D.: What did Marianne give you for your birthday?

F.: A new bicycle, because we sold our second car.

D.: How come?

F.: It was kaput anyway, and since we've moved to the city, I can ride my bike to work.

D.: Then you're saving a lot of money.

F.: Yes, and it also feels good to be doing something about air pollution.

Do You Play Sports?

BOY: Hey, do you like to play sports?

GIRL: Sure. I spend all weekend on the tennis court. Do you play tennis too?

BOY: Yes, that's my favorite sport, but I'm not a good player.

GIRL: Then I can recommend a wonderful tennis instructor to you.

Verben

empfehlen (empfiehlt), hat empfohlen to recommend

mit·machen to participate, cooperate

sammeln to collect *(recycle) (Sammle)*

schleppen (*colloq.*) to drag, lug (along), haul

treffen (trifft), hat getroffen to meet

treiben, hat getrieben to drive, force, propel

Sport treiben to play sports

um·ziehen, ist umgezogen to move, change residence

Substantive

der **Container,** - large trash container

der **Fortschritt, -e** progress

der **Geburtstag, -e** birthday

zum Geburtstag for (your/her/my/etc.) birthday

der **Junge, -n, -n** boy

der **Keller,** - cellar, basement

der **Müll** trash, refuse

der **Sack, ¨e** sack

der **Sport** sport

der **Tennisplatz, ¨e** tennis court

der **Zweitwagen,** - second car

das **Gefühl, -e** feeling

das **Geschenk, -e** present

das **Mädchen,** - girl

das **Papier, -e** paper

das **Recycling** recycling; recycling center

das **Tennis** tennis

das **Wohnhaus, ¨er** apartment building

die **Treppe** staircase, stairs

auf der Treppe on the stairs

die **Umwelt** environment

die **Verschmutzung** pollution

Adjektive und Adverbien

ganz whole, entire

das ganze Wochenende all weekend, the whole weekend

kaputt (*colloq.*) broken, kaput; exhausted

klar clear; (*colloq.*) sure, of course

nötig necessary

schmutzig dirty

sportlich athletic

umweltfreundlich environmentally safe, non-polluting

zweit- second

The word **kaputt** comes from a French cardplaying term, *être capot*: "*to lose all the tricks, be wiped out.*"

zweit- must have an adjective ending. See pp. 257–260 below. It can also be a prefix, as in **Zweitwagen.**

mach mit . . .

Aktion Saubere Landschaft e. V.
Oskar-Walzel-Straße 17, 5300 Bonn

Variationen

A Persönliche Fragen

1. Ist man in Ihrem Studentenwohnheim umweltfreundlich? Was macht man da für die Umwelt?
2. Auch als Hobby kann man Dinge sammeln, z.B. Briefmarken (*stamps*), Münzen (*coins*) oder CDs. Sammeln Sie etwas? Was?
3. Frau Berg hat früher ihren Müll zum Recycling geschleppt. Was müssen Sie jeden Tag (z.B. in Ihrem Rucksack) mitschleppen?
4. Zum Geburtstag hat Frank ein neues Fahrrad bekommen. Was würden Sie gern zum Geburtstag bekommen?
5. Besitzt Ihre Familie einen Zweitwagen? Braucht sie wirklich zwei Wagen?
6. Fährt jemand in Ihrer Familie mit dem Rad zur Arbeit? Wenn nicht, warum nicht?
7. Meinen Sie, daß die Luftverschmutzung hier ein Problem ist? Wie ist die Luft bei Ihnen zu Hause?
8. Treiben Sie Sport? Wie oft in der Woche?
9. Was ist Ihr Lieblingssport? Lieblingsfilm? Lieblingsbuch? Und Ihre Lieblingsstadt?

B Warum ich Geld brauche.

Sagen Sie, warum Sie Geld brauchen.

BEISPIEL: Warum brauchen Sie Geld?
Ich brauche Geld, *um* ein Rad *zu* kaufen.

C Welche Farbe hat das?

Sagen Sie, welche Farbe diese Dinge haben.

> BEISPIEL: Welche Farbe hat Georgs Hemd?
> Es ist rot.

Welche Farbe hat / haben . . .

der Wald?	der Wein?
der Kaffee?	das Hemd dieses Jungen?
das Meer?	diese Landkarte?
die Wände dieses Zimmers?	die Bäume im Sommer? im Herbst?
die Bluse dieser Studentin?	Ihr Pulli?

Lyrik zum Vorlesen

Um diese Parodie zu verstehen, muß man „Die Loreley" von Heinrich Heine schon kennen. Lesen Sie noch einmal Heines Gedicht *(poem)* auf Seite 222 und dann diesen Text.

Lab Manual Kap. 9, Lyrik zum Vorlesen.

Many words are not glossed here because they are the same as in Heine's poem. Some new active vocabulary comes from **Wortschatz 2** of this chapter.

Alptraum (*nightmare*) is an old word related to English *elf* and suggesting a terrifying vision. It has nothing to do with the mountains (**die Alpen**).

Die Lorelei 1973

Ich weiß nicht, was soll es bedeuten,
daß ich so traurig bin;
ein Alptraum° aus unseren Zeiten,   nightmare
er geht mir nicht aus dem Sinn.

Die Luft ist schwül° und verdunkelt,   close, heavy
und dreckig fließt der Rhein;
kein Gipfel des Berges funkelt,
wo sollt' auch die Sonne sein?

Am Ufer° des Rheines sitzt sie,   bank
die deutsche Chemie-Industrie;
dort braut° sie gefährliche Gifte,°   brews / poisons
die Luft macht erstickend° sie.   suffocating

Sie kümmert sich nicht um° den Abfall,°   **kümmert...** = doesn't care about
der° aus den Rohren° fließt;   garbage / that / pipes
er kommt aus dem chemischen Saustall,°   pigsty
wo er in den Rhein sich ergießt.°   **sich...** = pours

Dem Schiffer im Tankerschiffe,
ihm macht das Atmen Müh';°   **ihm...** = has trouble breathing
er schaut nicht die Felsenriffe,
er schaut nur die dreckige Brüh'.°   slop

Ich weiß, die Wellen verschlingen
einst° nicht nur Schiffer und Kahn;   some day
und das hat mit ihren Giften
die Industrie getan.

> Jürgen Werner (geboren 1939)

Predicate Adjectives versus Attributive Adjectives

Adjectives in both English and German are used in one of two ways:

- They may follow "linking" verbs such as *to be, to become, to remain,* and *to seem* (**sein, werden, bleiben, scheinen**), in which case they are called *predicate adjectives* because they constitute the second part of the predicate. Most of the adjectives you have encountered in this book have been predicate adjectives.

Das Rad ist **neu.**	*The bicycle is **new.***
Meine Großeltern werden **alt.**	*My grandparents are getting **old.***
Der Kaffee ist **heiß.**	*The coffee is **hot.***

  Predicate adjectives in German have *no endings.*

- Adjectives may also occur *before* a noun. In this position they are called *attributive adjectives.*

das **neue** Rad	*the **new** bicycle*
meine **alten** Großeltern	*my **old** grandparents*
heißer Kaffee	***hot** coffee*

  German attributive adjectives *always* have endings.

The Noun Phrase

Attributive adjectives occur in noun phrases. A noun phrase consists of a noun and the words directly associated with it. English and German noun phrases have similar structures. They typically consist of three types of words: *limiting words, attributive adjectives,* and *nouns.*

Limiting words are the **der**-words and **ein**-words you already know:

der-*words*	ein-*words*	
der	ein	
dieser	kein	
jeder	mein	⎫
welcher	dein	⎪
alle	sein	⎬ possessive adjectives
	ihr	⎪
	unser	⎪
	euer	⎪
	ihr	⎭

These words are called "limiting words" because they *limit* the noun in some way rather than describing it: ***dieses** Fahrrad* (***this** bicycle, not that one*), ***meine** Großeltern* (***my** grandparents, not yours*).

Here are some examples of noun phrases. Note that the noun phrase does not necessarily contain both a limiting word and an attributive adjective.

limiting word	+	attributive adjective	+	noun	
das		neue		Fahrrad	*the new bicycle*
jede				Woche	*every week*
alle		deutschen		Studenten	*all German students*
		heißer		Kaffee	*hot coffee*
meine		kleine		Schwester	*my little sister*

Alle is usually plural and takes the primary plural endings. Adjectives that follow it take the secondary plural endings: **alle deutschen Studenten.** When **alle** is followed by a second limiting word, however, they both take the same primary ending: **alle meine Freunde, alle diese Leute.**

German adjective endings have acquired the reputation of being a formidable obstacle for the learner. However, the system is conceptually quite simple and just requires practice until it becomes automatic in spoken German. To be able to use attributive adjectives, you need to know only two sets of endings—called the *primary endings* and the *secondary endings*—and three rules for their use. Half of the system is already familiar to you: the primary endings are simply the endings of the **der**-words that show gender, number, and case.

Primary Endings				
	masc.	*neut.*	*fem.*	*plur.*
nom.	-er	-es	-e	-e
acc.	-en	-es	-e	-e
dat.	-em	-em	-er	-en
gen.	-es	-es	-er	-er

There are only two secondary endings, **-e** and **-en**. They occur in the following pattern:

Secondary Endings				
	masc.	*neut.*	*fem.*	*plur.*
nom.	-e	-e	-e	-en
acc.	-en	-e	-e	-en
dat.	-en	-en	-en	-en
gen.	-en	-en	-en	-en

Note that the **-en** occurs *throughout the plural* as well as *throughout the dative and genitive cases.*

Rules for the Use of Adjective Endings

1. Noun phrases with adjectives must have a primary ending, either on the limiting word, or on the adjective itself. When the limiting word takes a primary ending, the adjective that follows it takes a secondary ending.

limiting word with primary ending		*attributive adjective with secondary ending*		*noun*	
dies**es**	+	schön**e**	+	Bild	*this beautiful picture*
mit mein**er**		gut**en**		Freundin	*with my good friend*

2. If the noun phrase has no limiting word or has an **ein**-word without an ending, then the attributive adjective takes the primary ending.[1]

no limiting word or ein-word without ending		*attributive adjective with primary ending*		*noun*	
		alt**e**		Häuser	*old houses*
		heiß**er**		Kaffee	*hot coffee*
ein		alt**es**		Haus	*an old house*

The following examples contrast noun phrases with and without limiting words. Note how the primary ending shifts from the limiting word to the adjective when there is no limiting word:

diese neu**en** Tennisplätze $\rightarrow$ neu**e** Tennisplätze
mit mein**em** österreichischen Geld $\rightarrow$ mit österreichisch**em** Geld
welch**es** deutsche Bier $\rightarrow$ deutsch**es** Bier

3. Attributive adjectives in succession have the same ending.

ein groß**es** alt**es** Haus	*a large old house*
groß**e** alt**e** Häuser	*large old houses*
gut**er** deutsch**er** Wein	*good German wine*

Pay special attention to the three instances in which **ein**-words have no endings. They are the *only* instances in which **ein**-word endings differ from **der**-word endings.

masculine nominative	*neuter nominative and accusative*
ein alt**er** Mann	ein klein**es** Kind
but	*but*
der alte Mann	dieses kleine Kind

---

[1] There is one exception to rule 2: In the masculine and neuter genitive singular, the attributive adjective not preceded by a limiting word takes the *secondary ending* **-en** rather than the primary ending.

trotz tief**en** Schnees	*in spite of deep snow*
wegen schlecht**en** Wetters	*because of bad weather*

Such phrases are quite rare. Moreover, note that the primary ending *is* present on the noun itself.

Adjectives whose basic forms end in unstressed **-er** (**teuer**) or **-el** (**dunkel**) drop the **-e-** when they take endings.

Die Theaterkarten waren **teuer**.	Das waren aber **teure** Karten!
Ist diese Farbe zu **dunkel**?	Ich mag **dunkle** Farben.

Let's summarize. The first table below shows the complete declension of an adjective following a **der**-word; the second, following an **ein**-word. The highlighted forms in the second table show the only instances in which the **ein**-word endings differ from the **der**-word endings. The third table shows adjective endings in noun phrases without a limiting word.

Adjective Endings Following a *der*-word			
masculine	*neuter*	*feminine*	*plural*
nom. dieser junge Mann	dieses junge Kind	diese junge Frau	diese jungen Leute
acc. diesen jungen Mann	dieses junge Kind	diese junge Frau	diese jungen Leute
dat. diesem jungen Mann	diesem jungen Kind	dieser jungen Frau	diesen jungen Leuten
gen. dieses jungen Mannes	dieses jungen Kindes	dieser jungen Frau	dieser jungen Leute

Adjective Endings Following an *ein*-word			
masculine	*neuter*	*feminine*	*plural*
nom. ein junger Mann	ein junges Kind	eine junge Frau	meine jungen Leute
acc. einen jungen Mann	ein junges Kind	eine junge Frau	meine jungen Leute
dat. einem jungen Mann	einem jungen Kind	einer jungen Frau	meinen jungen Leuten
gen. eines jungen Mannes	eines jungen Kindes	einer jungen Frau	meiner jungen Leute

Adjective Endings Without a Limiting Word			
masculine	*neuter*	*feminine*	*plural*
nom. kalter Wein	kaltes Wasser	kalte Milch	kalte Suppen
acc. kalten Wein	kaltes Wasser	kalte Milch	kalte Suppen
dat. kaltem Wein	kaltem Wasser	kalter Milch	kalten Suppen
gen. kalten Weines	kalten Wassers	kalter Milch	kalter Suppen

Neue Mode: Alte Häuser

1 Übung: Welcher Tisch ist das? (Mit offenen Büchern)

Below is a list of some people and classroom objects, arranged by gender, as well as a list of adjectives that you can use to describe them. Your instructor will ask you about them. Describe them with adjectives as in the example.

BEISPIEL: Welches Bild ist das?
Das ist *das neue Bild.*

masc.	neut.	fem.	plur.	adjectives
Bleistift	Bild	Gruppe	Bücher	alt
Junge	Buch	Hose	Jeans	billig
Kugelschreiber	Fenster	Jacke	Schuhe	blau, rot,
Mantel	Foto	Kamera	Studenten	grün usw.
Pulli	Glas	Landkarte		bunt
Radiergummi	Heft	Studentin		fleißig
Stadtplan	Hemd	Tafel		freundlich
Student	Kleid	Tasche		groß
Stuhl	Mädchen	Tür		herrlich
	Papier	Uhr		höflich
	Poster	Zeitschrift		kaputt
	Wörterbuch	Zeitung		kurz
				langweilig
				neu
				schrecklich
				toll
				typisch
				wunderbar

meki's basar

SCHÖNE ALTE MÖBEL

BERLIN-WILMERSDORF
KONSTANZER STRASSE 14
TEL. 030 - 87 04 61

2 Übung: Sehen Sie den Tisch?

Now your instructor asks whether you see certain objects or people. You're not sure which ones are meant, so you ask for more information.

> BEISPIEL: Sehen Sie den Tisch?
> Meinen Sie den *grünen* Tisch?

Was für can also introduce exclamations: **Was für ein schöner Wagen!** (*What a beautiful car!*)

Fragewort

Was für . . . ?   *What kind of . . . ?*

Was für ein Artikel ist das?	*What kind of article is that?*
Was für einen Wagen hast du?	*What kind of car do you have?*
Mit **was für** Menschen arbeitest du zusammen?	*What kind of people do you work with?*

3 Übung: Was für ein Buch ist das?

Jetzt fragt Ihr Professor zum Beispiel, was für ein Buch das ist. Sie beschreiben das Buch.

> BEISPIEL: Was für ein Buch ist das?
> Das ist ein interessantes Buch.

4 Partnerarbeit: Nicht wahr?

Take turns confirming each other's impressions. One partner asks the question and the other responds. Then switch roles.

> BEISPIEL: Das Haus ist schön, nicht wahr?
> Ja, das ist ein schönes Haus.

1. Die Kneipe ist alt, nicht?
2. Der Junge ist klug, nicht wahr?
3. Das Hotel ist teuer, nicht wahr?
4. Der Automechaniker ist gut, nicht?
5. Das Kind ist müde, nicht wahr?
6. Die Buchhandlung ist phantastisch, nicht?
7. Das Bett ist bequem, nicht?
8. Der Tag ist warm, nicht?

Now create your own sentences on the same pattern.

5 Übung: Was für ein Buch brauchen Sie?

Jetzt möchte Ihre Professorin wissen, was für Sachen Sie brauchen, tragen usw. Sagen Sie es ihr.

> BEISPIELE: A: Was für ein Buch brauchen Sie?
> B: Ich brauche ein neues Buch.
>
> A: Was für Schuhe tragen Sie heute?
> B: Heute trage ich alte Turnschuhe.

Schwerindustrie im Ruhrgebiet.

6 Übung: Wir haben keinen neuen Wagen.

Ihr Professor fragt Sie nach (*about*) etwas. Sie antworten, daß Sie es nicht haben.

BEISPIEL: Ist Ihr Wagen neu?
Nein, ich habe keinen neuen Wagen.

1. Ist Ihr Fahrrad neu?
2. Sind diese Bücher langweilig?
3. Ist der Tennislehrer wunderbar?
4. Ist der Kaffee heiß?
5. Ist die Wurst frisch?
6. Sind Ihre Freunde sportlich?
7. Sind diese Kleider schmutzig?
8. Ist Ihr Zimmer groß?

7 Übung: Was machen Sie lieber?

Der Professor fragt Sie, was Sie lieber machen.

BEISPIEL: Dieser Zug fährt langsam, aber dieser fährt schnell.
Mit welchem Zug fahren Sie lieber?
Ich fahre lieber mit dem langsamen Zug.

1. Dieser Kaffee ist heiß, aber dieser ist kalt. Welchen trinken Sie lieber?
2. Dieses Hemd ist rot, und dieses ist gelb. Welches gefällt Ihnen besser?
3. Diese Kartoffeln sind groß, aber diese sind klein. Welche nehmen Sie?
4. Dieser See ist warm, aber dieser ist kühl. In welchem würden Sie lieber schwimmen?
5. Diese Stadt ist schön, aber diese ist häßlich. In welcher würden Sie lieber wohnen?
6. Dieses Zimmer ist hell, aber dieses ist dunkel. Welches gefällt Ihnen?
7. Dieses Hotel ist alt, aber dieses ist neu. In welchem würden Sie lieber übernachten?
8. Diese Brezeln sind frisch, aber diese sind alt. Welche würden Sie lieber essen?

Word Order of Adverbs: Time / Manner / Place

You learned in **Kapitel 1** that adverb sequence in German is time before place.

Place can be either location (**zu Hause**) or destination (**nach Kopenhagen**). Notice that prepositional phrases such as these function as adverbs.

	time	*place*
Ich fahre	**morgen**	**nach Kopenhagen.**
Wir bleiben	**heute**	**zu Hause.**

If an adverb or adverbial phrase of manner (answering the question **wie?** or **mit wem?**) is also present, the sequence is *time—manner—place*.

	time	*manner*	*place*
Ich fahre	morgen	**mit der Bahn**	nach Kopenhagen.
Sie bleibt	heute	**allein**	zu Hause.

A good mnemonic device is that adverbs answer the following questions in alphabetical order:

wann? (morgen),   **wie?** (mit der Bahn),   **wo(hin)?** (nach Kopenhagen)

 Workbook Kap. 9, I.

8 Gruppenarbeit: Wie? Mit wem?

Create your own answers to these questions. Follow the example sentences.

1. Wie können wir morgen nach Berlin fahren?
   Wie viele Möglichkeiten gibt es für eine Reise nach Berlin?

   BEISPIEL: Wir können morgen <u>mit der Bahn</u> nach Berlin fahren.

2. Mit wem gehen Sie abends ins Kino?

   BEISPIEL: Ich gehe abends <u>mit meinem Freund</u> ins Kino.

Ordinal Numbers and Dates

The ordinal numbers (i.e., *first, second, third*, etc.) are adjectives and in German take the usual adjective endings.

German numbers up to **neunzehn** add **-t-** to the cardinal number and then the appropriate adjective ending. Note the three irregular forms in boldface.

der, das, die			
erste	1st	elfte	11th
zweite	2nd	zwölfte	12th
dritte	3rd	dreizehnte	13th
vierte	4th	vierzehnte	14th
fünfte	5th	fünfzehnte	15th
sechste	6th	sechzehnte	16th
siebte	7th	siebzehnte	17th
achte	8th	achtzehnte	18th
neunte	9th	neunzehnte	19th
zehnte	10th		

German numbers **zwanzig** and above add **-st-** and the adjective ending to the cardinal number.

der, das, die {	zwanzigste	20th
	einundzwanzigste	21st
	zweiundzwanzigste	22nd
	dreiundzwanzigste	23rd
	usw.	
	dreißigste	30th
	vierzigste	40th
	hundertste	100th
	tausendste	1000th

In German, an ordinal number is seldom written out in letters. It is usually indicated by a period after the numeral.

der **10.** November = der zehnte November

9 **Kettenreaktion: Ich bin die erste. Ich bin der zweite.**

Count off using ordinal numbers. Males say **der . . .** , females say **die . . .**

Immer auf der richtigen Höhe – damit die Kleinen am Tisch der Großen sitzen können.

Fürs vierte Jahr

Fürs erste Jahr

Dates in German

In German, the full date is given in the order: day, month, year.

den 1.2.1996 *February 1, 1996*

To tell in what year something happened, English uses the phrase *in 1996*. The German equivalent is **im Jahre 1996** or simply **1996** (no **in**).

Here is how to say on what date something occurs or occurred:

Das war **am zehnten** August.   *That was on the tenth of August.*
Wir fliegen **am achtzehnten**.   *We're flying on the eighteenth.*

Here is how to ask for and give the date:

Den wievielten haben wir heute?
or
Der wievielte ist heute?
}   *What's the date today?*
(literally: *"The how manyeth do we have today/is today?"*)

Heute haben wir **den dreizehnten**.
or
Heute ist **der dreizehnte**.
}   *Today is the thirteenth.*

Lab Manual Kap. 9, Üb. 10, 11.

Workbook Kap. 9, J.

Giving the date is a communicative goal.

10 Übungen

A. Der wievielte ist heute?
    Heute ist der . . .

    3. August
    9. Februar
    1. Mai
    20. Juli
    2. Januar
    8. April

B. Den wievielten haben wir heute?
    Heute haben wir den . . .

    5. März
    13. Juni
    11. November
    19. September
    7. Dezember
    28. Oktober

11 Übung

Wann kommt Frank? Er kommt am . . .

4. Januar
30. September
5. April
25. Juli
31. Oktober
20. Februar
24. März

12 Partnerarbeit: Wann reist Susanne nach München?

Sie sehen auf Seite 267 Susannes Terminkalender für Februar. Fragen Sie einander, wann sie alles macht.

BEISPIEL: A: Wann besucht sie Heinz?
            B: Sie besucht ihn am ersten.

FEBRUAR	
1 Heinz besuchen	**9** im Computerzentrum arbeiten
2	**10**
3 ins Theater gehen („Mutter Courage")	**11** ins Kino („Das schreckliche Mädchen")
4	**12** zum Recycling gehen
5	**13** Referat schreiben
6 mit Jörg und Katja essen gehen	. . .
7 schwimmen gehen (19 Uhr)	**20** Reise nach München
8	**21** in die Berge fahren

Unsere Umwelt in Gefahr

Tips zum Lesen und Lernen

Tips zum Vokabelnlernen

Identifying Noun Gender Now that you have acquired a German vocabulary of several hundred words, you can begin to recognize some patterns in the gender and formation of nouns. You have already learned that agent nouns ending in **-er** are always masculine (**der Lehrer**) and that the ending **-in** always designates a female (**die Lehrerin**).

The gender of many nouns is determined by a suffix. Here are some of the most common suffixes that form nouns.

- Nouns with the following suffixes are *always feminine* and *always* have the plural ending **-en**:

    -ung, -heit, -keit, -schaft, -ion, -tät

- **-ung** forms nouns from verb stems:

    lösen (*to solve*) → **die Lösung, -en** (*solution*)
    zerstören (*to destroy*) → **die Zerstörung** (*destruction*)
    verschmutzen (*to pollute*) → **die Verschmutzung** (*pollution*)

- **-heit** and **-keit** form nouns from adjective stems and from other nouns:

    frei → **die Freiheit, -en** (*freedom*)
    freundlich → **die Freundlichkeit** (*friendliness*)
    gesund → **die Gesundheit** (*health*)
    Mensch → **die Menschheit** (*humanity*)

- **-schaft** forms collective and more abstract nouns from concrete nouns:

    Studenten → **die Studentenschaft** (*student body*)
    Land → **die Landschaft, -en** (*landscape*)
    Freund → **die Freundschaft, -en** (*friendship*)

Unsere Umwelt

- **-ion** and **-tät**: Words with these suffixes are borrowed from French or Latin. Most have English cognates:

die Diskussion, -en   **die Generation, -en**
die Universität, -en   **die Elektrizität**

- The suffixes **-chen** and **-lein** form diminutives. The stem vowel of the noun is umlauted wherever possible, and the noun automatically becomes *neuter*. The plural and singular forms are always identical.

die Karte →	**das Kärtchen, -**	(*little card*)
das Stück →	**das Stückchen, -**	(*little piece*)
das Brot →	**das Brötchen, -**	
die Magd (archaic: *maid*) →	**das Mädchen, -**	
die Frau →	**das Fräulein, -**	(*Miss; young woman*)
das Buch →	**das Büchlein, -**	(*little book*)

Übung: Raten Sie mal! *(Take a guess!)*

Was bedeuten diese Wörter?

1. die Möglichkeit
2. die Wanderung
3. die Ähnlichkeit
4. die Mehrheit
5. die Meinung
6. die Lehrerschaft
7. die Wohnung
8. die Schönheit
9. die Dummheit
10. die Studentenschaft
11. die Radikalität
12. die Gesundheit
13. die Schwierigkeit
14. das Brüderlein
15. das Liedchen
16. das Städtchen
17. das Würstchen
18. das Häuschen
19. die Kindheit
20. die Menschheit

Lab Manual Kap. 9, Üb. zur Betonung.

Leicht zu merken

aktiv	akt<u>iv</u>
akut	
das **Atom, -e**	At<u>o</u>m
die **Basis**	
demonstrieren	demonstr<u>ie</u>ren
die **Elektrizität**	Elektriz<u>i</u>tät
die **Energie**	Energ<u>ie</u>
enorm	
die **Konsequenz, -en**	Konsequ<u>enz</u>
der **Lebensstandard**	
die **Natur**	Nat<u>u</u>r
das **Ökosystem**	
das **Plastik**	
politisch	
produzieren	produz<u>ie</u>ren
das **Prozent** (%)	
radikal	radik<u>al</u>
sortieren	sort<u>ie</u>ren
sowjetisch	sowj<u>e</u>tisch
der **Supertanker, -**	

The following text discusses environmental problems. These issues concern people all over the globe. They are particularly crucial in densely populated Europe.

Look over **Wortschatz 2**, then read the following hypotheses about the environment. Do you agree or disagree with them? Compare your responses to the opinions expressed in the reading.

	Das stimmt.	**Das stimmt nicht.**
1. Wir sind heute immer noch sehr abhängig von der Natur.	☐	☐
2. Die Schwerindustrie ist für die Umweltverschmutzung verantwortlich.	☐	☐
3. Die Atomenergie ist eine gute Alternative zum Öl.	☐	☐
4. Der Durchschnittsbürger (*average citizen*) kann im Alltag viel gegen die Umweltverschmutzung tun.	☐	☐
5. Die Politiker müssen viel mehr für die Umwelt tun.	☐	☐

Wortschatz 2

Verben

führen to lead
lösen to solve
retten to rescue, save
verschmutzen to pollute; to dirty
verschwenden to waste
werfen (wirft), hat geworfen to throw
  weg·werfen to throw away, discard

Substantive

der **Fisch, -e** fish
der **Politiker, -** politician
der **Unfall, ∸e** accident
der **Vogel, ∸** bird
das **Beispiel, -e** example

das **Kraftwerk, -e** power plant
  das **Atomkraftwerk** atomic power plant
das **Öl** oil
das **Tier, -e** animal
die **Chance, -n** chance
die **Dose, -n** (tin) can
die **Gefahr, -en** danger
die **Gesellschaft, -en** society
die **Gesundheit** health
die **Jugend** (*sing.*) youth; young people
die **Kraft, ∸e** power, strength
die **Lösung, -en** solution
die **Menschheit** mankind, human race
die **Partei, -en** political party
die **Pflanze, -n** plant
die **Politik** politics; policy

die **Technik** technology
die **Ware, -n** product

Adjektive und Adverbien

bereit prepared, ready
eigen- own
erstaunlich astounding
gefährlich dangerous
gesund healthy
hoch (*predicate adj.*), **hoh-** (*attributive adj.*) high
  Das Gebäude ist **hoch**.
    aber
    Das ist ein **hohes** Gebäude.
jährlich annually
sauer sour; acidic
  der **saure Regen** acid rain
stark strong

KATZEN würden GREENPEACE wählen!

Unsere Umwelt in Gefahr

 Lab Manual Kap. 9, Lesestück.

Learning about German environmental issues is the cultural goal of this chapter.

Das Problem: Der Mensch gegen die Natur?

Wir leben heute in Europa und Nordamerika in einer hochindustrialisierten° Welt. Wir lieben unseren Luxus° und brauchen die Technik, denn sie ist die Basis unseres hohen Lebensstandards. Aber unseren

5 erstaunlichen Fortschritt haben wir teuer bezahlt.° Manchmal vergessen wir, daß wir immer noch von der Natur abhängig° sind.

    Um unsere Lebensweise° möglich zu machen, brauchen wir enorm viel Energie. Obwohl die Nordamerikaner und Westeuropäer nur zirka 15% der Weltbevölkerung° sind, verbrauchen° sie zirka 65%

10 aller produzierten Energie. Spätestens° seit der Katastrophe im sowjetischen Atomkraftwerk in Tschernobyl am 26. April 1986 weiß man aber, wie gefährlich diese Energiequelle° für unser Ökosystem sein kann. Ein zweites Beispiel ist die Exxon-Valdez-Katastrophe vom Jahre 1989; das Öl aus diesem verunglückten° Supertanker hat das

15 Meer verschmutzt und Fische und Vögel weit und breit° in Gefahr gebracht. Die schlimmen Folgen° von solchen Unfällen können jahrelang fortdauern.° Leider aber sind alle unsere Hauptenergiequellen (Öl, Kohle,° Atomkraft) schädlich° für die Natur und für unsere Gesundheit.

20   Aber nicht nur die Schwerindustrie muß für die Umwelt verantwortlich sein, sondern auch jeder einzelne° Mensch. Wir fahren zu viel Auto, wir essen zu viel in Fast-Food-Restaurants, wir benutzen zu viele Spraydosen° und produzieren zu viel Müll. Die Konsequenzen sind: der saure Regen, Müllhalden° voll von unnötigen Plastikver-

25 packungen° und die Zerstörung der Ozonschicht.° Das Problem ist im dicht besiedelten° Deutschland besonders akut. Dort wirft jeder Bürger jährlich zirka 300 bis 400 kg Müll weg! Man möchte wirklich fragen: Sind wir Menschen denn die Feinde° der Natur?

highly industrialized / luxury

teuer... = paid a high price for
von... = dependent on
way of life

world population / consume
at the latest

energy source

grounded
far and wide
consequences
jahrelang... = persist for years
coal / harmful

individual

aerosol cans
trash dumps
plastic packaging / ozone layer
dicht besiedelt = densely populated
enemies

(*links*) Im Schwarzwald. (*rechts*) Waldsterben.

Die Lösung: aktiv umweltfreundlich sein!

30 Besonders die junge Generation in Deutschland zeigt für diese Probleme starkes Engagement.° Manche finden bei den Grünen² eine   commitment
radikale Alternative zu der Umweltpolitik der großen Parteien. Viele
demonstrieren gegen neue Atomkraftwerke und suchen auch in ihrem
eigenen Leben Alternativen zu der Wegwerfgesellschaft. Aber nicht
35 nur die umweltbewußte° Jugend, sondern Deutsche aus allen Alters-   environmentally conscious
gruppen° sind heute bereit, ihr Leben zu ändern,° um Meere, Wälder,   age groups / change
Tiere und Pflanzen zu retten.³

    Wie kann man denn ein umweltfreundliches Leben führen? Man
kann z.B. mehr radfahren und zu Fuß gehen und weniger° Auto   less
40 fahren. Man sollte° nur Waren ohne unnötige Verpackung kaufen und   should
den Hausmüll sortieren und zum Recycling bringen. Man kann auch
so wenig Wasser und Elektrizität wie° möglich verschwenden. Diese   **so . . . wie** = as . . . as
Vorschläge° für den Alltag sind nur ein Anfang. Man muß natürlich   suggestions
auch von den Politikern mehr Umweltbewußtsein° fordern.° Die   environmental awareness /
45 Menschheit hat nicht mehr viel Zeit. Nur wenn alle Länder politisch   demand
zusammenarbeiten, haben wir noch eine Chance, unsere Umwelt zu
retten.

---

²**Die Grünen**, the environmental and anti-nuclear party, first won seats in the Bundestag in 1983. Although they lost these seats in the 1990 federal elections, they
regained them in 1994 and are also represented at the state level in some **Länder**.

³In 1990 the Federal Republic became the first nation to ban the production and
use of ozone-depleting chlorofluorocarbons.

**Die Wälder sterben-
nach den Wäldern
sterben die Menschen.**

Discussing ecology and recycling
is a communicative goal.

Fragen zum Lesestück

1. Von welchen Umweltkatastrophen haben Sie schon gehört?
2. Wann war die Katastrophe in Tschernobyl?
3. Wie können Umweltkatastrophen für die Natur gefährlich sein?
4. Wer soll denn für die Umwelt verantwortlich sein?
5. Nennen Sie unsere Hauptenergiequellen.
6. Kennen Sie alternative Energiequellen?
7. Wie kann unser modernes Alltagsleben für die Umwelt gefährlich sein?
8. Wie können wir ein umweltfreundliches Leben führen?

Situationen aus dem Alltag

Der Sport   Talking about sports is a communicative goal.

„Wer Sport treibt, bleibt fit!" hört man oft. Was meinen Sie? Treiben Sie Sport, um fit und gesund zu bleiben, oder nur, weil es Ihnen Spaß macht? Hier sind einige nützliche Wörter für eine Diskussion über Sport.

Substantive	*Verben*
das **Spiel**, -e *game*	**gewinnen, hat gewonnen** *to win*
die **Mannschaft**, -en *team*	**schlagen, hat geschlagen** *to beat*
die **Konkurrenz** *competition*	**trainieren** *to train*

Gruppenarbeit: Was spielst du gern?

Hier sind einige Piktogramme aus den Olympischen Spielen. Welchen Sport treiben Sie gern?

BEISPIEL: A: Ich schwimme gern. Und du?
B: Ich _____ .

laufen
der **Läufer**
die **Läuferin**

schwimmen
der **Schwimmer**
die **Schwimmerin**

skifahren
der **Skifahrer**
die **Skifahrerin**

boxen
der **Boxer**

Volleyball spielen
der **Volleyballspieler**
die **Volleyballspielerin**

Fußball spielen
der **Fußballspieler**
die **Fußballspielerin**

radfahren
der **Radfahrer**
die **Radfahrerin**

(Eis)hockey spielen
der **Hockeyspieler**

Gruppenarbeit: Sprechen wir über Sport (2 oder 3 Personen)

1. Welchen Sport treibst du?
2. Warum gefällt dir dieser Sport?
3. Treibst du an der Uni Sport? Hast du auch in der Schule Sport getrieben?

Klassendiskussion: Was meinen Sie?

1. Kann man fit bleiben, ohne Sport zu treiben?
2. In Deutschland gibt es viele Sportklubs, aber nur wenige (*few*) Universitätsmannschaften. Finden Sie es gut, daß es solche Mannschaften an amerikanischen Unis gibt? Warum?

Sprechen wir miteinander

A Gruppenarbeit: Beschreiben wir das Klassenzimmer.

BEISPIEL: Dort hängt ein großes Bild an der Wand.
Dort steht ein kleiner Tisch.

Was sehen Sie sonst? Benutzen Sie Adjektive!

B Gruppenarbeit: Wer trägt was?

Benutzen Sie Adjektive, um die Kleider eines Studenten oder einer Studentin im Zimmer zu beschreiben. Die anderen müssen raten (*guess*), wen Sie meinen. Sie können auch Ihre eigenen Kleider beschreiben.

BEISPIEL: A: Wer trägt heute eine alte Hose und ein häßliches Hemd?
B: Meinst du Rick?

Using adjectives to describe things is a communicative goal.

C Übung: Ich habe ein interessantes Bild gefunden.

Suchen Sie in einem Bilderbuch oder einer Zeitschrift ein interessantes Bild oder Foto. Beschreiben Sie es vor der Klasse. Benutzen Sie viele Adjektive!

BEISPIEL: Ich habe dieses schöne Bild in einem alten Buch gefunden. Hier sieht man viele Häuser in einem kleinen Dorf. In der Mitte des Bildes steht eine alte Kirche, und vor dieser schönen Kirche geht ein alter Mann mit einem jungen Kind spazieren. Hinter dem Dorf sieht man auch einen dunklen Wald usw.

D Gruppenarbeit: Es gibt eine Alternative!

Hier sind einige Beispiele der Umweltverschmutzung. Können Sie Alternativen geben?

BEISPIEL: Einen Plastiklöffel wirft man meistens weg.
Alternative: Aber ich muß nicht mit Plastiklöffeln essen.

1. Meine Familie wirft jede Woche viele Flaschen weg.
2. Sonntags fahre ich gern im eigenen Auto aufs Land.
3. Im Supermarkt sind die Lebensmittel alle in Plastik verpackt.
4. Manchmal werfen Menschen Papier auf die Straße.
5. Wenn mein Kugelschreiber keine Tinte (*ink*) mehr hat, werfe ich ihn weg.
6. In unserem Studentenwohnheim gibt es keine Recyclingcontainer.

Jeden Tag benutzen wir viele Sachen. Aber wir verschwenden auch eine Menge, besonders Dinge aus Plastik. Machen Sie eine Liste von solchen Dingen aus Ihrem Alltag. Was haben Sie in den letzten Tagen wegwerfen müssen? Warum?

Liste: „Das haben wir in letzter Zeit weggeworfen."

Schreiben Sie zu Hause

F Combine elements of your choice from the following lists to write ten sentences that describe activities. Create both statements and questions and use both present and perfect tense.

Wann?	*Wie?*	*Wo(hin)?*	*Verben*
am 10. Oktober	mit meinen	ins Ausland	reisen
letzten Dienstag	Freunden	im Bett	liegen
morgen	allein	in der Bibliothek	lesen
gestern	mit dem Zug	ins Kino	übernachten
1993	mit dem Auto	in die Bibliothek	gehen
heute	ziemlich schnell	in der Jugendherberge	essen
am Mittwoch	gerne	im Tennisklub	joggen
nächsten Monat	fleißig	an der Uni	Sport treiben
dieses Semester	zusammen	in der Mensa	Tennis spielen
	ohne mich		

BEISPIELE: Am Mittwoch esse ich mit meinen Freunden in der Mensa.

Wann habt ihr zusammen in der Jugendherberge übernachtet?

G Rewrite this narrative, filling in each blank with an appropriate adjective. Don't forget to add the endings where they are needed.

Heute ist der _____ Mai, und es ist ein _____ Tag. Ich bin mit meiner _____ Freundin Laura im _____ Wald spazierengegangen. Die Sonne war _____ , und im Wald war es sehr _____ . Wir haben unser Mittagessen mitgebracht, und um ein Uhr waren wir schon hungrig. Aber wir haben vergessen, eine Flasche Wein mitzubringen. Wir haben gewußt, daß es im Wald ein _____ Restaurant gibt, und bald haben wir es gefunden. Dort haben wir also eine _____ Flasche Wein gekauft. Die Kellnerin war eine sehr _____ Frau. Mit ihr haben wir über das _____ Wetter gesprochen. Sie hat auch ein _____ Kind gehabt, und wir haben ein bißchen mit diesem _____ Mädchen gespielt. Später haben wir meinen _____ Freund Hannes getroffen. Er hat uns seinen _____ Wagen gezeigt. Am Ende dieses _____ Tages sind wir dann mit der Straßenbahn in die _____ Stadt zurückgefahren.

H Construct sentences from the elements provided. Be prepared to translate your sentences into English.

1. mein / umweltfreundlich / Mitbewohner / tragen / Müll / in / Keller

2. alle / neu / Einwohner / unser- (*gen.*) / Studentenwohnheim- / mitmachen

3. nach / unser / lang / Wanderung / können / wir / in / ein / billig / Restaurant / ein / kalt / Bier / trinken

4. das / riesengroß / Zimmer / ist / sonnig, / und / ich / haben / mein / eigen / Schreibtisch

5. die / klein / Schüler / aus / d- / dritt- / Klasse / sammeln / leer / Flaschen / für / d- / Umweltaktion

6. ich / war / in / ein / phantastisch / Jugendherberge / in / d- / Schweiz / wo / ich / in / ein / altmodisch / Bett / schlafen (*perfect tense*)

7. um / ein / lang, / gesund / Leben / haben, / sollen / jed- / Mensch / aktiv / bleiben

8. bei / dies- / schön / Wetter / wir / wollen / zusammen / zum / neu / Tennisplatz / gehen

9. ich / haben / ein / gut / Gefühl, / wenn / ich / mein- / schmutzig / alt / Dosen / zum / Recycling / schleppen

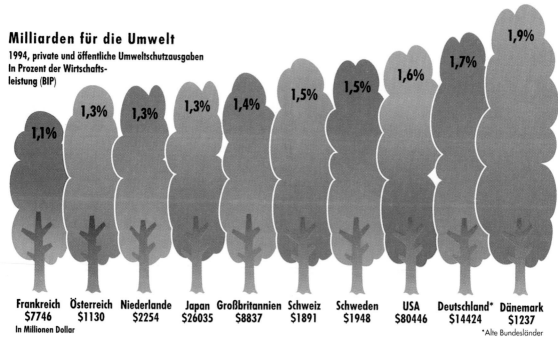

Milliarden für die Umwelt

1994, private und öffentliche Umweltschutzausgaben
In Prozent der Wirtschaftsleistung (BIP)

Land	Wert
Frankreich $7746	1,1%
Österreich $1130	1,3%
Niederlande $2254	1,3%
Japan $26035	1,3%
Großbritannien $8837	1,4%
Schweiz $1891	1,5%
Schweden $1948	1,5%
USA $80446	1,6%
Deutschland* $14424	1,7%
Dänemark $1237	1,9%

In Millionen Dollar

*Alte Bundesländer

Quelle: Institut der deutschen Wirtschaft (iw)

I Wie sagt man das auf deutsch?

1. What's the date today?
2. It's April 5th. Why do you ask?
3. My old friend Markus has a birthday today, and I haven't called him up yet.

4. Can you recommend a good restaurant to me?
5. Do you like to eat French food?
6. Of course. Do you know a good French restaurant?
7. Yes. My favorite restaurant is in the old part of town (**Altstadt**).

8. Are you throwing these old bottles away, Frau Schuhmacher?
9. Yes, I don't have time to carry them to the cellar.
10. May I have them? I'm collecting bottles to earn money.

BITTE VERLASSEN SIE DIESEN PLANETEN SO, WIE SIE IHN VORZUFINDEN WÜNSCHEN!

Es geht auch **OHNE PVC**

PVC = Polyvinylchlorid.

Seid ihr schlaue Umweltfüchse?

Der „Bund für Umwelt und Naturschutz Deutschland" ist eine Lobby von umweltfreundlichen Menschen. In einer Broschüre geben sie Tips zum Schutz (*protection*) der Umwelt.

Umweltfüchse wissen, . . .

- daß Wasser ein Lebensmittel ist.
- daß jeder Deutsche pro Tag zirka 150 Liter Trinkwasser benutzt.

Schlaue Umweltfüchse . . .

- werfen keine Medikamente in die Toilette, sondern bringen sie zur Sammelstelle für Giftmüll.
- duschen lieber, als ein Vollbad zu nehmen, weil sie beim Duschen nur 50 bis 100 Liter Wasser benutzen, statt 200 Liter beim Baden.

Umweltfüchse wissen, . . .

- daß die Bundesrepublik jedes Jahr einen Müllberg produziert, der so groß wie die Zugspitze ist.
- daß nur 11 Prozent dieses Mülls echter Müll sind. 98 Prozent wäre recyclebar.

Schlaue Umweltfüchse . . .

- kaufen Recyclingprodukte, z.B. Umweltschutzpapier.
- sortieren ihren Müll und bringen Glasflaschen, Metall und Papier zu Containern oder direkt zum Recycling.

Recyclingcontainer. (Garmisch-Partenkirchen, Bayern)

UMWELTTIPS
für jeden Tag
Haus · Garten · Verkehr

Bund für
Umwelt und
Naturschutz
Deutschland
e. V.

BUND

Deutschland im 20. Jahrhundert

Communicative Goals

- Narrating events in the past
- Describing objects
- Telling how long ago something happened
- Telling how long something lasted

Cultural Goal

- Learning about the Weimar Republic

Lab Manual Kap. 10, Dialoge, Fragen, Hören Sie gut zu!

Damals

Zwei Senioren sitzen nachmittags auf einer Bank.

HERR ZIEGLER: Wie lange wohnen Sie schon hier, Frau Planck?

FRAU PLANCK: Seit letztem Jahr. Vorher habe ich in Mainz gewohnt.

HERR ZIEGLER: Ach, das wußte ich ja gar nicht. Als ich ein Kind war, habe ich immer den ganzen Sommer dort bei meinen Großeltern verbracht.

FRAU PLANCK: Damals vor dem Krieg war die Stadt natürlich ganz anders.

Was ist denn los?

The tag question . . . **oder?** (here = *Did you?*) can follow either positive or negative statements. **Nicht wahr?** (p. 87) follows positive statements only.

JÜRGEN: Heinz, was ist denn los? Du siehst so besorgt aus.

HEINZ: Ach, Barbara hat mir vor zwei Wochen ihren neuen Kassettenrecorder geliehen . . .

JÜRGEN: Na und? Du hast ihn doch nicht verloren, oder?

HEINZ: Keine Ahnung. Ich hatte ihn in meiner Tasche, aber vor zehn Minuten konnte ich ihn dann plötzlich nicht mehr finden.

JÜRGEN: So ein Mist! Meinst du, jemand hat ihn dir geklaut?

HEINZ: Nee, denn mein Geldbeutel fehlt nicht.

Schlimme Zeiten

Als Hausaufgabe muß Steffi (10 Jahre alt) ihre Oma interviewen.

STEFFI: Oma, für die Schule sollen wir unsere Großeltern über die Kriegszeit interviewen.

OMA: Nun, was willst du denn wissen, Steffi?

STEFFI: Also . . . wann bist du eigentlich geboren?

Remember: English *in 1935* = **1935** (no *in*) or **im Jahre 1935**.

OMA: 1935. Als der Krieg anfing, war ich noch ein kleines Mädchen.

STEFFI: Erzähl mir bitte, wie es euch damals ging.

Note the restricted meaning of **fallen** in this context: *to die in combat*. Proverb: **Generale siegen, Soldaten fallen** (siegen = *to be victorious*).

OMA: Gott sei Dank lebten wir auf dem Land, und zuerst ging es uns relativ gut, obwohl wir nicht reich waren.

STEFFI: Was ist dann passiert?

OMA: Das dauerte nur bis 1943. Dann ist mein Bruder in Rußland gefallen, und ein Jahr später starb meine Mutter.

Note on Usage: *doch*

In **Kapitel 4**, you learned that **doch** can soften a command to a suggestion. In a statement, **doch** adds emphasis in the sense of *surely*, *really*. In the second dialogue, Jürgen fears the worst and says to Heinz:

Du hast ihn **doch** nicht verloren, oder?

(Surely) you haven't lost it, have you?

Back Then

Two senior citizens are sitting on a bench in the afternoon.

Z.: How long have you lived here, Mrs. Planck?

P.: Since last year. Before that, I lived in Mainz.

Z.: Oh, I didn't know that. When I was a child, I always spent the whole summer there with my grandparents.

P.: Of course back then before the war the city was very different.

What's wrong?

J.: Heinz, what's wrong? You look so worried.

H.: Oh, Barbara loaned me her new cassette player two weeks ago . . .

J.: So? You haven't lost it, have you?

H.: No idea. I had it in my bag, but then ten minutes ago I suddenly couldn't find it.

J.: What a drag! You think somebody ripped it off?

H.: Nope, because my wallet's not missing.

Tough Times

As a homework assignment, Steffi (age 10) has to interview her grandmother.

S.: Grandma, for school we're supposed to interview our grandparents about the war years.

O.: Well, what do you want to know, Steffi?

S.: Let's see . . . when were you born, anyway?

O.: In 1935. When the war began I was still a little girl.

S.: Please tell me what it was like for you back then.

O.: Thank goodness we lived in the country, and at first things were relatively good, although we weren't rich.

S.: What happened then?

O.: That lasted only until 1943. Then my brother was killed in action in Russia and my mother died a year later.

Wortschatz 1

Verben

dauern to last; to take (time)

fallen (fällt), fiel, ist gefallen to fall; to die in battle

fehlen to be missing; to be absent

interviewen, hat interviewt to interview

leihen, lieh, hat geliehen to lend, loan; to borrow

passieren, passierte, ist passiert to happen

stehlen (stiehlt), stahl, hat gestohlen to steal

verlieren, verlor, hat verloren to lose

Substantive

der **Geldbeutel**, - wallet, change purse

der **Kassettenrecorder**, - cassette player

der **Monat**, -e month

der **Nachmittag**, -e afternoon

  am Nachmittag in the afternoon

der **Senior**, -en, -en senior citizen

die **Bank**, ̈-e bench

Adjektive und Adverbien

besorgt worried, concerned

damals at that time, back then

letzt- last

plötzlich sudden(ly)

reich rich

vorher before that, previously

Andere Vokabeln

als (*sub. conj.*) when, as

doch (*flavoring particle, see p. 281*)

nachdem (*sub. conj.*) after

nun now; well; well now

Nützliche Ausdrücke

(Ich habe) keine Ahnung. (I have) no idea.

den ganzen Sommer (Tag, Nachmittag usw.) all summer (day, afternoon, etc.)

Na und? And so? So what?

So ein Mist! (*crude, colloq.*) What a drag!; What a lot of bull!

Wann sind Sie geboren? When were you born?

Gegensätze

besorgt ≠ **unbesorgt** concerned ≠ carefree

reich ≠ **arm** rich ≠ poor

vorher ≠ **nachher** before that ≠ after that

Mit anderen Worten

klauen (*colloq.*) = **stehlen**

Variationen

A Persönliche Fragen

1. Heinz sieht besorgt aus, weil er etwas verloren hat. Haben Sie je etwas verloren? Was?
2. Was machen Sie, wenn Sie etwas nicht finden können?
3. Würden Sie jemand Ihren Kassettenrecorder leihen? Warum oder warum nicht?
4. Wissen Sie, wann und wo Ihre Eltern geboren sind? Ihre Großeltern?
5. Wie lange wohnen Sie schon in dieser Stadt?
6. Herr Ziegler hat als Kind seine Sommerferien bei seinen Großeltern verbracht. Was haben Sie als Kind im Sommer gemacht?

Describing objects is a communicative goal.

B Partnerarbeit: Fundbüro *(Lost and found)*

Sie gehen zum Fundbüro, weil Sie etwas verloren haben. Unten ist eine Liste von Dingen im Fundbüro. Sagen Sie, was Sie verloren haben. Dann beschreiben Sie es.

> BEISPIEL: A: Was haben Sie verloren?
> B: Ich habe meine Kamera verloren.
> A: Können Sie sie beschreiben?
> B: Es war eine _____ Kamera.

Fahrrad	Koffer	Pulli
Kassettenrecorder	Tasche	Turnschuhe
Jacke	Wörterbuch	Geldbeutel

C Übung: Was ist passiert?

Gestern war sehr viel los. Sagen Sie, was passiert ist.

> BEISPIEL: Können Sie uns sagen, was gestern passiert ist?
> Ja, gestern . . .

D Übung: Den ganzen Tag

How long did you do certain things? Answer that you did them all morning, all day, all week, all semester, and so on.

> BEISPIEL: Wie lange sind Sie in Europa gewesen?
> Ich war *den ganzen Sommer* da.

1. Wie lange haben Sie gestern Tennis gespielt?
2. Wie lange waren Sie in der Bibliothek?
3. Wie lange waren Sie mit Ihren Freunden zusammen?
4. Wie lange sind Sie im Bett geblieben?
5. Wie lange haben Sie an Ihrem Referat gearbeitet?

Bertolt Brecht fled Germany in 1933 to settle first in France, then in Scandinavia. This poem, written in Finland during World War II, is the sixth of the short cycle "1940." It reflects events of that year.

Mein junger Sohn fragt mich

Mein junger Sohn fragt mich: Soll ich
    Mathematik lernen?
Wozu,° möchte ich sagen. Daß zwei   *what for?*
    Stück Brot mehr ist als eines
Das wirst du auch so merken.°   **Das . . .** = you'll notice that anyway
Mein junger Sohn fragt mich: soll
    ich Französisch lernen?
Wozu, möchte ich sagen. Dieses Reich
    geht unter.° Und   **Reich . . .** = empire will collapse
Reibe° du nur mit der Hand den Bauch°   rub / belly
    und stöhne°   groan
Und man wird dich schon verstehen.
Mein junger Sohn fragt mich: Soll
    ich Geschichte lernen?
Wozu, möchte ich sagen. Lerne du nur
    deinen Kopf in die Erde stecken°   **deinen . . .** = to stick your head in the
Da wirst du vielleicht übrig bleiben.°   sand
                                 wirst . . . = will survive

Ja, lerne Mathematik, sage ich
Lerne Französisch, lerne Geschichte!

              Bertolt Brecht (1898–1956)

>Der Klassiker der Vernunft‹

Bertolt Brecht
Große kommentierte Berliner und
Frankfurter Ausgabe in 30 Bänden
Suhrkamp

Simple Past Tense

Narrating events in the past is a communicative goal.

The simple past tense is used in written German to narrate a series of events in the past. Most literary texts are written in the simple past. In spoken German, however, the *perfect* tense is more commonly used to relate past events. Exceptions are **sein, haben,** and the modal verbs, which are used most frequently with the simple past in both conversation and writing. You learned the simple past tense of **sein** in **Kapitel 6.**

Weak verbs and strong verbs form the simple past tense in different ways. About 90 percent of German verbs are weak, but the strong verbs introduced in *Neue Horizonte* occur very frequently.

Simple Past of Weak Verbs

The marker for the simple past of weak verbs is **-te.** Weak verbs form the simple past by adding endings to the verb stem as follows:

First- and third-person singular forms are identical: **ich wohnte, er wohnte.**	ich wohn- **te** *I lived*	wir wohn- **ten** *we lived*
	du wohn- **test** *you lived*	ihr wohn- **tet** *you lived*
	er/es/sie wohn- **te** *he/it/she lived*	sie, Sie wohn- **ten** *they, you lived*

Verbs whose stems end in **-d** or **-t** add **-e-** between the stem and these endings:

ich arbeit- **ete** *I worked*	wir arbeit- **eten** *we worked*
du arbeit- **etest** *you worked*	ihr arbeit- **etet** *you worked*
er/es/sie arbeit- **ete** *he/it/she worked*	sie, Sie arbeit- **eten** *they, you worked*

For weak verbs, the only form you need to know to generate all other possible forms is the infinitive: **wohnen, wohnte, hat gewohnt; arbeiten, arbeitete, hat gearbeitet.**

Lab Manual Kap. 10, Var. zur Üb. 1, 2, 4–6.

Workbook Kap. 10, A–E.

In short narratives like this, German uses the simple past rather than the perfect.

1 Übung: Doras Einkaufstag

Here is a present-tense narrative of Dora's day in town. Retell it in the simple past tense.

Dora **braucht** Lebensmittel. Sie **wartet** bis zehn Uhr, dann **kauft** sie in einer kleinen Bäckerei ein. Sie **bezahlt** ihre Brötchen und **dankt** der Verkäuferin. Draußen **schneit** es, und sie **hört** Musik auf der Straße. Sie **sucht** ein Restaurant. Also **fragt** sie zwei Studenten. Die Studenten **zeigen** ihr ein gutes Restaurant gleich in der Nähe. Dort **bestellt** sie etwas zu essen und eine Tasse Kaffee. Es **schmeckt** ihr sehr gut, aber die Menschen am nächsten Tisch **quatschen** zu laut, und das **ärgert** sie ein bißchen.

Simple Past of Strong Verbs

Page 287 lists the 50 strong verbs introduced so far. The new simple past tense forms are boldfaced. Give yourself plenty of time to learn these and practice them aloud with a friend.

Strong verbs do *not* have the marker **-te**. Instead, the verb stem is changed. The changed stem is called the *simple past stem*, e.g., nehmen, **nahm**, hat genommen. This new stem takes the following personal endings in the simple past tense:

ich	nahm	*I took*	wir	nahm-**en**	*we took*
du	nahm-**st**	*you took*	ihr	nahm-**t**	*you took*
er/es/sie	nahm	*he/it/she took*	sie, Sie	nahm-**en**	*they, you took*

Note that the **ich-** and the **er/es/sie-**forms of strong verbs have *no* endings in the simple past: **ich nahm, er/es/sie nahm.**

Principal Parts of Strong Verbs

The simple past stem is one of the *principal parts* of a strong German verb. The principal parts are the three (or sometimes four) forms you must know in order to generate all other forms of a strong verb. You have now learned all of them.

infinitive	*3rd-person sing. present*	*simple past stem*	*auxiliary + past participle*
nehmen	**(nimmt)**	**nahm**	**hat genommen**

The table on p. 287 contains the principal parts of all the strong verbs you have learned so far. As an aid to memorization, they have been arranged into groups according to the way their stem-vowels change in the past tenses. Memorize their simple past stems and review your knowledge of the other principal parts. Verbs formed by adding prefixes to these stems are not included in the table, e.g., **abfahren, aufstehen, beschreiben, verstehen.**

Wahlplakat der Grünen, Rheinland - Pfalz.

Principal Parts of Strong Verbs

Infinitive	3rd-sing. pres.	Simple past	Perfect	English
anfangen	fängt an	**fing an**	hat angefangen	*to begin*
fallen	fällt	**fiel**	ist gefallen	*to fall; to die in battle*
halten	hält	**hielt**	hat gehalten	*to hold; to stop*
schlafen	schläft	**schlief**	hat geschlafen	*to sleep*
verlassen	verläßt	**verließ**	hat verlassen	*to leave*
einladen	lädt ein	**lud ein**	hat eingeladen	*to invite*
fahren	fährt	**fuhr**	ist gefahren	*to drive*
tragen	trägt	**trug**	hat getragen	*to carry; to wear*
essen	ißt	**aß**	hat gegessen	*to eat*
geben	gibt	**gab**	hat gegeben	*to give*
lesen	liest	**las**	hat gelesen	*to read*
sehen	sieht	**sah**	hat gesehen	*to see*
vergessen	vergißt	**vergaß**	hat vergessen	*to forget*
empfehlen	empfiehlt	**empfahl**	hat empfohlen	*to recommend*
helfen	hilft	**half**	hat geholfen	*to help*
nehmen	nimmt	**nahm**	hat genommen	*to take*
sprechen	spricht	**sprach**	hat gesprochen	*to speak*
stehlen	stiehlt	**stahl**	hat gestohlen	*to steal*
sterben	stirbt	**starb**	ist gestorben	*to die*
treffen	trifft	**traf**	hat getroffen	*to meet*
werfen	wirft	**warf**	hat geworfen	*to throw*
bleiben		**blieb**	ist geblieben	*to stay*
entscheiden		**entschied**	hat entschieden	*to decide*
leihen		**lieh**	hat geliehen	*to lend*
scheinen		**schien**	hat geschienen	*to shine; to seem*
schreiben		**schrieb**	hat geschrieben	*to write*
steigen		**stieg**	ist gestiegen	*to climb*
treiben		**trieb**	hat getrieben	*to drive, propel*
beginnen		**begann**	hat begonnen	*to begin*
finden		**fand**	hat gefunden	*to find*
klingen		**klang**	hat geklungen	*to sound*
schwimmen		**schwamm**	ist geschwommen	*to swim*
singen		**sang**	hat gesungen	*to sing*
trinken		**trank**	hat getrunken	*to drink*
liegen		**lag**	hat gelegen	*to lie*
sitzen		**saß**	hat gesessen	*to sit*
fliegen		**flog**	ist geflogen	*to fly*
fließen		**floß**	ist geflossen	*to flow*
schließen		**schloß**	hat geschlossen	*to close*
verlieren		**verlor**	hat verloren	*to lose*
ziehen		**zog**	hat/ist gezogen	*to pull; to move*
anrufen		**rief an**	hat angerufen	*to call up*
gehen		**ging**	ist gegangen	*to go*
hängen		**hing**	hat gehangen	*to be hanging*
heißen		**hieß**	hat geheißen	*to be called*
kommen		**kam**	ist gekommen	*to come*
laufen	läuft	**lief**	ist gelaufen	*to run*
sein	ist	**war**	ist gewesen	*to be*
stehen		**stand**	hat gestanden	*to stand*
tun		**tat**	hat getan	*to do*

Change the following sentences to the simple past tense.

In sentence 3, the infinitive construction **um fit zu bleiben** does not change tense.

1. Mir gefällt sein neues Fahrrad.
2. Barbara ruft um halb fünf an.
3. Sie schwimmt das ganze Jahr, um fit zu bleiben.
4. Stefan findet seinen Geldbeutel nicht.
5. Jede Woche schreibt sie uns eine Postkarte.
6. Der Film beginnt um 20.30 Uhr.
7. Er hilft mir gern mit meinen Hausaufgaben.
8. Sie heißt Dora Schilling.
9. Um acht gehen die Senioren miteinander essen.
10. Er liegt immer gern im Bett und liest die Zeitung.
11. Ich finde es komisch, daß er nichts trinkt.
12. Am Montag kommt Bert zurück.
13. Sie kommt um 10 Uhr an und bleibt den ganzen Tag da.
14. Sie sieht ihren Freund und läuft schnell zu ihm.

3 Übung: Ein Brief

Complete this letter by filling in the verbs in the simple past tense. Some of the verbs are strong and some are weak.

Liebe Martine,

weißt du, was dem armen Ulrich vorgestern passiert ist? Er hat mich gestern angerufen und _____ (erzählen) es mir. Er _____ (kennenlernen) im Park eine sympathische junge Studentin _____ . Sie _____ (aussehen) ganz elegant und reich _____ . Zusammen _____ (sitzen) sie auf einer Bank und _____ (sprechen) über das Studium. Ulrich _____ (tragen) eine Jacke, aber weil es sehr heiß war, _____ (legen) er sie auf die Bank. Alles _____ (scheinen) gut zu gehen, und Ulrich _____ (einladen) sie in ein Konzert _____ . Sie _____ (sagen) ja und _____ (geben) ihm ihre Adresse und Telefonnummer. Nach einer Stunde _____ (stehen) die Studentin auf und _____ (gehen) in die Bibliothek zurück. Am Abend _____ (kommen) er nach Hause und _____ (suchen) seinen Hausschlüssel in der Tasche seiner Jacke. Aber dort _____ (finden) er keinen Schlüssel, und auch sein Geld _____ (sein) weg. Er _____ (rufen) die Nummer der Studentin an, aber sie _____ (wohnen) gar nicht da. So ein Mist, nicht?

Jetzt muß ich gehen. Viele Grüße,

Deine

Annelies

Simple Past of Modal Verbs

The modal verbs form their simple past with the **-te** marker, like the weak verbs. But those modals that have an umlaut in the infinitive *drop* it in the past tense.

müssen, **mußte**					
ich	mußte	*I had to*	wir	mußten	*we had to*
du	mußtest	*you had to*	ihr	mußtet	*you had to*
er/es/sie	mußte	*he/it/she had to*	sie, Sie	mußten	*they, you had to*

Similarly:

dürfen	ich **durfte**	*I was allowed to*
können	ich **konnte**	*I was able to*
mögen	ich **mochte**	*I liked*
sollen	ich **sollte**	*I was supposed to*
wollen	ich **wollte**	*I wanted to*

*Note that **mögen** drops the umlaut and also has a consonant change in the simple past.*

4 Übung

1. Sagen Sie, was Sie gestern machen mußten.

   BEISPIEL: Ich mußte gestern zwei Bücher lesen.

2. Jetzt sagen Sie, was Sie und Ihre Freunde gestern machen wollten.

   BEISPIEL: Wir wollten gestern skifahren gehen.

3. Was durften Sie als Kind nicht machen?

   BEISPIEL: Ich durfte nie allein schwimmen gehen.

Simple Past of Mixed Verbs

The mixed verbs (see p. 167) use the **-te** marker for the simple past but attach it to the *changed* stem, which you have already learned for the past participles:

wissen, **wußte**, hat gewußt					
ich	wußte	*I knew*	wir	wußten	*we knew*
du	wußtest	*you knew*	ihr	wußtet	*you knew*
er/es/sie	wußte	*he, / it, / she knew*	sie, Sie	wußten	*they, you knew*

*Remember that **wissen** is irregular in the present-tense singular: ich **weiß**, du **weißt**, er **weiß**.*

Similarly:

bringen, **brachte**, hat gebracht
kennen, **kannte**, hat gekannt

Simple Past of *haben and* werden

Only **haben** and **werden** are irregular in the simple past tense.

haben, **hatte**, hat gehabt				
ich	hatte	*I had*	wir hatten	*we had*
du	hattest	*you had*	ihr hattet	*you had*
er	hatte	*he had*	sie, Sie hatten	*they, you had*

werden, **wurde**, ist geworden				
ich	wurde	*I became*	wir wurden	*we became*
du	wurdest	*you became*	ihr wurdet	*you became*
sie	wurde	*she became*	sie, Sie wurden	*they, you became*

5 Übung

Retell the following short narrative in the simple past.

Andreas **kennt** Mainz sehr gut, weil seine Großeltern dort **wohnen.** Als er 11 Jahre alt **wird, darf** er allein mit dem Zug nach Mainz fahren. Er **verbringt** jeden Sommer dort. Die Großeltern **wissen** alles über die Stadt, denn sie **leben** seit Jahren in Mainz. Er **bringt** ihnen immer ein Geschenk mit, und das **haben** sie immer gern.

Use of the Simple Past Tense

In English there is a difference in *meaning* between past tense and perfect tense. Compare these sentences:

> *I saw Marion in the restaurant.*
> *I have seen Marion in the restaurant.*

I saw Marion refers to a unique event in the past, while *I have seen Marion* implies that Marion has been in the restaurant on several occasions and may be there again.

In German, there is *no* difference in meaning between simple past and perfect tense. They both simply convey that the action is in the past:

> Ich **sah** Marion im Restaurant.
> Ich **habe** Marion im
>   Restaurant **gesehen.**   *I saw Marion in the restaurant.*

The difference between German simple past and perfect tense is mainly one of *usage:* they are used under different circumstances. As you have already learned, the perfect tense is the *conversational past*, used in conversation to refer to events in the past. The simple past tense is regularly used in conversation only with frequently occurring verbs such as **sein, haben,** and the modal verbs.

A: Wo **warst** du denn gestern? *Where were you yesterday? I*
   Ich habe auf dich gewartet.   *waited for you.*
B: Ich **hatte** kein Geld mehr   *I didn't have any more money*
   und **mußte** nach Hause.   *and had to go home.*

The primary use of simple past tense is in *written* German (in letters, newspaper reports, short stories, novels, etc.) to narrate a series of events in the past. Here, for example, is the beginning of the fairy tale „Hänsel und Gretel":

Es war einmal . . . is the formulaic beginning for most German fairy tales.

Es **war** einmal ein armer   *Once upon a time there was a*
   Holzhacker. Er **wohnte** mit   *poor woodcutter. He lived at*
   seinen zwei Kindern vor   *the edge of a forest with his*
   einem Wald. Sie **hießen**   *two children. Their names*
   Hänsel und Gretel. Sie   *were Hansel and Gretel. They*
   hatten wenig zu essen, und   *had little to eat and their*
   ihre Stiefmutter **wollte** sie   *stepmother wanted to get rid of*
   los werden.   *them.*

Simple Past after the Conjunction *als*

Clauses introduced by the subordinating conjunction **als** (*when* or *as* referring to a point or stretch of time in the past) require the simple past tense.

Hans hat uns oft besucht, **als**   *Hans often visited us when he*
   er in New York **wohnte**.   *lived in New York.*

Als ich meinen Geldbeutel   *When I looked for my wallet I*
   suchte, konnte ich ihn   *couldn't find it.*
   nicht finden.

6 Übung: Es war schon spät

Sagen Sie, daß es schon spät war, als etwas passierte.

BEISPIEL: Das Konzert fing an.
   Es war schon spät, als das Konzert anfing.

1. Ich fand den Laden.   4. Sie fuhr ab.
2. Er ging endlich.   5. Das Telefon klingelte.
3. Wir kamen in München an.   6. Meine Freunde kamen vorbei.

7 Partnerarbeit: Wie geht's weiter?

Take turns completing the following sentences with an **als**-clause.

1. Jürgen konnte seinen Schlüssel nicht finden, als . . .
2. Herr Ziegler hat jeden Sommer seine Großeltern besucht, als . . .
3. Es ging der Großmutter nicht gut, als . . .
4. Ute lief schnell ins Haus, als . . .
5. Alle Schüler lachten, als . . .

Now restate the sentences, beginning with your **als**-clause.

BEISPIEL: *Als* Jürgen nach Hause kam, konnte er seinen
   Schlüssel nicht finden.

Equivalents for *when:* als, wenn, wann

It is important to distinguish among three German subordinating conjunctions, each of which may be translated by English *when.*

- **als** = *when* (in the past); *as*   **Als** refers to an event or state *in the past* and requires the simple past tense.

Als wir in Wien waren, haben wir Andreas besucht.	*When we were in Vienna, we visited Andreas.*

- **wenn** = *when/if; whenever*   **Wenn** means *when* in reference to an event *in the present or future.* Since it can also mean *if,* clauses with **wenn** can be ambiguous.

Wenn wir in Wien sind, besuchen wir Andreas.	*When (If) we're in Vienna, we'll visit Andreas.*

  Wenn also means *whenever* in reference to repeated action in the past or present. To avoid confusion between *whenever* and *if,* add the adverb **immer** if you mean *whenever.*

Wenn Hans nach Wien kommt, geht er **immer** ins Kaffeehaus.	*Whenever Hans comes to Vienna, he always goes to a coffee house.*

  Note carefully the difference in meaning between **als** and **wenn** used with simple past tense.

Als sie das sagte, wurde er rot.	*When she said that, he turned red.*

Wenn sie das sagte, wurde er immer rot.	*Whenever she said that, he always turned red.*

- **Wann** = *when, at what time*   **Wann** is always a question word, used both in direct questions and in indirect questions:

  Wann ist das passiert?
  When did that happen?

  Ich weiß nicht, **wann** das passiert ist.
  I don't know when that happened.

> **Rule of thumb:** For cases in which English *when = at what time,* use German **wann.** If *when = if* or *whenever,* use **wenn.**

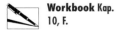

Workbook Kap. 10, F.

8 Übung: Als, wenn oder wann? (Mit offenen Büchern)

1. Mutti, _____ darf ich spielen?
   _____ du das Altglas in den Keller getragen hast.

2. _____ fängt das Konzert an?
   Ich weiß nicht, _____ es anfängt.
   Karl kann es uns sagen, _____ er zurückkommt.
   Wir haben viele Konzerte gehört, _____ wir Berlin besuchten.
   Das möchte ich auch tun, _____ ich nächstes Jahr in Berlin bin.

Die ersten freien Wahlen in der
ehemaligen DDR.

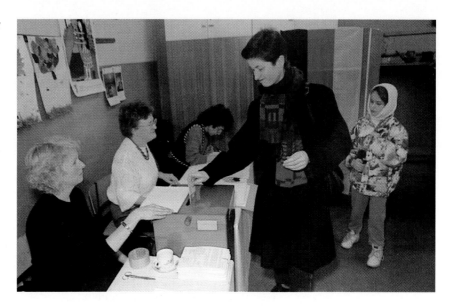

3. _____ ich gestern an der Uni war, habe ich Angelika getroffen. Sie hat
gesagt, sie kommt heute abend mit.
Gut! _____ Angelika mitkommt, macht es mehr Spaß.
Sag mir bitte noch einmal, _____ die Party beginnt.

9 Partnerarbeit: Wie sagt man das auf deutsch?

Sagen Sie diese Dialoge auf deutsch.

1. A: When did you meet Claudia?
   B: I met her when I was studying in Vienna. Whenever I'm there, I
   always write her a postcard.
   A: I don't know when I'll go to Vienna again.

2. A: When I was young I hitchhiked a lot.
   B: When I go to Europe, I'll do that too.
   A: When are you going to Europe?
   B: When I have enough money.

Past Perfect Tense

The past perfect tense is used for an event in the past that *preceded* another event in the past.

> Als Hans aufstand, **hatte** Ulla   *When Hans got up, Ulla **had***
> schon **gefrühstückt.**   *already **eaten breakfast**.*

The form of the past perfect tense is parallel to that of the perfect tense, but the auxiliary verb (**haben** or **sein**) is in the *past tense* instead of the present (**haben** → **hatte, sein** → **war**).

ich **hatte gegessen**	*I had eaten*
du **hattest gegessen**	*you had eaten*
er **hatte gegessen**	*he had eaten*
wir **hatten gegessen**	*we had eaten*
ihr **hattet gegessen**	*you had eaten*
sie **hatten gegessen**	*they had eaten*
ich **war aufgestanden**	*I had gotten up*
du **warst aufgestanden**	*you had gotten up*
sie **war aufgestanden**	*she had gotten up*
wir **waren aufgestanden**	*we had gotten up*
ihr **wart aufgestanden**	*you had gotten up*
sie **waren aufgestanden**	*they had gotten up*

Look at the following timetable of morning events at Hans and Ulla's house, then at how they are combined in the sentences that follow.

> 8.00 Uhr: Ulla hat gefrühstückt.
> 9.00 Uhr: Hans ist aufgestanden.
> 10.00 Uhr: Ulla ist zur Uni gegangen.
> 11.00 Uhr: Hans hat gefrühstückt.

> **event 1 (8.00 Uhr)   event 2 (9.00 Uhr)**

Ulla **hatte** schon **gefrühstückt,**   als Hans aufstand.
Ulla had already eaten,   *when Hans got up.*

The order of the clauses may of course be reversed:

> **event 2 (9.00 Uhr)   event 1 (8.00 Uhr)**

Als Hans aufstand,   **hatte** Ulla schon **gefrühstückt.**
When Hans got up,   *Ulla had already eaten.*

The subordinating conjunction **nachdem** (*after*) is often used with the past perfect tense.

> **Nachdem** Ulla gefrühstückt   *After Ulla had eaten breakfast,*
> hatte, ging sie zur Uni.   *she went to the university.*

10 Übung: Als Ulla nach Hause kam

Sie spielen die Rolle von Hans. Sie sind heute vor Ulla nach Hause gekommen und hatten viel Zeit, eine Menge zu machen. Sagen Sie, was Sie schon gemacht hatten, als Ulla um 23.00 Uhr endlich nach Hause kam.

> BEISPIEL: Lebensmittel eingekauft
> Als Ulla nach Hause kam, hatte ich schon
> Lebensmittel eingekauft.

1. nach Hause gekommen
2. Kartoffeln gekocht
3. alles sauber gemacht
4. die Kinder abgeholt
5. einkaufen gegangen
6. den Kindern das Essen gegeben

Distinguish between the preposition **nach** (+ noun in the dative) and the conjunction **nachdem** (+ clause with the verb in final position). Both are translated *after*. **Nach der Deutschstunde . . .** (*after German class*); **Nachdem wir das Essen bestellt hatten . . .** (*After we had ordered the meal . . .*).

Lab Manual Kap. 10, Var. zur Üb. 10.

Workbook Kap. 10, G.

7. die Zeitung gelesen
8. ein Glas Wein getrunken
9. die Kinder ins Bett gebracht
10. ein paar Briefe geschrieben
11. meine Kusine angerufen
12. ins Bett gegangen

Telling how long ago something happened is a communicative goal.

More Time Expressions

vor + dative = ago

The preposition **vor** is used with various time expressions in the dative case to mean *ago*.

vor fünf Minuten	*five minutes ago*
vor einer Stunde	*an hour ago*
vor drei Tagen	*three days ago*
vor vielen Wochen	*many weeks ago*
vor einem Monat	*a month ago*
vor hundert Jahren	*a hundred years ago*

11 Übung: Wann war das?

Sagen Sie auf deutsch, wann etwas passiert ist.

BEISPIEL: Wann ist das passiert?
(*two days ago*): Vor zwei Tagen.

1. a minute ago
2. an hour ago
3. three years ago
4. five months ago
5. ten days ago
6. a couple of weeks ago

[handwritten annotations: Vor fünf Monate ich über; Vor zehn Tagen; Vor ein paar Woche]

12 Partnerarbeit: Wann hast du zuletzt . . . gemacht?

Ask each other when you last did these things.

BEISPIEL: A: Wann hast du zuletzt deine Großeltern besucht?
B: Ich habe sie vor drei Monaten besucht.

deine Oma besuchen	in ein neues Haus umziehen
Geld ausgeben	Sport treiben
einen Stadtbummel machen	etwas für die Umwelt tun
einen langen Roman lesen	einen Brief bekommen

Duration Ending in the Past

German and English differ in the way they show an action ending in the past versus an action continuing into the present. English makes this distinction by using different verb tenses:

We ***lived*** in Berlin *for three years.*	*Past tense* for a state ending in the past (i.e., we don't live there any more).
We ***have lived*** in Berlin *for three years.*	*Perfect tense* for a state continuing at the moment of speaking (i.e., we're *still* living there).

In German, however, both *the simple past and the perfect tense* are used
for a state ending in the past.

Wir **wohnten** drei Jahre in Berlin.	We *lived* in Berlin
Wir **haben** drei Jahre in Berlin **gewohnt.**	for three years.

Duration Beginning in the Past but Continuing in the Present

For a state beginning in the past but continuing at the moment of speaking,
German uses *present tense* and one of these adverbial phrases:

schon (+ accusative)	→	**schon drei Jahre**
seit (+ dative)	→	**seit drei Jahren**

Wir **wohnen schon drei Jahre** in Berlin.	We *have lived* in
Wir **wohnen seit drei Jahren** in Berlin.	Berlin for three years.

Note carefully the difference between verb tenses in the two languages!

Note on Usage: *for a long time*

Notice the different ways to express *for a long time*.

Ich hoffe, du kannst **lange** bleiben.	*I hope you can stay for a long time.* (continuing into the future)
Ich wohne **schon lange** hier.	*I've lived here for a long time.*
Ich wohne **seit langem** hier.	(continuing from the past)

 Lab Manual Kap.
10, Üb. 13.

 Workbook Kap.
10, H.

13 Übung: Wie lange schon?

Ihre Professorin möchte wissen, wie lange Sie etwas schon machen. Sagen
Sie, Sie machen es schon zwei Jahre.

> BEISPIEL: Wie lange arbeiten Sie schon hier?
> Ich arbeite schon zwei Jahre hier.

Antworten Sie mit **schon**.

1. Wie lange studieren Sie schon hier?
2. Wie lange lernen Sie schon Deutsch?
3. Wie lange treiben Sie schon Sport?
4. Wie lange wohnen Sie schon im Studentenwohnheim?
5. Wie lange fahren Sie schon Rad?

Antworten Sie mit **seit**.

6. Seit wann kennen Sie mich?
7. Seit wann haben Sie kurze Haare?
8. Seit wann studieren Sie hier?
9. Seit wann sammeln Sie Altglas?
10. Seit wann spielen Sie ein Musikinstrument?

14 Partnerarbeit: Wie sagt man das auf deutsch?

Übersetzen Sie diese Sätze mit Ihrem Partner.

1. We've known him for a year.
2. She's lived here for two weeks.
3. He's been lending me money for a long time.
4. Barbara has already been here five days.
5. She has studied in Halle for two semesters.
6. For ten years there's been an excellent restaurant here.
7. Michael has been interviewing her for three hours.
8. I've been hungry for two days.

15 Partnerarbeit: Wie lange machst du das schon?

Fragen Sie einander, wie lange oder seit wann Sie etwas machen. Unten (*below*) sind einige Ideen, aber Sie können auch Ihre eigenen Fragen stellen.

1. Wie lange studierst du schon hier?
2. Seit wann lernst du Fremdsprachen?
3. Wie lange lernst du schon Deutsch?
4. Seit wann gibt es diese Uni?
5. Wie lange kannst du schon Auto fahren?
6. Seit wann arbeitest du mit dem Computer?
7. Wie lange sind wir heute schon in der Deutschstunde?

Lesestück

Other examples: Katholizismus, Protestantismus, Kapitalismus, Protektionismus, Sozialismus, Anarchismus, Modernismus, Expressionismus, Futurismus.

This is the origin of words like *hamburger, wiener, frankfurter, Budweiser,* and *pilsner* (from *Budweis* and *Pilsen,* German names for the Czech cities **České Budejovice** and **Plzeň**). Two German bakery items: **der Amerikaner** (*round flat cakes with half white and half chocolate frosting*), **der Berliner** (*jelly doughnut*).

Eine Ausstellung historischer Plakate aus der Weimarer Republik

Tips zum Lesen und Lernen

Tips zum Vokabelnlernen

The following reading mentions several concepts such as National Socialism, Communism, and anti-Semitism. English words ending in *-ism* denote a system of belief, a doctrine, or a characteristic. Their German equivalents end in the suffix **-ismus**. These words are all masculine in German and the stress is always on the penultimate syllable (**Optimismus**).

der Antisemitismus	der Kommunismus
der Extremismus	der Optimismus
der Idealismus	der Pessimismus

City Names as Adjectives   The reading also mentions the *Weimar* Republic, the *Versailles* Treaty, and the *New York* Stock Exchange. When the names of cities are used as adjectives in German, they are capitalized and simply add the ending **-er** in all cases: **die Weimarer Republik, der Versailler Vertrag, die New Yorker Börse.**

Leicht zu merken

die **Demokratie**, -n	Demokra<u>tie</u>
demokratisch	
der **Direktor**, -en	
die **Epoche**, -n	E<u>po</u>che
extrem	
die **Form**, -en	
ideologisch	
illegal	<u>il</u>legal
die **Inflation**	<u>In</u>flation
manipulieren	mani<u>pu</u>lieren
die **Methode**, -n	Me<u>tho</u>de
die **Monarchie**, -n	Mon<u>ar</u>chie
die **Opposition**, -en	Oppo<u>si</u>tion
die **Republik**, -en	Repu<u>blik</u>
die **Situation**, -en	Situa<u>tion</u>
symbolisch	
terroristisch	terro<u>ris</u>tisch

Einstieg in den Text

In the following reading, you will encounter quite a bit of factual historical information about an important period in modern German history: the Weimar Republic. Much of the information will probably be new to you, but you already know enough German to be able to understand complex issues.

When reading the text through for the first time, keep the following basic information questions in mind as a guide:

Was war die Weimarer Republik?
Wann war diese historische Epoche?
Wer hat damals eine Rolle gespielt?
Warum war diese Zeit so wichtig?

Before reading, also examine the illustrations that accompany and are referred to in the reading. These convey an impression of the content of the reading and will help you to understand the issues discussed.

Was für Plakate sind das?
Aus welcher Zeit kommen sie?
Was zeigen die Bilder?
Welche Wörter oder Namen können Sie schon verstehen?

Wortschatz 2

Verben
erklären to explain
nennen, nannte, hat genannt
    to name, call
stören to disturb

unterbrechen (unterbricht), unterbrach, hat unterbrochen to interrupt

versuchen to try, attempt
wachsen (wächst), wuchs, ist gewachsen to grow

wählen   to choose; to vote
zählen   to count

Substantive

der **Arm**, -e   arm
der **Schriftsteller**, -   writer (*m.*)
der **Staat**, -en   state
der **Wähler**, -   voter
das **Plakat**, -e   poster
das **Reich**, -e   empire, realm
das **Volk**, ¨er   people, nation,
   folk
die **Arbeitslosigkeit**
   unemployment
die **Ausstellung**, -en
   exhibition
die **Bedeutung**, -en
   meaning, significance

die **Dame**, -n   lady
die **Idee**, -n   idea
die **Schriftstellerin**, -nen
   writer (*f.*)
die **Wahl**, -en   choice;
   election

Idee: die **Idee** is the most general equivalent: **Das ist eine gute Idee.** Ahnung
means *inkling*: **Ich habe keine Ahnung.**

Adjektive und Adverbien

arbeitslos   unemployed
ausländisch   foreign
bekannt   known; well known
hart   hard; tough; harsh
unruhig   restless, uneasy,
   troubled

Andere Vokabeln

bevor (*sub. conj.*)   before

Nützliche Ausdrücke

zu Ende sein   to end, be
   finished, be over
**1918 war der Krieg zu
   Ende.**   The war ended
   in 1918.
eine Frage stellen   to ask a
   question

Fragen takes a direct object of person (**Ich
habe ihn gefragt**).

Gegensätze

bekannt ≠ **unbekannt**
   known ≠ unknown
unruhig ≠ **ruhig**
   restless ≠ calm, peaceful

German equivalents for *people*: **das Volk** (a people defined by a common language and culture: **das deutsche Volk**); **Menschen** (people in general: **die Menschen in dieser Stadt**); **Leute** (more restricted grouping: **die Leute hier im Zimmer**).

Eine Ausstellung historischer Plakate aus der Weimarer Republik

Plakat is the term for informational posters, **Poster** for decorative posters (performers, vacation spots, etc.).

 Lab Manual Kap. 10, Lesestück.

Learning about the Weimar Republic is the cultural goal of this chapter.

Im Hessischen Landesmuseum° gab es vor einiger Zeit° eine Ausstellung politischer Plakate aus der Weimarer Republik (1919–1933). Der Museumsdirektor führte eine Gruppe ausländischer Studenten durch die Ausstellung.

Hessian State Museum / **vor...** = a while ago

5   „Meine Damen und Herren, herzlich willkommen im Landesmuseum! Bevor wir in die Ausstellung gehen, möchte ich Ihnen ein paar Worte über die Geschichte der Weimarer Republik sagen. Vielleicht ist Ihnen diese Epoche schon bekannt, aber wenn Ihnen etwas nicht klar ist, können Sie jederzeit° Fragen stellen—das stört mich gar nicht.

at any time

10   Was war das eigentlich, die Weimarer Republik? So nennen wir den deutschen Staat in der Zeit zwischen dem Ende des Ersten Weltkrieges 1918 und dem Anfang des Dritten Reiches[1] im Januar 1933. Es war Deutschlands erster Versuch,° eine demokratische Staatsform zu entwickeln.° Unsere Plakate zeigen die extremen

attempt

develop

---

[1] **Das Dritte Reich:** The Nazis' own name for their regime (1933–1945). The first empire was the Holy Roman Empire (962–1806). The second empire (**das Deutsche Reich,** 1871–1918), collapsed at the end of the First World War.

15 ideologischen Gegensätze° dieser Epoche. Aber sie zeigen auch, wie
man gegensätzliche° Ideen oft mit ähnlichen Bildern darstellen° kann.“

    Hier unterbrach ein Student mit einer Frage: „Entschuldigung,
aber können Sie uns erklären, warum es die ‚Weimarer‘ Republik
hieß? War Berlin nicht damals die Hauptstadt Deutschlands?“

20   „Sicher. Berlin blieb auch die Hauptstadt, aber die Politiker
kamen 1919 in der Stadt Weimar zusammen, um die neue demokratische Verfassung zu beschließen.° In Berlin war die politische Situation damals sehr unruhig, und außerdem° hatte Weimar wichtige
symbolische Bedeutung als die Stadt, wo die großen Schriftsteller
25 Goethe und Schiller[2] früher gelebt und gearbeitet hatten.

    Die ersten Jahre der Republik waren eine Zeit der Arbeitslosigkeit
und der hohen Inflation. Deutschland hatte den Ersten Weltkrieg verloren, und die Monarchie war zu Ende.[3] Unter dem harten Versailler
Friedensvertrag mußte der neue demokratische Staat 20 Milliarden°
30 Goldmark an die Siegermächte° (besonders an Frankreich) zahlen.
Unser erstes Plakat, aus der Zeit vor 1925, zeigt den deutschen Reichs-
adler° durch den Versailler Vertrag gefesselt.°

    Als die New Yorker Börse° 1929 stürzte,° wurde die Wirtschafts-
krise° in den Industrieländern Europas katastrophal. Man zählte im
35 Februar 1930 schon mehr als° 3,5 Millionen arbeitslose Menschen in
Deutschland.

polarities	
contradictory / represent	
Verfassung... = ratify the constitution	
moreover	
billion	
victors	
imperial eagle / fettered	
stock market / crashed	
economic crisis	
mehr als = more than	

The symbols on the snakes from left to right identify the following parties: the
Social Democrats (SPD), the Nazis (NSDAP), and the Communists (KPD). The
fourth snake behind the others probably represents the right-wing German
National People's Party (DNVP).

---

[2] Johann Wolfgang von Goethe (1749–1832); Friedrich von Schiller (1759–1805).

[3] Kaiser Wilhelm II abdicated in November 1918 and went into exile in the Nether-
lands. The Peace Treaty of Versailles officially ended the First World War in 1919.

SPD poster for the Reichstag election of May 1924 ("The Answer to the Hitler Trial")

After the failed Nazi putsch in Munich in November 1923, Hitler received a light prison sentence of 5 years, and his National Socialist Party was officially banned. The SPD made a weak showing in the election, while both the Communists and the radical Right gained strength.

Diese Wirtschaftskrise brachte die junge deutsche Demokratie in Gefahr, denn schon 1932 waren sieben Millionen Menschen arbeitslos. Es gab damals mehr als dreißig politische Parteien, und besonders
40 die antidemokratischen konnten schnell wachsen. Auf diesem zweiten Plakat sieht man, wie die ‚starke Hand' der katholischen Zentrumspartei[4] die extremen Parteien erwürgt.° In den Wahlen nach 1930   strangles
stieg aber die Macht der Nationalsozialistischen Deutschen Arbeiterpartei (NSDAP)—der Nazis—bis sie die stärkste° im Reichstag[5] wurde.   strongest
45 Ihr Führer Adolf Hitler benutzte den Antisemitismus und Antikommunismus, um die Ängste des Volkes zu manipulieren. Ein Plakat der

---

[4] The conservative Center Party, consisting mainly of Catholic voters.

[5] The name of the German Parliament until 1945, now called **der Bundestag.** The parliament building in Berlin is still called the **Reichstag.**

Deutschland im 20. Jahrhundert

Nazis zeigt den symbolischen ‚starken Mann,' der° Deutschland retten soll. Die Opposition sehen Sie noch auf diesem Plakat von 1931, wo starke Arme versuchen, das Hakenkreuz° der Nazis zu zerreißen.“°

who

swastika / rip apart

Eine Studentin stellte eine Frage: „Ist denn Hitler nicht illegal an die Macht gekommen?“°

an... = came to power

„Eigentlich nicht“, antwortete der Museumsdirektor. „Nachdem die Wähler den Nazis die meisten Stimmen° gegeben hatten, mußte man Hitler zum Reichskanzler ernennen.° Erst als er Kanzler geworden war, konnte er mit terroristischen Methoden die Republik in eine Diktatur verwandeln.° Deutschland ist also ein gutes Beispiel für die Zerstörung einer schwachen Demokratie durch wirtschaftliche Not° und politischen Extremismus.“

(here) votes
zum... = appoint chancellor

in... = transform into a dictatorship
wirtschaftliche Not = economic hardship

Fragen zum Lesestück

1. Warum besuchte die Studentengruppe das Museum?
2. Aus welcher Zeit waren die Plakate dieser Ausstellung?
3. Wer führte die Gruppe durch die Ausstellung?
4. Was für Plakate haben die Studenten im Museum gesehen?
5. Was zeigen die Bilder auf den Plakaten?
6. Warum hieß der deutsche Staat damals die „Weimarer“ Republik?
7. Wie war die Situation in Deutschland nach dem Ersten Weltkrieg? Beschreiben Sie die Probleme.
8. Warum war die junge Demokratie in Gefahr?
9. Wann wurde Hitler Reichskanzler?
10. Wie ist er an die Macht gekommen?

Die Politik

In dem Lesestück haben Sie nicht nur etwas über Geschichte, sondern auch etwas über Politik gelernt. Was hat denn diese politische Diskussion mit unserem Leben zu tun? Wir sind alle politische Menschen, und die Politik spielt eine Rolle in unserem Alltag, ob wir es wollen oder nicht.

Spielen wir jetzt ein bißchen mit der Sprache und den Bildern der Politik. Zuerst einige Wörter (viele sind Ihnen schon bekannt):

Politik also means *policy*:
Außenpolitik (*foreign policy*),
Energiepolitik,
Umweltpolitik usw.

die Freiheit
der Frieden
der Krieg, -e
die Politik
der Politiker/die Politikerin
die Regierung, -en   *government in power,*
                                    administration

der Staat, -en
die Umwelt
das Volk, ¨er
die Wahl, -en
wählen
der Wähler, -

Über Klimaschutz reden viele.
Wir tun etwas.

Gruppenarbeit: Wir sind politisch aktiv (in kleinen Gruppen)

Gründen Sie (*found*) eine neue politische Partei.

Der Name unserer Partei: _____

Unser Parteiprogramm:

    Wir sind für _____ , _____ usw.

    Wir sind gegen _____ , _____ usw.

Wir sehen viele Probleme in der modernen Welt:

_____

Unsere Lösungen sind:

_____

Unsere Parole (*slogan*) für die Wahlen:

_____

Gruppenarbeit

Ihre politische Partei braucht auch ein Symbol für ihr Wahlplakat. Wie Sie gerade gelesen haben, waren Tiere wichtige Symbole auf den Plakaten in der Weimarer Republik. Sie können ein Tier als Symbol Ihrer Partei wählen, denn Tiere können Ideen symbolisieren.

der Adler, -	*eagle*
der Bär, -en, -en	*bear*
der Elefant, -en, -en	*elephant*
der Esel, -	*donkey*
der Fuchs, ̈e	*fox*
der Löwe, -n, -n	*lion*
die Schlange, -n	*snake*
die Taube, -n	*dove*

Gruppenarbeit: Wahlkampagne *(Election campaign)*

Jetzt zeigen Sie den anderen Studenten Ihr Wahlplakat. Erklären Sie, warum man Ihre Partei wählen soll. Die „Wähler" können natürlich Fragen stellen oder kritisieren.

Unser Plakat zeigt . . .

Wählt unsere Partei, weil . . .

Gruppenarbeit: Zur Diskussion

Ist es wichtig für Politiker, die Geschichte ihres Landes zu kennen? Was meinen Sie?

Zum Schluß

Sprechen wir miteinander

Lab Manual Kap. 10, Diktat.

Workbook Kap. 10, Üb. I–K.

A Kettenreaktion: Ich suche . . . (Mit offenen Büchern)

Wählen Sie ein Adjektiv und ein Substantiv und sagen Sie dann, was Sie suchen. Der nächste Student sagt, er hat das nicht. Dann geht's weiter.

BEISPIEL: A: Ich suche deutsche Zeitungen.
B: Leider habe ich keine deutschen Zeitungen. *Ich suche . . .*

Adjektive		Substantive	
amerikanisch	bunt	Romane	Fahrräder
kurz	frisch	Menschen	Alternativen
bekannt	freundlich	Pullis	Politiker
gesund	kostenlos	Geschenke	Restaurants
toll	leer	Brötchen	Arbeiter
deutsch	nagelneu	Rucksäcke	Gebäude
lang	riesengroß	Flaschen	Kleider
ehrlich	sportlich	Bücher	Wälder
besser	umweltfreundlich	Professoren	Plakate
interessant		Ideen	

B Gruppenspiel: Wer war ich?

Wählen Sie eine bekannte historische Person. Spielen Sie diese Person vor der Klasse. Geben Sie genug Information, so daß man Ihre Identität erraten (*guess*) kann.

BEISPIEL: Ich war im 18. Jahrhundert eine österreichische Prinzessin. Später wurde ich die Frau des Königs von Frankreich. Eigentlich habe ich nie gesagt: „Wenn das Volk kein Brot hat, dann soll es Kuchen essen." Während der Revolution verlor ich dann meinen Kopf. Wer war ich?

C Partnerarbeit: Als meine Großeltern jung waren

Interviewen Sie einander über die Jugend Ihrer Großeltern. Füllen Sie den Fragebogen aus (*fill out the questionnaire*).

1. Wo sind deine Großeltern geboren? _____
2. Wo lebten sie als Kinder? _____
3. Kamen sie aus großen Familien? _____
4. Wo und wie lernten sie einander kennen? _____
5. Wie war ihre Kindheit und Jugend anders als heute? _____

Narrating events in the past is a communicative goal.

A useful phrase when composing your stories: **eines Tages** = *one day.*

D Gruppenarbeit: Schreiben wir eine Geschichte zusammen (4–5 Personen)

Unten finden Sie eine Wortliste. Benutzen Sie diese Verben, um zusammen eine kurze Geschichte zu schreiben. Sie brauchen einen Sekretär oder eine Sekretärin. Er oder sie soll die Geschichte aufschreiben (*write down*). Der erste Satz der Geschichte ist: „Vor vielen Jahren lebte ein armer Student in einem alten Gebäude in der Altstadt." Student A wählt ein Verb von der Liste und sagt den zweiten Satz. Studentin B sagt einen dritten Satz usw. Sie dürfen natürlich auch andere Verben benutzen und sollen auch viele Adjektive benutzen.

aufstehen	aufmachen	aussehen	beginnen
benutzen	besitzen	bleiben	einkaufen
essen	dauern	frühstücken	heißen
hoffen	kochen	bekommen	liegen
machen	nehmen	schlafen	trinken
sitzen	spazierengehen	klauen	lernen
verdienen	verlieren	sagen	zahlen
versuchen	helfen	sterben	übernachten

Lesen Sie einander Ihre Geschichten vor. (**vorlesen** = *to read aloud*)

Schreiben Sie zu Hause

E Create sentences with a verb from column 1, an indirect object from column 2, and a direct object from column 3. Don't forget to change adjective endings where necessary.

> BEISPIEL: Ich habe meinem lieben Onkel einen langen Brief geschrieben.

1	**2**	**3**
geben	mein lieber Onkel	ein langer Brief
schenken	die nette Austauschstudentin	das neue Restaurant
kaufen	die kleinen Kinder	unsere schöne Altstadt
zeigen	unsere neuen Freunde	unser großer Straßenatlas
erzählen	meine Großeltern	ein Geburtstagsgeschenk
schreiben	das sympathische Mädchen	neue Turnschuhe
beschreiben	mein sportlicher Freund	ein neuer Kassettenrekorder
empfehlen	die ausländischen Touristen	das alte Märchen
leihen	meine gute Freundin	dieser neue Roman

F Write a friend a note about your visit to the poster exhibition. Use the simple past and the past perfect tenses.

1. nachdem / ich / essen (*past perfect tense*) // ich / treffen / mein / Freunde / vor / Museum
2. dort / es / geben / interessant / Ausstellung / von / politisch / Plakate
3. wir / wollen / sehen / Ausstellung // um ... zu / lernen / über / modern / Geschichte
4. wir / unterbrechen / der Museumsdirektor // um ... zu / Fragen / stellen
5. Plakate / zeigen / die / viel / Partei / während / dies- / Zeit
6. nachdem / wir / verbringen / ganz / Nachmittag / dort (*past perfect tense*) // gehen / miteinander / in / Café

G Freies Schreiben

1. Können wir aus der Geschichte der Weimarer Republik etwas lernen? Finden Sie Parallelen zu unserer Zeit?
2. Take the story you composed orally with your classmates in exercise D and polish it as a written assignment.

H Wie sagt man das auf deutsch?

1. How long have you lived in this house?
2. We've been here for two years. We like it a lot.
3. When we worked in Rostock, we only had a small apartment.

4. You look worried. Did something happen to you?
5. I think that somebody stole my new backpack.
6. I had it beside me in the restaurant and suddenly it was gone.
7. I hope you had your ID and your wallet in your pocket.

8. When were you in Heidelberg?
9. Two years ago, when I was an exchange student in Germany.
10. I tried all year to find an old friend of my parents, but he had died.

VIDEOECKE

5 Treibst du gern Sport? (18:18)

Stefan und Su-Sin machen eine Pause.

Stefan fährt mit dem Fahrrad zum Park, wo Su-Sin wartet. Sie wollen zusammen joggen gehen. Während Stefan sein Rad abschließt (locks), fällt ihm der Geldbeutel (wallet) aus der Tasche. Aber er merkt (notices) es nicht, und sie laufen durch den Wald. Später machen sie eine Pause, und Stefan merkt, daß sein Geldbeutel fehlt (is missing). Sie laufen schnell zurück und finden zwei ältere (older) Frauen bei den Rädern. Eine Frau hat den Geldbeutel gefunden, will aber wissen, ob er wirklich Stefan gehört. Also fragt sie ihn, was in seinem Geldbeutel war. Da er es ihr sagen kann, gibt sie ihm das Portemonnaie (= Geldbeutel) zurück.

Wortschatz zum Video

verlieren, hat verloren	*to lose*
der Geldbeutel, -	*wallet*
bestimmt	**= sicher**
Los!	*Let's go!*
Schau mal, wie . . .	*Look at how . . .*
Keine Ahnung.	*(I have) no idea.*
Wie ist Ihr Name?	**= Wie heißen Sie?**
Passen Sie auf.	*Be careful. Pay attention.*

Watch the first minute of video Module 5 showing recreational activities (18:35–19:09). Then check off what you've seen in the video.

Das habe ich gesehen:

———— 1. Ein Vater spielt Fußball mit seinem Sohn.
———— 2. Eine Frau geht mit ihrem Dachshund spazieren.
———— 3. Kinder klettern (are climbing) auf einem Baum.
———— 4. Junge Leute fahren auf Fahrrädern.
———— 5. Ein Mann spielt Tennis.
———— 6. Zwei alte Menschen sprechen miteinander.

B Was hat Stefan in seinem Geldbeutel gehabt?

Now watch the rest of video Module 5 (19:10–21:52). Check off the items that are in Stefan's wallet.

———— 1. Geld   ———— 4. ein Foto von Katrin
———— 2. eine Einkaufsliste   ———— 5. sein Studentenausweis
———— 3. ein Schlüssel   ———— 6. eine Kreditkarte

C Wer sagt das?

Choose the person who says the following.

a. Su-Sin   b. Stefan   c. Jogger   d. ältere Frau

1. ——— sagt: „Ich fahre jeden Tag mit dem Rad zur Uni."
2. ——— sagt: „Ich hab' einen gefunden, drüben bei den Rädern."
3. ——— sagt: „Ich bin jedes Wochenende auf dem Tennisplatz."
4. ——— sagt: „Schau mal, wie die Leute den Wald verschmutzen."
5. ——— sagt: „Ach, tut mir leid. Keine Zeit!"
6. ——— sagt: „Wir nehmen sie mit und werfen sie weg."

D Wie sehen sie aus?

Beschreiben Sie die Menschen im Video.

1. Su-Sin hat ——————— Haare und trägt eine ——————— Hose und einen ——————— Pulli.
2. Stefan trägt ——————— Schuhe und ein ——————— Sweatshirt.
3. Die Frau mit dem Geldbeutel trägt einen ——————— Mantel und einen ——————— Pulli. Sie hat ——————— Haare. Sie ist ungefähr (about) ——————— Jahre alt und sieht ——————— aus.
4. Die andere Frau trägt einen ——————— Pulli und einen ——————— Mantel.

Am Ende des Videos sehen Sie sich das Welle Magazin an (Sport in Berlin, 21:53–22:41). Sie sehen einige Sportarten. Sagen Sie jeweils (*in each case*), ob Sie einen Sport gern treiben, nicht gern treiben oder noch nie probiert (*tried*) haben.

Sportart	gern	nicht gern	nie probiert
Fußball	————	————	————
Rugby	————	————	————
Speerwurf (*javelin*)	————	————	————
Geländelauf (*cross-country*)	————	————	————
Tennis	————	————	————
Schwimmen	————	————	————
Rudern (*rowing*)	————	————	————
Windsurfing	————	————	————

»Radln is halt ganz was anders«

The Bundestag and German Political Parties Today

On December 2, 1990, with the addition of the five new **Länder** (*states*) from the former German Democratic Republic, a united Germany held its first free elections in 58 years. The last had been in November 1932, when Hitler's National Socialist Party (the Nazis) received a plurality of 33.1% of the votes. In January 1933 Hitler was appointed chancellor by President von Hindenburg and seized dictatorial powers soon thereafter.

Stimmzettel

für die Wahl zum Deutschen Bundestag im Wahlkreis 191 Konstanz
am 16. Oktober 1994

Sie haben 2 Stimmen

Ⓧ   Ⓧ

hier 1 Stimme
für die Wahl
eines/einer Wahlkreis-
abgeordneten

hier 1 Stimme
für die Wahl
einer Landesliste (Partei)
maßgebende Stimme für die Verteilung der
Sitze insgesamt auf die einzelnen Parteien

Erststimme   Zweitstimme

#	Erststimme				Zweitstimme	#
1	**Repnik,** Hans-Peter Jurist Radolfzell-Markelfingen, Ländlestraße 13	**CDU**	Christlich Demokratische Union Deutschlands	○	○ **CDU** — Christlich Demokratische Union Deutschlands Dr. Wolfgang Schäuble, Matthias Wissmann, Bernd Schmidbauer, Anton Pfeifer, Brigitte Baumeister	1
2	**Gawron,** Sigurd Diplom-Finanzwirt Konstanz, Eichhornstraße 31	**SPD**	Sozialdemo- kratische Partei Deutschlands	○	○ **SPD** — Sozialdemokratische Partei Deutschlands Dr. Herta Däubler-Gmelin, Dr. Hermann Scheer, Dr. Konstanze Wegner, Klaus Kirschner, Gernot Erler	2
3	**Stahnke-Bohnhardt,** Ursel Diplom-Betriebswirtin Konstanz, Max-Stromeyer-Straße 9	**FDP/ DVP**	Freie Demokratische Partei/Demokratische Volkspartei	○	○ **FDP/DVP** — Freie Demokratische Partei/Demokratische Volkspartei Dr. Klaus Kinkel, Dr. Wolfgang Weng, Roland Kohn, Gisela Frick, Dr. Helmut Haussmann	3
4	**Auhagen,** Hendrik Lehrer Konstanz, Gartenstraße 46 b	**GRÜNE**	BÜNDNIS 90/ DIE GRÜNEN	○	○ **GRÜNE** — BÜNDNIS 90/DIE GRÜNEN Dr. Ursula Eid-Simon, Rezzo Schlauch, Rita Grießhaber, Dr. Jürgen Rochlitz, Monika Knoche	4
5	**Niedermayr,** Romuald Wirtschaftsberater Konstanz, Max-Stromeyer-Straße 7 B	**REP**	DIE REPUBLIKANER	○	○ **REP** — DIE REPUBLIKANER Christian Käs, Dr. med. Rolf Schlierer, Rüdiger Helfer, Dieter Lieberwirth, Nikolaus Holzner	5
					○ **PDS** — Partei des Demokratischen Sozialismus Dr. Winfried Wolf, Andrea Schmidt, Reinhard Neudorfer, Ulrike Küstler, Birgit Pelc	6
					○ **APD** — AUTOFAHRER- und BÜRGER-INTERESSEN PARTEI DEUTSCHLANDS Konrad Kujau, Manfred Ullmann, Rolf Berreth, Dr. Peter Alber, Albert Butz	7
					○ — Bürgerrechtsbewegung Solidarität Renate Rumpf, Hartmut Cramer, Bernd Schulz, Stefan Blassauer, Edmund Belle	8
					○ **CM** — CHRISTLICHE MITTE – Für ein Deutschland nach GOTTES Geboten Michael Platt, Reinhard Förderer, Markus Iwersen, Sigrid Ganter, Marga Daffner	9
					○ **GRAUE** — DIE GRAUEN – Graue Panther Martha-Elisabeth Fischer, Günther Pohl, Margarethe Edele, Erich Waldner, Elisabeth Jäckel	10
					○ **NATUR-GESETZ** — DIE NATURGESETZ-PARTEI, AUFBRUCH ZU NEUEM BEWUSSTSEIN Dr. Günther Hermann, Herbert Groschup, Michael Floymayr, Andreas Müller, Günther Boss	11
					○ **MLPD** — Marxistisch-Leninistische Partei Deutschlands Christiana Grein, Martin Schlesinger, Dorothea Jauernig, Peter Bäuerle, Ulrike Riedel	12
13	**Stocker,** Axel Student Konstanz, Neugasse 42	**ÖDP**	Ökologisch- Demokratische Partei	○	○ **ÖDP** — Ökologisch-Demokratische Partei Bernd Richter, Verena Föttinger, Ulrich Davidsson, Ruth Bärenweiler, Dierk Lisdorf	13
					○ **PBC** — Partei Bibeltreuer Christen Martina Balzer, Dieter Indlekofer, Markus Schübel, Dieter Egert, Sigrid Lutz	14

ALTERNATIVE DIE GRÜNEN

Ergebnisse der Bundestagswahl am 16 Oktober 1994.
Sitzverteilung (bisherige Verteilung in Klammern).

CDU/CSU
294 (319)

PDS
30 (17)

FDP
47 (79)

Bündnis 90/
Grüne 49 (8)

SPD
252 (239)

In order to prevent the proliferation of small parties that had weakened the Weimar Republic, the framers of the 1949 **Grundgesetz** (*Basic Law* or constitution of the Federal Republic of Germany) added a requirement that a party must receive at least 5% of the popular vote to be represented in the **Bundestag** (*Federal Parliament*). This provision has effectively excluded extremist parties at the national level.

The victors in the 1990 election were the conservative and liberal coalition partners already in power, who had backed speedy unification of the two Germanies. Helmut Kohl's CDU (**Christlich-Demokratische Union**) with its Bavarian sister party the CSU (**Christlich-Soziale Union**) form the conservative end of the German political spectrum and have consistently received 45–50% of the popular vote. Their coalition partner is the liberal FDP (**Freie Demokratische Partei**) which has in the past received 5–10% of the popular vote. This coalition was again victorious in the elections of 1994, but by a much narrower margin.

The opposition in the Bundestag is currently made up of parties left of center. The SPD (**Sozialdemokratische Partei Deutschlands**) is the oldest party in Germany with a history stretching back to the beginnings of socialism in the 19th century. It typically receives 35–45% of the national vote from a constituency that includes many industrial workers, students, and intellectuals. The environmental and anti-nuclear party known as the Greens (**Die Grünen**) first won parliamentary representation in 1983. This forced the traditional parties to adopt more environmentally conscious platforms. Finally, the PDS (**Partei des Demokratischen Sozialismus**), the former East German Communist Party, garners votes largely from the new eastern states where voters are dissatisfied with the high unemployment and social disruption brought about by the unification process.

Dieses CDU-Wahlplakat zeigt
Bundeskanzler Helmut Kohl.

Communicative Goals

- Learning the parts of the body
- Describing morning routines
- Designating nationalities and saying where people are from

Cultural Goal

- Understanding Germany's role in Europe today

Chapter Outline

Lyrik zum Vorlesen Hoffmann von Fallersleben, „Das Lied der Deutschen"

Grammatik Reflexive Verbs • Dative Pronouns with Clothing and Parts of the Body • Adjectives and Pronouns of Indefinite Number: *einige, mehrere, etc.* • Adjectival Nouns • More on *bei*: Setting a Scene • Designating Decades: The 90s, etc.

Lesestück Deutschland im europäischen Haus

Situationen aus dem Alltag Morgens nach dem Aufstehen

Almanach Zeittafel zur deutschen Nachkriegsgeschichte

Das Brandenburger Tor: The Brandenburg Gate is a triumphal arch built in the late 18th century. From 1961–1989 the Berlin Wall ran just west of it.

die neuen Bundesländer: The 5 new federal States created, after unification, from the former German Democratic Republic: Sachsen-Anhalt, Mecklenburg-Vorpommern, Sachsen, Thüringen, Brandenburg. More information on unification is found in the **Lesestück** in this chapter. See also map of Germany on p. 23.

Am Brandenburger Tor   aus den USA: Note dative plural.

Helen aus den USA war 1989 in Berlin. Jetzt besucht sie wieder ihre Bekannte Anke in Berlin. Zusammen stehen sie am Brandenburger Tor.

ANKE: Weißt du noch, wie es am 9. November 1989 hier an der Mauer aussah?

HELEN: Als die DDR die Grenze öffnete? Das vergess' ich nie!

ANKE: Die Menschen haben sich so gefreut, sogar die Polizeibeamten waren freundlich!

HELEN: Du, von dieser Begeisterung merkt man aber heute nichts mehr. Man hört fast nur, wie schwierig und teuer die Vereinigung ist.

ANKE: Es stimmt: Deutschland ist wieder *ein* Land, aber es gibt noch starke Unterschiede zwischen den alten und den neuen Bundesländern.

Ein Unfall: Stefan bricht sich das Bein

23.00 Uhr. Stefans Vater liegt schon im Bett. Seine Mutter spricht am Telefon. Plötzlich läuft sie ins Schlafzimmer.

MUTTER: Markus, zieh dich schnell an und komm mit! Etwas Schlimmes ist passiert!

VATER: Was ist denn los?

MUTTER: Stefan hat sich beim Radfahren verletzt! Ich fürchte, er hat sich das Bein gebrochen.

VATER: Um Gottes Willen! Beeilen wir uns!

Anna besucht Stefan im Krankenhaus

ANNA: Wie geht's dir denn, du Armer?

STEFAN: Hallo Anna! Schön, daß du gekommen bist.

ANNA: Fühlst du dich heute besser, oder tut dir das Bein noch weh?

STEFAN: Ach, es geht. Ich kann mich schon selber waschen, aber ich darf noch nicht aufstehen.

ANNA: Schade! Schau mal, ich habe dir Schokolade und Blumen mitgebracht.

STEFAN: Oh, die sind hübsch! Danke, das ist aber lieb von dir!

ANNA: Nichts zu danken! Gute Besserung!

Gute Besserung

> **Note on Usage:** The definite article as pronoun
>
> In colloquial spoken German, the definite article can replace the personal pronoun. This is somewhat more emphatic than the personal pronoun and usually comes at the beginning of the sentence.
>
> **Die** (= sie) sind hübsch! *Those are pretty.*

At the Brandenburg Gate

Helen from the USA was in Berlin in 1989. Now she's again visiting her friend Anke in Berlin. They're standing together at the Brandenburg Gate.

A.: Do you remember what it looked like here at the Wall on November 9, 1989?

H.: When the GDR opened the border? I'll never forget it!

A.: People were so happy, even the police officers were friendly.

H.: You know, these days you don't see that enthusiasm anymore. Almost all you hear is how difficult and expensive unification is.

A.: You're right: Germany is one country again, but there are still great differences between the old and the new *Bundesländer*.

An Accident: Stefan Breaks His Leg

11:00 P.M. Stefan's father is already in bed. His mother is talking on the telephone. Suddenly she runs into the bedroom.

M.: Markus, get dressed quickly and come along! Something bad has happened.

F.: What's wrong?

M.: Stefan hurt himself riding his bike! I'm afraid he's broken his leg.

F.: For heaven's sake! Let's hurry!

Anna Visits Stefan in the Hospital

A.: How are you, you poor guy?

S.: Hi, Anna! Nice of you to come.

A.: Do you feel better today or does your leg still hurt?

S.: Oh, it's all right. I can wash myself already, but they won't let me get up yet.

A.: Too bad. Look, I've brought you chocolate and flowers.

S.: Oh, those are pretty. Thanks, that's really nice of you!

A.: Don't mention it. Get well soon!

Wortschatz 1

Verben

sich[1] etwas an·sehen (sieht an), sah an, hat angesehen   to take a look at something

sich an·ziehen, zog an, hat angezogen   to get dressed

sich beeilen   to hurry

brechen (bricht), brach, hat gebrochen   to break

sich erkälten   to catch a cold

sich freuen   to be happy

sich fühlen   to feel (*intrans.*)

fürchten   to fear

sich etwas leisten können   to be able to afford something

   Das kann ich mir nicht leisten.   I can't afford that.

merken   to notice

öffnen   to open

schauen   to look

schneiden, schnitt, hat geschnitten   to cut

sich setzen   to sit down

sich verletzen   to injure oneself, get hurt

sich verspäten   to be late

sich etwas vor·stellen   to imagine something

waschen (wäscht), wusch, hat gewaschen   to wash

weh tun, tat weh, hat weh getan (+ *dat. of person*)   to hurt

   Das tut (mir) weh.   That hurts (me).

Compare: **Das tut mir weh** (*That hurts me*) with **Es tut mir leid** (*I'm sorry*).

Substantive

der Arzt, ¨e   doctor (*m.*)

der Beamte, -n (*adj. noun*)   official, civil servant (*m.*)

der/die[2] Bekannte, -n (*adj. noun*)   acquaintance, friend

der Finger, -   finger

der Kopf, ¨e   head

der Mund, ¨er   mouth

der Unterschied, -e   difference

der/die Verwandte, -n (*adj. noun*)   relative

der Zahn, ¨e   tooth

das Auge, -n   eye

das Bein, -e   leg

das Bundesland, ¨er   federal state (*in Germany and Austria*)

das Gesicht, -er   face

das Krankenhaus, ¨er   hospital

das Licht, -er   light

das Ohr, -en   ear

das Schlafzimmer, -   bedroom

das Tor, -e   gate

die Ärztin, -nen   doctor (*f.*)

die Beamtin, -nen   official, civil servant (*f.*)

die Begeisterung   enthusiasm

die Blume, -n   flower

die Deutsche Demokratische Republik (DDR)   the German Democratic Republic (GDR)

die Grenze, -n   border

die Mauer, -n   (*freestanding or outside*) wall

---

[1] **Sich** is a reflexive pronoun. This will be explained on p. 318.

[2] Inclusion of both masculine and feminine articles indicates that this is an adjectival noun. See pp. 327–328.

die **Polizei** (*sing. only*) police
die **Schokolade** chocolate
die **Vereinigung** unification

Contrast **die Mauer** (*free-standing wall*) with **die Wand** (*interior wall*). The two words tell the cultural story of Roman innovations in building techniques. **Mauer** (from the Latin *murus*) was made of stone and capable of having windows (**Fenster** from Latin *fenestra*), whereas the Germanic **Wand** is related to the verb **winden**, and described a wall of woven twigs.

Adjektive und Adverbien

ander- other, different
genau exact, precise
hübsch pretty, handsome
mehrere several, a few
wenige few

Andere Vokabeln

sich (*third-person reflexive pronoun, see p. 318*)

Nützliche Ausdrücke

Gute Besserung! Get well soon!
schade too bad
  Das ist schade! That's a shame! Too bad! What a pity!
Schau mal. Look. Look here.
Weißt du noch? Do you remember?

Gegensätze

sich anziehen ≠ **sich aus-ziehen** to get dressed ≠ to get undressed

Mit anderen Worten

schnell machen (*colloq.*) = **sich beeilen**

Variationen

A Persönliche Fragen

1. Helen besucht ihre Bekannte in Berlin. Haben Sie Bekannte oder Verwandte im Ausland? Wo leben sie? Haben Sie sie schon einmal besucht?
2. Helen sagt, sie vergißt den 9. November 1989 nie. Gibt es einen Tag, den Sie nie vergessen können? Was ist an diesem Tag passiert?
3. Stefan hatte einen Unfall beim Radfahren. Haben Sie je einen Unfall gehabt? Mit dem Rad oder dem Auto?
4. Er hat sich verletzt. Ist Ihnen so was als Kind passiert? Wenn ja, wie?
5. Sind Sie je im Krankenhaus gewesen? Warum? Haben Ihnen Ihre Freunde etwas mitgebracht? Was denn?
6. Anna bringt Stefan Schokolade und Blumen mit. Was bringen Sie mir, wenn ich im Krankenhaus bin?

B Übung: Ich habe etwas Interessantes gemacht!

Choose from the list of adjectives below to characterize something you have done. Then say what it was you did.

BEISPIEL: A: Ich habe einmal etwas _____-es gemacht.
  B: Wieso? Was hast du denn gemacht?
  A: Ich habe (*oder*) bin _____ .

blöd	toll	wahnsinnig	intelligent
interessant	gefährlich	neu	furchtbar
wunderbar	schwierig	langweilig	schlimm

C Partnerarbeit: Wie geht's denn weiter?

Take these two lines from the second dialogue and compose your own continuation. Then perform your dialogue for the class.

A: Zieh dich schnell an und komm mit!

B: Was ist denn los?

A: _____

B: _____

A: _____

B: _____

The famous "Lied der Deutschen," also known as the "Deutschlandlied," is one of the most fervently nationalistic—and controversial—political songs ever composed. Although the first stanza is commonly associated with German military expansionism, the author was, ironically, an opponent of repressive government. His anti-authoritarian sentiments cost him his post as professor at the University of Breslau. The text proclaims abstract concepts ("unity, law, freedom") and calls for a unification of all German-speaking territories into one state. The idealistic dreams of unity were appropriate for Hoffmann's generation, which had survived the ravages of the Napoleonic Wars and was frustrated by the division of Germany into many small states.

Hoffmann wrote the text in 1841 to a favorite popular tune by Joseph Haydn in praise of the Austrian Emperor, "Gott erhalte Franz den Kaiser" (*God Preserve Kaiser Franz*, [1797]). Haydn also used this melody in his magnificent *Kaiserquartett* (Opus 76, No. 3, second movement). The song did not become the German national anthem until 1922, when it was chosen by the young Weimar Republic. In 1945 it was banned by the allied military government. In 1952, when no satisfactory substitute could be found, the third stanza alone became the national anthem of the Federal Republic of Germany.

Lab Manual Kap. 11, Lyrik zum Vorlesen.

die Maas = the Meuse River (Belgium); **die Memel** = the Nemunas River in Lithuania; **die Etsch** = the Adige River in South Tirol (Italy); **der Belt** = strait between two Danish islands in the Baltic Sea.

Das Lied der Deutschen

Deutschland, Deutschland über alles,
Über alles in der Welt,
Wenn es stets° zu Schutz und Trutze°   = immer / **Schutz...** = protection and
Brüderlich zusammenhält;   defiance
Von der Maas bis an die Memel,
Von der Etsch bis an den Belt:
Deutschland, Deutschland über alles,
Über alles in der Welt!

Deutsche Frauen, deutsche Treue,°   loyalty
Deutscher Wein und deutscher Sang°   song
Sollen in der Welt erhalten°   preserve
Ihren alten, schönen Klang,°   sound
Uns zu edler Tat begeistern°   **Uns . . . begeistern** = inspire us to noble
Unser ganzes Leben lang: deeds
Deutsche Frauen, deutsche Treue,
Deutscher Wein und deutscher Sang!

Einigkeit° und Recht° und Freiheit   unity / justice
Für das deutsche Vaterland!
Danach laßt uns alle streben°   **laßt...** = let us strive
Brüderlich mit Herz und Hand!
Einigkeit und Recht und Freiheit
Sind des Glückes Unterpfand:°   **des...** = guarantees of happiness
Blüh° im Glanze° dieses Glückes,   flourish / glow
Blühe, deutsches Vaterland!

August Heinrich Hoffmann
von Fallersleben (1798–1874)

„Berliner Mauer zu verkaufen!"
Mauerspecht (*wall-woodpecker*)
mit Brandenburger Tor im
Hintergrund.

Grammatik

Reflexive Verbs

Reflexive Verbs and Pronouns

In most sentences with objects, the subject and the object are two different people or things.

   subj.   *obj.*

Ich habe **ihn** verletzt.   *I injured **him**.*

Sometimes, however, a verb's subject and object are the *same* person or thing. The verb is then called *reflexive*. The object of a *reflexive verb* is always a pronoun called a *reflexive pronoun*.

   subj.   *obj.*

Ich habe **mich** verletzt.   *I hurt **myself**.*

Reflexive pronouns in English end in *-self* or *-selves*, e.g., *myself, himself, herself, themselves*. German has both accusative and dative reflexive pronouns. Reflexive pronouns are identical to personal pronouns except in the third person and the formal second person, where the reflexive pronoun is **sich**.

Note on spelling: sich is not capitalized when used with the polite **Sie: Fühlen Sie sich heute besser?**

Reflexive Pronouns		
	Singular	**Plural**
	acc. **dat.**	**acc. & dat.**
1st person	mich mir	uns
2nd person (fam.)	dich dir	euch
2nd person (form.)	sich sich	sich
3rd person	sich sich	sich

In the plural, the reflexive pronouns often denote reciprocity and are the equivalent of English *each other.*

Wir treffen **uns** morgen.	*We'll meet **each other** tomorrow.*
Kennt ihr **euch**?	*Do you know **each other**?*
Sie kennen **sich** seit langem.	*They've known **each other** for a long time.*
Wir verstehen **uns** gut.	*We understand **each other** well (= We're on the same wavelength).*

Note on Usage: einander (each other)

Plural reflexive pronouns used reciprocally may be replaced by the reciprocal pronoun **einander** (*each other*).

Kennt ihr **euch**? = Kennt ihr **einander**?

Remember that **einander** can also combine with prepositions.

miteinander	*with each other*
zueinander	*to each other*

Verbs with Accusative Reflexive Pronouns

*A transitive verb is a verb that takes a direct object (e.g., **sehen, tragen, verletzen**). An intransitive verb cannot take a direct object (e.g., **sein, werden, schlafen**).*

Any transitive verb may be used reflexively. Here is a sample conjugation using **sich verletzen**.

Ich habe **mich** verletzt.	*I hurt **myself**.*
Du hast **dich** verletzt.	*You hurt **yourself**.*
Sie hat **sich** verletzt.	*She hurt **herself**.*
Wir haben **uns** verletzt.	*We hurt **ourselves**.*
Ihr habt **euch** verletzt.	*You hurt **yourselves**.*
Sie haben **sich** verletzt.	*They hurt **themselves**. (You hurt yourself/yourselves.)*

Lab Manual Kap. 11, Var. zur Üb. 1, 5, 8, 10.

Workbook Kap. 11, A–E.

1 **Übung: Wer hat sich verletzt?**

Die ganze Klasse war im Bus, als der Busfahrer einen kleinen Unfall hatte. Sagen Sie, wer sich verletzt hat.

BEISPIEL: Ich habe mich verletzt.

Note on Usage: selber and selbst as intensifiers

The words **selber** and **selbst** are often used to intensify or emphasize a reflexive pronoun:

Soll ich das Kind waschen?	*Should I wash the child?*
Nein, sie kann sich **selber** waschen.	*No, she can wash herself.*

Answer these questions by saying that the person knows, sees, etc. only him- or herself.

> BEISPIEL: Wen kennt er denn?
> Er kennt nur sich selbst.

Proverb: Liebe dich selbst, so hast du keine Rivalen.

1. Wen sieht sie denn?
2. Wen versteht er denn?
3. Wen lieben Sie denn?
4. Wen brauche ich denn?

5. Wen haben Sie denn verletzt?
6. Wen hat er geärgert?
7. Wen haben sie gerettet?

3 Partnerarbeit: Wir verstehen uns.

Use each of the verbs below in the following routine:

> BEISPIEL: A: *Verstehst* du mich?
> B: Ja, ich verstehe dich. Verstehst du mich?
> A: Ja, ich verstehe dich auch.
> A & B: Wir verstehen uns! (Wir verstehen einander!)

verstehen	brauchen	morgen treffen
sehen	kennen	am Wochenende besuchen

German Reflexive Verbs That Are Not Reflexive in English

Many German reflexive verbs are not reflexive in English. Their English equivalents often use *get*. Here are some examples.

sich anziehen	*to get dressed*
sich waschen	*to get washed*
sich setzen	*to sit down*

Sie wäscht **sich**.	*She's getting washed.*
Er zog **sich** an.	*He got dressed.*
Bitte, setzen Sie **sich**.	*Please sit down.* (literally: *Please seat yourselves.*)

Täglich sich waschen

4 Übung: Bitte, setzen Sie sich!

Your instructor will tell you to stand up or sit down. Then say what you have done.

> BEISPIEL: A: Bitte stehen Sie auf!
> B: (*Student/in steht auf.*) Ich bin aufgestanden.
> A: Bitte setzen Sie sich.
> B: (*Student/in setzt sich.*) Ich habe mich gesetzt.

Verbs Requiring the Accusative Reflexive

Verbs like **anziehen** and **waschen** may be used either reflexively (**ich wasche mich**) or nonreflexively (**ich wasche den Wagen**). Some German verbs, however, must *always* be used with an accusative reflexive pronoun. Their English equivalents are *not* reflexive.

An analogous English verb is to enjoy oneself. I enjoyed myself at the party means I enjoyed the party, not literally myself. German: **sich amüsieren.**

sich beeilen	*to hurry*	**sich fühlen**	*to feel*
sich erkälten	*to catch cold*	**sich verspäten**	*to be late*
sich freuen	*to be happy*		

5 **Gruppenarbeit: Wann freust du dich besonders? (3 oder 4 Personen)**

Alle müssen sagen, wann sie sich besonders freuen. Die Bilder geben Ihnen einige Ideen, aber Sie dürfen auch frei antworten.

BEISPIEL: Ich freue mich, wenn die Sonne scheint. Wann freust du dich?

6 **Gruppenarbeit: Warum mußt du dich beeilen?**

Jetzt sind Sie alle in Eile. Sagen Sie einander warum.

BEISPIEL: Ich muß mich beeilen, weil ich zur Uni muß. Warum mußt du dich beeilen?

Jeder verspätet sich manchmal. Erzählen Sie der Klasse, warum Sie sich einmal verspätet haben. Unten sind einige Möglichkeiten, aber Sie dürfen auch frei antworten.

> BEISPIEL: Ich habe mich einmal verspätet, weil . . .

krank sein	Fahrrad kaputt
spät aufstehen	die Deutschstunde vergessen
sich verletzten	die Uhr verlieren
einen Unfall haben	einen Freund im Krankenhaus besuchen

Verbs with Dative Reflexive Pronouns

Verbs with Dative Objects   Verbs such as **helfen** that require a dative object take a dative reflexive pronoun when they are used reflexively.

> Ich kann **mir selber** helfen.   *I can help **myself**.*

Reflexive Indirect Object   The subject and *indirect* object of a verb can be the same person. In this case the indirect object is a *dative* reflexive pronoun.

Note: Except for **mir** and **dir**, the dative reflexive pronouns are identical in form to the accusative reflexive pronouns.

Ich kaufe **mir** Blumen.	*I'm buying **myself** flowers.*
Du kaufst **dir** Blumen.	*You're buying **yourself** flowers.*
Sie kaufen **sich** Blumen.	
Er kauft **sich** Blumen.	*He's buying **himself** flowers.*
Wir kaufen **uns** Blumen.	*We're buying **ourselves** flowers.*
Ihr kauft **euch** Blumen.	*You're buying **yourselves** flowers.*
Sie kaufen **sich** Blumen.	
Sie kaufen **sich** Blumen.	*They're buying **themselves** flowers.*

Was kaufst du dir?

The dative reflexive makes explicit the fact that the subject is the beneficiary of its own action. It may be omitted without changing the basic meaning of the sentence.

Ich kaufe mir eine Jacke.	*I'm buying myself a jacket.*
Ich kaufe eine Jacke.	*I'm buying a jacket.*

EIN TOLLER TAG

8 Übung: Einkaufsbummel

Jetzt gehen wir zusammen einkaufen. Jeder hat DM 200 und darf sich etwas kaufen. Erzählen Sie den anderen, was Sie sich kaufen. Die Bilder geben Ihnen einige Ideen, aber Sie dürfen sich natürlich auch andere Sachen kaufen.

> BEISPIEL: A: Was kaufen Sie sich, Robert?
> B: Ich kaufe mir ein neues Hemd und eine Zeitung.

Verbs Requiring the Dative Reflexive

There are some German verbs that must *always* be used with the dative reflexive pronoun. They all require a *direct object* (in the accusative) as well. Their English equivalents are *not* reflexive.

German: dative reflexive	English: not reflexive

sich etwas ansehen
  Ich wollte **mir** den Wagen
  ansehen.
	to take a look at, look over
	  I wanted to take a look at the
	  car.

sich etwas leisten können
  Kannst du **dir** ein neues
  Fahrrad leisten?
	to be able to afford
	  Can you afford a new
	  bicycle?

sich etwas vorstellen
  Das kann ich **mir** nicht
  vorstellen.
	to imagine
	  I can't imagine that.

Since the pronoun **sich** is both accusative and dative, how do you know which it should be with any particular reflexive verb? When a **Wortschatz** entry in this book includes the direct object **etwas**, it indicates that the reflexive pronoun is dative. If you look up **ansehen**, for example, you find **sich etwas ansehen**. This tells you that **etwas** is accusative and **sich** is dative. Any noun or pronoun in the accusative can replace **etwas**.

sich (*dative*) **etwas** (*accusative*) **ansehen**

Ich möchte mir das Auto ansehen.

A parallel English structure is *to cook oneself something* (**sich etwas kochen**). I'm cooking myself (*ind. obj.*) an egg (*dir. obj.*). = **Ich koche mir ein Ei.**

9 Kettenreaktion: Die armen Studenten

Wie alle Studenten haben Sie nie genug Geld. Sagen Sie, was Sie sich nicht leisten können, und dann fragen Sie weiter.

BEISPIEL: A: Ich kann mir keine Europareise leisten. Was kannst du dir nicht leisten?
B: Ich kann mir . . .

10 Partnerarbeit: Was wollen wir uns heute nachmittag ansehen?

Sehen Sie sich den Stadtplan auf Seite 241 an. Sie verbringen den Nachmittag zusammen in dieser Stadt. Sagen Sie einander, was Sie sich ansehen möchten.

BEISPIEL: A: Ich möchte mir den Dom und _____ ansehen. Und du?
B: Ich möchte mir lieber _____ ansehen.

Dative Pronouns with Clothing and Parts of the Body

Learning the parts of the body is a communicative goal.

Unlike English, German does not usually use possessive forms with parts of the body, or with articles of clothing when they are being put on or taken off. German uses the personal dative instead.

Die Mutter wäscht **dem Kind** die Hände.	*The mother washes **the child's** hands.*
Meine Freundin schneidet **mir** die Haare.	*My girlfriend cuts **my** hair.*
Sie zog **ihm** den Mantel an.	*She put **his** coat on him.*

Note that plural **die Haare** is more common than singular: **Sie hat dunkle Haare.**

If the subject is performing the action on itself, the dative pronoun is of course *reflexive*.

Ich habe **mir** die Hände gewaschen.	*I washed **my** hands.*
Sie zog **sich** den Mantel an.	*She put on **her** coat.*
Ich schneide **mir** selber die Haare.	*I cut **my** hair myself.*
Stefan hat **sich** das Bein gebrochen.	*Stefan broke **his** leg.*

11 Übung: Körperteile

Review your knowledge of parts of the body by identifying them in the picture below.

Rätsel (*Riddle*)

Was ist das? Hat Arme aber keine Hände, läuft und hat doch keine Füße.

die **Katze, -n**   *cat*   der **Hund, -e**   *dog*

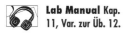

Lab Manual Kap. 11, Var. zur Üb. 12.

12 Übung: Wo tut es Ihnen weh?

Stefan tut das Bein noch ein bißchen weh. Wo tut es Ihnen weh?

BEISPIEL: Wo tut es Ihnen weh?
Mir tut der Kopf weh.

13 Übung

Sagen Sie Ihrem Professor, **wann** Sie sich heute angezogen haben, und dann, **was** Sie sich angezogen haben.

Ich ziehe **mich** an. = *I'm getting dressed.*
Ich ziehe **mir** ein Hemd an. = *I'm putting on a shirt.*

BEISPIEL: A: Um wieviel Uhr haben Sie sich heute angezogen?
B: Ich habe mich um halb acht angezogen.
A: Was haben Sie sich angezogen?
B: Ich habe mir _____ , _____ und _____ angezogen.

Adjectives and Pronouns of Indefinite Number

You have already learned as individual vocabulary words a group of adjectives used with plural nouns to indicate indefinite amounts.

wenige	*few*
einige	*some*
mehrere	*several*
andere	*other(s)*
viele	*many*

For **limiting words**, see p. 257; for **primary and secondary endings**, see p. 258.

These adjectives are *not* limiting words. They are treated just like descriptive adjectives: when not preceded by a limiting word, they take *primary* endings.

Andere Leute waren da.	*Other people were there.*
Ich habe **viele** Freunde in Bonn.	*I have a lot of friends in Bonn.*

When a limiting word precedes them, they take *secondary* endings.

Die anderen Leute waren da.	*The other people were there.*
Meine vielen Freunde schreiben mir oft.	*My many friends often write to me.*

Remember that descriptive adjectives following the adjective of indefinite number *always* have the *same* ending as the adjective of indefinite number.

Andere junge Leute waren da.	*Other young people were there.*
Die anderen jungen Leute waren da.	*The other young people were there.*

14 Gruppenarbeit: Viele oder wenige?

Choose a word from each column and state your opinion about a group of people. Begin with **Ich würde sagen,** . . .

BEISPIEL: Ich würde sagen, viele sportliche Frauen sind gesund.

A	B	C	D
viele	jung	Menschen	Sport treiben
wenige	sportlich	Amerikaner	gesund sein
	reich	Professoren	Müll recyclen
	arm	Studenten	glücklich sein
	stark	Frauen	Deutsch sprechen
	sympathisch	Männer	gut verdienen
	verrückt	Eltern	gern trampen
	kreativ		

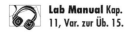

Lab Manual Kap.
11, Var. zur Üb. 15.

Workbook Kap. 11,
F.

15 Übung

Supply the correct adjective endings.

1. Darf ich mir einig_er_ schön_en_ Postkarten ansehen?
2. Sie hat schon mehrer____ deutsch____ Bücher gelesen.
3. Viel_e_ jung_e_ amerikanisch_e_ Schüler verstehen das nicht.
4. Haben Sie auch die ander____ neu____ Arbeiter kennengelernt?
5. Ich habe mit viel_en_ interessant_en_ Menschen gesprochen.
6. Deine viel____ neu____ Ideen gefallen mir sehr.
7. Das sind die Probleme der ander_en_ jung_en_ Journalisten.
8. Ich kenne einig____ gut____ Restaurants in Hamburg.

Indefinite Pronouns

When these words are not followed by nouns, they function as indefinite pronouns referring to human beings:

Viele sagen das.	*Many (people) say that.*
Einige gehen ins Kino, **andere** ins Theater.	*Some (people) are going to the movies, others to the theater.*

16 Übung: Einige und andere

Not everyone in your class likes doing the same things. Answer the following questions by saying that *some* of you (**einige**) like doing one thing, *others* (**andere**) prefer something else.

BEISPIEL: A: Gehen Sie gern ins Kino?
           B: *Einige* gehen gern ins Kino.
           C: *Andere* gehen lieber _____ .

1. Spielen Sie gern Tennis?
2. Sprechen Sie gern über Politik?
3. Essen Sie gern Wurst?
4. Fahren Sie gern Ski?
5. Lesen Sie gern Zeitung?
6. Arbeiten Sie gern in der Bibliothek?
7. Trinken Sie gern Kaffee zum Frühstück?
8. Sitzen Sie gern vor dem Fernseher?

Adjectival Nouns

Adjectival Nouns Referring to People

In English, adjectives such as *sick*, *rich*, and *famous* occasionally function as nouns referring *collectively* to a group of people.

> *Florence Nightingale cared for **the sick**.*
> *Life styles of **the rich and famous**.*

Adjectival nouns are more frequent in German than in English. Moreover, they can refer to individuals, not just to collective groups as in English. Masculine adjectival nouns denote men, feminine ones denote women, while plural adjectival nouns are not gender specific.

Colloquial **mein Alter/meine Alte** can mean *my father/my mother* or *my husband/my wife* (compare English *my old man/old lady*).

der Alte	the old man
die Alte	the old woman
die Alten	the old people

Like other nouns in German, adjectival nouns are capitalized, but they *receive adjective endings* as though they were followed by the nouns **Mann, Frau,** or **Menschen.** Here are some examples that include these nouns in brackets to make the structure clear. *Note the adjective endings!* As in any noun phrase, these endings will change depending on whether or not the adjectival noun is preceded by a limiting word.

Die Alte [Frau] lag im Bett.	*The old woman was lying in bed.*
Kennst du **den Großen** [Mann] da?	*Do you know that tall man there?*
Hier wohnt **ein Reicher** [Mann].	*A rich man lives here.*
Er wollte **den Armen** [Menschen] helfen.	*He wanted to help the poor.*

In principle, any adjective can be used as an adjectival noun. Here are some common ones you should learn:

Only the masculine form **der Beamte** is an adjectival noun. The feminine form is **die Beamtin.**

der/die Deutsche is the *only* noun of nationality that is adjectival.

der/die **Alte, -n**	*old man/woman*
der/die **Arme, -n**	*poor man/woman*
der **Beamte, -n**	*official, civil servant*
der/die **Bekannte, -n**	*acquaintance, friend*
der/die **Deutsche, -n**	*German (man/woman)*
der/die **Grüne, -n**	*member of the Greens (the environmental political party)*
der/die **Kleine, -n**	*little boy/girl or short man/woman*
der/die **Kranke, -n**	*sick man/woman*
der/die **Verwandte, -n** (from **verwandt** = *related*)	*relative*

 Lab Manual Kap. 11, Üb. 17.

 Workbook Kap. 11, G, H.

17 Übung

Complete each sentence with the appropriate form of **mein Bekannter** (*my acquaintance, friend* [*m.*]).

BEISPIEL: Das ist _____ .
Das ist *mein Bekannter.*

1. Heute zum Mittagessen treffe ich _____ .
2. Ich gehe oft mit _____ Volleyball spielen.
3. Das ist die Frau _____ .
4. _____ heißt Robert.

Now use a form of **meine Bekannten** (*my friends*).

5. Das sind _____ .
6. Kennen Sie _____ ?
7. Helfen Sie bitte _____ !
8. Das sind die Kinder _____ .

Now use a form of **die Deutsche** (*the German* [f.]).

9. Wie heißt denn _____ ?
10. Meinst du _____ ?
11. Ich trampe mit _____ nach Italien.
12. Ist das der Rucksack _____ ?

Now use a form of **die Alten** (*the old people*).

13. Das haben wir von _____ gelernt.
14. Morgen kommen _____ .
15. Wer trägt denn die Koffer _____ ?
16. Machen wir etwas Schönes für _____ .

Now use a form of **unser Verwandter** (*our relative* [m.]).

17. Helmut ist _____ .
18. Kennst du _____ ?
19. Du sollst mit _____ sprechen.
20. Die Tochter _____ besucht uns morgen.

Neuter Adjectival Nouns Referring to Qualities

Neuter adjectival nouns are abstract nouns designating qualities (e.g., *something good*, *nothing new*). They occur only in the singular, most frequently after the indefinite pronouns **etwas**, **nichts**, **viel**, and **wenig**. Note that since these pronouns are *not* limiting words, the following adjectival noun has the *primary* neuter ending **-es**.

etwas Herrliches	*something marvelous*
nichts Neues	*nothing new*
viel Gutes	*much that is good*
wenig Interessantes	*little of interest*

18 Rollenspiel: Was haben Sie mir mitgebracht? (Mit offenen Büchern)

Ihre Professorin hatte einen Unfall und liegt im Krankenhaus. Sie besuchen sie und bringen ihr Geschenke mit. (*First choose an adjective from the left-hand column to describe your present, then tell her what it is.*)

BEISPIEL: A: Ich habe Ihnen etwas _____ -es mitgebracht.
            B: O wie schön! Was denn?
            A: Ein-_____ .

neu	Pflanze
schön	Kassettenrecorder
teuer	frische Brötchen
interessant	Schokolade
herrlich	Fotos von unserer Reise
klein	Stück von der Berliner Mauer
lecker	Flasche Wein
umweltfreundlich	Zeitschriften
wunderbar	Blumen

Neuter adjectival nouns can also occur after the definite article **das**. In this case, they are abstract nouns signaling the *quality* designated by the adjective. There are several English equivalents for this.

Das Moderne gefällt mir.	*I like modern things.*
	I like what is modern.
Sie sucht immer **das Gute**.	*She's always seeking the good.*
	She's always seeking what's good.

More on *bei*

In **Kapitel 5** you learned that the dative preposition **bei** has the spatial meanings *in the home of* or *at*. Frequently, however, **bei** is used to set a scene. It then has the meanings *during, while . . . ing,* or *at* (an activity or someone's home or business). In this meaning, **bei** is often used with verbal nouns (p. 207).

Er hat sich **beim Radfahren** verletzt.	*He injured himself while riding his bicycle.*
Marion ist jetzt **bei der Arbeit**.	*Marion's at work now.*
Ich lese oft **beim Essen**.	*I often read while eating.*
Ich war gestern **beim Arzt**.	*I was at the doctor's yesterday.*

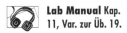

Lab Manual Kap. 11, Var. zur Üb. 19.

19 Übung: Wann passiert das?

Sagen Sie, wann etwas passiert oder nicht passiert. Benutzen Sie **bei** in Ihrer Antwort.

> BEISPIEL: Ich falle nie, wenn ich skifahre.
> Ich falle nie beim Skifahren.

1. Mein Mitbewohner stört mich, wenn ich lese.
2. Wir treffen uns oft, wenn wir radfahren.
3. Höfliche Kinder singen nicht, wenn sie essen.
4. Wenn wir spazierengehen, können wir miteinander sprechen.
5. Ich höre gern Musik, wenn ich Auto fahre.
6. Wenn ich arbeite, ziehe ich mir die Schuhe aus.

20 Übung

Antworten Sie mit **bei**.

> BEISPIEL: Wie hat er sich denn verletzt? (*while skiing*)
> Beim Skifahren.

1. Wie haben Sie sich erkältet? (*while swimming*)
2. Wo sind Sie morgens um zehn? (*at work*)
3. Wann lernt man viele Menschen kennen? (*while hitchhiking*)
4. Wann sprechen Sie nicht viel? (*when driving a car*)
5. Wo ist denn Ihre Frau? (*at the doctor's*)
6. Wie hast du so viel Geld verloren? (*playing cards*)

These examples show how German designates decades (**das Jahrzehnt, -e**).

<table>
<tr><td>die 20er (Zwanziger) Jahre</td><td>the 20s (Twenties)</td></tr>
<tr><td>aus den 60er Jahren</td><td>from the 60s</td></tr>
<tr><td>in den 90er Jahren</td><td>in the 90s</td></tr>
</table>

Note that the cardinal number adds the ending **-er**. No other adjective ending is used, regardless of case.

21 Übung: Alte Briefmarken *(stamps)*

Aus welchen Jahrzehnten kommen diese deutschen Briefmarken?

Lesestück — Deutschland im europäischen Haus

Tips zum Lesen und Lernen

Designating nationalities and talking about where people are from are communicative goals.

Tips zum Vokabelnlernen

Country Names; Nouns and Adjectives of Nationality   The only designation of nationality that is an adjectival noun is **der/die Deutsche**. Some other nouns of nationality have a masculine form ending in **-er** and a feminine in **-erin**. You already know some of these:

country	male native	female native	adjective
Amerika	der Amerikaner	die Amerikanerin	amerikanisch
England	der Engländer	die Engländerin	englisch
Italien	der Italiener	die Italienerin	italienisch
Kanada	der Kanadier	die Kanadierin	kanadisch
Österreich	der Österreicher	die Österreicherin	österreichisch
die Schweiz	der Schweizer	die Schweizerin	schweizerisch

Other nouns of nationality are N-nouns in the masculine that add **-in** (and sometimes an umlaut) in the feminine.

country	male native	female native	adjective
China	der Chinese, -n, -n	die Chinesin	chinesisch
Frankreich	der Franzose, -n, -n	die Französin	französisch
Rußland	der Russe, -n, -n	die Russin	russisch

Remember that when stating a person's nationality, Germans do *not* use the indefinite article.

Sind Sie Deutsche?	*Are you a German?*
Nein, ich bin Französin.	*No, I'm French.*

Gruppenarbeit: Woher kommst du?

Sie sind auf einer internationalen Studentenkonferenz. Sie bekommen vom Professor ein Stück Papier. Auf dem Papier steht der Name Ihrer Heimat (*native country*). Jetzt fragen Sie einander, woher Sie kommen.

BEISPIEL: A: Woher kommst du denn?
B: Ich komme aus England.
A: Ach, du bist Engländerin!

Lab Manual Kap. 11, Üb. zur Betonung.

Leicht zu merken

die **Demokratisierung**	
die **Demonstration, -en**	Demonstration
existieren	existieren
die **Integration**	Integration
investieren	investieren
der **Kapitalismus**	Kapitalismus
der **Kommunismus**	Kommunismus
der **Manager, -**	
die **Million, -en**	Million
modernisieren	modernisieren
Osteuropa	
der **Protest**	Protest
die **Reform, -en**	
reformieren	reformieren
das **Regime, -s**	
die **Revolution, -en**	Revolution
separat	separat
die **Sowjetunion**	Sowjetunion
stabil	stabil
das **Symbol, -e**	Symbol
zentral	zentral
die **Zone, -n**	

Word features such as prefixes and suffixes can help you build on your existing vocabulary and recognize new words in context.

The Negating Prefix *un-* The prefix **un-** attached to a noun or adjective forms the antonym of that word. Guess the meanings of these words from the **Lesestück**:

> die **Unsicherheit** (line 4)
> **ungelöste Probleme** (line 42)

The Suffix *-los* The suffix **-(s)los** is attached to nouns and forms adjectives and adverbs, e.g., **arbeitslos**. It is the equivalent of the English suffix *-less*. Guess the meanings of these words from the **Lesestück**:

> **gewaltlos** (from **Gewalt:** *force, violence*) line 32
> **hoffnungslos** (from **Hoffnung:** *hope*) line 45

Past Participles as Adjectives Past participles of verbs are often used as attributive adjectives. They take regular adjective endings.

> **bauen** → **gebaut-**   *to build* → *built*
> Das ist das neu **gebaute**   *That's the newly built dormitory*
>   Studentenwohnheim.

The reading contains the following participles used as adjectives:

> **besiegen** *to defeat*   → **besiegt-** (line 10)
> **entnazifizieren** *to denazify* → **entnazifiziert-** (line 11)
> **vereinen** *to unite*   → **vereint-** (line 38)
> **lösen** *to solve*   → **ungelöst-** (line 42)

Übung

Wie heißt das Adjektiv (mit Endung!)? Und wie heißt der neue Satz auf englisch?

> BEISPIEL: Jemand hat diese Waren gestohlen.
>   Die Polizei hat die *gestohlenen* Waren gefunden.
>   *The police found the stolen goods.*

1. Ich habe Altpapier gesammelt, und jetzt schleppe ich das _____ Altpapier zum Recycling.

2. Eine Fabrik hat diesen Fluß verschmutzt, und jetzt darf man in dem _____ Wasser nicht schwimmen.

3. Der Krieg hat viele deutsche Städte zerstört. Jetzt hat Deutschland seine _____ Städte wiederaufgebaut.

4. Wir hatten eine schöne Reise nach Schottland geplant, aber leider konnten wir uns die _____ Reise nicht leisten.

5. Ich habe meiner Mutter ein schönes Zimmer reserviert, aber das _____ Zimmer war ihr zu klein.

Verben

ändern to change (*trans.*)
　Sie hat ihr Leben geändert. She changed her life.
sich ändern to change (*intrans.*)
　Ihr Leben hat sich geändert. Her life changed.
auf·geben (gibt auf), gab auf, hat aufgegeben to give up
aus·wandern to emigrate
rufen, rief, hat gerufen to call, shout
vereinen to unite
verschwinden, verschwand, ist verschwunden to disappear

Substantive

der Haß hatred
der Nachbar, -n, -n neighbor
der Schlüssel, - key
der Teil, -e part
der Tod death

das Mitglied, -er member
die Brücke, -n bridge
die Bundesrepublik Deutschland (BRD) the Federal Republic of Germany (FRG)
die Heimat homeland; native country
die Macht, ¨e power, might
die Regierung, -en government in power, administration
die Wirtschaft economy
die Zukunft future

Compare **verschieden** (*various, different*) and **ander-** (*other, different*): **Ich kenne viele verschiedene Lieder** (*I know many different songs*) vs. **Ich kenne andere Lieder als du** (*I know different songs than you*).

Adjektive und Adverbien

beid- both
berühmt famous
europäisch European
offen open
tief deep
tot dead
verschieden various, different
wirtschaftlich economic

Gegensätze

auswandern ≠ einwandern to emigrate ≠ to immigrate
der Haß ≠ die Liebe hatred ≠ love
offen ≠ geschlossen open ≠ closed
der Tod ≠ das Leben death ≠ life
die Zukunft ≠ die Vergangenheit future ≠ past

Understanding Germany's role in Europe today is the cultural goal of this chapter.

 Lab Manual Kap. 11, Lesestück.

Deutschland im europäischen Haus

Im Jahre 1989 ging mit dem Fall° der Berliner Mauer eine Epoche der europäischen Geschichte zu Ende: Die Nachkriegszeit war endlich vorbei.° Besonders für die Länder Osteuropas sind die 90er Jahre eine Zeit der Unsicherheit aber auch der neuen Hoffnungen. Mit seiner

5　zentralen Lage° zwischen Ost und West und seiner starken Wirtschaft ist Deutschland in vieler Hinsicht° der Schlüssel zum neuen „europäischen Haus".³

　　　fall

　　　over

　　　location
　　　in . . . in many respects

---

³ The common "European House" was envisioned by the former Soviet President Mikhail Gorbachev.

Historischer Hintergrund:° 1945 bis 1989

1945 teilten die vier Alliierten° Amerika, England, Frankreich und die
10 Sowjetunion das besiegte° Hitlerreich in vier Zonen auf,° mit dem
Ziel, später einen neuen entnazifizierten° Staat zu bilden.° Aber bald
änderte sich das politische Klima. Es begann der sogenannte° Kalte
Krieg zwischen dem Kommunismus im Osten und dem Kapitalismus
im Westen. Anstatt eines vereinten Landes gründete° man 1949 die
15 Bundesrepublik Deutschland (BRD) und die Deutsche Demokratische
Republik (DDR), zwei separate und sehr verschiedene Staaten.

     Weil die Grenze zwischen Ost- und West-Berlin bis 1961 offen
blieb, konnten zirka 2,7 Millionen Menschen aus der DDR in den
Westen auswandern.[4] Die DDR verblutete.° Um einen langsamen Tod
20 zu verhindern,° baute die ostdeutsche Regierung 1961 eine Mauer
mitten durch° Berlin. Die Berliner Mauer, das berühmte Symbol des
Kalten Krieges, existierte 28 Jahre, bis die zwei Supermächte USA und
die Sowjetunion endlich ihre Feindschaft° aufgaben.

25 November 1989: Die Grenze öffnet sich

In den 80er Jahren leitete die „Glasnost-Politik"[5] Michael Gor-
batschows in der Sowjetunion eine Reform ein,° die° sich schnell auf die
anderen Länder Osteuropas ausweitete.° Im Sommer 1989 gab es in
Leipzig, Dresden und vielen anderen Städten der DDR riesengroße
30 friedliche° Demonstrationen gegen den kommunistischen Staat. „Wir
sind das Volk", riefen die Demonstranten,° und später: „Wir sind *ein*

Seitennotizen (rechte Spalte):
background
allies
defeated / **teilten . . . auf** = divided
denazified / form
so-called

founded

was bleeding to death
to prevent
mitten... through the middle of

enmity

leitete . . . ein = initiated / that
sich . . . ausweitete = spread

peaceful
demonstrators

DDR-Wagen kurz vor der Wieder-
vereinigung. Was bedeutet „BRDDR"?

---

[4]Although Berlin was located in the middle of the Soviet Occupation Zone, it too was divided among the Allies because of its importance as the capital. Air and highway corridors
linked it to the West.

[5]Mikhail Gorbachev initiated the internal reforms in the former Soviet Union known as
perestroika (restructuring) and *glasnost* (openness). These changes eroded the Communist Party's centralized control and hegemony.

35 Volk". Diese Demonstrationen leiteten die erste erfolgreiche gewaltlose
Revolution der deutschen Geschichte ein.° Die Regierung mußte die   **leiteten . . . ein** = started
Grenze öffnen. 1990 kamen dann die ersten freien Wahlen in der DDR
und im nächsten Jahr die Vereinigung der beiden Teile Deutschlands.

Deutschland im neuen Europa

40 Als Wirtschaftsmacht und größtes° Mitglied der Europäischen Union[6]   biggest
spielt das vereinte Deutschland eine wichtige Rolle als Brücke zwischen Ost und West. Deutschland ist selber ein Spiegel der großen Unterschiede in Europa. Wie sieht denn die Zukunft des europäischen
Hauses aus?

45   Es gibt natürlich noch ungelöste Probleme. Die Umwelt ist in Osteuropa durch die Industrie viel mehr beschädigt° als° im Westen.   damaged / than
Auch sind die meisten° Fabriken in den neuen Bundesländern und in   most
anderen osteuropäischen Ländern hoffnungslos veraltet° und können   hopelessly antiquated
nicht mit der westeuropäischen Industrie konkurrieren.° Man muß sie   compete
50 entweder schließen oder° sehr viel investieren, um sie zu moderni-   **entweder... =** either . . . or
sieren und umweltfreundlicher zu machen. Das bedeutet im Osten
mehr Arbeitslosigkeit und Ressentiments° gegen die Manager aus dem   resentment
Westen, die° die Marktwirtschaft° einführen° sollen.   who / market economy /
      introduce
    Weil die wirtschaftliche Situation in Osteuropa immer noch
55 prekär° ist, versuchen viele Menschen, ihre Heimat zu verlassen und   precarious
nach Deutschland auszuwandern. Sie stellen sich vor, daß sie dort ein
besseres° Leben finden können. Hinzu° kommen Flüchtlinge° aus   better / in addition / refugees
armen Ländern der ganzen Welt. Sie hoffen, politisches Asyl° oder Ar-   asylum
beit in Deutschland zu finden.[7] Obwohl die meisten° Deutschen   most
60 diesen Menschen helfen wollen, gibt es auch eine rechtsradikale
Minderheit,° die° Haß und Gewalt gegen Ausländer propagiert.° Im   radical right minority / that /
Ausland erwecken° solche Neonazis natürlich alte Ängste und Erin-   spreads
nerungen an° die Hitlerzeit.   awaken
      memories of
    Es dauert wahrscheinlich noch lange, bis diese alten Ängste und
65 die neuen politischen Probleme überwunden° sind. Aber die Demo-   overcome
kratisierung und Integration Osteuropas mit dem Westen sind wohl
nicht mehr aufzuhalten.° Zwischen den neuen Nachbarn im Osten   **sind wohl...** = can probably no
und den reichen Demokratien im Westen steht die politisch stabile   longer be stopped
und wirtschaftlich starke Bundesrepublik. Es ist sicher, daß sie im
70 neuen europäischen Haus eine zentrale Rolle zu spielen hat.

---

[6] The European Union, a political and economic alliance of European nations.

[7] Until 1993 Germany had the most liberal asylum laws in the world. In January 1993
alone, 36,000 foreigners applied for asylum. Through a constitutional amendment that re-
defined application criteria, applications were reduced to 13,000 in January 1994.

Fragen zum Lesestück

1. Wer hat zuerst von einem „europäischen Haus" gesprochen? Was bedeutet das?
2. Warum ist Deutschlands Rolle so wichtig im neuen Europa?
3. Wie kam es zu zwei deutschen Staaten?
4. Warum waren die beiden deutschen Staaten so verschieden?
5. Warum hat die Regierung der DDR die Mauer mitten durch Berlin gebaut?
6. Wie hat die friedliche Revolution in der DDR begonnen?
7. Wann hat die DDR-Regierung die Grenze ganz geöffnet?
8. Warum kommen Menschen aus Osteuropa und der Dritten Welt nach Deutschland?
9. Welche ungelösten Probleme gibt es noch in Osteuropa und in den neuen Bundesländern?

Situationen aus dem Alltag

Morgens nach dem Aufstehen

Das Wochenende war herrlich, aber jetzt ist es wieder Montag. Sie müssen sich für den Tag fertig machen und gehen ins Badezimmer. Sie müssen eine Menge Reflexivverben benutzen, um die Morgenroutine zu beschreiben.

Übung: Welcher Satz gehört zu welchem Bild?

Er kämmt sich die Haare.   Er rasiert sich.   Sie schminkt sich.
Sie badet sich.   Sie putzt sich die Zähne.   Er duscht sich.

Übung: Was ist Ihre Morgenroutine?

In welcher Reihenfolge (*order*) machen Sie sich morgens fertig? Antworten Sie mit ganzen Sätzen.

frühstücken
Sachen in die Tasche packen
aufstehen
zur Uni gehen
sich rasieren oder sich schminken
sich die Zähne putzen
eine zweite Tasse Kaffee trinken
sich anziehen
sich duschen oder baden
sich die Haare kämmen

1. Zuerst stehe ich auf.
2. Dann _____
3. _____
4. _____
5. _____
6. _____
7. _____
8. _____
9. _____
10. _____

Mit Inter Rail eröffnen sich neue Horizonte.

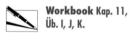 **Zum Schluß**

Sprechen wir miteinander!

 Lab Manual Kap. 11, Diktat.

Workbook Kap. 11, Üb. I, J, K.

A Rollenspiel: Schade, daß du im Krankenhaus bist! (3 Personen)

Lesen Sie zusammen diese Situation, und dann spielen Sie sie miteinander:

Ein Student spielt einen Verletzten. Er ist in einem Unfall gewesen und liegt jetzt im Krankenhaus. Die anderen zwei sind Freunde und besuchen ihn dort. Sie haben noch nichts Genaues über den Unfall gehört (Sie wissen z.B. nicht, wie er sich verletzt hat). Sie stellen ihm Fragen. Sie haben ihm natürlich auch Geschenke mitgebracht.

B Gruppenarbeit: Sprechen wir über die Fotos in diesem Kapitel.

Man sagt, ein Bild ist tausend Worte wert. Die Fotos in diesem Kapitel zeigen die menschliche Seite der Geschichte unserer Zeit. Sehen Sie sich diese Fotos noch einmal an, und versuchen Sie, so viel wie möglich auf dem Foto zu beschreiben. Dann stellen Sie sich vor, wie die Menschen auf diesen Fotos sich fühlen, was sie denken oder sagen.

Was hat sich geändert? Was muß sich noch ändern?

1. In Kapiteln 10 und 11 haben Sie eine ganze Menge über deutsche Geschichte im 20. Jahrhundert gelesen. Versuchen wir mal, eine kurze Liste von einigen Tatsachen (*facts*) aus dieser Epoche an die Tafel zu schreiben. Was scheint Ihnen besonders wichtig zu sein? Warum?

2. Sie haben in diesem Kapitel über viele große Änderungen gelesen. Das Jahr 1989 bedeutete das Ende des Kalten Krieges. Müssen die USA heute immer noch so viel Geld wie früher für das Militär (*the military*) ausgeben? Stellen Sie sich mal vor, Sie sind Berater (*advisors*) des amerikanischen Präsidenten. Was würden Sie ihm sagen? Soll man dieses Geld jetzt für etwas anderes ausgeben? Was soll sich in unserem Land oder in der Welt ändern?

John F. Kennedy und Konrad Adenauer (Bundeskanzler der BRD) in Berlin.

Schreiben Sie zu Hause

D Gute Besserung!

Schreiben Sie diese Anekdote als Dialog zwischen Dr. Büchner und seinem Patienten Herrn Lenz. Der arme Herr Lenz liegt im Krankenhaus.

Dr. Büchner läuft morgens um 10.00 Uhr ins Krankenzimmer und sagt Herrn Lenz, es tut ihm leid, daß er sich verspätet hat. Er würde gern wissen, wie es Herrn Lenz geht und ob er sich besser fühlt. Er fragt, wo es ihm noch weh tut, und was er sonst noch braucht. Der Arzt sagt, daß er sich schon vorstellen kann, wie langweilig es ist, so lange im Bett liegen zu müssen.

Herr Lenz antwortet, daß es ihm nicht so gut geht, daß er noch sehr krank ist, daß es ihm überall weh tut, daß ihm das Essen im Krankenhaus nicht schmeckt und daß er das Fernsehen langweilig findet und einige neue Romane haben möchte.

Dr. Büchner sagt, es freut ihn zu sehen, daß Herr Lenz so viel besser aussieht. Er soll sich anziehen, denn er darf heute nach Hause.

Write as a series of natural exchanges, beginning like this:

DR. BÜCHNER: Guten Morgen, Herr Lenz!
HERR LENZ: Morgen, Herr Doktor.
DR. BÜCHNER: Es tut mir leid, daß ich mich verspätet habe . . .

E Complete the three mini-dialogues with appropriate nouns formed from adjectives. Choose from the following list:

gut	schön	verwandt	bekannt
deutsch	einfach	altmodisch	interessant
neu	kalt	toll	modern
besonder-	schlimm	herrlich	

1. A: Hast du etwas _____ zu berichten?
   B: Ja, in der Stadt habe ich heute etwas ganz _____ gesehen!
   A: Wirklich? In unserer langweiligen Stadt? Das ist schon etwas _____!

The first sentence in dialogue 2 requires a designation of nationality (without article, see p. 332).

2. A: Kennst du Steffi Hartmann? Sie ist _____ und ist gerade aus Stuttgart angekommen.
   B: Wie nett, dich kennenzulernen, Steffi! Eine alte _____ von mir aus der Schulzeit heißt Hartmann und wohnt auch in Stuttgart.
   C: Ja, dann ist sie vielleicht sogar eine _____ von mir. Unsere Familie ist ziemlich groß.

3. A: Das _____ bei uns im Sommer ist nicht nur das Wetter, sondern auch die hohen Berge und die schöne Natur.
   B: Super. Für mich ist das etwas _____. Ich bin in der Großstadt zu Hause.
   A: Aber in unserem kleinen Dorf auf dem Lande ist das Leben manchmal noch wie im 19. Jahrhundert. Da gibt es wenig _____ zu tun.
   B: Das ist mir ja egal! So was gibt's in der Großstadt! Ich bin zu euch gekommen, um das _____ zu sehen.

F Machen Sie ganze Sätze. Vergessen Sie die Endungen nicht! (// = Komma)

1. (*perfect tense*) wegen / dies- / Situation / auswandern / viel- / Menschen
2. (*first clause: past perfect tense*) nachdem / man / Mauer / bauen // (*second clause: simple past tense*) können / wenig- / Menschen / nach Westen / reisen
3. (*simple past tense*) Mauer / müssen / 28 Jahre / existieren // bis / politisch / Situation / sich ändern
4. (*present tense*) nach / Vereinigung / beid- (*genitive*) / deutsch- / Staaten / aussehen / Zukunft / anders
5. (*present tense*) all- / Menschen / sich freuen // wenn / Völker / Europa (*genitive*) / in Frieden / miteinander / leben / können

G **Wie sagt man das auf deutsch?**

1. When did your relatives immigrate to America?
2. Some emigrated from Germany sixty years ago.
3. Others arrived at the beginning of the nineteenth century.

4. Ute told me that you got hurt.
5. Yes, I broke my arm last week.
6. How did that happen?
7. I had an accident with my new bicycle.

8. Hurry up or we'll be late!
9. I still have to wash and get dressed.
10. Thank goodness we can afford a taxi.
11. Have the children already eaten?
12. Yes, and they've washed and are in bed already.

Zeittafel, 1945–heute

1948 Währungsreform im Western. Berlin-Blockade durch die Sowjets, Berliner Luftbrücke.

1945 9. Mai: Kapitulation Deutschlands. Der Zweite Weltkrieg ist zu Ende.

1949 Gründung der BRD und der DDR, Deutschland in zwei Staaten geteilt.

1955 BRD wird Mitglied der NATO, DDR wird Mitglied des Warschauer Paktes

1950

1960

1953 Protestdemonstrationen in Ostberlin gegen zu hohe Arbeitsnormen.

1947 Marshall-Plan bringt den Westzonen ökonomische Hilfe. Der Wiederaufbau beginnt.

1946 Erste demokratische Kommunalwahlen seit 1933.

1989 Spätsommer: tägliche Flucht vieler DDR-Bürger über Ungarn. Erich Honecker tritt zurück. Millionen demonstrieren in Ost-Berlin, Leipzig und anderen Städten.
9. November: Die Regierung öffnet die Grenzen.

1990 März: erste demokratische Wahlen in der DDR.
Juli: Währungsunion der beiden deutschen Staaten.
Oktober: deutsche Vereinigung.
Dezember: erste gesamtdeutsche demokratische Wahlen seit 1932.

1961 Bau der Mauer zwischen Ost- und West-Berlin

70er Jahre: Willi Brandts Ostpolitik. Normalisierung der Beziehungen zwischen BRD and DDR.

1994 Die letzten alliierten Truppen verlassen Berlin.

1970   1980   1990   1994 1995

1963 Besuch des US-Präsidenten John F. Kennedy an der Mauer.

1982 Beginn der Kanzlerschaft Helmut Kohls.

1987 750-Jahre-Feier in beiden Teilen der Stadt Berlin.

1991 Berlin wird wieder die Hauptstadt Deutschlands.

1995 Österreich wird Mitglied der Europäischen Union.

Communicative Goals

- Comparing things
- Saying how often things happen
- Talking about memories

Cultural Goal

- Applying your knowledge of twentieth-century Germany to an authentic German literary text

Schreibmaschine oder Computer?

HANS-PETER: Du, Karin, hast du das Buch mit, das ich dir geliehen habe?

KARIN: Ach, tut mir leid. Ich hab's wieder zu Hause gelassen. Ich arbeite noch an meinem Referat.

HANS-PETER: Ist ja egal. Du darfst es ruhig noch behalten. Willst du auch meine Schreibmaschine benutzen?

KARIN: Danke, aber ich schreibe die Arbeit zum ersten Mal auf dem Computer. Ich hab' gehört, die Software ist idiotensicher.

Here **Arbeit** = **schriftliche** (*written*) **Arbeit, Referat.**

Klatsch

PETRA: Wer war denn der Typ, mit dem Rita gestern weggegangen ist?

JÖRG: Der Mann, der so komisch angezogen war?

PETRA: Genau, den meine ich.

JÖRG: Das war der Rudi. Stell dir vor, sie hat sich mit ihm verlobt!

PETRA: Wenigstens sah er intelligenter aus als ihr letzter Freund.

Vor der Haustür

Notice two N-nouns: **Nachbar** and **Herr.**

Frau Schwarzer, die neulich ins Haus eingezogen ist, redet nach der Arbeit mit ihrem Nachbarn Herrn Beck.

FRAU SCHWARZER: Ach Herr Beck, ich wollte Sie etwas fragen. Wo kann ich am billigsten meinen VW reparieren lassen?

HERR BECK: In der nächsten Querstraße gibt's den besten Mechaniker in der Gegend, aber der ist leider nicht der billigste.

FRAU SCHWARZER: Hmm . . . Im Augenblick bin ich etwas knapp bei Kasse. Ich glaub', ich mache es diesmal lieber selber.

HERR BECK: Na, viel Spaß. Also, dann wünsche ich Ihnen einen schönen Abend noch.

FRAU SCHWARZER: Danke, gleichfalls!

Guten Abend is a greeting. **(Ich wünsche Ihnen einen) schönen Abend noch** is said when parting.

Notes on Usage: *es* and *etwas*

In spoken German, the pronoun **es** is often contracted to **'s**.

Ich **hab's** wieder zu Hause gelassen.
In der nächsten Querstraße **gibt's** den besten Mechaniker.

etwas Note three different meanings:

Ich habe **etwas** vergessen.	*something*
Ich bin **etwas** müde.	*somewhat, a little*
Hast du **etwas** Geld?	*some*

Typewriter or Computer?

H.-P.: Karin, do you have the book with you that I lent you?

K.: Oh, sorry. I left it at home again. I'm still working on my paper.

H.-P.: Doesn't matter. Go ahead and keep it. Do you want to use my typewriter too?

K.: Thanks anyway, but I'm writing the paper on the computer for the first time. I've heard that the software is foolproof.

Gossip

P.: Who was the guy Rita left with yesterday?

J.: The man who was dressed so funny?

P.: Exactly. He's the one I mean.

J.: That was Rudi. Just imagine, she's gotten engaged to him!

P.: At least he looked more intelligent than her last boyfriend.

At the Front Door

Ms. Schwarzer, who has recently moved into the building, is talking after work to her neighbor, Mr. Beck.

MS. S.: Oh Mr. Beck, I wanted to ask you something. Where can I get my VW repaired most cheaply?

MR. B.: In the next cross street there's the best mechanic in the area, but he's unfortunately not the cheapest.

MS. S.: Hmm . . . At the moment I'm somewhat short of cash. I think I'll do it myself this time.

MR. B.: Well, have fun. Then I'll wish you a good evening.

MS. S.: Thanks, you too.

Verben

behalten (behält), behielt, hat behalten to keep, retain

erinnern an (+ *acc.*) to remind of

sich erinnern an (+ *acc.*) to remember

lassen (läßt), ließ, hat gelassen to leave (something or someone), leave behind; to let, allow; to cause to be done

reden to talk, speak

reparieren to repair

sich verloben mit to become engaged to

weg·gehen, ging weg, ist weggegangen to go away, leave

wünschen to wish

der Typ: Used colloquially for males (**ein sympathischer Typ**). For both male and female: **Er/sie ist nicht mein Typ.**

Substantive

der Augenblick, -e moment

  im Augenblick at the moment

der Besuch, -e visit

der Computer, - computer

der Klatsch gossip

der Typ, -en (*slang*) guy

das Mal, -e time (*in the sense of "occurrence"*)

  zum ersten Mal for the first time

die Erinnerung, -en memory

die Gegend, -en area, region

die Maschine, -n machine

die Nacht, ̈e night

  in der Nacht at night

Gute Nacht. Good night.

die Querstraße, -n cross street

die Schreibmaschine, -n typewriter

die Software software

Remember the basic meaning of **ruhig**: peaceful, calm. Cf. the cartoon on p. 80.

Adjektive und Adverbien

diesmal this time

einmal once

etwas somewhat, a little

idiotensicher foolproof

intelligent intelligent

jedesmal every time

knapp scarce, in short supply

  knapp bei Kasse short of money

komisch peculiar, odd; funny

mit along with (someone)

nächst- nearest; next

neulich recently

ruhig (*as sentence adverb*) feel free to, go ahead and

  Du kannst ruhig hier bleiben. Feel free to stay here.

übermorgen the day after tomorrow

vorgestern the day before yesterday

Andere Vokabeln

als (*with adj. or adv. in comparative degree*) than

  intelligenter als more intelligent than

na well . . .

Variationen

A Persönliche Fragen

1. Schreiben Sie Ihre Referate immer noch auf einer Schreibmaschine oder benutzen Sie einen Computer?
2. Leihen Sie Ihren Freunden Bücher, oder nicht? Wie ist es mit CDs, Ihrem Fahrrad, oder mit Kleidern?
3. Was haben Sie heute zu Hause gelassen?
4. Jörg sagt, daß Rudi komisch angezogen war. Ziehen Sie sich manchmal komisch an? Was tragen Sie dann?
5. Wie alt soll man sein, bevor man sich verlobt? Was meinen Sie?
6. Besitzen Sie einen Wagen? Was für einen?
7. Sind Sie ein guter Mechaniker? Können Sie Ihr Auto selber reparieren?

B Übung: Was braucht man?

Um ihr Referat zu schreiben, braucht Karin Bücher eine Schreibmaschine oder einen Computer, und vielleicht auch ein Wörterbuch. Was braucht man, um . . .

einen Brief zu schreiben?
das Frühstück zu machen?
eine Urlaubsreise zu machen?
eine Fremdsprache zu lernen?
einkaufen zu gehen?
eine Radtour zu machen?
eine Wanderung in den Bergen zu machen?

C **Übung: Das Beste in der Gegend**

Herr Beck weiß, wer der beste Mechaniker in der Gegend ist. Wissen Sie, wo man das Beste in der Gegend findet? Wo ist hier in unserer Gegend . . .

> das beste griechische Restaurant? das beste französische Restaurant?
> das beste Kleidergeschäft?
> das beste Hotel?
> die beste Kneipe?
> die beste Pizza?
> das beste Sportgeschäft?
> der beste Supermarkt?

D **Übung: Sie dürfen das ruhig machen.**

Sie sagen, Sie würden gern etwas machen. Der/Die nächste sagt, Sie dürfen es ruhig machen (oder) Sie können es ruhig machen.

> BEISPIEL: Ich würde gern deinen Kuli benutzen.
> Klar, du darfst ihn *ruhig* benutzen.

The sentence adverb **ruhig** *goes immediately after the inflected verb and all personal pronouns.*

1. Ich würde gerne deinen Wagen behalten.
2. Heute abend würde ich dich gerne besuchen.
3. Ich würde gern etwas Wichtiges sagen.
4. Ich würde meine Freunde gerne einladen.
5. Ich würde gern etwas essen.
6. Meinen Wagen würde ich gerne hier lassen.
7. Ich würde mir gerne die Kirche ansehen.
8. Ich würde gern meine Freundin Gertrud mitbringen.

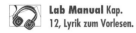

Joseph von Eichendorff was one of the foremost poets of the Romantic movement in Germany. Reverence for nature, longing for one's beloved, and nostalgia for one's homeland are all typical themes for the Romantics. The poem "Heimweh" (*Homesickness*) is from Eichendorff's story *Aus dem Leben eines Taugenichts* (*From the Life of a Good-for-Nothing*), in which the hero, in Italy, yearns for Germany and his beloved.

Lab Manual Kap. 12, Lyrik zum Vorlesen.

Heimweh

Wer in die Fremde° will wandern	= ins Ausland
Der muß mit der Liebsten° gehn,	beloved
Es jubeln° und lassen die andern	rejoice
Den Fremden alleine stehn.	
Was wisset ihr, dunkele Wipfel°	treetops
Von der alten, schönen Zeit?	
Ach, die Heimat hinter den Gipfeln,°	peaks
Wie liegt sie von hier so weit!	
Am liebsten° betracht° ich die Sterne,°	most of all / contemplate / stars
Die schienen, wie° ich ging zu ihr,	= als
Die Nachtigall° hör ich so gerne,	nightingale
Sie sang vor der Liebsten Tür.	
Der Morgen, das ist meine Freude!°	joy
Da steig ich in stiller° Stund'	quiet
Auf den höchsten° Berg in die Weite,°	highest / distance
Grüß dich, Deutschland, aus Herzens Grund!°	aus... from the bottom of my heart

Joseph von Eichendorff
(1788–1857)

Zeichnung (*drawing*) von Ludwig Richter (19. Jhdt.)

Comparison of Adjectives and Adverbs

Comparing things is a communicative goal.

When adjectives or adverbs are used in comparisons, they can occur in three stages or degrees.

- Positive degree (*basic form*)

  so interessant wie = *as interesting as*

Jörg ist **so interessant wie** Dieter.	*Jörg is **as interesting as** Dieter.*
Jutta läuft **schnell**.	*Jutta runs **fast**.*

- Comparative degree (*marker:* **-er**)

  interessanter als = *more interesting than*

Jörg ist **interessanter als** Helmut.	*Jörg is **more interesting than** Helmut.*
Jutta läuft **schneller als** ich.	*Jutta runs **faster than** I do.*

- Superlative degree of attributive adjectives (*marker:* **-st**)

  der interessanteste Schüler = *the most interesting pupil*
  die schnellste Läuferin = *the fastest runner*

- Superlative degree of adverbs and predicate adjectives

  (*marker:* **am _____ -(e)sten**)

  am interessantesten = *most interesting*

Von allen Schülern ist Jörg **am interessantesten**.	*Of all the pupils, Jörg is **most interesting**.*
Jutta läuft **am schnellsten**.	*Jutta runs **fastest**.*

> ## Die schnellsten Männer
> ## der Welt starten nicht in Monza,
> ## sondern im Büro.

Formation of Comparative Degree

- To form the comparative degree of any adjective or adverb, add the marker **-er** to the basic form:

Spelling note: Adjectives ending in **-el** and **-er** drop the **-e-** in the comparative:
dunkel → dunkler
teuer → teurer.

basic form	+	-er	=	*comparative degree*
schnell-		-er		**schneller**
dunkel-		-er		**dunkler**
interessant-		-er		**interessanter**

English adjectives longer than two syllables form their comparative with *more: interesting—more interesting*. German does not follow this pattern. Simply add **-er** to make the comparative, no matter how long the adjective is: **interessant—interessanter**.

- Attributive adjectives add the regular adjective endings *after* the comparative **-er-** ending.

basic form	+	-er-	+	*adjective ending*
schnell-		-er-		-en
interessant-		-er-		-es

> Wir fuhren mit dem **schnelleren** Zug. *We went by the faster train.*
> Ich lese ein **interessanteres** Buch. *I'm reading a more interesting book.*

- **als** = *than* when used with the comparative.

> Das Buch ist interessanter **als** der Artikel. *The book is more interesting than the article.*

Lab Manual Kap. 12, Üb. 1 and Var. zur Üb. 3, 4, 6–11.

Workbook Kap. 12, A–F.

 1 **Übung**

Everyone is praising Jörg, but you respond that you are *more* everything than he is.

> BEISPIEL: A: Jörg ist interessant.
> B: Aber ich bin interessanter als er.

1. Jörg ist hübsch.
2. Er ist ruhig.
3. Er läuft schnell.
4. Er ist ehrlich.
5. Jörg ist fleißig.
6. Er ist freundlich.
7. Er steht früh auf.
8. Er ist sportlich.

2 **Übung: Vergleichen wir!** *(Let's compare!)*

Antworten Sie mit einem ganzen Satz.

> BEISPIEL: A: Was fährt schneller als ein Fahrrad?
> B: Ein Auto fährt schneller als ein Fahrrad.

1. Was fährt langsamer als ein Zug?
2. Was schmeckt Ihnen besser als Salat?
3. Was ist moderner als eine Schreibmaschine?
4. Wer ist reicher als Sie?
5. Welches Auto ist teurer als ein Volkswagen?
6. Welche Energiequelle (*energy source*) ist umweltfreundlicher als Öl?
7. Welche Stadt ist sauberer als New York?
8. Welche Länder sind kleiner als Deutschland?

Hier sehen Sie einen der größten Kohlendioxidfresser der Welt.

Sie sind Verkäufer im Kaufhaus. Ihr Professor spielt einen Kunden. Nichts scheint ihm zu gefallen. Sie versuchen, ihm etwas Schöneres, Billigeres usw. zu zeigen.

> BEISPIEL: A: Dieses Hemd ist mir nicht dunkel genug.
> B: Hier haben wir dunklere Hemden.

1. Diese Blumen sind mir nicht schön genug.
2. Diese Brötchen sind mir nicht frisch genug.
3. Diese Taschen sind mir nicht leicht genug.
4. Diese Bücher sind mir nicht billig genug.
5. Diese Fahrräder sind mir nicht leicht genug.
6. Diese Computer sind mir nicht schnell genug.

Formation of the Superlative

The superlative is formed in the following ways:

Adverbs   All adverbs form their superlative using the following pattern:

am _____-(e)sten
am schnellsten   *most quickly*

Note on spelling: An extra **-e-** is added when the basic form ends in **-d, -t, -s, -ß,** or **-z: am mildesten, am heißesten.**

Jutta läuft **am schnellsten.**	*Jutta runs **fastest**.*
Hans hat **am schönsten** gesungen.	*Hans sang **most beautifully**.*

German has no superlative marker like English *most*. No matter how long an adverb is, simply add **-sten: am interessantesten** = *most interestingly*.

Attributive Adjectives   With attributive adjectives, add the regular adjective endings after the superlative **-(e)st-**, for example:

basic form	+	*-(e)st-*	+	*adjective ending*
interessant-		-est-		-e
schnell-		-st-		-en

Die **interessanteste** Studentin heißt Marianne.	*The **most interesting** student is named Marianne.*
Wir fuhren mit dem **schnellsten** Zug.	*We took the **fastest** train.*

Predicate Adjectives   Predicate adjectives in the superlative may occur either in the **am _____-sten** pattern or with the definite article and regular adjective endings.

You can use the superlative only with the *definite* article, never with the *indefinite* article: **der tiefste See,** but not **ein tiefster See.**

Albert ist **am interessantesten.**	*Albert is **most interesting**.*
Albert ist **der interessanteste.**	*Albert is **the most interesting**.*
Diese Bücher sind **die interessantesten.**	*These books are **the most interesting** (ones).*

4 Übung: Ich mache das am besten!

A visitor is praising the whole class. You then praise yourself in the superlative.

> BEISPIEL: A: Sie laufen alle schnell.
> B: Aber ich laufe am schnellsten.

1. Sie sind alle freundlich.
2. Sie sind alle sehr fleißig.
3. Sie singen alle sehr schön.
4. Sie sind alle elegant angezogen.
5. Sie sind alle sehr sportlich.
6. Sie denken alle sehr kreativ.

5 Gruppenarbeit: Ich bin der/die _____-ste!

Here are some adjectives you can use to describe yourself. Choose the one that you think you exemplify the best of anyone in the class. (Don't take this too seriously!) Then say, **Ich bin der/die** _____**-ste.**

> BEISPIEL: Ich bin der/die schönste hier!

aktiv	elegant	hungrig
altmodisch	faul	modern
blöd	fleißig	radikal
clever	höflich	wahnsinnig

clever in German means *sly, ingenious.*

6 Übung: Im Laden

Sie sind wieder Verkäufer, und Ihre Professorin spielt eine Kundin. Sie sucht etwas, und Sie sagen, Sie haben das Neueste, Billigste usw.

> BEISPIEL: A: Ich suche billige Weine.
> B: Hier sind die *billigsten* Weine.

1. Ich suche neue Schuhe.
2. Ich suche schöne Bilder.
3. Ich suche interessante Bücher.
4. Ich suche moderne Stühle.
5. Ich suche leichte Fahrräder.
6. Ich suche elegante Kleider.

Umlaut in Comparative and Superlative

Some comparative and superlative adjectives have two possible forms: **roter/röter, nasser/nässer, gesunder/gesünder. Gesund** is the only two-syllable adjective where umlaut is possible.

Many one-syllable adjectives and adverbs whose stem vowels are **a, o,** or **u** (but *not* **au**) are umlauted in the comparative and superlative degrees. Here is a list of adjectives and adverbs you already know. Some occur in easy-to-remember pairs of opposites.

old	alt	älter	am ältesten
young	jung	jünger	am jüngsten
dumb	dumm	dümmer	am dümmsten
smart	klug	klüger	am klügsten
cold	kalt	kälter	am kältesten
warm	warm	wärmer	am wärmsten
short	kurz	kürzer	am kürzesten
long	lang	länger	am längsten

strong	stark	stärker	am stärksten
weak	schwach	schwächer	am schwächsten
sick	krank	kränker	am kränksten
healthy	gesund	gesünder	am gesündesten
poor	arm	ärmer	am ärmsten
hard, harsh	hart	härter	am härtesten
often	oft	öfter	am öftesten
red	rot	röter	am rötesten
black	schwarz	schwärzer	am schwärzesten

7 Gruppenarbeit: kalt / kälter / am kältesten

The first student reads a sentence, and the next two respond with the comparative and superlative.

BEISPIEL: A: Meine Wohnung ist kalt.
B: Meine Wohnung ist noch kälter.
C: Aber meine Wohnung ist am kältesten.

1. Mein Bruder ist stark.
2. Mein Auto ist alt.
3. Mein Referat ist lang.
4. Mein Freund ist krank.

5. Meine Schwester ist jung.
6. Mein Zimmer ist warm.
7. Mein Besuch war kurz.
8. Mein Beruf ist hart.

Irregular Comparatives and Superlatives

Some of the most frequently used adjectives and adverbs in German have irregular forms in the comparative and superlative.

Note: The superlative of **groß** adds **-t (größt-)** rather than **-est** to the stem.

positive	*comparative*	*superlative*	
groß	größer	am größten	*big/bigger/biggest*
gut	besser	am besten	*good, well/better/best*
hoch, hoh-	höher	am höchsten	*high/higher/highest*
nahe	näher	am nächsten	*near/nearer/nearest; next*
viel	mehr	am meisten	*much, many/more/most*
gern	lieber	am liebsten	*like to/prefer to/most of all like to*

• The three degrees of **gern** are used to say how much you like to do things.

Ich gehe **gern** ins Kino.   *I like to go to the movies.*
Ich gehe **lieber** ins Theater.   *I'd rather (or) I prefer to go to the theater.*
Ich gehe **am liebsten** ins Konzert.   *Most of all, I like to go to concerts.*

Wenig, the antonym of **viel**, functions in the same way:
Ich esse **wenig** Brot.
Ich habe **wenige** Freunde.
Ich habe **weniger** Freunde als du.

• **Viel** means *much* or *a lot of* and it has *no adjective endings*. **Viele** means *many* and *does* have regular plural endings.

Ich esse **viel** Brot.   *I eat a lot of bread.*
Ich habe **viele** Freunde.   *I have many friends.*

The comparative degree **mehr** *never* has adjective endings.

Du hast **mehr** Freunde als ich.	*You have more friends than I.*

The superlative degree **meist-** *does* take endings; in addition, it is used with the definite article, in contrast to English *most*.

Die meisten Studenten essen in der Mensa.	***Most** students eat in the cafeteria.*

8 Übung: gut, besser, am besten

Rank the items on the right according to the criteria on the left.

BEISPIEL: schnell fahren   Bus, Fahrrad, Zug
Ein Fahrrad fährt schnell, ein Bus fährt schneller, und ein Zug fährt am schnellsten.

1. gut schmecken   Schokolade, Wurst, Kartoffelsalat
2. hoch sein   Berg, Haus, Dom
3. nahe sein   Studentenwohnheim, Mensa, Bibliothek
4. viel wissen   Schüler, Professoren, Studenten

9 Gruppenarbeit: Was sind Ihre Präferenzen?

Rank your preferences, as in the example.

BEISPIEL: trinken   Tee, Kaffee, Milch
Ich trinke gern Milch. Ich trinke lieber Kaffee. Aber am liebsten trinke ich Tee.

1. lesen   Zeitungen, Gedichte, Romane
2. hören   Rockmusik, Jazz, klassische Musik
3. wohnen   in der Stadt, auf dem Land, am Meer
4. spielen   Fußball, Tennis, Volleyball
5. bekommen   Briefe, Geschenke, gute Noten
6. essen   Pommes frites, Sauerkraut, Bauernbrot
7. schreiben   Briefe, Referate, Postkarten

Comparisons

genauso . . . wie = *just as . . . as*
nicht so . . . wie = *not as . . . as*

Heute ist es **genauso kalt wie** gestern.	*Today is **just as cold as** yesterday.*
Stuttgart ist **nicht so groß wie** Berlin.	*Stuttgart is **not as large as** Berlin.*

immer _____-er (shows progressive change)

Das Kind wird **immer größer**. *The child's getting **bigger and bigger**.*

Sie liest **immer mehr** Bücher. *She's reading **more and more** books.*

Proverb: **Je stärker der Wein, desto schwächer das Bein.**

je _____-er, desto _____-er = the _____-er, the _____-er

Je schneller, desto besser. *The faster the better.*
Je länger ich lebe, **desto weniger** weiß ich. *The longer I live, the less I know.*

10 Gruppenarbeit: Damals und jetzt

Vergleichen wir (*Let's compare*) damals und jetzt. Jeder sagt, wie es früher war, und wie sich alles immer mehr ändert.

BEISPIEL: Früher hatte man mehr Zeit, heute ist man immer mehr in Eile.
Früher war das Lebenstempo langsamer, jetzt wird es immer schneller.
Früher kostete das Studium . . .

11 Übung: Vergleiche (*Comparisons*)

Bring in pictures or photos that you have drawn, taken, or found in books or magazines. Find similarities and differences in these pictures and compare them in German for the class.

BEISPIELE: Diese Bäume sind höher als diese hier, aber dieser Berg ist genauso hoch wie der andere.

Diese Mutter sieht nicht so jung aus wie diese hier, aber dieses Kind ist genauso alt wie das Kind da. Das dritte Kind ist das älteste.

Relative Pronouns and Relative Clauses

A relative clause is a subordinate clause that modifies or further clarifies a noun. Relative clauses are introduced by relative pronouns. Compare the following sentences:

Das ist das **neue** Buch. *That's the **new** book.*

rel. pron.
Das ist das Buch, ***das*** du mir geliehen hast.
*That's the book **that** you lent me.*

The relative clause **das du mir geliehen hast**, like the descriptive adjective **neue**, modifies **Buch** by telling *which* book is being talked about.

The relative pronouns in English are *who, whom, whose, that,* and *which.* The German relative pronoun is identical in most cases to the definite article, which you already know. Study the following table and note especially the forms in bold, which are *different* from the definite article.

Compare declension of definite article on p. 231. There are only three relative pronouns that are not identical to forms of the definite article: **denen, dessen,** and **deren.** These forms are bolded in the table.

Relative Pronouns				
	masc.	**neut.**	**fem.**	**plur.**
nom.	der	das	die	die
acc.	den			
dat.	dem	dem	der	**denen**
gen.	**dessen**	**dessen**	**deren**	**deren**

Sentences having a relative clause can be thought of as a combination of two separate sentences that share a common element (a noun and the pronoun representing it). This element in the main clause is called the *antecedent* because it *antecedes* (i.e., precedes) the relative pronoun. In the relative clause, the relative pronoun *relates* (i.e., refers) back to the antecedent. Here are some examples. Note how the antecedent and the relative pronoun always denote the same person or thing.

                              masc.
                              sing.
         antecedent   *nom.*

1. Das ist **der Typ.**   **Er** war im Kino.

   Das ist der Typ, **der** im Kino war.
               rel. pron.
   That's the guy who was at the movies.

                              fem.
                              sing.
        antecedent   *dat.*

2. Kennst du **die Frau?**   Ich arbeite mit **ihr.**

   Kennst du die Frau, mit **der** ich arbeite?
               rel. pron.
   Do you know the woman [whom] I work with?

                              masc.
                              sing.
        antecedent   *gen.*

3. Das ist **der Autor.**   Die Romane **des Autors** sind berühmt.

   Das ist der Autor, **dessen** Romane berühmt sind.
               rel. pron.
   That's the author whose novels are famous.

4. Hast du **die Bücher**?   *antecedent*   *acc.* *plur.*   Ich habe **sie** dir geliehen.

Hast du die Bücher, **die** ich dir geliehen habe?
rel. pron.

Do you have the books [that] I lent you?

Rules for Relative Clauses

1. The relative pronoun is *never* omitted in German, as it often is in English (examples 2 and 4 above).

2. The relative pronoun *always* has the same gender and number as its antecedent.

3. The case of a relative pronoun is determined by its function in the relative clause.

fem. *fem.*
sing. *sing.*
nom. *dat.*

Das ist **die Frau**, mit **der** ich arbeite.

4. If the relative pronoun is the object of a preposition, the preposition *always precedes* it in the relative clause (example 2 above). In English the preposition often comes at the end of the relative clause (e.g., *the woman I work* **with**). This is *never* the case in German (die Frau, **mit** der ich arbeite).

5. The relative clause is *always a subordinate clause* with verb-last word order. The relative clause is *always* set off from the rest of the sentence by commas.

6. The relative clause is usually placed immediately after its antecedent.

Das Buch, das du mir geliehen hast, hat mir geholfen.

The book that you lent me helped me.

Lab Manual Kap. 12, Üb. 12, 14, and Var. zur Üb. 17, 18.

Workbook Kap. 12, G–K.

12 Kettenreaktion

Student A liest den ersten Satz auf deutsch vor. Studentin B gibt eine englische Übersetzung und liest dann den nächsten Satz vor, usw.

1. Das ist der Mann, der hier wohnt.
2. Das ist der Mann, den ich kenne.
3. Das ist der Mann, dem wir helfen.
4. Das ist der Mann, dessen Frau ich kenne.

Der Man, der alles kann.

5. Das ist das Fahrrad, das sehr leicht ist.
6. Das ist das Fahrrad, das sie gekauft hat.
7. Das ist das Fahrrad, mit dem ich zur Arbeit fahre.
8. Das ist das Fahrrad, dessen Farbe mir gefällt.

9. Das ist die Frau, die Deutsch kann.
10. Das ist die Frau, die wir brauchen.
11. Das ist die Frau, der wir Geld geben.
12. Das ist die Frau, deren Romane ich kenne.

13. Das sind die Leute, die mich kennen.
14. Das sind die Leute, die ich kenne.
15. Das sind die Leute, denen wir helfen.
16. Das sind die Leute, deren Kinder wir kennen.

> # Informationen, die Sie nicht über Ihr Telefon bekommen:
> ## Frankfurter Allgemeine

13 Übung

Lesen Sie jeden Satz mit dem richtigen Relativpronomen vor.

In Europa ist nur die Wolga in Rußland länger als die Donau (2.850 k). Die Zugspitze (2.692 m) ist der höchste Berg Deutschlands.

1. Die Donau ist ein Fluß, _____ durch Österreich fließt.   (*that*)
2. Der Berg, _____ man am Horizont sieht, ist die Zugspitze.   (*that*)
3. Kennst du den Herrn, _____ dieser Wagen gehört?   (*to whom*)
4. Der Professor, _____ Bücher dort liegen, kommt gleich zurück.   (*whose*)
5. Das ist ein Schaufenster, _____ immer bunt aussieht.   (*that*)
6. Mir schmeckt jedes Abendessen, _____ du kochst.   (*that*)
7. Das Kind, _____ ich geholfen habe, ist wieder gesund.   (*whom*)
8. Sie kommt aus einem Land, _____ Regierung undemokratisch ist.   (*whose*)
9. Die Studentin, _____ neben mir saß, war im zweiten Semester.   (*who*)
10. Beschreiben Sie mir die Rolle, _____ ich spielen soll.   (*that*)
11. Christa, _____ die Schreibmaschine gehört, leiht sie dir gerne.   (*to whom*)
12. Die Touristengruppe, _____ Gepäck dort steht, ist aus England.   (*whose*)
13. Wer sind die Leute, _____ dort vor der Mensa stehen?   (*who*)
14. Da sind ein paar Studenten, _____ du kennenlernen sollst.   (*whom*)
15. Es gibt viele Menschen, _____ dieser Arzt geholfen hat.   (*whom*)
16. Sind das die Kinder, _____ Hund gestorben ist?   (*whose*)

Antworten Sie wie im Beispielsatz.

> BEISPIEL: Arbeiten Sie für *diesen* Chef?
> Ja, das ist der Chef, für den ich arbeite.

1. Sind Sie durch *diese* Stadt gefahren?
2. Haben Sie in *diesem* Hotel übernachtet?
3. Haben Sie mit *diesen* Amerikanern geredet?
4. Haben Sie an *dieser* Uni studiert?
5. Erinnern Sie sich an *diesen* Roman?
6. Kommen Sie aus *dieser* Stadt?
7. Wohnen Sie bei *dieser* Familie?
8. Spricht er mit *diesen* Menschen?
9. Steht unser Wagen hinter *diesem* Gebäude?
10. Bekommst du Briefe von *diesen* Freunden?
11. Spielst du für *diese* Mannschaft?

15 Übung

Machen Sie aus den zwei Sätzen *einen* Satz. Machen Sie aus dem zweiten Satz einen Relativsatz.

> BEISPIEL: Ich kenne die Frau. (Du meinst sie.)
> Ich kenne die Frau, die du meinst.

These sentences are paired as conversational exchanges. The relative clauses in numbers 4 and 10 begin with prepositions. In numbers 11 and 14, the relative pronoun is in the genitive case.

1. Suchst du die Schokolade? (Sie war hier.)
2. Nein, ich habe selber Schokolade. (Ich habe sie mitgebracht.)

3. Ist das die Geschichte? (Horst hat sie erzählt.)
4. Ja, er erzählt Geschichten. (Man muß über seine Geschichten lachen.)

5. Das ist ein Buch. (Ingrid hat es schon letztes Jahr gelesen.)
6. Meinst du das Buch? (Es ist jetzt sehr bekannt.)

Rosen an einer alten Mauer (Schloß Langenburg).

7. Ist das der Mann? (Sie haben ihm geholfen.)
8. Nein, ich habe einem anderen Mann geholfen. (Er war nicht so jung.)

9. Kennst du die Studenten? (Sie wohnen in der Altstadt.)
10. Ja, das sind die Studenten. (Ich esse in der Mensa zusammen mit ihnen.)

11. Wie heißt der Junge? (Sein Vater ist Professor.)
12. Er hat einen komischen Namen. (Ich habe ihn vergessen.)

13. Ist die Frau berufstätig? (Du wohnst bei ihr.)
14. Ja, sie ist eine Frau. (Ihre Kinder wohnen nicht mehr zu Hause.)

16 Partnerarbeit: Ist das ein neuer Mantel?

Fragen Sie einander, ob Ihre Kleider und andere Sachen neu sind. Antworten Sie, daß Sie alles letztes Jahr gekauft haben. Benutzen Sie einen Relativsatz in Ihrer Antwort.

BEISPIEL: Ist das ein neuer Mantel?
Nein, das ist ein Mantel, *den* ich letztes Jahr kaufte.

The Relative Pronoun *was*

A relative clause following the pronoun antecedents **das, etwas, nichts, viel, wenig,** and **alles** begins with the relative pronoun **was.** Note again that English often leaves out the relative pronoun, whereas German *requires* it.

Stimmt **das, was** er uns erzählte?	*Is what he told us right?* (literally: *Is that right what he told us?*)
Gibt es noch **etwas, was** Sie brauchen?	*Is there something else [that] you need?*
Nein, Sie haben **nichts, was** ich brauche.	*No, you have nothing [that] I need.*
Alles, was er sagt, ist falsch.	*Everything [that] he says is wrong.*

Was must also begin a relative clause whose antecedent is a neuter adjectival noun (see p. 329–330):

Was war **das Interessante, was** du mir zeigen wolltest?	*What was the interesting thing [that] you wanted to show me?*
Ist das **das Beste, was** Sie haben?	*Is that the best [that] you have?*

Was also begins a relative clause whose antecedent is an entire clause (English uses *which*):

Rita hat sich verlobt, was ich nicht verstehen kann.	*Rita got engaged, which I can't understand.*

17 Übung: Etwas, was mir gefällt. / Etwas, was mich ärgert.

Ihre Professorin sagt etwas und möchte Ihre Reaktion hören. Ist das etwas, was Sie ärgert, oder etwas, was Ihnen gefällt?

> BEISPIEL: Die Umwelt ist sehr verschmutzt.
> Das ist etwas, was mich ärgert!

1. Das Studium wird immer teurer.
2. Der Kalte Krieg ist zu Ende.
3. Ihr Mitbewohner spielt abends laute Rockmusik.
4. Heute abend in der Mensa gibt es Pizza zum Abendessen.
5. Die Ferien beginnen bald.
6. Morgen kommen viele Verwandte zu Besuch.

18 Partnerarbeit: Was war das Tollste, was du je gemacht hast?

Below are cues for asking each other questions such as, "What's the greatest thing you've ever done?" Take turns asking each other the questions.

> BEISPIEL: toll / machen
> A: Was war das Tollste, was du je gemacht hast?
> B: Ich habe 1989 auf der Berliner Mauer gesessen.

1. schwierig / machen
2. schön / sehen
3. gefährlich / machen
4. dumm / sagen
5. erstaunlich / hören
6. gut / essen
7. interessant / lesen
8. toll / bekommen

The Verb *lassen*

Caution! Do not confuse these principal parts: **lassen (läßt), ließ, hat gelassen** and **lesen (liest), las, hat gelesen** (*to read*).

The verb **lassen** has several meanings in German:

- *to leave (something or someone), leave behind*

Lassen Sie uns bitte allein.	*Please leave us alone.*
Hast du deinen Mantel im Restaurant **gelassen**?	*Did you leave your coat in the restaurant?*

- *to allow, let:* **lassen** + infinitive

Man **läßt** uns **gehen**.	*They're letting us leave.*
Laß doch die Kinder **spielen**!	*Let the children play!*

- *to have or order something done:* **lassen** + infinitive

In the following sentences **lassen** shows that the subject is not performing an action, but rather having it done by someone else.

Sie **läßt** ihren Wagen **reparieren**.   *She's having her car fixed.*

The accusative case shows who performs the action:

Sie läßt **den Mechaniker** ihren Wagen reparieren.   *She's having the mechanic fix her car.*

A dative reflexive pronoun shows explicitly that one is having something done for one's own benefit.

Ich lasse **mir** ein Haus bauen.   *I'm having a house built (for myself).*

When **lassen** is used with a dependent infinitive, it takes the double infinitive construction in the perfect tense. The structure is parallel to that of the modal verbs (see page 205).

double infinitive

Die Beamtin hat mich nicht **reden lassen.**
The official didn't let me speak.

Ich habe den Wagen **reparieren lassen.**
I had my car repaired.

Lab Manual Kap. 12, Var. zur Üb. 19, 21.

Workbook Kap. 12, L, M.

19 Übung: Warum ist das nicht hier?

Sagen Sie, wo Sie diese Menschen oder Dinge gelassen haben. Rechts gibt es einige Möglichkeiten, aber Sie können auch frei antworten.

BEISPIEL: Warum haben Sie heute keine Jacke?
Ich habe sie zu Hause gelassen.

1. Warum sind Ihre Kinder nicht hier?   in der Schweiz
2. Warum tragen Sie heute keine Brille (*glasses*)?   im Rucksack
3. Warum haben Sie Ihr Referat nicht mit?   bei der Großmutter
4. Warum haben sie Ihren Ausweis nicht mit?   auf dem Bett
5. Warum haben Sie Ihren Wagen nicht mit?   zu Hause
6. Warum ist Ihre Tochter nicht hier?   in der Manteltasche

20 Partnerarbeit: Wo hast du das gelassen?

Hat Ihre Partnerin heute etwas nicht mitgebracht? Fragen Sie sie, wo sie es gelassen hat.

BEISPIEL: A: Wo hast du heute deine grüne Jacke gelassen?
B: Ich habe sie im Zimmer gelassen.

21 Übung: Er hat es machen lassen.

Manchmal will man etwas nicht selber machen, sondern man will es lieber machen lassen. Was haben diese Leute machen lassen?

BEISPIEL: Hat Fritz das Mittagessen selber gekocht?
Nein, er hat es kochen lassen.

1. Hat Herr von Hippel sein Haus selber gebaut?
2. Hat Frau Beck ihren Wagen selber repariert?
3. Hat Oma ihren Koffer selbst getragen?
4. Hat deine Freundin sich die Haare selber geschnitten?
5. Hat Frau Schwarzer den Brief selbst abgeschickt (*sent off*)?
6. Hat Günter das Referat selbst geschrieben?
7. Hat Robert seine Schuhe selber geputzt (*cleaned*)?

The equivalent you choose for the English verb *to leave* depends on whether it means *to go away* (intransitive) or *to leave something behind* (transitive), and also on what or whom you are leaving.

- Intransitive: **gehen, weggehen, abfahren** (= *leave by vehicle*)

Ich muß jetzt **gehen**.	*I have to leave now.*
Er **ging weg**, ohne etwas zu sagen.	*He left without saying anything.*
Um elf **fuhr** sie mit dem Zug **ab**.	*She left by train at eleven.*

- Transitive: **lassen** (= *leave something somewhere*); **verlassen** (= *leave a person or place for good*)

Ich habe meine Tasche zu Hause **gelassen**.	*I left my bag at home.*
Viele wollten ihre Heimat nicht **verlassen**.	*Many did not want to leave their homeland.*

22 Übung: Wie sagt man das auf deutsch?

1. Jörg left the house at seven.
2. Jörg left at seven.
3. Jörg's train left at seven.
4. Jörg left his book in the Mensa.
5. Jörg, please leave the room.
6. Jörg left his car in front of the hotel.
7. Jörg wants to leave school.

Time Phrases with *Mal*

The English word *time* has two German equivalents, **die Zeit** and **das Mal**.

Zeit denotes time in general.

Ich brauche mehr **Zeit**.	*I need more time.*

Mal denotes an occurrence.

wie viele Male = wie oft

Das erste **Mal** habe ich das Buch nicht verstanden.	*I didn't understand the book the first time.*
Wie viele **Male** hast du es gelesen?	*How many times did you read it?*

Learn the following idioms with **Mal**.

das erste Mal	*the first time*
zum ersten Mal	*for the first time*
zum zweiten Mal	*for the second time*
zum letzten Mal	*for the last time*
diesmal	*this time*
jedesmal	*every time*
das nächste Mal	*(the) next time*

Note on Usage: The suffix **-mal**

Note that **-mal** added as a suffix to cardinal numbers forms adverbs indicating repetition.

einmal	*once*
zweimal	*twice*
zwanzigmal	*twenty times*
hundertmal	*a hundred times*
zigmal	*umpteen times*

Workbook Kap. 12, N.

23 Übung: Wie oft haben Sie das schon gemacht?

Fragen Sie einander, wie oft Sie etwas schon gemacht haben.

> BEISPIEL: A: John, wie oft hast du schon dein Lieblingsbuch
> gelesen?
> B: Ich habe es schon viermal gelesen.

1. Wie oft hast du schon deinen Wagen reparieren lassen?
2. Wie oft bist du dieses Jahr schon nach Hause gefahren?
3. Wie oft bist du dieses Semester schon ins Kino gegangen?
4. Wie oft hast du dieses Semester schon Referate schreiben müssen?
5. Wie oft hast du dieses Semester schon deinen besten Freund angerufen?
6. Wie oft bist du schon am Wochenende weggefahren?

24 Übung: Wie sagt man das auf deutsch?

1. Please give me more time.
   Unfortunately, I don't have more time for you.

2. I'm trying it for the first time.
   The next time it's easier.

3. I need time and money.
   You say that every time.

25 Gruppenarbeit: Was haben Sie zum ersten Mal hier erlebt?

Wenn man Student wird, erlebt und lernt man viel Neues. Sagen Sie, was Sie hier an der Uni oder am College zum ersten Mal getan, erlebt, gelernt, gesehen, angefangen oder versucht haben.

> BEISPIEL: Ich habe *zum ersten Mal* etwas über Astronomie gelernt.
> Ich habe *zum ersten Mal* über Politik diskutiert.

Maurice Lacroix

ZEIT IN IHRER SCHÖNSTEN FORM.

Erinnerungen

Parts of the Day

Proverb: **Morgenstund' hat Gold im Mund** (*The early bird catches the worm*).

Note that these are all adverbial phrases and therefore written lowercase.

German divides up the day in the following way:

$$
\text{gestern} \begin{cases} \text{früh } \textit{oder } \text{morgen} \\ \text{nachmittag} \\ \text{abend} \end{cases} \qquad \textit{yesterday} \begin{cases} \textit{morning} \\ \textit{afternoon} \\ \textit{evening} \end{cases}
$$

$$
\text{heute} \begin{cases} \text{früh } \textit{oder } \text{morgen} \\ \text{nachmittag} \\ \text{abend} \end{cases} \qquad \textit{this} \begin{cases} \textit{morning} \\ \textit{afternoon} \\ \textit{evening} \end{cases}
$$

$$
\text{morgen} \begin{cases} \text{früh} \\ \text{nachmittag} \\ \text{abend} \end{cases} \qquad \textit{tomorrow} \begin{cases} \textit{morning} \\ \textit{afternoon} \\ \textit{evening} \end{cases}
$$

In addition, remember:

Workbook Kap. 12, O.

26 Übung: gestern, heute und morgen

Fragen Sie einander, wann Sie verschiedene Dinge zum letzten Mal gemacht haben.

> BEISPIEL: A. Wann hast du zum letzten Mal Kaffee getrunken?
> B. Gestern abend. (*oder*) Heute früh.

1. Wann hast du zum letzten Mal deinen besten Freund gesehen?
2. Wann bist du zum letzten Mal einkaufen gegangen?
3. Wann hast du zum letzten Mal Hausaufgaben gemacht?
4. Wann bist du zum letzten Mal ins Kino gegangen?
5. Wann hast du zum letzten Mal telefoniert?

Jetzt fragen Sie, wann Sie verschiedene Dinge das nächste Mal machen.

6. Wann besuchst du das nächste Mal deine Eltern?
7. Wann gehst du das nächste Mal ins Konzert?
8. Wann gehst du das nächste Mal ins Museum?
9. Wann fährst du das nächste Mal Rad?
10. Wann triffst du das nächste Mal deine Freunde?

Lesestück   Zwei Denkmäler

Tips zum Lesen und Lernen

Tips zum Vokabelnlernen

The Prefix *irgend-* With question words like **wo, wie,** and **wann,** the prefix **irgend-** creates indefinite adverbs as does the English word *some* in *somewhere, somehow, sometime,* etc.

Similarly: **irgendwer (=
irgend jemand),
irgendwas (= irgend
etwas), irgendwohin,
irgendwoher.**

irgendwo	*somewhere (or other), anywhere*
irgendwie	*somehow (or other)*
irgendwann	*sometime (or other), any time*

Hast du meine Zeitung **irgendwo** gesehen? — *Have you seen my newspaper anywhere?*

Kommen Sie **irgendwann** vorbei? — *Will you come by sometime?*

Meinen Schlüssel habe ich **irgendwie** verloren. — *Somehow or other I've lost my key.*

Im Lesetext für dieses Kapitel schreibt Anna Seghers:

Der Dom hat die Luftangriffe . . . **irgendwie** überstanden. — *The cathedral survived the air raids somehow or other.*

Einstieg in den Text

Like the poems in **Lyrik zum Vorlesen,** the following reading, "Zwei Denkmäler" by Anna Seghers, was written not for students learning German but rather for an audience of German speakers. Nonetheless, you have now learned enough German to read an authentic text with a little help from marginal glosses.

„Zwei Denkmäler" is not a story, but rather an essay *about* a story that Seghers never finished but could not "get out of her head" (**Das geht mir heute nicht aus dem Kopf**). She focuses on two monuments (**Denkmäler**)—one of grand cultural significance, the other of individual suffering.

Now that you have learned how relative clauses work in German, you will notice how frequent they are in expository prose like „Zwei Denkmäler." During your first reading of the text, be on the lookout for the eight relative clauses it contains. List each antecedent and relative clause. Here is the first one:

1. . . . eine Erzählung, die der Krieg unterbrochen hat.
   . . . *a story that the war interrupted.*

2. _____

3. _____

etc.

Wortschatz 2

Verben

holen to fetch, get
vergleichen, verglich, hat
    verglichen to compare
wieder·sehen (sieht wieder),
    sah wieder, hat
    wiedergesehen to see
    again, meet again
    Auf Wiedersehen!
    Goodbye.

On the telephone one says **auf
Wiederhören.**

Substantive

der Stein, -e stone
das Denkmal, ¨er monument
das Schiff, -e ship
die Erde earth
die Erzählung, -en story,
    narrative
die Freude, -n joy
die Größe, -n size; greatness
die Milch milk

Adjektive und Adverbien

einzig- single, only
fern distant, far away
grausam terrible, gruesome;
    cruel
jüdisch Jewish

Nützliche Ausdrücke

**Das geht mir nicht aus dem
    Kopf. = Das kann ich
    nicht vergessen.**
werden aus to become of
    **Was ist aus ihnen
    geworden?** What has
    become of them?

Zwei Denkmäler

Lab Manual Kap. 12,
Lesestück.

Applying your knowledge of twentieth-century Germany to an
authentic German literary text is the cultural goal of this chapter.

Anna Seghers

*Anna Seghers is the pseudonym of Netty Reiling, who was born in
Mainz in 1900. She studied art history and sinology. Because of her
membership in the Communist Party, she was forced to flee Germany in 1933. She sought asylum in France and Mexico. Much of
her writing in exile reflects the turbulent existence of a refugee and
committed antifascist. In 1947 she moved to the GDR, where she
died in 1983.*

    *The opening sentence of Seghers's essay establishes the historical context of an exile from Hitler's Germany, writing during World
War II about the horrors of World War I. The writer addresses loss
on many levels: of human life during wartime, of a literary manuscript, and of the memory of one woman's sacrifice. She suggests,
however, that in the story she wanted to write, Frau Eppstein's
daughter would have preserved that memory.*

In der Emigration° begann ich eine Erzählung, die der Krieg unterbrochen hat. Ihr Anfang ist mir noch in Erinnerung geblieben. Nicht
Wort für Wort, aber dem Sinn nach.° Was mich damals erregt° hat,
geht mir auch heute nicht aus dem Kopf. Ich erinnere mich an eine

5 Erinnerung.

    In meiner Heimat, in Mainz am Rhein, gab es zwei Denkmäler, die
ich niemals° vergessen konnte, in Freude und Angst, auf Schiffen, in
fernen Städten. Eins° ist der Dom. Wie ich als Schulkind zu meinem
Erstaunen° sah, ist er auf Pfeilern° gebaut, die tief in die Erde

10 hineingehen°—damals kam es mir vor,° beinahe° so hoch wie der

here: in exile

dem... = the sense of it / *excited*

niemals = nie
one of them
astonishment / pillars
go into / **kam...** = it seemed to
  me / **beinahe = fast**

Dom hochragt.° Ihre Risse sind auszementiert worden° sagte man, in vergangener° Zeit, da, wo das Grundwasser Unheil stiftete.° Ich weiß nicht, ob das stimmt, was uns ein Lehrer erzählte: Die romanischen[1] und gotischen[2] Pfeiler seien haltbarer° als die jüngeren.

15 Dieser Dom über der Rheinebene° wäre mir in all seiner Macht und Größe geblieben,° wenn ich ihn auch nie wieder gesehen hätte.° Aber ebensowenig° kann ich ein anderes Denkmal in meiner Heimatstadt vergessen. Es bestand nur aus° einem einzigen flachen Stein, den man in das Pflaster° einer Straße gesetzt hat. Hieß die Straße Bonifaziusstraße? Hieß sie Frauenlobstraße? Das weiß ich nicht
20 mehr. Ich weiß nur, daß der Stein zum Gedächtnis° einer Frau eingefügt wurde,° die im Ersten Weltkrieg durch Bombensplitter umkam,° als sie Milch für ihr Kind holen wollte. Wenn ich mich recht erinnere, war sie die Frau des jüdischen Weinhändlers° Eppstein. Menschenfresserisch,° grausam war der Erste Weltkrieg, man begann aber erst
25 an seinem Ende mit Luftangriffen° auf Städte und Menschen. Darum hat man zum Gedächtnis der Frau den Stein eingesetzt, flach wie das Pflaster, und ihren Namen eingraviert.°

Der Dom hat die Luftangriffe des Zweiten Weltkriegs irgendwie
30 überstanden,° wie auch° die Stadt zerstört worden ist.° Er ragt° über Fluß und Ebene. Ob der kleine flache Gedenkstein° noch da ist, das weiß ich nicht. Bei meinen Besuchen habe ich ihn nicht mehr gefunden.

In der Erzählung, die ich vor dem Zweiten Weltkrieg zu schreiben begann und im Krieg verlor, ist die Rede von° dem Kind, dem die
35 Mutter Milch holen wollte, aber nicht heimbringen° konnte. Ich hatte die Absicht,° in dem Buch zu erzählen, was aus diesem Mädchen geworden ist.

looms up / Risse... = cracks have been patched
past / Grundwasser... = groundwater caused damage
seien haltbarer = were more durable
Rheinebene = Rhine plain
wäre... = would have remained / **wenn...** = even if I had never seen it again
ebensowenig = no less
bestand... = consisted of only
Pflaster = pavement
zum Gedächtnis = in memory of
eingefügt wurde = had been set in / **durch...** = was killed by shrapnel
Weinhändler = wine merchant
Menschenfresserisch = cannibalistic
Luftangriffe = air raids
engraved

survived / **wie auch = obwohl** / **zerstört...** = was destroyed / **ragt** = looms
Gedenkstein = commemorative stone
ist... = the story is about
heimbringen = nach Hause bringen
Absicht = intention

Fragen zum Lesestück

1. Was hat Anna Seghers' Erzählung unterbrochen?
2. Welche Stadt war Anna Seghers' Heimatstadt?
3. Was konnte sie nie vergessen?
4. Über welche Denkmäler schreibt sie?
5. Vergleichen Sie diese zwei Denkmäler.
6. An wen sollte der Stein erinnern?
7. Hat Anna Seghers den Stein wieder gefunden?
8. Wann begann sie, die Erzählung zu schreiben?
9. Was wollte sie erzählen?

---

[1]**romanisch** Romanesque style (mid-11th to mid-12th century), characterized by round arches

[2]**gotisch** Gothic style (mid-12th to mid-16th century), characterized by pointed arches.

„Das geht mir nicht aus dem Kopf"

In der kurzen Erzählung „Zwei Denkmäler" erinnert sich die Schriftstellerin an etwas, was vor vielen Jahren passiert ist. Sie sagt, sie erinnert sich „an eine Erinnerung." Am Anfang dieses Kapitels haben Sie das Gedicht „Heimweh" von Eichendorff gelesen, in dem er auch über Erinnerungen an die Heimat und die Geliebte spricht.

Jeder Mensch hat Erinnerungen, nicht nur Dichter und Schriftsteller. Jetzt sprechen wir ein bißchen über unsere eigenen Erinnerungen.

Neue Vokabeln

die **Erfahrung, -en**	*experience*
die **Gegenwart**	*present (time)*
das **Heimweh**	*homesickness*
der **Ort, -e**	*place; small town*

Diese Wörter und Ausdrücke kennen Sie schon.

Ich bin in _____ (Heimatort) geboren.
sich erinnern an
alte Freunde
umziehen
die Vergangenheit
verlassen
wiedersehen

Berlin um 1900.

Gruppendiskussion: Wo haben Sie als Kind gewohnt?

Leben Sie noch in der Stadt, wo Sie geboren sind, oder sind Sie umgezogen? Gefällt es Ihnen besser, wo Sie jetzt wohnen? Besuchen Sie manchmal Ihren Geburtsort? Was wollen Sie dort sehen? Was hat sich dort geändert?

Discussing personal memories is a communicative goal.

Partnerarbeit: Ich erinnere mich an etwas Besonderes.

Erzählen Sie einander eine wichtige Erinnerung aus Ihrer Kindheit.
Gibt es z.B. einen besonderen Menschen, an den Sie sich erinnern? Oder einen Lieblingsort oder ein Gebäude, wo Sie gewohnt haben oder Zeit verbracht haben? Warum geht es Ihnen nicht aus dem Kopf?

Zum Schluß

Sprechen wir miteinander Lab Manual Kap. 12, Diktat.

A Gruppenarbeit: Vergleichen wir.

Sechs oder sieben Studenten kommen nach vorne (*to the front*). Zuerst sagen sie auf deutsch, wann sie geboren sind. Dann antworten die anderen auf die folgenden (*following*) Fragen.

1. Wer ist der/die älteste?
2. Wer ist der/die jüngste?
3. Wer ist der/die größte?
4. Wer ist der/die kleinste?
5. Wer hat die längsten/kürzesten Haare?
6. Wer ist heute am schönsten angezogen?

B Partnerarbeit: Ich bin älter als du.

Jetzt vergleichen Sie sich mit Ihrem Partner. Seien Sie nicht zu ernst (*serious*)!

> BEISPIEL: A: Ich bin intelligenter als du!
> B: Vielleicht, aber ich habe schönere Augen als du!

Wer ist gesünder? müder? optimistischer? pünktlicher? sportlicher? usw.

C Weltrekorde

Jeder von Ihnen stellt den anderen eine Frage über einen Weltrekord. Die anderen müssen die Antwort erraten (*guess*).

> BEISPIEL: Wie heißt der höchste Berg der Welt?
> Wer ist die beste Tennisspielerin der Welt?

D Gruppenarbeit: Was machen Sie selber? Was lassen Sie machen?

Sagen Sie, ob Sie etwas selber machen, oder ob Sie es lieber machen lassen.

> BEISPIEL: den Wagen reparieren
> Ich repariere den Wagen selber. *oder*
> Ich lasse den Wagen lieber reparieren.

sich die Haare schneiden
must have a dative reflexive,
which is optional with the other
verbs.

den Wagen reparieren
die Haare schneiden
das Mittagessen kochen

den Kaffee machen
Lebensmittel einkaufen
Referate schreiben

E Spiel: Ratet mal, wen ich meine!

Choose another student in the room to describe, but don't tell anyone who it is. When your turn comes, say **Ich kenne eine Studentin, die . . .** or **Ich kenne einen Studenten, der . . .** and then add some description. The others must guess whom you mean.

> BEISPIEL: Ich kenne eine Studentin, die heute eine gelbe Hose
> trägt.

Schreiben Sie zu Hause

F Antworten Sie mit Ihren eigenen Worten. Benutzen Sie in Ihrer Antwort einen Relativsatz (*relative clause*).

> BEISPIEL: Mit was für Menschen verbringen Sie gern Ihre
> Freizeit?
>
> *Mögliche Antwort:* Ich verbringe gern meine Freizeit
> mit Menschen, mit denen ich Sport treiben kann.

1. Was für Erzählungen würden Sie gern lesen?
2. Mit was für Menschen leben Sie gern zusammen?
3. Aus was für einer Familie kommen Sie?
4. Was für Städte gefallen Ihnen besonders gut?
5. In was für einem Gebäude wohnen Sie?
6. Mit was für Menschen verbringen Sie gern Ihre Freizeit?

With this chapter you have completed the third quarter of *Neue Horizonte*. For a concise review of the grammar and idiomatic phrases in chapters 9–12, you may consult the **Zusammenfassung und Wiederholung 3** (*Summary and Review 3*) on pages 129–144 of your Workbook. The review section is followed by a self-correcting test.

G **Aufsatzthemen** Anna Seghers hat eine Erzählung über das Mädchen begonnen, dessen Mutter im Ersten Weltkrieg Milch holen wollte, aber sie hat diese Erzählung nie zu Ende geschrieben. Wie würden Sie diese Geschichte erzählen? Schreiben Sie entweder den Anfang oder das Ende der Erzählung aus der Perspektive der Tochter.

1. Wie würde die Geschichte anfangen?
2. Schreiben Sie das Ende der Geschichte. Was ist aus dem Mädchen geworden?

H **Wie sagt man das auf deutsch?**

1. Can you repair your car yourself?
2. No, I never learned that. I always have it repaired.
3. A German I know is the best mechanic in the city.

4. Are German trains really more punctual than American trains?
5. Yes, but French trains are the fastest.

6. Have you heard the newest gossip?
7. Not yet. What's going on?
8. Rita went away with the richest guy in the office.
9. She left poor Rudi, who was always short of cash.

VIDEOECKE

6 Das vergesse ich nie. (22:44)

Herzlichen Glückwunsch zum Geburtstag!

Stefan und Katrin fahren zu Stefans Tante Waltraud, die heute Geburtstag feiert. Tante Waltraud wohnt in einem Dorf in der Nähe von Berlin. Bis 1990 lag dieser Ort in der DDR. Stefan und Katrin bringen der Tante Blumen und Geschenke mit. Sie sitzen zusammen im Wohnzimmer und sehen sich Familienfotos an, während ihnen Tante Waltraud über ihr Leben erzählt. Nachher kommt Stefans Familie auch zu Besuch, um ihr zum Geburtstag zu gratulieren (congratulate).

Wortschatz zum Video

Herzlichen Glückwunsch!	*Congratulations! Best wishes!*
die **Decke, -n**	*blanket*
zufrieden	*satisfied*
Ich bin zufrieden.	*I can't complain.*
die **Hochzeit, -en**	*wedding*
die **Trümmer** (*pl.*)	*ruins, rubble*
der **Enkel,-**	*grandson*
die **Banane, -n**	*banana*

A Tante Waltrauds Fotoalbum

Kreuzen Sie die Fotos an, die Sie in dem Fotoalbum sehen.

—— 1. das Geburtshaus
—— 2. der erste Schultag
—— 3. Tante Waltrauds zwei Brüder
—— 4. Tante Waltrauds Mutter
—— 5. Tante Waltraud an der Uni
—— 6. Fotos von ihrer Hochzeit
—— 7. das zerstörte Berlin
—— 8. Tante Waltraud auf Urlaub in Moskau
—— 9. der Enkel Markus
—— 10. Menschen auf der Berliner Mauer am 9. November 1989

B Richtig oder falsch?

Indicate whether each statement is **richtig (R)** or **falsch (F)**.

1. Stefan und Katrin fahren mit dem Bus zu Tante Waltraud.	R	F
2. Tante Waltraud freut sich sehr, sie zu sehen.	R	F
3. Sie bringen ihr Schokolade und Wein mit.	R	F
4. Tante Waltrauds Lieblingsfarbe ist grün.	R	F
5. Katrin schenkt ihr einen Pullover zum Geburtstag.	R	F
6. Katrin möchte wissen, was für ein Buch auf dem Tisch liegt.	R	F

C Wer sagt das?

Choose the person who says the following.

a. Katrin   b. Stefan   c. Tante Waltraud   d. Frau Bachmann

1. —— sagt: „Bitte, kommt 'rein ins Wohnzimmer."
2. —— sagt: „Die Eltern kommen später."
3. —— sagt: „Ich stelle die Blumen in die Vase."
4. —— fragt: „Wie geht es deinem Bein?"
5. —— fragt: „Ist das nicht ein Bild vom 9. November?"
6. —— sagt: „Hallo, liebes Geburtstagskind, hallo!"

D Wie geht's weiter?

Choose the best completion for each sentence, based on the video episode.

1. Markus hat sich Bananen gekauft, . . .
   a. weil er Hunger hatte.
   b. weil sie billig waren.
   c. weil sie für ihn etwas Herrliches waren.

2. Die Familie Bachmann kommt später zu Besuch, . . .
   a. denn sie wollen bei Tante Waltraud übernachten.
   b. weil sie zusammen feiern wollen.
   c. um Stefan und Katrin mit dem Wagen abzuholen.

3. Tante Waltraud zeigt Katrin und Stefan ihr Fotoalbum und erzählt ihnen . . .

   a. Erinnerungen aus ihrer Kindheit.
   b. von dem Krieg.
   c. von ihren Kindern.

4. Tante Waltraud ist sehr munter, . . .

   a. aber sie hat sich erkältet.
   b. obwohl sie nicht gut geschlafen hat.
   c. obwohl ihr das Bein ein bißchen weh tut.

E Welle Magazin: Was sehen Sie?

Read through the list below. Then watch the **Welle Magazin** (Das Dorf-leben, 26:34–27:31) and check off the people and things you see in the video.

Ich sehe . . .

_____ 1. eine Bushaltestelle
_____ 2. einen Traktor
_____ 3. eine alte Kirche
_____ 4. Kinder auf einem Spielplatz
_____ 5. einen Bauern bei der Arbeit
_____ 6. Schweine und Kühe (*pigs and cows*)
_____ 7. eine alte Frau auf einem Fahrrad
_____ 8. ein Blumengeschäft
_____ 9. einen Supermarkt

Gestern nachmittag haben wir das Baby bei Oma gelassen.

Erinnerungen

Four Modern Writers

A particular kind of memory has haunted German and Austrian writers of the past fifty years: the refusal to forget the Third Reich and the Second World War. For contemporary Germans, the act of recalling and interpreting this painful history has been termed **Vergangenheitsbewältigung:** *surmounting (or) overcoming* the past. These four writers all experienced National Socialism and war as children. They began writing after 1945 and earned international reputations. For them, there can be no question of repressing the past, for their literary works honor its memory, confront German guilt, and engage in **Trauerarbeit**, the *work of mourning*.

Günter Grass (b. 1927)

Günter Grass, the son of a grocer in Danzig (today Gdansk, Poland), was drafted out of school at the very end of the war and served briefly as a tank gunner. After the war he apprenticed to a stonecutter in Düsseldorf, and then studied graphic art and sculpture in Berlin. His first novel, *Die Blechtrommel* (*The Tin Drum*, 1959), was an instant international success. In it, the dwarf narrator Oskar Matzerath recounts with an outsider's black humor and wicked satire his life among the lower middle class of Danzig before, during, and after the war. Grass has continued to use his native city of Danzig/Gdansk as a setting for his fiction and to be an active voice for German-Polish reconciliation.

Ingeborg Bachmann (1926–1973)

Ingeborg Bachmann was born in Klagenfurt, Austria, and studied philosophy at the University of Vienna. Although she first gained fame as a lyric poet, she also wrote radio plays and short stories, an opera libretto, and the novel *Malina* (1972), which is the first volume of an unfinished trilogy entitled *Todesarten* (*Kinds of Death*). In her late prose Ingeborg Bachmann brilliantly exposes the tyranny and psychic violence that continue to lurk beneath the cultivated exterior of post-war Viennese society.

Jurek Becker (b. 1937)

Jurek Becker, born in Lodz, Poland, to Jewish parents, managed to survive imprisonment in Nazi concentration camps along with his father. Believing that anti-Semitism had been eliminated in Germany but not in Poland, they remained in what was to become the German Democratic Republic after the war. Becker's first novel, *Jakob der Lügner* (*Jakob the Liar*, 1969), is the story of a Jew who owns a clandestine radio and sustains the hopes of his fellow ghetto inhabitants by inventing stories of Allied victories. In *Bronsteins Kinder* (1986) he explores the complex relationship between a Holocaust survivor and his son.

Christa Wolf (b. 1929)

Christa Wolf's parents were shopkeepers in Landsberg, today Gorzów (Poland). She worked as an editor in the German Democratic Republic before publishing her first fiction in 1961. Since then, her works have been widely translated. Her autobiographical novel *Kindheitsmuster* (*Patterns of Childhood*, 1976) is an extended reflection on the psychic damage done to a child educated as a true believer in Nazism. *Kassandra* (1983) retells the story of the Trojan War from a feminist and antiheroic point of view.

Die Schweiz

Communicative Goals

- Talking about the future
- Telling people you'd like them to do something
- Introducing yourself and others

Cultural Goal

- Learning about Switzerland

DIALOGE   Skifahren in der Schweiz

Lab Manual Kap. 13, Dialoge, Fragen, Hören Sie gut zu!

Kurz vor dem Semesterende sprechen zwei Studentinnen über ihre Ferienpläne.

BRIGITTE: Ich freue mich sehr auf die Semesterferien!

JOHANNA: Hast du vor, wieder Ski zu fahren?

BRIGITTE: Ja, ich werde zwei Wochen in der Schweiz verbringen. Morgen früh flieg' ich nach Zürich.

JOHANNA: Da bin ich ja ganz baff! Früher hast du doch immer Angst vorm Fliegen gehabt!

BRIGITTE: Stimmt, aber ich habe mich einfach daran gewöhnt.

Ski is pronounced (and alternatively spelled) **Schi**. Note the colloquial contraction **vorm** = **vor dem**.

In der WG: Bei Nina ist es unordentlich.

UTE: Nina, hör mal zu, wann wirst du deine Sachen endlich aufräumen?

NINA: Ich mach' das gleich. Seid mir nicht böse—ich mußte mich heute morgen wahnsinnig beeilen.

LUTZ: Ja, das sagst du immer. Jetzt haben wir aber die Nase voll. Alle müssen doch mitmachen.

NINA: Ihr habt recht. Von jetzt an werde ich mich mehr um die Wohnung kümmern.

Am Informationsschalter in Basel

TOURIST: Entschuldigung. Darf ich Sie um Auskunft bitten?

BEAMTIN: Gerne. Wie kann ich Ihnen helfen?

TOURIST: Ich bin nur einen Tag in Basel und kenne mich hier nicht aus. Was können Sie mir empfehlen?

BEAMTIN: Es kommt darauf an, was Sie sehen wollen. Das Kunstmuseum lohnt sich besonders. Wenn Sie sich für das Mittelalter interessieren, dürfen Sie die neue Ausstellung nicht verpassen.

TOURIST: Das interessiert mich aber sehr. Wie komme ich denn dahin?

BEAMTIN: Direkt vor dem Bahnhof ist die Haltestelle. Dort müssen Sie in die Straßenbahnlinie 2 einsteigen. Am Museum steigen Sie dann aus.

TOURIST: Das werde ich schon finden. Vielen Dank für die Hilfe.

BEAMTIN: Bitte sehr.

Note on Usage: nicht dürfen

The equivalent for English *must not* is **nicht dürfen**.

Die Ausstellung dürfen Sie nicht verpassen.	*You mustn't (really shouldn't) miss the exhibit.*

Die Schweiz

Skiing in Switzerland

Shortly before the end of the semester, two students are talking about their vacation plans.

B.: I'm really looking forward to the semester break!

J.: Do you plan to go skiing again?

B.: Yes, I'll spend two weeks in Switzerland. Tomorrow morning I fly to Zürich.

J.: I'm flabbergasted! Before, you were always afraid of flying!

B.: True, but I've simply gotten used to it.

In the Group Apartment: Nina's Place is Messy

U.: Listen, Nina, when are you finally going to straighten up your things?

N.: I'll do it right away. Don't be mad at me—I was in a big rush this morning.

L.: Yeah, you always say that. Now we're really fed up. Everybody has to pitch in.

N.: You're right. From now on I'll take more care of the apartment.

At the Information Window in Basel

T.: Excuse me. May I ask you for information?

O.: Sure. How can I help you?

T.: I'm only in Basel for a day, and I don't know my way around here. What can you recommend to me?

O.: It depends on what you want to see. The art museum is especially worthwhile. If you're interested in the Middle Ages, you mustn't miss the new exhibit.

T.: That interests me a lot. How do I get there?

O.: Right in front of the station is the streetcar stop. You have to get the number 2 streetcar. Then get out at the museum.

T.: I'll find it all right. Thank you for the help.

O.: You're welcome.

Wortschatz 1

Verben

Angst haben vor (+ *dat.*) to be afraid of

auf·räumen to tidy up, straighten up

sich aus·kennen to know one's way around

Ich kenne mich hier nicht aus. I don't know my way around here.

bitten, bat, hat gebeten um to ask for, request

sich freuen auf (+ *acc.*) to look forward to

sich gewöhnen an (+ *acc.*) to get used to

interessieren to interest

sich interessieren für to be interested in

sich kümmern um to look after, take care of; to deal with

sich lohnen to be worthwhile, worth the trouble

verpassen to miss (*an event, opportunity, train, etc.*)

sich vor·bereiten auf (+ *acc.*) to prepare for

vor·haben to plan, have in mind

warten auf (+ *acc.*) to wait for

zu·hören (+ *dat.*) to listen (to)

Hören Sie gut zu! Listen carefully.

Hör mir zu. Listen to me.

Substantive

der Schalter, - counter, window

das Mittelalter the Middle Ages

die Auskunft information

die Haltestelle, -n (streetcar or bus) stop

die Hilfe help

die Linie, -n (streetcar or bus) line

die Straßenbahn, -en streetcar

Adjektive und Adverbien

böse (+ *dat.*) angry, mad (at); bad, evil

Sei mir nicht böse. Don't be mad at me.

direkt direct(ly)

unordentlich disorderly, messy

Nützliche Ausdrücke

von jetzt an from now on

Es kommt darauf an. It depends.

Es kommt darauf an, was Sie sehen wollen. It depends on what you want to see.

Wie komme ich dahin? How do I get there?

Gegensätze

böse ≠ gut evil ≠ good

sich interessieren ≠ sich langweilen to be interested ≠ to be bored

unordentlich ≠ ordentlich disorderly, messy ≠ orderly, neat

Die Museen in Basel

Variationen

A Persönliche Fragen

1. Brigitte freut sich auf die Semesterferien. Freuen Sie sich auf etwas?
2. Sie hat vor, Ski zu fahren. Was haben Sie am Wochenende vor?
3. Fahren Sie in den Semesterferien irgendwohin?

4. Bei Nina sieht's schlampig aus. Wie sieht es bei Ihnen im Zimmer aus?
5. Die anderen in der WG sind Nina böse, weil sie nicht aufräumt. Wann werden Sie böse?

6. Der Tourist kennt sich in Basel nicht aus, aber zu Hause kennt er sich natürlich sehr gut aus. In welcher Stadt kennen Sie sich besonders gut aus?
7. Der Tourist interessiert sich für das Mittelalter. Wann war denn das Mittelalter?
8. Der Tourist will die Austellung im nicht verpassen. Haben Sie je etwas Gutes verpaßt? Was denn?
9. Was machen Sie, wenn Sie sich in einer fremden Stadt nicht auskennen?

B Übung: Wie sagt man das mit anderen Worten?

1. Wenn man sehr wenig Geld hat, ist man _____ .
2. Wenn man zu viel von etwas gehabt hat, sagt man: „Ich habe _____ voll."
3. Jemand, der besonders müde ist, nennt man _____ .
4. Wenn Sie sich bei einer Vorlesung sehr gelangweilt haben, dann haben Sie sie _____ gefunden.
5. Etwas, was sehr groß ist, kann man auch _____ nennen.
6. Ein anderes Wort für *dumm* ist _____ .

Ihr Professor spielt die Rolle eines Freundes, dem Sie verschiedene Dinge empfehlen sollen. Sie sagen ihm jedesmal, es kommt darauf an.

> BEISPIEL: Können Sie mir *etwas in der Stadt* empfehlen?
> Es kommt darauf an, *was Sie sehen wollen.*

1. etwas auf der Speisekarte
2. ein gutes Buch
3. eine neue CD
4. ein Reiseziel
5. ein ruhiges Hotel
6. einen guten Wein
7. einen guten Kassettenrecorder
8. einen neuen Beruf

D Rollenspiel: Am Informationsschalter **(Gruppen von 3 Studenten)**

Zwei von Ihnen sind Touristen und kennen sich in dieser Stadt nicht aus. Der/die dritte arbeitet am Infoschalter und gibt Auskunft. Vergessen Sie nicht, „Sie" zueinander zu sagen. Fangen Sie so an:

> TOURISTEN: Entschuldigung. Dürfen wir Sie um Auskunft bitten?
>
> BEAMTER/BEAMTIN: Gerne. Wie kann ich Ihnen helfen?

Alpendorf im Winter (Kanton Graubünden).

Lyrik zum Vorlesen

Eugen Gomringer was born to Swiss parents in Bolivia. True to his typically polyglot Swiss background, he has written poems in German, Swiss-German dialect, French, English, and Spanish. Gomringer is a leading exponent of concrete poetry (**konkrete Poesie**), which rejects metaphor, radically simplifies syntax, and considers the printed page a visual as much as a linguistic experience. The following poem consists entirely of nouns followed by relative clauses in strict parallelism. Readers must work out the interrelationships for themselves. Pay particular attention to the verb tenses as you read this poem aloud.

Lab Manual Kap. 13, Lyrik zum Vorlesen.

nachwort°   afterword

das dorf,° das ich nachts hörte   village
der wald, in dem ich schlief

das land, das ich überflog°   flew across
die stadt, in der ich wohnte

das haus, das den freunden gehörte
die frau, die ich kannte

das bild, das mich wach hielt°   kept awake
der klang,° der mir gefiel   sound

das buch, in dem ich las
der stein, den ich fand

der mann, den ich verstand
das kind, das ich lehrte°   taught

der baum, den ich blühen° sah   blooming
das tier, das ich fürchtete

die sprache, die ich spreche
die schrift,° die ich schreibe   writing

Eugen Gomringer
(*geboren 1925*)

Grammatik

Verbs with Prepositional Complements

Many verbs use a prepositional phrase to complete, expand, or change their meaning. Such phrases are called *prepositional complements*.

Ich spreche.	*I'm speaking.*
Ich spreche **mit ihm**.	*I'm speaking **with him**.*
Ich spreche **gegen ihn**.	*I'm speaking **against him**.*

In the examples above, English and German happen to use parallel prepositions. In many cases, however, they do not. For example:

Er wartet **auf** seinen Bruder.	*He's waiting for his brother.*
Sie bittet **um** Geld.	*She's asking for money.*

For this reason, you must learn the verb and the preposition used with it *together*. For instance, you should learn **bitten (bat, hat gebeten) um**, *to ask for*.

Here is a list of the verbs with prepositional complements that you have already learned in this and previous chapters.

Sometimes the complete verbal idea also involves a noun, as in **Angst haben vor**. Notice that most equivalent English verbs also have prepositional complements (*to look forward to, to wait for*), but some do not (*to remember, to request*).

Angst haben vor (+ *dat.*)   *to be afraid of*

Hast du Angst vorm Fliegen?	*Are you afraid of flying?*

bitten um   *to ask for, request*

Sie bat mich um Geld.	*She asked me for money.*

erinnern an (+ *acc.*)   *to remind of*

Das erinnert mich an etwas Wichtiges.	*That reminds me of something important.*

sich erinnern an (+ *acc.*)   *to remember*

Sie hat sich an meinen Geburtstag erinnert.	*She remembered my birthday.*

sich freuen auf (+ *acc.*)   *to look forward to*

Ich freue mich auf die Ferien!	*I'm looking forward to the vacation!*

sich gewöhnen an (+ *acc.*)   *to get used to*

Sie konnte sich nicht an das kalte Wetter gewöhnen.	*She couldn't get used to the cold weather.*

sich interessieren für   *to be interested in*

Interessieren Sie sich für moderne Kunst?	*Are you interested in modern art?*

sich kümmern um   *to look after, take care of; to deal with*

Ich werde mich mehr um die Wohnung kümmern.	*I'll take more care of the apartment.*

sprechen (schreiben, lesen, lachen usw.) über (+ *acc.*)   *to talk (write, read, laugh, etc.) about*

Er hat über seine Heimat gesprochen.	*He talked about his home.*

sich verloben mit   *to get engaged to*

Rita hat sich mit Rudi verlobt.	*Rita got engaged to Rudi.*

Notice: Perfect tense of **sich vorbereiten** is **hat sich vorbereitet** (no **-ge-**).

sich vor·bereiten auf (+ *acc.*)   *to prepare for*

Wir haben uns auf seinen Besuch gut vorbereitet.	*We prepared well for his visit.*

warten auf (+ *acc.*)   *to wait for*

Auf wen warten Sie denn?	*Whom are you waiting for?*

Notes on Verbs with Prepositional Complements

1. When a prepositional phrase is a verbal complement, it constitutes the second part of the predicate (see p. 79) and therefore comes at the end of the sentence or clause.

Sie **schrieb** mir letzte Woche **über ihre neue Stelle**.	*She wrote me about her new job last week.*

2. When the preposition used with a verb is a two-way preposition, you must memorize the verb and the case it takes (dative or accusative). Don't just learn **warten auf**, *to wait for*, but rather **warten auf** + *accusative, to wait for*.

3. The two-way prepositions **auf** and **über** almost always take the accusative case when used as verbal complements in a non-spatial sense.

spatial	*non-spatial*
Er wartet auf **der** Straße. *He's waiting on the street.*	Er wartet auf **die** Lehrerin. *He's waiting for the teacher.*
Das Bild hängt über **meiner** Tür. *The picture hangs above my door.*	Ich sprach über **meine** Heimat. *I talked about my homeland.*

4. Some verbs have both a direct object *and* a prepositional complement.

d.o. *prep. compl.*	
Er bittet **die Beamtin um Auskunft.**	*He asks the official for information.*

d.o. *prep. compl.*	
Das erinnert **mich an meine Heimat.**	*That reminds me of my home.*

Be careful not to confuse prepositional complements (**erinnern *an***) and separable prefixes (***ankommen***). Although separable prefixes sometimes look like prepositions, they are not, because they have no object.

prepositional complement   *separable prefix*

object
Er erinnert mich **an meinen Bruder**.   Der Zug kommt um 9 Uhr **an**.

object
Wartest du **auf mich**?   Wann stehst du **auf**?

Fragewörter

To ask a question using a verb with a prepositional complement, German forms a question word by attaching the prefix **wo-** to the preposition: **wo-** + **vor** = **wovor**. (If the preposition begins with a vowel, the prefix is **wor-**: **wor-** + **auf** = **worauf**.)

Wovor hast du Angst?   ***What*** are you afraid ***of***?
Worauf wartest du denn?   ***What*** are you waiting ***for***?
Wofür interessieren Sie sich? ***What*** are you interested ***in***?

Lab Manual Kap. 13, Var. zur Üb. 1–4, 5, 6.

Workbook Kap. 13, A, B.

1 **Kettenreaktion: Wovor hast *du* denn Angst?**

Jeder hat manchmal Angst. Es gibt viele Sachen, vor denen man Angst haben kann. Sagen Sie, wovor Sie Angst haben, und fragen Sie dann weiter. Die Liste gibt Ihnen einige Beispiele, aber Sie können auch frei antworten.

BEISPIEL: A: Ich habe Angst vor großen Hunden. Wovor hast *du* denn Angst?
           B: Ich habe Angst vor . . .

große Hunde   komplizierte Technik
tiefes Wasser   Klausuren
ein Besuch beim Zahnarzt   das Leben in der Großstadt
das Fliegen   eine Umweltkatastrophe

2 Übung: Darf ich Sie um etwas bitten?

Jeder braucht etwas und bittet die Professorin darum. Was brauchen Sie?

> BEISPIEL: A: Darf ich Sie um Hilfe bitten?
>   B: Natürlich. Ich helfe Ihnen gerne.

3 Kettenreaktion: Worauf wartest *du* denn?

Sie stehen an einer Straßenecke und warten auf etwas. Sagen Sie, worauf Sie warten, und dann fragen Sie weiter.

> BEISPIEL: A: Ich warte auf die Staßenbahn, Linie 2. Worauf wartest *du* denn?
>   B: Ich warte auf _____ .

4 Kettenreaktion: Worauf freust *du* dich?

Sagen Sie, worauf Sie sich besonders freuen, und dann fragen Sie weiter.

> BEISPIEL: A: Ich freue mich auf die Semesterferien. Worauf freust *du* dich?
>   B: Ich freue mich auf _____ .

5 Kettenreaktion: Wofür interessierst *du* dich?

Nicht alle interessieren sich für die gleichen Dinge. Sagen Sie, wofür Sie sich besonders interessieren, und dann fragen Sie weiter.

> BEISPIEL: A: Ich interessiere mich für das Mittelalter. Wofür interessierst *du* dich?
>   B: Ich interessiere mich für _____ .

6 Übung: Woran konnten Sie sich nicht gewöhnen?

Wenn man anfängt zu studieren, ist es manchmal schwer, sich an das Neue zu gewöhnen. Sagen Sie, woran Sie sich am Anfang nicht so leicht gewöhnen konnten.

> BEISPIEL: A: Woran konnten Sie sich hier am Anfang nicht gewöhnen?
>   B: Ich konnte mich nicht an das Klima gewöhnen.

Pronouns as Objects of Prepositions: *da*-compounds and *wo*-compounds

da-compounds

When noun objects of prepositions are replaced by pronouns (e.g., **für meinen Freund** → **für ihn**), a distinction is made in German between nouns referring to people and nouns referring to inanimate objects.

- Nouns referring to people are replaced by personal pronouns, as in English.

Steht Christof hinter Gabriele?	*Is Christof standing behind Gabriele?*
Ja, er steht **hinter ihr**.	*Yes, he's standing **behind her**.*
Sprichst du oft mit den Kindern?	*Do you often talk with the children?*
Ja, ich spreche oft **mit ihnen**.	*Yes, I often speak **with them**.*
Wartet ihr auf Manfred?	*Are you waiting for Manfred?*
Ja, wir warten **auf ihn**.	*Yes, we're waiting **for him**.*

Da-compounds simplify things: they do not reflect case, number, or gender of the nouns they replace.

- Nouns referring to inanimate objects, however, are *not* replaced by personal pronouns. Instead, they are replaced by the prefix **da-** attached to the preposition (**da- + mit = damit**). If the preposition begins with a vowel, the prefix is **dar-** (**dar- + auf = darauf**).

Steht dein Auto vor oder hinter dem Haus?	*Is your car in front of the house or behind it?*
Es steht **dahinter**.	*It's **behind it**.*
Was machen wir mit diesen alten Maschinen?	*What shall we do with these old machines?*
Ich weiß nicht, was wir **damit** machen.	*I don't know what we'll do **with them**.*
Wie lange warten Sie schon auf den Zug?	*How long have you been waiting for the train?*
Ich warte schon 10 Minuten **darauf**.	*I've been waiting **for it** for 10 minutes.*

Reiseschecks von der Post: Alles, was Sie darüber wissen sollten.

Lab Manual Kap. 13, Üb. 7, 8, and Var. zur Üb. 9.

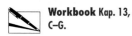

Workbook Kap. 13, C–G.

7 Übung

Antworten Sie wie im Beispielsatz.

> BEISPIEL: A: Stand er neben dem Fenster?
> B: Ja, er stand daneben.

1. Interessieren Sie sich für Fremdsprachen?
2. Hast du nach dem Konzert gegessen?
3. Fangt ihr mit der Arbeit an?
4. Hat er lange auf die Straßenbahn gewartet?
5. Hat sie sich an das Wetter gewöhnt?
6. Hat sie wieder um Geld gebeten?
7. Bereitest du dich auf die Deutschstunde vor?
8. Liegt meine Zeitung unter deinem Rucksack?
9. Erinnerst du dich an die Ferien?
10. Haben Sie vor der Bibliothek gewartet?

8 Partnerarbeit

Diesmal kommt es darauf an, ob das Objekt ein Mensch ist. Wenn nicht, dann müssen Sie mit **da-** antworten.

> BEISPIEL: A: Steht Ingrid neben Hans-Peter?
> B: Ja, sie steht *neben ihm.*
>
> A: Steht Ingrid neben dem *Wagen?*
> B: Ja, sie steht *daneben.*

1. Hast du dich an das Wetter gewöhnt?
2. Bist du mit Ursula gegangen?
3. Erinnerst du dich an deine Großeltern?
4. Können wir über dieses Problem sprechen?
5. Wohnst du bei Frau Lindner?
6. Demonstrierst du gegen diesen Politiker?
7. Demonstrierst du gegen seine Ideen?
8. Interessierst du dich für Sport?
9. Gehst du mit Karin essen?
10. Hat er dir für das Geschenk gedankt?

wo-compounds

With questions beginning with a prepositional phrase, the same distinction between animate and inanimate objects is made. To ask a question about a person, German uses the *preposition* + **wen** or **wem.**

Auf wen warten Sie denn?	***Whom*** *are you waiting **for**?*
Mit wem spielen die Kinder?	***Whom*** *are the children playing **with**?*

When asking about a thing, use the **wo**-compounds you have already learned.

Worauf warten Sie denn?	***What*** *are you waiting **for**?*
Womit spielt das Kind?	***What*** *is the child playing **with**?*

Only student A has an open book. A reads each sentence aloud; B asks C for information about what was said, as in the examples.

> BEISPIELE: A: Ich habe auf einen Brief gewartet.
> B: Worauf hat sie gewartet?
> C: Auf einen Brief.
>
> A: Ich habe auf meine Kusine gewartet.
> B: Auf wen hat er gewartet?
> C: Auf seine Kusine.

1. Ich freue mich auf die Semesterferien.
2. Ich habe mit Professor Hauser gearbeitet.
3. Ich habe mich mit Rita/Rudi verlobt.
4. Ich muß mich um die Wohnung kümmern.
5. Ich interessiere mich für deutschen Wein.
6. Ich habe keine Angst vor Polizeibeamten.
7. Ich erinnere mich an meinen komischen Onkel.
8. Ich kann mich nicht an diese harte Arbeit gewöhnen.

10 **Partnerarbeit: Persönliche Fragen**

Stellen Sie einander diese Fragen.

> BEISPIEL: Wofür interessierst du dich besonders?
> Für das Mittelalter. Und du?
> Für _____ .

1. Wofür interessierst du dich besonders?
2. Wovor hast du manchmal Angst?
3. Worauf freust du dich besonders?
4. Worauf mußt du dich im Moment vorbereiten?
5. Woran kannst du dich nicht gewöhnen?

Hildegard von Bingen
1098–1179

Future Tense

Formation: *werden* + infinitive

Talking about the future is a communicative goal.

The future is a compound tense, using an inflected form of the verb **werden** plus a dependent infinitive in final position:

ich	**werde schlafen**	*I shall sleep*	wir	**werden schlafen**	*we shall sleep*
du	**wirst schlafen**	*you will sleep*	ihr	**werdet schlafen**	*you will sleep*
sie	**wird schlafen**	*she will sleep*	sie, Sie	**werden schlafen**	*they, you will sleep*

Note: **Werden** as the auxiliary (helping) verb for future tense corresponds to *shall* or *will* in English. Do not confuse it with the modal verb **wollen**.

Er **wird** schlafen.	*He **will** sleep.*
Er **will** schlafen.	*He **wants to** sleep.*

Here is how the future tense of a modal verb is formed. Note that the order of the modal and its dependent infinitive is the *reverse* of English.

Wir werden es **tun müssen**.

We *will **have to do** it.*

Use of Future Tense

As you already know, German usually uses *present tense* to express future meaning, especially when a time expression makes the future meaning clear.

Sie kommt morgen zurück.   *She's coming back tomorrow.*

Future tense makes the future meaning explicit, especially in the absence of a time expression such as **morgen**.

Sie wird selbstverständlich   *Of course she will come back.*
zurückkommen.

Lab Manual Kap. 13, Var. zur Üb. 11.

Workbook Kap. 13, H.

11 Übung: Noch nicht, aber bald.

Sagen Sie, daß etwas noch nicht passiert ist, aber bald passieren wird.

BEISPIEL: A: Hast du schon gegessen?
B: Noch nicht, aber ich werde bald essen.

1. Hat es schon geregnet?
2. Hast du schon aufgeräumt?
3. Seid ihr schon skigefahren?
4. Ist er schon aufgestanden?
5. Haben sie sich schon vorbereitet?
6. Haben Sie das schon machen müssen?
7. Hat Susi schon angerufen?
8. Seid ihr schon essen gegangen?

Wanting *X* to Do *Y*

Telling people you'd like them to do something is a communicative goal.

To express the idea that a person wants something to happen or be done, English uses a direct object and an infinitive phrase.

d.o.	*infin. phrase*

*She would like **the music to stop**.*
*I don't want   **him**   **to think that**.*

German uses **wollen** or **möchten** followed by a **daß**-clause to express the same idea.

Sie möchte, **daß die Musik aufhört**.
Ich will nicht, **daß er das glaubt**.

Lab Manual Kap. 13, Üb. 12 and Var. zur Üb. 13.

Workbook Kap. 13, I.

12 Übung: Der Chef will das so.

Sie arbeiten für einen Chef, der sehr streng (*strict*) ist. Heute zeigen Sie einem neuen Lehrling das Büro. Er fragt immer, ob man alles so machen *muß*. Sagen Sie ihm, der Chef *will*, daß man es so macht.

> BEISPIEL: *Müssen* wir schon um acht im Büro sein?
> Ja, der Chef will, daß wir schon um acht im Büro sind.

1. *Müssen* wir den ganzen Tag hier bleiben?
2. *Muß* ich immer pünktlich sein?
3. *Dürfen* wir erst um *zehn* Kaffee trinken?
4. *Müssen* wir diese alten Computer benutzen?
5. *Müssen* wir auch samstags arbeiten?
6. *Muß* man immer eine Krawatte tragen?

13 Übung: Ich möchte etwas ändern.

Diese Situationen gefallen Ihnen nicht. Sagen Sie, wie Sie sie ändern möchten. Mehrere Antworten sind möglich.

> BEISPIEL: Die Musik ist Ihnen zu laut.
> Ich möchte, daß sie leiser wird.
> . . . , daß sie aufhört.

1. Draußen regnet es.
2. Das Wetter ist Ihnen zu kalt.
3. Ihre Mitbewohner quatschen zu viel.
4. Ihr kleiner Bruder stört Sie bei der Arbeit.
5. Man verschwendet zu viel Glas und Papier.
6. Ihre Mitbewohner sind Ihnen zu schlampig.

Lesestück

Zwei Schweizer stellen ihre Heimat vor

Tips zum Lesen und Lernen

Tips zum Vokabelnlernen

German Equivalents for *only*   When *only* is an adjective (meaning *sole* or *unique*), use **einzig-**. Otherwise use **nur**.

Er ist der **einzige** Mechaniker in der Gegend.	He's the **only** mechanic in the area.
Ich habe **nur** fünf Mark in der Tasche.	I have **only** five marks in my pocket.

Übung: Wie sagt man das auf deutsch?

1. I have only one pencil.
2. My only pencil is yellow.
3. A cup of coffee costs only DM 1,00.
4. That was the only restaurant that was open.

Leicht zu merken

die **Barriere, -n**	Barriere
(das) **Chinesisch**	
der **Dialekt, -e**	Dialekt
konservativ	konservativ
neutral	neutral
die **Neutralität**	Neutralität
offiziell	offiziell
das **Prozent**	
romantisch	
stabil	stabil
die **Stabilität**	Stabilität

Einstieg in den Text

In dem Lesestück auf Seite 394 sagt der Schweizer Dr. Anton Vischer, daß er sich manchmal über die Klischees ärgert, die er im Ausland über seine Heimat hört. Wenn man an die Schweiz denkt, denkt man z.B. automatisch an Schokolade, Schweizerkäse und gute Uhren. Diese Klischees sind Ihnen vielleicht auch bekannt. Aber interessanter ist sicher das Neue, was er über seine Heimat erzählt.

Nachdem Sie den Text gelesen haben, machen Sie sich eine Liste von wenigstens fünf neuen Dingen, die Sie über die Schweiz gelernt haben.

Wortschatz 2

Verben

antworten auf (+ *acc.*)   to answer (something); to respond to

sich ärgern (**über** + *acc.*)   to get annoyed (at), be annoyed (about)

auf·wachsen (**wächst auf**), **wuchs auf, ist aufgewachsen**   to grow up

denken, dachte, hat gedacht   to think

denken an (+ *acc.*)   to think of

Use **antworten** + *dat.* for answering people (Antworten Sie mir.). Use **antworten auf** for answering questions (Antworten Sie auf meine Frage.).

sich erholen (**von**)   to recover (from); to get well; to have a rest

reagieren auf (+ *acc.*)   to react to

sich etwas überlegen   to consider, ponder, think something over

Das muß ich mir überlegen.   I have to think it over.

vor·stellen   to introduce; to present

Darf ich meine Tante vorstellen?   May I introduce my aunt?

sich wundern (**über** + *acc.*)   to be surprised, amazed (at)

Substantive

der **Ort**, -e   place; town
der **Rechtsanwalt**, ⸚e
   lawyer (*m.*)
der **Schweizer**, -   Swiss (*m.*)
das **Gespräch**, -e
   conversation
das **Werk**, -e   work (of art),
   musical composition
die **Firma**, die **Firmen**   firm,
   company
die **Rechtsanwältin**, -nen
   lawyer (*f.*)
die **Schweizerin**, -nen   Swiss
   (*f.*)
die **Schwierigkeit**, -en
   difficulty

Adjektive und Adverbien

froh   happy
stolz auf (+ *acc.*)   proud of

Andere Vokabel

beides (*sing.*)   both things

Nützliche Ausdrücke

eines Tages   some day (*in
   the future*); one day (*in
   the past or future*)
in Zukunft   in the future

Gegensätze

froh ≠ **traurig**   happy ≠ sad

Zwei Schweizer stellen ihre Heimat vor

 Lab Manual Kap. 13, Lesestück.

Dr. Anton Vischer (45 Jahre alt), Rechtsanwalt aus Basel[1]

„In meinem Beruf bin ich für die Investitionen° ausländischer Firmen
verantwortlich und reise darum viel im Ausland. Dort höre ich oft die
alten Klischees über meine Heimat. Wenn man sagt, daß man aus der
5 Schweiz kommt, denken viele Menschen automatisch an saubere
Straßen, Schokolade, Uhren, Käse und an die Schweizergarde° im
Vatikan. Darüber ärgere ich mich immer ein bißchen. Ich möchte
lieber, daß andere wissen, was für eine politische Ausnahme° die
Schweiz in Europa bildet.° Ich werde versuchen, Ihnen etwas davon
10 zu beschreiben.

   Schon seit dem 13. Jahrhundert hat die Schweiz eine demokratische Verfassung.°[2] Sie gehört also zu° den ältesten und stabilsten
Demokratien der Welt. In beiden Weltkriegen ist die Schweiz neutral
geblieben, und sie hat ihre Neutralität und ihre politische Stabilität bis
15 heute bewahrt.°

Learning about Switzerland is the cultural goal of this chapter.

investments

Swiss Guard

exception
constitutes

constitution / **gehört... = ist
   also eine von**

hat... bewahrt = preserved

---

[1] Basel (*French* Bâle), Swiss city on the Rhine.

[2] In 1991, Switzerland celebrated the 700th anniversary of the Oath of Rütli, the defense
pact among the three original cantons against the Austrian Habsburgs. Wilhelm Tell is the
legendary hero of this period of Swiss resistance to foreign power.

Einige werden unsere Gesellschaft wohl zu konservativ finden. In einem Kanton³ war das Wahlrecht° der Frauen sogar bis 1992 beschränkt.° Aber man darf nicht vergessen, daß es in der Schweiz durchaus° auch einen Platz für soziale Kritik° gibt. Das zeigen die Werke unserer bekann-
20 testen Schriftsteller wie Max Frisch und Friedrich Dürrenmatt.⁴

   Jemand fragte mich einmal, ob ich stolz bin, Schweizer zu sein. Darauf habe ich sofort mit „ja" reagiert, aber in Zukunft werde ich mir die Antwort genauer überlegen. Ich werde einfach sagen, ich bin *froh*, Schweizer zu sein, denn meine Heimat ist das schönste Land,
25 das ich kenne. Da ich meine Freizeit immer auf Bergtouren verbringe, ist mein Leben mit der Alpenlandschaft eng verbunden.° Für mich sind die Alpen der einzige Ort, wo ich mich körperlich und seelisch° erholen kann. Das klingt vielleicht romantisch, aber eigentlich bin ich ein ganz praktischer Mensch."

30 Nicole Wehrli (24 Jahre alt), Dolmetscherin° aus Biel

   „Ich bin in der zweisprachigen° Stadt Biel — auf französisch Bienne — aufgewachsen, direkt an der Sprachgrenze zwischen der französi-schen und der deutschen Schweiz. Bei uns können Sie manchmal auf der Straße Gespräche hören, in denen die Menschen beides —
35 Französisch *und* Deutsch — miteinander reden. In der Schule habe

suffrage / restricted

definitely

criticism

eng verbunden = closely connected
körperlich... = physically and emotionally

interpreter

bilingual

„In den Bergen kann man sich körperlich und seelisch erholen."

³Switzerland is composed of twenty cantons, each with considerable autonomy. Women in the canton of Appenzell could not vote in local elections until 1992.

⁴Max Frisch (1911–1991) and Friedrich Dürrenmatt (1921–1990) both wrote novels, essays, and plays.

Kinder mit Schlitten (*sleds*) in der Altstadt von Basel.

ich dann Latein,° Englisch und Italienisch gelernt. Sie werden sich   Latin
also nicht wundern, daß ich mich für Fremdsprachen interessiere.
Eines Tages möchte ich sogar mit Chinesisch anfangen.

    Die Eidgenossenschaft[5] ist wohl ein Unikum° in Europa, denn sie   something unique
40 ist viersprachig. Die Sprachbarrieren waren lange Zeit ein großes Hin-
dernis° für die politische Vereinigung der Kantone und machen uns   obstacle
heute noch manchmal Schwierigkeiten. 69% der Bevölkerung° hat   population
Deutsch als Muttersprache, 18% spricht Französisch, 12% Italienisch
und etwa° ein Prozent Rätoromanisch.[6] Unser „Schwyzerdütsch"[7]   approximately

[5]**Eidgenossenschaft** = Confederation. *Confoederatio Helvetica*: the official (Latin) name
for modern Switzerland, hence CH on Swiss cars.

[6]Rhaetoromansch, or simply Romansch. It is a Romance language, a linguistic remnant of
the original Roman occupation of the Alpine territories, spoken by about 40,000 rural
Swiss in the canton of Grisons (**Graubünden**). Long under threat of extinction, it was de-
clared one of the four national languages in 1938.

[7]**Schweizerdeutsch** (*Swiss-German dialect*). **Hochdeutsch** (*High German*) is the official, standardized language of German-speaking countries. It is the language of the media,
the law, and education, and is based on written German (**Schriftdeutsch**). Educated native speakers are bi-dialectal, knowing their local dialect and High German, which they
may speak with a regional accent.

45 können die meisten Deutschen nicht verstehen. Da unsere Kinder Schriftdeutsch° erst in der Schule lernen müssen, ist es für sie oft so schwer wie eine Fremdsprache. Die geschriebene und offizielle Sprache in den Schulen bleibt Schriftdeutsch, aber nach dem Unterricht° reden Lehrer und Schüler Schwyzerdütsch miteinander."

standard written German

nach... = after class

„Mi Wält"

Fragen zum Lesestück

1. Was ist Dr. Vischer von Beruf?
2. Wofür ist er verantwortlich?
3. Welche Klischees hört er über die Schweiz, wenn er im Ausland ist?
4. Wie reagiert er darauf?
5. Seit wann hat die Schweiz eine demokratische Verfassung?
6. Was macht Herr Vischer in seiner Freizeit?
7. Warum ist die Stadt Biel, wo Nicole Wehrli aufgewachsen ist, besonders interessant?
8. Was war eine große Schwierigkeit bei der Vereinigung der Schweiz?
9. Wie viele Schweizer sind deutschsprachig?
10. Warum haben manche Deutsche Schwierigkeiten, die Schweizer zu verstehen?
11. Warum haben die Kinder in der Schweiz Schwierigkeiten mit Schriftdeutsch?

Situationen aus dem Alltag

Wie stellt man sich vor?

Wie stellt man sich oder einen Bekannten auf deutsch vor? Es kommt auf die Situation an. Unten sind vier verschiedene Situationen, aber zuerst ein paar Bemerkungen (*comments*).

Introducing yourself and others is a communicative goal.

Unter jungen Menschen ist es nicht so formell: Man sagt einfach seinen Namen und **Hallo** oder **Tag**, wie zum Beispiel in *Situation 1* (unten). Wie Sie schon wissen, sagen Studenten sofort **du** zueinander.

Wenn man ältere Menschen zum ersten Mal kennenlernt, ist es formeller (*Situationen 2* und *3*). Man sagt **angenehm** oder **freut mich** oder **sehr erfreut** (alle drei = *pleased to meet you*). Natürlich sagt man **Sie** statt **du**.

In allen Situationen ist es höflich, einander die Hand zu geben (*shake hands*). Das machen die Europäer viel öfter als die Amerikaner.

1. Die Studentin Sonja stellt ihrem Freund Wolfgang ihre Freundin Margaret aus Amerika vor.

   SONJA: Hallo Wolfgang! Darf ich vorstellen? Das ist meine Freundin Margaret aus Chicago.

   WOLFGANG: (*gibt ihr die Hand*) Hallo Margaret!

   MARGARET: Hallo Wolfgang.

   WOLFGANG: Nett, dich kennenzulernen.

   MARGARET: Danke, gleichfalls.

2. Bernd, 20, stellt seiner Mutter einen Freund vor.

   BERND: Mutter, ich möchte dir meinen Freund Theo vorstellen.

   FRAU RINGSTEDT: Freut mich, Sie kennenzulernen, Theo.

   THEO: Angenehm, Frau Ringstedt. (*Sie geben sich die Hände.*)

3. Der amerikanische Austauschstudent Michael Hayward stellt sich einem Professor in der Sprechstunde (*office hour*) vor.

   MICHAEL HAYWARD: Guten Tag, Professor Mohr. Darf ich mich vorstellen? Mein Name ist Hayward. (*Gibt ihm die Hand.*)

   PROF. MOHR: Guten Tag, Herr Hayward. Bitte nehmen Sie Platz.

4. Zwei Geschäftsleute treffen sich auf einer Konferenz.

   FRAU MÜLLER: Guten Tag, mein Name ist Müller.

   HERR BEHRENS: Freut mich, Frau Müller. Behrens.

Gruppenarbeit: Rollenspiele

1. **Darf ich mich vorstellen?**
   Sie sind alle zusammen auf einer Studentenparty, wo sie einander noch nicht kennen. Stehen Sie alle auf, und stellen Sie sich einander vor.

2. **Ich möchte euch meine Freunde vorstellen.**
   Zwei Studenten spielen die Rollen der Eltern. Ein dritter Student bringt zwei Freunde nach Hause und stellt sie den Eltern vor.

3. Now pretend that you're all business people at a convention. Introduce yourselves to each other. (In this kind of situation, people usually give only their last names.)

Zum Schluß

Sprechen wir miteinander

Lab Manual Kap. 13, Diktat.

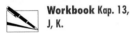

Workbook Kap. 13, J, K.

A Partnerarbeit: Was wird sein?

Lesen Sie die Zukunft Ihres Partners oder Ihrer Partnerin aus der Hand. Wie sieht die Zukunft aus?

> BEISPIEL: Du wirst lange leben. Du wirst dich oft verloben und dreimal heiraten (*get married*). Du wirst . . .

B Gruppenarbeit: Seid ihr optimistisch oder pessimistisch?

Wie wird die Welt in fünfzig Jahren aussehen? Wird das Leben besser sein oder nicht? Werden die Menschen glücklicher sein? Sagen Sie Ihre eigene Meinung.

C Partnerarbeit: Woran denkst du denn?

Stellen Sie einander Fragen mit diesen Verben.

> BEISPIEL: A: Woran denkst du denn?
> B: Ich denke an unser Gespräch von gestern.

1. denken an
2. sich freuen auf
3. sich interessieren für
4. sich ärgern über
5. sich kümmern um
6. sich erinnern an
7. warten auf
8. Angst haben vor
9. sich wundern über
10. sich vorbereiten (müssen) auf

D Gruppenarbeit: Was ist Ihr Hobby?

Wie verbringen Sie Ihre Freizeit? Haben Sie ein Hobby? Sprechen wir ein bißchen darüber. Machen wir zuerst eine Liste von Möglichkeiten.

1. Was kann man sammeln? Zum Beispiel: Briefmarken (*stamps*).
2. Spielen Sie ein Musikinstrument? Welches? Zum Beispiel: Klavier (*piano*).
3. Machen Sie gern etwas Kreatives? Zum Beispiel: Fotografieren.
4. Spielen Sie gern etwas oder treiben Sie Sport? Zum Beispiel: Schach (*chess*).
5. Jetzt sprechen wir über unsere Hobbies. Stellen Sie einander Fragen darüber. Hier sind einige Möglichkeiten:

> A: Wofür interessierst du dich?
> B: Ich interessiere mich für _____ .
> A: Warum interessierst du dich dafür? usw.
>
> A: Wie lange sammelst du schon _____ ?
> B: Seit _____ .
> A: Kostet das viel Geld? usw.

E Gruppenarbeit: Reaktionen: Das lohnt sich. / Das lohnt sich nicht.

Wer hat etwas Interessantes vor? Sagen Sie, was Sie vorhaben. Die anderen müssen dann darauf reagieren.

> BEISPIEL: A: Am Wochenende habe ich vor, den neuen Film „_____" zu sehen.
> B: Ja, das lohnt sich! Ich habe ihn schon letzte Woche gesehen. *oder*
> Das lohnt sich nicht. Ich habe gehört, er ist blöd.

F Partnerarbeit: Ich will, daß du dich änderst.

Sagen Sie Ihrem Partner, wie er sein Leben ändern soll. Dann antwortet er darauf. (Das ist nur ein Spiel. Nehmen Sie es also nicht zu ernst!)

> BEISPIEL: A: Ich will, daß du früher aufstehst!
> B: Warum denn? Ich schlafe doch gern. *Ich* möchte, daß *du . . .*

Schreiben Sie zu Hause

G For each pair of sentences below, fill in the past participle cued in English in the first sentence. In the second sentence, it is used as an attributive adjective. Don't forget the adjective ending!

1. Wer hat im Zimmer _____? (*straightened up*)
   Es ist schön, in einem _____ Zimmer zu sitzen.
2. Letztes Jahr habe ich sehr viel Geld _____ . (*saved*)
   Mit meinem _____ Geld will ich eine Reise ins Ausland machen.

3. Hat man dir den Rucksack _____? (*stolen*)
   Ja, und meine neue Kamera war leider im _____ Rucksack.

4. Ich habe meine Hemden _____. (*washed*)
   Die _____ Hemden hängen draußen hinter dem Haus.

5. Der Mann, mit dem sie sich verlobt hat, ist immer schön _____.
   (*dressed*)
   Nur schön _____ Männer gehen mit ihr aus.

6. Frau Schwarzer hat ihren Wagen selber _____. (*repaired*)
   Ihr _____ Wagen läuft jetzt gut.

H **Aufsatzthemen**   Wählen Sie eine Frage, und schreiben Sie eine Seite darüber.

1. Gibt es Sprachbarrieren in Ihrer Heimat? Beschreiben Sie einige.

2. Kennen Sie Ausländer, die in Amerika leben und deren Muttersprache nicht Englisch ist? Was für Schwierigkeiten gibt es wohl für solche Menschen? Vielleicht sind Sie selber Ausländer. Welche Schwierigkeiten haben Sie gehabt?

I **Wie sagt man das auf deutsch?**

1. Are you looking forward to the end of the semester?
2. Yes, I'm planning to go skiing in Switzerland.
3. That sounds good. Have a good trip.

4. What do you think of when you hear the word "Switzerland"?
5. I remember my father's aunt who came from Switzerland.

6. Excuse me, do you know your way around in the library?
7. A bit. How can I help you?
8. I'm interested in books on Switzerland. Do you know where they are?
9. Just a moment, please. I'll have to think it over.

10. What are you so annoyed about?
11. My roommate asked me for money again this morning.
12. Will you give it to her/him?

Profile of Switzerland

Area:	41,288 square kilometers; 15,941 square miles (approximately the same area as the states of Massachusetts, Connecticut, and Rhode Island combined)
Population:	6,700,000; density 162 people per square kilometer (420 per square mile)
Currency:	Swiss franc (**Schweizer Franken**); 1 sfr = 100 Rappen or Centimes
Major Cities:	Berne (**Bern**, capital, pop. 134,400), Zürich (largest city, pop. 346,900), Basel, Geneva (**Genf**), Lausanne
Religions:	48% Roman Catholic, 44% Protestant, 8% other

Switzerland has one of the highest per capita incomes in the world, as well as one of the highest standards of living. The literacy rate is 99.5%. The beauty of the Swiss Alps has made tourism Switzerland's main service industry; the alpine rivers provide inexpensive hydroelectric power.

Switzerland has not sent troops into foreign wars since 1515. It guards its neutrality even to the extent of staying out of the European Union and the United Nations. It is, however, a member of several special U.N. agencies. The second headquarters of the U.N. are in Geneva, which is also the seat of the International Red Cross and the World Council of Churches.

Marktplatz und altes Rathaus. (Basel)

In der zweisprachigen Stadt Biel / Bienne.

SPRACHREGIONEN

Deutsch
Französisch
Italienisch
Rätoromanisch

Bodensee

BRD

Basel

der Rhein

St. Gallen

Zürich

Zürchersee

LIECHTENSTEIN
ÖSTERREICH

Biel / Bienne

Luzern

Vierwaldstättersee

Bern

SCHWEIZ

der Rhein

Lausanne

Montreux

St. Moritz

die Rhone

Genfer See

Locarno

Genf
(Genève)

Lugano

FRANKREICH

Matterhorn

Zermatt

0   45 Km.

0   30 Mi.

ITALIEN

Die Schweiz

Österreich

Vienna, Karlsplatz subway
station (architect: Otto Wagner).

Communicative Goals

- Getting a room in a hotel
- Expressing wishes contrary to fact
- Talking about contrary-to-fact situations
- Making suggestions
- Making polite requests

Cultural Goal

- Learning about Austria

Chapter Outline

Lyrik zum Vorlesen Ernst Jandl, „ottos mops"

Grammatik General Subjunctive: Present Tense • Other Uses of the General Subjunctive (Conditions Contrary to Fact • Wishes Contrary to Fact • Hypothetical Statements and Questions • Polite Requests)

Lesestück Zwei Österreicher stellen sich vor

Situationen aus dem Alltag Im Hotel

Almanach Profile of Austria

Auf Urlaub in Österreich

Nach einem langen Tag in Salzburg will das Ehepaar Dietrichs aus Potsdam zum Abendessen ausgehen.

RICHARD: Ursula, hast du noch österreichisches Geld?

URSULA: Nein. Wieso, hast du auch keine Schillinge mehr?

RICHARD: Leider nicht. Wenn es nicht so spät wäre, könnte ich noch bei der Bank wechseln.

URSULA: Das macht ja nichts. An der Hotelkasse kannst du wechseln, oder wir zahlen im Restaurant entweder mit Kreditkarte oder mit Reiseschecks.

heute nacht = *tonight*, but also *last night* if said early in morning.

An der Rezeption

TOURIST: Grüß Gott! Hätten Sie noch ein Zimmer frei für heute nacht?

ANGESTELLTER: Wünschen Sie ein Einzelzimmer oder ein Doppelzimmer?

TOURIST: Am liebsten hätte ich ein Einzelzimmer mit Dusche.

ANGESTELLTER: Das könnte ich Ihnen erst morgen geben. Im Moment ist nur ein Doppelzimmer mit Bad frei.

TOURIST: Was würde das denn kosten?

ANGESTELLTER: 500 Schilling mit Frühstück.

TOURIST: Dürfte ich mir das Zimmer ansehen?

ANGESTELLTER: Selbstverständlich. (*Gibt ihm den Schlüssel.*) Das wäre Zimmer Nummer 14 im ersten Stock.

Getting a room in a hotel is a communicative goal of this chapter. Most hotels in Europe include breakfast in the room price. Note: **im ersten Stock** is the equivalent of American *on the second floor.*

Ausflug zum Heurigen

Zwei Freunde im ersten Semester in Wien wollen den neuen Wein probieren.

ANDREAS: Hast du heute abend etwas Besonderes vor?

ESTHER: Nein, warum?

ANDREAS: Dann könnten wir endlich nach Grinzing zum Heurigen fahren.

ESTHER: Ja, höchste Zeit! Und es wäre auch schön, dort zu essen.

ANDREAS: Gute Idee! Ich hab' schon Riesenhunger.

ESTHER: Dann sollten wir gleich losfahren.

Heurige are taverns in and around Vienna, each originally belonging to a vineyard and serving wine (called **Heuriger**) pressed from the current harvest (**heuer** = *this year*). **Grinzing**, a suburb of Vienna, has many **Heurige**.

WEINGUT GRINZING HEURIGER

GRINZING, SANDGASSE 9, TEL. 32 24 39

MUSIK

BUFFET PRÄMIERTE FLASCHENWEINE

On Vacation in Austria

After a long day in Salzburg, Mr. and Mrs. Dietrichs from Potsdam want to go out to dinner.

R.: Ursula, do you have any more Austrian money?

U.: No. Why? Don't you have any more schillings either?

R.: Unfortunately not. If it weren't so late, I could still change money at the bank.

U.: That doesn't matter. You can change money at the hotel cashier, or we'll pay in the restaurant, either with credit card or with traveler's checks.

At the Reception Desk

T.: Hello, would you still have a room free for tonight?

E.: Do you want a single or a double room?

T.: I'd prefer a single room with shower.

E.: I couldn't give you that until tomorrow. At the moment there is only a double room with bath available.

T.: What would that cost?

E.: Five hundred schillings with breakfast.

T.: May I please have a look at the room?

E.: Of course. (*Hands him the key*). That would be room number 14 on the second floor.

Outing to a Heuriger

Two friends in their first semester in Vienna want to try the new wine.

A: Have you got anything special planned for tonight?

E: No, why?

A: Then we could finally go to Grinzing to a *Heuriger*.

E: Yes, high time! And it would be nice to eat there too.

A: Good idea! I'm already famished.

E: Then we ought to leave right away.

Wortschatz 1

Verben

aus·gehen ging aus, ist ausgegangen to go out
los·fahren (fährt los), fuhr los, ist losgefahren to depart, start, leave
probieren to sample, try
wechseln to change (money)

Substantive

der/die **Angestellte, -n** employee
der **Ausflug, ⸚e** outing, excursion
der **Scheck, -s** check
  der **Reisescheck, -s** traveler's check
der **Schilling** Austrian shilling
der **Stock** floor (*of a building*)
  der **erste Stock** the second floor
  im ersten Stock on the second floor
das **Bad, ⸚er** bath
  ein Bad nehmen to take a bath
das **Badezimmer, -** bathroom
das **Doppelzimmer, -** double room
das **Ehepaar, -e** married couple

das **Einzelzimmer, -** single room
das **Erdgeschoß** first floor, ground floor
die **Bank, -en** bank
die **Dusche, -n** shower
die **Kasse, -n** cash register; cashier's office
die **Kreditkarte, -n** credit card
die **Nummer, -n** number
die **Rezeption** (hotel) reception desk

Adjektiv

österreichisch Austrian

Andere Vokabeln

entweder . . . oder (*conj.*) either . . . or

Nützlicher Ausdruck

höchste Zeit high time

Gegensätze

entweder . . . oder ≠ **weder . . . noch** either . . . or ≠ neither . . . nor

Mit anderen Worten

der **Riesenhunger** = **sehr großer Hunger**

Variationen

A Persönliche Fragen

1. Haben Sie je Geld wechseln müssen? Wo?
2. Zahlen Sie im Restaurant mit Kreditkarte, Scheck oder Bargeld (*cash*)?
3. Haben Sie je in einem Hotel übernachtet? Wo war das?
4. Würden Sie lieber in Jugendherbergen oder in Hotels übernachten, wenn Sie nach Österreich reisen? Warum?
5. Haben Sie ein Doppel- oder ein Einzelzimmer im Studentenwohnheim?
6. Grinzing ist ein Ausflugsort in der Nähe von Wien. Kennen Sie in Ihrer Gegend einen schönen Ausflugsort?

German dormitories have only singles and doubles. A triple would be called **ein Dreibettzimmer.**

B Übung: Was ist ein Riese?

Ein berühmter Riese in der Bibel hieß Goliath. Sie kennen schon das Wort „riesengroß." So nennt man etwas sehr Großes. Jetzt wissen Sie auch, wenn man sehr hungrig ist, sagt man: „Ich habe Riesenhunger!" Also:

1. Einen riesengroßen Hunger nennt man auch *einen Riesenhunger.*
2. Einen sehr sehr großen Koffer nennt man auch _____ .
3. Eine ganz große Freude ist _____ .
4. Wenn viele Menschen zusammen demonstrieren, dann hat man

   _____ .
5. Wenn ein Supertanker einen Unfall hat und sein Öl ins Meer fließt, dann ist das _____ .
6. Ein sehr großes Hotel kann man auch _____ nennen.

Das Wiener Riesenrad

C Partnerarbeit: Wie wäre das? *(How would that be?)*

Ihr Partner schlägt Ihnen etwas vor. Reagieren Sie darauf mit Ihren eigenen Worten: **Das wäre . . . !** (Switch roles for second column.)

BEISPIEL: A: Sollen wir einen Ausflug machen?
B: Ja, das wäre toll!

ins Kino gehen?	uns die Stadt ansehen?
Geld wechseln?	zu Hause sitzen?
Freunde einladen?	das Zimmer aufräumen?
skifahren gehen?	im Restaurant essen?
Theaterkarten kaufen?	eine Radtour machen?

Sagen Sie, Sie machen entweder **dies** oder **das**.

> BEISPIEL: Was trinken Sie heute abend?
> Ich trinke entweder Tee oder Kaffee.

1. Wohin fahren Sie im Sommer?
2. Was möchten Sie gern essen?
3. Mit wem wollen Sie Tennis spielen?
4. Welche Fremdsprache werden Sie nächstes Jahr lernen?
5. Wer war denn das?
6. Wissen Sie, in welchem Stock Ihr Hotelzimmer ist?
7. Wie kann man im Hotel zahlen?
8. Wann wollen Sie das nächste Mal skifahren gehen?

Lyrik zum Vorlesen

The Austrian poet Ernst Jandl was born in Vienna. In the following poem, he shows that it is possible to tell a whole story using only one vowel. Reading it aloud will be a good review of the German long and short **o**! Like many other modern poets, Jandl does not capitalize nouns.

Lab Manual Kap. 14, Lyrik zum Vorlesen.

ottos mops°   mutt

ottos mops trotzt°   won't obey
otto: fort° mops fort   go away
ottos mops hopst° fort   hops
otto: soso

otto holt koks°   charcoal briquettes
otto holt obst°   fruit
otto horcht°   listens
otto: mops mops
otto hofft

ottos mops klopft°   knocks
otto: komm mops komm
ottos mops kommt
ottos mops kotzt°   pukes
otto: ogottogott

> Ernst Jandl
> (geboren 1925)

General Subjunctive: Present Tense

In addition to general subjunctive, German also has a "special" subjunctive that you will learn in Kap. 16.

The *imperative* (Kap. 4) is also a grammatical mood.

Language offers you the possibility of presenting information in various ways. On the one hand, you can present something as a fact. On the other hand, you can present it as hypothetical, conjectural, or contrary to fact. Both German and English have two different sets of verb forms for these two possibilities, called the *indicative* and the *subjunctive moods* (from Latin *modus*, "manner, mode, way").

Up to now, you have been using the *indicative mood* to talk about what is definite, certain, and real.

Barbara **ist** nicht hier.	*Barbara **isn't** here.*
Ich **habe** Zeit.	*I **have** time.*

The *subjunctive mood* (**der Konjunktiv**) is used to talk about hypothetical, uncertain, or unreal situations, and also to make polite statements and requests.

Wenn Barbara nur hier **wäre!**	*If only Barbara **were** here!*
Wenn ich mehr Zeit **hätte** . . .	*If I **had** more time . . .*
Würden Sie mir bitte helfen?	***Would** you please help me?*

You've been using **würde**, the subjunctive form of **werden**, since Kap. 7.

A common subjunctive form in English is *were* in *if I were you.*

English *present* subjunctive is signalled by what look like *past-tense* forms or by **would** + a verb.

*If they **lived** nearby, we **would visit** them.*	(condition contrary to fact)
*If only I **had** more time!*	(wish contrary to fact)
*I **would like** to have a room.*	(polite request)

Note that the verbs *lived* and *had* in the examples above are identical to the past in *form*, but have present-tense meaning.

*If they **lived** nearby . . .*	(right now)
*If only I **had** more time!*	(right now)

Present Subjunctive of Weak Verbs

The present tense of the general subjunctive in German is also based on past indicative forms. In the case of *weak* verbs (see p. 285), the present subjunctive is *identical* to the simple past indicative you have already learned.

wenn ich	wohn**te**	*if I lived*	wenn wir	wohn**ten**	*if we lived*
wenn du	wohn**test**	*if you lived*	wenn ihr	wohn**tet**	*if you lived*
wenn sie	wohn**te**	*if she lived*	wenn sie, Sie	wohn**ten**	*if they, you lived*

Servus in Österreich®

> ### *Note on Usage:* Wishes Contrary to Fact
>
> A contrary-to-fact wish is expressed in German by a **wenn**-clause in the subjunctive (verb last) with an added **nur**.
>
> Wenn ich **nur** näher **wohnte**!   *If only I lived closer!*
>
> The **nur** is placed after all personal and reflexive pronouns, but before **nicht**:
>
> Wenn du es mir **nur** sagtest!   *If only you'd tell it to me!*
> Wenn es **nur** nicht so spät wäre.   *If only it weren't so late.*

Lab Manual Kap. 14, Üb. 1, 3, 5, and Var. zur Üb. 4, 7–9.

Workbook Kap. 14, A–D.

1 **Übung: Wenn es nur anders wäre!**

Sie hören eine Situation im Indikativ. Sie wünschen im Konjunktiv, daß es anders wäre.

BEISPIEL: A: Hans-Peter wohnt nicht hier.   *Hans-Peter doesn't live here.*

B: Wenn er nur hier wohnte!   *If only he lived here!*

1. Petra kauft das nicht.
2. Georg beeilt sich nicht.
3. Der Urlaub dauert nicht länger.
4. Ich erhole mich nicht.
5. Die Gäste setzen sich nicht.
6. Maria macht die Tür nicht zu.
7. Robert bestellt nicht genug Bier.
8. Meine Freunde besuchen mich nicht.
9. Meine Großeltern wohnen nicht bei uns.
10. Inge wechselt ihr Geld nicht.

Present Subjunctive of Strong Verbs

The present subjunctive of strong verbs is also based on their past indicative forms (see pp. 286–287), but these forms are *modified* according to the following three-step procedure.

Remember that you can only add umlaut to **a, o, u,** and **au.**

Step 1: Take the simple past stem of the verb:

fahren → **fuhr-**   gehen → **ging-**   laufen → **lief-**   sein → **war-**

Step 2: Add an umlaut to the stem vowel whenever possible:

führ-   **ging-**   **lief-**   **wär-**

Step 3: Add the following personal endings:

ich	wäre	*I would be*	wir	wär**en**	*we would be*
du	wär**est**	*you would be*	ihr	wär**et**	*you would be*
er	wäre	*he would be*	sie, Sie	wär**en**	*they, you would be*

Note the difference between the present subjunctive endings and the past indicative endings of strong verbs:

present subjunctive (would go)		past indicative (went)	
ich	ginge	ich	ging
du	gingest	du	gingst
sie	ginge	sie	ging
wir	gingen	wir	gingen
ihr	ginget	ihr	gingt
sie, Sie	gingen	sie, Sie	gingen

Only the **wir-** and the plural **sie-**endings are the same.

A complete list of the principal parts of strong and irregular verbs is in Appendix 2, p. 493–494.

2 Übung

Review the simple past stems of these strong verbs.

BEISPIEL: laufen *lief*

scheinen	finden
kommen	gehen
anfangen	fahren
gefallen	sein
tun	schlafen
aussteigen	bekommen

3 Übung: Wenn es nur anders wäre!

Jetzt hören Sie eine Situation im Indikativ. Sie wünschen im Konjunktiv, daß es anders wäre.

BEISPIEL: Meine Gäste gehen nicht nach Hause.
Wenn sie nur nach Hause gingen!

1. ~~Gabi~~ läuft nicht schnell.
2. Die Sonne scheint nicht.
3. Robert kommt nicht um zwölf.
4. Karin geht nicht mit uns spazieren.
5. Wir sind nicht alt genug.
6. Das Kind schläft nicht länger.
7. Wir bekommen kein Doppelzimmer.
8. Laura findet ihre Kreditkarte nicht.
9. Die Uhr geht nicht richtig.
10. Unsere Freunde fahren nicht nach Australien.
11. Er fängt nicht an.
12. Die Wohnung gefällt uns nicht.
13. Das tut Marie nicht gern.
14. Hier steigen wir nicht aus.

Present Subjunctive of Modal Verbs

To form the present subjunctive of modal verbs, take the past indicative, *including endings* (see p. 289), and add an umlaut to the stem vowel of *only* those verbs that have an umlaut in their infinitive.

infinitive		past indicative	
dürfen	*to be allowed*	**ich durfte**	*I was allowed*

ich	**dürfte**	*I would be allowed*	wir	**dürften**	*we would be allowed*
du	**dürftest**	*you would be allowed*	ihr	**dürftet**	*you would be allowed*
er	**dürfte**	*he would be allowed*	sie, Sie	**dürften**	*they, you would be allowed*

Similarly:

past indicative			*present subjunctive*		
ich konnte	*I was able to*		ich **könnte**	*I could, would be able to*	
ich mochte	*I liked*		ich **möchte**	*I would like to*	
ich mußte	*I had to*		ich **müßte**	*I would have to*	

The present subjunctive of **sollen** and **wollen**, however, is *not* umlauted, and so looks just like the past indicative.

| ich sollte | *I was supposed to* | ich **sollte** | *I ought to* |
| ich wollte | *I wanted to* | ich **wollte** | *I would want to* |

4 Übung: Hören Sie gut zu! (Mit geschlossenen Büchern)

Listen to each pair of sentences, then say which one is past indicative and which present subjunctive. Then, with open books, repeat each sentence aloud and give the English equivalent.

1. Durfte sie das machen? / Dürfte sie das machen?
2. Wir könnten ihn abholen. / Wir konnten ihn abholen.
3. Sie müßte das wissen. / Sie mußte das wissen.
4. Mochte er das Frühstück? / Möchte er das Frühstück?

5 Übung: Wenn es nur anders wäre!

Ihre Professorin beschreibt wieder eine Situation im Indikativ. Sie wünschen im Konjunktiv, daß es anders wäre.

BEISPIEL: Christine kann kein Englisch.
Wenn sie nur Englisch *könnte!*

1. Wir können kein Französisch.
2. Die Gäste müssen nach Hause.
3. Wir dürfen nicht länger bleiben.
4. Esther will nicht nach Grinzing.
5. Die Kinder können nicht mitfahren.
6. Unsere Freunde müssen abfahren.
7. Sie dürfen nicht alles sagen.
8. Andreas will nicht helfen.

Making suggestions is a communicative goal.

Note on Usage: Using the Subjunctive to Make Suggestions

| Wir **könnten** zusammen ausgehen. | We **could** go out together. |
| Wir **sollten** eigentlich hier bleiben. | We really **ought** to stay here. |

6 Partnerarbeit: Was könnten wir heute machen?

Partner A sagt etwas Schönes, was Sie machen **könnten**. Partner B sagt aber, Sie **sollten** eigentlich etwas anderes machen.

BEISPIEL: A: Wir *könnten* zusammen spazierengehen.
 B: Aber wir *sollten* eigentlich das Zimmer aufräumen.

Hier sind einige Möglichkeiten:

etwas Schönes	*etwas Wichtiges*
spazierengehen	das Zimmer aufräumen
Karten spielen	Hausaufgaben machen
italienisch essen	Lebensmittel einkaufen
Musik hören	uns auf die Klausur vorbereiten

Present Subjunctive of *haben, werden,* and *wissen*

To form the present subjunctive of the verbs **haben**, **werden**, and **wissen**, take the past indicative, *including endings* (see pp. 289–290), and add an umlaut to the stem vowel:

past indicative		*present subjunctive*	
ich hatte	*I had*	ich **hätte**	*I would have*
ich wurde	*I became*	ich **würde**	*I would become, I would*
ich wußte	*I knew*	ich **wüßte**	*I would know*

Making polite requests is a communicative goal.

> ***Note on Usage:*** Polite Requests: Subjunctive + *gern*
>
> **Ich hätte gern** ein Einzelzimmer mit Bad.
> **Ich wüßte gern**, wo die Kasse ist.
>
> *I would like to have a single room with bath.*
> *I would like to know where the cashier is.*

7 Kettenreaktion: Was hätten Sie gern?

Sagen Sie, was Sie gern hätten.

BEISPIEL: Ich hätte gern ein frisches Brötchen. Und du?
 Ich hätte gern ein-_____ .

8 Kettenreaktion: Was wüßten Sie gern?

Sagen Sie, was Sie gern wüßten.

BEISPIEL: Ich wüßte gern, wo ich Geld verdienen könnte. Und du?
 Ich wüßte gern, _____ .

Ohne Zeitung hätten Sie weniger zu sagen.

DIE ZEITUNGEN IN DEUTSCHLAND.

In **Kapitel 7** you learned how to use the subjunctive construction **würde** + *infinitive* to express intentions, opinions, preferences, and polite requests. This construction is an alternative to the one-word present subjunctive forms you have been learning in this chapter.

There is no difference in meaning between the following clauses:

Er **käme** . . .
Er **würde kommen** . . . } *He would come* . . .

The present subjunctive with **würden** often replaces the one-word form of weak verbs which is indistinguishable from the past indicative:

Ich kaufte das nicht. { *I didn't buy that. (past indic.)*
I wouldn't buy that. (pres. subj.)

is replaced by:

Ich **würde** das nicht **kaufen**.   *I wouldn't buy that.*

Spoken German also replaces the one-word form of many strong verbs with **würden** + *infinitive* (but *not* in the case of the frequently used verbs **sein**, **haben**, and the modals).

Ich **tränke** Wein . . .   is replaced by
Ich **würde** Wein **trinken** . . .   *I'd drink wine* . . .

9 Übung: Was würden Sie machen?

Sagen Sie, was Sie in diesen Situationen machen würden.

BEISPIEL: Was würden Sie machen, wenn Sie diese Woche frei
             hätten?
             Ich würde nach Hause fahren.

Was würden Sie machen . . .

1. wenn Sie 500 Schilling hätten?
2. wenn Sie Hunger hätten?
3. wenn Sie Durst hätten?
4. wenn Sie Musik hören wollten?
5. wenn Sie Wanderlust hätten?
6. wenn Sie knapp bei Kasse wären?
7. wenn Sie Spaß haben wollten?
8. wenn Sie sich das Studium nicht leisten könnten?

Talking about contrary-to-fact situations is a communicative goal.

Conditions Contrary to Fact: "If X were true, then Y would be true."

In **Kapitel 8** you learned about conditional sentences containing a **wenn**-clause (see p. 225). When the conditional sentence is describing a situation that is contrary to fact, the verbs must be in the subjunctive. Note the difference between the following sentences:

Indicative

Wenn der Junge schon dreizehn **ist**, **darf** er den Film sehen.	*If the boy is already thirteen he's allowed to see the movie.*

(*Implication:* The speaker doesn't know whether the boy is thirteen or not.)

Subjunctive

Wenn der Junge schon dreizehn **wäre**, **dürfte** er den Film sehen.	*If the boy were already thirteen, he would be allowed to see the movie.*

(*Implication:* The speaker knows the boy is not yet thirteen.)

A **wenn**-clause states the condition contrary to fact: "If X were true . . ."

Wenn wir jetzt in Deutschland wären . . .	*If we were in Germany now . . .*
Wenn ich mehr Geld hätte . . .	*If I had more money . . .*

The main clause (with an optional **dann** as the first word) draws the unreal conclusion: ". . . then Y would be true."

. . . (dann) würden wir sehr schnell Deutsch lernen.	*. . . (then) we would learn German very quickly.*
. . . (dann) müßte ich nicht so viel arbeiten.	*. . . (then) I wouldn't have to work so much.*

Putting them together:

> **Wenn wir jetzt in Deutschland wären, würden wir sehr schnell Deutsch lernen.**
> **Wenn ich mehr Geld hätte, dann müßte ich nicht so viel arbeiten.**

Conditional sentences may begin either with the **wenn**-clause (as in the two previous examples) *or* with the conclusion clause.[1]

> **Wir würden** sehr schnell Deutsch lernen, wenn wir jetzt in Deutschland **wären.**
> **Ich müßte** nicht so viel arbeiten, wenn ich mehr Geld **hätte.**

---

[1] The **wenn** is sometimes omitted from the **wenn**-clause. Its verb is then placed at the *beginning* of the clause. Compare the similar structure in English that omits *if*:

Hätte er das Geld, (dann) **würde** er mehr kaufen. ***Had** he the money, he would buy more.*

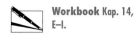
Lab Manual Kap. 14, Üb. 10, 14, and Var. zur Üb. 12–14.

Workbook Kap. 14, E–I.

10 Übung: Wenn es anders wäre . . . (Mit offenen Büchern)

Ihr Professor beschreibt eine Situation im Indikativ. Sie sagen im Konjunktiv, wie es wäre, wenn die Situation *anders* wäre. (Note that the logic of these sentences demands changing positive to negative and vice versa).

> BEISPIEL: Weil es so kalt ist, können wir nicht schwimmen.
>> Wenn es *nicht* so kalt *wäre*, *könnten* wir schwimmen.

1. Weil es so weit ist, können wir nicht zu Fuß gehen.
2. Weil ich keine Lust habe, mache ich es nicht.
3. Weil dieses Buch langweilig ist, lesen wir es nicht.
4. Weil der Dom geschlossen ist, können Sie ihn nicht besuchen.
5. Weil ich keine Zeit habe, kann ich keine Dusche nehmen.
6. Weil sie nicht aus Österreich kommt, sagt sie nicht „Grüß Gott".
7. Weil ich keinen Hunger habe, bestelle ich nichts.
8. Weil sie sich nicht für diesen Film interessiert, geht sie nicht mit.

11 Übung (Mit offenen Büchern)

Wiederholen Sie, was Sie schon in **Übung 10** gemacht haben, aber diesmal beginnen Sie *nicht* mit **wenn**.

> BEISPIEL: Wir kommen zu spät, weil du nicht schneller fährst.
>> Wir würden nicht zu spät kommen, wenn du schneller fahren würdest.

1. Wir bleiben hier, weil er uns braucht.
2. Ich muß jetzt wechseln, weil ich kein österreichisches Geld habe.
3. Wir gehen spazieren, weil die Sonne scheint.
4. Wir trampen nach Italien, weil wir keinen Wagen haben.
5. Ich lese die Zeitung nicht, weil ich so müde bin.
6. Er kann mir nicht danken, weil er meinen Namen nicht weiß.
7. Wir sehen uns nicht, weil er nicht mehr vorbeikommt.

Wenn ich fliegen könnte...

Wishes Contrary to Fact

There are two ways to form contrary-to-fact wishes:

Wenn sie nur hier wäre!	*If only she were here!*
Ich wünschte, sie wäre hier.	*I wish she were here.*

When you use the second expression, notice that *both* verbs are in the subjunctive (**wünschte, wäre**). The second clause of this construction *never* begins with **daß** but *always* has verb-second word order.

12 Gruppenarbeit: Buttje, Buttje, in der See

Es gibt ein bekanntes norddeutsches Märchen („Der Fischer und seine Frau"), in dem ein großer Butt (*flounder*) einem Fischer seine Wünsche erfüllt (*grants*). Der Fischer ruft ihn immer wieder aus der See mit den Worten: „Buttje, Buttje, in der See", und sagt ihm, was er sich wünscht. Jetzt sagen Sie einander, was Sie sich wünschen. Antworten Sie, ob Sie den Wunsch erfüllen können oder nicht.

> BEISPIEL: A: Ich wünschte, ich könnte wie ein Vogel fliegen!
> B: Das kann ich dir leider nicht erfüllen!

Hypothetical Statements and Questions

German also uses subjunctive for hypothetical statements and questions, where English uses *would*, *could*, or *ought to*.

Du **solltest** daran denken.	*You **ought to** think of that.*
Wir **könnten** nach Grinzing fahren.	*We **could** drive to Grinzing.*
Das **wäre** schön!	*That **would be** nice!*
Was **würde** das kosten?	*What **would** that cost?*

13 Partnerarbeit: Wie wäre das?

Sie wollen heute irgendetwas zusammen machen. Partner A macht einen Vorschlag (*suggestion*). Partner B reagiert darauf.

> BEISPIEL: A: Wir **könnten** eine Wanderung machen.
> B: Ja, das **wäre** schön! *oder* Nein, das **wäre** zu schwierig.

Polite Requests

Note the difference in the tone of the following two requests:

Can *you do this for me?* vs. **Could** *you do this for me?*

It is more polite to soften the request with the subjunctive, as in the second sentence.

German uses the subjunctive in the same way as English to make polite requests. These are sometimes in the statement form you have already used.

Ich **hätte** gern eine Tasse Kaffee.	*I'd like to have a cup of coffee.*
Ich **wüßte** gern, wo der Bahnhof ist.	*I'd like to know where the train station is.*

Sometimes polite requests are questions.

Könnten Sie mir bitte helfen?	*Could you please help me?*
Würden Sie mir bitte den Koffer tragen?	*Would you please carry my suitcase?*
Dürfte ich eine Frage stellen?	*Might I ask a question?*

14 Übung: Könnten Sie das bitte machen?

Benutzen Sie den Konjunktiv statt des Indikativs, um höflicher zu sein.

BEISPIEL: Können Sie mir bitte ein Einzelzimmer zeigen?
Könnten Sie mir bitte ein Einzelzimmer zeigen?

1. Können Sie mir bitte sagen, wann der Zug nach Berlin abfährt?
2. Haben Sie Zeit, eine Tasse Kaffee mit mir zu trinken?
3. Darf ich mich hier setzen?
4. Tragen Sie mir bitte die Koffer? (Benutzen Sie *würden*!)

5. Ist es möglich, eine Zeitung zu kaufen?
6. Können Sie mir meinen Platz zeigen?
7. Haben Sie ein Einzelzimmer mit Dusche?
8. Wissen Sie, wo man Karten kaufen kann?

Lesestück | Zwei Österreicher stellen sich vor

Tips zum Lesen und Lernen

Tips zum Vocabelnlernen: Adverbs of Time

The suffix *-lang* To form the German equivalents of the English adverbial phrases *for days*, *for hours*, etc., add the suffix **-lang** to the plural of the noun.

minuten**lang**	*for minutes*	monate**lang**	*for months*
stunden**lang**	*for hours*	jahre**lang**	*for years*
tage**lang**	*for days*	jahrhunderte**lang**	*for centuries*
wochen**lang**	*for weeks*		

You can guess the meaning of **jahrzehntelang.**

Compare the Note on Usage on p. 296.

Also learn the phrase

eine Zeitlang   *for a time, for a while*

In diesem Kapitel lesen Sie über Österreich. Das Lesestück spricht von der historischen Rolle Österreichs als Weltreich:

„Die Habsburger Dynastie regierte **jahrhundertelang** über Deutsche, Ungarn, Tschechen, Polen, Italiener, Serben und **eine Zeitlang** sogar über Mexikaner."

Übung: Wie lange hat's gedauert?

Ihre Professorin möchte wissen, ob etwas lange gedauert hat. Wählen Sie ein Zeitadverb mit **-lang** für Ihre Antwort.

BEISPIEL: A: Haben Sie lange im Zug zwischen Paris und Berlin gesessen?
            B: Ja, *stundenlang.*

Hat das elegante Abendessen lange gedauert?
Haben Sie lange auf den Bus warten müssen?
War's letzten Sommer sehr heiß?
War der Chef lange am Telefon?
Sind Sie manchmal schlechter Laune?
Waren die alten Römer lange Zeit in Nordeuropa?

Leicht zu merken

analysieren	analy<u>s</u>ieren
die **Dynastie, -n**	Dyna<u>s</u>tie
der **Humor**	Hu<u>mor</u>
die **Ironie**	Iro<u>n</u>ie
der **Kontakt**	Kon<u>takt</u>
kreativ	krea<u>tiv</u>
literarisch	lite<u>rar</u>isch
die **Melancholie**	Mela<u>ncholie</u>
der **Patient, -en, -en**	Pa<u>tient</u>
philosophieren	philoso<u>ph</u>ieren
produktiv	produk<u>tiv</u>
die **Psychoanalyse**	Psychoana<u>ly</u>se

Einstieg in den Text

The two Austrians in the following reading selection use subjunctive mood
mainly for conjectural and hypothetical statements. Below is one example
of each type. After reading through the text once, write down other examples of subjunctive mood used for these purposes; be sure you understand
them and can give English equivalents.

hypothetical statements

Ich . . . könnte . . . bei meinen Eltern wohnen und an der
    Musikhochschule in Wien studieren.

conjecture

. . . ohne Johann Strauß würde die Welt wahrscheinlich keine Walzer
    tanzen.

Die Wiener Oper.

Verben

erwarten to expect
sich konzentrieren auf (+ *acc.*) to concentrate on
statt·finden, fand statt, hat stattgefunden to take place
tanzen to dance
träumen to dream

Substantive

der **Künstler, -** artist (*m.*)
der **Spiegel, -** mirror
der **Witz, -e** joke; wit
das **Klavier, -e** piano
die **Gegenwart** present (time)
die **Gelegenheit, -en** opportunity, chance
die **Hochschule, -n** university; institution of higher learning

die **Künstlerin, -nen** artist (*f.*)

Hochschule corresponds roughly to college, not high school (generically called **die Oberschule**). **Musikhochschule** = *conservatory*; **Technische Hochschule** = *engineering college.*

Adjektive und Adverbien

außerdem (*adv.*) besides, in addition
begeistert von enthusiastic about, ecstatic about
ernst serious
 etwas ernst nehmen to take something seriously
gemütlich cozy, comfortable; quiet, relaxed
witzig witty, amusing
zunächst first (of all), to begin with

Andere Vokabel

beide (*pl. pronoun*) both (people)

Nützlicher Ausdruck

eine Zeitlang for a time, for a while

Gegensätze

ernst ≠ heiter serious ≠ cheerful
gemütlich ≠ ungemütlich cozy ≠ unpleasant, not cozy

Zwei Österreicher stellen sich vor

Marie-Therese Werdenberg, Musikstudentin in Salzburg

„Ich heiße Marie-Therese Werdenberg und bin Musikstudentin. Ich komme aus Wien und könnte freilich° dort bei meinen Eltern wohnen und an der Musikhochschule in Wien studieren. Aber ich studiere lieber in Salzburg, weil ich mich hier besser auf das Klavierspielen
5 konzentrieren kann. In Wien gäbe es zwar mehr Konzerte, in die man gehen könnte, aber hier ist es ruhiger und gemütlicher. Außerdem finden hier im Sommer die berühmten Festspiele² statt, und da habe ich die Gelegenheit, mit vielen Musikern° in Kontakt zu kommen.
  Ja, was wäre Österreich ohne seine Musiktradition? Und umge-
10 kehrt.° Was wäre die Musikgeschichte ohne Österreich? Salzburg ist

Lab Manual Kap. 14, Lesestück.

= **natürlich**

Learning about Austria is the cultural goal of this chapter.

= **Menschen, die Musik spielen**

vice versa

---

²The **Salzburger Festspiele** are an annual summer festival of drama and classical music.

Oskar Kokoschka (1886–1980), Selbstbildnis (self-portrait, 1917).

Mozarts Geburtsort.° Auch Haydn, Schubert, Bruckner, Mahler und Schönberg sind alle in Österreich geboren. Beethoven und Brahms — beide deutsche Komponisten° — haben in Wien ihre wichtigsten Werke geschrieben. Und ohne Johann Strauß würde die Welt wahr-
15 scheinlich keine Walzer° tanzen.

    Aber ich sollte nicht nur über Musik reden, bloß° weil das meine Leidenschaft° ist. Die Kulturgeschichte Österreichs hat der Welt eine ganze Menge gegeben. In Wien um 1900 gab es z.B. ein besonders produktives und faszinierendes° Kulturleben. Die literarischen Werke von
20 Hugo von Hofmannsthal und Arthur Schnitzler sind ein Spiegel dieser sehr kreativen Zeit. In der Malerei° arbeiteten Künstler wie Gustav Klimt und Oskar Kokoschka. Um diese Zeit gründete° Sigmund Freud die Psychoanalyse. Ich könnte noch viele Namen nennen, aber dann müßten wir fast den ganzen Tag hier sitzen.“

25 Dr. Ulrich Kraus, Psychologe° aus Wien

„Mein Name ist Kraus, und ich bin Psychologe. Mit meinen Patienten und ihren Problemen habe ich mehr als genug zu tun; erwarten Sie also nicht von mir, daß ich den Durchschnittsösterreicher° analysiere. Ich könnte aber mindestens° versuchen, diesen Menschen — den
30 homo austriacus — ein bißchen zu beschreiben.

    Zunächst etwas Geschichte: Ich möchte Sie daran erinnern, daß wir Österreicher auf eine sehr alte und große Tradition stolz sind. Die Habsburger Dynastie regierte° jahrhundertelang über Deutsche, Ungarn, Tschechen, Polen, Italiener, Serben und eine Zeitlang sogar über
35 Mexikaner.[3] Was man vom englischen Weltreich sagt, könnte man auch von Österreich sagen: Die Sonne ging nicht unter° über diesem Reich.

	= Ort, wo man geboren ist
	= Menschen, die Musik komponieren
	waltzes
	= nur
	passion
	= sehr sehr interessantes
	painting
	founded
	psychologist
	average Austrian
	= wenigstens
	ruled
	ging . . . unter = set

---

[3]The Habsburgs ruled the Holy Roman Empire from 1278 to 1806, and Austria (later Austria-Hungary) from 1815 to 1918. The empire came to include Germans, Hungarians, Czechs, Poles, Italians, and Serbs. In 1864 Archduke Maximilian, brother of the Austrian Emperor, was made Emperor of Mexico. He was executed in 1867 by republican troops.

Blick auf Salzburg.

Heute spielt unser kleines Land eine viel bescheidenere° politische Rolle. Und dieser Kontrast zwischen Vergangenheit und Gegen-
40 wart hat zu unserem Humor und unserer Selbstironie beigetragen.°
Manchmal habe ich das Gefühl, wir Österreicher sind unglücklich
über unsere verlorene Größe, aber wir sind wenigstens glücklich, daß
wir unglücklich sind. Verstehen Sie diese witzige Melancholie, die sich
selbst nicht ganz ernst nimmt?
45 Viele Österreicher würden den Unterschied zwischen sich und
den Deutschen so ausdrücken: Die Deutschen sind fleißig, aber die
Österreicher gemütlich. Die Wiener Kaffeehäuser könnten nicht existieren, wenn der Österreicher nicht gern stundenlang vor seinem
Mokka[4] säße und träumte. Er philosophiert gern darüber, wie die Welt
50 sein könnte. Darum nennt man Österreich manchmal das Land des
Konjunktivs: ‚Alles würde hier besser gehen, wenn wir nur . . .‘ oder
‚Das wäre möglich, wenn . . .‘ "

more modest

contributed

Im Wiener Kaffeehaus.

---

[4]A strong aromatic coffee served in demitasse cups, named after a city in Yemen. The
drink was introduced into Vienna during the Turkish siege of the city in 1683. Viennese
cafés serve dozens of different types of coffee, each with its own name.

Fragen zum Lesestück

1. Woher kommt die Musikstudentin im ersten Teil des Textes, und was macht sie in Salzburg?
2. Warum studiert sie lieber dort als in Wien?
3. Was könnte sie öfter in Wien machen, wenn sie dort wohnte?
4. Nennen Sie einen berühmten Menschen, der in Salzburg geboren ist.
5. Kennen Sie andere berühmte Namen aus der Musikgeschichte Österreichs?
6. Warum war Wien um 1900 besonders interessant? Wer hat damals dort gelebt und gearbeitet?
7. Was wissen Sie von der Geschichte Österreichs?
8. Beschreiben Sie den größten Unterschied für die Österreicher zwischen der Vergangenheit und der Gegenwart ihres Landes.
9. Welche Unterschiede findet Dr. Kraus zwischen den Deutschen und seinen Landsleuten in Österreich?
10. Warum nennt man Österreich manchmal das Land des Konjunktivs?

Situationen aus dem Alltag

Im Hotel

Auf Seite 425 sehen Sie die Rezeption in einem Hotel. Hier ist eine Liste von Vokabeln, die Ihnen zum größten Teil (*for the most part*) schon bekannt sind.

Die Hotelgäste

sich an·melden	*to register*
das **Gepäck**	
der **Koffer, -**	
der **Reisepaß, -pässe**	
ein Zimmer reservieren	
ein Taxi bestellen	

An der Rezeption

der/die **Angestellte**	
die **Kasse**	
der **Zimmerschlüssel, -**	
der **Stadtplan, ¨e**	
der **Stadtführer, -**	*city guidebook*
der **Speisesaal**	*dining room*
der **Lift**	*elevator*

Im Hotelzimmer

das **Bad**	
die **Dusche**	
das **Telefon (telefonieren)**	
sich um·ziehen	*to change clothes*

Gruppenarbeit

Beschreiben Sie dieses Bild. Wer steht wo? Wer tut was?

Rollenspiele (Gruppen von 3 Personen)

Spielen Sie diese Situationen zusammen. Improvisieren Sie frei.

1. *An der Rezeption*
   Zwei Touristen kommen gerade vom Flughafen im Hotel an. Sie haben
   ein Zimmer schon reserviert. Sie melden sich an der Rezeption an und
   stellen Fragen über das Zimmer.

2. *Eine Stunde später*
   Die Touristen haben sich jetzt geduscht und umgezogen. Jetzt wollen
   sie ausgehen und sich die Stadt ansehen. An der Rezeption bitten sie um
   Auskunft. Der Angestellte gibt Ihnen viel Information über die Stadt,
   z.B. über das kulturelle Leben, Verkehrsmittel, Restaurants usw. Bei
   ihm bekommen sie auch Stadtführer, Stadtpläne und Broschüren
   (*brochures*). Sie müssen auch Geld wechseln.

Sprechen wir miteinander

A Partnerarbeit: Was würdest du tun?

Unten sind einige Situationen. Besprechen Sie miteinander, was Sie in diesen Situationen tun würden.

> BEISPIEL: krank sein
> Was würdest du tun, wenn du krank wärest?
> Ich würde zunächst ins Bett gehen. Dann . . .

reich sein   viel Zeit haben
in Europa sein   jetzt Ferien haben
kein Student sein   Hunger haben
wenig Geld haben   Politiker sein

B Gruppenarbeit: Studentenreise nach Österreich (4–5 Personen)

Sie reisen nächstes Jahr mit einer Studentengruppe nach Österreich. Sie müssen sich jetzt darauf vorbereiten.

1. Was sollte man mitbringen?
2. Was für Bücher könnte man über Österreich lesen?
3. Was sollte man dort sehen? (Die Fotos in diesem Kapitel geben Ihnen vielleicht einige Ideen.)
4. Was würden Sie am liebsten in Österreich machen?

C Partnerarbeit: Rollenspiele

Spielen Sie diese Situation zusammen. Seien Sie höflich, und benutzen Sie den Konjunktiv! Seien Sie bereit, Ihren Dialog vor der Klasse zu spielen.

Kellner und Gast im Lokal

Der Kellner fragt den Gast, was er (*oder*) sie bestellen möchte. Der Gast fragt, ob man verschiedene Gerichte (*dishes*) hat und bestellt dann ein großes Essen. (You can use some food vocabulary from **Kapitel 8**, p. 243).

> KELLNER/IN: Bitte sehr? Was hätten Sie gern?
>
> GAST: Hätten Sie vielleicht . . . ? Könnten Sie mir sagen . . . ?
> Ich hätte gern . . .

D Gruppendiskussion: Wie könnten wir das ändern?

An Ihrer Uni gibt es sicher Sachen, die Sie gern ändern würden. Machen Sie eine Liste von diesen Sachen. Dann diskutieren Sie, wie man sie ändern oder anders machen könnte.

> BEISPIEL: Die Bibliothek schließt zu früh. Das müßte man ändern. Sie sollte länger offen bleiben, besonders am Semesterende. Ja, das wäre viel besser. Dann hätte man mehr Zeit zu lernen. Aber natürlich würde das mehr kosten. Wer würde das bezahlen?

Prepare by reviewing
"Specifying time" on Workbook
pp. 136–138.

E **Übung: Eine witzige Anekdote aus Österreich**

Provide the missing time word or phrase (in parentheses) in the following anecdote.

_____ (*Many years ago*), _____ (*when*) noch relativ wenige Touristen nach Österreich kamen, erzählte man eine Anekdote über eine reiche Amerikanerin, die _____ (*one month*) in den Österreichischen Alpen verbrachte. Sie wohnte in einem gemütlichen Hotel in einem kleinen Dorf, wo die Menschen sie sehr interessant fanden. _____ (*Each morning*), _____ (*when*) sie Frühstück aß, bestellte sie nur wenig zu essen: ein weich gekochtes Ei [*soft-boiled egg*] und eine Tasse Kaffee. _____ (*Whenever*) das Wetter gut war, verbrachte sie _____ (*the whole day*) draußen, und aß Brot und Käse aus ihrem Rucksack, _____ (*when*) sie Hunger hatte. _____ (*When*) die Dame endlich wieder nach Hause mußte, sagte sie dem Wirt [*innkeeper*] _____ (*on Sunday*), sie würde _____ (*day after tomorrow*) abfahren. _____ (*On Tuesday*) bestellte sie nach dem Frühstück die Rechnung [*bill*]. Zunächst las sie die Rechnung und sagte _____ (*for a while*) nichts. Darauf stand „für 28 Eier: 300 Schilling". Es stimmte, sie hatte _____ (*for weeks*) _____ (*every morning*) ein weiches Ei gegessen, aber sie konnte sich nicht erinnern, _____ (*when*) sie je in ihrem Leben so teure Eier gegessen hatte. Sie ließ sofort den Wirt kommen und bat ihn um eine Erklärung. „ _____ (*When*) ich _____ (*every morning*) mein Ei bestellte," sagte sie, „wußte ich nicht, daß sie bei Ihnen so selten [*rare*] sind." Der Wirt antwortete: „Ja, wissen Sie, gnädige Frau [*Madame*], die Eier sind bei uns *nicht* so selten, aber *Amerikanerinnen* sehr." Sie lachte, bezahlte die Rechnung und sagte, sie würde _____ (*next year*) wiederkommen. „Hoffentlich sind _____ (*then*) Amerikanerinnen _____ (*no longer*) so selten und die Eier weniger teuer!"

Schreiben Sie zu Hause

F Schreiben Sie diese Sätze zu Ende.

1. Wenn ich Künstler/in wäre . . .
2. Ich würde dich ernst nehmen, wenn . . .
3. Wenn ich die Gelegenheit hätte, dann . . .
4. Die Party könnte heute abend stattfinden, wenn . . .
5. Wenn du mit mir tanzen wolltest, . . .
6. Wir würden in diesem Hotel übernachten, wenn . . .
7. Wenn wir knapp bei Kasse wären, . . .
8. Wenn ich morgen nichts Besonderes vorhätte, dann . . .

G Machen Sie ganze Sätze mit diesen Vokabeln. Vergessen Sie die Endungen nicht. (// = Komma)

1. wenn / ich / nur / können / Klavier / spielen! (*wish contrary to fact*)
2. wir / würd- / gemütlich / sitzen / zusammen // wenn / wir / haben / mehr Zeit (*condition contrary to fact*)

3. wenn / ich / haben / Zimmer / im / erst- / Stock // Straßenbahn / würd- / mich / stören (*condition contrary to fact*)
4. wenn / wir / können / nicht / wechseln / Geld // wir / können / immer / zahlen / mit / Reisescheck (*conditional sentence in the indicative*)
5. ich / wissen / gern // wie / kommen / man / zum Museum (*first clause: polite subjunctive*)
6. ich / wünschen // ich / sein / bei / mein- / Freunde / auf / Land (*wish contrary to fact*)

H Wenn ich ein Vöglein wär'   You have learned that the subjunctive is used to express wishes contrary to fact. As you might expect, this use of subjunctive occurs frequently in poems about love and longing. A well-known German folk song begins like this:

Wenn ich ein Vöglein wär'
Und auch zwei Flüglein° hätt'   little wings
Flög' ich zu dir.
Weil's aber nicht kann sein,
Bleib' ich allhier.°   = hier

Try creating a short poem of your own (either rhymed or not) in which you express such an unfulfillable wish.

Wenn ich . . .
. . .
Dann . . .

I Aufsatzthema: Wenn ich die Welt regieren könnte   Stellen Sie sich vor, Sie könnten eine Woche lang die Welt regieren. Was würden Sie für die Völker der Erde tun? Was würden Sie ändern? Schreiben Sie eine Seite darüber.

J Wie sagt man das auf deutsch?

1. Would you like to go dancing with us tomorrow night?
2. That would be great, but unfortunately I've broken my leg.
3. That's a shame! You could come along anyway.
4. Your old friend Rainer will be there.

5. Max has been in Leipzig for weeks.
6. It would be nice to write him a postcard.
7. If only I knew where he is living now.
8. He's either in the Hotel Europa or somewhere in a youth hostel.

9. Can't you concentrate on your paper?
10. No, Marie always disturbs me with her loud music.
11. If you didn't have a piano in your room, you wouldn't have a problem.
12. That's right, but then I would have to look for a new roommate.

7 Fährst du mit in die Schweiz? (27:32)

Fährst du mit in die Schweiz?

Katrin will in den Semesterferien in die Schweiz. Dort möchte sie ihre Tante in Zürich besuchen und auch ein bißchen in den Bergen wandern. Weil sie das Alpenland noch nicht gut kennt, geht sie zum Reisebüro. Die Angestellte im Reisebüro gibt ihr Auskunft darüber. Später ruft sie Su-Sin an, um sie zu fragen, ob sie Lust hätte, mitzukommen. Su-Sin muß sich diesen Plan überlegen, aber ruft dann bei Bachmanns an, um zu sagen, daß sie gerne mitkommen würde.

Wortschatz zum Video

das **Reisebüro, -s**	*travel agency*
zunächst . . . danach	*first . . . after that*
die **Ermäßigung**	*discount*
buchen	*to book (a flight, hotel, etc.)*
preiswert	**= billig**
die **Geduld**	*patience*
das **Bargeld**	*cash*

Österreich

429

Verkehrsmittel *(Means of transportation)*

Sehen Sie sich den Anfang des Abschnitts *(section)* (27:40–28:27) an. Welche öffentlichen *(public)* und privaten Verkehrsmittel sehen Sie? Kreuzen Sie sie an.

——— 1. Flugzeug
——— 2. Fahrräder
——— 3. Taxis
——— 4. die U-Bahn
——— 5. Autos
——— 6. Bus
——— 7. Straßenbahn
——— 8. Mopeds

B **Wörter im Kontext: Was könnte das bedeuten?**

Jetzt sehen Sie sich die ganze Episode (28:27–31:34) Sie sehen oder hören die folgenden *(following)* Wörter. Wählen Sie das beste englische Äquivalent im Kontext.

1. Bahnsteig
   a. train information   b. railroad crossing   c. station platform
2. Reiseladen
   a. travel agency   b. souvenir shop   c. luggage shop
3. das Berner Oberland
   a. express train to Bern   b. mountainous region in Switzerland
   c. a dog used for mountain rescue
4. Flugkarten
   a. flight itineraries   b. postcards of airplanes   c. airline tickets

C **Wer macht das? Wer sagt das?**

Choose the person who does or says the following.

   a. Katrin   b. die Angestellte im Reisebüro
   c. ein Kunde im Reisebüro

1. ——— „Darf ich um Auskunft bitten?"
2. ——— „Da braucht man dann einen internationalen
          Jugendherbergsführer."
3. ——— unterbricht das Gespräch.
4. ——— findet einen Zettel *(note)* an der Tür.
5. ——— „Wie war Ihr Name bitte?"
6. ——— „Toll!"

D **Wie geht's weiter?**

Wählen Sie die beste Möglichkeit, den Satz zu ergänzen *(complete)*.

1. Katrins Tante lebt . . .
   a. im Berner Oberland.   b. in Leipzig.   c. in Zürich.
2. Katrin hat es vor, . . .
   a. allein zu reisen.   b. ihre Ferien mit einer Freundin zu verbringen.
   c. mit ihrer Tante zu wandern.

3. Die Angestellte sagt Katrin, sie kann Geld sparen, wenn sie . . .
   a. in Jugendherbergen übernachtet.   b. per Autostop reist.
   c. nur Reiseschecks benutzt.
4. Der Kunde im Hintergrund . . .
   a. spricht nur Französisch.   b. scheint in Eile zu sein.
   c. will auch in die Schweiz.
5. Als Katrin auf dem Zettel liest, daß Su-Sin mitkommt, . . .
   a. freut sie sich sehr.   b. will sie sofort mit ihr telefonieren.
   c. ärgert sie sich.

E **Im Gespräch**

For each sentence in the left column, find the appropriate response in the right column.

_____ 1. Haben Sie vielleicht was zu schreiben?

_____ 2. Entschuldigung, darf ich bitte unterbrechen?

_____ 3. Dieser Prospekt informiert Sie über Sonderfahrkarten.

_____ 4. Was empfehlen Sie, soll ich mir Reiseschecks kaufen?

_____ 5. Ich fürchte, ich kann's mir nicht leisten.

a. Den nehme ich mit.
b. Ach, überleg's dir doch! Es ist bestimmt nicht teuer.
c. Da haben Sie Papier und einen Kugelschreiber.
d. Ja, das ist wohl sicherer als Bargeld.
e. Kleinen Moment Geduld bitte!

Das Hundertwasserhaus, Wien.

Österreich

Almanach

Profile of Austria

Area:	83,855 square kilometers; 32,376 square miles (slightly smaller than the state of Maine)
Population:	7,950,000; density 95 people per square kilometer (246 people per square mile)
Currency:	Schilling; 1 öS = 100 Groschen
Major Cities:	Vienna (**Wien**, capital, pop. 1,550,000), Graz, Linz, Salzburg, Innsbruck
Religion:	85% Roman Catholic, 6% Protestant, 9% other

Austria consists of nine states (**Bundesländer**). It became a member of the European Union in 1995. In addition to basic industries such as machinery, iron and steel, and textiles and chemicals, tourism provides an important source of income. The literacy rate is 98%.

Austria plays a vital role in the United Nations, and Vienna is an important point of contact between eastern and western Europe. With the opening of the "UNO City" in 1979, Vienna became the third seat of the United Nations. It is also the headquarters for OPEC (the Organization of Petroleum Exporting Countries).

Straßenkonzert vor dem Stefansdom, Wien.

Endlich ist der Frühling da. (Innsbruck mit Blick auf die Nordkette)

Burgenland · Kärnten · Niederösterreich · Oberösterreich · Salzburg · Steiermark · Tirol · Vorarlberg · Wien

Ausländer in Deutschland

Communicative Goals

- Using the post office
- Talking about what could or might have happened in the past
- Talking about houses and apartments

Cultural Goal

- Learning about the situation of foreigners in Germany

Wo liegt die Heimat?

Lab Manual Kap. 15, Dialoge, Fragen, Hören Sie gut zu!

Demetra, Schülerin aus einer Gastarbeiterfamilie, wird für die Schüler-zeitung interviewt.

Ich bin doch hier geboren: See p. 281 for flavoring particle **doch.**

INTERVIEWER: Es überrascht mich, daß du als Ausländerin so perfekt Deutsch kannst.

DEMETRA: Kein Wunder, ich bin doch hier geboren. Viele halten mich sogar für eine Deutsche.

INTERVIEWER: Aber ihr kommt doch aus Griechenland, nicht? Wo fühlst du dich eigentlich zu Hause?

DEMETRA: Das frag' ich mich auch. Hier kenne ich mich besser aus, aber mir ist klar, daß ich nicht von allen Deutschen akzeptiert werde.

Die verpaßte Geburtstagsfeier

verpaßte: Notice the adjectival use of past participle.

LILLI: Bist du nicht zu Sonjas Geburtstagsfeier eingeladen worden?

FELIX: Doch, und ich wünschte, ich wäre dabei gewesen. Aber ich war auf Urlaub in Spanien.

LILLI: Du hättest wenigstens anrufen können, um ihr zu gratulieren.

FELIX: Da hast du recht. Das hätte ich machen sollen.

Vor der Post   Using the post office is a communicative goal.

Vor der Hauptpost sehen Herr und Frau Becker einen Briefkasten.

FRAU BECKER: Da kannst du deinen Brief einwerfen.

drauf (*colloq.*) = **darauf.**

HERR BECKER: Augenblick. Hab' ich genug Briefmarken drauf? Vielleicht sollte ich hineingehen und ihn wiegen lassen.

FRAU BECKER: Zeig mal her . . . Aber Hartmanns sind doch umgezogen. Das ist ihre alte Adresse.

HERR BECKER: Verflixt nochmal! Das hätte ich nicht vergessen sollen.

FRAU BECKER: Ach, reg dich nicht auf! Wir kaufen schnell einen neuen Umschlag.

Hans Becker
Kieler Straße 314
22083 Hamburg

Frau
Annemarie Hartmann
Vogelsangstraße 17
60327 Frankfurt

Where Is Home?

Demetra, a student from a family of foreign workers, is being interviewed for the school newspaper.

I.: I'm surprised that you, as a foreigner, speak such perfect German.

D.: No wonder. After all, I was born here. Many people even think I'm a German.

I.: But your family comes from Greece, don't they? Where do you actually feel at home?

D.: I ask myself that too. I know my way around here better, but it's clear to me that I'm not accepted by all Germans.

The Missed Birthday Party

L.: Weren't you invited to Sonja's birthday party?

F.: Yes I was, and I wish I had been there. But I was on vacation in Spain.

L.: At least you could have phoned to congratulate her.

F.: You're right. I should have done that.

In Front of the Post Office

Mr. and Mrs. Becker see a mailbox in front of the main post office.

MRS.B: You can mail your letter there.

MR.B: Just a second. Do I have enough stamps on it? Maybe I should go in and have it weighed.

MRS.B: Let me see . . . But the Hartmanns have moved. That's their old address.

MR.B: Darn it all! I shouldn't have forgotten that.

MRS.B: Oh, don't get upset! We'll just buy a new envelope.

Wortschatz 1

Verben

akzeptieren to accept

sich auf·regen (über + *acc.*) to get upset (about), get excited (about)

dabei sein to be present, attend

ein·werfen to mail (a letter) (*literally*: to throw in)

sich fragen to wonder, ask oneself
  Ich frage mich, ob . . . I wonder if . . .

gratulieren (+ *dat.*) to congratulate
  Ich gratuliere dir zum Geburtstag! Happy birthday!

halten für to take for, regard as, think X is
  Ich halte es für möglich. I think it's possible.

überraschen to surprise

wiegen, wog, hat gewogen to weigh (*trans. and intrans.*)

Substantive

der **Ausländer, -** foreigner (*m.*)

der **Briefkasten, ⸚** mailbox

der **Gastarbeiter, -** foreign worker, guest worker (*m.*)

der **Umschlag, ⸚e** envelope

(das) **Griechenland** Greece

(das) **Spanien** Spain

die **Adresse, -n** address

die **Ausländerin, -nen** foreigner (*f.*)

die **Briefmarke, -n** stamp

die **Feier, -n** celebration, party

  die **Geburtstagsfeier** birthday party

  die **Gastarbeiterin, -nen** foreign worker, guest worker (*f.*)

die **Post** post office; postal service; mail

Adjektiv oder Adverb

perfekt perfect(ly)

Andere Vokabeln

hinein- (*prefix*) in, into (see pp. 448–450)

Nützliche Ausdrücke

Kein Wunder! No wonder!

Zeig mal her. Let's see. Show it to me.

Mit anderen Worten

Verflixt nochmal! (*colloq.*) = **So ein Mist!** (Das sagt man, wenn man sich über etwas sehr ärgert.)

Gastarbeiter: Official designation of foreign workers is **ausländische Arbeitnehmer.**

Spanien: adj. **spanisch.** Idiom: **Das kommt mir spanisch vor** (*It's Greek to me*). The expression recalls the elaborate customs introduced by Emperor Karl V to the Habsburg court from Spain in the 16th century.

Variationen

A Persönliche Fragen

1. Der Interviewer ist überrascht, daß Demetra so perfekt Deutsch spricht. Sind Sie auch manchmal überrascht? Was hat Sie zum Beispiel an dieser Uni überrascht, als Sie hier neu waren?
2. Die junge Griechin weiß nicht genau, wo sie sich eigentlich zu Hause fühlt. Wo fühlen Sie sich zu Hause: wo Sie jetzt wohnen, wo Ihre Eltern wohnen oder wo Sie geboren sind?
3. Felix hat Sonjas Geburtstagsfeier verpaßt. Haben Sie je etwas Wichtiges verpaßt? Erzählen Sie davon.
4. Schreiben Sie oft Briefe? An wen? Telefonieren Sie lieber, oder benutzen Sie E-mail?
5. Wo ist hier der nächste Briefkasten?
6. Gehen Sie oft zur Post? Wann gehen Sie zur Post? Was lassen Sie dort machen?

Üb. A, 4: If students ask, Man schickt oder bekommt *eine* E-mail.

Telefonieren = *to use the phone, talk on the phone* (intrans.): **Es ist billiger, abends zu telefonieren.** **Anrufen** = *to call up, telephone* (trans.): **Rufe mich morgen vor zehn an.**

B Gruppenarbeit: Reg dich nicht auf! *(Take it easy!)*

Manchmal regt man sich unnötig auf. In welchen Situationen regen Sie sich besonders auf? Wenn Sie etwas vergessen haben? Wenn Sie etwas Wichtiges vorhaben? Machen Sie zusammen eine Liste von solchen Situationen.

BEISPIEL: Ich rege mich auf, wenn ich ein Referat halten muß.

C Klassendiskussion: Geburtstagstraditionen

Was macht man in Ihrer Familie, wenn jemand Geburtstag hat? Gibt es bestimmte Familientraditionen? Feiern Sie zu Hause oder im Restaurant? Lädt man viele Gäste ein, oder ist es nur eine kleine Feier? Darf sich das Geburtstagskind (die Person, die Geburtstag hat) sein Lieblingsessen bestellen?

In diesen Gedichten beschreiben zwei Lyriker ihre Gefühle als Fremde in Deutschland. Obwohl diese Lyriker nicht in Deutschland geboren sind, leben sie jetzt dort und schreiben auf deutsch. Clara Tauchert-da Cruz ist in Portugal geboren und studierte Germanistik. Şadi Üçüncü ist in der Türkei geboren und kam 1974 zum Studium der politischen Wissenschaften nach Deutschland.

Über Grenzen

Draußen
ist es leicht
die Grenzen zu überschreiten.°   cross

Tief drinnen°   within
aber
sind die eigenen Grenzen
nicht zu überwinden.°   **sind . . . nicht zu uberwinden** = can't be conquered

Zu spät
kommt die Erkenntnis°   insight
— die Heimat ist schon
verloren
und keine neue gewonnen.°   gained

Clara Tauchert-da Cruz
(geboren 1938)

Integration

ich bin glücklich,
wenn du mir „Guten Tag" oder „Hallo" sagst;

ich bin froh,
wenn du mir freundlich
begegnest;°   **mir begegnest = mich grüßt**

ich freue mich,
wenn du mich fragst:
„Wie geht es dir";

ich finde es gut,
wenn du mit mir solidarisch°   supportive
und brüderlich° bist;   **brüderlich = wie ein Bruder**

es ist sehr nett
von dir,
wenn du mir hilfst;

es ist willkommen,
wenn du mich besuchst
ab und zu;°   now and then

dann fühle ich mich
in dieser fremden Gesellschaft,
in der Du und Ich
nebeneinander, miteinander
und
füreinander
leben,
nicht mehr
als Fremder, als Ausländer.

Şadi Üçüncü
(geboren 1945)

Grammatik

General Subjunctive: Past Tense

Talking about what could or might have happened in the past is a communicative goal.

Past subjunctive is used to talk about hypothetical or contrary-to-fact situations *in the past* (e.g., "*I would have waited* for you yesterday"). Now that you have learned how to use present-tense subjunctive, past subjunctive will prove quite easy. Its form is similar to the *perfect tense* of the indicative. The only difference is that the auxiliary verb is in the *present subjunctive* (a form of **hätten** or **wären** instead of **haben** or **sein**).

Past Subjunctive			
ich **hätte** gewartet	*I would have waited*	wir **hätten** gewartet	*we would have waited*
du **hättest** gewartet	*you would have waited*	ihr **hättet** gewartet	*you would have waited*
sie **hätte** gewartet	*she would have waited*	sie, Sie **hätten** gewartet	*they, you would have waited*
ich **wäre** gekommen	*I would have come*	wir **wären** gekommen	*we would have come*
du **wärest** gekommen	*you would have come*	ihr **wäret** gekommen	*you would have come*
er **wäre** gekommen	*he would have come*	sie, Sie **wären** gekommen	*they, you would have come*

Caution! Note that English uses the word *would* in both the present and past subjunctive, while German uses **würden** *only* in the present subjunctive, *not* in the past.

| **present** | Er **würde** mitkommen. | *He **would** come along.* |
| **past** | Er **wäre** mitgekommen. | *He **would have** come along.* |

Note also that the subjunctive mood has *only this one past tense*, unlike the indicative which has three past tenses (simple past, perfect, past perfect).

Lab Manual Kap. 15, Var. zur Üb. 1, 3, 4, 7.

Workbook Kap. 15, A–D.

1 Übung: Aber *ich* hätte das gemacht.

Ihre Professorin sagt Ihnen, was sie nicht gemacht hat. Sie sagen, daß *Sie* es gemacht hätten.

> BEISPIEL: Ich habe keinen Ausflug gemacht.
> Aber *ich* hätte einen Ausflug gemacht.

1. Ich habe nicht um Auskunft gebeten.
2. Ich habe Anna nicht geholfen.
3. Ich habe die Adresse nicht gewußt.
4. Ich bin nicht Ski gefahren.
5. Ich habe mir die Haare nicht gekämmt.
6. Ich bin nicht lange geblieben.
7. Ich habe den Plan nicht verstanden.
8. Ich bin nicht tanzen gegangen.
9. Ich habe mich nicht verspätet.
10. Ich habe die Briefe nicht eingeworfen.

2 Übung

Wie sagt man das auf deutsch?

1. I would have hated that.
2. Bernd wouldn't have waited.
3. We would have bought stamps.
4. I would have gotten up earlier.
5. That would have lasted a long time.
6. That would have cost too much.
7. You wouldn't have been happy.
8. I would have gotten used to it.
9. They would have stayed longer.
10. They would have shown us a double room.
11. She would have congratulated me.
12. We would have gladly flown to Greece.

3 Gruppenarbeit (Phantasiediskussion): Was hätten Sie gemacht?

Sagen Sie, was *Sie* gemacht hätten . . .

- wenn Sie letzten Sommer 20 000 Dollar im Lotto (*lottery*) gewonnen hätten.

- wenn Ihr Professor sich gestern das Bein gebrochen hätte.
- wenn Sie vor 100 Jahren gelebt hätten.

DEUTSCHE BUNDESPOST

Past Subjunctive of Modal Verbs

Review the double-infinitive construction in perfect indicative of modals, p. 205, and in perfect tense of **lassen**, pp. 362–363.

The past subjunctive of modal verbs is also similar to the perfect indicative tense. Because modal verbs always use **haben** as their auxiliary, their past subjunctive is formed with **hätten** plus the *double infinitive.*

Du **hättest** doch **anrufen können.**	*You could have called.*
Das **hätte** ich **machen sollen.**	*I should have done that.*

In English, the past subjunctive of modal verbs uses *would have, could have* or *should have.* Notice how simple and consistent German modals are compared to English.

Ich **hätte** kommen **dürfen.**	*I would have been allowed to come.*
Ich **hätte** kommen **können.**	*I could have come.*
Ich **hätte** kommen **müssen.**	*I would have had to come.*
Ich **hätte** kommen **sollen.**	*I should have come.*
Ich **hätte** kommen **wollen.**	*I would have wanted to come.*

Note: When the double-infinitive structure occurs in a *subordinate* clause, the inflected auxiliary (**hätte** in the sentences above) must come *before* the double infinitive.

Er sagte mir, daß ich mehr Geld **hätte** wechseln sollen ▬ .

Ich fragte, wie ich das **hätte** wissen sollen ▬ .

This is the *only* case in German where the inflected verb is not in final position in a subordinate clause.

4 Übung: Das hätten Sie machen sollen

Ihr Professor hat vergessen, viele wichtige Dinge zu machen. Sagen Sie ihm, er hätte sie machen sollen.

BEISPIEL: Ich habe vergessen, meinen Regenschirm mitzubringen.
Sie hätten ihn mitbringen sollen.

1. Ich habe vergessen, mein Bett zu machen.
2. Ich habe vergessen, meine Bücher mitzubringen.
3. Ich habe vergessen, meine Frau anzurufen.
4. Ich habe vergessen, eine Zeitung zu kaufen.
5. Ich habe vergessen, das Fenster zu schließen.
6. Ich habe vergessen, den Witz zu erzählen.

5 Übung

Wie sagt man das auf deutsch?

1. We could have flown.
2. We would have had to buy tickets.
3. Frank should have come along.
4. He wouldn't have wanted to come along.
5. He wouldn't have been allowed to come along.

6 Gruppenarbeit (Phantasiediskussion): Was hätten Sie machen müssen?

Was hätten Sie machen müssen . . .

- wenn Sie heute zu spät aufgestanden wären?
- wenn Sie Ihren Bus verpaßt hätten?
- wenn Ihr Wagen kaputt gewesen wäre?
- wenn Sie sich das Bein gebrochen hätten?

7 Gruppenarbeit: Ich wünschte, ich hätte das nicht gemacht.

Als Kinder haben wir alle viel gemacht, was wir lieber nicht gemacht hätten. Sagen Sie, was Sie lieber gemacht oder nicht gemacht hätten.

BEISPIELE: Ich wünschte, ich hätte meine ältere Schwester nicht so oft geärgert.
Ich wünschte, ich hätte mehr Klavier geübt.
Ich wünschte, ich wäre . . .

Passive Voice

Compare the following sentences:

Die meisten Studenten lesen diesen Roman.	*Most students read this novel.*
Dieser Roman wird von den meisten Studenten gelesen.	*This novel is read by most students.*

Both sentences say essentially the same thing, but the first is in the *active voice* while the second is in the *passive voice*. The passive voice is used to emphasize that something is being *acted upon* (the *novel* is being read) rather than to emphasize the agent performing that action (the *students* are reading it).

In active sentences, the grammatical subject is also the agent or performer of the action.

Die Studenten lesen.   *The students read.*

Since passive voice emphasizes the thing acted upon, most passive sentences do not express the agent at all. For passive sentences with an agent, see p. 447.

In passive sentences, the grammatical subject is the *object* of the action.

Der Roman wird gelesen.   *The novel is read.*

Every passive sentence can be thought of as the transformation of an active sentence *with a transitive verb and a direct object*. The direct object (*acc.*) of the active sentence becomes the *subject* (*nom.*) of the passive sentence.

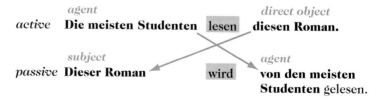

Formation of the German Passive Voice

The passive voice in English consists of the auxiliary verb *to be* plus a past participle.

active voice	→	*passive voice*		
			aux.	*part.*
They see him.	→	*He*	**is**	**seen.**
We never do that.	→	*That*	**is** *never* **done.**
They drank coffee.	→	*Coffee*	**was**	**drunk**.

The passive voice in German consists of the auxiliary verb **werden** plus a past participle.

Das wird nie gemacht.
Alternate translation: *That never gets done.* Gets conveys the passive voice in such sentences.

active voice	→	*passive voice*		
			aux.	*part.*
Sie sehen ihn.	→	Er	**wird**	**gesehen.**
Wir machen das nie.	→	Das	**wird** nie **gemacht.**
Man trank Kaffee.	→	Kaffee	**wurde**	**getrunken.**

Here is a table showing the formation of all tenses of **gesehen werden** (*to be seen*).

Passive Voice				
passive infinitive		**gesehen** werden	*to be*	*seen*
present	Er wird	**gesehen.**	*He is*	*seen.*
past	Er wurde	**gesehen.**	*He was*	*seen.*
future	Er wird	**gesehen** werden.	*He will be*	*seen.*
perfect	Er ist	**gesehen** worden.	*He has been*	*seen.*
			or:	
			He was	*seen.*
past perfect	Er war	**gesehen** worden.	*He had been*	*seen.*

Use Appendix 2, pp. 493–494, to review the past participles of strong transitive verbs.

Note:

- In both German and English passive, the past participle (**gesehen**/*seen*) appears in all tenses. The auxiliary verb (**werden**/*to be*) is conjugated.
- The normal past participle of **werden** (**geworden**) is contracted to **worden** in the perfect tenses of the passive voice.
- The German passive infinitive is in the reverse order of English.

You should be able to understand the two passive structures in this advertisement.

Ausländer in Deutschland

Lab Manual Kap. 15, Üb. 9, 12, and Var. zur Üb. 8, 10.

Workbook Kap. 15, E–G.

Üb. 8, 9, 10: Each of these sentences in active voice has a personal pronoun or **man** as subject. These pronoun subjects disappear in the passive voice. Do not try to express agent in these passive sentences.

8 Übung

Change the sentences from the active to the passive. Be careful to keep the same tense as in the active sentence.

present tense

1. Man liest diese Romane oft.
2. Morgens kaufen wir die Zeitung.
3. Bei uns sieht man nicht viele Deutsche.
4. Ich rufe meine Eltern jedes Wochenende an.
5. Man versteht mich nicht!
6. Wir feiern morgen deinen Geburtstag.
7. Wir räumen die Schlafzimmer jeden Samstag auf.
8. Ich schicke dieses Paket nach Australien.

simple past tense

9. Im 18. Jahrhundert schrieb man viele Briefe.
10. In der ganzen Welt las man seinen ersten Roman.
11. Man zeigte den Film in jedem Kino.
12. Man kaufte viele Bananen.

future tense

13. Was wird man sagen?
14. Man wird dieses Wahlplakat nicht sehen.
15. Man wird neue Wohnungen für die Armen bauen.
16. Man wird dieses Thema besprechen.

perfect tense

17. Man hat die alte Wohnung verkauft.
18. Man hat die Briefe eingeworfen.
19. Man hat den jungen Künstler eingeladen.
20. Man hat unsere Umwelt verschmutzt.

Welches Haus wurde früher gebaut? Fachwerk-(*half-timbered*) und modernes Einfamilienhaus.

9 Übung: Das wird sofort gemacht!

Sie sind Hotelangestellte/r. Ihre Professorin ist Gast im Hotel und bittet Sie, verschiedene Sachen für sie zu machen. Sie sagen, alles wird sofort gemacht.

BEISPIEL: Können Sie mir bitte diese Uhr reparieren?
Ja, sie wird sofort repariert!

1. Können Sie mir bitte einen Brief einwerfen?
2. Können Sie mir bitte einen Tisch reservieren?
3. Können Sie mir bitte die Schuhe putzen?
4. Können Sie mir bitte das Zimmer aufräumen?
5. Können Sie mir bitte meine Kleider aufhängen?
6. Können Sie mir bitte das Bett machen?
7. Können Sie mir bitte das Frühstück bringen?
8. Können Sie mir bitte ein Taxi bestellen?

Passive Voice with a Modal Verb

Often you need to say that something *must* be done, *should* be done, *can* be done, or *may* be done. In such cases, you must use the modal verb with the passive voice. Just keep in mind that the dependent infinitive is the two-word *passive infinitive* (e.g., **getan werden**) rather than the one-word active infinitive (**tun**).

active	Er mußte es **tun**.	*He had to do it.*
passive	Es mußte **getan werden**.	*It had to be done.*

Here is a table showing the formation of all tenses of a modal verb with the passive voice.

Passive with a Modal Verb		
present	Das muß **getan werden.**	*That has* **to be done.**
past	Das mußte **getan werden.**	*That had* **to be done.**
future	Das wird **getan werden** müssen.	*That will have* **to be done.**
perfect	Das hat **getan werden** müssen.	*That had* **to be done.**
past perfect	Das hatte **getan werden** müssen.	*That had had* **to be done.**

Note that it is the modal verb that gets inflected. The passive infinitive remains unchanged throughout all tenses.

10 Übung

Change the sentences from active to passive voice. Be sure to use the same tense as in the active sentence.

present

1. Wir müssen die Wohnung aufräumen.
2. Wir müssen noch den Wein kaufen.
3. Du darfst deine Freunde einladen.
4. Ich muß Oma nach Hause bringen.
5. Ich soll diese Briefe wiegen.

past

6. Man mußte die Fenster schließen.
7. Man mußte die Kinder abholen.
8. Man konnte das Mädchen nicht interviewen.
9. Man durfte nichts kochen.
10. Ich durfte diesen Witz nicht erzählen.

11 Gruppenarbeit: Was muß gemacht werden? (Mit offenen Büchern)

Sie diskutieren, was gemacht werden muß, um die Umwelt zu retten. Unten sind einige Möglichkeiten zum Kombinieren, aber Sie sollen auch Ihre eigenen Ideen benutzen.

BEISPIEL: Der Müll muß zum Recycling gebracht werden.

der Müll	schließen
das Altglas	finden
Alternativen	organisieren
Atomkraftwerke	zum Recycling bringen
Demonstrationen	ändern
unser Denken	bauen
umweltfreundliche Autos	sammeln

Passive Voice with an Agent

Most passive sentences make no mention of the agent performing the action.

Diese Häuser wurden sehr schnell gebaut.	*These houses were built very quickly.*
Das wird oft gesagt.	*That is often said.*

When an animate agent *is* expressed, **von** + *dative* is used.

Diese Häuser wurden **von türkischen Gastarbeitern** gebaut.	*These houses were built by Turkish foreign workers.*
Das wird **von vielen Menschen** gesagt.	*That is said by many people.*

12 Übung

Restate the following sentences in the passive. Use the same tense as in the active sentence.

> BEISPIEL: Meine Freundin liest jetzt den Roman.
> Der Roman wird jetzt von meiner Freundin gelesen.

1. Fast alle Physikstudenten belegen dieses Seminar.
2. Viele deutsche Schüler tragen gern Turnschuhe.
3. Unser Professor empfahl dieses Buch.
4. Alle Schüler in der Schweiz müssen Fremdsprachen lernen.
5. Michael hat mich eingeladen.
6. Die Gruppe hat das Referat besprochen.
7. Mein Freund hat die Gäste abgeholt.
8. Die Kinder singen immer dieses Lied.
9. Der Gepäckträger schleppte den Koffer zum Taxi.
10. Die ganze Familie feiert Omas Geburtstag.

13 Übung: Von wem?

Sagen Sie, von wem diese verschiedenen Dinge gemacht werden (oder gemacht wurden).

> BEISPIEL: Von wem werden Brötchen gebacken?
> Sie werden vom Bäcker gebacken.

1. Von wem wird das Essen im Restaurant gebracht?
2. Von wem werden Autos repariert?
3. Von wem werden Romane geschrieben?
4. Von wem wurde die Psychoanalyse gegründet?
5. Von wem wurde „Hamlet" geschrieben?
6. Von wem wurde Beethovens Neunte Symphonie komponiert?
7. Von wem wird eine Vorlesung an der Uni gehalten?
8. Von wem werden Zeitungsartikel geschrieben?

Die schwimmende Brücke
über den Bodensee

The Present Participle

To form the present participle (English: *sleeping*, *reading*, etc.) of a German verb, simply add **-d** to the infinitive.

schlafend	*sleeping*
feiernd	*celebrating*
denkend	*thinking*
lesend	*reading*

Remember that past participles can also be used as adjectives. See p. 333.

The present participle is used

- as an attributive adjective with the standard adjective endings:

Wir wollen das **schlafende** Kind nicht stören.	*We don't want to disturb the sleeping child.*
Lesen Sie die **folgenden** Seiten.	*Read the following pages.*

- occasionally as an adverb:

Sie sah mich **fragend** an.	*She looked at me questioningly.*

The German present participle is *not* used as a verbal noun. German uses the infinitive for this purpose: *No Parking* = **Parken verboten** (see p. 207)

Lab Manual Kap. 15, Üb. 14.

Workbook Kap. 15, H.

14 Übung

Add the present participle of the cued verb as an adjective to each sentence.

BEISPIEL: Wir können die Preise nicht mehr zahlen. (steigen)
Wir können die steigenden Preise nicht mehr zahlen.

1. Jeder Mensch weiß das. (denken)
2. Was meinen die Politiker? (führen)
3. Die Arbeitslosigkeit ist ein Problem. (wachsen)
4. Sie hörte die Kinder. (lachen)
5. Bitte stören Sie meinen Mitbewohner nicht. (schlafen)

Directional Prefixes: *hin-* and *her-*

German has two separable prefixes that combine with verbs of motion to show whether that motion is *toward the speaker* (**her-**) or *away from the speaker* (**hin-**). You are already familiar with these directional indicators from the question words **woher**? (*from where?*) and **wohin?** (*to where?*).

Können wir nicht **hin**fahren?	*Can't we go **there**?*
Komm doch mal **her**.	*Come **here** a minute.*
Wie komme ich (da)**hin**?	*How do I get **there**?*

Recall Herr Becker's line in the third dialogue, p. 435: **Vielleicht sollte ich hineingehen . . .**

These directional indicators are often used in combination with other separable prefixes that indicate direction. Two sets of these are **auf und unter** (*up and down*) and **ein und aus** (*in and out*). The two elements combine to make one separable prefix that can be attached to any verb of motion.

hinausgehen

herauskommen

hereinkommen

hineingehen

heraufsteigen

hinuntergehen

Notice that the preposition **in** becomes the prefix **ein:** hineingehen = *to go in.*

The prefixes **hin-** and **her-** must be used when the sentence does not contain a directional phrase such as **in die Post** or **ins Haus**. It is *incorrect* to say „Gehen wir ein." Correct is: **Gehen wir hinein.**[1]

Da ist die Hauptpost. Gehen wir **hinein.**

There's the main post office. Let's go in.

Draußen scheint die Sonne. Gehen wir **hinaus.**

The sun is shining outside. Let's go out.

Note: When someone knocks at the door, Germans simply say

Herein! *Come in!*

Workbook Kap. 15, I.

In spoken German, both directional prefixes are often replaced by initial **'r: Raus mit dir! Gehen wir rein / rauf / runter.**

15 Gruppenarbeit: Gehen wir hinein!

Complete these sentences by filling in the missing words.

*You're standing **outside** the house.*

1. Gehen wir _____ . (in)
2. Karl, komm doch _____ ! (out)
3. Anna ist vor einer Minute _____ . (gone in)
4. Bald kommen die Kinder aus dem Haus _____ . (out)

*You're standing **inside** the house.*

5. Kommt Grete bald _____ ? (in)
6. Es ist so schön, ich möchte jetzt _____ . (go out)
7. Wir sollten alle _____ . (go out)
8. (*Es klingelt.*) _____ ! ("Come in!")

*You're standing **at the top** of the steps.*

9. Warum kommt ihr nicht _____ ? (up)
10. Jörg ist gerade _____ . (gone down)

*You're standing **at the bottom** of the steps.*

11. Susi, ich brauche Hilfe! Komm mal schnell _____ ! (down here)
12. Ich bin jetzt müde. Ich gehe _____ und lege mich aufs Bett. (up)

Alle Menschen sind Ausländer.

---

[1]Even when a prepositional phrase *is* used, the directional prefixes are sometimes added:

Er ist aus dem Haus **heraus**gekommen.

He came **out** of the house.

Sie ging in die Kirche **hinein.**

She went **into** the church.

16 Partnerarbeit: Wo kommt sie her? Wo geht er hin?

Beschreiben Sie, was diese Menschen machen.

Wer ist ein Türke?

Tips zum Lesen und Lernen

Tips zum Vokabelnlernen

German Equivalents for *to think* The English verb *to think* has several meanings, for which German has various verbs (rather than just one). You have already learned most of these verbs as separate vocabulary items.

- When *think = to have an opinion*, use **glauben, meinen,** or **finden.**

Ich **finde** das toll.	*I think that's great.*
Ich **meine**, das stimmt nicht.	*I think that's incorrect.*
Ich **glaube** schon.	*I think so.*
Ich **glaube** nicht.	*I don't think so.*

- When *think = to think of, keep in mind*, use **denken an.**

Er **dachte an** seine Jugend.	*He was thinking of his youth.*
Denken Sie **an** die anderen.	*Think of the others.*

- When *think = to think x is . . ., to take x for . . .*, use **halten für.**

Ich **hielt** sie **für** eine Deutsche.	*I thought she was a German.*
Ich **halte** das **für** zu schwer.	*I think that's too difficult.*

  Synonyms for **halten für:** Ich **finde** das zu schwer. Ich **meine**, das ist zu schwer.

- When *think = to think about, ponder*, use **sich etwas überlegen.**

Das muß ich mir **überlegen.**	*I have to think about that.*
Ich werde mir die Alternativen **überlegen.**	*I'll think about the alternatives.*

Übung: Wie sagt man das auf deutsch?

1. I often think of you.
2. I think she's a good doctor.
3. What do *you* think?
4. I have to think about the answer.
5. I think that's a great idea!
6. Do you think I'm crazy?
7. I don't think so.

Leicht zu merken

 Lab Manual Kap. 15, Üb. zur Betonung.

die **Anekdote, -n**	Anek<u>do</u>te
die **Arroganz**	Arro<u>ganz</u>
die **Klinik, -en**	
die **Nationalität, -en**	Nationali<u>tät</u>

Einstieg in den Text

Recognizing the Passive Voice in Context   The following text contains five passive constructions. You will recognize them by the fact that they all have some form of **werden** plus a past participle. Here is the first occurrence of passive voice (ll. 8–9):

> . . . der wegen seiner Nationalität nicht überall akzeptiert wird.

As you encounter the others, jot them down and make sure you understand them.

Leitfragen   Im folgenden Lesestück beschreibt der Autor — ein Türke, der in Deutschland lebt — was er eines Tages in einem Zugabteil erlebte (*experienced*). Die deutschen Mitreisenden halten ihn für einen Deutschen. Wenn dann ein „richtiger" Türke ins Abteil will, ist ihre Reaktion ganz anders. Die Sprache dieser Anekdote ist relativ einfach und direkt, aber auch witzig. Suchen Sie Antworten auf die folgenden Fragen, während Sie lesen:

1. Warum fühlt sich der Autor als Türke, obwohl er in Deutschland lebt und arbeitet?
2. Welche Klischees über die Türken und die Deutschen finden Sie in dieser Anekdote?
3. Was ist der Unterschied zwischen dem Erzähler und dem „richtigen" Türken? Zum Beispiel, wie sehen diese zwei Türken aus?

Wortschatz 2

Verben

an·schauen   to look at
diskutieren   to discuss
kontrollieren   to check, inspect

Anschauen and its synonym **ansehen** = *to look at*. Contrast **sich etwas ansehen** = *to take a (good) look at something.*

schreien, schrie, hat geschrieen   to shout, yell
teil·nehmen (nimmt teil), nahm teil, hat teilgenommen an (+ *dat.*)   to take part in

sich unterhalten (unterhält), unterhielt, hat sich unterhalten (mit)   to converse with, talk to

452   Kapitel 15

Substantive

der **Paß**, die **Pässe**   passport
der **Türke**, -n, -n   Turk (*m.*)
das **Abteil**, -e   railway
   compartment
das **Thema**, die **Themen**
   topic, subject, theme
(das) **Türkisch**   Turkish
   (language)
die **Fahrt**, -en   trip, ride
die **Türkei**   Turkey

die **Türkin**, -nen   Turk (*f.*)
die **Tüte**, -n   (paper, plastic)
   bag

Die Türkei takes article, like **die
Schweiz: Wir fahren in** *die* **Türkei.
Er kommt aus** *der* **Türkei.**

Adjektive

angenehm   pleasant
richtig   true; real
türkisch   Turkish

Andere Vokabeln

so ein (*demonstrative*)   such
   a

Gegensätze

angenehm ≠ **unangenehm**
   pleasant ≠ unpleasant
richtig ≠ **falsch**   correct ≠
   incorrect

Wer ist ein Türke?

Lab Manual Kap. 15,
Lesestück.

*Şinasi Dikmen ist 1945 in Ladik/Samsun in der Türkei geboren. Er
besuchte in der Heimat eine Berufsschule für Gesundheitswesen.° Er
arbeitete vier Jahre als Gesundheitsberater° in der Türkei. Dikmen
lebt seit 1972 in der BRD. Dort arbeitete er zunächst als Fach-*
5 *krankenpfleger° auf der chirurgischen° Intensivstation der Univer-
sitäts-Kliniken Ulm. Heute ist er freier Schriftsteller.°*

    *In der folgenden Anekdote schreibt Dikmen mit Humor über ein
ernstes soziales Thema. Als Ausländer, der wegen seiner Nationalität nicht überall akzeptiert wird, muß er sich fragen, was es denn*
10 *bedeutet, ein Türke in Deutschland zu sein.*

Wer ist ein Türke? Wie erkennt° man ihn, woher weiß man, ob jemand ein Türke ist? Diese Fragen beschäftigen° mich, seit ich in
Deutschland bin. (. . .) Viele glauben, ein Türke sei[2] der,° der einen
schwarzen Schnurrbart° und einen türkischen Paß hat. Es gibt in Eu-
15 ropa aber viele Türken, die keinen türkischen Paß haben, darunter
sogar etliche, denen gar der Schnurrbart fehlt.° Nichtsdestoweniger°
sind es[3] Türken, denn sie sprechen Türkisch. Viele von ihnen
sprechen aber auch Deutsch. Sind es[3] darum Deutsche? (. . .)

    Ich bin in der Türkei geboren, mit türkischer Erziehung° aufge-
20 wachsen. Meine Eltern sind Türken wie meine Geschwister und meine
Verwandten. Ich habe die türkische Schule besucht, als türkischer
Gastarbeiter bin ich nach Deutschland gekommen, als Türke habe ich
mich beim Ausländeramt gemeldet.° Meine Krankenversicherung,°
meine Rente° und meine Autoversicherung° laufen unter der Nationali-
25 tät „Türke", und ich spreche mit meinen Kindern, soweit° es möglich

health professions
health consultant

nurse-specialist / surgical

freier... = free-lance writer

Dikmen berichtet in heiterem Ton von
Vorurteilen gegen Ausländer. Der
Almanach (S. 461) behandelt (*treats*)
die ernste Seite dieses Themas.

recognize
concern
sei der = ist jeder Mann
mustache

darunter... = among them even
   many who have no mustache
nichtsdestoweniger = trotzdem

upbringing

habe... = registered with the
   Resident Alien Office / health
   insurance
pension / car insurance
as far as

---

[2]**sei** (line 13): special subjunctive form of **sein** used to report speech and thoughts
indirectly (= *is* or *was*).

[3]**sind es Türken . . . Sind es Deutsche?** The singular pronoun **es** used with plural
sind is parallel to the phrase **das sind** (*those are*) and refers to people collectively.

Ausländer in Deutschland

ist, zu Hause Türkisch, ich liebe türkisch,° ich hasse türkisch, ich esse türkisch (. . .), und ich glaubte fest daran, daß° ich ein Türke sei° — bis mir dieser Vorfall° passierte.

    Vor zwei Jahren nahm ich an einer Lesung° in Hameln teil und
30 stieg in Hannover in den Zug Richtung° Ulm.[4] Es war eine gute Lesung in Hameln. Das Publikum° war nett, wir unterhielten uns angenehm, diskutierten über die Situation der Türken und über die Deutschen, über Gott und die Welt.° Nach der Lesung gingen wir in ein griechisches Lokal, wo wir fast türkisch aßen. Am nächsten Tag wurde ich
35 von einer Dame bis zum Bahnhof in Hannover gefahren. Ich betrat° ein Abteil, in dem nur ein älteres Ehepaar saß. Ich fragte sie höflich, ob ein Platz frei sei,° und sie antworteten höflich, ja, bitte; ich setzte mich hin, schlug „Die Zeit"[5] auf° und tat, was in Deutschland bei einer solchen° Fahrt verlangt° wird, nämlich° schweigen, schweigen,
40 schweigen, nie etwas fragen, solange° du selbst nicht gefragt wirst. (. . .)

    Ich (. . .) las weiter „Die Zeit", stellte niemandem Fragen, wurde auch nichts gefragt. (. . .) In Fulda[6] stieg ein richtiger Türke zu,° fragte das Ehepaar kurz und knapp:° „Frei?" Bevor er ausgesprochen
45 hatte schrie die Dame schon: „Nein, nichts frei!" Der Türke, klein, gedrungen,° mit handgestrickter Weste,° grün, ich würde sagen, Türkengrün,[7] in beiden Händen Plastiktüten, ging nach dieser barschen° Antwort weiter.

---

[4]**Hameln, Hannover:** Städte in Niedersachsen. Dikmen wohnt in **Ulm.**

[5]**Die Zeit:** weekly newspaper with educated readership.

[6]**Fulda:** Stadt im Bundesland Hessen.

[7]**Türkengrün:** Wortspiel auf **Türkisgrün** (*turquoise*). Dieser Stein wurde zuerst in der Türkei gefunden.

türkisch (*adv.*) = als Türke
glaubte... = firmly believed that
/ = war
incident
reading
in the direction of
Publikum = Menschen, die zur Lesung gekommen waren
über Gott und die Welt = über alles

= **ging in . . . hinein**

= war

schlug . . . auf = machte . . . auf
einer solchen = such a / required
/ namely
as long as

stieg . . . zu = stieg auch ein
kurz und knapp = ohne viele Worte
stocky / hand-knit vest

= **unhöflich**

Ich schaute ihn an, er schaute mich an, so als frage er,° hier sind
50 doch drei Plätze frei; ich hatte das alles nicht richtig mitbekommen,°
so schnell ging es. Der Zug war, soviel° ich sehen konnte, voll. Der
Türke stellte sich genau vor unsere Tür — wie zum Trotz.° Ich fragte
die Dame, „Hier sind doch noch drei Plätze frei. Warum sagten Sie dem
Mann, daß nichts frei sei?"° Wie stets,° wenn Deutsche sich gegensei-
55 tig° taxieren,° antwortete die Dame mit einer Stimme, die zwar höflich
war, aber° vom Gesprächspartner Abstand verlangte,° daß sie mit so
einem Typen[8] nicht zusammen in einem Abteil fahren möchte.

Ich hakte nach°: „Was meinen Sie mit Typen? Mit einem türkischen Typen? Woher wissen Sie, daß er ein Türke ist?" „Das merkt
60 man doch gleich", antwortete sie, ich solle° mal richtig hinschauen,°
dieser finstere Blick° und diese Arroganz. Ich erwiderte:° „Der Mann
hat doch nur höflich gefragt." „Das meinen Sie! Ich aber kenne diese
Türkenblicke!"° Nein, ich könne° von der Dame nicht verlangen,° daß
sie sich die Fahrt durch die Anwesenheit° eines Türken verderbe.° Sie
65 möchte auf keinen Fall° mit einem Türken im Abteil sitzen. Ich ließ
nicht locker:° „Sie fahren aber mit einem Türken im Abteil." „Nein",
sagte sie, „nein, der ist mein Mann, ich fahre nicht und ich werde
auch nicht fahren." „Doch, Sie fahren mit einem Türken, und zwar°
mit mir!" Sie wußte zunächst nicht, was sie sagen sollte. Sie schaute
70 ihren Mann an, bat ihn um Hilfe, aber der verlor kein Wort,° er kon-
trollierte seine Fußspitze,° tat so, als höre er nichts.° (. . .)

„Ich bin aber Türke, und Sie fahren leider mit einem Türken
zusammen." „Sie können doch kein Türke sein." „Warum nicht?"
„Nur so."° „Ich bin Türke, soll ich Ihnen meinen Paß zeigen?" „Das
75 brauchen Sie nicht, weil Sie kein Türke sind." „Warum sind Sie so
sicher?" „Erstens,° ja, hmm, erstens, ich weiß nicht, aber, hmm, Sie
sind auf alle Fälle kein° Türke." „Warum nicht?" „Weil, hmm, weil,
wie soll ich sagen, hmm, weil Sie ‚Die Zeit' lesen."

Ich weiß nicht, wie viele „Zeit"-Leser es in Deutschland gibt, ein-
80 hundert-, zweihundert-, drei-, vier-, fünfhunderttausend oder eine
Million. In Deutschland leben 60 Millionen vermeintliche° Deutsche.
Da nicht alle „Die Zeit" lesen, denke ich, daß die Deutschen, die keine
„Zeit" lesen, keine Deutschen sind, sondern Türken.

so...	= as if to ask
	= verstanden
	as far as
zum Trotz	= out of defiance
	= ist / = immer
	= einander / "check out"
	zwar . . . aber = to be sure . . . but / Abstand verlangte = Distanz erwartete
	hakte nach = followed up
	= sollte / take a look
	finsterer Blick = scowl / erwiderte = antwortete
	"the way the Turks look at you" / = konnte / = erwarten
	presence / ruin
	auf... = nie
	ließ... = didn't let go
	namely
	verlor... = sagte nichts
	tip of his foot / tat... = acted as if he didn't hear anything
	"Just because."
	first of all
	auf... = gar kein
	putative, supposed

Fragen zum Lesestück

1. Wo und wann ist Şinasi Dikmen geboren?
2. Was hat er als Beruf gelernt? Wo wohnt er jetzt?
3. Was halten viele Deutsche für „typisch türkisch"?
4. Was definiert den Autor als Türken?
5. Was für einen Eindruck macht das deutsche Ehepaar im Abteil auf
   Dikmen? Was für einen Eindruck macht er auf sie?
6. Was hält er für „typisch deutsch"?
7. Warum wird der „richtige Türke" von der deutschen Dame nicht
   akzeptiert?
8. Warum hält die Dame den Autor für einen Deutschen?
9. Wo ist der Humor im Text? Geben Sie ein paar Beispiele.

---

[8]Alternative usage of **Typ** as N-noun.

Refer to p. 181 for furniture vocabulary.

Wohnen und Wohnungen

Hier ist der Grundriß (*floorplan*) vom Erdgeschoß einer typischen deutschen Wohnung. Wahrscheinlich gibt es auch noch einen ersten Stock mit mehr Schlafzimmern. Wie ist diese deutsche Wohnung anders als eine amerikanische? In Deutschland gibt es zum Beispiel keine eingebauten Schränke (*built-in closets*) wie in Amerika, sondern man hat einen großen Kleiderschrank (*wardrobe*) im Schlafzimmer. Merken Sie andere Unterschiede?

der Garten

die Terrasse

das Wohnzimmer

die Toilette

das Badezimmer

das Arbeitszimmer

die Kuche

das Schlafzimmer

die Garage

das Eßzimmer

die Treppe

Übung: Zimmernamen

Um diese Übung zu machen, müssen Sie zuerst die Namen der Zimmer wissen.

1. Wo wird das Essen vorbereitet?
2. Wo wird das Auto geparkt?
3. Wo werden Referate, Briefe usw. geschrieben?
4. Wo könnte man fernsehen und die Zeitung lesen?
5. Wo spielen die Kinder bei schönem Wetter?
6. Wo putzt man sich die Zähne?
7. Wo schläft man?
8. Wo nimmt man ein Bad?
9. Wo ißt die Familie zusammen?
10. Wo könnte man bei gutem Wetter sitzen und Kaffee trinken?

Partnerarbeit: Ich möchte dir unsere Wohnung zeigen.

Partner A zeigt Partner B seine Wohnung.

A: Komm bitte herein. Gehen wir zuerst ins Eßzimmer.
B: Oh, wie schön! Was ist denn das in der Ecke?

Gruppenarbeit: Zur Diskussion

1. Wie wohnen Sie zu Hause? Beschreiben Sie das Haus oder die Wohnung Ihrer Familie.
2. Wie würde Ihr Traumhaus aussehen? Beschreiben Sie es.

Zum Schluß

Sprechen wir miteinander

Lab Manual Kap. 15, Diktat.

A Partnerarbeit: Was hättest du lieber gemacht?

In den Sommerferien hat man nie genug Zeit, alles zu machen, was man machen möchte. Sagen Sie einander zuerst, was Sie letzten Sommer gemacht haben, und dann was Sie lieber gemacht hätten.

BEISPIEL: Ich mußte den ganzen Tag im Büro arbeiten, aber ich hätte lieber eine lange Radtour gemacht.

B Gruppenarbeit: Was hätten Sie gemacht, wenn . . .

So ist es *nicht* gewesen, aber es hätte anders sein können. Was hätten Sie gemacht, . . .

1. wenn Sie dieses Semester nicht studiert hätten?
2. wenn Sie letztes Jahr eine Million Dollar gewonnen hätten?
3. wenn Sie vor 10 000 Jahren gelebt hätten?
4. wenn Sie Beethoven gewesen wären?
5. wenn Sie gestern einen Autounfall gehabt hätten?

C Übung

Erzählen Sie die „Lebensgeschichten" der folgenden Dinge im Passiv. Das wird so gemacht:

BEISPIEL: Zeitung: Journalisten / schreiben
Die Zeitung wird zuerst von Journalisten geschrieben.
(usw.)

You can connect your sentences with **dann: Die Zeitung wird zuerst von Journalisten geschrieben,** *dann* wird sie . . .

1. die Zeitung: Journalisten / schreiben
am Morgen auf der Straße / kaufen
zwischen sieben und halb acht / lesen
im Zug / vergessen
alter Mann / finden und lesen
2. der Roman: Schriftsteller / schreiben
in der Buchhandlung / kaufen
zu Hause / lesen
einem Freund / leihen
vom Freund / verlieren
3. die Wurst: Metzger (*butcher*) / machen
Hausfrau / kaufen
im Wasser / kochen
zum Mittagessen / essen
4. die Postkarte: in Italien / kaufen
Barbara / schreiben
zur Post / bringen
in den Briefkasten / einwerfen
Familie / lesen

Erzählen Sie weiter von den folgenden Gegenständen (*objects*): der Tisch, das Auto, das Brötchen, das Frühstück, das Gepäck, die Weinflasche, das Foto.

D Gruppenarbeit: Trivial Pursuit (2 Mannschaften)

Jetzt spielen Sie ein bißchen „Trivial Pursuit". Jede Mannschaft stellt der anderen Fragen über Geschichte, berühmte Personen, Kunst, Literatur usw. Benutzen Sie den Passiv.

BEISPIELE: Von wem wurde *Faust* geschrieben?
Wo wurde Jazzmusik zuerst gespielt?

Schreiben Sie zu Hause

E Rewrite these sentences in passive voice. Keep the same tense.

1. Man akzeptiert mich fast überall.
2. Robert interviewt eine italienische Schülerin.
3. Man warf den Brief in den Briefkasten ein.
4. Die Studenten haben eine Europareise geplant.
5. Hat jemand die Wohnung im ersten Stock schon gekauft?
6. Dort sprach man nur Türkisch.
7. Man muß dieses Problem verstehen.
8. Die Gäste haben meine Großmutter überrascht.
9. Der Beamte muß das Gepäck kontrollieren.
10. Am Montag soll man dieses Thema diskutieren.

F Aufsatzthemen

1. Was für Schwierigkeiten hätten Sie in einem Land, wo kein Englisch gesprochen wird? Beschreiben Sie die Situation.
2. Gibt es Gastarbeiter in Nordamerika? Wie ist die Situation anders als in Europa?

G Phantasiefrage Wählen Sie eine historische Person und stellen Sie sich vor, Sie wären dieser Mensch gewesen. Wie hätten Sie gelebt? Hätten Sie etwas anderes gemacht?

BEISPIEL: Wenn ich Einstein gewesen wäre . . .

1. Would you like to have lived in the 19th century?
2. I have to think about that.
3. How would life have been different back then?
4. You would not have been able to work with a computer.

5. My paper has to be written soon.
6. When do you need my new typewriter?
7. Either today or the day after tomorrow.
8. What are you writing about?
9. About foreign workers in Austria and Switzerland.
10. A lot of books have been written about that.

11. There is the post office. Didn't you want to mail your letter?
12. Yes, let's go in. I could also buy some stamps.

Das Leben hätte zürich davon gewechselt.

Foreigners Living and Working in Germany

During the past 50 years, Germany has attracted large numbers of foreigners. In the economic recovery after World War II, manpower shortages existed in the industrialized countries of northern Europe. From the 1960s to the early 1970s, workers from Turkey, Yugoslavia, Italy, Greece, Spain, and Portugal were brought to West Germany. The Federal Republic still has the largest number of such so-called guest workers (**Gastarbeiter**) in Europe (1.9 million in West Germany in 1991), but has discouraged more from coming since the end of the labor shortage. Although many of these workers and their families have lived in Germany for years, German law makes it difficult for them to become citizens.

Another large class of foreigners in Germany are those seeking asylum from political persecution in their native countries. The German Basic Law (**Grundgesetz**) of 1949 stated that "those being persecuted politically have a right to asylum." But by the early 1990s, the densely populated country was finding it increasingly difficult to support large numbers of political refugees (438,000 in 1992). In 1993 the Basic Law was amended to make the requirements for asylum seekers much more strict.

The most acute immigration problem in the late 1980s and early 1990s resulted from the liberalization of Eastern Europe and the opening of what used to be called the "Iron Curtain." Ethnic Germans (**Volksdeutsche**) from Eastern European countries such as Poland, the Soviet Union, and Romania are entitled to citizenship under the German constitution. In 1992, over 230,000 of these Eastern European immigrants (the so-called **Aussiedler**) entered Germany. The government helps integrate these immigrants into German society with stipends, language courses, and temporary housing.

Im BMW-Werk (München).

Die Frau: neue Wege und Rollen

Communicative Goals

- Reporting what others have said
- Expressing feelings

Cultural Goal

- Learning about women in Germany and the changing social roles of both men and women

Chapter Outline

Lyrik zum Vorlesen **Vier Gedichte von Mascha Kaléko**

Grammatik **Subjunctive with** als ob • **Indirect Quotation and Special Subjunctive** • **Impersonal Passive** • **Subjective Use of Modal Verbs** • **Extended Modifiers**

Lesestück **Gedanken über die Emanzipation der Frau**

Situationen aus dem Alltag **Mit Gefühl! (Wie drückt man Gefühle aus?)**

Almanach **Legal Protection During Pregnancy and Maternity**

Kind oder Beruf?

Margarete ist bei ihrer alten Schulfreundin Martha zu Besuch. Sie sitzen im Garten bei einer Tasse Kaffee.

MARTHA: Wie schafft ihr das, wenn euer Kind da ist? Wirst du deine Stelle aufgeben?

MARGARETE: Nee, eine so gut bezahlte Stelle ist schwer zu finden. Rolf kann vormittags auf das Baby aufpassen und nachmittags an seiner Diss arbeiten.

MARTHA: Wer paßt *dann* auf das Baby auf?

MARGARETE: Dann bin ich da. Ich habe meine Chefin schon gefragt, ob es möglich sei, halbtags zu arbeiten.

MARTHA: Was sagte sie dazu?

MARGARETE: Sie meinte, das ginge. Die ist ja selber verheiratet mit Kindern.

Goldene Hochzeit

Am Morgen vor der Vorlesung treffen sich Heinrich und Liese im Studentencafé.

HEINRICH: Liese, du siehst aus, als ob du kaum geschlafen hättest.

LIESE: Stimmt schon. Bei uns wurde bis halb vier gefeiert.

HEINRICH: Was wurde denn gefeiert?

LIESE: Die goldene Hochzeit meiner Großeltern.

HEINRICH: Sagenhaft! Und sie sehen noch so jung aus!

Mädchen in „Männerberufen": Berufe für Männer und Frauen

Child or Career?

Margarete is visiting her old school friend Martha. They're having coffee in the garden.

M.: How are you going to manage when your child is born? Will you quit your job?

M.: No, such a well-paying job is hard to find. Rolf can look after the baby in the mornings and work on his dissertation in the afternoons.

M.: Who'll look after the baby then?

M.: Then I'll be here. I've already asked my boss whether it's possible to work part-time.

M.: What did she say to that?

M.: She thought it would work. She's married and has kids herself.

Golden Wedding Anniversary

In the morning before their lecture, Heinrich and Liese meet in the student café.

H.: Liese, you look as though you had hardly slept.

L.: That's right. Our party went on until 3:30.

H.: What were you celebrating?

L.: My grandparents' golden wedding anniversary.

H.: Incredible! And they still look so young!

Verben

arbeiten an (+ *dat.*)   to work on

auf·passen   to pay attention; to look out

  aufpassen auf (+ *acc.*)   to look after

heiraten   to marry, get married

verheiratet sein   to be married

Hochzeit, which originally meant *celebration*, has become more specific since the Middle Ages and now refers to the "high times" enjoyed at a *wedding*.

Substantive

das **Baby, -s**   baby

die **Hochzeit, -en**   wedding

  die **goldene Hochzeit** golden wedding anniversary

Adjektive und Adverbien

golden   golden

halbtags (*adv.*)   half days

  halbtags arbeiten   to work part-time

kaum   hardly, barely

vormittags   (in the) mornings

Andere Vokabeln

als ob (+ *subjunctive*)   as if, as though

Nützliche Ausdrücke

Was sagen/meinen Sie dazu?   What do you say to that?

sagenhaft   incredible, marvelous

Gegensätze

verheiratet ≠ unverheiratet/ ledig   married ≠ unmarried / single

Mit anderen Worten

die Diss = die Dissertation = die Doktorarbeit

Variationen

A Persönliche Fragen

1. Margarete sagt, sie wird ihre Stelle nicht aufgeben, um auf das Baby aufzupassen. Was würden Sie in dieser Situation machen, wenn Sie gerade ein Kind bekommen hätten?
2. Haben Sie je eine gute Stelle aufgegeben? Warum?
3. Wollen Sie eines Tages Kinder haben? Wie stellen Sie sich Ihr Leben mit Kindern vor?
4. Liese sagt, daß sie bis halb vier gefeiert hat. Haben Sie je so lange gefeiert? Was wurde gefeiert?
5. Lieses Großeltern haben ihre goldene Hochzeit gefeiert. Nach wievielen Jahren feiert man goldene Hochzeit?
6. Leben Ihre Großeltern noch? Wenn ja, wissen Sie, wie lange sie schon verheiratet sind?

Review high-frequency idiomatic phrases like these in each **Zusammenfassung und Wiederholung** section. They are important for authentic conversational German.

B Gruppenarbeit: Was sagen Sie dazu?

Reagieren Sie auf die Sätze links mit einem passenden (*appropriate*) Ausdruck von der rechten Seite.

Heute habe ich Geburtstag.	Das wäre nett!
Du sprichst perfekt Deutsch.	Gott sei Dank!
Gehen wir zusammen Ski fahren?	Doch.
Möchten Sie etwas trinken?	Natürlich.
Darf ich meinen Freund Gerd vorstellen?	Kein Wunder!
Morgen früh wasche ich mir die Haare.	Lieber nicht.
Stefan hat sich das Bein gebrochen.	Sehr angenehm.
Wollt ihr viele Kinder haben?	Höchste Zeit!
Wir bekommen einen neuen Professor.	Gerne!
Ich war bis halb vier auf.	Wie schade!
Kannst du mich nicht verstehen?	Verflixt nochmal!
Ich hab meinen Geldbeutel verloren!	Ich gratuliere!
	Danke gleichfalls!
	Bist du verrückt?

C Übung: Das ist schwer zu finden

Margarete sagt, eine gute Stelle ist schwer zu finden. Antworten Sie auf die folgenden Fragen.

1. Was ist in dieser Gegend schwer zu finden?
2. Was ist manchmal schwer zu wissen?
3. Was ist für Sie schwer zu verstehen?

Die Frau: neue Wege und Rollen   **465**

Mascha Kaléko wurde 1907 als Tochter eines russischen Vaters und einer österreichischen Mutter geboren. Nach dem Ersten Weltkrieg zog die Familie nach Marburg. Kaléko studierte in Berlin, wo sie in den frühen 30er Jahren begann, für führende Zeitungen zu schreiben. 1938 verließ sie Hitlers Drittes Reich und ging nach New York ins Exil. 1966 zog sie nach Israel. Sie starb 1975.

Kalékos Gedichte, die oft in der Alltagssprache der Großstadt geschrieben sind, zeigen Witz, Ironie und manchmal etwas Melancholie. Diese vier kurzen Gedichte erschienen (*appeared*) zuerst in der Sammlung *Kleines Lesebuch für Große* (1934).

Von Mensch zu Mensch

Nun, da du fort° bist, scheint mir alles trübe.°   = **weg** / = **traurig**
Hätt' ich's geahnt,° ich ließe dich nicht gehn.   foreseen
Was wir vermissen,° scheint uns immer schön.   = **was uns fehlt**
Woran das liegen mag° —. Ist das nun Liebe?   **woran...** = I wonder why that is.

Von Elternhaus und Jugendzeit

Jetzt bin ich groß. Mir blüht kein Märchenbuch.°   **Mir...** = Life's not going to be a fairy tale.
Ich muß schon oft „Sie" zu mir selber sagen.
Nur manchmal noch, an jenen° stillen Tagen,   those
Kommt meine Kindheit heimlich° zu Besuch.   in secret

Von den Jahreszeiten

Der Frühling fand diesmal im Saale° statt.   = **im Zimmer**
Der Sommer war lang und gesegnet.°   blissful
—Ja, sonst gab es Winter in dieser Stadt.
Und sonntags hat's meistens geregnet . . .

Von Reise und Wanderung

Einmal sollte man seine Siebensachen°   possessions
Fortrollen aus diesen glatten Geleisen.°   **Fortrollen...** = roll off of these smooth tracks
Man sollte sich aus dem Staube machen°   **sich...** = hit the road
Und früh am Morgen unbekannt verreisen.°   = **wegreisen**

Mascha Kaléko (1907–1975)

Masha Kaléko als junges Mädchen.

Grammatik

Subjunctive with *als ob* (*as if, as though*)

The subordinating conjunction **als ob** (*as if, as though*) must be followed by a verb in the subjunctive.[1] Clauses with **als ob** are preceded by introductory phrases such as the following (note the special meaning of **tun** in the first example).

Du tust (so), als ob . . .	*You act as though . . .*
Du siehst aus, als ob . . .	*You look as if . . .*
Es war, als ob . . .	*It was as if . . .*
Es klingt, als ob . . .	*It sounds as if . . .*

Er tut, **als ob** er nichts **wüßte**.	*He acts as if he didn't know anything.*
Du siehst aus, **als ob** du krank **wärest**.	*You look as though you're ill.*
Es war, **als ob** wir uns immer **gekannt hätten**.	*It was as if we had always known each other.*
Es klingt, **als ob** du viel zu tun **hättest**.	*It sounds as if you have a lot to do.*

Lab Manual Kap. 16, Var. zur Üb. 1.

Workbook Kap. 16, A.

1 Übung: Aber Sie tun doch, als ob Sie gesund wären!

Ihr Professor erzählt Ihnen etwas über sich selbst. Sagen Sie ihm, er tut, als ob das Gegenteil stimmte.

BEISPIEL: Ich fühle mich heute krank.
Aber Sie tun doch, als ob Sie gesund wären.

1. Ich bin traurig.
2. Ich bin knapp bei Kasse.
3. Ich bin von Natur aus (*by nature*) faul.
4. Ich bin relativ altmodisch.
5. Ich bin eigentlich ein schlampiger Mensch.
6. Ich bin fast immer ernst.
7. Eigentlich bin ich dumm.

---

[1]Either general *or* special subjunctive may be used. Sometimes this conjunction is used in the abbreviated form of **als** alone (without **ob**). In this case, the verb immediately follows it rather than coming at the end of the clause: Du siehst aus, als **wärest** du krank.

2 Gruppenarbeit: Sie sehen aus, als ob . . .

Sehen Sie sich die Menschen auf diesen Fotos an. Wie sehen sie aus? (Gefühle, Berufe usw.)

BEISPIEL: Sie sieht aus, *als ob* sie viel zu tun hätte.

1.

2.

Sicher

3.

Sie sieht aus,
als ob
sie müde wäre.

entschlossen

4.

traurig

Indirect Quotation and Special Subjunctive

Direct versus Indirect Quotation

Reporting what others have said is a communicative goal.

Note on punctuation: German uses a colon before a direct quotation, while English uses a comma.

There are two basic ways to report what someone has said: directly or indirectly. One can quote directly, repeating the original speaker's exact words.

Bernd sagte: „Ich muß heute in die Bibliothek."

Bernd said, "I have to go to the library today."

It is much more common, however, to report speech in *indirect* quotation, either without a conjunction:

Bernd sagte, er muß heute in die Bibliothek.

Bernd said he had to go to the library today.

or with the conjunction **daß** (*that*):

Bernd sagte, daß er heute in die Bibliothek muß.	*Bernd said that he had to go to the library today.*

Note that in indirect quotation, pronouns often have to be changed: „**Ich muß** in die Bibliothek." — Er sagte, **er** muß in die Bibliothek.

In conversation many Germans simply use the indicative for indirect quotation, as in the previous examples and as we have done up to this point in this book. But it is also quite common to use *subjunctive* for indirect quotation.

Bernd sagte, er **müßte** in die Bibliothek.	*Bernd said he had to go to the library.*
Meine Chefin meinte, das **ginge**.	*My boss thought it would work.*

In formal written and spoken German, however (for example, in a term paper, newspaper article, television news report, or speech), indirect quotation *must* be expressed with forms called the *special subjunctive*.

Notice that *thoughts* (**Die Chefin** *meinte* . . .) can also be reported in indirect quotation.

Er sagte, er **müsse** in die Bibliothek.
Die Chefin meinte, das **gehe**.

Formation of the Special Subjunctive

To form the special subjunctive, add the endings from the general subjunctive of strong verbs (**-e, -est, -e; -en, -et, -en**) to the *unchanged infinitive stem* of the verb.

er/es/sie **gehe, laufe, könne, wisse, müsse, sehe** usw.

In practice, the special subjunctive occurs *almost exclusively* in the third person singular.[2] This form is immediately recognizable for the following reasons:

- It is built on the *infinitive* stem (**geh-, lauf-**), not on the past stem (**ging-, lief-**) like the general subjunctive.
- Special subjunctive ends in **-e** (**er/es/sie gehe**), not in the indicative ending **-t** (**er/es/sie geht**).

---

[2]A note about forms. There are two reasons why special subjunctive occurs most often in the third person singular. First, any special subjunctive form that would be identical to an indicative form *does not exist*. Forms of the general subjunctive are used instead, as in the following paradigm:

ich **liefe** (laufe)	wir **liefen** (laufen)
du **laufest**	ihr **laufet**
er/es/sie **laufe**	sie, Sie **liefen** (laufen)

Thus there is *no* **wir-** or **sie-**form in special subjunctive, because they would *always* be identical to indicative. An **ich-**form exists only for verbs with an irregular indicative singular, such as the modal verbs and **wissen: ich könne, ich wisse.**

The second reason for the high frequency of the third person singular is that special subjunctive is the *most formal* method for indirect quotation. As such, it is seldom used in the **ich-, du-,** or **ihr-**forms. It is usually used instead to quote formally some third person.

The *only* German verb with a complete set of forms in the special subjunctive is **sein**. Note that the **ich-** and **er-**forms lack endings.

ich	**sei**	wir	**seien**
du	**seiest**	ihr	**seiet**
er/es/sie	**sei**	sie, Sie	**seien**

The special subjunctive has only two additional tenses, future and past, each formed using the special subjunctive of the auxiliary verb.

future	sie **werde** das **sagen**	*she will say that*
past	er **habe** das **gewußt**	*he knew that*
	sie **sei** dort **gewesen**	*she was there*

Fanny Mendelssohn-Bartholdy (1805–1847) Child prodigy at the piano, composer, diarist; sister of Felix Mendelssohn. Her music includes works for solo voice, chorus, piano, and chamber ensemble.

Use of Special Subjunctive

You will encounter indirect quotation in special subjunctive introduced by a verb of saying or asking in the *indicative*. Once an environment of indirect quotation has been thus established, the economy of special subjunctive becomes evident: it makes explicit that the person is still being quoted indirectly, and no further verbs saying who is speaking are required, as they sometimes are in English. Here are some examples of the kind you might hear on the evening news or read in the paper:

Bei seinem Besuch in Rostock sagte der Bundeskanzler, er **wisse** noch nicht, wie man dieses Problem lösen **werde**, aber er **glaube**, daß etwas bald entschieden werden **müsse**. Man **habe** nicht mehr viel Zeit.

On his visit to Rostock, the Chancellor said he didn't know yet how they would solve this problem, but he believed that something had to be decided soon. (He continued that) there wasn't much time left.

In einem exklusiven Interview mit unserem Reporter sagte der junge Tennisstar, sie **hoffe**, noch eine lange Karriere vor sich zu haben. Sie **sei** noch jung und **fühle** sich sehr fit, besonders seit sie sich von einer schlimmen Erkältung erholt **habe**.

In an exclusive interview with our reporter, the young tennis star said that she hoped to have a long career still ahead of her. (She said) she was still young and felt very fit, especially since recovering from a bad cold.

As you can see from the examples above, there is a difference in the way English and German handle tenses in indirect quotation. In English, the tense of the introductory verb of saying influences the tense of the indirect quotation.

> ***Direct Quotation***
>
> *Barbara said, "I have to go to the library."*
>
> ***Indirect Quotation:*** *Introductory Verb in the Present*
>
> *She **says** she **has** to go to the library.*
>
> ***Indirect Quotation:*** *Introductory Verb in the Past*
>
> *She **said** she **had** to go to the library.*

In German, the tense of the introductory verb of saying has *no influence* on the tense of the indirect quotation. The tense of the indirect quotation is *always the same as the tense of the direct quotation* from which it derives. If the tense of the direct quotation was *present*, use *present subjunctive* for the indirect quotation.

> Bundeskanzler: „Ich **muß** mir das überlegen."
>
> Der Bundeskanzler sagt, ⎫
> Der Bundeskanzler sagte, ⎭ er **müsse** sich das überlegen.

If the tense of the direct quotation was *future*, use *future subjunctive*.

> Tennisstar: „Ich **werde** mehr spielen."
>
> Der Tennisstar sagt, ⎫
> Der Tennisstar sagte, ⎭ sie **werde** mehr spielen.

If the tense of the direct quotation was *any past tense*, use *past subjunctive*.

> Tennisstar: „Ich **habe** mich von der Erkältung **erholt**."
>
> Der Tennisstar sagt, ⎫
> Der Tennisstar sagte, ⎭ sie **habe** sich von der Erkältung **erholt**.

If the original quotation is *already* in the subjunctive, the indirect quotation simply *remains* in the subjunctive.

> Bundeskanzler: „Ich **möchte** nichts mehr darüber sagen."
>
> Der Bundeskanzler sagt, ⎫
> Der Bundeskanzler sagte, ⎭ er **möchte** nichts mehr darüber sagen.

Lab Manual Kap. 16, Üb. 5 and Var. zur Üb. 3, 5.

Workbook Kap. 16, B–E.

3 Übung: Zeitungsartikel

Here are two examples of indirect quotation one might encounter in a news report. Reconstruct the original direct quotations, changing pronouns as necessary.

1. Eine führende Politikerin berichtete, die Barrieren zur europäischen Vereinigung **seien** gefallen. Man **könne** jetzt beginnen, dem

Europa-Parlament in Straßburg mehr Autorität zu geben. Es **werde** wahrscheinlich noch ein paar Jahre dauern, bis alle Probleme gelöst **seien**. Sie persönlich **glaube** aber, daß man schon große Fortschritte gemacht **habe**.

2. Die Polizei meldete (*announced*) heute, ein schwerer Unfall auf der Autobahn zwischen Stuttgart und Heidelberg **habe** acht Verletzte und zwei Tote gekostet. Die Ursache (*cause*) des Unfalls **sei** das neblige Wetter im Neckartal gewesen. Alle Autofahrer **sollten** sich andere Routen nach Norden aussuchen.

4 Schriftliche Übung: Bericht über ein Interview

The most polite form of address to someone with a professional title is **Frau Doktor Edenhof, Herr Professor Nolden**.

As a reporter for the student newspaper, you interview Frau Dr. Edenhof, a visiting lecturer on international affairs. Below is a transcript from your tape recorder. Now report what she said to you in indirect quotation. Begin your report with „Frau Dr. Edenhof sagte, . . . “ and be careful to change pronouns and possessive adjectives as necessary.

„Ich freue mich sehr, hier an der Uni zu sein. Ich war vor zehn Jahren zum letzten Mal hier und habe damals viele nette Menschen kennengelernt. Ich finde diese Stadt wunderschön. Ich hoffe, ich werde diesmal mehr Zeit haben, um mir die Stadt anzusehen. Mein Thema für heute abend ist die Zukunft der NATO im neuen Europa. Ich weiß, daß es hier sehr viel Interesse für dieses aktuelle Problem gibt. Man kann natürlich in einer Stunde nicht alles darüber sagen. Ich hoffe, am Ende meines Vortrags (*lecture*) eine gute Diskussion mit Ihnen zu haben.“

Questions and Commands in Indirect Quotation

- Yes/no questions become **ob**-clauses in indirect quotation.

  Karin: „Hat Hans genug Geld?“

  Karin fragte, **ob** Hans genug Geld hat (habe, hätte).

- Information questions become subordinate clauses introduced by a question word.

  Tourist: „Wo ist der Bahnhof, bitte?“

  Der Tourist fragte, **wo** der Bahnhof ist (sei, wäre).

- Commands become statements with the verb **sollen**, with or without **daß**.

  Frau Henning: „Paß doch auf, Heinz!“

  Frau Henning sagte ihrem Mann, er **soll** (solle, sollte) aufpassen.

  Frau Henning sagte ihrem Mann, **daß** er aufpassen **soll** (solle, sollte).

Übung: Was hat sie denn gesagt?

Ihre Professorin fragt Sie etwas oder sagt, Sie sollen etwas machen. Erzählen Sie dem nächsten Studenten, was die Professorin gesagt hat.

BEISPIELE:
A. Bitte leihen Sie mir einen Bleistift.
B. Sie sagte, ich soll ihr einen Bleistift leihen.

A. Wo ist Ihr Regenschirm?
B. Sie fragte, wo mein Regenschirm sei.

1. Wie fühlen Sie sich heute?
2. Arbeiten Sie oft mit dem Computer?
3. Was haben Sie zum Frühstück gegessen?
4. Empfehlen Sie mir bitte etwas Neues.
5. Helfen Sie mir bitte heute nachmittag.
6. Können Sie sich auf Ihre Arbeit konzentrieren?
7. Können Sie sich ein neues Fahrrad leisten?
8. Haben Sie Ihren Studentenausweis mit?
9. Passen Sie gut auf!
10. Seien Sie froh!

Impersonal Passive

One use of the German passive voice has no precise English equivalent. It is used to say that some human activity is going on, without mentioning who performs it. No subject is expressed at all, and the verb is *always* in the third person singular.

Bis halb vier **wurde gefeiert**.
Hier **wird** bis zwei Uhr morgens **getanzt und gesungen**.

The party went on until 3:30.
There's dancing and singing here until 2:00 A.M.

If no other element occupies first position in the sentence, an impersonal **es** is used to fill it. This **es** is not a real subject and disappears if any other element occupies first position.[3]

Es wurde bis halb vier gefeiert.
Es wird hier bis zwei Uhr morgens getanzt.

---

[3]Similarly, when verbs with dative objects (see p. 199) are used in the passive voice, their objects *remain* in the dative case and the passive is *always* in the third-person singular. An impersonal **es** is in the first position if no other element occupies it.

active
Man hilft dem Alten. *They're helping the old man.*

passive
Dem Alten wird geholfen
Es wird dem Alten geholfen. } *The old man is being helped.*

Die Frau: neue Wege und Rollen

Lab Manual Kap.
16, Var. zur Üb. 6.

Workbook Kap. 16,
F–H.

Note that impersonal passive is
only passive in *structure,* not in
meaning. The verb does not need
to be transitive, but must
designate a human activity.
Impossible: **Hier wird
geregnet** (not a human
activity).

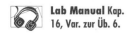

6 Übung: Anders gesagt

Diese Sätze mit **man** kann man auch als unpersönliche Passivsätze
formulieren.

> BEISPIEL: Heute ißt man um neun Uhr.
> Heute wird um neun Uhr gegessen.

1. Hier singt man zu laut.
2. Beim Bäcker fängt man früh an.
3. In Leipzig demonstrierte man.
4. Damals arbeitete man schwer.
5. Morgen liest und schreibt man viel.
6. Jetzt kauft man ein.
7. Gestern tanzte man bis zwei Uhr.
8. In unserer Stadt baut man immer mehr.

Was wird hier gemacht?

7 Übung: Wo wird das in der Wohnung gemacht?

Antworten Sie auf diese Fragen.

> BEISPIELE: Wo wird in der Wohnung oder im Haus gekocht?
> In der Küche.
>
> Was wird im Arbeitszimmer gemacht?
> Bücher werden dort gelesen.

1. Wo wird gegessen?
2. Was wird im Schlafzimmer gemacht?
3. Wo wird ferngesehen?
4. Was wird im Garten gemacht?
5. Wo wird der Wagen geparkt?

Und jetzt stellen Sie einander ähnliche Fragen.

Subjective Use of Modal Verbs

The modal verbs are sometimes used to show speakers' subjective attitudes toward what they are saying. By and large, this subjective use of the modal verbs is parallel to English.

- **mögen** expresses *possibility*

Das **mag** sein.	*That may be.*

- **müssen** expresses *strong probability*

Die Menschen drüben **müssen** Touristen sein.	*The people over there must be tourists.*

- **sollen** expresses *hearsay*

Sie **soll** eine gute Lehrerin sein.	*She's supposed to be a good teacher.*
Sie **sollen** so glücklich sein.	*They are said to be so happy.*

- **können** expresses *fairly strong possibility*

Kann das Richard sein?	*Can that be Richard?*
Es **kann** sein, daß sie drei Wochen bleibt.	*It could be that she'll stay three weeks.*

- **wollen** casts *doubt on someone else's claim* (no parallel in English)

Er **will** viel über Musik wissen.	*He claims to know a lot about music.*

Moderne „Zusammenarbeit": so wird das Essen vorbereitet.

Sehen Sie sich das Foto genau an. Was weiß man über das Ehepaar?

Die Frau: neue Wege und Rollen

Übung: Kann das sein?

Lesen Sie die folgenden Sätze laut vor. Dann geben Sie ein Äquivalent auf englisch, und sagen Sie, ob das Modalverb objektiv oder subjektiv gebraucht wird.

1. Kann das Utes Wagen sein?
2. Nein, das muß Richards Wagen sein.
3. Wieso, Ute wollte sich doch einen roten Wagen kaufen, nicht?
4. Mag sein. Wir müssen Ute fragen.
5. Ja, sie soll um drei wieder da sein.
6. Dann müssen wir zusammen in die Vorlesung.

9 Übung: Wie sagt man das auf deutsch?

1. She is supposed to be very famous.
2. That may be.

3. Hans-Peter must know a lot about politics.
4. He claims to know everything about politics.

5. It may be that they don't love each other any more.
6. But they are supposed to be so happy together!

Extended Modifiers

Look at the following phrases:

diese deutsche Schriftstellerin	*this German writer*
diese bekannte deutsche Schriftstellerin	*this well-known German writer*
diese sehr bekannte deutsche Schriftstellerin	*this very well-known German writer*

Both German and English can extend noun phrases by inserting a series of adjectives and adverbs between a limiting word (**diese**, *this*) and its noun (**Schriftstellerin**, *writer*). In German, however, such a series can be continued much further than in English.

diese unter jungen Lesern sehr bekannte deutsche Schriftstellerin	*this German writer who is very well known among young readers*
diese unter jungen Lesern in Europa sehr bekannte deutsche Schriftstellerin	*this German writer who is very well known among young readers in Europe*
diese heute unter jungen Lesern in Europa sehr bekannte deutsche Schriftstellerin	*this German writer who is very well known among young readers in Europe today*

Such extended modifiers are encountered primarily in written German, and their use or avoidance is a matter of stylistic preference. You should *not* try to use this construction actively until you have had more experience with German, but you *should* be able to recognize and understand it.

The extended modifier is a substitute for a relative clause.

diese unter Studenten bekannte Schriftstellerin =
diese Schriftstellerin, **die unter Studenten bekannt ist**

Extended modifiers often contain a present or past participle functioning as an attributive adjective. This participle would be the conjugated verb in the corresponding relative clause.

Die Schüler freuen sich auf **die in zwei Tagen *beginnenden* Ferien**. =
Die Schüler freuen sich auf die Ferien, **die in zwei Tagen *beginnen***.

Eine so gut *bezahlte* Stelle ist schwer zu finden. =
Eine Stelle, **die so gut *bezahlt* wird**, ist schwer zu finden.

Schauen Sie sich diese Briefmarken an. Was wird darauf als Beruf gewürdigt (*commemorated*)? Was meinen Sie: Kann man das einen Beruf nennen? Warum?

Beruf:

75 Jahre Deutscher Hausfrauen-Bund — Deutsche Bundespost 100

Beruf:

75 Jahre Deutscher Hausfrauen-Bund — Deutsche Bundespost 100

10 Übung: Die Schriftstellerin

First read these sentences aloud. Then give their English equivalents. Finally, transform the extended modifiers into relative clauses.

> BEISPIEL: Die in Hamburg geborene Schriftstellerin wohnt heute in Berlin.
> *The writer, who was born in Hamburg, lives in Berlin today.*
> Die Schriftstellerin, die in Hamburg geboren ist, wohnt heute in Berlin.

1. Ihr erstes, im Ausland kaum gelesenes Buch machte sie in Deutschland berühmt.
2. Ihre zwei Jahre jüngere Schwester ist Lehrerin in Düsseldorf.
3. In Berlin wohnt sie in einem alten, von Touristen kaum besuchten Stadtteil.
4. Aus ganz Deutschland bekommt sie Briefe von ihren oft sehr jungen Lesern.
5. Von ihr erwartet man Antworten auf viele für die Jugend immer ernster werdende Probleme.

Gedanken über die Emanzipation der Frau

Lab Manual Kap.
16, Üb. zur Betonung.

Tips zum Lesen und Lernen

Leicht zu merken

die **Emanzipation**	Emanzipation
ideal	ideal
industriell	industriell
die **Karriere, -n**	Karriere
parallel	parallel
das **Phänomen, -e**	Phänomen
die **Position, -en**	Position
psychologisch	

Einstieg in den Text

Leitfragen   Das Lesestück in diesem Kapitel hat als Thema die Emanzipation der Frau. Dieses Thema ist nicht nur für Frauen, sondern auch für Männer wichtig. Als Vorbereitung auf das Lesen sollen Sie über Ihre eigenen Meinungen zu diesem Thema nachdenken. Hier sind einige Fragen, die Sie sich stellen könnten.

Heute muß man sich im Büro mit dem Computer auskennen.

1. Ist Ihre Mutter Hausfrau?
2. Ist sie auch berufstätig?
3. Wie war es mit Ihrer Großmutter?
4. Wie ist das Leben Ihrer Mutter anders als das Leben Ihrer Großmutter?
5. Wollen Sie heiraten und Kinder haben? Wenn ja, wie stellen Sie sich Ihr Leben als Vater oder als Mutter vor?

Identifying Special Subjunctive and Extended Modifiers in Context   The following reading contains several examples of both indirect quotation in the special subjunctive and extended modifiers. After reading it through once, first see if you understand why special subjunctive is used in lines 7 and 31–32. Then look closely at the two examples of extended modifiers and see if you can translate them into English (the marginal glosses will help you).

(line 27)   Heutige Frauen haben auch gelernt, **die trotz aller Schwierigkeiten errungenen Leistungen** dieser früheren Frauengeneration zu schätzen.

(line 43)   **Die auch in Amerika bekannte Schriftstellerin** Christa Wolf schrieb über dieses Phänomen . . .

Wortschatz 2

Verben

bieten, bot, hat geboten   to offer; to provide
erledigen   to attend to, take care of, finish
frustrieren   to frustrate

Substantive

der **Erfolg, -e**   success
der **Gedanke, -ns,**[4] **-n**   thought
der **Lohn, ⸚e**   wage
der **Weg, -e**   way, path
das **Geschlecht, -er**   sex, gender
das **Gesetz, -e**   law
   vor dem Gesetz   under/in the eyes of the law

die **Aufgabe, -n**   task, assignment
die **Gleichberechtigung** (*sing.*)   equal rights
die **Küche, -n**   kitchen

Adjektive und Adverbien

deutlich   clear
gebildet   educated
gesellschaftlich   social
gleich   equal
gleichberechtigt   enjoying equal rights
kritisch   critical
öffentlich   public

Remember that **gleich** also means *right away:* **Ich muß gleich losfahren.**

Nützlicher Ausdruck

es geht um   it's a question of . . . ; it's about . . .
   (*subject is always* **es**)
Worum geht es in dieser Diskussion?   What's this discussion about?
Es geht um die Gleichberechtigung.
   It's about equal rights.

Idiom: **Es geht um die Wurst.**
(*Something important is at stake*).

Gegensätze

gebildet ≠ ungebildet
   educated ≠ uneducated
öffentlich ≠ privat   public ≠ private

---

[4]The nouns **Gedanke** and **Name** take an **-n** in every case except the nominative (Kennst du meinen Namen?) *and* add **-s** in the genitive. Proverb: **Der Wunsch ist Vater des Gedankens.**

Gedanken über die Emanzipation der Frau

 Lab Manual Kap. 16, Lesestück.

Learning about the changing social roles of men and women in Germany is the cultural goal of this chapter.

Die Rolle der Frau in der Gesellschaft ist in Deutschland wie fast überall in der Welt in den letzten Jahren zum heißen Diskussionsthema geworden. Es wird sowohl über soziale als auch° über psychologische Fragen diskutiert. Es geht um gleichen Lohn für gleiche Arbeit, aber
5 auch um das Selbstbewußtsein° der Frau und um die Beziehungen° zwischen den Geschlechtern.

    Ein altes Klischee sagt, die Frau solle sich nur um „Kinder, Küche und Kirche" kümmern. Für manche Frauen mag das noch stimmen, aber für die meisten jungen Frauen nicht mehr. Es ist das Ziel der
10 Frauenbewegung, solche Klischees zu bekämpfen° und allen Frauen neue Wege zu eröffnen.° Heute versuchen viele Frauen, aus dieser traditionellen sozialen Rolle auszubrechen.

    In früheren Zeiten wurden fast alle jungen Mädchen auf eine Zukunft als Mutter und Hausfrau vorbereitet. Sie mußten früh lernen,
15 wie die „ideale" Frau sein sollte: bescheiden,° ordentlich und kinderlieb.° Dieses traditionelle Bild hatte sich nach und nach als selbstverständlich etabliert.°

    Im industriellen Zeitalter° wurde es aber immer deutlicher, daß die Industrie die Arbeitskraft° der Frau brauchte. Es waren die unge-
20 bildeten und armen Frauen aus der Arbeiterklasse, die in gefährlichen, ungesunden Fabriken arbeiten mußten, weil ihre Familien sonst verhungert° wären. Die Damen der Oberschicht° aber konnten zu Hause Herrin° sein, wo es ihre Aufgabe war, den Haushalt° zu führen und gesellschaftliche Unterhaltung° zu bieten. Natürlich gab es
25 schon im 18. und 19. Jahrhundert auch sehr gebildete und aktive

Glossar (Randspalte):
- sowohl . . . als auch = both . . . and
- self-esteem / relationships
- = kämpfen gegen
- = neue Chancen zu geben
- modest
- = lieb zu Kindern
- established
- = Epoche
- labor
- = an Hunger gestorben / = der oberen Klasse
- mistress / household
- entertainment

Rita Süssmuth (CDU), Präsidentin des Bundestags.

Frauen, wie z.B. Bettina von Arnim oder Rahel Varnhagen, die Berliner Salons führten.[5] Heutige° Frauen haben auch gelernt, die trotz aller Schwierigkeiten errungenen Leistungen° dieser früheren Frauengenerationen zu schätzen.°

30 Und wie ist es heute? Im Grundgesetz[6] der BRD (Artikel 3) steht zwar, daß alle Menschen vor dem Gesetz gleich seien. Männer und Frauen seien gleichberechtigt. Aber ist die offizielle Gleichberechtigung schon Wirklichkeit? Manche berufstätigen Frauen müssen noch die ganze Hausarbeit erledigen, obwohl sie den gleichen Arbeitstag 35 haben wie ihre Männer. Jeder Mensch, der so überfordert° ist, wird natürlich frustriert.

Trotzdem hat sich viel im Leben der Frauen geändert. Jungen Frauen stehen heute viel mehr Türen offen als vor fünfzig Jahren. Immer mehr Frauen nehmen aktiv und kritisch am öffentlichen 40 Leben ihres Landes teil. In der BRD haben Frauen führende Positionen in den Parteien und in der Regierung.

Viele Frauen wollen traditionelle Männerrollen nicht einfach übernehmen, sondern auch ändern. Die auch in Amerika bekannte

= **moderne**

errungenen Leistungen = gained achievements appreciate

overtaxed

---

[5] The novelist and essayist Bettina von Arnim (1785–1859) and the prolific letter writer Rahel Varnhagen von Ense (1771–1833) presided over influential literary salons in Berlin.

[6] The *Basic Law* or constitution of the Federal Republic of Germany.

Schriftstellerin Christa Wolf[7] schrieb über dieses Phänomen: „Die
45 Möglichkeit, die unsere Gesellschaft [den Frauen] gab: zu tun, was die
Männer tun, hat sie . . . zu der Frage gebracht: Was *tun* die Männer
überhaupt?° Und will ich das eigentlich?“

anyway, after all

Aber parallel zu den Verbesserungen° im Leben der Frau ändert
sich auch die Rolle des Mannes. Heute wollen viele Männer mehr
50 Zeit mit ihren Familien verbringen und sich weniger um Karriere und
Erfolg kümmern. Die Frauenemanzipation bringt also viel mehr als
nur bessere Berufschancen für Frauen. Sie könnte auch eines Tages zu
einem besseren Leben für beide Geschlechter führen.

improvements

Fragen zum Lesestück

1. Was sind die Ziele der Frauenbewegung?
2. Wie heißt das alte Klischee über das Leben der Frau?
3. Beschreiben Sie die traditionelle Rolle der Frau.
4. Wie wurde die soziale Rolle der Frau durch die Industrialisierung geändert?
5. Was für Frauen arbeiteten in den Fabriken?
6. Welche Möglichkeiten haben junge Frauen von heute, die die Frauen vor fünfzig Jahren nicht hatten?
7. Wie könnte die Frauenbewegung auch das Leben der Männer ändern?

Sophie Scholl (1921–1943): leader of Munich student resistance
to Hitler, executed with her brother Hans by the Nazis.
Nellie Sachs (1891–1970): poet, shared 1966 Nobel Prize for
Literature.
Hannah Arendt (1906–1975): German-born political theorist,
emigrated to the United States in 1941.

[7] The novelist and essayist Christa Wolf (b. 1929) is an important figure in the literary culture of the former East Germany. After unification she became the focus of a fierce debate
about the role of intellectuals in that state.

Situationen aus dem Alltag

Mit Gefühl!

Expressing feelings is a communicative goal.

Sie haben schon viele Ausdrücke gelernt, mit denen Sie Gefühle und Reaktionen ausdrücken können. Die folgende Liste wiederholt solche Ausdrücke aus früheren Kapiteln.

sich freuen (*die Freude*, joy)

Wunderbar!
Ich bin heute so glücklich!
Das ist ja wunderschön!
Ich gratuliere (dir)!
Ich bin begeistert!

Mitleid ausdrücken (*das Mitleid*, sympathy)

Das tut mir leid.
Gute Besserung!
Schade!
Du siehst traurig aus.
Was ist denn los?
Du Arme! Du Armer!

sich ärgern (*der Ärger*, annoyance, anger)

Ich habe die Nase voll.
So ein Mist!
Verflixt nochmal!
Ich bin frustriert!

enttäuscht sein (*die Enttäuschung*, disappointment)

Schade!
Ich habe Pech gehabt.
So ein Mist!

überrascht sein (*die Überraschung*, surprise)

Um Gottes Willen!
Mensch!
So was!
Ich bin ganz baff!
Ich bin erstaunt!

Angst haben

Ich habe Angst vor . . .
Ich fürchte . . .
Hilfe!

Gruppenarbeit: Mensch, bin ich . . . !

Diese Zeichnungen zeigen Menschen, die starke Gefühle haben. Beschreiben Sie die Emotion, die jedes Bild zeigt. (Es gibt natürlich verschiedene Möglichkeiten.)

Gruppendiskussion: Da war ich sehr aufgeregt.

Alle Menschen haben manchmal starke Gefühle. Beschreiben Sie eine Situation aus Ihrem Leben, in der Sie ein Gefühl von Ärger, Freude, Überraschung, Enttäuschung, Mitleid oder Angst gehabt haben.

BEISPIEL: Ich war einmal besonders überrascht, als . . .

Partnerarbeit: Mini-Dialoge

Unten werden verschiedene Situationen beschrieben. Erfinden Sie (*make up*) zu jeder Situation einen Mini-Dialog, in dem Sie Gefühle und Reaktionen aus- drücken. Spielen Sie dann einen von Ihren Dialogen vor der ganzen Klasse.

1. Sie wollen zusammen ausgehen. Ihre Freundin kann aber ihren Geldbeutel nicht finden.
2. Ein Partner ruft den anderen an und sagt, er müsse heute leider zu Hause bleiben, weil er plötzlich sehr krank geworden sei.
3. Ein Partner arbeitet für die Lotterie (*lottery*) und ruft den anderen an, um ihm zu gratulieren: Er habe DM 100 000 gewonnen.
4. Sie freuen sich schon seit Monaten auf eine Reise nach Spanien. Jetzt hören Sie plötzlich, daß die Reise nicht mehr stattfinden kann, weil die Reisegesellschaft (*travel agency*) bankrott (*bankrupt*) ist.
5. Sie verbringen einen langweiligen Nachmittag vor dem Fernseher, und plötzlich klingelt es. Sie gehen an die Haustür, und da steht Ihr Lieblingsonkel Max, den Sie seit vier Jahren nicht mehr gesehen haben.

Zum Schluß

Workbook Kap. 16, K.

Casablanca (1942) was directed by Austrian emigré Michael Curtiz. It starred Humphrey Bogart, Ingrid Bergman, and Claude Rains as well as the German emigrés Peter Lorre and Conrad Veidt.

Sprechen wir miteinander

Lab Manual Kap. 16, Diktat.

A Worum geht es?

Nennen Sie zuerst Filme oder Bücher, die Ihnen besonders gefallen. Dann sagen Sie bei jedem Werk, worum es geht.

BEISPIEL: Mein Lieblingsfilm heißt „Casablanca". In dem Film geht es um Liebe, aber auch um Politik.

B Gruppenarbeit: Was wird hier gemacht?

Sagen Sie, was auf diesen Bildern gemacht wird.

BEISPIEL: Hier werden Bücher gelesen. *oder*
Hier wird gelesen.

C Partnerarbeit: Rollenspiel

Wählen Sie eine Situation aus, und seien Sie bereit, sie vor der ganzen Klasse zu spielen.

1. **Abends um 18 Uhr**
   Margarete, die vor vier Monaten ein Baby bekommen hat, arbeitet wieder in ihrer alten Stelle. Ihr Mann Rolf schreibt an seiner Diss und bleibt bei dem Kleinen zu Hause. Margarete kommt nach einem harten Arbeitstag nach Hause.

2. **Umziehen oder hierbleiben?**
   Monika und Harald sind Studenten in ihrem letzten Semester an der Uni in München. Sie haben vor, bald zu heiraten. Harald hat gerade eine gut bezahlte Stelle an einem Gymnasium in Frankfurt bekommen. Monika hat noch keine Stelle gefunden, und sie will München nicht verlassen.

3. **Mutter und Tochter**
   Anita (19 Jahre alt) fragt ihre Mutter (50), wie es damals war, als sie jung war. Frau Baumann erzählt ihrer Tochter, was sie als junge Frau gern gemacht hätte, oder was sie heute anders machen würde.

D Klassendiskussion: Unterschiede und Ähnlichkeiten

1. Besprechen Sie einige Unterschiede und Ähnlichkeiten
   - in der Erziehung (*upbringing*) von Mädchen und Jungen.
   - im Leben von Studenten und Studentinnen an dieser Uni.

2. An einigen privaten Hochschulen in Amerika studieren *nur* Frauen (ohne Männer). Halten Sie das für gut? Warum oder warum nicht?

Schreiben Sie zu Hause

E Fernsehinterview Im Fernsehen gab es neulich ein Gespräch zwischen einem Interviewer und der bekannten Feministin Elisabeth Schmidt-Dengler. Lesen Sie diesen Bericht über das Interview, und schreiben Sie das Gespräch, das die beiden geführt haben, als Dialog.

Der Interviewer fragte Frau Schmidt-Dengler, wie lange sie wohl noch für die Emanzipation der Frau kämpfen müsse. Das sei schwer zu sagen, meinte sie. Sie werde einfach nicht aufgeben, bis alle Frauen gleichberechtigt seien. Der Interviewer unterbrach und sagte, daß die Gleichberechtigung schon seit Jahren im Grundgesetz stehe. Frau Schmidt-Dengler lachte und sagte, ja, das stimme schon, und das sei auch wichtig. Auf der anderen Seite seien das Grundgesetz und die Wirklichkeit leider oft zwei verschiedene Sachen. Die Frauenemanzipation dürfe nicht nur im Gesetz stehen. Man müsse auch das traditionelle Denken über die Rollen von Mann und Frau ändern. Der Interviewer dankte Frau Schmidt-Dengler für das Gespräch.

With this chapter you have completed the fourth quarter of **Neue Horizonte.** For a concise review of the grammar and idiomatic phrases in chapters 13–16, you may consult the **Zusammenfassung und Wiederholung 4** (*Summary and Review 4*) on pages 179–192 of your Workbook. The review section is followed by a self-correcting test.

F Aufsatzthemen

1. Für Studenten: Was wäre in Ihrem Leben anders, wenn Sie eine Frau wären?
   Für Studentinnen: Was wäre in Ihrem Leben anders, wenn Sie ein Mann wären?
2. Wählen Sie ein Thema aus der Klassendiskussion D (S. 485), und schreiben Sie darüber.

G Wie sagt man das auf deutsch?

1. Max told me that there was a new restaurant around the corner.
2. Yes, the food is supposed to be very good.
3. But the prices could be lower.
4. Max has eaten there three times already. He recommended it to me.

5. Did you ask Mimi whether she were coming to the wedding?
6. Yes, but she acted as if she had never heard about it.
7. Brigitte says she invited her last month.

8. Hello, Ruth! Why weren't you at Lina's birthday party on Friday night?
9. I'm sorry, but I was simply too tired.
10. You know, I've found a new job and I had a lot to attend to.
11. Too bad you missed it.
12. We celebrated until 3:30. (Use impersonal passive.)

VIDEOECKE

8 Ich bezahle das Abendessen! (32:33)

Katrin bezahlt das Essen.

Stefan und Katrin sind im Restaurant in Kreuzberg, einem Stadtteil Berlins, wo viele Türken leben. Stefan hat Katrin ein Halstuch (scarf) geschenkt, und sie dankt ihm dafür. Sie sprechen über die Türken, die sie heute auf dem Markt gesehen haben.

Sie schauen sich die Speisekarte an und bestellen dann etwas zu essen und zu trinken. Während der Mahlzeit kommt das Gespräch auf die Rolle der Frau. Katrin sagt, sie finde es normal, wenn Frauen nicht nur Kinder haben, sondern auch berufstätig sind. So habe es ihre Mutter gemacht.

Dann erzählen sie einander über ihre Ferienpläne. Katrin wird heute bei Su-Sin übernachten, denn sie fahren morgen zusammen in die Schweiz. Sie rufen den Kellner, um zu zahlen. Jeder möchte den anderen einladen (treat), aber endlich gibt Stefan nach (gives in) und läßt Katrin zahlen.

das **Getränk**, -e	*drink*
die **Rechnung**, -en	*bill, check*
die **Speise**, -n	*food, dish (menu item)*
die **Nachspeise**	= **der Nachtisch**
das **Tuch**, ¨er	*scarf*
jemand anders	*someone else*
Prost! (*or*) **Prosit!**	*Cheers!*
Wie kommt das?	*How come? What's the reason for that?*

A Was sehen Sie im Video?

Sehen Sie sich den Anfang des Abschnitts an (32:42–33:20). Hier sehen Sie den Kreuzberger Türkenmarkt am Maibachufer in Berlin. Kreuzen Sie in der Liste unten an, was Sie im Video sehen. Wenn Sie einen Preis sehen, schreiben Sie ihn auf.

_____ 1. Bananen
_____ 2. Würste
_____ 3. Äpfel
_____ 4. Salat
_____ 5. Brötchen
_____ 6. Gurken (*cucumbers*), Preis: DM _____
_____ 7. Orangen
_____ 8. Käse

B Wer macht das? Wer sagt das?

Now watch the rest of video Module 8 (33:21–36:46). Choose the person who does or says the following.

    a. Stefan   b. Katrin   c. der Kellner

1. _____ „Das letzte Mal hatte ich hier Eisbein mit Sauerkraut.“
2. _____ „Getränke vielleicht erstmal?“
3. _____ bestellt sich ein Knoblauchrippchen (*pork chop with garlic*) mit Salat und Zwiebelbrot.
4. _____ „Ich würd' den Apfelstrudel empfehlen.“
5. _____ trinkt Apollinaris (Mineralwasser).
6. _____ „Ich lade dich ein, zum Semesterabschluß.“

C Wie geht's weiter?

Wählen Sie die beste Möglichkeit, um jeden Satz zu vervollständigen (*complete*).

1. Das Tuch, das Stefan Katrin geschenkt hat, . . .
    a. ist ihr zu groß.
    b. gefällt ihr sehr.
    c. hat eine schöne rote Farbe.

2. Heute will Katrin das essen bezahlen, denn . . .
   a. Stefan hat kein Geld.
   b. es geht ihr um die Gleichberechtigung.
   c. das Essen war nicht sehr teuer.
3. Beide nehmen zum Nachtisch warmen Apfelstrudel, weil . . .
   a. es sonst nichts Gutes gibt.
   b. sie immer noch Riesenhunger haben.
   c. es ihnen der Kellner empfohlen hat.
4. Katrins Mutter hat den ganzen Tag gearbeitet, während Katrin . . .
   a. bei der Oma blieb.
   b. im Kindergarten war.
   c. in einer Fabrik arbeitete.

D Im Gespräch

For each sentence in the left column, find the appropriate response in the right column.

_____ 1. Heute abend möchte ich dich zum Abendessen einladen.

_____ 2. Was darf's denn sein?

_____ 3. Viele Gastarbeiter bleiben in der Bundesrepublik, nicht wahr?

_____ 4. Herr Ober, zahlen bitte!

_____ 5. Das macht zusammen D.M. 33,85 bitte.

a. Augenblick bitte, ich komme gleich.

b. Natürlich, viele sind sogar hier geboren.

c. Nee, heute bezahle _ich_ das Abendessen.

d. Nehmen Sie bitte fünfunddreißig.

e. Wir möchten zweimal Espresso und zwei Stück Apfelstrudel bestellen.

Legal Protection During Pregnancy and Maternity

The laws known collectively as **Mutterschutz** (*Maternity Protection*) are a good example of the extensive social services available to German citizens. In 1992 this safety net served as a model for all countries in the European Union.

Mutterschaftsgeld: A pregnant woman continues to receive the full amount of her previous pay (or disability pay, or a lump sum).

Mutterschaftsvorsorge: All expenses for prenatal care and delivery are covered.

Gefahrenschutz: A pregnant woman may not be forced to undertake tasks that would endanger her or her child.

Kündigungsschutz: A woman cannot be fired during her pregnancy or in the four months following delivery (eight months if she chooses to take maternity leave).

Beschäftigungsverbot: A pregnant woman cannot be forced to work in the six weeks prior to her delivery date, and may not work for eight weeks after delivery (twelve weeks for premature deliveries or multiple births).

Mutterschaftsurlaub: Maternity leave at reduced salary for up to four months may be taken after the 8–12 week protective period has expired. 93 percent of mothers take advantage of this leave to care for their newborn children.

Answer Key to *Videoecke* Exercises

Videoecke 1: *Ist das Zimmer noch frei?*

A. 1, 2, 4, 5, 6, 7, 8
B. 2, 3, 4, 7
C. 1. b;   2. c;   3. a;   4. b
D. 1. F;   2. R;   3. F;   4. F;   5. F;   6. R
E. 2, 3, 4, 5, 6, 7, 9, 11

Videoecke 2: *Ohne Frühstück geht's nicht!*

A. 1, 3, 4, 5, 6, 9
B. 2, 4, 5, 8
C. 1. b;   2. b;   3. c;   4. b;   5. b
D. 1. F;   2. R;   3. F;   4. R;   5. F;   6. F
E. 1. c;   2. b;   3. c;   4. c.;   5. c
F. 1, 4, 5, 6

Videoecke 3: *Wie war deine Vorlesung?*

A. 1, 2, 5, 6
B. 1. in der Uni-Bibliothek;   2. aus China (aus Beijing);   3. Mathematik (Mathe); 4. langweilig;   5. ins Kino gehen
C. 1. a;   2. c.;   3. c.;   4. b.;   5. b.; 6. c
D. 1. R;   2. F;   3. R;   4. F;   5. F; 6. R
E. 1. b;   2. d;   3. a;   4. e;   5. c

Videoecke 4: *Gehen wir doch einkaufen!*

A. 1, 2, 4, 7, 8
B. 1. b;   2. a;   3. c;   4. b;   5. a;   6. b; 7. d
C. 1 Pfund Brot (*500 grams—about 1 pound—of bread*), 100 g Leberwurst (*100 grams of liverwurst*), 200 g Käse (*200 grams of cheese*), eine Flasche Orangensaft (*1 bottle of orange juice*), 1 gegrilltes Hähnchen (*1 grilled chicken*)
D. 1. sonntags und montags;   2. um 7.00 Uhr;   3. am Samstag;   4. bis 18 Uhr
E. 1, 2, 3, 4, 5, 8

Videoecke 5: *Treibst du gern Sport?*

A. 1, 3, 4, 6
B. 1, 3, 5
C. 1. a;   2. d;   3. b;   4. b.;   5. c;   6. a
D. *Answers may vary.*
    1. schwarze / dunkle / lange Haare; eine graue Hose; einen roten Pulli
    2. weiße Schuhe; ein blaues Sweatshirt
    3. einen roten Mantel; einen weißen / hellen Pulli; kurze / graue Haare; 60 bis 70 Jahre alt; sieht sympathisch / freundlich aus
    4. einen roten Pulli; einen grauen Mantel
E. *Answers will vary.*

Videoecke 6: *Das vergesse ich nie.*

A. 1, 2, 4, 6, 7, 9, 10
B. 1. F;   2. R;   3. F;   4. F;   5. F;   6. R
C. 1. c;   2. b;   3. c;   4. b;   5. a;   6. d
D. 1. c;   2. b;   3. a;   4. c
E. 2, 3, 5, 7, 8

Videoecke 7: *Fährst du mit in die Schweiz?*

A. 1, 2, 3, 5, 6, 7
B. 1. c;   2. a;   3. b;   4. c
C. 1. a;   2. b;   3. c;   4. a;   5. b;   6. a
D. 1. c;   2. b;   3. a;   4. b;   5. a
E. 1. c;   2. e;   3. a;   4. d;   5. b

Videoecke 8: *Ich bezahle das Abendessen!*

A. 3; 5; 6 (Preis: DM 1,00 pro Stück); 7
B. 1. a;   2. c;   3. a;   4. c;   5. b;   6. a
C. 1. b;   2. b;   3. c;   4. b
D. 1. c;   2. e;   3. b;   4. a;   5. d

Principal Parts of Strong and Irregular Verbs

The following table contains the principal parts of all the strong, mixed, and irregular verbs in *Neue Horizonte*. With a few exceptions, only the basic stem verbs are listed, e.g., **fahren**, **bringen**, and **kommen**. Verbs formed by adding a prefix—e.g., **radfahren**, **verbringen**, and **ankommen**—change their stems in the same way as the basic verb.

infinitive	3rd person sing. present	simple past	perfect	English
anfangen	fängt an	fing an	hat angefangen	*begin*
beginnen		begann	hat begonnen	*begin*
bieten		bot	hat geboten	*offer*
bitten		bat	hat gebeten	*ask for, request*
bleiben		blieb	ist geblieben	*stay*
brechen	bricht	brach	hat gebrochen	*break*
bringen		brachte	hat gebracht	*bring*
denken		dachte	hat gedacht	*think*
dürfen	darf	durfte	hat gedurft	*may, be allowed to*
einladen	lädt ein	lud ein	hat eingeladen	*invite*
empfehlen	empfiehlt	empfahl	hat empfohlen	*recommend*
entscheiden		entschied	hat entschieden	*decide*
essen	ißt	aß	hat gegessen	*eat*
fahren	fährt	fuhr	ist gefahren	*drive*
fallen	fällt	fiel	ist gefallen	*fall*
finden		fand	hat gefunden	*find*
fliegen		flog	ist geflogen	*fly*
fließen		floß	ist geflossen	*flow*
geben	gibt	gab	hat gegeben	*give*
gehen		ging	ist gegangen	*go*
gewinnen		gewann	hat gewonnen	*win*
haben	hat	hatte	hat gehabt	*have*
halten	hält	hielt	hat gehalten	*hold, stop*
hängen[1]		hing	hat gehangen	*be hanging*
heißen		hieß	hat geheißen	*be called*
helfen	hilft	half	hat geholfen	*help*
kennen		kannte	hat gekannt	*know, be acquainted with*
klingen		klang	hat geklungen	*sound*
kommen		kam	ist gekommen	*come*
können	kann	konnte	hat gekonnt	*can, be able to*
lassen	läßt	ließ	hat gelassen	*leave; let; allow to; cause to be done*
laufen	läuft	lief	ist gelaufen	*run*

[1]When it is transitive, **hängen** is weak: **hängte, hat gehängt.**

infinitive	3rd person sing. present	simple past	perfect	English
leihen		lieh	hat geliehen	*lend*
lesen	liest	las	hat gelesen	*read*
liegen		lag	hat gelegen	*lie*
mögen	mag	mochte	hat gemocht	*like*
müssen	muß	mußte	hat gemußt	*must, have to*
nehmen	nimmt	nahm	hat genommen	*take*
nennen		nannte	hat genannt	*name, call*
raten	rät	riet	hat geraten	*guess*
rufen		rief	hat gerufen	*call, shout*
scheinen		schien	hat geschienen	*shine, seem*
schlafen	schläft	schlief	hat geschlafen	*sleep*
schlagen	schlägt	schlug	hat geschlagen	*hit, beat*
schließen		schloß	hat geschlossen	*close*
schneiden		schnitt	hat geschnitten	*cut*
schreiben		schrieb	hat geschrieben	*write*
schreien		schrie	hat geschrie(e)n	*shout, yell*
schweigen		schwieg	hat geschwiegen	*be silent*
schwimmen		schwamm	ist geschwommen	*swim*
sehen	sieht	sah	hat gesehen	*see*
sein	ist	war	ist gewesen	*be*
singen		sang	hat gesungen	*sing*
sitzen		saß	hat gesessen	*sit*
sollen	soll	sollte	hat gesollt	*should*
sprechen	spricht	sprach	hat gesprochen	*speak*
stehen		stand	hat gestanden	*stand*
stehlen	stiehlt	stahl	hat gestohlen	*steal*
steigen		stieg	ist gestiegen	*climb*
sterben	stirbt	starb	ist gestorben	*die*
tragen	trägt	trug	hat getragen	*carry, wear*
treffen	trifft	traf	hat getroffen	*meet*
treiben		trieb	hat getrieben	*drive, propel*
trinken		trank	hat getrunken	*drink*
tun		tat	hat getan	*do*
vergessen	vergißt	vergaß	hat vergessen	*forget*
vergleichen		verglich	hat verglichen	*compare*
verlassen	verläßt	verließ	hat verlassen	*leave*
verlieren		verlor	hat verloren	*lose*
verschwinden		verschwand	ist verschwunden	*disappear*
wachsen	wächst	wuchs	ist gewachsen	*grow*
waschen	wäscht	wusch	hat gewaschen	*wash*
werden	wird	wurde	ist geworden	*become*
werfen	wirft	warf	hat geworfen	*throw*
wiegen		wog	hat gewogen	*weigh*
wissen	weiß	wußte	hat gewußt	*know (a fact)*
wollen	will	wollte	hat gewollt	*want to*
ziehen		zog	hat/ist gezogen	*pull; move*

The following list contains all the words introduced in *Neue Horizonte* except for personal and relative pronouns, possessive adjectives, cardinal and ordinal numbers, and words glossed in the margins of the **Lesestücke**. The code at the end of each entry shows where the word or phrase is introduced in the text:

12-1	Kapitel 12, Wortschatz 1
9-2	Kapitel 9, Wortschatz 2
Einf.	Einführung (Introductory Chapter)
2-G	Kapitel 2, Grammatik
5-TLL	Kapitel 5, Tips zum Lesen und Lernen (*in the section* Leicht zu merken)
10-SA	Kapitel 10, Situationen aus dem Alltag
2-VID	Video segment following Kapitel 2

Strong and irregular verbs are listed with their principal parts: **nehmen (nimmt), nahm, hat genommen.** Weak verbs using **sein** as their auxiliary are shown by inclusion of the perfect: **reisen, ist gereist.**

Separable prefixes are indicated by a raised dot between prefix and verb stem: **ab·fahren.** This dot is *not* used in German spelling.

When a verb has a prepositional complement, the preposition follows all the principal parts. If it is a two-way preposition, the case it takes with this verb is indicated in parentheses: **teil·nehmen (nimmt teil), nahm teil, hat teilgenommen** *an* (+ *dat.*).

Adjectival nouns are indicated thus: der/die **Verwandte, -n.**

Masculine N-nouns like **der Student** and irregular nouns like **der Name** are followed by both the genitive singular and the plural endings: der **Student, -en, -en;** der **Name, -ns, -n.**

Adjectives followed by a hyphen may only be used attributively: **eigen-.**

If an adjective or adverb requires an umlaut in the comparative and superlative degrees, or if these forms are irregular, this is indicated in parentheses: **arm (ärmer); gern (lieber, am liebsten).**

The following abbreviations are used here and throughout *Neue Horizonte.*

acc.	accusative	*m.*	masculine
adj.	adjective	*neut.*	neuter
adj. noun	adjectival noun	*pers.*	person
adv.	adverb	*pl.*	plural
colloq.	colloquial	*prep.*	preposition
conj.	conjunction	*sing.*	singular
coor. conj.	coordinating conjunction	*sub. conj.*	subordinating conjunction
dat.	dative		
f.	feminine	*trans.*	transitive
gen.	genitive	*usw.*	(= und so weiter) etc.
intrans.	intransitive		

der **Abend, -e** evening, 7-2
   am Abend in the evening, 7-2
   Guten Abend! Good evening, *Einf.*
das **Abendessen, -** supper, evening meal, 8-1
   zum Abendessen for supper, 8-1
abends (in the) evenings, 5-2
aber (1) but (*coor. conj.*), 1-1; (2) (*flavoring particle*), 9-1
ab·fahren (fährt ab), fuhr ab, ist abgefahren to depart, leave (by vehicle), 7-1
ab·holen to pick up, fetch, get, 5-2
das **Abi** (*slang*) = **Abitur**, 5-1
das **Abitur** final secondary school examination, 5-1
das **Abteil, -e** railway compartment, 15-2
ach oh, ah, 2-1
das **Adjektiv, -e** adjective
der **Adler, -** eagle, 10-SA
die **Adresse, -n** address, 15-1
das **Adverb, -ien** adverb
ähnlich (+ *dat.*) similar (to), 3-2
   Sie ist ihrer Mutter ähnlich. She's like her mother.
die **Ähnlichkeit, -en** similarity, 11-2
die **Ahnung** notion, inkling, hunch
   (Ich habe) keine Ahnung. (I have) no idea. 10-1
aktiv active, 9-TLL
aktuell current, topical, 5-2
akut acute, 9-TLL
akzeptieren to accept, 15-1
alle (*pl.*) all; everybody, 2-2
allein alone, 4-1
alles everything, 6-2
der **Alltag** everyday life, 8-2
der **Almanach, -e** almanac
die **Alpen** (*pl.*) the Alps, 4-TLL
als (1) when (*sub. conj.*), 10-1; (2) as a, 5-1; (3) than (*with comparative degree*), 12-1

als ob (+ *subjunctive*) as if, as though, 16-1
also (1) well . . . 1-1; (2) thus, 3-2
alt (älter) old, 2-2
die **Alternative, -n** alternative, 2-TLL
altmodisch old-fashioned, 4-2
die **Altstadt, ⸚e** old city center, 8-TLL
(das) **Amerika** America, 3-2
der **Amerikaner, -** American (*m.*), 1-2
die **Amerikanerin, -nen** American (*f.*), 1-2
amerikanisch American, 3-2
an (*prep. + acc. or dat.*) to, toward; at, alongside of, 6-1
analysieren to analyze, 14-TLL
ander- other, different, 11-1
ändern to change (*trans.*), 11-2
   sich ändern to change (*intrans.*), 11-2
anders different, 2-2
die **Anekdote, -n** anecdote, 15-TLL
der **Anfang, ⸚e** beginning, 6-1
   am Anfang at the beginning, 6-1
an·fangen (fängt an), fing an, hat angefangen to begin, start, 5-1
der **Anfänger, -** beginner, 5-TLL
angenehm pleasant, 15-2; "pleasure to meet you," 13-SA
der/die **Angestellte, -n** (*adj. noun*) employee, 14-1
die **Anglistik** English studies, 6-SA
die **Angst, ⸚e** fear, 3-2
   Angst haben to be afraid, 3-2
   Angst haben vor (+ *dat.*) to be afraid of, 13-1
an·kommen, kam an, ist angekommen to arrive, 5-1
an·kommen auf (+ *acc.*) to depend on, be contingent on

Es kommt darauf an. It depends. 13-1
sich an·melden to register (at a hotel, at the university, etc.), 14-SA
an·rufen, rief an, hat angerufen to call up, 5-1
an·schauen to look at, 15-2
sich etwas an·sehen (sieht an), sah an, hat angesehen to take a look at something, 11-1
anstatt (*prep. + gen.*) instead of, 8-G
die **Antwort, -en** answer, 6-2
antworten (+ *dat.*) to answer (a person), 6-2
   antworten auf (+ *acc.*) to answer (something), respond to, 13-2
an·ziehen, zog an, hat angezogen to dress, 11-1
   sich anziehen to get dressed, 11-1
   sich etwas anziehen to put something on
der **Anzug, ⸚e** suit, 3-SA
die **Apotheke, -n** pharmacy, 8-SA
der **Appetit** appetite
   Guten Appetit! *Bon appétit!* Enjoy your meal! 8-SA
(der) **April** April, *Einf.*
die **Arbeit** work, 2-2
arbeiten to work, 1-1
   arbeiten an (+ *dat.*) to work on, 16-1
der **Arbeiter, -** worker (*m.*), 5-2
die **Arbeiterin, -nen** worker (*f.*)
arbeitslos unemployed, 10-2
die **Arbeitslosigkeit** unemployment, 10-2
das **Arbeitszimmer, -** study, 15-SA
der **Ärger** annoyance, anger, 16-SA
ärgern to annoy; offend, 8-2
   sich ärgern (über + *acc.*) to get annoyed (at), be annoyed (about), 13-2

der **Arm, -e** arm, 10-2

arm (ärmer) poor, 10-1

die **Armbanduhr, -en** wrist watch

die **Arroganz** arrogance, 15-TLL

der **Artikel, -** article, 2-1

der **Arzt, ¨e** doctor (*m.*), 5-SA; 11-1

die **Ärztin, -nen** doctor (*f.*), 5-SA; 11-1

der **Aspekt, -e** aspect, 8-TLL

das **Atom, -e** atom, 9-TLL

das **Atomkraftwerk** atomic power plant, 9-2

auch also, too, 1-1

auf (*prep. + acc. or dat.*) onto; on, upon, on top of, 6-1

die **Aufgabe, -n** task, assignment, 16-2

auf·geben (gibt auf), gab auf, hat aufgegeben (*trans. & intrans.*) to give up, quit, 11-2

auf·hängen to hang up, 7-1

auf·hören (mit) to cease, stop (doing something), 5-1

auf·machen to open, 5-1

auf·passen to pay attention; to look out, 10-VID; 16-1

auf·passen auf (+ *acc.*) to look after, 16-1

auf·räumen to tidy up, straighten up, 13-1

sich auf·regen (über + acc.) to get upset (about), get excited (about), 15-1

der **Aufsatz, ¨e** essay

das **Aufsatzthema, -themen** essay topic

auf·stehen, stand auf, ist aufgestanden (1) to stand up; to get up; (2) to get out of bed, 4-VID; 5-1

auf·wachen, ist aufgewacht to wake up (*intrans.*), 7-1

auf·wachsen (wächst auf), wuchs auf, ist aufgewachsen to grow up, 13-2

das **Auge, -n** eye, 11-1

der **Augenblick, -e** moment, 12-1

(Einen) Augenblick, bitte. Just a moment, please. 12-1

im Augenblick at the moment, 12-1

(der) **August** August, *Einf.*

aus (*prep. + dat.*) out of; from, 5-1

aus·brechen (bricht aus), brach aus, ist ausgebrochen to break out

der **Ausdruck, ¨e** expression

der **Ausflug, ¨e** outing, excursion, 14-2

aus·geben (gibt aus), gab aus, hat ausgegeben to spend (money), 6-2

aus·gehen, ging aus, ist ausgegangen to go out, 14-1

ausgezeichnet excellent, 8-1

sich aus·kennen, kannte aus, hat ausgekannt to know one's way around, 13-1

die **Auskunft** information, 13-1

das **Ausland** (*sing.*) foreign countries, 7-2

im Ausland abroad (*location*), 7-2

ins Ausland abroad (*destination*), 7-2

der **Ausländer, -** foreigner (*m.*), 15-1

die **Ausländerin, -nen** foreigner (*f.*), 15-1

ausländisch foreign, 10-2

aus·packen to unpack, 11-SA

aus·sehen (sieht aus), sah aus, hat ausgesehen to appear, look (like), 5-2

außer (*prep. + dat.*) besides; in addition to, 5-1

außerdem (*adv.*) besides, in addition, 14-2

aus·steigen, stieg aus, ist ausgestiegen to get out (of a vehicle), 7-2

die **Ausstellung, -en** exhibition, 10-2

der **Austauschstudent, -en, -en** exchange student, 6-1

aus·wandern, ist ausgewandert to emigrate, 11-2

der **Ausweis, -e** I.D. card, 6-2

aus·ziehen, zog aus, ist ausgezogen to move out, 6-1

sich ausziehen to get undressed, 11-1

das **Auto, -s** car, 2-2

die **Autobahn, -en** expressway, high-speed highway, 7-SA

automatisch automatic, 6-TLL

der **Automechaniker, -** auto mechanic, 5-1

der **Autostop** hitchhiking

per Autostop reisen to hitchhike, 7-2

B

das **Baby, -s** baby, 16-1

der **Bäcker, -** baker, 5-1

die **Bäckerei, -en** bakery, 5-1

das **Bad** bath, 14-1

ein Bad nehmen to take a bath, 14-1

sich baden to take a bath, 11-SA

das **Badezimmer, -** bathroom, 14-1

baff sein to be flabbergasted, speechless, 13-1

die **Bahn** railroad, railway system, 7-2

der **Bahnhof, ¨e** train station, 7-1

bald soon, 3-1

die **Banane, -n** banana, 12-VID

die **Bank, ¨e** bench, 10-1

die **Bank, -en** bank, 14-1

der **Bär, -en, -en** bear, 10-SA

barbarisch barbaric, 4-TLL

das **Bargeld** cash, 14-VID

die **Barriere, -n** barrier, 13-TLL

die **Basis** basis, 9-TLL

bauen to build, 8-2

der **Bauer, -n, -n** farmer, 5-1

das **Bauernbrot** dark bread, 5-1

der **Baum, ⸚e** tree, 4-2

der **Beamte, -n** (*adj. noun*) official, civil servant (*m.*), 11-1

die **Beamtin, -nen** official, civil servant (*f.*), 11-1

bedeuten to mean, signify, 1-2

die **Bedeutung, -en** meaning, significance, 10-2

sich beeilen to hurry, 11-1

begeistert von enthusiastic about, 14-2

die **Begeisterung** enthusiasm, 11-1

beginnen, begann, hat begonnen to begin, 4-1

behalten (behält), behielt, hat behalten to keep, retain, 12-1

bei (*prep. + dat.*) (1) at the home of; near; at, 5-1; (2) during, while -ing, 11-G

beid- (*adj.*) both, 11-2

beide (*pl. pronoun*) both (people), 14-2

beides (*sing. pronoun*) both things, 13-2

das **Bein, -e** leg, 11-1

das **Beispiel, -e** example, 9-2
   zum Beispiel for example, 1-2

bekannt known; well known, 10-2

der/die **Bekannte, -n** (*adj. noun*) acquaintance, friend, 11-1

bekommen, bekam, hat bekommen to receive, get, 4-1

belegen to take (a university course), 6-2

benutzen to use, 7-2

bequem comfortable, 7-2

bereit prepared, ready, 9-2

der **Berg, -e** mountain, 3-1

bergig mountainous, 4-SA

berichten to report, 5-2

der **Beruf, -e** profession, vocation, 2-2

Was sind Sie von Beruf? What is your profession? 5-SA

berufstätig employed, 2-2

berühmt famous, 11-2

beschreiben, beschrieb, hat beschrieben to describe, 4-2

besitzen, besaß, hat besessen to own, 2-2

besonders especially, 5-2

besorgt worried, concerned, 10-1

besprechen (bespricht), besprach, hat besprochen to discuss, 3-2

besser better, 12-G

die **Besserung**
   Gute Besserung! Get well soon! 11-1

best- best, 12-G

bestellen to order, 8-1

bestimmt certainly, surely, 10-VID

der **Besuch, -e** visit, 12-1

besuchen to visit, 3-1

die **Betriebswirtschaft** management, business, 6-SA

das **Bett, -en** bed, 2-VID; 6-1
   ins Bett gehen to go to bed, 7-1

bevor (*sub. conj.*) before, 10-2

bezahlen to pay, 6-2

die **Bibliothek, -en** library, 6-1

das **Bier, -e** beer, 4-2

bieten, bot, hat geboten to offer; to provide, 16-2

das **Bild, -er** picture; image, 5-2

billig inexpensive, cheap, 6-2

die **Biologie** biology, 6-SA

bis (*prep. + acc.*) until, *Einf.*; by, 1-1
   bis dann until then, 1-1

ein bißchen a little; a little bit; a little while, 3-1

bitte (sehr) (1) you're welcome, 2-1; (2) please, 3-2; (3) here it is, there you are, 5-1

bitten, bat, hat gebeten um to ask for, request, 13-1
   Er bittet mich um das Geld. He's asking me for the money.

blau blue, 3-2

bleiben, blieb, ist geblieben to stay, remain, 2-2

der **Bleistift, -e** pencil, *Einf.*

blitzschnell quick as lightning, 3-2

blöd dumb, stupid, 5-1

die **Blume, -n** flower, 11-1

die **Bluse, -n** blouse, 3-SA

böse (*+ dat.*) angry, mad (at); bad, evil, 13-1

boxen to box, 9-SA

brauchen to need, 2-1

braun brown, 3-2

die **BRD** (= **Bundesrepublik Deutschland**) the FRG (= the Federal Republic of Germany), 2-2

brechen (bricht), brach, hat gebrochen to break, 11-1

die **Brezel, -n** soft pretzel, 5-1

der **Brief, -e** letter, 6-2

der **Briefkasten, ⸚** mailbox, 15-1

die **Briefmarke, -n** postage stamp, 15-1

der **Briefträger, -** letter carrier, mailman, 5-TLL

die **Brille** (*sing.*) (eye)glasses, 3-SA

bringen, brachte, hat gebracht to bring, 6-1

das **Brot, -e** bread, 5-1

das **Brötchen, -** roll, 4-1

die **Brücke, -n** bridge, 8-SA; 11-2

der **Bruder, ⸚** brother, 2-1

das **Buch, ⸚er** book, *Einf.*

buchen to book (a flight, hotel, etc.), 14-VID

das **Bücherregal, -e** bookcase, 6-SA

die **Buchhandlung, -en** bookstore, 5-2

die **Bude, -n** (rented) student room, 6-2

der **Bummel, -** stroll, walk, 8-1
  einen Bummel machen to take a stroll, 8-1
das **Bundesland, ¨er** federal state (in Germany and Austria)
die **Bundesrepublik Deutschland** the Federal Republic of Germany, 2-2
bunt colorful, multicolored, 3-2
der **Bürger, -** citizen, 6-2
das **Büro, -s** office, 1-1
der **Bus, -se** bus, 7-SA
die **Butter** butter, 4-VID; 8-SA

C

das **Café, -s** café, 8-SA
campen to camp, 5-TLL
die **CD, -s** CD (compact disk), 6-SA
  der **CD-Spieler** CD player
die **Chance, -n** chance, 9-2
der **Chef, -s** boss (*m.*), 5-1
die **Chefin, -nen** boss (*f.*), 5-1
die **Chemie** chemistry, 6-SA
(das) **China** China, 11-TLL
der **Chinese, -n, -n** Chinese (*m.*), 11-TLL
die **Chinesin, -nen** Chinese (*f.*), 11-TLL
chinesisch Chinese (*adj.*), 11-TLL
der **Computer, -** computer, 6-SA; 12-1
der **Container, -** container, 9-1

D

da (1) there, 1-1; (2) then, in that case, 9-1; (3) since (*sub. conj., causal*), 8-G
  da drüben over there, 2-1
dabei sein to be present, be there, 15-1
dahin: Wie komme ich dahin? How do I get there? 13-1
damals at that time, back then, 10-1
die **Dame, -n** lady, 10-2

danach (*adv.*) after that, 14-VID
der **Dank** thanks
  vielen Dank thanks a lot, 2-1
danke thanks, thank you, *Einf.*; 1-1
  Danke, gleichfalls. You too. Same to you. *Einf.*; 12-1
danken (+ *dat.*) to thank, 7-1
  Nichts zu danken! Don't mention it! 2-1
dann then, 1-1
darum therefore, for that reason, 3-2
das sind (*pl. of* **das ist**) those are, 2-2
daß that (*sub. conj.*), 8-1
dauern to last; to take (time), 10-1
die **DDR (= Deutsche Demokratische Republik)** the GDR (= the German Democratic Republic), 11-1.
die **Decke, -n** blanket, 12-VID
die **Demokratie, -n** democracy, 10-TLL
demokratisch democratic, 10-TLL
die **Demokratisierung** democratization, 11-TLL
die **Demonstration, -en** demonstration, 11-TLL
demonstrieren to demonstrate, 9-TLL
denken, dachte, hat gedacht to think, 13-2
  denken an (+ *acc.*) to think of, 13-2
das **Denkmal, ¨er** monument, 12-2
denn (1) (*flavoring particle in questions*), 2-1; (2) (*coor. conj.*) for, because, 7-G
desto *see* **je . . . desto**
deutlich clear, 16-2
deutsch German, 2-2
  auf deutsch in German, 1-2
(das) **Deutsch** German language, 3-2
der/die **Deutsche, -n** (*adj. noun*) German (person), 1-2

die **Deutsche Demokratische Republik** German Democratic Republic (GDR), 11-1
die **Deutsche Mark (DM)** German mark, 5-1
(das) **Deutschland** Germany, 1-2
die **Deutschstunde, -n** German class, 3-1
(der) **Dezember** December, *Einf.*
der **Dialekt, -e** dialect, 13-TLL
der **Dialog, -e** dialogue
der **Dichter, -** poet
(der) **Dienstag** Tuesday, *Einf.*
dieser, -es, -e; (*pl.*) **diese** this, these, 5-1
diesmal this time, 12-1
das **Ding, -e** thing, 7-2
direkt direct(ly), 12-1
der **Direktor, -en** director, 10-TLL
die **Diskussion, -en** discussion, 2-2
diskutieren to discuss, 15-2
die **Diss** (*university slang*) dissertation, 16-1
die **Dissertation, -en** dissertation, 16-1
DM *see* **Deutsche Mark**
doch (1) (*stressed, contradictory*) yes I do, yes I am, yes he is, etc., 3-1; (2) (*unstressed flavoring particle with commands*), 4-1; (3) (*unstressed flavoring particle with statements*), 10-1
die **Doktorarbeit, -en** dissertation, 16-1
der **Dom, -e** cathedral, 8-1
(der) **Donnerstag** Thursday, *Einf.*
das **Doppelzimmer, -** double room, 14-1
das **Dorf, ¨er** village, 5-2
dort there, 2-1
die **Dose, -n** (tin) can, 9-2
draußen outside, 1-1

dreckig (*colloq.*) dirty, 9-1

dritt- third, 9-G

drüben over there, 2-1

dumm (dümmer) dumb, 5-1

dunkel dark, 3-2

durch (*prep. + acc.*) through, 4-1

dürfen (darf), durfte, hat gedurft may, to be allowed to, 3-1

Was darf es sein? What'll it be? May I help you? 5-1

der **Durst** thirst

Durst haben to be thirsty, 8-1

die **Dusche, -n** shower, 14-1

sich duschen to take a shower, 11-SA

die **Dynastie, -n** dynasty, 14-TLL

E

echt? (*slang*) really? 6-VID

die **Ecke, -n** corner, 8-2

an der Ecke at the corner, 8-2

um die Ecke around the corner, 8-2

egal wo, wer, warum usw. no matter where, who, why, etc., 7-2

Das ist (mir) egal. It doesn't matter (to me). I don't care. 7-1

das **Ehepaar, -e** married couple, 14-1

ehrlich honest, 3-2

das **Ei, -er** egg, 4-VID; 8-SA

eigen- own, 9-2

eigentlich actually, in fact, 3-2

die **Eile** hurry

in Eile in a hurry, 1-1

einander (*pronoun*) each other, 1-2

der **Eindruck, ⁀e** impression, 8-2

einfach simple, easy, 5-1

einige some, 6-2

ein·kaufen to shop for; to go shopping, 5-2

ein·laden (lädt ein), lud ein, hat eingeladen to invite, 8-1

einmal once, 4-1

noch einmal once again, once more, 4-1

eins one, 1-2

ein·schlafen (schläft ein), schlief ein, ist eingeschlafen to fall asleep, 7-1

ein·steigen, stieg ein, ist eingestiegen to get in (a vehicle), 7-2

der **Einstieg, -e** entrance, way in

einverstanden Agreed. It's a deal. O.K. 5-1

ein·wandern, ist eingewandert to immigrate, 11-2

ein·werfen (wirft ein), warf ein, hat eingeworfen to throw in; to mail (a letter), 15-1

das **Einzelzimmer, -** single room, 14-1

ein·ziehen, zog ein, ist eingezogen to move in, 6-1

einzig- single, only, 12-2

das **Eis** (1) ice; (2) ice cream, 8-SA

das **Eishockey** ice hockey, 9-SA

der **Elefant, -en, -en** elephant, 10-SA

elegant elegant, 8-TLL

die **Elektrizität** electricity, 9-TLL

die **Elektrotechnik** electrical engineering, 6-SA

der **Elektrotechniker, -** electrician; electrical engineer (*m.*), 5-SA

die **Elektrotechnikerin, -nen** electrician; electrical engineer (*f.*), 5-SA

die **Eltern** (*pl.*) parents, 2-1

die **Emanzipation** emancipation, 16-TLL

empfehlen (empfiehlt), empfahl, hat empfohlen to recommend, 8-VID; 9-1

das **Ende, -n** end, 6-2

am Ende at the end, 6-1

Ende Februar at the end of February, 6-2

zu Ende sein to end, be finished, be over, 10-2

endlich finally, 1-1

die **Energie, -n** energy, 9-TLL

der **Engländer, -** Englishman, 11-TLL

die **Engländerin, -nen** Englishwoman, 11-TLL

englisch English, 11-TLL

(das) **Englisch** English language, 3-2

der **Enkel, -** grandson, 12-VID

enorm enormous, 9-TLL

entscheiden, entschied, hat entschieden to decide, 3-2

Entschuldigung! Pardon me! Excuse me. 1-1

enttäuschen to disappoint, 6-2

die **Enttäuschung, -en** disappointment, 16-SA

entweder . . . oder either . . . or, 14-1

die **Epoche, -n** epoch, 10-TLL

die **Erdbeermarmelade** strawberry jam, 4-VID

die **Erde** earth, 12-2

das **Erdgeschoß** ground floor, first floor, 14-2 (*see* **Stock**)

die **Erfahrung, -en** experience, 12-SA

erfinden, erfand, hat erfunden to invent

der **Erfolg, -e** success, 16-2

erfreut pleased

Sehr erfreut. Pleased to meet you. 13-SA

sich erholen (von) (1) to recover (from), get well; (2) to have a rest, 13-2

erinnern an (*+ acc.*) to remind of, 12-1

sich erinnern an (*+ acc.*) to remember, 12-1

die **Erinnerung, -en** memory, 12-1

sich erkälten to catch a cold, 11-1

erklären to explain, 10-2

erledigen to attend to, take care of, finish, 16-2

die **Ermäßigung, -en** discount, 14-VID

ernst serious, 14-2

etwas ernst nehmen to take something seriously, 14-2

erst (*adv.*) not until; only, 5-1

erst- (*adj.*) first, 9-G

erstaunlich astounding, 9-2

erwarten to expect, 14-2

erzählen to tell, recount, 6-2

die **Erzählung, -en** story, narrative, 12-2

der **Esel, -** donkey, 10-SA

das **Essen** food; meal, 2-2

essen (ißt), aß, hat gegessen to eat, 2-1

das **Eßzimmer, -** dining room, 15-SA

etwas (1) (*pronoun*) something, 3-1; (2) (*adj. & adv.*) some, a little; somewhat, 12-1

(das) **Europa** Europe, 3-2

der **Europäer, -** European, 3-2

europäisch European, 11-2

existieren to exist, 11-TLL

extrem extreme, 10-TLL

F

die **Fabrik, -en** factory, 5-2

das **Fach, ¨er** area of study; subject, 6-SA

fahren (fährt), fuhr, ist gefahren to drive, go (by vehicle), 3-1

die **Fahrkarte, -n** ticket (for bus, train, streetcar, etc.), 7-2

das **Fahrrad, ¨er** bicycle, 8-2

die **Fahrt, -en** trip, ride, 15-2

fallen (fällt), fiel, ist gefallen (1) to fall; (2) to die in battle, 10-1

falsch false, incorrect, wrong, *Einf.*; 15-2

die **Familie, -n** family, 2-1

die **Farbe, -n** color, 3-2

fast almost, 2-2

faul lazy, 5-2

(der) **Februar** February, *Einf.*

fehlen to be missing; to be absent, 10-1

die **Feier, -n** celebration, party, 15-1

feiern to celebrate, 6-2

das **Fenster, -** window, *Einf.*

die **Ferien** (*pl.*) (university and school) vacation, 6-2

fern distant, far away, 12-2

fern·sehen (sieht fern), sah fern, hat ferngesehen to watch TV, 5-2

der **Fernseher, -** television set, 2-2

fertig (mit) (1) done, finished (with); (2) ready, 5-1

der **Film, -e** film, movie, 6-TLL

finanzieren to finance, 6-TLL

finden, fand, hat gefunden to find, 2-2

Das finde ich auch. I think so, too. 3-2

der **Finger, -** finger, 11-1

die **Firma, die Firmen** firm, company, 13-2

der **Fisch, -e** fish, 9-2

fit in shape, *Einf.*; 3-1

flach flat, 4-2

die **Flasche, -n** bottle, 7-1; 8-VID

das **Fleisch** meat, 2-1

fleißig industrious, hardworking, 5-2

fliegen, flog, ist geflogen to fly, 1-1

fließen, floß, ist geflossen to flow, 4-2

der **Flughafen, ¨** airport, 7-SA

das **Flugzeug, -e** airplane, 7-2

der **Fluß, die Flüsse** river, 4-2

folgen, ist gefolgt (+ *dat.*) to follow, 9-2

die **Form, -en** form, 10-TLL

formell formal, 1-TLL

formulieren to formulate

der **Fortschritt, -e** progress, 9-1

das **Foto, -s** photograph, 6-TLL; 7-2

ein Foto machen to take a picture, 7-2

die **Frage, -n** question, 2-1

eine Frage stellen to ask a question, 10-2

der **Fragebogen** questionnaire

fragen to ask, 1-1

fragen nach to inquire, ask about, 8-SA

sich fragen to wonder, ask oneself, 15-1

(das) **Frankreich** France, 5-2

der **Franzose, -n, -n** Frenchman, 11-TLL

die **Französin, -nen** Frenchwoman, 11-TLL

französisch French, 5-2

die **Frau, -en** woman; wife, 1-1

Frau Kuhn Mrs./Ms. Kuhn, *Einf.*

das **Fräulein, -** young (unmarried) woman

Fräulein Schmidt Miss Schmidt, *Einf.*

frei free; unoccupied, 2-1

die **Freiheit, -en** freedom, 7-2

(der) **Freitag** Friday, *Einf.*

die **Freizeit** free time, leisure time, 5-2

fremd (1) strange; (2) foreign, 3-2

die **Fremdsprache, -n** foreign language, 3-2

die **Freude, -n** joy, 12-2

freuen

Das freut mich. I'm glad. *Einf.*

(Es) freut mich. Pleased to meet you. *Einf.*; 13-SA

sich freuen to be happy, 11-1

sich freuen auf (+ *acc.*) to look forward to, 13-1

der **Freund, -e** friend (*m.*), 2-1

die **Freundin, -nen** friend (*f.*), 3-1

freundlich friendly, 1-2

der **Frieden**   peace, 6-2
frisch   fresh, 5-1
froh   happy, glad, 13-2
früh   early, 3-1
der **Frühling**   spring, 4-2
das **Frühstück**   breakfast, 4-1
  zum Frühstück   for
    breakfast, 4-1
frühstücken   to eat breakfast,
  4-1
frustrieren   to frustrate, 16-2
sich **fühlen**   to feel (*intrans.*),
  11-1
führen   to lead, 9-2
für (*prep. + acc.*)   for, 1-1
furchtbar   terrible, *Einf.*
fürchten   to fear, 11-1
der **Fuchs**, ⸚e   fox, 10-SA
der **Fuß**, ⸚e   foot, 3-2
  zu Fuß   on foot, 3-2
der **Fußball**   soccer;
    soccer ball, 5-2
der **Fußgänger**, -   pedestrian,
  8-2
die **Fußgängerzone**, -n
    pedestrian zone, 8-2

G

die **Gabel**, -n   fork, 8-SA
ganz   entire, whole, 9-1
  ganz gut   pretty good, 1-1
  den ganzen Sommer (Tag,
    Nachmittag usw.)   all
    summer (day, afternoon,
    etc.)
gar
  gar nicht   not at all, 3-2
  gar kein   no . . . at all, not a
    . . . at all, 8-2
die **Garage**, -n   garage, 15-SA
der **Garten**, ⸚   garden, 2-VID;
  15-SA
der **Gast**, ⸚e   guest; patron, 8-1
der **Gastarbeiter**, -   foreign
    worker (*m.*), 15-1
die **Gastarbeiterin**, -nen
    foreign worker (*f.*), 15-1
das **Gebäude**, -   building, 8-1
geben (gibt), gab, hat gegeben
    to give, 2-2

es gibt (+ *acc.*)   there is,
    there are, 2-2
gebildet   educated, 16-2
das **Gebirge**, -   mountain range,
  4-TLL
geboren   born
  Wann sind Sie geboren?
    When were you born? 10-1
der **Geburtstag**, -e   birthday, 9-1
  Wann hast du Geburtstag?
    When is your birthday?
    Einf.
  zum Geburtstag   for (one's)
    birthday, 9-1
der **Gedanke**, -ns, -n   thought,
  16-2
das **Gedicht**, -e   poem
die **Geduld**   patience, 14-VID
die **Gefahr**, -en   danger, 9-2
gefährlich   dangerous, 9-2
gefallen (gefällt), gefiel, hat
    gefallen (+ *dat. of person*)
    to please, appeal to, 7-1
das **Gefühl**, -e   feeling, 9-1
gegen (*prep. + acc.*)
    (1) against, (2) around,
    about (*with time*), 4-1
die **Gegend**, -en   area, region,
  12-1
der **Gegensatz**, ⸚e   opposite
der **Gegenteil: im Gegenteil**
    on the contrary, 8-2
die **Gegenwart**   present (time),
  12-SA; 14-2
gehen, ging, ist gegangen
    (1) to go; (2) to walk, 1-1
  Es geht.   It's all right. 4-1
  Es geht nicht.   Nothing
    doing. It can't be done.
  es geht um   it's a question of
    . . . ; it's about . . . (*subject
    is always es*), 16-2
  Wie geht es Ihnen/dir?   How
    are you? *Einf.*
  Wie geht's?   How are you?
    Einf.
gehören (+ *dat. of person*)   to
    belong to (a person), 7-1
gelb   yellow, 3-2
das **Geld**   money, 2-2

der **Geldbeutel**, -   wallet,
    change purse, 10-1; 10-VID
die **Gelegenheit**, -en
    opportunity, chance, 14-2
das **Gemüse**   vegetables, 2-1
gemütlich   cozy, comfortable;
    quiet, relaxed, 14-2
genau   exact, precise, 11-1
genauso . . . wie   just as . . . as,
  12-G
die **Generation**, -en
    generation, 8-TLL
genug   enough, 3-1
die **Geographie**   geography,
  4-TLL
geographisch   geographical,
  4-TLL
das **Gepäck**   luggage, 7-1
gerade   just, at this moment, 6-2
geradeaus   straight ahead, 8-2
die **Germanistik**   German
    studies, 6-SA
gern(e) (lieber, am liebsten)
    gladly, with pleasure,
    2-VID; 4-1
  etwas gern haben   to like
    something, 4-1
  gern + *verb*   like to, 4-1
  lieber + *verb*   prefer to,
    would rather, 4-1
  Lieber nicht.   I'd rather not.
    No thanks. Let's not. 4-1
das **Geschäft**, -e   business;
    store, 5-2
die **Geschäftsfrau**, -en
    businesswoman, 5-SA
der **Geschäftsmann**, die
    Geschäftsleute
    businessman, 5-SA
das **Geschenk**, -e   present
    (*gift*), 9-1
die **Geschichte**, -n   (1) story;
    (2) history, 6-2
das **Geschlecht**, -er   sex,
    gender, 16-2
geschlossen   closed (*see*
    schließen), 11-2
die **Geschwister** (*pl.*)   siblings,
  2-SA
die **Gesellschaft**, -en   society,
  9-2

gesellschaftlich   social, 16-2

das **Gesetz, -e**   law, 16-2

  vor dem Gesetz   under the law, in the eyes of the law, 16-2

das **Gesicht, -er**   face, 11-1

das **Gespräch, -e**   conversation, 13-2

gestern   yesterday, 6-1

  gestern abend   yesterday evening, 12-G

  gestern früh   yesterday morning, 12-G

gesund   healthy, 9-2

die **Gesundheit**   health, 9-2

das **Getränk, -e**   drink, 16-VID

gewinnen, gewann, hat gewonnen   to win, 9-SA

sich gewöhnen an (+ *acc.*)   to get used to, 13-1

das **Glas, ̈er**   glass, 8-1

glauben (+ *dat. of person*) (1) to believe; (2) to think, 4-1

  Ich glaube nicht.   I don't think so. 8-1

  Ich glaube schon.   I think so. 8-1

gleich   (1) right away, immediately, 5-1; (2) equal, 16-2

gleichberechtigt   enjoying equal rights, 16-2

die **Gleichberechtigung** (*sing.*) equal rights, 16-2

das **Gleis, -e**   track, 7-1

das **Glück**   (1) happiness; (2) luck, 6-2

  Glück haben   to be lucky, 6-2

glücklich   happy, *Einf.*

der **Glückwunsch: Herzlichen Glückwunsch!** Congratulations! Best wishes! 12-VID

golden   golden, 16-1

  die **goldene Hochzeit** golden wedding anniversary, 16-1

der **Gott, ̈er**   god

  Gott sei Dank   thank goodness, 4-1

Grüß Gott   hello (in southern Germany and Austria), *Einf.*

Um Gottes Willen!   For heaven's sake! Oh my gosh! 3-1

das **Gramm**   gram, 8-1

die **Grammatik**   grammar

gratulieren   (+ *dat. of person*) to congratulate, 15-1

grau   gray, 3-2

grausam   terrible, gruesome; cruel, 12-2

die **Grenze, -n**   border, 11-1

(das) **Griechenland**   Greece, 15-1

griechisch   Greek, 8-1

groß (größer, am größten) big, tall, 2-1

die **Größe, -n**   size; greatness, 12-1

die **Großeltern** (*pl.*) grandparents, 2-2

die **Großmutter, ̈** grandmother, 2-2

die **Großstadt, ̈e**   large city (over 500,000 inhabitants), 8-2

der **Großvater, ̈**   grandfather, 2-2

grün   green, 3-2

der **Grund, ̈e**   reason

die **Gruppe, -n**   group, 1-2

grüßen   to greet, say hello, 1-2

  Grüß Gott   hello (in southern Germany and Austria), *Einf.*

gut (besser, am besten)   good, well, *Einf.*; 1-1

  ganz gut   pretty good, 1-1

  Guten Abend!   Good evening! *Einf.*

  Guten Morgen!   Good morning! *Einf.*

  Gute Reise!   Have a good trip! 1-1

  Guten Tag!   Hello! *Einf.*

  Ist gut. (*colloq.*)   OK. Fine by me. 5-1

das **Gymnasium, die Gymnasien** secondary school (prepares pupils for university), 3-2

H

das **Haar, -e**   hair, 6-2

  sich die Haare kämmen   to comb one's hair, 11-SA

haben (hat), hatte, hat gehabt to have, *Einf.*; 2-1

  Ich hätte gern . . .   I'd like to have . . . 6-VID

der **Hafen, ̈**   port, harbor, 8-2

halb (*adv.*)   half

  halb acht   seven-thirty, *Einf.*

halbtags (*adv.*)   half days, 16-1

  halbtags arbeiten   to work part time, 16-1

Hallo!   Hello! *Einf.*

halten (hält), hielt, hat gehalten   (1) to stop (*intrans.*); (2) to hold, 3-1

  halten für (+ *acc.*)   to take for, regard as, think X is, 15-1

die **Haltestelle, -n**   (streetcar or bus) stop, 8-SA; 13-1

die **Hand, ̈e**   hand, 5-1

der **Handschuh, -e**   glove, 3-SA

hängen (*trans.*)   to hang, 7-1

hängen, hing, hat gehangen (*intrans.*)   to be hanging, 7-1

hart (härter)   hard; tough; harsh, 10-2

der **Haß**   hatred, 11-2

hassen   to hate, 3-2

häßlich   ugly, 1-1

Haupt- (*noun prefix*)   main, chief, primary, most important, 4-TLL

das **Hauptfach, ̈er**   major field (of study), 6-2

die **Hauptstadt, ̈e**   capital city, 4-TLL

das **Haus, ̈er**   house; building, 1-2

  nach Hause   home (as destination of motion), 3-1

  zu Hause   at home, 2-2

die **Hausaufgabe, -n** homework assignment, 3-2

die **Hausfrau, -en**   housewife, 2-2

das **Heft, -e** notebook, *Einf.*

die **Heimat** native place or country, homeland, 11-2

das **Heimweh** homesickness, 12-SA

heiraten to marry, get married, 16-1

heiß hot, *Einf.*

heißen, hieß, hat geheißen to be called, 2-1

  das heißt that means, in other words, 6-2

  Ich heiße . . . My name is . . . *Einf.*

  Wie heißen Sie? What's your name? *Einf.*

heiter cheerful, 14-2

hektisch hectic, 7-TLL

helfen (hilft), half, hat geholfen (+ *dat.*) to help, 7-1

hell bright, light, 2-VID; 3-2

das **Hemd, -en** shirt, 3-2

her- (*prefix*) *indicates motion toward the speaker*, 15-G

der **Herbst** fall, autumn, 4-2

der **Herr, -n, -en** gentleman, 1-1

  Herr Lehmann Mr. Lehmann, *Einf.*

herrlich great, terrific, marvelous, *Einf.*

Herzlich willkommen! Welcome! Nice to see you! 6-2

heute today, *Einf.*

  heute abend this evening, tonight, 1-1

  heute morgen this morning, 5-1

  heute nachmittag this afternoon, 12-G

hier here, 1-1

die **Hilfe** help, aid, 13-1

hin- (*prefix*) *indicates motion away from speaker*, 15-G

hinein- (*prefix*) in, into, 15-1

hinter (*prep. + acc. or dat.*) behind, 6-1

historisch historic, 8-TLL

hoch (*predicative adj.*), **hoh-** (*attributive adj.*) **(höher, am höchsten)** high, 4-2

  höchste Zeit high time, 14-1

das **Hochland** highlands, 4-TLL

die **Hochschule, -n** university, institute of higher learning, 14-2

die **Hochzeit, -en** wedding, 12-VID; 16-1

  die **goldene Hochzeit** golden wedding anniversary, 16-1

hoffen to hope, 7-2

hoffentlich (*adv.*) I hope, 4-1

höflich polite, 1-2

holen to fetch, get, 12-2

hören to hear, 3-2

der **Horizont, -e** horizon, 7-TLL

die **Hose, -n** trousers, pants, 3-2

das **Hotel, -s** hotel, 4-1

hübsch pretty, handsome, 11-1

der **Hügel, -** hill, 4-2

hügelig hilly, 4-SA

der **Humor** humor, 14-TLL

der **Hund, -e** dog, 11-G

hundert hundred, 2-G

der **Hunger** hunger, 8-1

  Hunger haben to be hungry, 8-1

hungrig hungry, 4-1

der **Hut, ⸚e** hat, 3-SA

I

ideal ideal, 16-TLL

die **Idee, -n** idea, 10-2

ideologisch ideological, 10-TLL

idiotensicher foolproof, 12-1

illegal illegal, 10-TLL

immer always, 1-2

  immer größer bigger and bigger, 12-G

  immer noch still, 4-2

in (*prep. + acc. or dat.*) in, into, 1-1

der **Indikativ** indicative

die **Industrie, -n** industry, 5-TLL

industriell industrial, 16-TLL

die **Inflation** inflation, 10-TLL

die **Informatik** computer science, 6-SA

der **Ingenieur, -e** engineer (*m.*), 5-SA

die **Ingenieurin, -nen** engineer (*f.*), 5-SA

die **Insel, -n** island, 4-TLL

das **Instrument, -e** instrument, 7-TLL

die **Integration** integration, 11-2

intelligent intelligent, 12-1

interessant interesting, 3-1

interessieren to interest, 13-1

  sich interessieren für (+ *acc.*) to be interested in, 13-1

international international, 3-TLL

interviewen to interview, 10-1

investieren to invest, 11-TLL

irgend- (*prefix*)

  irgendwann sometime or other, any time, 12-G

  irgendwie somehow or other, 12-G

  irgendwo somewhere or other, anywhere, 12-G

die **Ironie** irony, 14-TLL

(das) **Italien** Italy, 4-2

der **Italiener, -** Italian (*m.*), 11-TLL

die **Italienerin, -nen** Italian (*f.*), 11-TLL

italienisch Italian, 11-TLL

J

ja (1) yes; (2) (*unstressed flavoring particle*), 1-1

die **Jacke, -n** jacket, 3-2

das **Jahr, -e** year, 5-1

  im Jahr(e) 1996 in 1996, 9-2

jahrelang (*adv.*) for years, 14-TLL

die **Jahreszeit, -en** season

das **Jahrhundert, -e** century, 8-2

jahrhundertelang (*adv.*) for centuries, 14-TLL

jährlich annually, 9-2

(der) **Januar** January, *Einf.*

je ever, 6-2

    je größer, desto besser the bigger, the better, 12-G

die **Jeans** (*pl.*) jeans, 3-TLL

jeder, -es, -e each, every, 5-1

    jeder (*pronoun*) everyone

jedesmal every time, 12-1

jemand somebody, someone, 2-2

    jemand anderes someone else, 16-VID

jetzt now, 3-1

    von jetzt an from now on, 13-1

der **Journalist, -en, -en** journalist, 5-TLL

jüdisch Jewish, 12-2

die **Jugend** (*sing.*) youth; young people, 9-2

die **Jugendherberge, -n** youth hostel, 7-2

(der) **Juli** July, *Einf.*

jung (jünger) young, 2-2

der **Junge, -n, -n** boy, 9-1

(der) **Juni** June, *Einf.*

Jura (study of) law, 6-SA

K

der **Kaffee** coffee, 8-1

kalt (kälter) cold, *Einf.*

die **Kamera, -s** camera, 7-TLL

kämmen to comb

    sich die Haare kämmen to comb one's hair, 11-SA

(das) **Kanada** Canada, 5-TLL; 6-1

der **Kanadier, -** Canadian (*m.*), 11-TLL

die **Kanadierin, -nen** Canadian (*f.*), 11-TLL

kanadisch Canadian (*adj.*), 11-TLL

das **Kännchen, -** small (coffee or tea) pot, 8-SA

der **Kapitalismus** capitalism, 11-TLL

das **Kapitel, -** chapter

kaputt (*colloq.*) (1) broken, kaput; (2) exhausted, 9-1

    kaputt·machen to break, 12-1

die **Karriere, -n** career, 16-TLL

die **Karte, -n** (1) card; (2) ticket; (3) map, 4-1

die **Kartoffel, -n** potato, 8-1

der **Käse** cheese, 2-1

die **Kasse, -n** cashier; cashier's office, 14-1

der **Kassettenrecorder, -** cassette player, 10-1

katastrophal catastrophic, 8-TLL

die **Katastrophe, -n** catastrophe, 6-2

die **Katze, -n** cat, 11-G

kaufen to buy, 4-1

das **Kaufhaus, ̈er** department store, 8-SA

kaum hardly, barely, 16-1

kein not a, not any, no, 3-1

    kein . . . mehr no more . . . , not a . . . any longer, 4-1

der **Keller, -** cellar, basement, 9-1

der **Kellner, -** waiter, 5-SA; 8-1

die **Kellnerin, -nen** waitress, 5-SA; 8-1

kennen, kannte, hat gekannt to know, be acquainted with, 2-1

kennen·lernen to get to know; to meet, 5-1

die **Kette, -n** chain

die **Kettenreaktion, -en** chain reaction

das **Kilo** (*short for* das **Kilogramm**), 8-1

das **Kilogramm** kilogram, 8-1

der **Kilometer, -** kilometer

das **Kind, -er** child, 1-1

die **Kindheit, -en** childhood, 9-TLL

das **Kino, -s** movie theater, 6-2

die **Kirche, -n** church, 8-SA

klar (1) clear; (2) (*colloq.*) sure, of course, 9-1

die **Klasse, -n** class; grade, 1-2

der **Klatsch** gossip, 12-1

klauen (*colloq.*) to rip off, steal, 10-1

die **Klausur, -en** written test, 6-2

das **Klavier, -e** piano, 14-2

das **Kleid, -er** dress (*pl.* = dresses *or* clothes), 3-2

der **Kleiderschrank, ̈e** clothes cupboard, wardrobe, 6-SA

die **Kleidung** clothing, 3-SA

klein little, small; short, 2-1

die **Kleinstadt, ̈e** town (5,000 to 20,000 inhabitants), 8-2

das **Klima** climate, 4-2

klingeln to ring, 7-1

klingen, klang, hat geklungen to sound, 8-1

die **Klinik, -en** clinic, 15-TLL

das **Klischee, -s** cliché, 2-2

klischeehaft (*adj.*) cliché, stereotyped, 13-SA

klug (klüger) smart, bright, 5-1

knapp scarce, in short supply, 12-1

    knapp bei Kasse short of cash, 12-1

die **Kneipe, -n** tavern, bar, 6-2

kochen to cook, 2-2

der **Koffer, -** suitcase, 7-1

(das) **Köln** Cologne, 8-1

die **Kolonie, -n** colony, 4-TLL

komisch peculiar, odd; funny, 12-1

kommen, kam, ist gekommen to come, *Einf.*; 1-1

    kommen aus to come from, *Einf.*

    Wie kommt das? How come? What's the reason for that? 16-VID der **Kommunismus** Communism, 11-TLL

die **Konditorei, -en** pastry café, 8-SA

der **Konflikt, -e** conflict, 2-TLL

der **Konjunktiv** subjunctive

die **Konkurrenz** competition, 9-SA

können (kann), konnte, hat gekonnt can, be able to, 3-1

Ich kann Deutsch. I can speak German. 3-G

die **Konsequenz, -en** consequence, 9-TLL

konservativ conservative, 13-TLL

der **Kontakt, -e** contact, 14-TLL

der **Kontrast, -e** contrast, 4-TLL

kontrollieren to check, inspect, 15-2

sich konzentrieren auf (+ *acc.*) to concentrate on, 14-2

das **Konzert, -e** concert, 6-TLL

der **Kopf, ̈e** head, 11-1

Das geht mir nicht aus dem Kopf. I can't forget that. 12-2

der **Korrespondent, -en, -en** correspondent, 5-TLL

(das) **Korsika** Corsica, 5-TLL

kosten to cost, 2-VID; 5-1

Wieviel kostet das bitte? How much does that cost, please? 5-1

kostenlos free of charge, 6-2

die **Kraft, ̈e** power; strength, 9-2

das **Kraftwerk, -e** power plant, 9-2

krank (kränker) sick, *Einf.*

das **Krankenhaus, ̈er** hospital, 11-1

der **Krankenpfleger, -** nurse (*m.*), 5-SA

die **Krankenschwester, -n** nurse (*f.*), 5-SA

die **Krankheit, -en** sickness, 9-2

die **Krawatte, -n** tie, 3-SA

kreativ creative, 14-TLL

die **Kreditkarte, -n** credit card, 14-1

die **Kreide** chalk, *Einf.*

der **Krieg, -e** war, 6-2

kritisch critical, 16-2

die **Küche, -n** kitchen, 15-SA; 16-2

der **Kuchen, -** cake, 8-SA

der **Kugelschreiber, -** ballpoint pen, *Einf.*

kühl cool, *Einf.*

die **Kultur, -en** culture, 4-TLL

sich kümmern um (+ *acc.*) to look after, take care of, deal with, 13-1

der **Kunde, -n, -n** customer (*m.*), 5-1

die **Kundin, -nen** customer (*f.*), 5-1

die **Kunst, ̈e** art, 8-1

die **Kunstgeschichte** art history, 6-SA

der **Künstler, -** artist (*m.*), 5-SA; 14-2

die **Künstlerin, -nen** artist (*f.*), 5-SA; 14-2

kurz (kürzer) short; for a short time, 4-1

die **Kusine, -n** cousin (*f.*), 2-SA

die **Küste, -n** coast, 4-TLL

L

das **Labor, -s** lab, 6-SA

lachen to laugh, 3-2

der **Laden, ̈** shop, store, 5-1

die **Lampe, -n** lamp, 6-SA

das **Land, ̈er** country, 4-2

auf dem Land in the country, 8-2

aufs Land to the country, 8-2

die **Landkarte, -** map, *Einf.*

die **Landschaft, -en** landscape, 4-2

die **Landsleute** compatriots

der **Landwirt, -e** farmer (*m.*), 5-SA

die **Landwirtin, -nen** farmer (*f.*), 5-SA

die **Landwirtschaft** agriculture, 6-SA

lang(e) (länger) long; for a long time, 4-1

langsam slow, *Einf.*; 3-2

sich langweilen to be bored, 13-1

langweilig boring, 3-1

lassen (läßt), ließ, hat gelassen (1) to leave (something or someone), leave behind; (2) to let, allow; (3) to cause to be done, 12-1

laufen (läuft), lief, ist gelaufen (1) to run; (2) (*colloq.*) to go on foot, walk, 3-1

die **Laune** mood

guter/schlechter Laune in a good/bad mood, *Einf.*

laut loud, *Einf.*

das **Leben** life, 4-2

leben to live, be alive, 2-2

die **Lebensmittel** (*pl.*) groceries, 5-2

der **Lebensstandard** standard of living, 9-TLL

die **Leberwurst, ̈e** liverwurst, 8-1

lecker tasty, delicious, 8-1

ledig single (= unmarried), 16-1

leer empty, 5-1

legen to lay, put down, 6-1

der **Lehrer, -** teacher (*m.*), *Einf.*

die **Lehrerin, -nen** teacher (*f.*), *Einf.*

der **Lehrling, -e** apprentice, 5-1

leicht (1) light (in weight); (2) easy, 3-1

leid: Das tut mir leid. I'm sorry about that. *Einf.*; 7-1

leider unfortunately, *Einf.*; 3-1

leihen, lieh, hat geliehen (1) to lend, loan; (2) to borrow, 10-1

leise quiet, soft, *Einf.*

leisten: sich etwas leisten können to be able to afford something, 11-1

die Leitfrage, -n guiding question

lernen to learn, 3-2

lesen (liest), las, hat gelesen to read, 2-1

lesen über (+ *acc.*) to read about, 2-1

das Lesestück, -e reading selection

letzt- last, 10-1

letzte Woche last week, 6-2

die Leute (*pl.*) people, 2-1

das Licht, -er light, 11-1

lieb dear; nice, sweet, 6-2

Lieber Fritz! Dear Fritz, (salutation in letter), 6-TLL

die Liebe love, 11-2

lieben to love, 3-2

lieber preferably, would rather (*see* **gern**)

Lieblings- (*noun prefix*) favorite, 9-1

am liebsten most like to, like best of all to (*see* **gern**), 4-1

das Lied, -er song, 4-2

liegen, lag, hat gelegen to lie; to be situated, 4-2

der Lift, -s elevator, 14-SA

lila violet, lavender, 3-SA

die Limnologie limnology

die Linguistik linguistics, 6-SA

die Linie, -n (streetcar or bus) line, 13-1

links to the left; on the left, 8-2

die Liste, -n list

der Liter liter, 8-1

literarisch literary, 14-TLL

der Löffel, - spoon, 8-SA

der Lohn, ⸚e wage, 16-2

sich lohnen to be worthwhile, worth the trouble, 13-1

das Lokal, -e neighborhood restaurant or tavern, 8-1

los! let's go! 10-VID

Was ist los? (1)What's the matter? (2)What's going on? 3-1

lösen to solve, 9-2

los·fahren (fährt los), fuhr los, ist losgefahren to depart, start, leave, 14-1

die Lösung, -en solution, 9-2

der Löwe, -n, -n lion, 10-SA

die Luft air, 4-SA; 8-2

die Luftverschmutzung air pollution, 8-2

die Lust desire

Ich habe keine Lust. I don't want to. 3-1

Lust haben (etwas zu tun) to want to do (something), 8-1

die Lyrik poetry

M

machen (1) to make; (2) to do, 1-1

Das macht (mir) Spaß. That is fun (for me). 7-1

Das macht zusammen . . . All together that comes to . . . 5-1

Es macht (doch) nichts. It doesn't matter. 7-1

die Macht, ⸚e power, might, 11-2

das Mädchen, - girl, 9-1

mag (*see* **mögen**)

(der) Mai May, *Einf.*

das Mal, -e time (in the sense of occurrence), 12-1

das nächste Mal (the) next time, 12-G

zum ersten Mal for the first time, 12-G

mal (*flavoring particle with commands, see p. 106*), 4-1

man one (*indefinite pronoun*), 1-2

der Manager, - manager, 11-TLL

mancher, -es, -e many a, 9-2

manche (*pl.*) some

manchmal sometimes, 2-2

manipulieren to manipulate, 10-TLL

der Mann, ⸚ (1) man; (2) husband, 2-1

die Mannschaft, -en team, 5-2

der Mantel, ⸚ coat, 3-2

das Märchen, - fairy tale, 4-2

die Mark (die Deutsche Mark— DM) mark (the German mark), 5-1

(der) März March, *Einf.*

die Maschine, -n machine, 12-1

die Mathe (*slang*) math, 6-VID

die Mathematik mathematics, 6-SA

die Mauer, -n (freestanding or exterior) wall, 11-1

der Mechaniker, - mechanic, 5-1

die Medizin (field of) medicine, 6-SA

das Meer, -e sea, 4-2

mehr more, 2-2

nicht mehr no longer, not any more, 2-2

mehrere several, 11-1

meinen (1) to be of the opinion, think, 1-2; (2) to mean, 2-1

Was meinen Sie dazu? What do you say to that? What do you think of that? 16-1

die Meinung, -en opinion

meist- most (*see* **viel**)

meistens mostly, usually, 5-2

die Melancholie melancholy, 14-TLL

die Menge, -n quantity; crowd

eine Menge a lot, lots of, 6-2

die Mensa university cafeteria, 1-1

der Mensch, -en, -en person, human being, 6-1

Mensch! Man! Wow! 3-1

die Menschheit mankind, human race, 9-2

merken to notice, 11-1

leicht zu merken easy to remember

das Messer, - knife, 8-SA

die **Methode, -n**   method, 10-TLL

mieten   to rent, 2-VID

die **Milch**   milk, 8-SA; 12-2

mild   mild, 4-TLL

die **Million, -en**   million, 11-TLL

die **Minute, -n**   minute, 3-1

minutenlang (*adv.*)   for minutes, 14-TLL

Mist: So ein Mist! (*crude & colloq.*)   (1) What a drag. (2) What a lot of bull. 10-1

mit   (*prep. + dat.*)   with, 2-1; (*adv.*) along with, 12-1

der **Mitbewohner, -**   fellow occupant, roommate, housemate (*m.*), 3-1

die **Mitbewohnerin, -nen**   fellow occupant, roommate, housemate (*f.*), 3-1

mit·bringen, brachte mit, hat mitgebracht   to bring along, take along, 6-1

miteinander   with each other, together, 1-2

das **Mitglied, -er**   member, 11-2

mit·kommen, kam mit, ist mitgekommen   to come along, 5-1

das **Mitleid**   sympathy, 16-SA

mit·machen   to participate, cooperate, pitch in, 9-1

mit·nehmen (nimmt mit), nahm mit, hat mitgenommen   to take along, 7-2

das **Mittagessen**   midday meal, lunch, 5-2

das **Mittelalter**   the Middle Ages, 13-1

(der) **Mittwoch**   Wednesday, *Einf.*

die **Möbel** (*pl.*)   furniture, 6-SA

möbliert   furnished, 6-SA

modern   modern, 4-2

modernisieren   to modernize, 11-TLL

mögen (mag), mochte, hat gemocht   to like, 4-1
  möchten   would like to, 3-1

Das mag sein.   That may be. 16-G

möglich   possible, 6-1

der **Moment, -e**   moment
  im Moment   at the moment, 1-1

die **Monarchie, -n**   monarchy, 10-TLL

der **Monat, -e**   month, 10-1

monatelang (*adv.*)   for months, 14-TLL

(der) **Montag**   Monday, *Einf.*

morgen   tomorrow, *Einf.*; 1-1
  morgen abend   tomorrow evening, 12-G
  morgen früh   tomorrow morning, 12-G
  morgen nachmittag   tomorrow afternoon, 12-G

der **Morgen, -**   morning, 1-1
  Guten Morgen!   Good morning! 1-1

morgens (*adv.*)   in the morning(s), 4-1

das **Motorrad, ˸er**   motorcycle, 5-1

müde   tired, weary, *Einf.*

der **Müll**   trash, refuse, 9-1

(das) **München**   Munich, 8-2

der **Mund, ˸er**   mouth, 11-1

munter   wide-awake, cheerful, *Einf.*

das **Museum, die Museen**   museum, 8-1

die **Musik**   music, 3-2

die **Musikwissenschaft**   musicology, 6-SA

müssen (muß), mußte, hat gemußt   must, to have to, 3-1

die **Mutter, ˸**   mother, 2-2

die **Muttersprache, -n**   native language, 5-2

die **Mutti, -s**   mama, mom, 2-2

die **Mütze, -n**   cap, 3-SA

N

na   well . . . 12-1
  Na endlich!   At last! High time! 9-1

Na und?   And so? So what? 10-1

nach (*prep. + dat.*)   (1) after, 5-1; (2) to (with cities and countries), 1-1
  nach Hause   home (as destination of motion), 3-1

der **Nachbar, -n, -n**   neighbor (*m.*), 11-2

die **Nachbarin, -nen**   neighbor (*f.*), 11-2

nachdem (*sub. conj.*)   after, 10-1

nachher (*adv.*)   later on, after that, 4-1

der **Nachmittag, -e**   afternoon, 10-1
  am Nachmittag   in the afternoon, 10-1

nachmittags   (in the) afternoons, 5-TLL

die **Nachspeise, -n**   dessert, 16-VID

nächst-   next; nearest, 12-1
  nächstes Semester   next semester, 2-1

die **Nacht, ˸e**   night, 1-1
  Gute Nacht.   Good night. 12-1
  in der Nacht   in the night, at night, 12-1

der **Nachtisch, -e**   dessert, 8-1
  zum Nachtisch   for dessert, 8-1

nachts   at night, 5-TLL

nah(e) (näher, am nächsten)   near, 8-1

die **Nähe**   nearness; vicinity
  in der Nähe (von or **+ gen.)**   near, nearby, 7-2

der **Name, -ns, -n**   name, 5-1
  Wie ist Ihr Name?   What's your name? 10-VID

die **Nase, -n**   nose, 5-1
  Ich habe die Nase voll.   I'm fed up. I've had it up to here. 5-1

naß   wet, damp, 4-2

die **Nationalität, -en**   nationality, 15-TLL

die **Natur**   nature, 9-TLL

natürlich   natural, naturally; of course, 1-1

der **Nebel**   fog, mist, 4-SA

neben (*prep. + acc. or dat.*) beside, next to, 6-1

das **Nebenfach, ¨er**   minor field (of study), 6-2

neblig   foggy, misty, *Einf.*

nee (*colloq.*)   no, 6-1

nehmen (nimmt), nahm, hat genommen   to take, 2-1

nein   no, *Einf.*

nennen, nannte, hat genannt to name, call, 10-2

nett   nice, 6-1

neu   new, 3-2

neulich   recently, 12-1

neutral   neutral, 13-TLL

die **Neutralität**   neutrality, 13-TLL

nicht   not, *Einf.*; 1-1

  gar nicht   not at all, 3-2

  nicht mehr   no longer, not any more, 2-2

  nicht nur . . . sondern auch not only . . . but also, 9-2

  nicht wahr?   isn't it? can't you? doesn't she? etc., 3-1

nichts   nothing, 3-1

  Nichts zu danken!   Don't mention it! 2-1

  Es macht nichts.   It doesn't matter. 7-1

nie   never, 1-2

niedrig   low, 6-2

niemand   nobody, no one, 2-2

noch   still, 2-2

  noch ein   another, an additional, 2-2

  noch einmal   once again, once more, 4-1

  noch etwas   something else, anything more, 8-1

  noch immer   still, 4-2

  noch jemand   someone else

  noch kein-   not a . . . yet, not any . . . yet, 4-1

  noch nicht   not yet, 4-1

(das) **Nordamerika**   North America, 2-TLL

der **Norden**   the north, 4-2

normal   normal, 2-TLL

die **Note, -n**   grade, 5-1

nötig   necessary, 9-1

(der) **November**   November, *Einf.*

die **Nummer, -n**   number, *Einf.*; 14-1

nun   (1) now; (2) well . . . , well now, 10-1

nur   only, 2-1

nützlich   useful

O

ob (*sub. conj.*)   if, whether, 8-1

oben (*adv.*)   above; on top

das **Obst**   fruit, 2-1

obwohl (*sub. conj.*)   although, 8-2

oder (*coor. conj.*)   or, 1-2

offen   open, 11-2

öffentlich   public, 16-2

offiziell   official, 13-TLL

öffnen   to open, 11-1

oft (öfter)   often, 1-2

ohne (*prep. + acc.*)   without, 4-1

  ohne . . . zu   without . . . -ing, 8-G

das **Ohr, -en**   ear, 11-1

das **Ökosystem, -e**   ecosystem, 9-TLL

(der) **Oktober**   October, *Einf.*

das **Öl**   oil, 9-2

die **Oma, -s**   grandma, 2-2

der **Onkel, -**   uncle, 2-2

der **Opa, -s**   grandpa, 2-2

die **Opposition, -en** opposition, 10-TLL

optimistisch   optimistic, 3-TLL

ordentlich   tidy, orderly, 13-1

der **Ort, -e**   (1) place; (2) small town, 12-SA; 13-2

der **Osten**   the east, 4-2

(das) **Österreich**   Austria, 4-1

der **Österreicher, -**   Austrian (*m.*), 11-TLL

die **Österreicherin, -nen** Austrian (*f.*), 11-TLL

österreichisch   Austrian, 14-1

(das) **Osteuropa**   Eastern Europe, 11-TLL

P

ein paar   a couple (of), a few, 6-2

packen   to pack, 7-TLL

die **Pädagogik**   (field of) education, 6-SA

das **Papier, -e**   paper, *Einf.*; 9-1

parallel   parallel, 16-TLL

die **Partei, -en**   political party, 9-2

der **Partner, -**   partner, 5-TLL

die **Party, -s**   party, 6-TLL

der **Paß**, die **Pässe**   passport, 7-SA; 15-2

passieren, ist passiert   to happen, 10-1

der **Patient, -en, -en**   patient, 14-TLL

pauken   (*student slang*) to cram, 6-VID

die **Pause, -n**   break; intermission, 3-1

  eine Pause machen   to take a break, 3-1

Pech haben   to have bad luck, be unlucky, 6-2

per   by (means of)

  per Autostop reisen   to hitchhike, 7-2

perfekt   perfect, 15-1

die **Person, -en**   person

persönlich   personal

pessimistisch   pessimistic, 3-TLL

die **Pflanze, -n**   plant, 9-2

das **Pfund**   500 grams, 8-VID

das **Phänomen, -e** phenomenon, 16-TLL

phantastisch   fantastic, 2-1

die **Philosophie**   philosophy, 6-TLL

philosophieren   to philosophize, 14-TLL

die **Physik**   physics, 6-SA

das **Plakat, -e**   (political) poster, 10-2

planen to plan, make plans, 7-1

das Plastik plastic, 9-TLL

der Platz, ⁻e (1) place; (2) space; (3) city square, 6-1; (4) seat, 7-2

plötzlich suddenly, 10-1

die Politik (1) politics; (2) policy, 9-2

der Politiker, - politician (*m.*), 5-SA; 9-2

die Politikerin, -nen politician (*f.*), 5-SA

die Politikwissenschaft political science, 6-SA

politisch political, 9-TLL

die Polizei (*sing. only*) the police

die Pommes frites (*pl.*) French fries, 3-2

die Portion, -en order, helping (of food), 8-SA

die Position, -en position, 16-TLL

die Post (1) post office; postal service; (2) mail, 8-SA; 15-1

das Poster, - poster, *Einf.*

die Postkarte, -n postcard, 5-2

praktisch practical, 6-TLL

der Präsident, -en, -en president, 10-SA

der Preis, -e price, 8-2

preiswert inexpensive, 14-VID

prima terrific, great, *Einf.*; 1-1

privat private, 6-TLL

probieren to sample, try, 8-VID; 14-1

das Problem, -e problem, 2-2

produktiv productive, 14-TLL

produzieren to produce, 9-TLL

der Professor, -en professor (*m.*), *Einf.*

die Professorin, -nen professor (*f.*), *Einf.*

das Programm, -e program, 6-TLL

der Programmierer, - programmer (*m.*), 5-SA

die Programmiererin, -nen programmer (*f.*), 5-SA

Prost! (*or*) **Prosit!** Cheers! 16-VID

der Protest, -e protest, 11-TLL

das Prozent percent, 13-TLL

die Prüfung, -en examination

die Psychoanalyse psychoanalysis, 14-TLL

die Psychologie psychology, 6-SA

psychologisch psychological, 16-TLL

der Pulli, -s (*short for* **Pullover**), 3-2

der Pullover, - pullover, sweater, 3-2

pünktlich punctual, on time, 7-2

putzen to clean, 11-SA

Q

Quatsch! Baloney! Nonsense! 5-1

quatschen (*colloq.*) (1) to talk nonsense; (2) to chat, 7-2

die Querstraße, -n cross street, 12-1

R

das Rad, ⁻er (1) wheel; (2) bicycle, 8-2

rad·fahren (fährt Rad), fuhr Rad, ist radgefahren to bicycle, 8-2

der Radiergummi eraser, *Einf.*

radikal radical, 9-TLL

das Radio, -s radio, 6-SA

sich rasieren to shave, 11-SA

raten (rät), riet, hat geraten to guess

Raten Sie mal! Take a guess!

das Rathaus, ⁻er town hall, 8-SA

reagieren auf (+ *acc.*) to react to, 13-2

die Reaktion, -en reaction

realistisch realistic, 5-TLL

die Rechnung, -en bill, check, 16-VID

recht: recht haben (hat recht), hatte recht, hat recht gehabt to be right, 4-1

rechts (*adv.*) to the right; on the right, 8-2

der Rechtsanwalt, ⁻e lawyer (*m.*), 5-SA; 13-2

die Rechtsanwältin, -nen lawyer (*f.*), 5-SA; 13-2

das Recycling recycling; recycling center, 9-1

reden to talk, speak, 12-1

das Referat, -e (1) oral report; (2) written term paper, 6-2

ein Referat halten to give a report, 6-SA

ein Referat schreiben to write a paper, 6-SA

die Reform, -en reform, 11-TLL

reformieren to reform, 11-TLL

das Regal shelf

der Regen rain, 4-SA

der Regenschirm, -e umbrella, 3-SA

die Regierung government in power, administration (U.S.), 10-SA; 11-2

das Regime regime, 11-TLL

die Region, -en region, 4-TLL

regnen to rain, *Einf.*; 1-1

regnerisch rainy, 4-SA

reich rich, 10-1

das Reich, -e empire; realm, 10-2

die Reise, -n trip, journey, 3-2

eine Reise machen to take a trip, 3-2

Gute Reise! Have a good trip! 1-1

das Reisebüro, -s travel agency, 14-VID

der Reiseführer, - guide book, 5-1

reisen, ist gereist to travel, 5-2

per Autostop reisen to hitchhike, 7-2

der Reisescheck, -s traveler's check, 14-1

das **Reiseziel, -e** destination, 7-2

relativ (*adj. and adv.*) relative, 2-TLL

reparieren to repair, 12-1

die **Republik, -en** republic, 10-TLL

reservieren to reserve, 7-1

das **Restaurant, -s** restaurant, 8-1

die **Restauration, -en** restoration, 8-TLL

retten to save, rescue, 9-2

die **Revolution, -en** revolution, 11-TLL

die **Rezeption** hotel reception desk, 14-1

der **Rhein** the Rhine River, 4-TLL

richtig right, correct, *Einf.*; true, real, 15-2

der **Riese, -n, -n** giant

riesen- (*noun and adj. prefix*) gigantic

  riesengroß huge, gigantic, 8-2

  Ich habe Riesenhunger. I'm famished (*or*) hungry as a bear. 14-2

der **Rock, ¨e** skirt, 3-SA

die **Rolle, -n** role, 2-2

der **Roman, -e** novel, 5-2

romantisch romantic, 13-TLL

rosa pink, 3-SA

rot (röter) red, 3-2

der **Rucksack, ¨e** rucksack, backpack, 7-2

rufen, rief, hat gerufen to call, shout, 11-2

ruhig (1) calm, peaceful, 10-2; (2) (*as sentence adverb*) "feel free to," "go ahead and," 12-1

der **Russe, -n, -n** Russian (*m.*), 11-TLL

die **Russin, -nen** Russian (*f.*), 11-TLL

russisch Russian, 11-TLL

(das) **Rußland** Russia, 8-2

S

die **Sache, -n** (1) thing; item, 8-1; (2) matter, affair

der **Sack, ¨e** sack, 9-1

der **Saft, ¨e** juice, 8-SA

sagen to say; to tell, 1-2

  Sag mal, . . . Tell me, . . .

  Was sagen Sie dazu? What do you say to that? What do you think of that? 16-1

sagenhaft! incredible! marvelous! 16-1

die **Sahne** cream, 8-SA

der **Salat, -e** (1) salad; (2) lettuce, 8-1

sammeln to collect, 9-1

(der) **Samstag** Saturday, *Einf.*

der **Satz, ¨e** sentence; clause

sauber clean, 9-1

sauer (*colloq.*) (1) ticked off, sore, *Einf.*; (2) sour, acidic, 9-2

schade too bad, 11-1

  Das ist schade! That's a shame! What a pity! 11-1

schaffen to handle, manage, get done, 3-1

der **Schalter, -** counter, window, 13-1

schauen to look, 11-1

  Schau mal. Look. Look here. 10-VID; 11-1

das **Schaufenster, -** store window, 5-2

der **Scheck, -s** check, 14-1

scheinen, schien, hat geschienen (1) to shine; (2) to seem, 1-1

schenken to give (as a gift), 5-1

schicken to send, 6-2

das **Schiff, -e** ship, 12-2

der **Schilling, -e** Austrian shilling, 14-1

der **Schinken** ham, 8-SA

schlafen (schläft), schlief, hat geschlafen to sleep, 3-1

das **Schlafzimmer, -** bedroom, 11-1

schlagen (schlägt), schlug, hat geschlagen (1) to hit; (2) to beat, 9-SA

schlampig (*colloq.*) messy, disorderly, 13-1

die **Schlange, -n** snake, 10-SA

schlecht bad, *Einf.*; 1-1

schleppen (*colloq.*) to drag, lug (along), haul, 9-1

schließen, schloß, hat geschlossen to close, 5-2

schließlich (*adv.*) after all, finally, 15-1

schlimm bad, 6-2

der **Schluß, die Schlüsse** end, conclusion

  zum Schluß in conclusion, finally

der **Schlüssel, -** key, 6-SA; 11-2

schmecken (1) to taste (*trans. and intrans.*); (2) to taste good, 8-1; 8-VID

sich schminken to put on make-up, 11-SA

schmutzig dirty, 9-1

der **Schnee** snow, 4-2

schneiden, schnitt, hat geschnitten to cut, 11-1

schneien to snow, *Einf.*

schnell fast, *Einf.*; 3-2

  schnell machen (*colloq.*) to hurry, 11-1

das **Schnitzel, -** cutlet, chop, 8-1

die **Schokolade** chocolate, 11-1

schon (1) already, yet; (2) (*flavoring particle, see p.75*), 3-1

  schon lange for a long time, 10-G

schön beautiful, 1-1

schrecklich terrible, 4-2

schreiben, schrieb, hat geschrieben to write, 3-2

  Wie schreibt man das? How do you write (spell) that? *Einf.*

die **Schreibmaschine, -n** typewriter, 12-1

der **Schreibtisch, -e**   desk, 6-1

schreien, schrie, hat geschrieen
to shout, yell, 15-2

der **Schriftsteller, -**   writer
(*m.*), 10-2

die **Schriftstellerin, -nen**
writer (*f.*), 10-2

der **Schuh, -e**   shoe, 3-2

die **Schule, -n**   school, 2-1

der **Schüler, -**   grade school
pupil or secondary school
student (*m.*), *Einf.*

die **Schülerin, -nen**   grade
school pupil or secondary
school student (*f.*), *Einf.*

das **Schulsystem, -e**   school
system, 3-TLL

schwach (schwächer)   weak,
9-2

schwarz (schwärzer)   black, 3-2

**schweigen, schwieg, hat
geschwiegen**   to be silent,
12-1

die **Schweiz**   Switzerland, 4-2

der **Schweizer, -**   Swiss (*m.*),
13-2

die **Schweizerin, -nen**   Swiss
(*f.*), 13-2

schweizerisch   Swiss, 11-TLL

schwer   (1) heavy; (2) hard,
difficult, 3-1

die **Schwester, -n**   sister, 2-1

schwierig   difficult, 5-1

die **Schwierigkeit, -en**
difficulty, 13-2

das **Schwimmbad, ⸚er**
swimming pool, 8-SA

**schwimmen, schwamm, ist
geschwommen**   to swim,
4-1

der **See, -n**   lake, 4-1
am See   at the lake

sehen (sieht), sah, hat gesehen
to see, 2-1

sehr   very, 1-1

sein (ist), war, ist gewesen   to
be, *Einf.*; 1-1
dabei sein   to be present,
attend, 15-1

seit (*prep. + dat., sub. conj.*)
since, 5-1

seit 5 Jahren   for (the past)
5 years, 5-1

seit langem   for a long time,
10-G

der **Sekretär, -e**   secretary
(*m.*), 5-SA

die **Sekretärin, -nen**   secretary
(*f.*), 5-SA

selber (*or*) **selbst** (*adv.*)   by
oneself (myself, yourself,
ourselves, etc.), 6-2

selbstverständlich   "It goes
without saying that . . ."
4-1

selten   seldom, 1-2

das **Semester, -**   semester, 2-1
nächstes Semester   next
semester, 2-1

die **Semesterferien** (*pl.*)
semester break, 6-2

das **Seminar, -e**   (university)
seminar, 4-1

der **Senior, -en, -en**   senior
citizen, 10-1

separat   separate, 11-TLL

(der) **September**   September,
Einf.

die **Serviette, -n**   napkin, 8-SA

setzen   to set (down), put, 7-1
sich setzen   to sit down,
11-1

sich (*3rd person reflexive
pronoun*)   himself,
herself, themselves,
(*formal 2nd person*)
yourself, yourselves, 11-1

sicher   certain, sure, 2-1

siebt-   seventh, 9-G

singen, sang, hat gesungen   to
sing, 3-2

die **Situation, -en**   situation,
10-TLL

sitzen, saß, hat gesessen   to
sit, 6-2

(das) **Skandinavien**
Scandinavia, 8-TLL

**ski·fahren (fährt Ski), fuhr Ski,
ist skigefahren**   to ski,
8-2

so   (1) like this, 1-2; (2) so, 7-2

so ein (*demonstrative*)   such
a, 15-2

so lange (*adv.*)   for such a
long time, 6-1

sofort   immediately, right away,
6-2

die **Software**   software, 12-1

sogar   even, in fact, 2-2

der **Sohn, ⸚e**   son, 2-1

solcher, -es, -e   such, such a,
9-2

die **Solidarität**   solidarity,
1-TLL

sollen (soll), sollte, hat gesollt
should, be supposed to, 3-1

der **Sommer**   summer, 4-2

das **Sommersemester**   spring
term (usually May-July),
6-SA

sondern (*coor. conj.*)   but
rather, instead, 7-1
nicht nur . . . sondern auch
not only . . . but also, 9-2

(der) **Sonnabend**   Saturday,
Einf.

die **Sonne**   sun, 1-1

sonnig   sunny, *Einf.*

(der) **Sonntag**   Sunday, *Einf.*

sonst (*adv.*)   otherwise, apart
from that, 6-2
Sonst noch etwas?   Will
there be anything else? 5-1

sortieren   to sort, 9-TLL

sowieso   anyway, 7-1

die **Sowjetunion**   Soviet Union,
11-TLL

sozial   social, 2-TLL

der **Sozialarbeiter, -**   social
worker, 8-TLL

die **Soziologie**   sociology, 6-SA

(das) **Spanien**   Spain, 15-1

sparen   to save (money *or*
time), 7-2

der **Spaß**   fun
Das macht (mir) Spaß.
That is fun (for me). 7-1
Viel Spaß.   Have fun. 12-1

spät   late, 3-1
Ich bin spät dran.   I'm late.
4-VID

Wie spät ist es? What time is it? *Einf.*

später later, 4-1

spazieren·gehen, ging spazieren, ist spazierengegangen to go for a walk, 5-2

die Speise, -n food, dish (menu item), 16-VID

die Speisekarte, -n menu, 8-SA

der Speisesaal (hotel) dining room, 14-SA

der Spiegel, - mirror, 14-2

das Spiel, -e game, 9-SA

spielen to play, 1-1

spontan spontaneous, 7-TLL

der Sport sport, 5-TLL; 9-1

  Sport treiben to play sports, 9-1

sportlich athletic, 9-1

die Sprache, -n language, 3-2

sprechen (spricht), sprach, hat gesprochen to speak, talk, 2-1

  sprechen über (+ *acc.*) to talk about, 2-1

der Staat, -en state, 10-2

stabil stable, 11-TLL

die Stabilität stability, 13-TLL

die Stadt, ⁀e city, 4-2

der Stadtbummel, - stroll through town, 8-1

der Stadtführer, - city guidebook, 14-SA

der Stadtplan, ⁀ city map, 5-2

stark (stärker) strong, 5-2

statt (*prep. + gen.*) instead of, 8-G

statt·finden, fand statt, hat stattgefunden to take place, 14-2

staunen to be amazed, surprised, 6-2

stehen, stand, hat gestanden to stand, 5-1

stehlen (stiehlt), stahl, hat gestohlen to steal, 10-1

steigen, stieg, ist gestiegen to climb, 8-2

steil steep, 3-1

der Stein, -e stone, 12-2

die Stelle, -n job, position, 2-2

stellen to put, place, 7-1

  eine Frage stellen to ask a question, 10-2

sterben (stirbt), starb, ist gestorben to die, 5-2

die Stimme, -n voice, 5-2

stimmen to be right (*impersonal only*), 1-2

  das stimmt that's right, that's true

  Stimmt schon. That's right. 3-2

stinklangweilig extremely boring, 3-1

das Stipendium, die Stipendien scholarship, stipend, 6-2

der Stock floor (of a building), 14-2

  der erste Stock the second floor (*see* **Erdgeschoß**)

  im ersten Stock on the second floor

stolz auf (+ *acc.*) proud of, 13-2

stören to disturb, 10-2

die Straße, -n street; road, 1-1

der Straßenatlas road atlas, 7-1

die Straßenbahn, -en streetcar, 8-SA; 13-1

der Streß, die Stresse stress, 5-2

stressig stressful, 5-2

das Stück, -e piece, 5-1

  ein Stück Kuchen a piece of cake, 8-G

  sechs Stück six (of the same item), 5-1

der Student, -en, -en university student (*m.*), *Einf.*; 1-2

der Studentenausweis, -e student I.D., 6-2

das Studentenwohnheim, -e student dormitory, 6-1

die Studentin, -nen university student (*f.*), *Einf.*; 1-2

studieren to attend a university; to study (a subject); to major in, 1-2

studieren an (+ *dat.*) to study at, 6-SA

das Studium university studies, 6-2

der Stuhl, ⁀e chair, *Einf.*

die Stunde, -n (1) hour; (2) class hour, 3-1

stundenlang (*adv.*) for hours, 14-TLL

das Substantiv, -e noun

suchen to look for, seek, 2-1

der Süden the south, 4-2

super super, 4-1

der Supermarkt, ⁀e supermarket, 5-TLL

der Supertanker, - super tanker, 9-TLL

die Suppe, -n soup, 1-1

süß sweet, 9-2

das Symbol, -e symbol, 11-TLL

symbolisch symbolic, 10-TLL

sympathisch friendly, congenial, likeable, 7-2

das System, -e system, 3-TLL

T

die Tafel, -n blackboard, *Einf.*

der Tag, -e day, 1-1

  eines Tages some day (in the future); one day (in the past or future), 13-2

  Guten Tag! Hello! *Einf.*

  jeden Tag every day, 5-2

  Tag! Hi! Hello! *Einf.*

tagelang (*adv.*) for days, 14-TLL

das Tal, ⁀er valley, 4-2

die Tante, -n aunt, 2-2

tanzen to dance, 14-2

die Tasche, -n (1) pocket, (2) shoulder bag, 3-SA; 7-2

die Tasse, -n cup, 8-1

  eine Tasse Tee a cup of tea, 4-VID

die Taube, -n dove, pigeon, 10-SA

tausend thousand, 2-G

das Taxi, -s taxicab, 8-SA

die Technik technology, 9-2

der **Tee** tea, 8-SA

der **Teil, -e** part, 11-2

teilen to divide, 11-2

teil·nehmen (nimmt teil), nahm teil, hat teilgenommen an (+ *dat.*) to take part in, 15-2

das **Telefon, -e** telephone, 6-SA; 7-2

telefonieren to telephone, make a phone call, 14-SA

die **Telefonnummer, -n** telephone number, *Einf.*

der **Teller, -** plate, 8-SA

das **Tempo** pace, tempo, 6-2

das **Tennis** tennis, 9-1

der **Tennisplatz, ⸚e** tennis court, 9-1

der **Teppich, -e** rug, 6-SA

der **Termin, -e** appointment, 6-2

die **Terrasse, -n** terrace, 15-SA

terroristisch terrorist (*adj.*), 10-TLL

teuer expensive, 6-2

der **Text, -e** text

das **Theater, -** theater, 6-TLL

das **Thema, die Themen** topic, subject, theme, 15-2

die **Thermosflasche, -n** thermos bottle, 7-1

das **Ticket, -s** (airline) ticket, 7-TLL

tief deep, 11-2

das **Tiefland** lowlands, 4-TLL

das **Tier, -e** animal, 9-2

der **Tip, -s** tip, hint, suggestion

der **Tisch, -e** table, *Einf.*

die **Tochter, ⸚** daughter, 2-2

der **Tod** death, 11-2

todmüde (*colloq.*) dead tired, 4-1

die **Toilette, -n** lavatory, 15-SA

toll (*colloq.*) great, terrific, 3-2

das **Tor, -e** gate, 11-1

tot dead, 11-2

die **Tour, -en** tour, 8-TLL

der **Tourist, -en, -en** tourist (*m.*), 1-TLL

die **Touristin, -nen** tourist (*f.*), 1-2

die **Tradition, -en** tradition, 11-TLL

traditionell traditional, 2-TLL

tragen (trägt), trug, hat getragen (1) to carry; (2) to wear, 3-1

trainieren to train, 9-SA

trampen, ist getrampt to hitchhike, 7-2

träumen to dream, 14-2

traurig sad, 13-2

treffen (trifft), traf, hat getroffen to meet, 9-1

treiben, trieb, hat getrieben to drive, force, propel, 9-1

Sport treiben to play sports, 9-1

die **Treppe** staircase, stairs, 9-1

auf der Treppe on the stairs, 9-1

trinken, trank, hat getrunken to drink, 4-2

trocken dry, 4-2

trotz (*prep. + gen.*) in spite of, despite, 8-G

trotzdem (*adv.*) in spite of that, nevertheless, 8-2

die **Trümmer** (*pl.*) ruins, rubble, 12-VID

Tschüs! So long! *Einf.*

das **T-Shirt, -s** T-shirt, 3-SA

das **Tuch, ⸚er** scarf; cloth, 16-VID

tun, tat, hat getan to do, 3-1

Das tut mir weh. That hurts (me). 11-1

Er tut, als ob . . . (+ *subjunctive*) He acts as if . . . 16-G

Es tut mir leid. I'm sorry (about that). 7-1

die **Tür, -en** door, *Einf.*

der **Türke, -n, -n** Turk (*m.*), 15-2

die **Türkei** Turkey, 15-2

die **Türkin, -nen** Turk (*f.*), 15-2

türkisch Turkish, 15-2

(das) **Türkisch** Turkish (language), 15-2

der **Turnschuh, -e** sneaker, gym shoe, 3-2

die **Tüte, -n** (paper, plastic) bag, 8-VID

der **Typ, -en** (1) type; (2) (*slang*) guy, 12-1

typisch typical, 1-1

U

die **U-Bahn** (= **Untergrundbahn**) subway train, 8-SA

üben to practice, *Einf.*

über (1) (*prep. + acc.*) about, 2-1; (2) (+ *acc. or dat.*) over, across; above, 6-1

überall everywhere, 2-2

sich etwas überlegen to consider, ponder, think something over, 13-2

übermorgen the day after tomorrow, 12-1

übernachten to spend the night, 7-2

überraschen to surprise, 15-1

die **Überraschung, -en** surprise, 16-SA

übersetzen to translate, *Einf.*

übrigens by the way, 1-1

die **Übung, -en** exercise

die **Uhr, -en** clock; watch, *Einf.*

9 Uhr 9 o'clock, *Einf.*; 5-1

Wieviel Uhr ist es? What time is it? 7-1

um (1) at (with times), 1-1; (2) around (the outside of), 4-1

um . . . zu in order to, 8-1

der **Umschlag, ⸚e** envelope, 15-1

um·steigen, stieg um, ist umgestiegen to transfer, change (trains, buses, etc.), 7-SA

die **Umwelt** environment, 3-2

umweltfreundlich environmentally safe, non-polluting, 9-1

um·ziehen, zog um, ist umgezogen to move, change residence, 9-1

sich um·ziehen, hat sich umgezogen to change clothes, 14-SA

unangenehm unpleasant, 15-2

unbekannt unknown, 10-2

unbesorgt unconcerned, carefree, 10-1

und (*coor. conj.*) and, 1-1

der **Unfall, ⸚e** accident, 9-2

ungebildet uneducated, 16-2

ungemütlich unpleasant, not cozy, 14-2

die **Uni, -s** (*colloq.*) university, 6-1

an der Uni at the university, 6-1

die **Universität, -en** university, 5-TLL; 6-1

an der Universität at the university, 6-1

unmöglich impossible, 6-1

unnötig unnecessary, 9-1

unordentlich messy, disorderly, 13-1

unruhig restless, troubled, 10-2

unten (*adv.*) below, on the bottom

unter (+ *acc.* or *dat.*) (1) under, beneath; (2) among, 6-1

unterbrechen (unterbricht), unterbrach, hat unterbrochen to interrupt, 10-2

sich unterhalten (unterhält), unterhielt, hat sich unterhalten mit to converse with, talk to, 15-2

der **Unterschied, -e** difference, 11-1

unterwegs on the way, en route; on the go, 4-1

unverheiratet unmarried, 16-1

unwichtig unimportant, 2-2

uralt ancient, 3-2

der **Urlaub, -e** vacation (from a job), 4-1

Urlaub machen to take a vacation, 5-2

in Urlaub gehen (*or*) **fahren** to go on vacation

die **USA** (*pl.*) the USA, 5-TLL

usw. (= **und so weiter**) etc. (= and so forth), 1-1

V

die **Variation, -en** variation

der **Vater, ⸚** father, 2-1

der **Vati, -s** papa, dad, 2-2

(das) **Venedig** Venice (Italy), 7-1

verantwortlich für responsible for, 6-2

das **Verb, -en** verb

verboten forbidden, prohibited

verbringen, verbrachte, hat verbracht to spend (time), 7-2

verdienen to earn, 2-2

vereinen to unite, 11-2

die **Vereinigung** unification, 11-1

Verflixt nochmal! (*colloq.*) Darn it all! 15-1

die **Vergangenheit** past (time), 11-2

vergessen (vergißt), vergaß, hat vergessen to forget, 5-2

vergleichen, verglich, hat verglichen to compare, 12-2

verheiratet sein to be married, 16-1

verkaufen to sell, 4-1

der **Verkäufer, -** salesman, 5-SA

die **Verkäuferin, -nen** saleswoman, 5-SA

der **Verkehr** traffic, 7-SA

das **Verkehrsmittel, -** means of transportation, 8-SA

verlassen (verläßt), verließ, hat verlassen to leave (a person or place), 5-1

sich verletzen to injure oneself, get hurt, 11-1

verlieren, verlor, hat verloren to lose, 10-1; 10-VID

sich verloben mit (+ *dat.*) to become engaged to, 12-1

verpassen to miss (an event, opportunity, train, etc.), 13-1

verrückt crazy, insane, 7-2

verschieden different, various, 11-2

verschmutzen to pollute; to dirty, 9-2

die **Verschmutzung** pollution, 9-1

verschwenden to waste, 9-2

verschwinden, verschwand, ist verschwunden to disappear, 11-2

sich verspäten to be late, 11-1

verstehen, verstand, hat verstanden to understand, 3-1

versuchen to try, attempt, 10-2

der/die **Verwandte, -n** (*adj. noun*) relative, 11-1

der **Vetter, -n** cousin (*m.*), 2-SA

viel (mehr, am meisten) much, a lot, 1-1

viele many, 1-2; (*pronoun*) many people, 8-2

vielen Dank many thanks, 2-1

vielleicht maybe, perhaps, 1-1

das **Viertel** quarter

Viertel vor/nach sieben quarter to/past seven, *Einf.*

der **Vogel, ⸚** bird, 9-2

die **Vokabel, -n** word

das **Volk, ⸚er** people, nation, folk, 10-2

das **Volkslied, -er** folk song, 4-2

voll full, 5-1

der **Volleyball** volleyball, 9-SA

von (*prep.* + *dat.*) from, 4-2; of; by, 5-1

vor (*prep.* + *acc.* or *dat.*) in front of, 6-1

vor einem Jahr   a year ago, 10-G

vorbei·kommen, kam vorbei, ist vorbeigekommen   to come by, drop by, 5-2

vor·bereiten   to prepare

sich vor·bereiten auf (+ *acc.*) to prepare for, 13-1

vorgestern   the day before yesterday, 12-1

vor·haben (hat vor), hatte vor, hat vorgehabt   to plan, have in mind, 13-1

vorher   before that, previously, 4-VID; 10-1

vor·lesen (liest vor), las vor, hat vorgelesen   to read aloud

die **Vorlesung, -en**   university lecture, 6-1

das **Vorlesungsverzeichnis, -se** university course catalogue, 6-1

vormittags (*adv.*)   (in the) mornings, 16-1

der **Vorschlag, ⸚e**   suggestion

vor·stellen   to introduce, present, 13-2

sich vor·stellen   to introduce oneself, 13-2

sich etwas vor·stellen   to imagine something, 11-1

das **Vorurteil, -e**   prejudice, 13-SA

W

wachsen (wächst), wuchs, ist gewachsen   to grow, 10-2

der **Wagen, -**   car, 3-1

die **Wahl, -en**   (1) choice; (2) election, 10-2

wählen   (1) to choose; (2) to elect, 10-2

der **Wähler, -**   voter, 10-2

wahnsinnig   (*adv. colloq.*) extremely, incredibly, 3-1

wahr   true, 3-1

nicht wahr?   isn't it? can't you? doesn't she? etc., 3-1

während (*prep. + gen.*)   during, 8-G

die **Wahrheit, -en**   truth, 13-SA

wahrscheinlich   probably, 1-2

der **Wald, ⸚er**   forest, 4-2

die **Wand, ⸚e**   (interior) wall, *Einf.*

die **Wanderlust**   wanderlust, 7-TLL

wandern, ist gewandert   to hike, wander, 4-2

die **Wanderung, -en**   hike, 5-2

der **Wandschrank, ⸚e** cupboard, 2-VID

wann?   when? *Einf.*

die **Ware, -n**   product, 9-2

warm (wärmer)   warm, *Einf.*

warten   to wait, 4-1

warten auf (+ *acc.*)   to wait for, 13-1

Warte mal!   Wait a second! Hang on! 4-1

warum?   why? 1-1

was?   what? *Einf.*

was für?   what kind of? 9-1

Was ist los?   What's the matter? What's going on? 3-1

waschen (wäscht), wusch, hat gewaschen   to wash, 11-1

das **Wasser**   water, 4-1

wechseln   to change (money), 14-1

wecken   to wake up (*trans.*), 4-VID

der **Wecker, -**   alarm clock, 6-SA

weder . . . noch   neither . . . nor, 14-1

der **Weg, -e**   way, path, 16-2

weg (*adv.*)   away, gone, 4-1

wegen (*prep. + gen.*)   because of, on account of, 8-G

weg·gehen, ging weg, ist weggegangen   to go away, leave, 12-1

weg·werfen (wirft weg), warf weg, hat weggeworfen   to throw away, 9-2

weh tun, tat weh, hat weh getan (+ *dat. of person*) to hurt, 11-1

weil (*sub. conj.*)   because, 8-G

der **Wein, -e**   wine, 4-2

weinen   to cry, 3-2

weiß   white, 3-2

weit   far, far away, 8-1

weiter·gehen, ging weiter, ist weitergegangen   to go on, continue

welcher, -es, -e   which, 7-1; 8-VID

die **Welt, -en**   world, 3-2

wem? (*dat.*)   to whom? for whom? 5-1

wen? (*acc.*)   whom? 2-1

wenig   little bit, not much, 1-1

wenige   few, 11-1

wenigstens   at least, 2-2

wenn (*sub. conj.*)   (1) if, 8-G; (2) when, whenever, 10-G

wer? (*nom.*)   who? *Einf.*

werden (wird), wurde, ist geworden   to become, get (*in the sense of* become), 4-1

werfen (wirft), warf, hat geworfen   to throw, 9-2

das **Werk, -e**   work (of art), musical composition, 13-2

wessen?   whose? 2-1

der **Westen**   the west, 4-2

das **Wetter**   weather, *Einf.*; 1-1

die **WG, -s** (= **Wohngemeinschaft**) communal living group, shared apartment, 6-1

wichtig   important, 2-2

wie   (1) how, *Einf.*; (2) like, as, 1-1

Wie bitte?   I beg your pardon? What did you say? *Einf.*

wie lange?   how long? 3-1

wieder   again, 1-1

wiederholen   to repeat, *Einf.*

die **Wiederholung, -en** repetition; review

wieder·sehen (sieht wieder), sah wieder, hat wiedergesehen   to see again, meet again, 12-2

Auf Wiedersehen! Good-bye! *Einf.*

wiegen, wog, hat gewogen (*trans. and intrans.*) to weigh, 15-1

(das) **Wien** Vienna, 1-1

wieso? How come? How's that?; What do you mean? 9-1

wieviel? how much? 5-1

  Wieviel Uhr ist es? What time is it? 7-1

wie viele? how many? 2-1

wievielt-: Den wievielten haben wir heute? What's the date today? 9-G

wild wild, 4-TLL

willkommen welcome, 6-2

  Herzlich willkommen! Welcome! Nice to see you!, 6-2

der **Wind** wind, 4-SA

windig windy, *Einf.*

der **Winter, -** winter, 4-1

  im Winter in the winter, 4-1

das **Wintersemester** fall term (usually Oct.–Feb.), 6-SA

wirklich real, 6-1

die **Wirtschaft** economy, 11-2

wirtschaftlich economic, 11-2

die **Wirtschaftswissenschaft** economics, 6-SA

der **Wischer, -** (blackboard) eraser, *Einf.*

wissen (weiß), wußte, hat gewußt to know (a fact), 2-1

  Weißt du noch? Do you remember? 11-1

die **Wissenschaft, -en** (1) science; (2) scholarship; field of knowledge, 6-SA

der **Witz, -e** (1) joke; (2) wit, 14-2

witzig witty, amusing, 14-2

wo? where? *Einf.*

die **Woche, -n** week, 5-1

das **Wochenende, -n** weekend, 5-2

  am Wochenende on the weekend, 5-2

Schönes Wochenende! (Have a) nice weekend! *Einf.*

wochenlang (*adv.*) for weeks, 14-TLL

woher? from where? *Einf.*

wohin? to where? 3-1

wohl probably, 6-2

wohnen to live, dwell, 1-1

die **Wohngemeinschaft, -en** communal living group, shared apartment, 6-1

das **Wohnhaus, ̈er** apartment building, 9-1

die **Wohnung, -en** apartment, 6-2

das **Wohnzimmer, -** living room, 15-SA

die **Wolke, -n** cloud, 4-SA

wolkig cloudy, *Einf.*

wollen (will), wollte, hat gewollt (1) to want to, intend to, 3-1; (2) to claim to, 16-G

worden (*special form of the past participle of* **werden** *used in the perfect tenses of the passive voice*)

das **Wort** word (*2 plural forms:* die **Worte** = words in context; die **Wörter** = unconnected words, as in a dictionary), 5-2

das **Wörterbuch, ̈er** dictionary, 5-2

der **Wortschatz** vocabulary

das **Wunder, -** miracle

  Kein Wunder! No wonder! 15-1

wunderbar wonderful, 7-1

sich wundern (über + *acc.*) to be surprised, amazed (at), 13-1

wunderschön very beautiful, 1-1

wünschen to wish, 8-VID; 12-1

die **Wurst, ̈e** sausage, 4-VID; 8-1

  Das ist mir Wurst (*or* **Wurscht**). I don't give a darn. 7-1

Z

zahlen to pay, 8-1

  Zahlen bitte! Check please! 8-1

zählen to count, 10-3

der **Zahn, ̈e** tooth, 11-SA

  sich die Zähne putzen to brush one's teeth, 11-SA

zeigen to show, 2-VID; 5-1

  Zeig mal her. Let's see. Show it to me. 15-1

die **Zeile, -n** line (of text)

die **Zeit, -en** time, 3-2

  höchste Zeit high time, 14-1

Zeitlang: eine Zeitlang for a time, for a while, 14-2

die **Zeitschrift, -en** magazine, 5-2

die **Zeitung, -en** newspaper, 2-1

zentral central, 11-TLL

zerstören to destroy, 8-2

die **Zerstörung** destruction

ziehen, zog, hat gezogen to pull, 6-1

das **Ziel, -e** goal, 7-2

ziemlich fairly, quite, 1-2

zigmal (*adv.*) umpteen times, 12-G

das **Zimmer, -** room, 2-1

zirka circa, 4-TLL

die **Zone, -n** zone, 11-TLL

zu to; too, 1-1; (*prep. + dat.*) to, 5-1

  zu Fuß on foot, 3-1

  zu Hause at home, 2-2

zuerst first, at first, 8-1

zufrieden satisfied

  Ich bin zufrieden. I can't complain. 12-VID

der **Zug, ̈e** train, 7-1

zu·hören (+ *dat.*) to listen (to), 13-1

die **Zukunft** future, 11-2

  in Zukunft in the future, 13-2

zuletzt last of all, finally, 8-1

zu·machen to close, 5-1

zunächst first (of all), to begin with, 14-2

zurück back, 1-1

zurück·bringen, brachte zurück, hat zurückgebracht to bring back

zurück·kommen, kam zurück, ist zurückgekommen to come back, 1-1

zusammen together, *Einf.*; 4-1

die **Zusammenfassung** summary

zweimal twice, 12-G

zweit- second, 9-1

der **Zweitwagen, -** second car, 9-1

zwischen (*prep. + acc. or dat.*) between, 2-2

ENGLISH–GERMAN VOCABULARY

Strong and irregular verbs are marked by an asterisk: *brechen, *können, *bringen. Their principal parts can be found in Appendix 2.

A

able: be able to *können
about über (*prep. + acc.*)
  it's about X es geht um X
above oben (*adv.*); über (*prep. + dat. or acc.*)
abroad im Ausland (*location*); ins Ausland (*destination*)
absent: be absent fehlen
accept akzeptieren
accident der Unfall, ¨e
account: on account of wegen (*+ gen.*)
acidic sauer
acid rain der saure Regen
acquaintance der/die Bekannte, -n (*adj. noun*)
acquainted: be acquainted with *kennen
across über (*prep. + dat. or acc.*)
act: He acts as if . . . Er tut, als ob . . .
active aktiv
actually eigentlich
acute akut
address die Adresse, -n
adjective das Adjektiv, -e
administration, government in power die Regierung, -en
adverb das Adverb, -ien
affair, matter die Sache, -n
afford: be able to afford something sich etwas leisten können
afraid: be afraid (of) Angst haben (vor + *dat.*)
after nach (*prep. + dat.*); nachdem (*sub. conj.*)
  after all schließlich
  after that danach (*adv.*)
afternoon der Nachmittag, -e

in the afternoon am Nachmittag
(in the) afternoons nachmittags
this afternoon heute nachmittag (*adv.*)
afterwards, after that nachher (*adv.*)
again wieder
against gegen (*prep. + acc.*)
ago vor (+ *dat.*)
  a year ago vor einem Jahr
agreed einverstanden
agriculture die Landwirtschaft
ah ach
aid die Hilfe
air die Luft
  air pollution die Luftverschmutzung
airplane das Flugzeug, -e
airport der Flughafen, ¨
alarm clock der Wecker, -
alive: be alive leben
all alle (*pl.*)
  all summer (day, afternoon, etc.) den ganzen Sommer (Tag, Nachmittag usw.)
allow *lassen
allowed: be allowed to *dürfen
almanac der Almanach, -e
almost fast
alone allein
along with mit (*adv.*)
alongside of an (*prep. + acc. or dat.*)
a lot viel (mehr, am meisten); eine Menge
Alps die Alpen (*pl.*)
already schon
also auch
alternative die Alternative, -n
although obwohl (*sub. conj.*)

always immer
amazed
  be amazed staunen
  be amazed (at) sich wundern (über + *acc.*)
America (das) Amerika
American amerikanisch (*adj.*); der Amerikaner, -; die Amerikanerin, -nen
among unter (*prep. + acc. or dat.*)
amusing witzig
analyze analysieren
ancient uralt
and und (*coor. conj.*)
anecdote die Anekdote, -n
anger der Ärger
angry (at) böse (+ *dat.*)
animal das Tier, -e
annoy ärgern
  get annoyed sich ärgern
annoyance der Ärger
annually jährlich
another, an additional noch ein
answer die Antwort, -en
answer (a person) antworten (+ *dat.*)
  answer (something) antworten auf (+ *acc.*)
anything
  Anything more? (Sonst) noch etwas?
  Will there be anything else? Sonst noch etwas?
anyway sowieso
anywhere irgendwo
apart from that sonst
apartment die Wohnung, -en
  apartment building das Wohnhaus, ¨er
appear *aus·sehen

appointment der Termin, -e
apprentice der Lehrling, -e
April (der) April
area die Gegend, -en
arm der Arm, -e
around, about (*with time*) gegen (*prep. + acc.*)
around (*the outside of*) um (*prep. + acc.*)
arrive °an·kommen
arrogance die Arroganz
art die Kunst, ¨e
  art history die Kunstgeschichte
article der Artikel, -
artist der Künstler, -; die Künstlerin, -nen
as wie
  as a als
ask fragen
  ask a question eine Frage stellen
  ask for °bitten um
  ask oneself sich fragen
aspect der Aspekt, -e
assignment die Aufgabe, -n
astounding erstaunlich
at bei (*prep. + dat.*); an (*prep. + acc. or dat.*); (*with times*) um (*prep. + acc.*)
athletic sportlich
At last! Na endlich!
at least wenigstens
atom das Atom, -e
atomic power plant das Atomkraftwerk, -e
attempt versuchen
attend to erledigen
attention: pay attention auf·passen
August (der) August
aunt die Tante, -n
Austria (das) Österreich
Austrian österreichisch (*adj.*); der Österreicher, -; die Österreicherin, -nen
automatic automatisch
auto mechanic der Automechaniker, -; die Automechanikerin, -nen

automobile das Auto, -s; der Wagen, -
autumn der Herbst
away weg (*adv.*)

B

baby das Baby, -s
back zurück (*adv.*)
backpack der Rucksack, ¨e
bad schlecht; schlimm; böse (*evil*)
bag die Tüte, -n
baker der Bäcker, -; die Bäckerin, -nen
bakery die Bäckerei, -en
ballpoint pen der Kugelschreiber, -
Baloney! Quatsch!
banana die Banane, -n
bank die Bank, -en
bar, tavern die Kneipe, -n
barbaric barbarisch
barely kaum
barrier die Barriere, -n
basement der Keller, -
basis die Basis
bath das Bad
  take a bath ein Bad °nehmen
bathroom das Badezimmer, -
be °sein
bear der Bär, -en, -en
beat °schlagen
beautiful schön
  very beautiful wunderschön
because weil (*sub. conj.*)
  because, for denn (*coor. conj.*)
  because of wegen (+ *gen.*)
become, get °werden
bed das Bett, -en
  get out of bed °auf·stehen
  go to bed ins Bett °gehen
bedroom das Schlafzimmer, -
beer das Bier, -e
before bevor (*sub. conj.*)
  before that vorher (*adv.*)
begin °an·fangen; °beginnen
  to begin with zunächst (*adv.*)

beginner der Anfänger, -
beginning der Anfang, ¨e
  at/in the beginning am Anfang
behind hinter (*prep. + acc. or dat.*)
believe glauben (+ *dat. of person*)
belong to (a person) gehören (+ *dat.*)
below unten (*adv.*); unter (*prep. + acc. or dat.*)
bench die Bank, ¨e
beneath unter (*prep. + acc. or dat.*)
beside neben (*prep. + acc. or dat.*)
besides außer (+ *dat.*)
best best-
  like best of all to am liebsten (+ *verb*)
better besser
between zwischen (*prep. + acc. or dat.*)
bicycle das Fahrrad, ¨er; das Rad, ¨er; °rad·fahren
big groß (größer, größt-)
bill die Rechnung, -en
biology die Biologie
bird der Vogel, ¨
birthday der Geburtstag, -e
  for one's birthday zum Geburtstag
  When is your birthday? Wann hast du Geburtstag?
black schwarz (schwärzer)
blackboard die Tafel, -n
blanket die Decke, -n
blouse die Bluse, -n
blue blau
book das Buch, ¨er; buchen (*verb*)
bookcase das Bücherregal, -e
bookstore die Buchhandlung, -en
border die Grenze, -n
bored: be bored sich langweilen
boring langweilig
  extremely boring stinklangweilig (*colloq.*)

born   geboren
borrow   °leihen
boss   der Chef, -s; die Chefin, -nen
both   beid-
  both (people)   beide (*pl. pronoun*)
  both (things)   beides (*sing. pronoun*)
bottle   die Flasche, -n
bottom: at the bottom   unten (*adv.*)
box   boxen
boy   der Junge, -n, -n
bread   das Brot, -e
  dark bread   das Bauernbrot
break, intermission   die Pause, -n
  take a break   eine Pause machen
break   °brechen; kaputt machen
  break out   °aus·brechen
breakfast   das Frühstück, -e
  eat breakfast   frühstücken
  for breakfast   zum Frühstück
bridge   die Brücke, -n
bright (light)   hell
  bright (smart)   klug (klüger)
bring   °bringen
  bring along   °mit·bringen
  bring back   °zurück·bringen
broken   kaputt (*colloq.*)
brother   der Bruder, ¨
brown   braun
brush one's teeth   sich die Zähne putzen
build   bauen
building   das Gebäude, -
bus   der Bus, -se
business   das Geschäft, -e
  business (field of study)   die Betriebswirtschaft
  business people   die Geschäftsleute
  businessman   der Geschäftsmann
  businesswoman   die Geschäftsfrau
but   aber (*coor. conj.*)

but rather   sondern (*coor. conj.*)
butter   die Butter
buy   kaufen
by
  by (a certain time)   bis (*prep. + acc.*)
  by oneself (myself, yourself, etc.)   selbst *or* selber (*adv.*)
  by the way   übrigens

C

café   das Café, -s
  pastry café   die Konditorei, -en
cafeteria (at the university)   die Mensa
cake   der Kuchen, -
call   °rufen
  be called   °heißen
  call up   °an·rufen
calm, peaceful   ruhig
camera   die Kamera, -s
camp   campen
can, be able to   °können
Canada   (das) Kanada
Canadian   kanadisch (*adj.*); der Kanadier, -; die Kanadierin, -nen
cap   die Mütze, -n
capitalism   der Kapitalismus
car   das Auto, -s; der Wagen, -
card   die Karte, -n
care
  I don't care.   Das ist mir egal.
  take care of   sich kümmern um
  take care of, finish   erledigen
career   die Karriere, -n
carefree   unbesorgt
carry   °tragen
cash   das Bargeld
cashier, cashier's office   die Kasse, -n
cassette player   der Kassettenrecorder, -

cat   die Katze, -n
catalogue (university)   das Vorlesungsverzeichnis, -se
catastrophe   die Katastrophe, -n
catastrophic   katastrophal
cathedral   der Dom, -e
cause to be done   °lassen (+ *infinitive*)
CD (compact disk)   die CD, -s
  CD player   der CD-Spieler, -
cease   auf·hören (mit)
celebrate   feiern
celebration   die Feier, -n
cellar   der Keller, -
central   zentral
century   das Jahrhundert, -e
  for centuries   jahrhundertelang
certain, sure   sicher; bestimmt
chain   die Kette, -n
  chain reaction   die Kettenreaktion, -en
chair   der Stuhl, ¨e
chalk   die Kreide
chance   die Gelegenheit, -en; die Chance, -n
change   ändern (*trans.*); sich ändern
  change (clothes)   sich °um·ziehen
  change (money)   wechseln
  change (trains, buses, etc.), transfer   °um·steigen
change purse   der Geldbeutel, -
chapter   das Kapitel, -
chat   quatschen (*colloq.*)
cheap   billig
check   der Scheck, -s (*bank check*); die Rechnung, -en (*restaurant bill*)
  Check please!   Zahlen bitte!
check   kontrollieren
cheerful   munter; heiter
Cheers!   Prost! *or* Prosit!
cheese   der Käse
chemistry   die Chemie
chief   Haupt- (*noun prefix*)
child   das Kind, -er
childhood   die Kindheit, -en
China   (das) China

Chinese (das) Chinesisch; der Chinese, -n, -n; die Chinesin, -nen

chocolate die Schokolade

choice die Wahl, -en

choose wählen

chop, cutlet das Schnitzel, -

church die Kirche, -n

circa zirka

citizen der Bürger, -

city die Stadt, ⸚e
   capital city die Hauptstadt, ⸚e
   city guidebook der Stadtführer, -
   city map der Stadtplan, ⸚e
   large city (over 500,000 inhabitants) die Großstadt, ⸚e
   old city center die Altstadt, ⸚e
   small city (5,000 to 20,000 inhabitants) die Kleinstadt, ⸚e

civil servant der Beamte (*adj. noun, m.*); die Beamtin, -nen (*f.*)

claim to °wollen

class die Klasse, -n
   class hour die Stunde, -n

clean sauber (*adj.*); putzen (*verb*)

clear klar; deutlich

clerk der Verkäufer, -; die Verkäuferin, -nen

cliché das Klischee, -s

cliché (*adj.*), **stereotyped** klischeehaft

climate das Klima

climb °steigen

clinic die Klinik, -en

clock die Uhr, -en

close °schließen, zu·machen
   closed geschlossen

cloth das Tuch

clothes die Kleider (*pl.*)
   clothes cupboard der Kleiderschrank, ⸚e

clothing die Kleidung

cloud die Wolke, -n

cloudy wolkig

coat der Mantel, ⸚

coffee der Kaffee

cold kalt (kälter)
   catch a cold sich erkälten

collect sammeln

Cologne (das) Köln

colony die Kolonie, -n

color die Farbe, -n

colorful bunt

comb kämmen
   comb one's hair sich die Haare kämmen

come °kommen
   All together that comes to . . . Das macht zusammen . . .
   come along °mit·kommen
   come back °zurück·kommen
   come by °vorbei·kommen
   I come from . . . Ich komme aus . . .
   Where do you come from? Woher kommst du?

comfortable bequem

communal living group die Wohngemeinschaft, -en; die WG, -s

Communism der Kommunismus

compare °vergleichen

compatriots die Landsleute (*pl.*)

competition die Konkurrenz

complain: I can't complain. Ich bin zufrieden.

computer der Computer, -
   computer science die Informatik

concentrate on sich konzentrieren auf (+ *acc.*)

concerned besorgt

concert das Konzert, -e

conclusion der Schluß, die Schlüsse
   in conclusion zum Schluß

conflict der Konflikt, -e

congenial sympathisch

congratulate gratulieren (+ *dat. of person*)

Congratulations! Herzlichen Glückwunsch!

consequence die Konsequenz, -en

conservative konservativ

consider something sich etwas überlegen

contact der Kontakt, -e

contingent: be contingent on, depend on °an·kommen auf (+ *acc.*)

contrary: on the contrary im Gegenteil

contrast der Kontrast, -e

conversation das Gespräch, -e

converse with sich °unterhalten mit

cook kochen

cool kühl

cooperate mit·machen

corner die Ecke, -n
   around the corner um die Ecke
   at/on the corner an der Ecke

correct richtig

correspondent der Korrespondent, -en, -en

Corsica (das) Korsika

cost kosten

count zählen

counter, window der Schalter, -

country das Land, ⸚er
   in the country auf dem Land
   to the country aufs Land

couple
   a couple (of) ein paar
   married couple das Ehepaar, -e

cousin die Kusine, -n (*f.*); der Vetter, -n (*m.*)

cozy, relaxed gemütlich

cram pauken (*student slang*)

crazy verrückt

cream die Sahne

creative kreativ

critical kritisch

cross street die Querstraße, -n

crowd die Menge, -n

cruel grausam

cry weinen

culture die Kultur, -en

cup   die Tasse, -n
current   aktuell (*adj.*)
customer   der Kunde, -n, -n; die Kundin, -nen
cut   °schneiden
cutlet   das Schnitzel, -

D

dad   der Vati, -s
damp   naß
dance   tanzen
danger   die Gefahr, -en
dangerous   gefährlich
dark   dunkel
darn
  Darn it all!   Verflixt nochmal!
  I don't give a darn.   Das ist mir Wurst (*or* Wurscht).
date: What's the date today?   Der wievielte ist heute? Den wievielten haben wir heute?
daughter   die Tochter, ⸚
day   der Tag, -e
  day after tomorrow   übermorgen
  day before yesterday   vorgestern
  for days   tagelang
  in those days   damals
  one day (in the past or future)   eines Tages
  some day (in the future)   eines Tages
dead   tot
deal with   sich kümmern um
dear   lieb
death   der Tod, -e
December   (der) Dezember
decide   °entscheiden
deep   tief
delicious   lecker
democracy   die Demokratie
democratic   demokratisch
democratization   die Demokratisierung
demonstrate   demonstrieren
demonstration   die Demonstration, -en

depart   °ab·fahren; °los·fahren
department store   das Kaufhaus, ⸚er
depend on   °an·kommen auf (+ *acc.*)
describe   °beschreiben
desire   die Lust
desk   der Schreibtisch, -e
despite   trotz (+ *gen.*)
dessert   der Nachtisch, -e; die Nachspeise, -n
  for dessert   zum Nachtisch
destination   das Reiseziel, -e
destroy   zerstören
destruction   die Zerstörung
dialect   der Dialekt, -e
dialogue   der Dialog, -e
dictionary   das Wörterbuch, ⸚er
die   °sterben
  die in battle   °fallen
difference   der Unterschied, -e
different, other   ander- (*attributive adj.*); anders (*predicate adj.*)
different, various   verschieden
difficult   schwer; schwierig
difficulty   die Schwierigkeit, -en
dining room   das Eßzimmer, -
  dining room (hotel)   der Speisesaal
direct(ly)   direkt
director   der Direktor, -en
dirty   schmutzig; dreckig (*colloq.*)
disappear   °verschwinden
disappoint   enttäuschen
disappointment   die Enttäuschung, -en
discount   die Ermäßigung, -en
discuss   diskutieren; °besprechen
discussion   die Diskussion, -en
disorderly   schlampig (*colloq.*); unordentlich
dissertation   die Dissertation, -en; die Diss (*university slang*); die Doktorarbeit
distant   fern
disturb   stören

divide   teilen
do   machen; °tun
doctor   der Arzt, ⸚e; die Ärztin, -nen
dog   der Hund, -e
done   fertig
donkey   der Esel, -
door   die Tür, -en
dove   die Taube, -n
drag   schleppen (*colloq.*)
dream   träumen
dress   das Kleid, -er
dress, get dressed   sich °an·ziehen
drink   das Getränk, -e; °trinken (*verb*)
drive (a vehicle)   °fahren
  drive, force   °treiben
drop by   °vorbei·kommen
dry   trocken
dumb, stupid   dumm (dümmer); blöd
during   während (+ *gen.*)
  during, while . . . -ing   bei . . .
dwell   wohnen
dynasty   die Dynastie, -n

E

each   jed-
  each other   einander
eagle   der Adler, -
ear   das Ohr, -en
early   früh
earn   verdienen
earth   die Erde
east   der Osten
easy, simple   einfach; leicht
eat   °essen
economic   wirtschaftlich
economics   die Wirtschaftswissenschaft
economy   die Wirtschaft
ecosystem   das Ökosystem, -e
educated   gebildet
education (as field of study)   die Pädagogik
egg   das Ei, -er
either . . . or   entweder . . . oder

elect wählen
election die Wahl, -en
electrical engineer der Elektrotechniker, -; die Elektrotechnikerin, -nen
electrical engineering die Elektrotechnik
electrician der Elektrotechniker, -; die Elektrotechnikerin, -nen
electricity die Elektrizität
elegant elegant
elephant der Elefant, -en, -en
elevator der Lift, -s
emancipation die Emanzipation
emigrate aus·wandern
empire das Reich, -e
employed berufstätig
employee der/die Angestellte, -n (*adj. noun*)
empty leer
end das Ende, -n; der Schluß, die Schlüsse
  at the end am Ende
  at the end of February Ende Februar
  end, be finished, be over zu Ende °sein
energy die Energie
engaged: become engaged to sich verloben mit
engineer der Ingenieur, -e; die Ingenieurin, -nen
English (*adj.*) englisch
  English (language) (das) Englisch
  English studies die Anglistik
Englishman der Engländer, -
Englishwoman die Engländerin, -nen
enormous enorm
enough genug
en route unterwegs
enthusiasm die Begeisterung
enthusiastic about begeistert von
entire ganz
entrance, way in der Einstieg, -e

envelope der Umschlag, ⸚e
environment die Umwelt
  environmentally safe, non-polluting umweltfreundlich
epoch die Epoche, -n
equal gleich
equal rights die Gleichberechtigung (*sing.*)
  enjoying equal rights gleichberechtigt
eraser der Radiergummi (*pencil*); der Wischer, - (*blackboard*)
especially besonders
essay der Aufsatz, ⸚e
  essay topic das Aufsatzthema, -themen
etc. usw. (= und so weiter)
Europe (das) Europa
  Eastern Europe (das) Osteuropa
European europäisch (*adj.*); der Europäer, -; die Europäerin, -nen
even, in fact sogar
evening der Abend, -e
  evening meal das Abendessen
  good evening guten Abend
  in the evening am Abend
  (in the) evenings abends
  this evening, tonight heute abend
ever je
every jed-
  every time jedesmal (*adv.*)
everybody alle (*pl. pron.*)
everyday life der Alltag
everyone jeder (*sing. pron.*)
everything alles
everywhere überall
evil böse (*adj.*)
exact genau
examination die Prüfung, -en; das Abitur (*final secondary school exam*); das Abi (*slang*)
example das Beispiel, -e
  for example zum Beispiel
excellent ausgezeichnet

exchange student der Austauschstudent, -en, -en
excursion der Ausflug, ⸚e
Excuse me. Entschuldigung.
exercise die Übung, -en
exhausted kaputt (*colloq.*)
exhibition die Ausstellung, -en
exist existieren
expect erwarten
expensive teuer
experience die Erfahrung, -en
explain erklären
expression der Ausdruck, ⸚e
expressway die Autobahn, -en
extreme extrem
extremely wahnsinnig (*colloq. adv.*)
eye das Auge, -n
eyeglasses die Brille (*sing.*)

F

face das Gesicht, -er
fact
  in fact eigentlich
  in fact, even sogar
factory die Fabrik, -en
fairly ziemlich
fairy tale das Märchen, -
fall, autumn der Herbst
  fall term das Wintersemester
fall °fallen
  fall asleep °ein·schlafen
false, incorrect falsch
family die Familie, -n
famous berühmt
fantastic phantastisch
far, far away weit; fern
farmer der Bauer, -n, -n; der Landwirt, -e; die Landwirtin, -nen
fast schnell
father der Vater, ⸚
favorite Lieblings- (*noun prefix*)
fear die Angst, ⸚e; Angst haben (vor + *dat.*); fürchten
February (der) Februar

Federal Republic of Germany (FRG) die Bundesrepublik Deutschland (BRD)

fed up: I'm fed up. Ich habe die Nase voll.

feel sich fühlen (*intrans.*)

feeling das Gefühl, -e

fetch holen

  fetch, pick up ab·holen

few wenige

  a few ein paar

film der Film, -e

finally endlich; schließlich; zum Schluß; zuletzt

finance finanzieren

find °finden

Fine by me. Ist gut. (*colloq.*)

finger der Finger, -

finish, take care of erledigen

finished with fertig mit

firm, company die Firma, die Firmen

first erst- (*adj.*); zuerst (*adv.*)

  at first zuerst

  first (of all) zunächst

fish der Fisch, -e

flabbergasted baff (*colloq.*)

flat flach

floor (of a building) der Stock

  ground floor, first floor das Erdgeschoß

  on the second floor im ersten Stock

  second floor der erste Stock

flow °fließen

flower die Blume, -n

fly °fliegen

fog der Nebel

foggy neblig

folk das Volk, ¨er

  folk song das Volkslied, -er

follow folgen, ist gefolgt (+ *dat.*)

food das Essen; die Speise, -n (*dish, menu item*)

foolproof idiotensicher

foot der Fuß, ¨e

  on foot zu Fuß

for für (*prep.* + *acc.*)

  for, because denn (*coor. conj.*)

for a long time lange; seit langem, schon lange

for years seit Jahren

forbidden verboten

force, propel °treiben

foreign ausländisch

  foreign, strange fremd

  foreign countries das Ausland (*sing.*)

  foreign language die Fremdsprache, -n

  foreign worker der Gastarbeiter, -; die Gastarbeiterin, -nen

foreigner der Ausländer, -; die Ausländerin, -nen

forest der Wald, ¨er

forget °vergessen

  I can't forget that. Das geht mir nicht aus dem Kopf.

fork die Gabel, -n

form die Form, -en

formal formell

formulate formulieren

fox der Fuchs, ¨e

France (das) Frankreich

free

  free, unoccupied frei

  free of charge kostenlos

  free time die Freizeit

freedom die Freiheit, -en

French (*adj.*) französisch

French fries die Pommes frites (*pl.*)

Frenchman der Franzose, -n, -n

Frenchwoman die Französin, -nen

fresh frisch

Friday (der) Freitag

friend der Freund, -e; die Freundin, -nen

friendly freundlich; sympathisch

from aus (+ *dat.*); von (+ *dat.*)

front: in front of vor (*prep.* + *dat.* or *acc.*)

fruit das Obst

frustrate frustrieren

full voll

fun der Spaß

  Have fun. Viel Spaß.

  That is fun (for me). Das macht (mir) Spaß.

funny, peculiar komisch

furnished möbliert

furniture die Möbel (*pl.*)

future die Zukunft

  in the future in Zukunft

G

game das Spiel, -e

garage die Garage, -n

garden der Garten, ¨

gate das Tor, -e

gender das Geschlecht, -er

generation die Generation, -en

gentleman der Herr, -n, -en

geographical geographisch

geography die Geographie

German deutsch (*adj.*); der/die Deutsche, -n (*adj. noun*)

  German class die Deutschstunde, -n

  German Democratic Republic (GDR) die Deutsche Demokratische Republik (DDR)

  German (language) (das) Deutsch

  German mark, Deutschmark die Deutsche Mark

  German studies die Germanistik

  in German auf deutsch

Germany (das) Deutschland

get, receive °bekommen

  get, become °werden

  get, fetch holen

  get, pick up ab·holen

  get in (a vehicle) °ein·steigen

  get out (of a vehicle) °aus·steigen

  get there: How do I get there? Wie komme ich dahin?

  get up, get out of bed °auf·stehen

giant der Riese, -n, -n

gigantic   riesengroß; riesen-
   (*noun and adj. prefix*)
girl   das Mädchen, -
give   °geben
   give (as a gift)   schenken
   give up   °auf·geben
glad   froh
   I'm glad.   Das freut mich.
gladly, with pleasure   gern(e)
   (*adv.*)
glass   das Glas, -̈er
glasses   die Brille (*sing.*)
glove   der Handschuh, -e
go   °gehen
   go (by vehicle)   °fahren
   go away   °weg·gehen
   go out   °aus·gehen
   let's go!   los!
   on the go   unterwegs
goal   das Ziel, -e
god   der Gott, -̈er
golden   golden
   golden wedding anniversary
   die goldene Hochzeit
gone   weg
good   gut (besser, best-)
   Good-bye!   Auf
   Wiedersehen!
   Good evening!   Guten
   Abend!
   Good morning!   Guten
   Morgen!
   Have a good trip!   Gute
   Reise!
   pretty good   ganz gut
gossip   der Klatsch
government in power   die
   Regierung, -en
grade, class   die Klasse, -n
   grade (on a test, paper, etc.)
   die Note, -n
gram   das Gramm
   500 grams   das Pfund
grammar   die Grammatik
grandfather   der Großvater, -̈
grandma   die Oma, -s
grandmother   die Großmutter, -̈
grandpa   der Opa, -s
grandparents   die Großeltern
   (*pl.*)
grandson   der Enkel, -

gray   grau
great, terrific   herrlich; prima,
   toll (*colloq.*)
greatness   die Größe
Greece   (das) Griechenland
Greek   griechisch (*adj.*)
green   grün
greet   grüßen
groceries   die Lebensmittel
   (*pl.*)
group   die Gruppe, -n
grow   °wachsen
   grow up   °auf·wachsen
gruesome   grausam
guess   °raten
   Take a guess!   Raten Sie
   mal!
guest   der Gast, -̈e
guide book   der Reiseführer, -
guy   der Typ, -en (*slang*)
gym shoe   der Turnschuh, -e

H

hair   das Haar, -e
half   halb (*adv.*)
   half days   halbtags (*adv.*)
ham   der Schinken
hand   die Hand, -̈e
handsome   hübsch
hang   hängen (*trans.*); °hängen
   (*intrans.*)
   hang up   auf·hängen
happen   passieren, ist passiert
happiness   das Glück
happy   glücklich, froh
   be happy   sich freuen
harbor   der Hafen, -̈
hard   hart (härter)
   hard, difficult   schwer
hardly   kaum
hard-working   fleißig
harsh   hart (härter)
hat   der Hut, -̈e
hate   hassen
hatred   der Haß
haul   schleppen
have   °haben
   have in mind   °vor·haben
   have to, must   °müssen

head   der Kopf, -̈e
health   die Gesundheit
healthy   gesund (gesünder)
hear   hören
heaven: For heaven's sake!
   Um Gottes Willen!
heavy   schwer
hectic   hektisch
hello   Grüß Gott! (*in southern
   Germany and Austria*);
   Guten Tag!; Hallo!
   say hello to   grüßen
help   die Hilfe; °helfen (+ *dat.*)
helping, portion   die Portion,
   -en
here   hier (*location*); her
   (*destination*)
   Here it is.   Bitte.
Hi!   Tag!
high   hoch (*pred. adj.*), hoh-
   (*attributive adj.*) (höher,
   höchst-)
   High time!   Höchste Zeit! Na
   endlich!
highway   die Autobahn, -en
hike   die Wanderung, -en;
   wandern
hill   der Hügel, -
hilly   hügelig
hint   der Tip, -s
historic   historisch
history   die Geschichte, -n
hit   °schlagen
hitchhike   per Autostop reisen;
   trampen
hitchhiking   der Autostop
hold   °halten
home (as destination of
   motion)   nach Hause
   at home   zu Hause
   in the home of   bei (+ *dat.*)
homeland   die Heimat
homesickness   das Heimweh
homework assignment   die
   Hausaufgabe, -n
honest   ehrlich
hope   hoffen
   I hope   hoffentlich (*adv.*)
horizon   der Horizont, -e
hospital   das Krankenhaus, -̈er
hot   heiß

hotel das Hotel, -s
hour die Stunde, -n
  for hours stundenlang
house das Haus, ⸚er
housemate der Mitbewohner, -;
  die Mitbewohnerin, -nen
housewife die Hausfrau, -en
how? wie?
  How come? Wieso? *or* Wie
    kommt das?
  how long? wie lange?
  how many? wie viele?
  how much? wieviel?
however aber
human being der Mensch, -en,
  -en
human race die Menschheit
humor der Humor
hunch die Ahnung, -en
hunger der Hunger
hungry hungrig
  be hungry Hunger haben
hurry die Eile; sich beeilen,
  schnell machen (*colloq.*)
  in a hurry in Eile
hurt weh °tun (+ *dat. of*
  person)
  get hurt sich verletzen
  That hurts (me). Das tut
    (mir) weh.
husband der Mann, ⸚er

I

ice das Eis
  ice cream das Eis
  ice hockey das Eishockey
idea die Idee, -n
  (I have) no idea. Ich habe
    keine Ahnung.
ideal ideal
I.D. card der Ausweis, -e
ideological ideologisch
if wenn (*sub. conj.*)
  if, whether ob (*sub. conj.*)
illegal illegal
image das Bild, -er
imagine something sich etwas
  vor·stellen
immediately gleich; sofort
immigrate ein·wandern

important wichtig
  most important Haupt-
    (*noun prefix*)
impossible unmöglich
impression der Eindruck, ⸚e
in, into in (*prep. + acc.* or
  dat.); hinein- (*prefix*)
incorrect, false falsch
Incredible! Sagenhaft!
incredibly wahnsinnig (*colloq.*
  adv.)
indicative der Indikativ
industrial industriell
industrious fleißig
industry die Industrie, -n
inexpensive billig, preiswert
inflation die Inflation
information die Auskunft
injure oneself sich verletzen
inkling die Ahnung, -en
insane verrückt
inspect kontrollieren
instead sondern (*coor.*
  conj.)
  instead of anstatt (+ *gen.*);
    statt (+ *gen.*)
instrument das Instrument, -e
integration die Integration
intelligent intelligent
intend to °wollen
interest interessieren
  be interested in sich
    interessieren für
interesting interessant
intermission die Pause, -n
international international
interrupt °unterbrechen
interview interviewen
into in (*prep. + acc.*); hinein-
  (*prefix*)
introduce vor·stellen
  introduce oneself sich
    vor·stellen
invent °erfinden
invest investieren
invite °ein·laden
irony die Ironie
Italian italienisch (*adj.*); der
  Italiener, -; die Italienerin,
  -nen
Italy (das) Italien

J

jacket die Jacke, -n
January (der) Januar
jeans die Jeans (*pl.*)
Jewish jüdisch
job, position die Stelle, -n
joke der Witz, -e
journalist der Journalist, -en,
  -en
journey die Reise, -n
joy die Freude, -n
juice der Saft, ⸚e
July (der) Juli
June (der) Juni
just, at the moment gerade
  just as . . . as genau so . . .
    wie

K

kaput kaputt (*colloq.*)
keep °behalten
key der Schlüssel, -
kilogram das Kilogramm; das
  Kilo (*colloq.*)
kilometer der Kilometer, -
kitchen die Küche, -n
knife das Messer, -
know (a fact) °wissen
  get to know kennen·lernen
  know, be acquainted with
    °kennen
  know one's way around
    sich °aus·kennen
known bekannt

L

lab(oratory) das Labor, -s
lady die Dame, -n
lake der See, -n
  at the lake am See
lamp die Lampe, -n
landscape die Landschaft, -en
language die Sprache, -n
last letzt-
  last of all zuletzt
  last, take time dauern
late spät
  be late sich verspäten
  I'm late. Ich bin spät dran.
later on nachher (*adv.*)

laugh lachen
lavatory die Toilette, -n
lavender lila
law das Gesetz, -e
   (study of) law Jura
   **under the law, in the eyes of
     the law** vor dem Gesetz
lawyer der Rechtsanwalt, ˸e;
   die Rechtsanwältin, -nen
lay, put down legen
lazy faul
lead ˚führen
learn lernen
**leave (something or someone),
   leave behind** ˚lassen
   leave (a person or place)
     ˚verlassen
   leave (by vehicle)
     ˚ab·fahren; ˚los·fahren
   leave, go away ˚weg·gehen
lecture (university) die
   Vorlesung, -en
left: to the left, on the left
   links (*adv.*)
leg das Bein, -e
leisure time die Freizeit
lend ˚leihen
let ˚lassen
let's go! los!
letter der Brief, -e
lettuce der Salat, -e
library die Bibliothek, -en
lie, be situated ˚liegen
life das Leben
light das Licht, -er
   light (in color) hell
   light (in weight) leicht
like ˚mögen; wie (*conj.*)
   I like that. Das gefällt mir.
   like something etwas gern
     haben; etwas mögen
   like this so
   like to (do something) gern
     (+ *verb*)
   would like to möchten
likeable sympathisch
limnology die Limnologie
line (of text) die Zeile, -n
   line (streetcar or bus) die
     Linie, -n
linguistics die Linguistik

lion der Löwe, -n, -n
list die Liste, -n
listen (to) zu·hören (+ *dat.*)
liter der Liter
literary literarisch
little klein (*adj.*); wenig
   (*pronoun*)
   a little etwas
   **a little; a little bit; a little
     while** ein bißchen
live leben
   live, dwell wohnen
lively munter
liverwurst die Leberwurst, ˸e
loan ˚leihen
long lang(e) (länger)
   for a long time lange;
     (*stretch of time continuing
     in the present*) schon
     lange, seit langem
   for such a long time so
     lange
   no longer nicht mehr
look schauen
   look after auf·passen auf
     (+ *acc.*); sich kümmern
     um
   look, appear ˚aus·sehen
   look at an·schauen
   look for, seek suchen
   look forward to sich freuen
     auf (+ *acc.*)
   Look here. Schau mal.
   look out (for) auf·passen
     (auf + *acc.*)
   take a look at something
     sich etwas ˚an·sehen
lose ˚verlieren
lots of eine Menge; viel
loud laut
love die Liebe; lieben
low niedrig
luck das Glück
   be lucky Glück haben
   be unlucky, have bad luck
     Pech haben
lug (along) schleppen
   (*colloq.*)
luggage das Gepäck
lunch, midday meal das
   Mittagessen

M

machine die Maschine, -n
magazine die Zeitschrift, -en
mail die Post
mail (a letter) ˚ein·werfen
mailbox der Briefkasten, ˸
mailman der Briefträger, -
main Haupt- (*noun prefix*)
major field (of study) das
   Hauptfach, ˸er
major in (a subject) studieren
make machen
make-up: put on make-up
   sich schminken
mama, mom die Mutti, -s
man der Mann, ˸er
  Man! Mensch!
manage schaffen (*colloq.*)
management (field of study)
   die Betriebswirtschaft
manager der Manager, -
manipulate manipulieren
mankind die Menschheit
many viele (*adj.*)
   many a manch-
   many people viele (*pl.
     pron.*)
   many things vieles (*sing.
     pron.*)
map die Karte, -n; die
   Landkarte, -n
March (der) März
mark (the German mark) die
   Mark
marry, get married heiraten
   be married verheiratet
     sein
marvelous herrlich; sagenhaft
math die Mathe (*slang*)
mathematics die Mathematik
   (*sing.*)
matter, affair die Sache, -n
matter
   It doesn't matter. Es macht
     (doch) nichts.
   It doesn't matter to me.
     Das ist mir egal.
   **no matter where, who, why,
     etc.** egal wo, wer, warum
     usw.

What's the matter? Was ist los?

May (der) Mai

may, be allowed to °dürfen

That may be. Das mag sein.

maybe vielleicht

meal das Essen

mean, signify bedeuten

mean, think meinen

that means, in other words das heißt

What do you mean? Wieso?

meaning die Bedeutung, -en

meat das Fleisch

mechanic der Mechaniker, -

medicine die Medizin

meet (for the first time) kennen·lernen

meet again °wieder·sehen

meet (by appointment) °treffen

melancholy die Melancholie

member das Mitglied, -er

mention

Don't mention it. Nichts zu danken.

menu die Speisekarte, -n

messy schlampig (*colloq.*); unordentlich

method die Methode, -n

Middle Ages das Mittelalter (*sing.*)

might die Macht

mild mild

milk die Milch

million die Million, -en

minor field (of study) das Nebenfach, ¨er

minute die Minute, -n

for minutes minutenlang

miracle das Wunder, -

mirror der Spiegel, -

Miss Fräulein

miss (an event, opportunity, train, etc.) verpassen

missing: be missing fehlen

mist der Nebel

misty neblig

modern modern

modernize modernisieren

mom, mama die Mutti, -s

moment der Augenblick, -e; der Moment, -e

at the moment im Augenblick; im Moment

at the moment, just gerade

Just a moment, please. (Einen) Augenblick, bitte.

monarchy die Monarchie, -n

Monday (der) Montag

money das Geld

month der Monat, -e

for months monatelang

monument das Denkmal, ¨er

mood die Laune, -n

in a good/bad mood guter / schlechter Laune

more mehr

not any more nicht mehr

morning der Morgen, -

Good morning! Guten Morgen!

in the morning(s) morgens (*adv.*); vormittags (*adv.*)

this morning heute morgen

most meist-

most like to am liebsten (+ *verb*)

mostly meistens

mother die Mutter, ¨

motorcycle das Motorrad, ¨er

mountainous bergig

mouth der Mund, ¨er

move, change residence °um·ziehen

move in °ein·ziehen

move out °aus·ziehen

movie der Film, -e

movie theater das Kino, -s

Mr. Herr

Mrs. Frau

Ms. Frau

much viel (mehr, meist-)

not much wenig

Munich (das) München

museum das Museum, die Museen

music die Musik

musicology die Musikwissenschaft

must °müssen

N

name der Name, -ns, -n; °nennen

My name is . . . Ich heiße . . .

What's your name? Wie heißen Sie? *or* Wie ist Ihr Name?

napkin die Serviette, -n

nation, folk das Volk, ¨er

nationality die Nationalität, -en

native

native language die Muttersprache, -n

native place or country die Heimat

natural natürlich

nature die Natur

near nah (näher, nächst-)

near, nearby in der Nähe (von *or* + *gen.*)

nearness die Nähe

necessary nötig

need brauchen

neighbor der Nachbar, -n, -n; die Nachbarin, -nen

neither . . . nor weder . . . noch

neutral neutral

neutrality die Neutralität

never nie

nevertheless trotzdem

new neu

newspaper die Zeitung, -en

next nächst-

nice nett; lieb

night die Nacht, ¨e

Good night. Gute Nacht.

in the night, at night in der Nacht; nachts

no nein; nee (*colloq.*)

no, not a kein (*negative article*)

no more X kein X mehr

nobody, no one niemand

Nonsense! Quatsch!

normal normal

north der Norden

North America (das) Nordamerika

nose die Nase, -n
not nicht
    not a kein (*negative article*)
    not a . . . at all gar kein
    not an X any longer kein X
      mehr
    not any kein
    not any more, no longer
      nicht mehr
    not any X yet noch kein X
    not at all gar nicht
    not much wenig
    not only . . . but also nicht
      nur . . . sondern auch
    not yet noch nicht
notebook das Heft, -e
nothing nichts
notice merken
notion die Ahnung, -en
noun das Substantiv, -e
novel der Roman, -e
November (der) November
now jetzt; nun
    from now on von jetzt an
number die Nummer, -n
nurse der Krankenpfleger, -;
    die Krankenschwester, -n

O

object, thing die Sache, -n
objective objektiv
o'clock Uhr (3 o'clock = 3
    Uhr)
October (der) Oktober
odd komisch
of von (*prep. + dat.*)
    of course natürlich
    of course, sure klar
      (*colloq.*)
offend ärgern
offer ˚bieten
office das Büro, -s
official offiziell (*adj.*); der
    Beamte (*adj. noun, m.*); die
    Beamtin, -nen (*f.*)
often oft (öfter)
oh ach
oil das Öl
OK Ist gut; okay (*colloq.*)
old alt (älter)

old-fashioned altmodisch
on auf (*prep. + acc.* or *dat.*)
once einmal
    once again, once more
      noch einmal
one (*indefinite pronoun*) man
oneself: by oneself (myself,
    yourself, etc.) selber,
    selbst
only nur (*adv.*)
    only, single einzig- (*adj.*)
onto auf (*prep. + acc.* or *dat.*)
open offen (*adj.*); öffnen
    (*verb*)
opinion die Meinung, -en
    be of the opinion, think
      meinen
opportunity die Gelegenheit,
    -en
opposite der Gegensatz, ¨e
opposition die Opposition, -en
optimistic optimistisch
or oder (*coor. conj.*)
order die Portion, -en
    (*of food*); bestellen
    in order to um . . . zu
orderly ordentlich
other ander-
otherwise sonst
outing der Ausflug, ¨e
out of aus (*prep. + dat.*)
outside draußen (*adv.*)
over über (*prep. + dat.* or
    acc.)
    over there drüben;
      da drüben
own ˚besitzen; eigen- (*adj.*)

P

pace das Tempo
pack packen
page die Seite, -n
pants die Hose, -n
papa der Vati, -s
paper das Papier, -e
    write a paper ein Referat
      schreiben
    written term paper das
      Referat
parallel parallel

Pardon me. Entschuldigung.
    I beg your pardon? Wie
    bitte?
parents die Eltern (*pl.*)
part der Teil, -e
    take part in ˚teil·nehmen an
      (+ *dat.*)
participate mit·machen
partner der Partner, -
party die Party, -s
    party (political) die Partei,
      -en
passport der Paß, die Pässe
past (time) die Vergangenheit
path der Weg, -e
patience die Geduld
patient der Patient, -en, -en
patron der Gast, ¨e
pay bezahlen; zahlen
    pay attention auf·passen
peace der Frieden
peaceful, calm ruhig
peculiar komisch
pedestrian der Fußgänger, -
pedestrian zone die
    Fußgängerzone, -n
pen (ballpoint) der
    Kugelschreiber, -
pencil der Bleistift, -e
people die Leute (*pl.*)
    people, nation, folk das
      Volk, ¨er
percent das Prozent
perfect perfekt
perhaps vielleicht
person der Mensch, -en, -en;
    die Person, -en
personal persönlich
pessimistic pessimistisch
pharmacy die Apotheke, -n
phenomenon das Phänomen,
    -e
philosophize philosophieren
philosophy die Philosophie
photograph das Foto, -s
physics die Physik (*sing.*)
piano das Klavier, -e
pick up ab·holen
picture das Bild, -er
    take a picture ein Foto
      machen

piece das Stück, -e
pigeon die Taube, -n
pink rosa
pity: What a pity! Das ist schade!
place der Ort, -e; der Platz, ¨e
place, put stellen
plan °vor·haben
  plan, make plans planen
plant die Pflanze, -n
plastic die Plastik
plate der Teller, -
play spielen
  play sports Sport °treiben
pleasant angenehm
please bitte
please, appeal to °gefallen (+ *dat.*)
Pleased to meet you. Sehr erfreut. *or* Es freut mich.
Pleasure to meet you. Angenehm.
pocket die Tasche, -n
poem das Gedicht, -e
poet der Dichter, -; die Dichterin, -nen
poetry die Lyrik
police die Polizei (*sing. only*)
policy die Politik
polite höflich
political politisch
  political science die Politikwissenschaft
politician der Politiker, -; die Politikerin, -nen
politics die Politik
pollute verschmutzen
  non-polluting, ecologically beneficial umweltfreundlich
pollution die Verschmutzung
ponder something sich etwas überlegen
poor arm (ärmer)
port der Hafen, ¨
portion die Portion, -en
position die Position, -en
  position, job die Stelle, -n
possible möglich
postage stamp die Briefmarke, -n

postal service die Post
postcard die Postkarte, -n
poster das Poster, -
  poster (political) das Plakat, -e
post office die Post
pot: small (coffee or tea) pot das Kännchen, -
potato die Kartoffel, -n
power die Kraft, ¨e; die Macht, ¨e
  power plant das Kraftwerk, -e
practical praktisch
practice üben
precise genau
prefer (to do something) lieber (+ *verb*)
preferably lieber
prejudice das Vorurteil, -e
prepared, ready bereit
prepare for sich vor·bereiten auf (+ *acc.*)
present (gift) das Geschenk, -e
  be present, be there °dabei·sein
  present (time) die Gegenwart
president der Präsident, -en, -en
pretty hübsch
pretzel die Brezel, -n
previously vorher
price der Preis, -e
primary Haupt- (*noun prefix*)
private privat
probably wahrscheinlich; wohl
problem das Problem, -e
produce produzieren
product, ware die Ware, -n
productive produktiv
profession der Beruf, -e
  What is your profession? Was sind Sie von Beruf?
professor der Professor, -en; die Professorin, -nen
program das Programm, -e
programmer der Programmierer, -; die Programmiererin, -nen
progress der Fortschritt, -e

prohibited verboten
propel °treiben
protest der Protest, -e
proud of stolz auf (+ *acc.*)
provide °bieten
psychoanalysis die Psychoanalyse
psychological psychologisch
psychology die Psychologie
public öffentlich
pull °ziehen
pullover der Pullover, -; der Pulli, -s (*colloq.*)
punctual pünktlich
pupil der Schüler, -; die Schülerin, -nen
put stellen
  put down, lay legen
  put down, set setzen

Q

quantity die Menge, -n
quarter das Viertel, -
  quarter to/past Viertel vor/nach
question die Frage, -n
  ask a question eine Frage stellen
  guiding question die Leitfrage, -n
  it's a question of es geht um
questionnaire der Fragebogen
quick as lightning blitzschnell
quiet leise
quit, to give up °auf·geben
quite ziemlich

R

radical radikal
radio das Radio, -s
railroad, railroad system die Bahn
railway compartment das Abteil, -e
rain der Regen; regnen
rainy regnerisch
rather
  I'd rather not. No thanks. Lieber nicht.

would rather (do something) lieber (+ *verb*)

reaction die Reaktion, -en

react to reagieren auf (+ *acc.*)

read °lesen

read aloud °vor·lesen

reading selection das Lesestück, -e

ready, finished fertig

ready, prepared bereit

real wirklich

really? echt? (*slang*)

realm das Reich, -e

reason der Grund, ⸚e

receive °bekommen

recently neulich

reception desk die Rezeption

recommend °empfehlen

recover (from) sich erholen von

recycling das Recycling

red rot (röter)

reform die Reform, -en; reformieren

refuse, trash der Müll

regard as °halten für

regime das Regime

region die Gegend, -en; die Region, -en

register (at a hotel, the university, etc.) sich an·melden

register for, take (a university course) belegen

relative der/die Verwandte, -n (*adj. noun*); relativ (*adj. and adv.*)

remain °bleiben

remember sich erinnern an (+ *acc.*)

Do you remember? Weißt du noch?

remind of erinnern an (+ *acc.*)

rent (from somebody) mieten

repair reparieren

repeat widerholen

repetition die Wiederholung, -en

report berichten

give a report ein Referat °halten

oral report das Referat, -e

republic die Republik, -en

request °bitten um

rescue retten

reserve reservieren

respond to antworten auf (+ *acc.*)

responsible for verantwortlich für

rest: have a rest sich erholen

restaurant das Restaurant, -s; das Lokal, -e

restauration die Restauration

restless unruhig

retain °behalten

review die Wiederholung

revolution die Revolution, -en

Rhine River der Rhein

rich reich

right, correct richtig

be right recht °haben (*with person as subject*); stimmen (*impersonal only*)

right away sofort; gleich

That's right. Das stimmt. Stimmt schon.

to the right, on the right rechts (*adv.*)

ring klingeln

rip off, steal klauen (*colloq.*)

river der Fluß, die Flüsse

road die Straße, -n

road atlas der Straßenatlas

role die Rolle, -n

roll das Brötchen, -

romantic romantisch

room das Zimmer, -

dining room das Eßzimmer, -

double room das Doppelzimmer, -

living room das Wohnzimmer, -

rented student room die Bude, -n (*colloq.*)

single room das Einzelzimmer, -

roommate der Mitbewohner, -; die Mitbewohnerin, -nen

rubble die Trümmer (*pl.*)

rucksack der Rucksack, ⸚e

rug der Teppich, -e

ruins die Trümmer (*pl.*)

run °laufen

Russia (das) Rußland

Russian der Russe, -n, -n; die Russin, -nen; russisch (*adj.*)

S

sack der Sack, ⸚e

sad traurig

salad der Salat, -e

salesman der Verkäufer, -

saleswoman die Verkäuferin, -nen

sample probieren

satisfied zufrieden

Saturday (der) Samstag, (der) Sonnabend

sausage die Wurst, ⸚e

save, rescue retten

save (money or time) sparen

say sagen

What did you say? Wie bitte?

What do you say to that? Was meinen/sagen Sie dazu?

scarce, in short supply knapp

scarf das Tuch, ⸚er

schilling (Austrian currency) der Schilling, -e

scholarship die Wissenschaft

scholarship, stipend das Stipendium, die Stipendien

school die Schule, -n; das Gymnasium, die Gymnasien (*prepares pupils for university*)

elementary school pupil or secondary school student der Schüler, -; die Schülerin, -nen

school system das Schulsystem, -e

science die Wissenschaft, -en

sea das Meer, -e

seat der Platz, ⸚e

second zweit-

   second car der Zweitwagen, -

secretary der Sekretär, -e; die Sekretärin, -nen

see °sehen

   Let's see. Zeig mal her.

   see again °wieder·sehen

seek, look for suchen

seem °scheinen

seldom selten

self: by oneself (myself, yourself, etc.) selbst *or* selber (*adv.*)

sell verkaufen

semester das Semester, -

   semester break die Semesterferien (*pl.*)

seminar das Seminar, -e

send schicken

senior citizen der Senior, -en, -en

sentence der Satz, ¨e

separate separat

September (der) September

serious ernst

   take something seriously etwas ernst °nehmen

set (down) setzen

seventh siebt-

several mehrere, einige

sex, gender das Geschlecht, -er

shame: That's a shame! Das ist schade!

shape: in shape fit

shared apartment die Wohngemeinschaft, -en; die WG, -s

shave sich rasieren

shine °scheinen

ship das Schiff, -e

shirt das Hemd, -en

shoe der Schuh, -e

shop, store der Laden, ¨

shop for, go shopping ein·kaufen

short kurz (kürzer); klein (*short in height*)

   short of cash knapp bei Kasse

should °sollen

shoulder bag die Tasche, -n

shout °schreien

show zeigen

   Show it to me. Zeig mal her.

shower die Dusche, -n

   take a shower sich duschen

siblings die Geschwister (*pl.*)

sick krank (kränker)

sickness die Krankheit, -en

significance die Bedeutung, -en

silent: be silent °schweigen

similar (to) ähnlich (+ *dat.*)

similarity die Ähnlichkeit, -en

simple, easy einfach; leicht

since (causal) da (*sub. conj.*)

   since (temporal) seit (*prep. + dat. & sub. conj.*)

sing °singen

single, only einzig- (*adj.*)

   single, unmarried ledig

sister die Schwester, -n

sit °sitzen

   sit down sich setzen

situated: be situated °liegen

situation die Situation, -en

size die Größe, -n

ski °ski·fahren

skirt der Rock, ¨e

sleep °schlafen

slow langsam

small klein

smart klug (klüger)

snake die Schlange, -n

sneaker der Turnschuh, -e

snow der Schnee; schneien

so so

   So long! Tschüs!

   So what? Na und?

soccer der Fußball

   soccer ball der Fußball, ¨e

social gesellschaftlich; sozial

   social worker der Sozialarbeiter, -; die Sozialarbeiterin, -nen

society die Gesellschaft, -en

sociology die Soziologie

soft, quiet leise

software die Software

solidarity die Solidarität

solution die Lösung, -en

solve lösen

some etwas (*sing.*); einige (*pl.*); manche (*pl.*)

somebody jemand

somehow or other irgendwie

someone jemand

   someone else jemand anderes

something etwas

sometime or other irgendwann

sometimes manchmal

somewhat etwas

somewhere or other irgendwo

son der Sohn, ¨e

song das Lied, -er

soon bald

sore, ticked off sauer (*colloq.*)

sorry: I'm sorry about that. Das tut mir leid.

sound °klingen

soup die Suppe, -n

sour, acidic sauer

south der Süden

Soviet Union die Sowjetunion

space der Platz, ¨e

Spain (das) Spanien

speak reden; °sprechen

   I can speak German. Ich kann Deutsch.

speechless baff (*colloq.*)

speed das Tempo

spell: How do you spell that? Wie schreibt man das?

spend (money) °aus·geben

   spend (time) °verbringen

   spend the night übernachten

spite

   in spite of trotz (+ *gen.*)

   in spite of that, nevertheless trotzdem (*adv.*)

spontaneous spontan

spoon der Löffel, -

sport der Sport

   play sports Sport °treiben

spring der Frühling

   spring term das Sommersemester

square: city square der Platz, ¨e

stability   die Stabilität
stable   stabil
staircase   die Treppe, -n
stairs   die Treppe, -n
stamp   die Briefmarke, -n
stand   °stehen
  stand up   °auf·stehen
standard of living   der
    Lebensstandard
start   °an·fangen
  start, depart (by vehicle)
    °los·fahren
state   der Staat, -en; das
    Bundesland, ¨er (federal
    state)
stay   °bleiben
steal   stehlen
  steal, rip off   klauen
    (colloq.)
steep   steil
stereotyped, cliché
    klischeehaft
still (adv.)   noch; noch immer;
    immer noch
stipend   das Stipendium, die
    Stipendien
stone   der Stein, -e
stop (for streetcar or bus)   die
    Haltestelle, -n
stop   °halten (intrans.)
  stop (doing something)
    auf·hören (mit)
store   das Geschäft, -e
  store, shop   der Laden, ¨
story   die Geschichte, -n
  story, narrative   die
    Erzählung, -en
straighten up   auf·räumen
strange, foreign   fremd
strawberry jam   die
    Erdbeermarmelade
street   die Straße, -n
streetcar   die Straßenbahn, -en
strength   die Kraft, ¨e
stress   der Streß, die Stresse
stressful   stressig
stroll   der Bummel, -
  stroll through town   der
    Stadtbummel, -
  take a stroll   einen Bummel
    machen

strong   stark (stärker)
student (at university)   der
    Student, -en, -en; die
    Studentin, -nen
  student dormitory   das
    Studentenwohnheim, -e
  student I.D.   der
    Studentenausweis, -e
studies (at university)   das
    Studium
study   das Arbeitszimmer, -
study (a subject), major in
    studieren
  study at   studieren an
    (+ dat.)
stupid   blöd; dumm
subject, area of study   das
    Fach, ¨er
  subject, topic   das Thema,
    die Themen
subjective   subjektiv
subjunctive   der Konjunktiv
subway train   die
    Untergrundbahn; die
    U-Bahn
success   der Erfolg, -e
such a   so ein(e)
suddenly   plötzlich
suggestion   der Vorschlag, ¨e;
    der Tip, -s
suit   der Anzug, ¨e
suitcase   der Koffer, -
summary   die
    Zusammenfassung, -en
summer   der Sommer
sun   die Sonne
Sunday   (der) Sonntag
sunny   sonnig
super   super
supermarket   der Supermarkt,
    ¨e
super tanker   der Supertanker, -
supper   das Abendessen
  for supper   zum Abendessen
supposed: be supposed to
    °sollen
sure, certain   sicher; bestimmt
  sure, of course   klar
    (colloq.)
surprise   die Überraschung,
    -en; überraschen

be surprised   staunen
be surprised (about)   sich
    wundern (über + acc.)
sweater   der Pullover, -; der
    Pulli, -s
sweet   süß
swim   °schwimmen
swimming pool   das
    Schwimmbad, ¨er
Swiss   schweizerisch (adj.); der
    Schweizer, -; die
    Schweizerin, -nen
Switzerland   die Schweiz
symbol   das Symbol, -e
symbolic   symbolisch
sympathy   das Mitleid
system   das System, -e

T

T-shirt   das T-Shirt, -s
table   der Tisch, -e
take   °nehmen
  take along   °mit·bringen;
    °mit·nehmen
  take (a university course)
    belegen
  take for   °halten für
  take part in   °teil·nehmen an
    (+ dat.)
  take place   °statt·finden
talk   reden; °sprechen
  talk nonsense   quatschen
    (colloq.)
  talk to   sich °unterhalten mit
tall   groß
task   die Aufgabe, -n
taste; taste good   schmecken
tasty   lecker
tavern   die Kneipe, -n; das
    Lokal, -e
taxicab   das Taxi, -s
tea   der Tee
teacher   der Lehrer, -; die
    Lehrerin, -nen
team   die Mannschaft, -en
technology   die Technik
telephone   das Telefon, -e;
    telefonieren

television set der Fernseher, -
  watch television °fern·sehen
tell sagen
  tell, recount erzählen
  tell me sag mal
tempo das Tempo
tennis das Tennis
  tennis court der Tennisplatz, ⁻e
term paper das Referat, -e
terrace die Terrasse, -n
terrible furchtbar; grausam; schrecklich
terrific herrlich; prima; toll (*colloq.*)
terrorist terroristisch (*adj.*)
test die Prüfung, -en
  written test die Klausur, -en
text der Text, -e
than (*with comparative degree*) als
thank danken (+ *dat.*)
  thank goodness Gott sei Dank
thanks der Dank
  thanks, thank you danke
  thanks a lot, many thanks vielen Dank
that daß (*sub. conj.*)
theater das Theater, -
theme das Thema, die Themen
then dann
  then, in that case da (*adv.*)
there da, dort
  How do I get there? Wie komme ich dahin?
  there is, there are es gibt (+ *acc.*)
therefore darum
thermos bottle die Thermosflasche, -n
thing das Ding, -e
  thing, item die Sache, -n
think °denken; meinen, glauben
  I don't think so. Ich glaube nicht.
  I think so. Ich glaube schon.
  I think so too. Das finde ich auch.
  think of °denken an (+ *acc.*)

think something over sich etwas überlegen
think X is °halten X für
What do you think of that? Was meinen/sagen Sie dazu?
third dritt-
thirst der Durst
thirsty Durst haben
this, these dies-
thought der Gedanke, -ns, -n
through durch (*prep. + acc.*)
throw °werfen
  throw away °weg·werfen
Thursday (der) Donnerstag
thus also
ticked off, sore sauer (*colloq.*)
ticket die Karte, -n; die Fahrkarte, -n (*bus, train, streetcar*); das Ticket, -s (*airline*)
tidy ordentlich
tidy up auf·räumen
tie die Krawatte, -n
time die Zeit, -en
  for a long time lange
  for a short time, briefly kurz
  for a time eine Zeitlang
  for such a long time so lange
  high time höchste Zeit
  on time, punctual pünktlich
  take time, last dauern
  What time is it? Wie spät ist es? *or* Wieviel Uhr ist es?
time (in the sense of "occurrence") das Mal, -e
  any time irgendwann
  at that time, back then damals
  for the first time zum ersten Mal
  the next time das nächste Mal
  this time diesmal (*adv.*)
  umpteen times zigmal
tin can die Dose, -n
tip der Tip, -s

tired, weary müde
  dead tired todmüde
to (*prep.*) an (*prep. + acc. or dat.*); nach (+ *dat., with cities and countries*); zu (+ *dat., with people and some places*)
today heute
together zusammen; miteinander
tomorrow morgen
  tomorrow afternoon morgen nachmittag
  tomorrow evening morgen abend
  tomorrow morning morgen früh
too auch; zu
  too bad schade
tooth der Zahn, ⁻e
top: on top oben (*adv.*)
topic das Thema, die Themen
topical aktuell
tough hart (härter)
tour die Tour, -en
tourist der Tourist, -en, -en; die Touristin, -nen
toward an (*prep. + acc. or dat.*)
town (5,000 to 20,000 inhabitants) die Kleinstadt, ⁻e
  small town der Ort, -e
  town hall das Rathaus, ⁻er
track das Gleis, -e
tradition die Tradition, -en
traditional traditionell
traffic der Verkehr
train der Zug, ⁻e
  train station der Bahnhof, ⁻e
train (for a sport) trainieren
transfer °um·steigen
translate übersetzen
trash der Müll
  trash container der Container, -
travel reisen
travel agency das Reisebüro, -s
traveler's check der Reisescheck, -s

tree der Baum, ⸚e

trip die Reise, -n; die Fahrt

Have a good trip! Gute Reise!

take a trip eine Reise machen

trousers die Hose, -n

true wahr; richtig

truth die Wahrheit, -en

try versuchen (*attempt*); probieren (*sample*)

Tuesday (der) Dienstag

Turk der Türke, -n, -n; die Türkin, -nen

Turkey die Türkei

Turkish türkisch

twice zweimal

type der Typ, -en

typewriter die Schreibmaschine, -n

typical typisch

U

ugly häßlich

umbrella der Regenschirm, -e

unconcerned unbesorgt

under unter (*prep.* + *acc.* or *dat.*)

understand ⸰verstehen

undress, get undressed sich ⸰aus·ziehen

uneducated ungebildet

unemployed arbeitslos

unemployment die Arbeitslosigkeit

unfortunately leider

unification die Vereinigung

unimportant unwichtig

unite vereinen

university die Universität, -en; die Uni, -s (*colloq.*); die Hochschule, -n

attend a university studieren

at the university an der Uni(versität)

university studies das Studium

unknown unbekannt

unmarried unverheiratet

unnecessary unnötig

unpack aus·packen

unpleasant ungemütlich; unangenehm

until bis

not until erst

upon auf (*prep.* + *acc.* or *dat.*)

upset: get upset (about) sich auf·regen (über + *acc.*)

USA die USA (*pl.*)

use benutzen

used to: get used to sich gewöhnen an (+ *acc.*)

useful nützlich

usually meistens

V

vacation (from university or school) die Ferien (*pl.*)

go on vacation in Urlaub gehen/fahren

take a vacation Urlaub machen

vacation (from a job) der Urlaub, -e

valley das Tal, ⸚er

variation die Variation, -en

various verschieden

vegetables das Gemüse (*sing.*)

Venice (Italy) (das) Venedig

verb das Verb, -en

very sehr

vicinity die Nähe

Vienna (das) Wien

village das Dorf, ⸚er

visit der Besuch, -e; besuchen

vocabulary der Wortschatz

voice die Stimme, -n

volleyball der Volleyball

voter der Wähler, -

W

wage der Lohn, ⸚e

wait (for) warten (auf + *acc.*)

Wait a second! Hang on! Warte mal!

waiter der Kellner, -

waitress die Kellnerin, -nen

wake up auf·wachen (*intrans.*); wecken (*trans.*)

walk der Bummel, -; ⸰gehen; ⸰laufen (*colloq.*)

go for a walk ⸰spazieren·gehen

wall (freestanding or exterior) die Mauer, -n

wall (interior) die Wand, ⸚e

wallet der Geldbeutel, -

wander wandern

wanderlust die Wanderlust

want to ⸰wollen

I don't want to. Ich habe keine Lust.

want to do something Lust haben, etwas zu tun

war der Krieg, -e

wardrobe der Kleiderschrank, ⸚e

warm warm (wärmer)

wash ⸰waschen

waste verschwenden

watch die Uhr, -en

watch television ⸰fern·sehen

water das Wasser

way der Weg, -e

on the way unterwegs

weak schwach (schwächer)

wear ⸰tragen

weary, tired müde

weather das Wetter

wedding die Hochzeit, -en

Wednesday (der) Mittwoch

week die Woche, -n

for weeks wochenlang (*adv.*)

weekend das Wochenende, -n

on the weekend am Wochenende

weigh ⸰wiegen

welcome willkommen (*adj.*)

Welcome! Nice to see you! Herzlich willkommen!

You're welcome. Bitte (sehr).

well . . . also . . . ; na . . . ; nun . . .

well (*adv.*) gut

get well sich erholen von

Get well soon. Gute
    Besserung.
well known bekannt
west der Westen
wet naß
what? was?
  what kind of? was für?
wheel das Rad, ˙er
when als (*sub. conj.*); wann
    (*question word*); wenn
    (*sub. conj.*)
whenever wenn (*sub. conj.*)
where? wo?
  from where? woher?
  to where? wohin?
whether, if ob (*sub. conj.*)
which? welch-?
while während (*sub. conj.*)
  for a while eine Zeitlang
  while . . . -ing bei . . .
white weiß
who? wer?
whole ganz
whose? wessen?
why? warum?
wild wild
win ˚gewinnen
wind der Wind
window das Fenster, -
  store window das
    Schaufenster, -
  window, counter der
    Schalter, -

windy windig
wine der Wein, -e
winter (der) Winter
  in the winter im Winter
wish wünschen
wit der Witz, -e
with mit
  with each other
    miteinander
without ohne
  without . . . -ing ohne . . .
    zu
witty witzig
woman die Frau, -en
  young unmarried woman
    das Fräulein, -
wonder, ask oneself sich
    fragen
  No wonder! Kein Wunder!
wonderful wunderbar
word das Wort, die Worte (*in
    context*), die Wörter
    (*unconnected*); die
    Vokabel, -n
work die Arbeit
  work (of art) das Werk, -e
work arbeiten
  work on arbeiten an
    (+ *dat.*)
  work part time halbtags
    arbeiten
worker der Arbeiter, -; die
    Arbeiterin, -nen

world die Welt, -en
worried besorgt
worthwhile: be worthwhile,
    worth the trouble sich
    lohnen
Wow! Mensch!
write ˚schreiben
writer der Schriftsteller, -; die
    Schriftstellerin, -nen
wrong falsch

Y

year das Jahr, -e
  for years jahrelang
yell ˚schreien
yellow gelb
yes ja
  yes I do, yes I am, etc. doch
yesterday gestern
  yesterday evening gestern
    abend
  yesterday morning gestern
    früh
young jung (jünger)
  young people die Jugend
    (*sing.*)
youth die Jugend
  youth hostel die
    Jugendherberge, -n

Z

zone die Zone, -n

Text

Page 408 "Ottos mops" by Ernst Jandl, from *Der künstliche Baum*, 1970. Reprinted by permission of Hermann Luchterhand Verlag, Germany.

Page 466 "Von Mensch zu Mensch," Von Elternhaus und Jugendzeit," "Von den Jahreszeiten," and "Von Reise und Wanderung" by Mascha Kaleko from *Das Lyrische Stenogrammheft*, copyright © 1956 by Rowohlt Verlag GmbH, Hamburg. Reprinted by permission.

Illustrations

Ruth J. Flanigan: 3–5, 7, 12, 13, 15, 17, 18, 28, 44, 54, 56, 57, 67, 73, 84, 89, 94, 117, 130, 163, 171–173, 181, 183, 204, 241, 242, 245, 321, 323–325, 337, 366, 425, 449, 451, 456, 483–485
Matthew Hansen: 130 bottom
Joseph Scharl: 417. From *Grimm's Fairy Tales*. Copyright 1944 by Pantheon Books, Inc. and renewed 1972 by Random House, Inc. Reprinted by permission of Pantheon Books, Inc., a division of Random House, Inc.

Photographs

Page 2: Farrell Grehan/Photo Researchers, Inc.; **8**: Judy Poe; **13** (*left*): Kevin Galvin/Stock Boston; **13** (*right*): Kevin Galvin; **16**: Andrew Brilliant; **17**: Andrew Brilliant; **24**: Ulrike Welsch; **25**: Andrew Brilliant; **30**: Ulrike Welsch; **40** (*left*): Owen Franken/Stock Boston; **40** (*right*): Beryl Goldberg; **43**: Ulrike Welsch; **48**: Bob Krist; **51**: Kees Van Den Berg/Photo Researchers, Inc.; **61** (*right*): Judy Poe; **64**: Andrew Brilliant; **72**: Ulrike Welsch; **74**: Ulrike Welsch; **93**: Ulrike Welsch; **100**: Wolfgang Kaehler; **101**: Tony Freeman/PhotoEdit; **108**: Mike Mazzaschi/Stock Boston; **115**: Wolfgang Kaehler; **118**: Vandystadt/Photo Researchers, Inc.; **119**: COMSTOCK/Sven Martsen; **120** (*left*): Judy Poe; **120** (*middle*): Ulrike Welsch; **120** (*right*): Wolfgang Kaehler; **126**: Jan Halaska/Photo Researchers, Inc.; **132**: Palmer & Brilliant; **143**: Owen Franken; **146**: Kevin Galvin/Stock Boston; **149**: Kevin Galvin; **158**: Beryl Goldberg; **166**: Ulrike Welsch; **175**: Helga Lade Fotoagentur; **178**: Kevin Galvin; **190**: Carol Palmer; **191**: Ulrike Welsch; **198**: Kevin Galvin; **206**: Ulrike Welsch; **209**: Andrew Brilliant/Carole Palmer; **210**: Stuart Cohen; **215**: Wolfgang Kaehler; **218**: Palmer & Brilliant; **224**: Wolfgang Kaehler; **238**: Kevin Galvin; **246**: Andrew Brilliant; **252**: Owen Franken/Stock Boston; **263**: Helga Lade Fotoagentur; **271** (*left*): Marvullo/The Stock Market; **271** (*right*): W. Geiersperger/Interfoto; **272** (*left*): Kevin Galvin/Stock Boston; **272** (*right*): Interfoto; **278**: Kevin Galvin; **280**: Owen Franken/Stock Boston; **284**: Kevin Galvin; **286**: Beryl Goldberg; **293**: Pierre Valette; **311**: Ulrike Welsch; **312**: J. Douglas Guy; **317**: Owen Franken; **335**: Margot Granitsas/The Image Works; **342** (*top left*): Keystone Photo/The Image Works;